19<u>50</u>

Mankind and Mother Earth

A NARRATIVE HISTORY OF THE WORLD

Arnold Toynbee

1976
OXFORD UNIVERSITY PRESS
NEW YORK AND LONDON

© 1976 Oxford University Press
Library of Congress Catalogue Card Number: 76-4651
Printed in the United States of America

CONTENTS

Contents

MAPS

(at end of book)

PREFACE

THE celebration of Queen Victoria's Diamond Jubilee in 1897 called to
mind the history of the preceding sixty years, and this retrospect opened
up a view of the whole of history which looked clear and simple.
Between 1837 and 1897 the West had completed the establishment of its
ascendancy over all the rest of the World. This was the consummation
of a process that had been started, four hundred years before 1897, by
Columbus's transit of the Atlantic and Vasco da Gama's voyage from
Portugal round the Cape of Good Hope to the west coast of India. In the
course of those four centuries, all but two of the non-Western countries,
Afghanistan and Abyssinia (Ethiopia), had either fallen under Western
domination or had salvaged their independence by voluntarily adopting
the triumphant Western civilization's way of life in some degree. Peter
the Great had started to Westernize Russia in 1694; the makers of the
Meiji Revolution in Japan had embarked on the same course in 1868.
In 1897, six of the seven existing Great Powers were Western states, and
the seventh, Russia, was a Great Power in virtue of her having Westernized herself to a considerable extent in the course of the last two centuries.
Japan had not yet acquired the status of a Great Power; she did not
wage and win her war with Russia till 1904–5.

Thus, though the establishment of the West's ascendancy was recent,
it looked as if it were going to be permanent. In 1897 the World appeared
to have settled down under a Western dispensation. Apparently history
had reached its denouement in the political unification of Italy and
Germany in 1871, if 'history' was synonymous, as, in 1897, many people
assumed that it was, with the alarums and excursions of the Western
civilization's turbulent past that, within living memory, had happily
been left behind. Accordingly, the year 1897 seemed to be a date at
which an observer could look back on the course of history and see it
'steadily and whole', from a point of time at which the observer himself
was no longer floundering in history's flux.

History, viewed in retrospect at that moment, appeared to have resulted in the attainment of a stable state that rested on the West's world-wide ascendancy, and on this view, the chart of history's course seemed to be manifest. History consisted, so it then seemed, of those particular past events that had led up to the West's present ascendancy. Other past events were irrelevant to history, and they could be ignored. It was true that the whole World had now been drawn into the West's ambit, and, in consequence, had been brought within history's scope, but this Westernization of the World was recent, and the Westernized countries were subordinate or at any rate were peripheral. India, for instance, had been drawn into the West's ambit through having become one of the arenas of competition between two Western Powers, Britain and France, in 1746, and India had a place in the World in 1897 as a portion of the British Empire. Russia had become one of the Great Powers thanks to the prescience of Peter the Great; yet Russia, though admittedly powerful, was not fully civilized; culturally, she was not a first-class member of the Western club. As for the Westernization of Japan, this was remarkable, but it was a freak.

History, defined as the series of events that had led up to the West's ascendancy, could now be rather accurately delimited. The Israelites and their heirs the Jews were unquestionably participants in history, at least down to the year A.D. 70; for their history was the prelude to the history of Roman Catholic and Protestant Christianity, and this was the West's religion. The participation in history of the Greeks of the Hellenic Age was likewise unquestionable. Hellenic-Age Greek philosophy had been enlisted for the formulation of Christian theology, and not only the philosophy but the literature, visual art, and architecture of Hellenism as well had given inspiration, since the Renaissance, to the Modern West's culture.

Judaism and Hellenism were the two principal sources of the Western civilization. This had been generated by the encounter between them, and, in a retrospective reconnaissance of the past, it was not strictly necessary for an historian to push his way any farther up the stream of time. However, within the sixty years of Queen Victoria's reign down to 1897, Western archaeologists had been bringing to light some forgotten pre-Israelite and pre-Hellenic civilizations: for instance, the Pharaonic Egyptian, the Assyrian, and, more recently, the Mycenaean. The archaeologists' reconstruction of these older civilizations was, so far, fragmentary and hazy, but these disinterred civilizations, too, would qualify for being included in history if it emerged that they had made contributions to the Western civilization's Jewish and Hellenic sources.

The ascent from Judaism and Hellenism to the Westernized World of 1897 seemed easy to trace. The Jews and the Greeks had been incorporated in the Roman Empire. This had been the political matrix of Christianity. The Roman Empire had been converted to Christianity before its collapse in its western provinces. The conversion to Christianity of the barbarian conquerors of this ex-Roman territory in the West had led on and up to the progressive expansion of Western Christendom that had started in the last decade of the fifteenth century of the Christian Era. Since then, the rest of the World had been brought within the scope of history as and when it had been drawn into the West's constantly widening ambit.

This retrospective view of history was plausible in 1897 because at that date it looked as if the global ascendancy that the West had attained by then was going to be permanent. In 1973 it still looked as if the West's ascendancy had been unprecedented in having been literally world-wide; but it now also looked as if this ascendancy was going to be as transitory as the previous less than world-wide ascendancies of the Mongols, Arabs, Huns, Romans, Greeks, Persians, Assyrians, and Akkadians. If the West's ascendancy, too, was likely to turn out to have been ephemeral, this could no longer be taken as being a consummation to which the whole of history had led, and the scope of history could no longer be limited to the Western civilization's historical antecedents. The expunging of this arbitrary limitation revealed the immensity of the amount of history that had been jettisoned in fashioning, out of the residue, the picture of history that, in 1897, had purported to include everything that was relevant to the state of human affairs in that year.

The picture presented in 1897 had excluded from history the history of Japan before 1868, of China before 1839, of India before 1746, of Russia before 1694. It had excluded the whole history of Buddhism, Hinduism, and Islam, though in 1897, as in 1973, these had been three of the four religions that had the largest number of adherents, while Buddhism and Islam had been two of the three principal missionary religions. Their range had been as wide as Christianity's. The picture presented in 1897 had also excluded three out of the four main branches of Christianity itself, namely Nestorianism, Monophysitism, and Eastern Orthodoxy, though in 1897 the number of adherents of the churches in the Eastern Orthodox communion was of the same order of magnitude as the number, at that date, of Protestants and Catholics.

Other features of the picture had been still more bizarre. The Jews had been excluded from history as from the year A.D. 70, the date of the temporary destruction of Jerusalem by the Romans, and the Greeks had been excluded as from the year A.D. 451, the date in which the Acts of the Council of Chalcedon had been drafted by Christian Greek theologians. (The Greeks had been re-admitted as from 1821, because in that

year they had revolted from the Ottoman Empire with the intention of
seeking admission to membership in the Western society.)

The treatment of the history of the Roman Empire in the fifth century
of the Christian Era had been the most bizarre of all. In that century the
Roman Empire had survived in the Levant, which had always been its
demographic and economic centre of gravity, but it had collapsed in its
relatively backward western provinces. Yet, as from the year A.D. 476, in
which the last of the impotent Roman Emperors in the western part of
the Empire had been deposed, the chart of the course of history that was
current in 1897 ignored the Roman Empire, though, in the Levant, the
Empire was still a going concern, and though it continued to play a
major part in human affairs till the close of the twelfth century. Indeed,
at the year A.D. 476, the chart that was in vogue in 1897 ignored the
whole of the civilized world of that date, from Greece to China and from
China to Meso-America and Peru. This fantastic chart concentrated
attention, as from A.D. 476 onwards, on the barbarian successor-states of
the Roman Empire in the Empire's derelict western provinces.

By 1973 it had become manifest that none of the enormous mass of
jettisoned history could be written off any longer as being irrelevant.
For instance, the Meso-American civilization, which had seemed to have
been obliterated by Cortés and his men, was now showing signs of re-
emerging in Mexico and Guatemala, from beneath a crumbling veneer
of Westernization. As for the history of Eastern Asia, anyone who looked
at China and Japan in 1973 was bound to conclude that the antecedents
of these two countries, as far back as the East Asian Neolithic Age, were
no less important than the antecedents of the contemporary West. In
1973 an historian could not afford to abandon the major part of history
that he might have been willing to jettison in 1897. He had now to
retrieve it all, and to re-integrate it with the residue, leading up to the
West in the year 1897, which the chart that was in vogue in 1897 had
retained.

In 1973 an integral survey of history was imperative, but this task
presented formidable problems of both selection and presentation.

Any account of anything is bound to be selective. The human intellect
has not the capacity for comprehending the sum of things in a single
panoramic view. Selection is unavoidable, but it is also inevitably
arbitrary; and, the greater the mass of information from which a selection has to be made, the more disputable will be the investigator's
choice. For instance, the selection of historical events that had seemed
plausible in 1897 looked grotesque already in 1973. In the present
narrative, I have refrained from giving to the Western civilization and
its antecedents the excessive prominence that has been given to them
customarily in Western surveys of world history, but I have also tried to

avoid falling into the opposite mistake of giving less to the West and its antecedents than their due. However, a Chinese reader of my narrative may judge that I have allowed the West still to loom too large, while a Western reader may judge that I have 'leaned over backwards' in my effort to put his and my ancestral civilization in its place.

In a narrative written in 1973, the opening and the closing phases of mankind's history were less difficult to handle than the intervening phase. In the Lower Palaeolithic Age (about fifteen-sixteenths of the time-span of human history, to date), life was uniform because, slow though communications were, the pace of change was slower still. Within the last five centuries, mankind's habitat has become a unity on the technological and economic, though not yet on the political, plane because the acceleration in the pace of change has been surpassed by an acceleration in the speed of communications. During the intervening phase, and especially during the four millennia and a half c. 3000 B.C.– A.D. 1500, change was more rapid than the means of communication, and consequently during this period the differentiation between regional ways of life was at its maximum.

There were moments, even within this period, at which large parts of man's habitat were linked together, and I have taken such moments as opportunities for trying to present a panoramic view. Examples of wider horizons in the Old World are the new departure in spiritual life in the sixth century B.C., the dissemination of the Hellenic civilization as a result of Alexander the Great's career, and the political unification of all but the extremities of the Old World by the Mongols' conquests in the thirteenth century of the Christian Era. Corresponding moments in Andean history are represented by the Chavín and Tiahuanáco 'horizons'. However, for most of the time between c. 3000 B.C. and A.D. 1500, each of the regions into which mankind's habitat was divided went its own way. Insulation and differentiation prevailed over intercourse and assimilation. The regional civilizations co-existed without coalescing.

This is an historical fact that has to be reflected in an historical narrative, and the narrator is confronted with the problem of having to record half-a-dozen simultaneous series of events. I have copied the conjuror's trick of keeping several balls in the air simultaneously. I have kept on throwing up and letting drop the history of each region in turn. At the cost of thus foregoing consecutiveness in my treatment of particular regions, I have been able to present in approximately chronological sequence the history of the World as a whole.

The narrational form of presentation and the analytical and comparative form have their own distinctive advantages and drawbacks. To give a comprehensive bird's-eye view of mankind's history in narrational form has been my objective in the present book.

A.J.T., 1974

[I]

RIDDLES IN THE PHENOMENA

AFTER a human being has been conceived and has then been born, the baby may die before it has awakened to consciousness. Until the twentieth century a cruelly high percentage of babies did die at the pre-conscious stage of life. Infant mortality used to be appallingly common, even in human communities that were relatively secure and affluent, and that were also relatively well-informed and well-equipped medically. For pre-modern humans, the rate of infant mortality was of the same order of magnitude as for rabbits. Moreover, if a child does survive long enough to experience the dawn of consciousness, its life may still be cut short at any stage deliberately or by some accident or by some disease or some injury that cannot be cured by the medical and surgical skill and equipment that are accessible at the particular time and place.

However, the length of the expectation of life has now increased sensationally in communities that are medically and socially precocious, and it has begun to increase appreciably in the relatively backward majority of communities as well. Nowadays a human being's conscious-ness may be awake continuously for seventy or eighty years before it is extinguished by death or is dimmed, before physical death, by mental senility. During those seventy or eighty years of consciousness, the human being is aware of phenomena. These phenomena present him with a number of riddles, and the ultimate riddles have not been eluci-dated by the advance of scientific knowledge and understanding—rapid and far-reaching though this advance has been in the Modern Age.

Scientists have recently been discovering the chemical composition and the structural configurations of matter that are the physical enabling conditions for bringing matter to life and for awakening a living organism to consciousness. The advance of science has also brought with it one negative finding that seems likely to stand, though, among the adherents of theistic religions, it meets with strong resistance because it runs counter to deeply-ingrained, though unverified and unverifiable, traditional beliefs. It is now hardly possible any longer to believe that the phenomena of which a human being is conscious have been called into existence by the fiat of a human-like creator god. This traditional way of accounting for the phenomena was based on an unwarrantable analogy with human activities. Human beings do shape already existing inanimate 'raw materials' into tools, machines, clothes, houses, and other artefacts, and they give their artefacts a function and a style that are not inherent in the 'raw materials'. Function and style are non-material; in terms of matter, they are created *ex nihilo*. The explanation of the existence of the phenomena as being accounted for by a human-like creative activity has ceased to be convincing because the existence of a human-like creator god is an hypothesis that is not confirmed by any evidence. But, so far, this no longer tenable traditional hypothesis has not been replaced by any convincing alternative.

The increase in our knowledge of the physical enabling conditions for the presence of life and of human consciousness and purposefulness has not brought with it an understanding of the nature or the purpose (if there is a purpose) of life and consciousness themselves. These are different modes of being both from each other and from the organically structured matter with which, in our experience, they are associated. Every live human being that a human being knows or knows of, including himself, is a conscious purposeful spirit that is physically alive in a material body. None of these components of a live human being have ever been encountered apart from the rest. They are always found in association with each other; yet their relation to each other is incomprehensible.

Why are some portions of the material phenomena associated temporarily with life (as they are in living beings of all species) and also with consciousness (as they are in human beings), while other portions (apparently by far the greater part of the sum total of matter in the cosmos) are permanently inanimate and unconscious? How, in the space-time stream, at one particular point-moment—i.e. in the tenuous 'biosphere' that temporarily envelops our ephemeral planet—have life and consciousness come to be associated with matter? Why does life, embodied in organically structured matter, strive to perpetuate itself or, in organisms that are sexual and mortal, to reproduce itself true to type? The maintenance of any species of living being manifestly costs an intense effort. Is this effort inherent in the nature of the species and of its specimens? If it is, why is it not inherent in the nature of the constituents of organic matter in the pre-organic and post-organic states of these constituents, whose organic configuration is such a brief episode in their history? And, if the effort is not inherent but is introduced, what is the agency that introduces it if we rule out the hypothesis of the operation of a creator god?

Next, let us grant the reality of mutations in the structure and the functioning of living organisms; and let us grant, further, the cogency of the Darwinian thesis that mutations, played upon by natural selection for a sufficient length of time, account adequately for the differentiation of life into diverse species and for the success of some species in surviving and for the failure of others. Even granting all this, the mutations themselves remain unexplained. Are mutations fortuitous, or are they designed, or are they infractions of a design, or are all these three questions inappropriate when they are asked apropos of phenomena that are not credited with the possession of consciousness and with the ability to make plans? Supposing that we do allow ourselves to consider non-human species in these anthropomorphic terms, we are then confronted with further questions. The proneness of a species to undergo mutations is a contrary tendency to the species's effort to maintain or reproduce itself true to type. Is keeping true to type the objective of a species, and are mutations just so many failures to achieve this objective? Or is a species designed to change, and is its practice of keeping true to type just an obstruction of change by inertia?

The differentiation of life into different species has brought with it both competition among some species and co-operation among others. Which, if either, of these two antithetical relations is the paramount law of nature? In the relations of non-conscious species with each other, neither co-operation nor competition is an act of deliberate choice; but the choice is deliberate in human beings, and in us it is bound up with the human sense of the difference and antithesis between right and wrong and between good and evil. What is the source of these ethical judgements, which apparently are intrinsic to human nature but are foreign to the nature of non-human species?

Finally, what is the situation and the significance in the Universe of a conscious, purposeful human being, imbued with this sense of the distinction between right and wrong and impelled (even if he resists this ethical impulse) to do what seems to him to be right? A human being feels as if he is the centre of the Universe because his own consciousness is, for him, the point from which he views the cosmic spiritual and material panorama. He is also self-centred in the sense that his natural impulse is to try to make the rest of the Universe serve his own purposes. At the same time, he is aware that, so far from being the Universe's true centre, he himself is ephemeral and expendable; and his conscience also tells him that, in so far as he gives way to his self-centredness, he is putting himself morally, as well as intellectually, in the wrong.

These are some of the riddles that are presented to a human being by

the phenomena of which he is conscious. Science may or may not continue to advance. Whether science is going to progress or to stagnate is
not a question of intellectual capacity. There does not seem to be any
limit to Man's intellectual ability to add to his scientific knowledge and
to apply this knowledge to the further advancement of his technology.
The future of science and technology partly depends on whether society
continues to value these activities as highly, and to reward them as
handsomely, as has been society's practice in recent times. It also partly
depends on whether individuals of the highest intellectual ability continue to concern themselves with science and technology. This cannot be
taken for granted. In all fields of human activity, fashions change. It is
conceivable that religion or art might become again the paramount
interest of the ablest minds, as they have been in the past at various
times and places. However, even if science were to continue to advance
at its present pace, it seems likely that its further achievements would
not carry it beyond its past and present confines. Our knowledge of the
way in which the phenomenal Universe works might increase, but
science does not seem likely in the future to succeed, any better than it
has succeeded in the past, in enabling us to understand the reason why
the Universe works as it does, or indeed the reason why the Universe
exists.

However, a human being has to live and to act during his psychosomatic life in the biosphere, and the demands of life and action force
him to provide himself with provisional answers to the riddles presented
to him by the phenomena, even if he cannot obtain these answers from
science and even if he believes that scientific knowledge is the only true
kind of knowledge. This belief is not impregnable. Nevertheless, it is true
that answers which are found outside the confines of science are unverifiable acts of faith. They are not intellectual demonstrations; they are
religious intuitions. Therefore it seems probable that in the future, as in
the past, life will compel human beings to answer the ultimate questions
in the intuitive unverifiable terms of religion. Superficially the post-
scientific and the pre-scientific expressions of religion may seem to be
poles apart from each other. Every past expression of religion has been
attuned to the intellectual outlook of the time and place at which each
particular expression was formulated. But the underlying essence of
religion is, no doubt, as constant as the essence of human nature itself.
Religion is, in fact, an intrinsic and distinctive trait of human nature. It
is a human being's necessary response to the challenge of the mysterious-
ness of the phenomena that he encounters in virtue of his uniquely
human faculty of consciousness.

[2]

THE BIOSPHERE

THE word 'biosphere' was coined by Teilhard de Chardin. It is a new word, required by our arrival at a new stage in the progress of our scientific knowledge and our material power. The biosphere is a film of dry land, water, and air enveloping the globe (or virtual globe) of our planet Earth. It is the sole present habitat—and, as far as we can foresee today, also the sole habitat that will ever be accessible—for all the species of living beings, including mankind, that are known to us.

The biosphere is rigidly limited in its volume, and therefore contains only a limited stock of those resources on which the various species of living beings have to draw in order to maintain themselves. Some of these resources are renewable; others are irreplaceable. Any species that overdraws on its renewable resources or exhausts its irreplaceable resources condemns itself to extinction. The number of extinct species that have left traces in the geological record is startlingly great by comparison with the number of those that are still extant.

The most significant characteristic of the biosphere is the relative smallness of its size and the exiguousness of the resources that it offers. In terrestrial terms the biosphere is fantastically thin. Its upper limit may be equated with the maximum altitude in the stratosphere at which a plane can remain air-borne; its lower limit is the depth, below the surface of its solid portion, to which engineers can mine and bore. The thickness of the biosphere, between these two limits, is minute by comparison with the length of the radius of the globe which it coats like a delicate skin. This globe is far from being the largest of our sun's planets, and it is also far from being the most distant of these planets from the sun round which they all 'circle' in orbits, that are, in truth, not circular but elliptical. Moreover, our sun is only one among the almost incredibly numerous suns that constitute our galaxy, and our galaxy is only one in a host of galaxies whose number is unknown (the known number of

galaxies increases with each increase in the range of our telescopes).
Thus, by comparison with the dimensions of the known portion of the
physical cosmos, the dimensions of our biosphere are infinitesimally
minute.

The biosphere is not as old as the planet that it now envelops. It is an
excrescence—one might call it alternatively either a halo or a rust—
that came into existence long after the crust of the planet had cooled
down sufficiently for parts of its originally gaseous components to
liquify and to solidify. It is almost certainly the only biosphere now
existing within our solar system, and it is possible that, within this
system, no other biosphere ever has come into existence or ever will. Of
course our solar system, like our biosphere, is only an infinitesimally
minute part of the known portion of the physical cosmos. It is possible
that other suns—perhaps numerous others—besides ours have planets,
and that, among these possibly existing other planets, there may be some
which, like ours, circle round their suns at a distance at which they, like
our planet, can grow biospheres round their surfaces. But if there are, in
truth, other potential biospheres, it cannot be taken for granted that
these are actually inhabited, as ours is, by living beings. In a potential
habitat for life, this potentiality is not bound to be actualized.

The physical configuration of organically structured matter has now
been discovered, but, as has been observed already, life's and consciousness's and purposefulness's physical container is not the same thing as
life and consciousness and purposefulness themselves. We do not know
how or why life and consciousness and purposefulness have come into
existence round the surface of our planet. We do now know, however,
that the material constituents of our biosphere have been re-distributed
spatially and have been re-compounded chemically as a result of the
interaction between living organisms and inorganic matter. We know
that one effect of the genesis of 'primitive' living organisms has been to
provide a filter through which the radiation that is constantly bombard-
ing our biosphere from our sun and from other external sources is now
admitted into our biosphere at a strength at which it is not only tolerable
but is hospitable to 'higher' forms of life (the term 'higher' meaning
nearer to the form taken by life in the species *homo sapiens*—a relative and
subjective use of the word 'higher').

We also know that the matter contained in our biosphere has been,
and is being, constantly interchanged or 're-cycled' between those
portions of this matter that, at a given moment, are inanimate and
animate, and that, in the portion that is animate at the given moment,
some sections are vegetable and some are animal and, in the animal
section, some specimens are non-human and some are human. The
biosphere exists and survives by means of a delicate self-regulating and

self-maintaining balance of forces. The constituents of the biosphere are interdependent, and Man is just as dependent on his relation with the rest of the biosphere as any of the biosphere's other present constituents. In an act of thought, a human being can distinguish himself from the rest of mankind, from the rest of the biosphere, and from the rest of the physical and spiritual Universe. Yet human nature, including human consciousness and conscience, as well as human physique, is also located in the biosphere, and we have no evidence that either individual human beings or mankind have, or could have, any existence beyond their life in the biosphere. If the biosphere were to cease to be any longer a possible habitat for life, mankind, so far as we know, would suffer the fate of extinction that would then overtake every other form of life.

Moreover, the nearest potential biosphere to ours (if any other, besides ours, is to be found anywhere in the physical cosmos) may be hundreds of millions of light-years distant from our planet. In our generation, a few human beings have been landed on the surface of our planet's moon and, after a brief stay there, they have been brought back again to Earth still alive in almost every case. This has been a magnificent feat of science applied to technology, but it has been a still more notable feat of sociality, considering that, so far, human beings have been far less successful in managing their relations with each other than they have been in mastering the non-human part of Nature. This feat has taught us some lessons which are of practical importance for estimating our prospects and choosing our policy on Earth.

The Moon is much closer to the Earth than is any other star; it is our planet's satellite. Yet to land a few men on the Moon for a few hours has required the precisely co-ordinated and enthusiastically co-operative work of several hundreds of thousands of human beings. It has also required a vast expenditure of material resources and a considerable draft on the courage and ability that are mankind's rarest and most precious assets. Even if the Moon were to prove to be as rich in resources for human life as the Americas, the exploitation of these resources would not be remunerative economically. A permanent colonization of the Moon by earthlings would be impracticable. Human bodies have a physical structure that enables them to withstand, without feeling the strain, the particular gravitational pull of the Earth's mass and the particular pressure of the Earth's envelope of air. They need food in the form of other organic substances, either vegetable or animal. All these features and necessities of human life were present in the Americas for those Europeans who reached the Americas by crossing the Atlantic in the tenth century of the Christian Era from Scandinavia and in the fifteenth century from Spain. Their meeting with other human beings who had anticipated the Europeans in reaching and occupying the Americas was evidence that these other parts of the Earth's dry land were habitable.

The Moon is not habitable for any form of life. The only lunar matter that could be a resource for human beings would be inanimate matter that has never been even temporarily organic. In order to be made useful, this lunar matter would have to be transported from the Moon to the Earth by human beings camping and working on the Moon under the handicap of extremely trying conditions. This would not pay, as it did pay to convey tobacco from America to Europe and to cultivate in Europe and in Asia other plants—for instance maize and potatoes—that had been domesticated in America by the Europeans' predecessors who had reached America from the opposite side.

Though neither the Moon nor the Earth's sister planets, which are far more remote from the Earth than the Moon is, are habitable for inhabitants of our biosphere, it is conceivable that some other sun than ours, perhaps a sun in some other galaxy, might have a planet that would be habitable for us; but, even if we could locate another habitable planet, it would hardly be feasible for travellers from our biosphere to reach it. Suppose we were to discover how to steer the course without being attracted, en route, into one of the burning fiery furnaces of the innumerable suns that are on the move through space; the journey might take a hundred years. We should therefore have to devise a spaceship on board of which the passengers could beget children who would be able to live on board and beget children and grandchildren there in their turn, before the conveyance could land and disembark the third or fourth generation. And, even if this arriving and landing generation could count on finding breathable air and drinkable water and edible food and tolerable air pressure and gravitational pull in this hypothetical replica of our biosphere, the conveyance (a modernized Noah's Ark) in which they had made the voyage from one habitable biosphere to another would have had to be stocked with rations of air and food and drink that would keep successive generations on board alive for a century. It seems most unlikely that this fabulous voyage will ever really be made.

Thus our present knowledge and experience point to the conclusion that the habitat of the denizens of the biosphere on the face of the planet Earth is going to continue to be confined to this capsule within which life, in the form known to us, has made its appearance. Though it is possible that other biospheres, habitable for denizens of our biosphere, may exist, it is so improbable that we could ever reach and colonize any of them that the possibility cannot reasonably be taken into account. This fantasy is, in fact, Utopian.

If we do conclude that our present biosphere, which has been our only habitat so far, is also the only physical habitat that we are ever likely to have, this conclusion will admonish us to concentrate our thoughts and efforts on *this* biosphere: to survey its history, to forecast its prospects, and to do everything that human action can do to ensure that *this*— which, for us, is *the*—biosphere shall remain habitable until it is made uninhabitable eventually by cosmic forces beyond human control.

Mankind's material power has now increased to a degree at which it could make the biosphere uninhabitable and will, in fact, produce this suicidal result within a foreseeable period of time if the human population of the globe does not now take prompt and vigorous concerted action to check the pollution and the spoliation that are being inflicted on the biosphere by short-sighted human greed. On the other hand, mankind's material power will not avail to ensure that the biosphere shall remain habitable so long as we ourselves refrain from wrecking it; for, though the biosphere is finite, it is not self-sufficient. Mother Earth has not engendered life by parthenogenesis. Life has been begotten on the biosphere through the fertilization of Mother Earth by a father: the Pharaoh Akhenaton's Aton, the sun-disk, who is 'the Unconquerable Sun', 'Sol Invictus', of the Illyrian Roman Emperors from Aurelian to Constantine the Great.

The biosphere's fund of physical energy—which is the material source of life and also the source of the physical power present in inanimate nature that Man has now harnessed—does not originate within the biosphere itself. This physical energy has been, and is constantly being, radiated into the biosphere from our sun, and also from other cosmic sources, and the biosphere's role in this vital reception of radiation from beyond its confines is merely selective. It has been mentioned already that the biosphere filters the radiation that impinges on it. It admits the life-giving rays and repels those that are lethal. But this beneficent play of radiation on the biosphere from external sources will continue to be beneficent only so long as the filter is not put out of action and so long as these sources of radiation remain unvarying; and our sun, like every other in the stellar cosmos, is undergoing change all the time. It is conceivable that, at some future date, some of these cosmic changes, either in our sun or in other stars, might so alter the incidence of the radiation received by our biosphere as to make what is now a biosphere uninhabitable, and, if and when our biosphere comes to be threatened with this disaster, it seems improbable that mankind's material power will be great enough to be able to counteract a deadly change in the play of cosmic forces.

Let us now consider the biosphere's components and the nature of their relations with each other. There are three components of the biosphere: first, matter that has never yet come to life through acquiring an organic structure; second, living organic matter; third, inanimate matter that has once been alive and organic and that still retains some organic qualities and powers. We know that the biosphere is younger than the planet that it envelops; we also know that, within the biosphere itself, life and consciousness have not been present for as long a time as the matter with which they have come to be associated. The film of matter that is now a biosphere was once wholly inanimate and unconscious, as the major part of the globe's matter still is. We do not know how or why a part of the material substance of the biosphere eventually became animate, nor how or why, at a still later stage, a part of this live matter became conscious. We can put the same question conversely: How and why did life and consciousness become incarnate? But, in this converse form too, the answer to the riddle still eludes us.

The ex-organic component of the biosphere is surprisingly large, and it has provided mankind with some of the most important resources for the maintenance of human life. By now it is common knowledge that coral reefs and islands have been produced by myriads of animalculae, each adding its tiny increment of solid and enduring artificial rock. In the course of aeons the work done by these animalculae has added appreciably to the area of dry land in the biosphere that is habitable for non-aquatic forms of life. These minute but multitudinous and indefatigable living beings have built a larger aggregate area of habitable insular terra firma than the mighty inanimate force of volcanic action, which has emulated the coral-making animalculae in piling up solid matter under water till an island has emerged above the surface of the sea.

It is also now common knowledge that coal is a product of the carcases of once live trees and that fertile soil derives part of its fertility from having been passed through the bodies of worms and through being populated by bacteria of kinds that enhance the soil's capacity for giving sustenance to vegetation; but the layman is still surprised if a geologist suggests to him that the limestone that now strikes the eye in the jagged sky-lines of some of the biosphere's present mountain ranges is a product of age-long deposits of the shells or bones of marine animals on the beds of vanished seas, and that these horizontal deposits of once live organic matter have been buckled—recently, in terms of the geologists' time-scale—by a contraction of the Earth's crust till the stuff has ruckled up into its present contorted shapes. The layman is still more surprised if it is suggested that the vast subterranean deposits of mineral oil may also be ex-organic matter—may, that is to say, be akin to coal and not to iron-ore or granite: substances that have never passed through an organic stage in the configuration of their constituent molecules.

The surprising magnitude of the amount of ex-organic matter in the biosphere calls our attention to some disconcerting aspects of the history of life (misnamed 'evolution', a word that means, not genuine change, but merely the 'unfolding' of something that has always been there latently). Life has come to be differentiated into a number of distinct genera and species, and each species is represented by a number of specimens. The multiplicity of species and specimens has been the enabling condition for the progression of life from relatively simple and weak to relatively complex and potent organisms, but the price of this progression through division and differentiation has been competition and strife. Each species, and each specimen of each species, has been in competition with others for appropriating those constituents of the biosphere, both inanimate and animate, that, for a particular species and for its specimens, are resources in the sense of being effective means for the maintenance of life. In some cases the competition has been indirect; one species, or one specimen of a species, has extinguished another, not by preying on it or by exterminating it, but by winning for itself the lion's share of some resource which, for both competitors, is one of the necessities of life. When the specimens of non-human species of animals contend with each other for food, or for water, or for mating, the losers are reputed to ask for quarter and to receive this from the winners in return for the losers' surrender. Human beings are reputed to be the only animals that fight each other to the death and that massacre 'the enemy's' women and children and old men as well as his combatant males. This distinctively human form of atrocity was being perpetrated in Vietnam at the moment at which I was writing these words in London, and it has been celebrated—and thus unintentionally execrated— in famous works of art created within the last 5,000 years: for instance, the palette of Narmer; the bas-relief of Eannatum; the stele of Naramsin and the monuments of his subsequent Assyrian emulators; the Homeric Greek epics; and Trajan's column.

Thus the progression of life has, at best, been parasitic, while, at worst, it has been predatory. The Animal Kingdom has been parasitic on the Vegetable Kingdom; animals (non-marine animals, at any rate) could not have come into existence if vegetation had not been in existence already as a source of life-giving air and food for animals; some species of animals maintain themselves by killing and devouring animals of other species; and Man has become one of these carnivores since the date at which he descended from his former shelter aloft in the trees and ventured on to the ground to take his chance there of slaying or being slain. The victims of life's progression are the species that have become extinct and the representatives of surviving species that are continually being slaughtered. Man has domesticated some species of non-human animals in order to rob them of their produce—milk or honey—while they are alive and to kill them ruthlessly in order to use their flesh for food and their bones and sinews and hides and fur as raw materials for making tools and clothes.

Human beings have also preyed on each other. Cannibalism and enslavement have been practised in highly sophisticated societies—both these enormities in pre-Columbian Meso-America, for instance, and slavery in the Graeco-Roman and Islamic and Modern Western societies. A slave is a human being who is treated as if he were a non-human domestic animal, and the shockingness of Man's treatment of non-human animals has been confessed implicitly in the movement during the last two centuries for abolishing the practice of enslaving human beings. Moreover, the juridical emancipation of slaves may not liberate them actually; for a juridical freeman can be exploited servilely. A nominally free fourth-century A.D. Roman colonus, and a contemporary Roman decurion too, was less free *de facto* than a first-century A.D. Roman slave-herdsman or slave-estate-manager or slave-clerk in the Emperor's household, or than an Islamic mamluk (this Arabic word means 'reduced to being a piece of property': yet, for a mamluk, juridical enslavement was the avenue to becoming the lord and master of a host of juridically free peasants). The Blacks in the United States who were emancipated juridically in 1862 are, with good reason, feeling now, more than a century later, that they are still being denied full human rights by the White majority of their fellow-citizens.

The distinctively human enormity that is dying hardest is murder in the ritual form of human sacrifice. Murder has been widely condemned when the motive has been personal covetousness or hatred. Murder as a punishment for murder has also been progressively discountenanced. Not only private blood-feuds but official executions have been abolished in some present-day states. Ritual murder too has been prohibited in cases in which the god to whom the human victim is sacrificed is a deification of one or other of the natural resources for the maintenance of human life—for instance, rain or crops or livestock. However, since the date at which Man gained the upper hand over non-human nature, the gods that have been most devoutly and fanatically and remorselessly worshipped have been deifications of the organized collective human power through which Man's victory over non-human nature has been won.

Sovereign states have been mankind's paramount objects of worship during the last 5,000 years; and these are goddesses which have demanded and received hecatombs of human sacrifices. Sovereign states go to war with each other, and in war they each require the choicest of their young male subjects to murder the subjects of the 'enemy' state at the risk of themselves being murdered by their intended victims. Till within living memory, all human beings except a few small minorities—for instance, the members of the Society of Friends—have looked upon killing and being killed in war as being not only legitimate but meritorious and glorious. Killing in war, as well as killing in the execution of a death sentence, has been condoned paradoxically as being 'no murder'.

Has the progression of life in the biosphere been worth its price in anguish? Is a human being more valuable than a tree, or a tree than an amoeba? The progression of life has produced an ascending series of species only if we assess ascent in terms of power. Mankind is the most potent species that has arisen so far, but mankind alone is evil. Human beings are unique in being able to be wicked, because they are unique in being conscious of what they are doing and in making deliberate choices. The poet William Blake, thinking of living creatures in traditional terms as being the handiwork of a human-like creator god, was rightly appalled by the creation of the tiger. But a tiger, unlike both a man and a hypothetical creator god, is innocent. When a tiger satisfies his hunger by killing and eating his victim, he suffers no pangs of conscience. On the other hand, it would have been a purposeless and unnecessary and supremely wicked act if a god had created the tiger to prey upon the lamb and had created the human being to slay the tiger and had created the bacillus and the virus to maintain its species by killing human beings *en masse*.

Thus, at first glance, the progression of life looks evil—evil objectively, even if we discard the belief that this evil has been deliberately created by a god who, if he has done his work deliberately, must be more wicked than any human being has ever yet had the power to be. However, this first judgment on the consequences of the progression of life testifies that, besides the evil in the biosphere, there is a conscience in the biosphere which condemns and abhors what is evil.

This conscience resides in Man. The human conscience's revolt against evil is evidence that Man is also capable of being good, and we know from experience that human beings can, and sometimes do, act unselfcentredly and disinterestedly to the point of sacrificing themselves completely for the sake of their fellows. We also know that self-sacrifice is not an exclusively human virtue. The classic motive for self-sacrifice is a mother's love for her children, and human mothers are not alone in sacrificing themselves in this cause. Self-sacrificing maternal love is found in other species of mammals, and also in birds.

Moreover, all those species that maintain themselves in existence by reproducing themselves obtain from their living specimens a co-operation between representatives of the two sexes which is not of direct benefit to the individuals themselves but is a service performed by them for the species. On a panoramic view, we can also see that the interplay between the various species of life does not solely take the form of competition and conflict. While the relation between the Vegetable Kingdom and the Animal Kingdom is in one aspect a relation between an exploited host and a predatory parasite, in another aspect the two kingdoms act as partners working in the common interest of keeping the biosphere habitable for plants and animals alike. This co-operative interplay secures, for instance, the distribution and circulation of oxygen and carbon dioxide in a rhythmic movement that makes life possible.

Thus the progression of life in the biosphere appears to reveal in itself two tendencies that are antithetical and contrary to each other. When a human being surveys the history of the biosphere as far as its present point, he finds that it has produced both evil and good and both wickedness and virtuousness. These are, of course, exclusively human concepts. Only a being that possesses consciousness can distinguish between evil and good and can choose between acting wickedly and acting virtuously. These concepts are non-existent for non-human living creatures, and they are deemed to be evil or good by human acts of judgment.

Does this mean that ethical standards are imposed arbitrarily by a human fiat, and that this fiat is irrelevant to the facts of life and is therefore Utopian? We might be constrained to draw this conclusion if Man were simply a spectator and a censor, viewing and appraising the biosphere from outside. Certainly Man is both a spectator and a censor. These roles of his are corollaries of his faculty of consciousness and of his consequent unavoidable power and need to make ethical choices and to pass ethical judgments. But mankind is also a branch of the tree of life; we are one of the products of life's progression; and this means that Man's ethical standards and judgments are inherent in the biosphere and therefore in the total reality of which the biosphere is a part. Thus life and consciousness and good and evil are no less real than the matter with which, in the biosphere, they are mysteriously associated. If we guess that matter is a primordial constituent of reality, we have no ground for supposing that these non-material manifestations of reality are not primordial likewise.

However, in the progression of life in the biosphere, consciousness has made its appearance here at the relatively recent date of the appearance of Man, and in our time we have become aware, belatedly and abruptly, that Man's presence is now presenting a threat to the habitability of the biosphere for all forms of life, including human life itself. Hitherto, the competition and conflict that have been one aspect of the progression of life have caused the extinction of numerous species of living beings, and have also inflicted premature, violent, and painful deaths on innumerable specimens of all species. Mankind has taken a toll of human sacrifice from itself, besides dealing death to rival species of predators and wiping out a number of species of plants. Even sharks and bacteria and viruses are no longer a match for their human antagonists. However, until our own time, this destruction of particular species and of individual specimens of species has not seemed to carry with it a threat to the survival of life itself. Hitherto, the extinction of some species of life has opened up opportunities for other species to flourish.

Man has been the most successful of all the species in mastering the other constituents of the biosphere, both animate and inanimate. At the dawn of his consciousness, Man found himself at the mercy of non-human nature; he set himself to make himself non-human nature's master, and he has advanced progressively towards the attainment of this objective. Within the last 10,000 years, he has challenged natural selection by substituting human selection for it, in so far as he has had the power. He has fostered the survival of plants and animals that he has domesticated for his own requirements, and he has set out to exterminate some other species that he has found obnoxious. He has labelled these unwanted species 'weeds' and 'vermin', and, in giving them these pejorative labels, he has served notice that he is going to do his utmost to exterminate them. In so far as Man has succeeded in substituting human selection for natural selection, Man has reduced the number of surviving species.

However, during the first stage of his career, which has been by far the longest stage so far, Man did not make as great a mark on the biosphere as was being made by some of his fellow living beings of other species. The pyramids at Gizah and at Teotihuacán, and the man-made mountains at Cholula and at Sakai, dwarf the temples and cathedrals and 'sky-scrapers' of later ages, yet Man's most massive monuments are puny by comparison with the work of the animalculae that have built the coral islands. By the date of the dawn of civilization, about 5,000 years ago, Man had become conscious of the pre-eminence of the power that he had acquired in the biosphere; before the beginning of the Christian Era he had discovered that the biosphere is a finite envelope round the surface of a star that is a globe; since the fifteenth century of the Christian Era, Europeans have been appropriating and populating the once sparsely populated portions of the biosphere's land-surface. Yet, until the present generation, mankind has continued to behave in practice as if the supply of the biosphere's non-replaceable resources, such as minerals, was inexhaustible, and as if the sea and air were unpollutable.

These constituents of the biosphere seemed, in fact, until lately, to be virtually infinite when measured in terms of Man's ability to use them up or to pollute them. In my childhood (I was born in 1889) it would still have seemed fantastic to imagine that Man would ever have the power to pollute the whole of the biosphere's circumambient atmosphere, though in London, where I grew up, and also in Manchester and in St. Louis and in an increasing number of other cities by then, the smoke generated by the domestic and industrial burning of coal was producing fogs that intercepted the sun's light and choked human lungs for several days on end. This menace to the purity of the atmosphere was discounted as being no more than a local and occasional nuisance. As for the possibility that human activities might pollute the sea, this would have been considered a ridiculous fantasy.

The truth is that, until the third quarter of the twentieth century A.D. mankind had underestimated the modern increase in its power to affect the biosphere. This increase has been produced by two new departures: first, the deliberate systematic pursuit of scientific research and the application of this to the advancement of technology; second, the harnessing, for application to human purposes, of the physical energy patent or latent in the inanimate constituents of the biosphere: for instance, the energy of the water that is perpetually flowing downwards towards sea-level after having been drawn up from sea-level into the atmosphere. Since the outbreak of the Industrial Revolution in Britain two hundred years ago, this gravitational water-power, which previously had been applied to little else than the grinding of corn, has been harnessed to drive machinery for the manufacture of many kinds of material commodities. Water-power has also been raised to higher degrees of potency by being converted into steam-power and into electric power. Electricity can be generated from the physical force of natural or artificial waterfalls, but water cannot be converted into steam without being heated by the combustion of fuels, and these have been used, not only for converting water-power into steam-power and electric power, but for superseding the use of water-power even in its most potent form. Moreover, charcoal, a replenishable fuel derived from wood, has been superseded by non-replaceable fuels: coal, mineral oil, and eventually uranium.

Uranium, the most recently exploited fuel, releases atomic energy, but, in venturing to manipulate this titanic force, Man, since 1945, has embarked on the adventure that ended fatally for the mythical demigod Phaethon when he usurped the chariot of his divine father the Sun. The steeds of Helios' chariot kicked over the traces when they found that the reins had been taken over by a weak mortal's hands. They plunged out of their proper course, and the biosphere would have been burnt to cinders if Zeus had not saved it from destruction by summarily thunderbolting the Sun's presumptuous mortal *remplaçant*. The myth of Phaethon is an allegory of the risk to which Man has exposed himself by playing with atomic energy. It remains to be seen whether Man will be able to utilize this mighty material force with impunity. Its power is unprecedentedly great, but so, too, is the poisonousness of its aftermath of radio-active waste. Man has now interfered with the process by which the biosphere—life's Mother Earth—has been impregnated with solar radiation on terms that are life-giving, not lethal. This portentous feat of human scientific technology, in conjunction with the effects of the lesser previous achievements of the Industrial Revolution, is now threatening to make the biosphere uninhabitable.

Thus we now stand at a turning-point in the history of the biosphere and in the shorter history of one of its products and denizens, mankind. Man has been the first of Mother Earth's children to subdue life's mother and to wrest out of the hands of life's father, the Sun, the fearful force of solar power. Man has now let this power loose in the biosphere, naked and untempered, for the first time since the biosphere became habitable for life. Today we do not know whether Man is going to be willing or able to avoid bringing Phaethon's fate on himself and on his fellow living beings.

Man is the first species of living being in our biosphere that has acquired the power to wreck the biosphere and, in wrecking it, to liquidate himself. As a psychosomatic organism, Man is subject, like every other form of life, to an inexorable law of Nature. Man, like his fellow living beings of other kinds, is an integral part of the biosphere, and, if the biosphere were to be made uninhabitable, Man, as well as all other species, would become extinct.

The biosphere has been able to harbour life because the biosphere has been a self-regulating association of mutually complementary components, and, before the emergence of Man, no single component of the biosphere—organic, ex-organic, or inorganic—ever acquired the power to upset the delicately adjusted balance of the play of forces by means of which the biosphere has become a hospitable home for life. Pre-human species of living beings that were either too incompetent or too aggressive to keep in tune with the biosphere's rhythm were liquidated by the play of this rhythm long before their incompetence or aggressiveness came anywhere near to threatening to derange the rhythm on which their life, and the life of all other species, depended. The biosphere was vastly more potent than any of its pre-human denizens.

Man is the first of the biosphere's denizens that is more potent than the biosphere itself. Man's acquisition of consciousness has enabled him to make choices and therefore to devise and to carry out plans that can prevent Nature from liquidating him as she has liquidated other species that have become a nuisance and a menace to the biosphere as a whole. Man can succeed in surviving till he has wrecked the biosphere if he chooses to wreck it, but, if he does make this choice, he cannot escape its nemesis. If Man wrecks the biosphere he will extinguish himself as well as all other forms of psychosomatic life on the face of life's mother, the Earth.

From this point, therefore, we can make a retrospective survey of the history, to date, of the encounter between Mother Earth and Man, the mightiest and most enigmatic of all her children. The enigma lies in the mysterious fact that Man, alone among the inhabitants of the biosphere, is also an inhabitant of another realm as well—a spiritual realm that is non-material and invisible. In the biosphere Man is a psychosomatic being, acting within a world that is material and finite. On this plane of human activity, Man's objective, ever since he became conscious, has been to make himself master of his non-human environment, and in our day he has come within sight of success in this endeavour—possibly to his own undoing. But Man's other home, the spiritual world, is also an integral part of total reality; it differs from the biosphere in being both non-material and infinite; and, in his life in the spiritual world Man finds that his mission is to seek, not for a material mastery over his non-human environment, but for a spiritual mastery over himself.

These two antithetical objectives, and the two different ideals by which they are inspired have been expounded in famous texts. The classical directive to Man to make himself master of the biosphere is given in verse 28 of the first chapter of the Book of Genesis:

Be fruitful and multiply and replenish the Earth and subdue it, and have dominion over the fish of the sea and over the fowl of the air and over every living thing that moveth upon the Earth.

This directive is clear and emphatic, but so, too, are the rejections of it. 'Lead us not into temptation but deliver us from evil' reads like a direct reply to the directive in the Book of Genesis, and the New Testament has been anticipated by the *Tao tê Ching* in declaring that Man's technological and organizational achievements are a snare.

> The more 'sharp weapons' there are,
> The more benighted will the whole land grow.
> The more cunning craftsmen there are,
> The more pernicious contrivances will be invented.
> The more laws are promulgated,
> The more thieves and bandits there will be.[1]
>
> Stretch a bow to the very full,
> And you will wish that you had stopped in time.[2]

He could bring it about that, though there should be among the people contrivances requiring ten times, a hundred times, less labour, they would

[1] *Tao tê Ching*, ch. 57, in Arthur Waley's translation, *The Way and its Power* (London, 1934, Allen and Unwin), p. 211.
[2] Op. cit., ch. 9, on p. 152.

not use them. . . . There might still be boats and carriages, but no one would go in them; there might still be weapons of war, but no one would drill with them.[1]

These passages of the *Tao tê Ching* have their counterpart in the Gospel according to St. Matthew:

Consider the lilies of the field, how they grow. They toil not, neither do they spin; and yet I say unto you that even Solomon in all his glory was not arrayed like one of these.[2]

These are repudiations of the call to dedicate ourselves to the acquisition of power and wealth. They clear the air for a call to embrace an opposite ideal.

Whosoever will come after me, let him deny himself and take up his cross and follow me. For whosoever will save his life shall lose it; but whosoever shall lose his life for my sake and the gospel's, the same shall save it. For what shall it profit a man if he shall gain the whole world and lose his own soul? Or what shall a man give in exchange for his soul?[3]

If a human being were to lose his soul, he would cease to be human; for the essence of being human is an awareness of a spiritual presence behind the phenomena, and it is as a soul, not as a psychosomatic organism, that a human being is in communication with this spiritual presence, or is even identical with it in the experience of the mystics.

Living, as he does live, in the biosphere and in the spiritual world simultaneously, Man is truly an amphibian, as he has aptly been called by Sir Thomas Browne, and, in each of the two elements in which he is at home, Man has an objective. But he cannot pursue each of two objectives, or serve each of two masters, whole-heartedly. One of his two objectives and one of his two allegiances must be given paramountcy, or must even be given exclusive devotion if the two turn out to be incompatible and irreconcilable. Which of the two alternatives is to be chosen? The debate over this question had become explicit in India in the Buddha's generation, about half way through the last millennium B.C. It was explicit in the West in the generation of St. Francis of Assisi in the thirteenth century A.D. On both these occasions, a taking of opposite choices led to a parting of the ways between a father and a son. The issue has probably been implicitly under debate since the dawn of consciousness; for one of the home truths that is revealed to a human being by consciousness is the moral ambivalence of human nature. However, at most times and places down to the present day, people have avoided bringing into the open the question that moved the Buddha and

[1] Op. cit., ch. 80, on p. 241.   [2] Matt. 6: 28–29.
[3] Mark 8: 34–37. Cp. Matt. 16: 24–26; Luke 9: 23–25.

St. Francis in turn to break away from their natural ties with their
families. It is only in our own generation that the choice has become
inescapable for mankind as a whole.

In our generation, Man's completion of his mastery over the whole of
the biosphere is threatening to defeat Man's intentions by wrecking the
biosphere and extinguishing life, including human life itself. Since the
thirteenth century Western Man has professedly honoured Francesco
Bernardone, the saint who renounced the inheritance of a lucrative
family business and who was rewarded with Christ's stigmata for his
espousal of the Lady Poverty. But the example that Western Man has
actually followed has not been St. Francis's; Western Man has emulated
the saint's father, Pietro Bernardone, the successful wholesale cloth-
merchant. Since the outbreak of the Industrial Revolution, Modern
Man has dedicated himself, more obsessively than any of his forebears,
to the pursuit of the objective set before him in the first chapter of the
Book of Genesis.

It looks as if Man will not be able to save himself from the nemesis of
his demonic material power and greed unless he allows himself to undergo a change of heart that will move him to abandon his present objective
and to espouse the contrary ideal. His present self-inflicted plight has
confronted him with a peremptory challenge. Can he bring himself to
accept, as necessary practical rules of conduct for people of ordinary
moral stature, those precepts, preached and practised by saints, that
hitherto have been regarded as being Utopian counsels of perfection for
l'homme moyen sensuel? The long-drawn-out debate over this issue that
seems to be approaching a climax in our day is the theme of the present
chronicle of Mankind's encounter with Mother Earth.

[3]

THE DESCENT OF MAN

THERE are at least three different senses in which the word 'descent' can be taken in relation to the word 'Man'. Our ancestors descended, in the literal physical sense, from living up aloft in the trees to living on the ground. They are descended genetically from pre-human forms of life. It has also been held (though this is a controversial thesis) that they descended morally when they awoke to consciousness.

The third of these three applications of the word 'descent' is surely unwarrantable. It is true that a conscious being can be wicked, whereas a non-conscious being cannot be. But the inability to be wicked is not tantamount to being virtuous. A conscious being can be virtuous, besides being able to be wicked; a non-conscious being cannot be either wicked or virtuous. For a non-conscious being the ethical distinction between wickedness and virtuousness does not, and cannot, exist. Ethics first appeared in the biosphere simultaneously with consciousness. Together, consciousness and ethics constitute a mode of existence—the spiritual mode—which had not been represented in the biosphere previously. Thus there is no basis for a comparison in ethical terms between Man and his pre-conscious ancestors. They can be compared with each other on the biological plane, and, on this plane, Man's affiliation to his forebears can be recognized and traced, but on the ethical plane there is no common ground, since the ethical plane exists for conscious beings only.

On the ethical plane the most conspicuous and enigmatic feature of human nature is the extent of Man's ethical gamut. The range of his ethical potentialities between the two poles of diabolism and saintliness is as remarkable a feature of human life as the ethical dimension itself. Both features are peculiar to Man among all the denizens of the biosphere. Now that Man has acquired the power to wreck the biosphere, we cannot be sure that he will not commit this suicidal crime; but we also cannot be sure that he will not redeem the biosphere from the state of nature in which, so far, love and strife have been at issue with each other inconclusively. It is conceivable that, instead of wrecking the biosphere, Man may use his power over the biosphere to replace the state of nature by a state of grace in which love will prevail. This would transfigure life from a pandemonium into a communion of saints.

When we take the word descent in its genetic meaning, it confronts us with the question of the age of *genus homo*. Manifestly there is a valid sense in which Man is coeval with all other surviving species of living beings and, in fact, with life itself; for, though evolution has proceeded by differentiation, the different species that evolution has produced are all related to each other like the branches of a tree. They all derive from a common root. If we seek to date the genesis of Man more distinctively, we shall single out the date at which the family of hominids branched off from other families within the order of primates among the mammals. This parting of the genetic ways marks a point of no return. For hominids, it cut off the possibility of their becoming *hylobatidae* (e.g. gibbons) or *pongidae* (e.g. orang-outangs, chimpanzees, gorillas). When once the progenitor of the hominids had passed this forking-point, and had passed it by taking the hominid road, the hominids were left with only two alternative possibilities. They could become human or alternatively they would fail to survive. Actually the only genus that has survived within the hominid family is *homo*, and, within *genus homo*, the only species that still survives is *homo sapiens* (an undeservedly flattering label which this sole surviving species of hominid has affixed to itself with naïve self-conceit). If we reckon Man to be as old as the date at which it had ceased to be possible for our ancestors, if they were to survive, to become anything other than human, then Man must be held to have originated, as a distinctive form of life, in the miocene age or even possibly as long ago as the latest phase of the oligocene; and, on this reckoning, Man would have been in existence for about twenty million to twenty-five million years by now.

Can we date the age of mankind still more closely by equating it with one or other of Man's distinctive anatomical features or distinctive habits and accomplishments? Can we say that our ancestors became human when they descended from the trees to the ground? Or when they acquired the capacity to walk and run by using only one pair of limbs for locomotion, thus liberating the other pair for manipulating tools? Or when they developed brains that were not only much larger than those of any other hominid, but also much more highly organized in the sense that the number of possible alternative patterns of inter-communication between the brain-cells was very much greater? Or can we date the genesis of human nature by its achievement of such accomplishments as sociality or as language (i.e. a code of sounds conveying meanings intelligible to all the members of a community, as contrasted with a set of ejaculations expressing emotions)? Or did Prometheus make our ancestors human by teaching them how, without burning their fingers, to keep fire alight and how to use it, for warming and cooking, and how to kindle it, instead of being terrified of this potentially useful but also potentially dangerous and destructive force?

The answer surely is that the event which dates the first appearance of human nature in the biosphere is neither the development of an anatomical feature nor the acquisition of an accomplishment; the historic event is Man's awakening to consciousness. The date of this event can only be inferred from the material traces left by our ancestors (e.g. bones and tools). There is not, and there could not have been, any contemporary awareness of the experience, and consequently there could not have been any record of it. A human being is aware of being awake when he is awake, but he cannot catch himself consciously experiencing the process of either waking up or going to sleep. Therefore, we can do no more than guess the date of Man's awakening to consciousness in terms of his anatomical development and his achievement of particular social and technological accomplishments.

We may guess, as an inference from our ancestors' survival after descending from the shelter of the trees to the comparatively dangerous ground-level that, by then, they were already social animals or that at least they had become such in the act of shifting their habitat. At ground-level, solitary hominids would have been an easy prey for non-hominid predators for whom, at that stage, our ancestors would have been no match if they had not banded together. Certainly Man must have been a social animal before he invented language; but his invention of language may have been a much more recent event than his achievement of sociality; for there are other kinds of social animals (e.g. the social insects) that communicate with each other effectively for the maintenance of their necessary social co-operation without possessing a vocal language. Bees, for instance, appear to communicate information and instruction to each other by physical miming which, if they were human beings, we should describe as 'dancing'.

As for the liberation of the hands for other uses than locomotion, and the elaboration of the brain, we may guess that the development of hand and brain was contemporaneous and that, at each stage, there was an interplay between them which assisted the further evolution of each of them. The full development of these two interacting organs was, we may also guess, the anatomical enabling condition for Man's awakening to consciousness. Man must surely have been conscious already by the time when he overcame the fear of fire that is still felt by many species of undomesticated non-human animals. And Man can no longer have been

afraid of spontaneously kindled fire when he discovered how to keep it
alight and to make use of it and eventually to kindle it artificially.

Can we date the dawn of consciousness, either in terms of geological
ages or, still more audaciously, in terms of years B.C.? To try to date it is
all the more difficult if we guess—and this seems a reasonable guess—
that it was a gradual process which, though perhaps rapid in terms of the
geological time-scale, may have taken aeons in terms of the time-scale of
recorded human history (a record that has been kept for no more than
about 5,000 years, so far). We can be sure that the sole now surviving
species of *genus homo*, the self-styled *homo sapiens*, is not the only variety of
hominid that has possessed consciousness. Neanderthal Man is believed
to have disposed of the dead ceremonially, instead of just treating their
carcases as rubbish, and, if the evidence is cogent, it tells us that Neanderthal Man shared with *homo sapiens* the notion that human nature has
a dignity that does not extend to other forms of life.

Neanderthal Man seems to have survived until as recently as the
transition from the Lower Palaeolithic to the Upper Palaeolithic Age
perhaps some 70,000 or 40,000 years ago. There are even indications
that there were mixed communities of Neanderthalers and 'Sapientes',
and, if there were, it seems likely that these two kinds of human being
were physically enough akin to be able to interbreed with each other, as
all varieties of *homo sapiens* can. If so *homo sapiens* and *homo neanderthalensis*
might be classified as two sub-species of a single species. However, Peking
Man, whose date is guessed to be about half a million years ago, must be
reckoned as being a different species; and, if it is true that Peking Man
had already mastered fire, his consciousness must have been well developed. It must also have required a glimmer of consciousness to think
of chipping stones in order to make them more effectively serviceable as
tools, instead of merely using, as tools, unmodified natural objects, and
tool-making by stone-chipping is attributed to *australopithecus*—a hominid
whose date is guessed to be about two or three million years ago.
Australopithecus is classified as a hominid but not as *homo*, and it is not
certain that he is *homo*'s ancestor. In the autumn of 1972 a skull that is
very like *homo sapiens*'s skull was unearthed from under a layer of volcanic
ash that is estimated to be 2,600,000 years old.

Even the estimated dates of *australopithecus*'s and this early *homo-sapiens*-
like skull are recent compared with the date at which our common
ancestors are reckoned to have become differentiated irrevocably from
the ancestors of our cousins the *hylobatidae* and the *pongidae*. On the other
hand, if the Lower Palaeolithic Age is coeval with the first appearance of
the now long since extinct *australopithecus*, this Lower Palaeolithic Age
accounts for perhaps fifty-nine-sixtieths of the duration, to date, of the
hominidae, and for perhaps fourteen-fifteenths of the duration, to date, of

homo, including Peking Man and Neanderthal Man as well as *homo sapiens*. Unintentional records, in the form of shaped tools, are as old as *australopithecus*; but the earliest records that were made intentionally to serve as such are only about 20,000 or 30,000 years old if the Upper-Palaeolithic-Age paintings on the walls of caves in France and Spain are the oldest intentional records of any kind.

Records in the form of pictograms that were the forerunners of non-representational scripts were not made, so far as we know, till the fifth millennium B.C., and at that date, so far as we know, in Sumer only. Yet the material relics of extinct human societies which do not include written documents that have been deciphered and translated give us only fragmentary information about the life of the people who have left these non-documentary material traces of their existence. Pre-documentary archaeological evidence is informative about technology, but technology is merely an enabling condition for the non-material constituents of Man's way of life: his feelings and thoughts, his institutions and ideas and ideals. These are more important manifestations of human nature than technology; it is one of Man's nobler distinctive characteristics that he does not live by bread alone; and, though the material debris of technology does throw light on some of the non-material facets of human life, this light is dim. Inferences from what is material to what is spiritual are, at best, shots in the dark, and, when the material evidence is all that we have, it leaves some aspects of spiritual life shrouded in complete obscurity.

Thus our information is far more copious and more illuminating for the last 5,000 years of history—the documented 5,000 years—than it is for the first million or half million years after the probably gradual dawn of consciousness. Is the significance of the later and shorter of these two periods proportionate to the degree of our knowledge of it? We must be on our guard against taking this for granted. What is nearest and clearest inevitably looms largest; yet this appearance may not correspond to the reality. The course of the so-called 'pre-historic age'—meaning the age before the making of written records that have survived and have also been deciphered and translated—was (in so far as we can discern it) monotonous, besides being enormously long, by comparison with the course of the subsequent documented age. Viewed against the background of 'pre-history', all documented history is virtually contemporary history in the literal sense, as well as in the subjective sense in which Benedetto Croce held that all history is contemporary history. Subjectively the past is inevitably seen by an observer as it looks to him on a retrospective view taken from the standpoint of the observer's own time and place.

Are we to conclude that these virtually contemporary last five millennia are the only fraction of history that counts? This conclusion would be paradoxical, and it is surely ruled out by the fact that the 'pre-historic' age was inaugurated by the most momentous event to date in human history, namely the dawn of consciousness in the biosphere. This achievement was so immense, and the effort demanded by it must have been so arduous, that it is not surprising that the dawn of consciousness should have been followed by a million or half a million years of torpor, before Man began to exercise actively the spiritual and material power with which his awakening to consciousness had endowed him. If we now look back from the present moment to the dawn, and if we regard the whole of human history since the dawn as being one single epoch, perhaps we may find the normal rhythm of this epoch in the relative torpor of the Lower Palaeolithic Age. Then the increasing speed and vehemence and variety of the subsequent 70,000 or 40,000 years, running from the outbreak of the Upper Palaeolithic Industrial Revolution to the harnessing of atomic energy, will look not so much like all that counts as like a grand finale that is heading towards a climax.

This climax might be the annihilation of life through the wrecking of the biosphere by human wickedness and folly now that the devil incarnate in Man has armed himself with sufficient technological power. Alternatively, the climax might prove to be a transition from the first epoch of human history to a second, or, more probably, to a long series of successive epochs; for the two million years that have passed since the first stone was chipped into a more useful shape by *australopithecus* is the twinkling of an eye compared with the 2,000 million years more, for which, so it has been estimated, the biosphere will continue to be habitable if Man permits. We cannot foresee the future, but we can augur that we are approaching an ethical parting of the ways that will be as decisive as the biological parting, twenty or twenty-five million years ago, between the way that has led to Man and the way that has led to the hominoid apes. Once again, the alternatives may be polar extremes. The narrative in the rest of this book carries the story up to the verge of the clarification of this still dark riddle.

[4]

THE OIKOUMENÊ

THE Oikoumenê is a Greek term which became current in the Hellenic
Age of Greek history after the Hellenic Greek World had expanded, first
westward and then eastward, from its original domain astride the Aegean
Sea. Its westward expansion carried it to the Atlantic coasts of Europe
and North-West Africa and into western Europe's largest off-shore island,
Britain. Its subsequent eastward expansion carried it into Central Asia
and India. The way for its eastward expansion was opened by Alexander
the Great's conquest and overthrow of the First Persian Empire, and the
post-Alexandrine Age of Hellenic history was the time when the term
'Oikoumenê' became current. Its literal meaning is 'the Inhabited (Part
of the World)'—ἡ οἰκουμένη νῆ—but in practice the Greek inventors
and users of the term restricted its application to the fraction of the
inhabited part of the World that was occupied by so-called 'civilized'
societies. The participants in the societies of this kind have called themselves 'civilized' till our own time, when our horrifying and humiliating
experience of the atrocities that we have committed has taught us that
civilization has never yet been an accomplished fact, but has merely been
an endeavour or aspiration that, hitherto, has always fallen far short
of its ambitious target.

Even in its original restricted usage, in which the barbarians on the
fringes of the civilizations were ignored, the post-Alexandrine Greek
Oikoumenê embraced only the domains of the civilizations with which
the Greeks themselves had become familiar. Since at least as early as the
generation of the historian Herodotus in the fifth century B.C., the Greeks
had been dimly aware of a 'Hyperborean' civilization that was in contact with the Greek colonial city-states along the north coast of the
Black Sea, via a trail running across the Eurasian steppe that was the
continental hinterland of these Greek maritime colonies. We may guess
that, notwithstanding the meaning of their name, the 'Hyperboreans'

lay, not 'beyond the North Wind', but to the east of the steppe, and that they were in truth the Chinese, who were known to the post-Alexandrine Greeks and Romans as 'Seres' or 'Sinae'.

By the time most of the Graeco-Roman World had been united politically in the Roman Empire, silk was being imported into the Graeco-Roman World both overland and by sea; but the so-called 'civilized' peoples at the east and the west ends of the Old World were still only faintly aware of each other's existence. The Chinese equivalent of the Greek 'Oikoumenê' is 'All that is under Heaven', but, for the Chinese, Ta Ch'in, the big replica of the Chinese Empire at the west end of the Continent, was as hazy as the Sinae or Seres or Hyperboreans were for the Greeks and Romans. The two extremities of the Continent were only belatedly brought into direct contact with each other—first temporarily, in the thirteenth century, by the incorporation of all the shores of the Eurasian steppe in the huge but ephemeral Mongol Empire, and then permanently, since before the close of the fifteenth century, by the West European peoples' conquest of the Ocean. As for the civilizations of Meso-America and of the Andean strip of South America, these were unknown to any of the inhabitants of the Old World until after Columbus had made his first landfall on the American side of the Atlantic. Yet the civilizations of Meso-America and Peru had blossomed into their 'classic' full flower perhaps as early as the beginning of the Christian Era, while the antecedent 'formative' period of these American higher cultures may have begun—in Meso-America, at any rate—as early as the beginning of any of the Old-World civilizations except the Sumero-Akkadian and the Pharaonic Egyptian.

If we use the term Oikoumenê in its literal meaning of the habitat of mankind, we can see that the true extent of the Oikoumenê is much larger than the area of the 'civilized' world known to the Greeks and Romans, but we can also see that this comprehensive Oikoumenê is nevertheless much smaller than the biosphere. The major part of the biosphere's surface is occupied by the sea, and the biosphere's air-envelope accounts for the major part of the biosphere's volume. The sea is believed to have been the original habitat of life, and it is still rich in both flora and fauna; but, since the date at which Man's ancestors became terrene animals, they have not made themselves at home again in the sea, as their fellow-mammals the whales and porpoises have. Human beings have not even become amphibians like their other fellow-mammals the seals and otters. They have discovered how to traverse the surface of rivers and seas in boats and ships, and how to dive—not very deep and not for very long at a time—below the sea's surface; but, on or in the water, human beings are only wayfarers; they are not inhabitants —they are, in fact, not an aquatic species.

In the twentieth century A.D., Man has also invented aircraft; but, in taking to the air, Man has been anticipated, ages ago, by insects and birds and bats, and no bat, bird, insect or human being can live in the air, as the fish and the marine species of mammals can live in the water. In the air, no species of living being can be more than a wayfarer. A winged species may depend on being air-borne for winning its livelihood, but it cannot dispense with having either a terrene or an aquatic base of operations. Even swallows perch on telegraph-wires and build nests of clay for rearing their young.

Mankind's Oikoumenê lies wholly on the land-surface of the biosphere, though the Oikoumenê's human inhabitants traverse the biosphere's water-surface, and now its air-envelope too, in travelling from one part of the Oikoumenê to another. But the Oikoumenê is far from being co-extensive even with the biosphere's land-surface, and the extent of its area, within the coasts of the dry land, has fluctuated, as is illustrated by the current lethal drought in the Sahel, i.e. the belt of Savannah country in Africa between the former southern edge of the Sahara and the northern edge of the tropical rain-forest. The fluctuations have been caused partly by physiographical and climatic changes that Man has not initiated and has not had the power even to modify, and partly by human action, either deliberate or unintended. The non-human agencies that have shaped the Oikoumenê have been predominant over human action till within the last 10,000–12,000 years.

In the course of the planet Earth's history, the physiographical and climatic changes in this planet's constitution have been immense. Probably they were most extreme and most violent during the first aeon of the Earth's existence, before the biosphere appeared on the surface of the globe. Fossilized relics of plants and animals in strata of the Earth's crust that were on the surface in geological ages before the date of the appearance of Man have revealed that regions which are now temperate or sub-arctic once had a tropical climate. For these regional changes of climate there are several possible alternative explanations. One possibility is that the globe's axis may have veered, and that the points on the Earth's surface which are now the poles may once have been on or near the Equator; but, if so, it is hard to see how the Earth has managed to maintain the regularity of its rotatory motion and its elliptical orbit, without being thrown off its course by the postulated shift in its stance. An alternative possibility is that the continents may have drifted across the surface of the Earth, as if they were rafts afloat on a quagmire, not flag-stones bedded on rock. The theory of continental drift, like the theory of a displacement of the poles, is disputable and is perhaps un-verifiable, but, in some form or other, it seems to be winning adherence, and it is commended by the consideration that, unlike the alternative theory, it postulates, not a re-orientation of the whole of the globe, but only a change in the configuration of the globe's crust.

However, the enigmatic presence of tropical fossils in what are now non-tropical zones is the problem of a geological age that antedates the first appearance of hominids by many millions of years. The climatic phenomenon that has been contemporaneous with the presence of hominids in the biosphere is the series of glacial periods, alternating with thaws, during the pleistocene age—that is to say, during the last two million years. The latest glaciation (it would be rash to assume that this is the last glaciation that there is ever going to be) gave way to the present thaw about 12,000 or 10,000 years ago.

During the glacial periods the ice-caps seem never to have covered more than a small part of the land-surface of the biosphere. The glaciated areas lay mostly within the two polar zones, with some isolated patches of glaciation on high mountains less distant from the Equator. However, this partial glaciation excluded temporarily from the Oikoumenê some fertile soils (for instance in Skåne, in the insular part of Denmark, in Midlothian, and in Caithness) which have been highly productive since they have been brought under cultivation. Moreover, the local glaciations changed the ratio between sea and dry land in the dry land's favour. So great a volume of water was temporarily piled up and immobilized in the ice-caps that the sea-level dropped appreciably all round the globe. The beds of shallow seas were left high and dry; narrow seas became narrower; some straits were even bridged by isthmuses. In terms of the sea's mean depth and of the ratio of sea to dry land in the configuration of the planet's surface, this global effect of local glaciations was small; but it was great in terms of the opportunity for the expansion of Man's Oikoumenê in an age in which Man's only means of locomotion on land were his own feet and in which the shipwright's and the navigator's arts were still in their infancy.

Even when we have allowed for the facilitation of migration thanks to the temporary lowering of the sea-level, the early hominids' prowess in expanding the Oikoumenê is amazing in the eyes of present-day Man. This is because, within the last century and a half, we have invented a series of mechanized means of conveyance, starting with mechanized ships and railway-trains and following these up with mechanized road-vehicles and with aeroplanes. We shall feel less surprise at the hominids' expansion when we recall the corresponding feats of the non-hominid primates. These have colonized the Americas, as well as Asia together with its peninsulas and its off-shore islands. On the other hand, no genus of the hominid family except *genus homo*, and no species of *genus homo* except *homo sapiens*, has ever reached the Americas by sea from equatorial and southern East Africa, which seems to be the region in which the hominids first became differentiated from their cousins the great apes. All the surviving pre-Columbian human inhabitants of the Americas are descended from representatives of *homo sapiens* who made their way over-land to the Americas from the Continent during the latest bout of glaciation. The pre-Columbian Americans arrived from the north-east corner of Asia via a temporary isthmus that has subsequently been sub-merged beneath the Behring Straits; only the post-Columbian Ameri-cans and their Norse precursors from the European north-west corner of Asia traversed the Atlantic.

If *homo sapiens*, like his now extinct fellow-hominids, made his first appearance in tropical East Africa, the geographical distance covered by his trek on foot from there to Tierra del Fuego was certainly long. So too, however, was this trek's time-span. Moreover, Man, like other fauna, is mobile; he is not rooted to the Earth, like most of the bio-sphere's flora; yet the flora has disseminated itself as widely as the fauna, though most of the flora is dependent for its dissemination on the action of insects and of winds. Yet, when all this has been said, the range of Stone-Age Man's expansion is remarkable. Man had reached Tierra del Fuego and also Australia by at least as early as *circa* 6000 B.C., though, even when sea-level was at its lowest, the overland route from Asia to Australia was interrupted by a thirty-mile-wide stretch of sea between Borneo and Celebes. Stone-Age Man's most amazing *tour de force* was the colonization of Polynesia, including Easter Island. Within the last five hundred years, West Europeans and their colonists overseas have explored the whole surface of the biosphere. They have reached both of the Poles. Yet, except for the two polar regions, they have found few places that have not already been occupied by pre-European human inhabitants.

Man is peculiar among the primates in having lost his coat of fur except for a few patches covering only a small part of the surface of his body. For living in tropical regions where there was no screen of foliage between the naked human body and the sun, human beings needed to clothe themselves in artificial fur; and they also needed clothing for living in temperate or sub-arctic regions where they were exposed to frost. The Eskimo seal-hunter and the Arab pastoral nomad both clothe themselves thickly, the Eskimo in skins and the badu in woollen gar-ments. Man's mastery of fire enabled him to expand his Oikoumenê still farther. At the present day, modern technology is being used to extend the area of exploitation, if not the area of habitation, into the far north of the Soviet Union and Canada.

The ice-caps that cover the interiors of Greenland and of the much larger antarctic continent still lie beyond the bounds of the Oikoumenê, and so do some enclaves of tropical rain-forest, of snow-covered mountain country, and of bone-dry desert. But Man seems to be able to live in a wider range of climates than any of the other primates. If you traverse one of the cañons that have been carved deep into the soft volcanic soil of Ethiopia, you descend from the temperate surface of the plateau to a level at which the cañon is habitable for monkeys; but, before you reach the bottom, you leave the monkey's habitat behind. You descend to a depth at which the cañon is too hot to hold monkeys; but there is no altitude, from temperate plateau to tropical river-bed, at which Ethiopia is not habitable for Man.

The extent and the configuration of the Oikoumenê have not changed greatly since the recession of the latest glaciation about 12,000 or 10,000 years ago. The habitable dry land surface of the biosphere consists of a single continent, Asia, together with its peninsulas and its off-shore islands. Asia's most prominent peninsulas are Europe, Arabia, India, and Indo-China. This last would have been the largest of the four if it had extended continuously from Malaya to Australia and New Zealand. Actually, its middle section has sagged and has partly foundered, and Australia is now sundered from the mainland of Asia by the narrow sea of the Indonesian archipelago—a maze of straits and islands. The three largest of Asia's off-shore islands are Africa and the two Americas. The most distant of the islands is Antarctica. Africa is linked to Asia by the isthmus of Suez, and South America to North America by the isthmus of Panama. These two isthmuses have been transformed into artificial straits since they have been pierced by man-made canals. The most important of the natural straits are the Straits of Malacca, which provide a sea passage between the Indian Ocean and the Pacific.

The best channels of communication for conveying passengers or freight from one part of the Oikoumenê to another are outside the bounds of the Oikoumenê; for the most conductive elements are air and water, and these are elements which human beings can traverse but cannot inhabit. Till the invention, in the nineteenth century, of steam-driven locomotives hauling trains along rails, water-transport, by navigable river and by sea, was both quicker and cheaper than overland transport. In the pre-railway age, the only motive-power at Man's command for overland travel and transport was the muscle-power of human beings and animals. On the other hand, on the water, human muscle-power, plying punting-poles and oars, had been supplemented, before the dawn of civilization, by the harnessing of wind-power in sails. Wind-power was the first inanimate physical force to be harnessed by Man; it has also been the first to be discarded. It became superfluous when other inanimate physical forces were harnessed for operating machines.

In the age of water-transport, the main lines of communication were determined by the configuration of the water-surface of the biosphere. The most precious maritime waterways were straits (e.g. besides the Straits of Malacca, the narrow waters linking the Black Sea with the Aegean, the Straits of Gibraltar, the Straits of Dover, and the narrow waters linking the Baltic with the North Sea). The useful inland waterways were slow-flowing navigable rivers. The classic example was the Nile below the First Cataract. On this stretch of the Nile, a sailing-boat could float downstream with the current and could travel upstream under sail, since the north wind is the prevailing wind in Egypt. Moreover, after the opening-up of Egypt, no human settlement or field or even quarry in Egypt was very far from a navigable waterway. Before the invention of railways, Egypt's means of communication were better than those of any other country of that size.

In the age of water-transport, the key pieces of the land-surface of the Oikoumenê were those that offered portages from one sea or from one navigable river to another. Egypt itself was a portage area, since the Nile debouches into the Mediterranean, and, from the Nile to the Red Sea coast, there is a short portage from the easternmost arm of the Delta to Suez via the Wadi Tumilat, and another via the Wadi Hammamat from Coptos, in Upper Egypt, to Old Qusayr (Leukos Limen). Indeed, the portage across the Isthmus of Suez between the Red Sea and the Mediterranean is part of a wider portage area that includes Egypt to the west and Iraq to the east. In this area the Mediterranean, which is a backwater of the Atlantic Ocean, and the Red Sea and the Persian Gulf, which are backwaters of the Indian Ocean, are separated from each other by the narrowest extent of intervening dry land, and the passage from the Mediterranean to the Red Sea via the Nile is duplicated by the passage to the Persian Gulf via the Euphrates.

These unique facilities for communication made Egypt and South-West Asia the 'geopolitical' hub of the Oikoumenê in the Old World. It is surely not just an accident that this region was also the birthplace, first of the Neolithic culture, and then of the two earliest civilizations. Two other portages have been of outstanding historical importance: the portage between the rivers debouching into the Baltic and those debouching into the Caspian and the Black Sea, and the portage across the North China plain between the lower courses of the Yangtse, the Hwai, the Yellow River, and the Pei Ho—a portage that has been turned into a waterway by the digging of the Grand Canal. However, the Chinese and Russian portages are on the fringe of the Old-World Oikoumenê; they are surpassed in historical importance by the central portage between the Mediterranean and the Indian Ocean.

Within this dominant Egyptian and South-West Asian portage, traffic has been focused on two 'roundabouts'. One of these is in northern

Syria, between the westward bulge of the River Euphrates and the north-east corner of the Mediterranean Sea; the other is in present-day Afghanistan, astride a section of the Hindu Kush Range that is pierced by passes connecting the upper basins of the Oxus and Jaxartes Rivers with the upper basin of the Indus. Northern Syria is linked both over-land and by sea with Egypt; by sea with all the shores of the Medi-terranean and its backwaters and, through the Straits of Gibraltar, with the Atlantic; overland, through the Cilician Gates and across the Dardanelles and the Bosphorus, with Europe; overland, up the valley of the more northerly of the two headwaters of the Euphrates, with the Caspian Gates and the Oxus–Jaxartes basin and India; and down the Euphrates to the Persian Gulf, the Indian Ocean, and, through the Straits of Malacca, with the Pacific. Afghanistan is linked with Meso-potamia and with northern Syria via the Caspian Gates: with the Volga basin down the River Jaxartes and across the Eurasian steppe; with China via Sinkiang; with India through the passes that pierce the Suleyman Range.

Before the successive inventions of railways and of aeroplanes the traffic converging on, and radiating out of, the two 'roundabouts' made use of water-transport, by river or by sea, wherever this was practicable. Where passengers and freight had perforce to travel overland in the age before the beginning of mechanization, Man was at the mercy of the terrain. Mountains could be circumvented or surmounted; forests, temperate as well as tropical, were particularly obstructive; steppes were exceptionally conductive. Indeed, the three largest continuous areas of steppe—the Eurasian, the Arabian, and the North-African—became almost as conductive as the sea itself when Man domesticated service-able animals: donkeys, horses, and, above all, camels. With the aid of riding-animals, pack-carrying-animals, and draft-animals, human beings could cross the steppe almost as rapidly as they could cross the sea; but the use of both elements required organization and discipline. A caravan, like a ship, had to have a captain, and his orders had to be obeyed.

Even when the steppes, as well as the seas and the navigable rivers, had been brought into use for providing channels of communication between different parts of the Oikoumenê, mankind's media of inter-course remained inadequate until the dawn of the Machine Age. Even with these inadequate means, empires were put together and were held together successfully, and religions whose missionaries set out to convert all mankind did win and retain adherents over a wider range than was ever attained by any secular empire. The First Persian Empire, the Chinese Empire, the Roman Empire, the Arab Caliphate, and the three principal missionary religions—Buddhism, Christianity, and Islam—are monuments to the triumph of human will-power over physical impediments. But the limits of their success also reveal the limits of the scale that was practicable for human societies without the aid of the mechanical means of communication that have been invented since the beginning of the nineteenth century.

The most striking evidence of the inadequacy of means of communication before the beginning of the machine age is the number of different languages, current locally in different parts of the Oikoumenê, that have no discernible relation with each other. Speech is a universal human faculty. A speechless human community is unheard-of. These two facts, taken together, suggest that, before *homo sapiens* spread over the land-surface of the biosphere from equatorial East Africa (if that was the region in which this species of the *genus homo* made its first appearance), mankind as a whole must already have been on the way towards becoming articulate, but had not yet fully developed this potentiality. This hypothesis would explain how it has come about that all human communities have languages, but that languages, unlike the human beings who speak them, are not all manifestly akin to each other. Of course, the only human beings that are known to us through any relics other than bones and tools are all representatives of the sole surviving species. We do not know, and we have no means of discovering, whether any other species of *genus homo* or any other genera of the family of hominids ever learnt to talk, or whether this accomplishment has been peculiar to *homo sapiens*.

The known languages spoken by different communities of our own species have had ranges of widely different extents.

In the tropical forests of West Africa, before these were opened up by invaders from outside the region, there used to be numerous languages, apparently unrelated to each other, in close juxtaposition. The range of each of these languages was minute. The inhabitants of two villages that were separated from each other by only a few miles of forest might be unable to communicate intelligibly with each other by word of mouth. Their lingua franca was dumb-show. The vocal languages that are now widely current in West Africa have come in from outside: the Hausa language, for instance, from the North African steppe and French and English from the coast.

In contrast to the relative imperviousness of the forest, the sea has conveyed the Malay languages north-eastwards to the Philippines and south-westwards to Madagascar. The sea has also carried the Polynesian language to all the islands of Oceania, as far from the Continent as Easter Island and New Zealand. The Mediterranean Sea once disseminated the Punic and Greek and Latin languages round its shores, and the Atlantic Ocean has conveyed the Spanish, Portuguese, English, and French languages from Western Europe to the Americas. The steppe has conveyed languages almost as far as the sea. First the Indo-European languages and then the Turkish languages have traversed the Eurasian steppe and have spread beyond its shores in opposite directions. The Arabic language has travelled from the Arabian peninsula across the North-African steppe to the shore of the Atlantic Ocean.

The dissemination of languages via conductive non-human media has been reinforced by deliberate human action in the forms of religious missionary activity, military conquest, political organization, and trade. The Aramaean tribes and principalities were impotent politically; they were subjugated by the Assyrians; yet the Aramaic language was disseminated throughout South-West Asia, and the Aramaic alphabet as far afield as Mongolia and Manchuria, as a result of the administrative use of Aramaic in the Assyrian and the First Persian Empires and its liturgical use by the Nestorian Christian and Manichaean churches. On the other hand, the Greek language's success in supplanting Aramaic as the lingua franca of South-West Asia and Egypt was a result of the military conquest of the First Persian Empire by Alexander the Great, and military conquest has also been the agency by which the Romance languages have been propagated eastward to Roumania and south-westward to Chile from the Latin language's tiny original domain astride the lower course of the Italian River Tiber.

In the history of the Oikoumenê, different regimes have played the leading role at different times. If equatorial and southern East Africa was in truth the cradle of the hominids and, among them, of the *sapiens* species of *genus homo*, East Africa and the Oikoumenê were originally conterminous with each other. Before the close of the Upper Palaeolithic Age the Oikoumenê had expanded from East Africa over the greater part of the Continent, and human beings were colonizing the Americas. At this stage the leading role appears to have passed to the southern fringes of the North-European ice-cap, where Upper Palaeolithic hunters found an abundance of big game before the onset of the present thaw. However, the apparent primacy of Europe in this age may be an illusion arising from the inadequacy of our information. If the traces left by Upper Palaeolithic Man are eventually explored as thoroughly in the rest of the World as they have been explored already in Europe, the picture may come to look different.

We can feel more sure that, in the Neolithic Age, the leading role was played by South-West Asia and by the margins of the northernmost section of the Nile Valley, and that Sumer—the alluvium in the lower basin of the Tigris and Euphrates—was the birthplace of the earliest of the civilizations, though, in the foregoing Neolithic Age, this piece of South-West Asia had been uninhabitable. The thirteenth century A.D. in which this alluvial cornucopia ceased, at last, to be productive, saw the leading role in the Oikoumenê played, during the brief time-span of two generations, by Mongolia, thanks to the conductivity of the Eurasian steppe and to the mobility and prowess and discipline of the Eurasian pastoral nomads. These, temporarily united under Mongol command, subjugated the whole heartland of the Continent; only the Continent's peninsulas and its off-shore islands remained immune. Then, in the fifteenth century A.D., the leading role in the Oikoumenê was taken over by Western Europe when her mariners had mastered the Ocean—a still vaster conductive medium than the Eurasian steppe.

When, in the twentieth century, Western Europe forfeited her ecumenical hegemony by waging two fratricidal wars, the leading role passed to the United States. At the time of writing, it looked as if the American ascendancy in the Oikoumenê would be as short-lived as the Mongol ascendancy had been. The future was enigmatic, but it seemed possible that, in the next chapter of the Oikoumenê's history, the lead might pass from America to Eastern Asia.

[5]

TECHNOLOGICAL REVOLUTIONS,

c. 70,000/40,000 B.C.—3000 B.C.

EVERY species of living being, and every specimen of each species, is affecting and modifying the biosphere by its efforts to keep itself alive during its brief lifetime. However, no pre-hominid species has ever had the power to dominate the biosphere or to wreck it. On the other hand, when a hominid chipped a stone with the intention of making it into a more serviceable tool, this historic act, performed perhaps two million years ago, made it certain that, one day, some species of some genus of the hominid family of primate mammals would not merely affect and modify the biosphere, but would hold the biosphere at its mercy. This mastery over the biosphere has been achieved, in our time, by *homo sapiens*.

During all but the last 70,000 or 40,000 years of these two million years of tool-making, the hominid family's potential command over the biosphere hardly began to be translated into accomplished fact. There was, of course, some technological progress during the Lower Palaeolithic Age, but in that age this progress was slow and feeble, and each of the successive technological innovations spread uniformly throughout the Oikoumenê (in the Lower Palaeolithic Age, the Oikoumenê did not yet include the Americas). The dissemination of Lower Palaeolithic technological innovations was slow; for the new type of tool had to be transmitted by pedestrians from one community to another, and, in this food-gathering stage of economy, human communities could not live close to each other, since each party required a large area to roam over in order to pick up its livelihood.

Moreover, we may guess that Lower Palaeolithic hominids, including the most successful species, *homo sapiens*, were conservative-minded, and that they were shy of adopting an innovation, even when they had the new pattern in their hands. The reason why, nevertheless, new types of tool spread uniformly throughout the Oikoumenê was that, though transmission was slow, innovation was infrequent. The time-intervals between successive innovations were long enough to allow each innovation to spread throughout the Oikoumenê before the next one followed.

In the history of technology the Upper Palaeolithic revolution, which broke out about 70,000/40,000 years ago, was epoch-making. From this time until the present day, improvements in tools of all kinds have accelerated, and, though there have been local and temporary pauses, and even relapses, acceleration has been the paramount tendency in the history of technology during this latest age.

During the period *c.* 3000 B.C.–A.D. 1500, the respective speeds of dissemination and innovation were reversed. New types of tools were invented before the previously current types had time to spread throughout the Oikoumenê. Consequently the ecumenical uniformity that was characteristic of the Lower Palaeolithic Age gave way, during the subsequent ages, to differentiation. New inventions did not have time to travel from their place of origin to the farthest extremities of the Oikoumenê before they were superseded regionally by further inventions. The speed of dissemination did not overtake and surpass the speed of invention again till after the fifteenth century A.D. when the conductivity of the Oikoumenê was suddenly increased by the West-European peoples' invention of a new type of sailing-ship which could stay at sea for months on end and could therefore reach every shore and could circumnavigate the globe.

Within the last five hundred years, the speed of both the dissemination and the invention of tools has become immensely greater than it was during the first two million years of tool-making. But the Modern Age and the Lower Palaeolithic Age have one feature in common with each other. In the Modern Age and the Lower Palaeolithic Age alike, the speed of invention has not kept pace with the speed of dissemination, and in both cases the consequence, on the technological plane, has been a high degree of ecumenical uniformity.

In the Upper Palaeolithic Age, *homo sapiens* made his way from north-eastern Asia to north-western North America, and spread from there to the southern tip of South America. The Upper Palaeolithic settlers in the Americas lost touch with Asia, except, perhaps, for the occupants of the Pacific coasts of present-day Oregon, Washington, and British Columbia. There was a time-interval of perhaps 20,000 years between the colonization of the Americas from north-eastern Asia and the second colonization of them from Asia's European peninsula. During this intervening period, society and culture in the Americas developed independently, and the stages of this development do not correspond to those in the contemporary history of Asia and its annexes. Moreover, the conventional labels and datings of stages in the history of the Old World since the close of the Lower Palaeolithic Age are misfits, here too, to some extent.

For instance, the Upper Palaeolithic Age was not distinguished solely by an advance in the technique of flaking and chipping stone tools. It also produced at least three pioneer inventions: the domestication of dogs, archery, and the painting and modelling of likenesses of animals and human beings. The Upper Palaeolithic hunters' feat of taming dogs from being Man's hostile competitors into becoming his obedient servants was the first of Man's successes in making non-human animals minister to human purposes. In inventing the bow, Upper Palaeolithic Man harnessed an inanimate physical force, the elasticity of wood, to enable his own muscle power, by drawing the bow, to shoot a missile farther than a human arm, unaided, could have hurled it. As for the paintings and modellings, they are the earliest known works of visual art. The painters of cave-walls in France and Spain took advantage of the unevenness of the surfaces in order to give to some of their likenesses of animals the form of bas-reliefs. At Lepenski Vir, on the right bank of the River Danube at the Iron Gates, other Upper Palaeolithic artists took the further step of modelling fully three-dimensional figures. The cave-paintings may have had a religious, or at any rate a magical, purpose. The ceremonial centre at Lepenski Vir was surely a sanctuary. The site of Lepenski Vir was a natural terminus for the trails of food-gatherers and hunters. We may infer that although, before the invention of agriculture, mankind had to keep constantly on the move in order to make its living, some Upper Palaeolithic communities already had fixed points which they visited at more or less regular intervals, probably for the purpose of performing communal rites. It looks as if such permanent ceremonial centres were the forerunners of permanent habitations.

'Palaeolithic' is thus an inadequate label for describing the activities and achievements of so-called 'Upper Palaeolithic' Man. *A fortiori*, the age which started soon after the beginning of the present thaw—that is to say, some 12,000 years or 10,000 years ago—is inadequately described by the label 'Neolithic'. It is true that the earliest technological invention in the Neolithic Age was the discovery of ways of grinding tools to the required shapes, instead of striking flakes off a flint or some other fissionable kind of stone. This not only made it possible to shape tools more exactly for serving their purpose; it also gave the tool-makers a much wider range of raw materials. However, the epoch-making achievement of the Neolithic Age was not the art of grinding tools; it was the domestication of a number of species of plants and animals. Moreover, the Neolithic-Age inventions of spinning and weaving and of pottery-manufacturing made almost as great a difference for human life as the inventions of agriculture and of animal-husbandry.

Agriculture and animal-husbandry have certainly been the most important of all human inventions to date. They have not ceased to be the economic foundations of human life, even at times and places at which they have been overshadowed by trade and manufacture. Viewed in retrospect, agriculture and animal-husbandry can be seen to have been felicitous devices for reconciling the development of Man's technological power with the preservation of the welfare of the biosphere—a welfare that is the condition for the survival of all kinds of life, including human life itself. In so far as Man has achieved the domestication of some species of plants and animals, he has, it is true, substituted human selection for natural selection and, in imposing his choice for his own specific purposes, he has impoverished the biosphere in order to enrich mankind. Man's crops and orchards and flocks and herds have supplanted many species, useless or inimical to Man, which, for Man, have been 'weeds' and 'vermin', condemned to extinction in so far as Man has been able to exterminate them. At the same time, Man has ensured the survival of those plants and animals that he has made his own. He has learnt to reserve part of his annual harvest for providing the next year's seed-corn, and he has recruited his flocks and herds by keeping alive some of each year's lambs and calves. Moreover, by selective breeding, he has changed some of the domesticated species both more rapidly and more radically than they would have been changed by Nature if she had been left to her own devices.

The invention of pottery has provided a visual record of the differentiation of culture. In pottery, the fashions of shape and decoration change almost as fast as in dress; and potsherds are indestructible, whereas old clothes perish except in the rare cases in which they have been preserved in dry sand or in air-tight peat-bogs. Thus, for all times between the invention of pottery and the invention of writing, the stratification of potsherds on a site of human habitation is the surest chronometer. It is also the surest demarcator of the geographical domains of distinctive cultures, and indicator of the intermingling or fusion of cultures through the dissemination of the arts and through migrations and conquests. Both in the Old World and in the Americas, the variety of styles of pottery is the key to the history of the development and differentiation of regional cultures in the Pre-civilizational Age—and also after the appearance of civilizations, where this has not been accompanied by the invention of scripts, or where scripts have been invented but have fallen out of use and have not been re-deciphered.

Regional Neolithic cultures superseded the Upper Palaeolithic culture in most of the Old-World portion of the Oikoumenê. (In the Americas, as has been noted already, the Upper Palaeolithic culture of the colonists from north-eastern Asia developed further on lines of its own.) In the Old World, the Neolithic culture of one particular region,

South-West Asia, developed gradually into a Copper-Age culture through a transitional phase that has been labelled 'Chalcolithic'. This means an age in which copper and stone were used contemporaneously as the raw materials for tool-making. Actually, stone continued to be used for making some kinds of tools—the commonest and most useful kinds—long after copper and bronze and iron in turn had come to be used for making weapons and ornaments. Thus the ages that have been labelled with the names of different materials for tool-making have actually overlapped with each other chronologically. The Neolithic Age did not really come to an end until eventually, at different dates in different regions, iron superseded stone as the material for making agricultural implements and non-ceramic household utensils.

While the domestication of wild plants and animals has become the staff of human life, the invention of metallurgy has been the _chef d'oeuvre_ of Man's technological virtuosity. Metallurgy is the end-product of a chain of successive discoveries, and the concatenation was not self-evident. Each link was added by a stroke of intellectual genius. Neolithic Man first noticed lumps of more or less pure metal exposed to view on the Oikoumenê's land-surface. He first treated these lumps of metal as stones and discovered that, unlike ordinary stones, they were malleable. He then discovered that, if heated, they became temporarily pliable and that they eventually liquefied if the temperature were raised to a high degree. Thus, in metal, Man had hit upon a raw material which, like clay, was much more amenable than stone was to being shaped. The next discovery was that metals were to be found, not only in a more or less pure state, but as ingredients in ores, and that, by heating metalliferous ore to a degree at which its metallic content liquefied, the latent metal could be disengaged from the slag. The final step was the discovery that the most copious supplies of ores were subterranean, and the invention of the techniques of mining.

By now, metallurgy has been practised for almost 6,000 years in the Old-World Oikoumenê and for perhaps 2,800 years in Peru, and it has had revolutionary effects on both the material and the social conditions of human life and on the interplay between Man and the biosphere that is Man's sole habitat. Metallurgy has raised mankind's material standard of living; but the social price of metallurgical expertise has been the division of labour, while the environmental price has been the progressive using up of a raw material that is both scarce and irreplaceable.

The smith and the miner were the earliest specialists. Each had to devote the whole of his working time to his craft instead of continuing to be a jack of all trades, like the Palaeolithic hunter and the Neolithic husbandman. The division of labour was the technological consequence. The social corollary of this was the exchange of the products of diverse kinds of work; and this in turn created a still unsolved, and perhaps insoluble, ethical problem. On what principle is the total product of society to be distributed among the various classes of producers? The total product is the fruit of the co-operative work of all participants in society, but their respective contributions are unequal in effectiveness and in value. The inequality is manifest. But can it be reflected in an allocation of shares that will be recognized by all parties as being equitable? Ought an attempt at an equitable allocation to be made? Or is it right, or, short of that, inevitable, that the lion's share shall be appropriated by those that have the preponderant power?

The invention of metallurgy sowed the seeds of class differentiation and class conflict. The once distinctive surname 'Smith' is evidence that, in a 'Chalcolithic' village, the smith was felt to be a villager of a different kind from the still unspecialized majority of the village's inhabitants. It is true that there may have been the rudiments of technological speciali-zation in the Palaeolithic Age. Palaeolithic Man learnt that different varieties of flint were of different value for him as raw materials for tool-making. He even mined for flint of the most desirable kind. But it is improbable that, before the invention of metallurgy, any worker became a full-time specialist who could earn his living wholly by exchange, without taking any direct part in the community's basic work of pro-viding itself with food.

The second of the two fateful changes that were introduced by the invention of metallurgy was the use of a non-replaceable and scarce raw material. The replacement of the husbandman's crops and livestock was guaranteed for him by the fact that these were living beings, and that life reproduces itself naturally if Nature is not thwarted. In order to ensure the perpetuation of domesticated plants and animals, all that is required of Man is foresight and consequent self-restraint. The husbandman must save enough of his harvest and of his lambs and calves to provide the next year's seed-corn and to maintain the numerical strength of his flocks and herds; and he must also refrain from the over-exploitation of Mother Earth. He must resist the temptation to exhaust her by over-cropping and over-grazing.

On condition that the husbandman exercises foresight and practises self-restraint, Nature will continue to be fertile for the husbandman's benefit. In fact, there is no reason why agriculture and animal hus-bandry, once invented, should not be carried on until the biosphere ceases to be habitable. By contrast, the history of metallurgy is a history of perpetual prospecting for virgin sources of ore to replace the sources that have already been discovered and exhausted. Metals, being in-animate, do not replenish Man's supplies of them by reproducing themselves; nor do ex-organic substances such as coal. In our time, the scale of the extraction of non-replaceable natural resources has increased to such a portentous degree that we have now come within sight of using up all the accessible supplies of them.

In agriculture and animal husbandry, Man's technological power and Nature's productivity are in equilibrium. With the invention of metallurgy, Man's technological ability began to make a demand on Nature that she is not capable of satisfying throughout the time for which the biosphere can still continue to be habitable. If we think of the last 10,000 years of human history in terms of the 2,000 million years of mankind's potential expectation of life, we may perhaps conclude that it would have been better for our descendants if metallurgy had never been invented, and if Man, after having attained the Neolithic level of technology, had not succeeded in raising himself higher in terms of technological achievement. If Man's progress in the technique of tool-making had stopped short of the utilization of metals, mankind's numbers and material wealth would, no doubt, today be only a fraction of what they actually are. On the other hand, mankind's survival would be far more secure; for we should be in no danger of exhausting irre-placeable resources. It is true that hard stone, like metal, is irreplaceable because it is inanimate and is therefore not self-renewing. On the other hand, stone is so abundant by comparison with even the least rare metals, that it seems virtually inexhaustible. It would have been less difficult and less painful for our Neolithic-Age ancestors to remain at the pre-metallic level than it would be for our descendants to revert to it, if, for them, this should come to be the only alternative to extinction.

Where, within the Oikoumenê, were agriculture and animal hus-bandry and metallurgy invented for the first time? The last four words in this question are of the essence of it, for we can never be sure that any of Man's inventions has been made at a single time and place only. An invention made at one particular time and place may, of course, be adopted, at some later date, elsewhere. There is also the indirect form of dissemination that is known as 'stimulus diffusion'. The sight or report of a foreign invention may stimulate people, not to adopt it as it stands, but to create a counterpart of it in a style of their own. However, an identical invention may be made at several places and times indepen-dently. This is possible because inventions are products of human nature, and human nature is uniform in the sense of having certain specific spiritual, psychological, and physiological characteristics that are com-mon to all specimens of the species, though each specimen will display these common characteristics in an individual way of its own. Any invention may have had any one of these three alternative possible histories, and in many cases there is no evidence to show whether a particular invention that has made its appearance at a particular time and place has been an independent creation or has been a response to a stimulus or has merely been adopted ready-made.

Subject to these provisos, we may guess, with some confidence, that, in the Old-World Oikoumenê agriculture and animal husbandry, metallurgy and also the techniques for quarrying and transporting huge and heavy blocks of stone, were all invented for the first time in South-West Asia, the central portage area of the Old-World portion of the Oikoumenê. We can even define the area of the region more exactly. It did not include the Arabian Peninsula except for its southern corner. When agriculture and animal husbandry were being invented, most of Arabia, including its northernmost fringe, the present-day Syrian desert, was too arid to provide a setting for the domestication of plants and animals. Only the southern corner of Arabia has been kept fertile by the monsoon rains, and the desiccation of the rest of Arabia insulated this corner of the Yemen before the invention of sea-faring ships and the subsequent domestication of the Arabian camel.

The South-West-Asian motherland of husbandry and metallurgy did not include the alluvium laid down by the Rivers Tigris and Euphrates along and around their lower courses. Before this alluvium was drained and irrigated for human occupation and cultivation, it was inhospitable to Man and to his domesticated plants and animals. It was a maze of waters threading their way through reed-beds—the marshland to which the district around the lower course of the Euphrates has now reverted. On the other hand, the area within which husbandry and then metallurgy were first invented included part, at least, of southern Asia Minor and western Iran and Türkmenistan besides Mesopotamia and Syria and Palestine. The cereals and animals that were domesticated in this region during the Neolithic chapter of this region's history seem to have been at home there already in their previous wild state. Elsewhere, the same domesticated plants and animals seem to have been introduced from South-West Asia either by colonists from South-West Asia itself or by autochthonous local peoples who borrowed these South-West-Asian inventions and, in borrowing them, made, in their turn, the cultural transition from the Palaeolithic to the Neolithic, and eventually to the Chalcolithic and to the Copper-Age and Bronze-Age ways of life.

At the time of writing, the Neolithic-Age strata had been excavated at only a few sites in South-West Asia and Egypt; and, as exploration continues, our picture of Neolithic life, in this region where it made its first appearance, may continue to change, as it has kept on changing already in the light of successive explorations and discoveries. Some points, however, are already clear. The beginnings of the settlements so far explored range in date from *c.* 10,000 B.C. (the estimated date of the pre-pottery-age settlement at Jericho) to the fifth millennium B.C. At sites other than Jericho, the settlements began in the seventh or the early sixth millennium B.C. We also know that the transition from food-gathering and hunting to agriculture and animal-husbandry was made in oases watered by springs, or in flood-plains of fertile soil deposited by small streams at the foot of the mountains from which these streams descend. All such potential fields are watered by natural irrigation. These sites, however, differ greatly from each other in altitude and climate. Jericho lies in a valley below sea-level which has a tropical climate; on the other hand, Çatal Hüyük on the plateau of Asia Minor, and Tepe Sialk on the Iranian plateau, are under snow for part of the year.

On flood-plains and in oases watered by springs, the exhaustion of the soil through cultivation is made good by Nature. She replenishes the fields' fertility by bringing deposits of silt. The oasis of Jericho and the Ghutah of Damascus are kept perpetually fertile by this natural process. However, this bounty is rare. Most of the South-West-Asian region within which agriculture was invented lies in what was, and still is, a rainfall zone. Some of the early South-West-Asian agricultural communities were dependent for their water-supply on rainfall only. Rain carries no silt, and the yield of solely rain-fed agriculture quickly diminishes. The line of least resistance is then to treat the temporarily exhausted soil as if it were a permanently exhausted mine, if the disappointed husbandman is aware that there is virgin soil, within reach, for him to occupy. Even in the modern age the West-European agricultural settlers in North America kept on moving westwards, and the Russian peasants in the Old World eastwards, though their ancestors had long since acquired the technique of renewing the fertility of rain-fed soil without Nature's help.

This technique was discovered only gradually. In woodlands the first step towards making sedentary rain-fed agriculture possible by artificial fertilization was to burn the trees that had been felled to make way for crops of domesticated cereals. The fertilizing ash then enabled the husbandman to snatch crops from his clearing for one or two seasons, and the process could be repeated if, after that, the trees were given time enough to cover the clearing again. By this 'slash-and-burn' technique, the same patch could be re-cultivated perhaps once in every ten years, and, if the cultivator had ten patches at his disposal for him to cultivate in turn, he could move round within a limited circuit. The problem of making a living from rain-fed agriculture without migrating even locally was finally solved by the device of manuring fallow land with cattle dung instead of waiting for a new growth of trees to provide a fresh supply of ash. But, pending this discovery, the husbandman was impelled, as the prospector for minerals has continued to be impelled down to the present day, to move on into still unexploited regions of the Oikoumenê.

Meanwhile, either through migration or through recultivation, husbandry, accompanied by the arts of spinning and weaving and pottery-making and followed by the arts of metallurgy and of hewing and hauling megaliths, spread from its earliest home in South-West Asia over most of the rest of the Old World. We shall find the various regional civilizations of the Old World rising, at different dates, from this common Neolithic foundation that had been extended—likewise at different dates—far and wide, from its original South-West-Asian base. However, the expansion of this latest form of pre-civilizational culture in the Old World was neither complete nor uniform.

Australia, for instance, remained the preserve of a pre-Neolithic food-gathering detachment of *homo sapiens* that had successfully crossed the geographical dividing-line between the respective realms of the continental and the Australian flora and fauna. These first human settlers in Australia and their dogs were the first non-marsupial mammals to arrive there. Their feat was not emulated by any Neolithic people, and they remained in unchallenged occupation of their secluded retreat till Australia was 'discovered' by modern West-Europeans in the eighteenth century A.D. Neolithic seafarers did succeed in occupying the Polynesian archipelago, but New Zealand, which was their biggest territorial prize, was occupied by them only about six centuries before they too were overtaken by the modern West-Europeans' world-wide expansion.

The differentiation of the Neolithic way of life in the course of its spread from its point of origin in South-West Asia is illustrated by the contrast between the regional variety of the shapes and decorations of Neolithic pots and the ecumenical uniformity of Palaeolithic tools. It has already been noted that potsherds are visual indications of ways of life. The differentiation of local styles of Neolithic pottery seems to have been due, for the most part, to local initiative, and it is questionable whether an inspiration from the Levant can be detected in the Megalithic monuments that were erected along the West-Mediterranean and Atlantic coasts of Continental Europe and its offshore islands, from southern Spain and Portugal to Denmark and from Malta to Stonehenge in Britain.

Like the Pyramids of the Pharaonic Age in Egypt, the megaliths in Europe seem likely to outlast all later local works of Man. Their dates appear to fall within two millennia, running from *c.* 2500 to *c.* 1500 B.C., during which Western Europe passed out of the Neolithic through the Chalcolithic into the Copper and Bronze Age. Though their builders were non-literate, these buildings themselves, and the associated works of visual art, testify dumbly that they were made to serve cults of ancestors and of a mother goddess that have Levantine counterparts. Yet the relation of the West-European megaliths to the Levant is doubly

enigmatic. In the first place, the region from which the megalithic
religion and technology spread along both the Mediterranean and the
Atlantic coast of Western Europe was southern Spain and Portugal—
that is to say, the extremity of Europe which is the most remote from
both Egypt and the Aegean. In the second place, some of the Levantine
works which the West-European megalithic monuments resemble are
younger, not older, than these. The beehive tombs at Los Millares, on
the Mediterranean coast of southern Spain, appear to be more than
2,000 years older than their counterparts at Mycenae; and, though
Stonehenge is nearly one thousand years younger than the pyramids of
the Fourth Dynasty of Egyptian Pharaohs, the less massive masonry of
the Los Millares tombs may be several centuries older than the comparable masonry of the Third-Dynasty Pharaoh Zoser's pyramid at
Saqqarah.

The differentiation of the last phases of pre-civilizational culture went
to the length of original feats of domestication. The vine, olive, fig, plum,
cherry, peach, apple, and pear, and also cattle, goats, and sheep, seem
to have been indigenous to South-West Asia, and to have been domesticated there in the Neolithic Age. But rice and roots and citrus-bearing
trees and bananas, and also humped cattle and elephants and camels,
both Arabian and Central Asian, were domesticated in regions outside
South-West Asia; and, for all we know, these feats of domestication may
have been entirely independent; they may not even have been inspired
from South-West Asia by stimulus diffusion. The date-palm may not
have been domesticated till sultry Sumer and Egypt had been opened
up. The earliest age for which we have a record of domesticated Arabian
camels is the latter part of the second millennium B.C. Our earliest
evidence for the domestication of the Central Asian camel is no earlier
than about 600 B.C., if 'with Golden Camels' is the correct interpretation
of the Prophet Zarathustra's name.

As for the Americas, the dog was the only domesticated animal that
the colonists from Asia brought with them, and the only native American
animals that were domesticated by the colonists were the llama, alpaca,
guinea-pig, and bee. On the other hand, the number of plants indigenous
to the Americas that were domesticated there is comparable to the
number of those that were domesticated in the Old World. The Americas
and the Old World had hardly any domesticated plants in common
before the arrival in the Americas of the modern West-Europeans.

This seems to indicate that agriculture was invented in the Americas
independently; and, if we come to this conclusion we may also guess that
the invention of bronze (i.e. copper alloyed with tin) in Peru was also
independent of any inspiration from the Old World. The question
whether the pre-Columbian American civilizations were or were not

independent creations is still being hotly debated. Perhaps few students of the subject would deny that some of the ingredients of the American civilizations were of Old-World origin, but the prevailing opinion now seems to be that these Old-World ingredients were of minor importance and that, in essence, the pre-Columbian American civilizations were created independently *in situ* by descendants of the Upper-Palaeolithic-Age immigrants.

The date of the dawn of the oldest civilizations in the Old World was *c.* 3000 B.C., and, at that date, those pre-Columbian American cultures that eventually blossomed into civilizations comparable to those of the Old World had perhaps already taken the first steps towards the domestication of maize, which was to become their staple cultivated food-plant. In Meso-America, in the Coxcatlán cave near Puebla in the Mexican highlands, in a deposit dated *c.* 4000 B.C., maize-cobs have been found which may be either from a wild maize-plant or, alternatively, from a plant slightly modified by the first steps towards its domestication. At Bat Cave in New Mexico, in a deposit dated *c.* 2500 B.C., cobs have been found in which the indications of domestication are clearer. Thus in Meso-America the dawn of agriculture was apparently coeval with the dawn of civilization in the Old World, and was at least 4,000 years later than the Old-World dawn of agriculture in South-West Asia.

Already the cultures of the Old World and of pre-Columbian America were developing along separate lines, and, within the confines of the Old World itself, the dawn of civilization inaugurated an age of increasing regional differentiation. About 4,500 years passed before the West-European conquest of the Ocean turned the tide back towards uniformity and also towards a unification that had been out of the question in the Lower Palaeolithic Age. At the time of writing, the divisive forces which had prevailed during the intervening ages were fighting a stubborn rear-guard action, and it could not yet be foreseen whether the movement that was making for unification would win the day. It could, however, already be seen that the inexorable condition for mankind's survival was now the unification of the whole of the Oikoumenê, and this not only on the technological level but on every plane of life.

[6]

THE OPENING-UP OF THE TIGRIS–EUPHRATES ALLUVIUM AND THE CREATION OF THE SUMERIAN CIVILIZATION

In the preceding chapter we have noted that the invention of agriculture created the problem of how to work out a technique for enabling cultivators of the soil to be sedentary, when once they had burst the bounds of the small and sparsely scattered South-West-Asian oases, watered by natural irrigation, in which the transition from food-collecting to food-producing appears to have been made.

In the vastly more extensive areas of the Old-World Oikoumenê in which the husbandman has to rely on rainfall alone for watering his crops, there was a gradual advance, by stages. Vagrant agriculture, in which an exhausted field was abandoned for ever, was first replaced by circuit agriculture, in which a field, fertilized temporarily by the 'slash-and-burn' technique, was eventually brought back into cultivation, but this only after a time-interval which would allow a sufficient new growth of wild trees for re-fertilizing the temporarily derelict field.

In the rainfall zone it took many generations, or perhaps even many centuries, to discover how to make an adequate living from a block of fields compact enough to be cultivated by the husbandman and his family from a fixed habitation. They could then hand on house and fields together to their descendants. To be thus anchored to a patch of cultivable soil was later to become a mark of servitude in societies that could provide a choice of alternative economic opportunities. Originally, however, the sedentary husbandman's anchorage to the soil must have been a long-desired social reward for having attained a long-pursued technological objective.

Some—perhaps a majority—of the emigrants from the South-West-Asian oases drifted far and wide over the face of the rainfall zone of the Oikoumenê before they learnt how to become sedentary without the aid of natural irrigation. There was, however, one region, close to the cradles of agriculture in the South-West-Asian oases, which, if it were opened up and were broken in by artificial drainage and irrigation, would provide the pioneer with much greater returns than he could win from his ancestral oasis, and this on a far larger territorial scale. This land of promise was the jungle-swamp in the lower Tigris–Euphrates basin: a chaotic mix of potentially fertile alluvium with potentially fertilizing water.

The mastering of the jungle-swamp was a social, far more than a technological, achievement. Of course, all mankind's technological achievements have been social achievements too. Man is a social being. Our pre-human ancestors would hardly have survived to become human if they had not been social animals already, and the limitedness of Man's sociality has always acted as a brake on his apparently unlimited techno-logical ability. Sociality is the necessary condition for the making and using of even the most rudimentary tools. The cultivators of the minor South-West-Asian oases had probably discovered already how to im-prove artificially on Nature's local gift of irrigation. In order to exploit the Twin Rivers' gift of alluvium, Man had to apply his already acquired technique of artificial irrigation on a scale that required the co-operation of a far larger number of human beings than had ever before co-operated in any enterprise. This difference in the scale of co-operation was tantamount to a difference, not just of degree, but of kind; and this was a social, not a technological, revolution.

The human conquest of the alluvium must have been planned by leaders who had the imagination, foresight, and self-control to work for returns that would be lucrative ultimately but not immediately. The leaders' plans would have been no more than unfulfilled dreams if they had not been able to induce large numbers of their fellow men to pursue objectives which were probably incomprehensible to them. The masses must have had faith in their leaders, and this faith in the leaders must have been founded on faith in gods whose potency and wisdom were realities for both the human leaders and their followers. The one in-dispensable new tool was a script. The leaders needed this instrument for organizing people and water and soil in quantities and magnitudes that were too vast to be handled efficiently by the unrecorded memorizing of oral arrangements and instructions. The invention of the Sumerian script was a masterpiece of creative genius, but this earliest known system of writing was complicated and clumsy, and it therefore remained eso-teric. It served the needs of society as a whole; at the same time it con-firmed the literate leaders' ascendancy over the illiterate majority.

In opening up for cultivation the alluvium in the lower basin of the Tigris and the Euphrates the Sumerians were creating the earliest of a new species of human society: the regional civilizations. This achieve-ment is attributable to the Sumerians because it is their language that we find conveyed in the Sumerian script at the stage in this script's evolution at which it becomes decipherable. But we cannot be sure that the Sumerians were the inventors of the first rudiments of their script, or that they were the earliest pioneers in the jungle-swamp that was eventually transformed into the land of Sumer. The Sumerian tamers of the jungle-swamp cannot have been autochthonous, for, before this wilderness was tamed, it had been uninhabitable for human beings. Some of the earliest Sumerian settlements—Ur, Uruk, Eridu—were planted on the south-western edge of the great swamp, adjoining Arabia; but it is unlikely that the Sumerians came from Arabia; their language has no affinity with the languages of the Semitic family, and the successive swarms of migrants who have streamed out of Arabia into adjoining regions of Asia and Africa have all been Semitic-speaking.

The Sumerian is the earliest of the regional civilizations of which we have a record. It is also the only one which was certainly derived from a pre-civilizational society or societies, and which was not copied from, or even inspired by, any pre-existing society of its own kind. (The Meso-American civilization was probably likewise derived direct from pre-civilizational antecedents; but the Meso-American civilization's originality is not universally admitted.) Modern archaeological exploration has brought to light the gradualness of the development of at least two of the Sumerian civilization's distinctive features: its script and its temple architecture.

We can follow the creation of the script out of pictographs (i.e. visual representations of people, things, events, and actions). The creative act was the invention of ideograms (i.e. conventional signs that are not necessarily representational, even vestigially, yet had an identical meaning for all literate members of the Sumerian society). The final stage is the invention of phonemes (i.e. conventional signs standing for sounds used in the spoken language). The Sumerians never went over to phonemes exclusively. Their script was an ambiguous and arbitrary combination of phonemes with ideograms. The disadvantage of ideograms is that they are inevitably numerous; their advantage over phonemes is that an idea and a sign can be associated with each other permanently, whereas a sound and a sign lose their pristine conventional correspondence as the sounds of the spoken language change in the course of time. Nevertheless, phonemes have the advantage over ideograms in being limited in number. There is a limit to the number of articulate sounds that can be emitted by the human voice, and each of mankind's languages actually uses only a selection from this potential repertory.

At the earliest stage of which we have pictorial and written records, the Sumerian civilization displays features that are shared by other members of the species of society of which it is the oldest known specimen.

In bringing the alluvium under cultivation, the Sumerians were the first society in the Old-World Oikoumenê to produce a surplus, over and above the annual requirements for bare subsistence. This surplus was not distributed equally among all the participants in the society who had contributed to the society's productivity in various ways and degrees. If the surplus had been shared out in equal portions, the bonus per head would have been minimal; for the surplus was small by comparison with the amount of the total produce that was required for subsistence, though the production of any surplus at all was a revolutionary new departure. Actually the surplus was reserved for the use of a privileged minority whose energy and time were thus released from the task of food-production which still occupied the whole of the working life of the majority. This assignment of the surplus to a minority was the economic basis of the differentiation of classes; but, though this was the enabling condition for the ruling class's enjoyment of its privilege, this privilege would have been too invidious to be tolerated by the masses if these had not believed that the ruling class earned its privilege by performing services for the society as a whole. These services were genuine, and they were indeed indispensable if the society was to survive in the remunerative but artificial conditions that had been created by the conquest of the alluvium. In any case, the ruling minority impounded the alluvial agriculture's economic surplus, and they spent the leisure thus acquired not only on performing public services but on enjoying private luxuries.

The rulers' primary public service was the administration of a community with an urban nucleus that dwarfed the antecedent Neolithic village-communities in magnitude and was incomparable in its complexity. In contrast to the Neolithic cultivator of the soil, the Sumerian peasant did not organize his own work. The maintenance of the irrigation-system was the necessary condition for the survival of the whole community; the public corvée of keeping the embankments and channels in order was as much a part of the peasant's duty as the cultivation of his own fields; and all his operations had to be carried out under the direction of the public authorities, since the distribution of the vital supply of irrigation-water in particular quantities at particular seasons required a single command, invested with irresistible power.

It has already been noted that the rulers' human authority was supported by a supernatural sanction. Besides administering the irrigation-system which, for living and working on the alluvium, was the all-important public utility, the rulers served the community as mediators between it and the gods, and the common belief in the gods' potency and wisdom was the spiritual force that moved the participants in a Sumerian city-state to act in concert, in spite of their numbers and their division into different social classes. The rulers also spent part of their wealth and leisure on private luxury: the personal service of attendants and the works of art that now make their appearance side by side with metallic tools. (The stone tools used by the peasants for cultivating the land were still mostly home-made.)

Another new feature of the Sumerian civilization was the local concentration, in cities, of the non-agricultural minority of the population who lived on the surplus of the majority's agricultural product. These cities may have started as ceremonial centres, at which the community assembled periodically for the performance of religious rituals and the closely related organization of utilitarian public works. Such ceremonial centres may have had few permanent residents, but they will have developed into cities, with dwelling-houses clustering round the shrines, as the non-agricultural minority increased in numbers and as its functions were distributed among priests and secular administrators (not differentiated from each other at first), together with their scribes, their personal attendants, and their artisans.

Class-differentiation, accentuated by the topographical segregation of classes between countryside and city, was the first of the social evils that were the price of the birth of civilization in Sumer. The second congenital evil of civilization was war; and the economic enabling condition for both evils was the production of a surplus. In a community in which the working time of every able-bodied participant is fully occupied by the task of producing food, there is no spare time for the maintenance of even part-time administrators, priests, artisans, or soldiers.

What was the fundamental innovation in the new species of society that the Sumerians created? Surplus production, class-differentiation, script, monumental architecture, urban settlements, and war were all new and distinctive features, but the crucial change was in the character and function of the gods.

The religion of extinct pre-literate societies has to be inferred from their visual art: Upper Palaeolithic cave-wall paintings, the three-dimensional figures at Lepenski Vir, the Neolithic-Age figurines portraying the fertile Mother. We can only guess at the corresponding rites and myths, but the earliest decipherable documents in the Sumerian script and language throw a flood of light on Sumerian religion, as well as on other aspects of Sumerian life. In these documents we encounter a pantheon of Sumerian gods, and we find that these gods have already entered on a second chapter of their history.

After the Sumerian civilization has come to birth, its gods still stand partly for forces of Nature, and we can see that originally this must have been the gods' exclusive function. By now, however, some of these gods have acquired a dual role; each of them now also stands for the collective human power of some particular Sumerian city-state. This duplication of the Sumerian gods' roles reflects a revolution in the relations between Man and Nature. At the time when the Sumerian gods first took shape in human minds, Man was still at Nature's mercy. The conquest of the alluvium for cultivation and settlement by concerted human action shifted the balance of power between Man and Nature to Man's advantage. Man, acting as a social animal, had now proved able to impose his will on a previously intractable province of Nature's realm, and Man had signalized his recognition of this exhilarating human triumph by taking to worshipping his own collective power alongside the non-human powers that he had previously felt to be omnipotent. The Sumerian tamers of the alluvium registered this change of fortunes by conscripting their ancestral nature-gods to serve as divine patrons—or divine servitors —of human sovereign states.

As representatives of the forces of Nature, the Sumerian gods had continued to be part of the common cultural heritage of the Sumerian society as a whole. As representatives of states, they stood severally for local Sumerian communities whose interests might conflict. In their political role the gods had become partly divisive and no longer wholly unitive. This new role, which the gods had already assumed by the date of the earliest surviving Sumerian written records, was ominous for the Sumerian civilization's future. The fruits of human society's victory over Nature might be forfeited if Man were to use his formidable collective power not only for dominating and exploiting non-human nature but also for fratricidal warfare between well-organized and well-armed local human 'powers'.

[7]

THE OPENING-UP OF THE NILOTIC ALLUVIUM AND THE CREATION OF THE PHARAONIC EGYPTIAN CIVILIZATION

In the preceding chapter the Sumerians have been credited with the creation of a society of a new species—a regional civilization—in virtue of a number of innovations that they made in the process of draining and irrigating the alluvial jungle-swamp in the lower basin of the Rivers Tigris and Euphrates. Judged by the same criteria, the Pharaonic Egyptians must be held to have created the second oldest of the regional civilizations in the process of opening up the jungle-swamp in the lower valley and in the delta of the River Nile.

The Egyptians, in their turn, achieved a surplus of production beyond what was required for bare subsistence, and in Egypt, as in Sumer, this economic achievement was accompanied by class-differentiation, literacy, monumental architecture, urban settlements, war, and a crucial change in the field of religion. Unlike the Sumerians, however, the Pharaonic Egyptians did not make this new departure unaided. Though they, too, built their civilization on foundations laid by their Neolithic and Chalcolithic ancestors, they were inspired by the example of an already existing society of the same species as the one that they were creating. There is a consensus among present-day Egyptologists that, at the birth of the Pharaonic Egyptian civilization, Sumerian influence can be discerned—for instance, in the practice of sealing with engraved cylinders, in a recessed style of building with bricks, in a Sumerian build of ship, in a number of artistic motifs, and in the formation of a script in which ideograms were supplemented, without being ousted, by phonemes.

This form of script is peculiar. It is unlikely that an identical structure was worked out for the second time independently in Egypt, where, in other fields, there is evidence of contemporary Sumerian influence at the time at which the Egyptian script took shape. Moreover, the archaeological evidence indicates that the Egyptian script was devised suddenly,

in contrast to the gradual evolution of the Sumerian script out of antecedent pictographs. The Sumerian structure of the Egyptian script, taken
together with the suddenness of its appearance, is the strongest single
piece of evidence indicating that Sumerian influence was one of the
factors that brought the Pharaonic Egyptian civilization to birth.

We have no indication of the route by which this Sumerian influence
made its way to the lower valley of the Nile. The evidence itself has been
found in Upper Egypt; but most of the rest of our archaeological
evidence for the history of the Pharaonic Egyptian civilization also
comes from Upper Egypt, not from the Nile delta, because the climate
of Upper Egypt favours the preservation of human artefacts, whereas the
climate and physiography of the Delta are inimical to this. The atmosphere in the latitude of the Delta is not as dry as it is in Upper Egypt,
even though rain is rare in the Delta, except in its extreme north-west
corner. Furthermore, the material relics of the Pharaonic Age are buried,
in the Delta, under a deposit of alluvium of an unknown depth, and this
deposit is surmounted by modern towns on most of the town-sites of the
Pharaonic Age. For these reasons, the Delta has not yielded up the
archaeological record of its history in the Pharaonic Age—in contrast to
the evidence for the pre-civilizational age of Egyptian history, in which
the Upper-Egyptian Neolithic sites on the high ground overhanging the
alluvium have a counterpart at Merimde, which overhangs the upper
part of the Delta from high ground to the west of it.

This blank in our archaeological record in respect of the Delta begins
when the record shows that, in Upper Egypt, the former inhabitants of
the high ground on either side of the valley ventured down on to the
alluvium and began to break it in; and the absence of comparable
archaeological information, positive or negative, about the contemporary history of the Delta reduces to guesswork any attempt to reconstruct
the antecedents of the birth of the regional civilization of Pharaonic
Egypt. The surviving archaeological record in Upper Egypt gives the
impression that, by comparison with the gradual emergence of civilization in Sumer, its emergence in Egypt was a sudden event. Is this
impression an illusion that would be dispelled if we could recover the
archaeological evidence for the history of the Delta during the prelude
to the flowering of the Pharaonic Egyptian civilization? Or would successful excavation here confirm our present impression by revealing that
the Delta, in contrast to Upper Egypt, was still to a large extent in its
pristine state of jungle-swamp when it was united politically with Upper
Egypt?

If this second of the two alternative possibilities corresponds to the
truth, the Delta may have been an impassable barrier for communication overland between Sumer and Egypt at the time when, in Egypt,

Sumerian influence was making itself felt. This time was brief; the influence ceased to make itself felt almost immediately after the political unification of Egypt; and, if the opening-up of the Delta was completed only during the ensuing Age of the Old Kingdom, the Sumerian influence cannot have reached Upper Egypt overland via the Delta; it must have come direct by sea. In that case, Sumerian ocean-going ships must have reached the Red-Sea ports of Upper Egypt, or, alternatively, Egyptian and Sumerian mariners must have met each other on some intermediate coast: perhaps the incense-exporting coast of the Yemen and Somaliland or the copper-exporting coast of the unidentified region known to the Sumerians as Magan. It has been noted already that, before the Railway Age, a long sea-voyage was quicker and easier than a shorter journey overland.

However, the blank in our archaeological record in respect of the Delta leaves room for a different guess that is equally legitimate and equally unverifiable. We may guess alternatively that, in the emergence of the civilization of Pharaonic Egypt, the Delta, not Upper Egypt, played the leading role. We may picture the Delta as having reached, before the close of the fourth millennium B.C., the same stage as contemporary Sumer—a stage in which the alluvium had already been partially mastered by Man, and in which there were already nascent cities. On that hypothesis, it would be probable that the Sumerian influence reached the Delta before it reached Upper Egypt, and that it travelled, not by sea round Arabia, but overland, via Syria.

In any case the Sumerian influence on the nascent Pharaonic Egyptian civilization was not only brief; it was also no more than an influence; it did not amount to a dissemination into Egypt of the Sumerian civilization itself, ready-made and unmodified. For instance, the Egyptian script, though it is Sumerian in structure, is distinctively Egyptian in style, and the hieroglyphs are original creations; they are not imitations of their Sumerian counterparts. In the field of Egyptian visual art, the Sumerian motifs faded out, while, in the field of architecture, the Egyptians, unlike the Sumerians, did not continue to use mud-brick as the material for their monuments. They translated their monumental architecture from mud brick into stone; their classic monuments are built of stone in massive blocks. Masonry in the grand style and on a colossal scale was an indigenous achievement for which the Egyptians were not indebted to the Sumerians or to any other outsiders. The mere size of the Sumerian brick-built ziggurats does not put them on a par with the Egyptian pyramids. These are unrivalled both in the masterlines of their design and in the precision of its execution.

The Sumerians' failure to match the Egyptians' masonry does not convict the Sumerians of being inferior to the Egyptians in imagination or in skill; it is simply a reminder that the transformation of the Tigris–Euphrates swamp into the home of a civilization was a greater, as well as an earlier, feat than the subsequent similar transformation of the Nilotic swamp. The taming of Upper Egypt was relatively easy. Here there was only one river to harness, and its valley was narrow. The belt of jungle-swamp in this section of the Nile basin was close to the bluffs on either side which had been the sites of the settlements of the Pharaonic Egyptians' Neolithic and Chalcolithic forerunners. In Egypt, only the Delta was a physiographical counterpart of the alluvial portion of the Tigris–Euphrates basin, and the Delta seems to have been opened up only gradually.

Moreover, Egypt as a whole, including the Delta, has, close at hand, some of the materials that are indispensable for the creation and maintenance of a civilization. There is an abundance of stone of the finest quality for the architect's and the sculptor's purposes; it is only a short haul from quarry to river-bank; and even an obelisk is easy to transport when once it is water-borne. The mines near the east coast of the Gulf of Suez—if these were, in truth, copper mines—are also within easy reach of Upper Egypt by sea, with a short overland haul through the Wadi Hammamat; and, if the Sinai Peninsula could not supply Egypt with all the copper that she needed, the island of Cyprus could, and both Cyprus and Syria were accessible by sea for the rulers of Upper Egypt when they had annexed the Delta, with its Mediterranean ports. Egypt could, and did, import timber from Mount Lebanon via the Phoenician port of Byblos; and the trading partnership between Egypt and Byblos may have been coeval with the establishment of the Egyptian United Kingdom. Thus sea-routes could bring timber and copper to Egypt's doors, and the Nile below the First Cataract provided Egypt with an internal waterway from end to end of the country. Besides, this waterway, though it was a river, could be used for traffic upstream as well as downstream; for the Nile here flows from south to north, whereas the prevalent wind in Egypt is the north wind, as has been mentioned already.

By comparison with Upper Egypt, Sumer was at a great disadvantage in respect both of means of communication and of access to raw materials; and it is surprising that the earliest of the civilizations that have been based economically on the taming of swamp land should have arisen, not in Upper Egypt, but in the lower basin of the Tigris and Euphrates. The Sumerians not only anticipated but surpassed the Egyptians in adventurousness. The Sumerians staked their future on the exploitation of a single raw material, the alluvium, and, in descending on it and opening it up, they were leaving behind them their ancestral sources for the supply of stone, as well as copper and timber. In the new land that they

had tamed and occupied and brought under cultivation, the fertile soil
was the only local asset. The Sumerians showed their resourcefulness by
performing a technological *tour de force*. They discovered how to make
agricultural implements of clay baked to an almost metallic degree of
hardness and sharpness. But this invention could not make copper superfluous for them; and they had to fetch their copper from as far afield as
the upper basin of the Euphrates and Tigris, and perhaps also even from
mines on the Black Sea side of the watershed between the Euphrates and
the rivers in eastern Asia Minor that debouch into the Black Sea along
its southern shore. The Sumerians had to fetch their timber from Mount
Amanus. As for the importation of stone, this was out of the question
for Sumerian architects; these had to do the best that they could with
bricks made of the local mud. They did import stone to serve as their
material for monumental sculpture, but in Sumer the sculptor's stone
was almost as costly an import as gold and silver.

The Sumerians not only had to import copper and timber; they had
to pay for these imports with exports of their own produce—for instance,
grain (a bulky commodity to transport) and textiles, for which the
earliest material in Sumer was wool. Sumerian trade was necessarily
more active than Egyptian trade, and it had to be carried farther afield.
It was promoted by the foundation of colonial Sumerian settlements.
As-Asshur, up the Tigris, and al-Tall Brak, in Mesopotamia (the Jazirah),
the earliest settlements, seem to have been Sumerian, not Semitic. This
commercial expansion up-river overland was matched by maritime trade
down the Persian Gulf and perhaps beyond as far as the Indus delta and
possibly even the Red-Sea coast of Upper Egypt; but the Sumerians'
greatest feat of transportation was their overland commercial expansion
north-westward.

When the timber felled on Mount Amanus had been hauled to the
west bank of the Euphrates, and the copper of Arghana Maden had been
hauled (a shorter haul) to the upper reaches of the Tigris, these bulky
and heavy commodities could be floated downstream on rafts, while
passengers could travel in coracles made of wickerwork sheathed in
hides. Conveyance by water downstream was easy and rapid, for both
the Tigris and the Euphrates flow with a stronger current than the Nile
in the lowest section of its course. But, for the same reason, the Sumerians
could not use the Twin Rivers for travel or transportation upstream. In
the Tigris–Euphrates basin there is not a prevalent south-east wind to
match the prevalent north wind that is one of Nature's precious gifts to
Egypt. Sumerian prospectors for copper and timber had to travel north-
westward laboriously overland; and the Sumerian merchants who followed the prospectors had to transport, in the same laborious way, the
exports with which they paid for their imports.

The only sumpter-animal that the Sumerians possessed in the age in which they were opening up their alluvium was the donkey. This was a domesticated onager (wild ass), and to break in this swiftest and shyest of all equines was as great a *tour de force* as the manufacture of agricultural implements out of clay. The Sumerians did not possess horses or camels; these were domesticated on the steppes by other peoples at later dates.

Thus, on the economic plane, the Sumerians surpassed their Egyptian pupils in the art of creating a civilization. On the other hand, on the political plane, the Egyptians shot ahead of the Sumerians. When the curtain rises on the first act of the tragedy of Sumerian history, we find the Sumerian society partitioned politically among a number of sovereign local city-states, and this political fission of the Sumerian World was incongruous with its unity on the cultural and economic and physiographical planes. The Sumerian civilization depended for its survival on an effective control and administration of the lower Tigris–Euphrates basin's waters; this control could not be fully effective unless and until it was brought under a unitary command; and, in Sumerian history, this ultimately indispensable political unification was achieved too late and at the cost of too much antecedent destruction and suffering, and, even then, it was not achieved by the Sumerians themselves; it was imposed on them eventually by their Akkadian neighbours.

On the other hand, Upper Egypt and the Delta were unified politically at the dawn of the Pharaonic Egyptian civilization. The grimness of the war in which the Delta was conquered and annexed by Upper Egypt is naïvely revealed in the scenes carved in relief on the Palette of Narmer, but, at this price, Egypt purchased political unity, and consequent internal peace and order, and these boons were preserved throughout the more than 3,000-year course of Pharaonic Egyptian history, save for some occasional and relatively brief 'intermediate periods' in which the normal state of unity and domestic peace was in abeyance.

The political unification of Upper and Lower Egypt was evidently a sudden dramatic event, but we are ignorant of its antecedents. In the subsequent ages, for which we have written records, the departments into which both parts of the United Kingdom of Pharaonic Egypt were divided were social realities. The inhabitants of each department had a local patriotism. But this is not evidence that, before the political unification of Egypt, these departments already existed as local sovereign states, corresponding to the Sumerian sovereign local city-states. The Greek rendering of the Egyptian word denoting these local territorial units was 'nomoí', and 'departments' is this Greek word's literal meaning. It is possible that the Egyptian 'nomes', so far from being pre-existing obstacles to unification, were, like the present-day departments of France, artificial creations designed to replace and obliterate previous historic territorial units which might have been a menace to the maintenance of political unity on a larger scale if the memory of them, and the emotional attachment to them, had been allowed to survive.

In Egypt, as in Sumer, the society's economic and political history is reflected in its religious history, and a comparison of the two histories on the religious plane bears out the classification of the Pharaonic Egyptian society as being a second specimen of the same species as the Sumerian, while at the same time it illustrates the Egyptian civilization's individuality.

In Egypt, as in Sumer, the gods stood for forces of Nature that held Man at their mercy; but, in Egypt too, this worship of Nature came to be supplemented by the worship of collective human power. To some extent this new religion found the same expression as in Sumer. In both Sumer and Pharaonic Egypt, some of the nature gods were conscripted to stand for Man's, as well as Nature's, power; and this addition to their functions was made easier by the fact that, though the Nature-gods, like Nature herself, were common to the whole society, they also came to be associated with particular places at which the local shrine had acquired ecumenical prestige. Even the Egyptian sun-god Re—a cosmic god *par excellence*—had a local habitation at Heliopolis on the east side of the Nile, near the head of the Delta.

Horus, the falcon son of the ecumenical vegetation-god Osiris, was appropriated by the rulers of the twin cities, Nekhen-Nekheb (Hieraconpolis), in the deep south of Upper Egypt. These were the political unifiers of Egypt at the outset of the history of the Pharaonic civilization *circa* 3100 B.C.; they achieved their conquest of the Delta under Horus' auspices, and this portentous political event gave an historical secondary meaning to the myth of Horus' battle with, and victory over, his evil kinsman Set. Originally this myth had symbolized a recurrent event in the course of Nature: the annual death and re-birth of vegetation—above all, the cereals which Neolithic Man had domesticated. The harvesting of the annual crops had become the condition for Man's survival now that Man had passed out of the food-collecting into the food-producing stage of economy. Osiris, the spirit of the vegetation, is murdered by his evil brother Set; the fratricide cuts up his victim's corpse and scatters the pieces; but these are then found and assembled by Osiris' devoted sister and wife Isis; Osiris comes to life again, and he hands over his kingdom to his loyal son Horus, who meanwhile has avenged Osiris' death by overcoming the murderer Set. After the annexation of the Delta to Upper Egypt, this nature-myth was turned to account for the commemoration of that historic political event. The focal point for the worship of Set happened to be the north-east corner of the Delta, at the opposite end of Egypt to Nekhen-Nekheb. Accordingly, Horus' victory over Set was made to stand for Upper Egypt's victory over Lower Egypt and for the consequent union of the two crowns.

The political unification of Egypt inaugurated the Pharaonic Egyptian civilization and continued to govern its 3,000-year history. This was an unprecedented manifestation of collective human power, and the worship of it took a novel form. The unifier and, after him, the successive wearers of the Double Crown were worshipped as incarnations of the overwhelming power concentrated in the two crowns that were now united on Pharaoh's head. Pharaoh (the Hebrew rendering of the Egyptian name for the palace at the United Kingdom's eventual capital, Memphis) was a live human god—present in the flesh side by side with the older gods who lived only a make-believe life in their ritually animated graven images.

The political union of Upper Egypt with the Delta by Narmer eventually had its counterpart in the Tigris–Euphrates basin in the union of Sumer with Akkad by Lugalzaggisi. But here the feat of unification was not achieved till the Sumerian civilization was more than seven centuries old, and it was accepted, without enthusiasm, as a lesser evil than a continuance of an agonizing international anarchy. Neither Lugalzaggisi nor Sargon, who wrested out of Lugalzaggisi's hands the empire that Lugalzaggisi had put together, was rewarded with deification, and though some of their successors—for instance, Naramsin (*c.* 2291–2255) and Shulgi (*c.* 2095–2048)—ventured to lay claim to divinity, they did not set a precedent. In Sumer and Akkad, live human gods were the exception, not the rule.

[8]

SUMER AND AKKAD, *c.* 3000–2230 B.C.

THE Sumerian civilization is rightly so named, for the opening-up and occupation of the alluvium of the lower Tigris–Euphrates basin—an achievement of collective human power which brought this civilization to birth—was the work of a single people, the Sumerians, who had a common language, religion, and culture. At the start, however, the Sumerians' collective human power was not embodied politically in an ecumenical state ruling over the whole of the alluvial domain that the Sumerians had won for themselves. The pioneering was done by a number of separate Sumerian communities, independent of each other politically, which attacked the alluvium at different points. We can infer this from the political structure of the Sumerian World which we find already in existence at the date of the earliest surviving decipherable and translatable documents in the Sumerian script. At the dawn of the history of the Sumerian civilization, Sumer was a mosaic of local sovereign city-states. The Sumerian World's cultural unity was not yet matched by unity on the political plane.

During the first five or six centuries of the Sumerian civilization's history (*c.* 3100–2500 B.C.) the city-states appear to have co-existed without colliding with each other. No doubt the alluvium was opened up only gradually, and, for a long time the irrigated fields and water-meadows created by the founders of each city amounted to no more than an oasis, insulated from the domains of other cities by stretches of still virgin swamp that, in the aggregate, were more extensive than the total area of all the oases together. During this earliest chapter of the history of the Sumerian civilization, the extent of the virgin swamp at the disposal of each community, beyond the edge of the territory that each had opened up, must have seemed virtually endless. Moreover, each community could control the waters within its own ambit without coming into competition with similar works that were being carried out contemporaneously by other communities in other patches.

The politically critical moment came when the expanding domains of the local city-states eliminated the insulating zones of swamp and became direct neighbours of each other. This consummation of Man's technological victory over Nature in Sumer created political problems on the plane of human relations; and the Sumerians did not respond to this social challenge promptly by the radical expedient of ecumenical unification which had been adopted in Egypt when the same social problem had presented itself there. When, in Sumer, the previously isolated pieces of the political mosaic came into contact with each other, they were not cemented together immediately, as they were in Egypt, into a single united kingdom. The city-states continued, after they had become contiguous, each to retain its local sovereign independence.

At this stage the productivity of the Tigris–Euphrates alluvium was so great that even a portion of it could provide the members of the 'establishment' of a Sumerian city-state with the means of living—and dying—in luxury. The excavation of the royal tombs of the First Dynasty of one city-state, Ur, has revealed that the sovereign had at his command artificers who could make exquisite jewelry for his queen, and that he could carry with him, not only the draft-oxen of the royal waggon, but also a cortège of human attendants of both sexes, to serve him in a presumptive after-life by being put to death, or by voluntarily committing suicide, as the climax of their sovereign's funeral rites. This extreme degree of class-differentiation, which we find at Ur in this early chapter of the history of the Sumerian civilization, seems likely to have been typical of social conditions in the whole of the contemporary Sumerian World.

In the next phase of Sumerian history, which opened about half way through the third millennium B.C., the salient feature is not the maintenance of the privileged status of the 'establishment' in each city-state; it is the collision of the city-states with each other. The bas-relief on which King Eannatum of Lagash celebrated his victory over Lagash's neighbour Umma shows that, by this time, inter-state warfare in Sumer had become highly organized and proportionately grim and lethal. Eannatum's troops were not only expensively equipped with helmets (perhaps metallic) and ample shields; they were also well drilled for fighting in phalanx formation. Eannatum's sculptor displays them, drawn up shoulder to shoulder and line behind line, with the pikes of several ranks protruding from the front rank's shield-wall. The corpses of the defeated enemy soldiers lie prone beneath the feet of the victorious army and its leader. By this date, the kings of Sumerian city-states may have ceased to demand human sacrifices at their graves, but they were now exacting human sacrifices on a far larger scale from the combatants on both sides in their wars with each other, and the victims of war were the choicest of the belligerent communities' young men.

The bone of contention between Lagash and Umma in Eannatum's day was the possession of a canal on the border between the two states—a prize that carried with it the enjoyment of the produce of the adjoining land, whose productivity depended on the irrigation and drainage that the coveted canal provided. In this war for the life-giving canal, Eannatum claims to have been the victor, but we may infer that, even if this victory was genuine, it was costly. At any rate, at Lagash the precarious domestic balance of social power seems to have been upset. The Sumerian peasantry's tolerance of the 'establishment's' privileges was conditional on the continuance of the unprivileged majority's belief that the privileged minority was performing effectively a social service that was indispensable for the welfare of the community as a whole. This belief must have been shaken by the time King Urukagina of Lagash (*c.* 2378–2371 B.C.) was able to challenge the authority of the priesthood.

If Urukagina did attempt to make a social revolution he was thwarted. He was overthrown by King Lugalzaggisi, who had already established his rule over two city-states, namely Umma and Uruk. Urukagina went on to incorporate in his dominions not only Lagash but all the other Sumerian city-states. He then expanded his empire beyond the bounds of Sumer till it stretched 'from sea to sea'—that is, from the head of the Persian Gulf to the Mediterranean coast of northern Syria.

Lugalzaggisi (*c.* 2371–2347 B.C.) conquered his empire by force of arms, yet his imperialistic wars were a lesser evil than the chronic inconclusive inter-state warfare which the Sumerians had been inflicting on themselves; and, indeed, forcible political unification was the only cure for this social malady. In the lower basin of the Tigris and Euphrates, the completed network of waterways, natural and artificial, was indivisible; and, so long as this network was not controlled by a single authority possessing the power to regulate and distribute the waters that were the means of life, the management of these waters could not be either efficient or peaceful. Inevitably it was a perpetual *casus belli* between local sovereign states, for these would be bound to compete and conflict with each other in striving each to win the maximum amount of water-control for itself. Lugalzaggisi's feat of unifying Sumer politically and then extending his empire north-westwards made a unitary control of the waters of the Tigris and Euphrates feasible for the first time; and it also put the ruler of Sumer in possession of Sumer's source of timber on Mount Amanus, and perhaps also of its sources of copper, still farther afield.

However, the fruits of Lugalzaggisi's empire-building were not harvested by Lugalzaggisi himself or by any other emperor of Sumerian nationality. The empire welded together by Lugalzaggisi was wrested out of his hands by an Akkadian Semitic-speaking officer, Sargon, who appears to have started his career by becoming the ruler of Kish. Sargon had seceded from Kish and had founded a city of his own at Agade. The site has not yet been identified, but evidently it was somewhere in the neighbourhood of the future site of Babylon, and the location was well chosen; for, lying, as it certainly did lie, towards the north-western extremity of the alluvium, where the courses of the Tigris and Euphrates swerve closest to each other, it gave its occupant the power to control all the water-network from end to end of the alluvium, down to the mouths of the Twin Rivers.

Sargon's seizure of Lugalzaggisi's empire is perhaps not the first appearance of a Semitic-speaker in recorded history. The people of Byblos may already have been Semitic-speaking when they first entered into commercial and cultural relations with Pharaonic Egypt; and this was 600–700 years before Sargon's day. However, Sargon's Empire of Sumer and Akkad was the first great power whose rulers spoke a Semitic language. Sargon's Akkad, with its imperial capital at Agade, lay astride the Tigris and Euphrates, upstream from Sumer, and it extended as far to the north-west as the points at which the alluvium begins. We do not know whether the establishment of a Semitic-speaking population in this strategic position was Sargon's doing, or whether the Akkadians had infiltrated into this section of the Tigris–Euphrates basin at some earlier date. In any case, it can be assumed that the Akkadians, and also the Canaanites, who are the earliest known Semitic-speaking occupants of Palestine and Syria, had come from Arabia; for this is the region from which subsequent successive waves of Semitic-speakers—the Amorite wave, the Hebrew–Aramaean–Chaldaean wave, and the Arab wave— swept over the northern shores of the Arabian steppe into the Fertile Crescent.

The languages of the Semitic family are closely related to each other, and the Semitic family itself is distantly related to groups of languages in North Africa—the Ancient Egyptian language (represented today by Coptic), the 'Kushite' languages of north-east Africa (Beja, Danākil, Galla, Somali), and the Berber dialects of north-west Africa. Thanks to the conductivity of the steppes, the Semitic languages have been more widely disseminated than any others except the Indo–European and the Turkish. Arabic, the latest of the Semitic languages to be carried out of Arabia in a *Völkerwanderung*, is spoken today right across South-West Asia and northern Africa from the western foot of the Zagros Range and the eastern shore of the Persian Gulf to the North-African shore of the Atlantic. Syriac, the modern form of Aramaic, is still spoken at a few spots in the Antilebanon Range and along the western shore of Lake Urmiyah, while Hebrew is now again spoken in Palestine.

Sargon of Agade reigned *c.* 2371–2316 B.C. and the dynasty he

founded lasted till *c.* 2230 B.C. The empire captured from Lugalzaggisi
by Sargon and handed on by Sargon to his descendants was the counterpart, in Sumero-Akkadian history, of the Old Kingdom in Pharaonic
Egyptian history; but the Old Kingdom had the advantage over the
Empire of Sumer and Akkad in two respects. It was established at the
dawn of the history of the Pharaonic Egyptian civilization, which was
the auspicious moment, and its founders were not aliens. Their place of
origin, the twin cities Nekhen-Nekheb, lay just within the southern
bounds of Egypt. Their rulers were the wardens of Egypt's southern
marches, and in playing this role they may have acquired the martial
prowess that they eventually displayed in the fratricidal war by which
they imposed political unity on the Egyptian World. By contrast, Akkad,
with its capital Agade, lay just outside the north-western bounds of
Sumer. The Akkadians were semi-barbarian interlopers, and Sargon
and his descendants, like Sargon's predecessor Lugalzaggisi, were men
of war, whereas the Pharaonic Egyptian United Kingdom, once established, gave Egypt nearly a thousand years of continuous peace.

Sargon himself is reported to have led an expeditionary force into
eastern Asia Minor in response to an appeal for help from a settlement
of traders—presumably Akkadians—who were being ill-treated by the
natives. This reputed exploit of Sargon's may be legendary. It may be
an antedating of the history of the authentic settlement of Assyrian
traders, from the twentieth to the late nineteenth century B.C., in a
suburb of the city of Kaneš, where their archives have been retrieved.
However, the historicity of the expedition of the Sargonid Naramsin
into the Zagros highlands is not in doubt. It is attested by the bas-relief
on Naramsin's stele—as grim a visual document as Eannatum's bas-
relief and as Narmer's palette.

Though brutal and ostensibly triumphal, Naramsin's expedition was
probably an offensive–defensive operation, to judge by the sequel; and,
if he was really on the defensive, he was defending not only Akkad but
also Sumer and the Sumerian civilization. This civilization had captivated its Akkadian conquerors. They had adopted it almost *en bloc*,
including its script and even its religion. Most of the Akkadian gods were
Sumerian gods thinly disguised under Semitic names; the Akkadian
language was put into writing in Sumerian characters, though these
were clumsy instruments for conveying a language of the Semitic family,
since the root-form of a Semitic word is not a string of syllables but a set
of three consonants.

The Sumerian civilization had already developed its two salient
features when the Akkadians took it over. One of these features was
religious devoutness; the other was business ability. The devoutness is
expressed vividly in the figurines of worshippers which were a major

genre of Sumero-Akkadian visual art. The suppliant's humbly folded hands and tensely staring eyes convey the vehemence of his prayer to a present-day viewer. The monuments of Sumero-Akkadian business ability are the hundreds of thousands of inscribed clay tablets recording business transactions of many kinds. The gods were the biggest property-owners, and the administrators of their temples may have been the pioneers in working out the Sumerian methods of doing business systematically on the grand scale; but the public sector of the Sumerian economy was balanced by a private sector. In business the Sumerians were as whole-hearted as they were in worship. In both fields of activity, the Akkadians emulated the Sumerians' practice and caught their spirit.

Circa 2230 B.C. the Sargonid dynasty was overthrown by Gutaean barbarian highlanders from the north-east, and from *c.* 2230 to *c.* 2120 B.C. both Sumer and Akkad were under Gutaean rule. During this period of Gutaean domination, the Semitic-speaking Amorites seeped into Akkad from the south-west and subsequently founded Babylon. The Gutaeans, detested by Akkadians and Sumerians alike, were eventually exterminated or evicted. The Amorite trespassers on Akkadian ground lived on to play a leading role in a later phase of Sumero-Akkadian history.

[9]

PHARAONIC EGYPT, *c.* 3000–2181 B.C.

SINCE the dawn in Sumer, toward the close of the fourth millennium B.C., of the earliest of the regional civilizations, a number of societies of this species have come and gone. Others still survive, though the oldest of these survivors, namely the Chinese, is at least 1,500 years younger than its Sumerian and Pharaonic Egyptian forerunners. Among all these regional civilizations the Pharaonic Egyptian in its first phase, the so-called 'Old Kingdom' (*c.* 3100–2181 B.C.) has distinguished itself by its relative stability. During its time-span of nearly a thousand years, the Old Kingdom was more stable than any subsequent dispensation in the history of either Egypt itself or any other region, and some of the Egyptian Old Kingdom's achievements survived the Old Kingdom's demise. The highly distinctive style of visual art and system of writing that the Pharaonic Egyptians created at the inauguration of the Old Kingdom, and the religion they inherited, retained their identity till the third century of the Christian Era as going concerns, and did not become extinct till the fifth century. Of course they underwent changes in the course of these three millennia and a half, but, within that time-span, there was no break in the continuity of the Pharaonic Egyptian cultural tradition. As for the regulation of the waters of the lower course of the Nile below the First Cataract, by which the Egyptians converted a former unproductive and inhospitable jungle-swamp into fertile fields and pastures, this has been maintained down to the present day.

In the former land of Sumer, an area along the lower course of the Euphrates has not been saved from reverting to its pristine state, and, throughout the alluvial south-eastern portion of the present-day state of Iraq, the work of water-control, carried out by the Sumerians five or six millennia ago, is now having to be started again *de novo*. The heirs of the Pharaonic Egyptian Old Kingdom have never allowed their predecessors' work for controlling the waters to be undone in any part of Egypt.

The fifth-century-B.C. Greek observer Herodotus asserted that Egypt was 'the gift of the Nile'. He was thinking of the alluvial soil which the river had deposited and which it continued to replenish with annual increments of silt till the completion in 1902 of the first barrage at Aswan. It would, however, be nearer to the truth to say that Egypt was the gift to posterity of the late pre-dynastic and early dynastic Egyptians. The Nile's gift had provided no more than the raw materials for the conversion of an alluvial jungle-swamp into an alluvial garden. This transformation of a wilderness into the land of Egypt was achieved by the sociality, industry, skill, and administrative ability of the Egyptians themselves.

The Pharaonic Egyptians' capital achievement was the organization of an effective centralized government for the whole of Egypt from the First Cataract to the sea. This political and administrative unification of Egypt was achieved at the beginning of the history of the Pharaonic Egyptian civilization. This was the political enabling condition for the maintenance of the irrigation-agriculture of Egypt, and, like this, it has been maintained down to the present day, with some brief temporary lapses into political disunity at intervals during the Pharaonic Age. Egyptologists label these lapses 'intermediate periods', because they rightly deem that effective unity has been the normal political dispensation in Egypt since the original unifier-Pharaoh's day. This enduring political achievement, which is unique in respect of the earliness of its date, was no doubt made possible by the excellence of Egypt's internal system of communications, which was likewise unique until the invention of railways a century and a half ago.

The collective human power concentrated in the hands of an effective ruler of the whole of Egypt produced an unprecedentedly large surplus of the material means of life, beyond the requirements of bare subsistence, when it was applied systematically and skilfully to the exploitation of the tamed Egyptian alluvium's potentiality for agricultural production. Applied to monumental architectural work, which was not productive in material terms, the same collective power, in combination with the release of part of the people's time from the primary task of food-production, gave Pharaoh the means of satisfying, for Pharaoh himself and for a privileged inner circle of his courtiers, a desire that was the paramount concern of every Egyptian, in all walks of life, throughout the Pharaonic Age.

The Egyptians were eager to secure everlasting life for themselves after death, and they pursued this posthumous objective more earnestly than any that would be attainable within a human life-time. They were materialist-minded. They enjoyed the material goods—food and property—that were obtainable in this life; they envisaged immortality after death in terms of an unending enjoyment of amenities of the same kind; and, since life before death is brief, whereas life after death might perhaps be made everlasting, they spent more wealth and effort on a tomb than on a house and on the mummification of the corpse than on the adornment of the living body. So far from shrinking from the thought of death, they took pleasure in anticipating it mentally by preparing for the far longer and more important phase of life which they believed that death would inaugurate for them if they took the necessary previous action.

The Egyptians' beliefs about the life after death were neither unitary nor consistent with each other. The physical preservation of a mummified corpse in a monumental tomb matched a belief that this would enable one part of the soul to keep the corpse company. They also believed that Pharaoh, at any rate, would join the other gods with another part of his soul. They even harboured a crude primitive belief that Pharaoh would actually devour his fellow gods and would thereby appropriate their powers. A third belief was that Osiris—the vegetation-spirit who had died and had come to life again—would enable his worshippers to achieve the same metamorphosis, and that he would receive them in a green paradise in the west, to dwell with him there blissfully for ever. The Egyptian Osiris-myth bears a striking resemblance to the Canaanite Adonis-myth and to the Attis-myth of Asia Minor, but, if it came to Egypt from abroad, it had lodged itself in the heart of the Egyptians' religious life at an early stage of the history of the Pharaonic Egyptian civilization. In the long course of this history, the worship of Osiris became increasingly popular, and eventually it also became ethical. Death, so it came to be believed, would be followed by judgment, and only those souls whose good deeds outweighed their evil deeds in the posthumous judges' balance would be admitted to Osiris' paradise.

Meanwhile, the belief that immortality could be acquired through being interred in a monumental tomb led to the invention of a massive style of architecture in stone. The development of the quarryman's and the mason's and builder's skills in Pharaonic Egypt has already been noticed. Masonry of the age of the First Dynasty has been unearthed, but the achievement of monumental work on the grand scale was as sudden as the previous political unification of Egypt and creation of the hieroglyphic script. The earliest stone pyramid was built at Saqqarah for King Zoser (c. 2668–2647 B.C.) by his minister and architect Imhotpe. This was an experimental piece of work. The stones were cut to the shape of bricks, and were put together like brickwork. Moreover, in the course of the work, there was more than one change of plan, and the ambitious final monument was larger than the more modest earlier essays that it incorporated.

Imhotpe was not only remembered by posterity; he was revered and was even deified, and his abiding prestige was well-deserved, for he was indeed the father of the Egyptian monumental architecture in stone. Within little more than half a century, King Snofru (*c.* 2613–2590 B.C.), the inaugurator of the Fourth Dynasty of Pharaohs, was building a pyramid (or possibly two pyramids) of massive stone blocks at Dahshur; and then in rapid succession the Great Pyramid at Gizah was built by Cheops (Khufu) (*c.* 2589–2567 B.C.), the Second at Gizah by Chephren (Khaef-Re) (*c.* 2558–2534 B.C.), and the Third at Gizah by Mycerinus (Menkaure).

Sculpture blossomed *pari passu* with architecture. The architects' mastery of stone for the building of colossal monuments was matched by the sculptors' mastery of it for carving portraits in which the traits of a personality were immortalized. In their magnificent portrait-statues, Cheops and Chephren still live for us forty-five centuries after the date of their ephemeral lives in the flesh. Their countenances, as portrayed, are majestic. These Pharaohs look as if they wielded their overwhelming power effortlessly, as befitted the gods that they claimed to be. Yet an Old-Kingdom Pharaoh could also be disarmingly human. Mycerinus (*c.* 2523–2496 B.C.) had his wife's statue carved side by side with his own, and their arms are round each other's waists. Evidently even a Pharaoh's relation with his wife could be one of mutual affection and esteem, and the humaneness of the relation is still more clearly manifest in the Old-Kingdom portrait-statues of non-Pharaonic husbands and wives seated side by side in the same posture of mutual embrace.

These three-dimensional representations of married couples are one of the genres of Old-Kingdom art. This suggests that, in that age of Egyptian history, marriage was an institution that satisfied the emotional needs of both partners. If so, it will have been a stable institution, and its stability might be one of the causes of the stability of the Old Kingdom itself.

However, even the Egyptian Old Kingdom was mortal, and, in the course of its long life, it suffered stresses and strains. During the first half of its millennium, there was a progressive centralization of the government and progressive concentration of power in Pharaoh's hands. Nekhen-Nekheb, the home of the original unifiers of Egypt, lay inconveniently close to the southern extremity of Upper Egypt. After the union of the two crowns, the capital was moved downstream, first to Thinis (a short way downstream below Abydos) and then to Memphis, a new city, just above the head of the Delta, which was the most convenient site for the capital of the United Kingdom. The absolutism of the Pharaonic monarchy reached its peak in the time of the Fourth Dynasty (*c.* 2613–2495 B.C.), but Cheops' air of effortless omnipotence is deceptive; for in reality his absolutism was not unchallenged. The deification of the wearer of the Double Crown was not the only form in which the political unification of Egypt was expressed on the plane of religion. Pharaoh had to reckon with a host of non-human gods who had been worshipped in Egypt before the first Pharaoh had been deified.

The political unification of Egypt had raised questions about the ancient gods who represented ubiquitous forces of Nature. Now that these gods' local shrines had all been brought within the bounds of a single political realm, the gods themselves had become members of a single divine society. What were the genealogical and the hierarchical relations between them? A theology, establishing these relations, was worked out at the Sun-god Re's holy city Heliopolis, and the Heliopolitan presentation of the godhead as a pantheon of nine non-human gods under Re's presidency seems to have clashed with the Fourth Dynasty's doctrine that the godhead was incarnate in Pharaoh.

The transition from the Fourth Dynasty to the Fifth Dynasty (*c.* 2494–2346 B.C.) signifies, not, apparently, a genealogical break of continuity, but a new departure in Pharaonic theology which was, in effect, a capitulation of the government at Memphis to the priesthood at Heliopolis. This change in the balance of power is reflected in a change in Pharaonic architecture. Instead of attempting to vie with their predecessors in building colossal pyramids, the Pharaohs of the Fifth and Sixth Dynasties built temples in honour of the supreme member of the Heliopolitan pantheon, the Sun-god Re (Ra). Pharaoh had always been deemed to be one of the gods, but, from the inauguration of the Fifth Dynasty onwards, his divinity was deemed to derive from his being the son of Re, begotten on Pharaoh's human mother, not by a sexual act of his human father, but by a non-physical act of the god.

The Fourth Dynasty had brought the Pharaonic Egyptian civilization to its apogee in all fields of achievement; the Fifth Dynasty had marked a theological turning-point; the Sixth Dynasty (*c.* 2345–2181 B.C.) saw a decline that ended in a fall. Pepi II, who was the last Pharaoh not only of the Sixth Dynasty but of the Old Kingdom itself, had the longest reign of any sovereign whose regnal dates are on record. He was on the throne for perhaps ninety-four years (*c.* 2278–2184 B.C.). Pepi II reigned, but he hardly governed. He came to the throne as a child, and he lived to see an accelerating disintegration of the realm that the first Pharaoh of the First Dynasty had welded together.

Three causes of the Old Kingdom's eventual decline and fall can be discerned. The direct political cause was the gradual transformation of the Crown's once amenable local officials into local princes who held office by *de facto* hereditary right and no longer by revocable appointment. These captured the control of the native Egyptian contingents of

the army, and the Pharaonic Government's counter-move—the enlist-
ment of Nubian mercenaries—failed to salvage Pharaoh's military
supremacy. The second cause of the Old Kingdom's decline and fall was
the cumulative economic burden of the Pharaoh's successive funerary
foundations and temples.

The burden was not imposed by the building of the physical monuments. Egypt's fertile fields produced a surplus, and the fertilizing Nile
made agricultural work impossible during the period of the annual
inundation. The current year's surplus product, together with the compulsory annual vacation from agricultural labour, liberated and fed the
seasonal man-power with which these mighty monuments were erected.
The cumulative burden was imposed by the assignment of land and its
produce for the upkeep, in perpetuity, of the rites on which the immortality of each immortalized Pharaoh was deemed to depend. This
meant, in practice, the economically unprofitable maintenance of an
increasing host of priests, who, unlike the seasonal workers on the
monuments, were parasites on Egypt's productivity.

The third cause of the fall was the increasing scepticism, and consequent restiveness, of the mass of the people. In Pharaonic Egypt in the
Age of the Old Kingdom the class-differentiation between the unprivileged majority and the privileged 'establishment' was even greater
than it had been in Sumer in the Age of the Warring City-States and of
the subsequent Sargonid Empire. The conscription of labour for the
building of the Pharaohs' mighty works would hardly have been
practicable if it had been entirely coercive. We may guess that the
conscripted workers had believed that they were working for something
of greater social and religious significance and value than merely
Pharaoh's personal aggrandisement. We may also guess that, when this
hypothetical faith was lost, the emotional reaction was on the scale of
the mountains which faith had once moved.

Our information about the breakdown of the Pharaonic Egyptian
society that followed the centenarian Pharaoh Pepi II's death is derived
from works of literature that seem to have been composed in the Age of
the Middle Kingdom (*c.* 2040–1730 B.C.). If this is in fact the date of our
evidence, this evidence is not contemporary, yet it gives the impression
of presenting a true picture of the social convulsions that it portrays
retrospectively. This first 'intermediate period' in the history of Pharaonic
Egypt seems to have witnessed a social revolution that was not nipped
in the bud, as Urukagina's abortive revolution at Lagash had been. The
image of the Egyptian revolution that imprinted itself on Egyptian folk-
memory was the impression of a raging tearing revolution in which the
tables had been turned and the roles had been reversed. The poor had
despoiled the rich; the former masters had become servants of their

former servants. The service of the ancient Pharaohs' funerary rites had been abandoned. Rites, Pharaohs, pyramids, and temples, with all the rest of the Old Kingdom's burdensome Pharaonic apparatus, had been discredited, scorned, and denounced. This is the earliest thorough-going social revolution of which we have a record.

There are indications that the Pharaonic Sixth Dynasty may have been actually overthrown, as the Sargonid dynasty certainly had been in the Sumero-Akkadian world half a century earlier, by a barbarian invasion from the north-east, but, unlike the unquestionably valid evidence for the occupation of Sumer and Akkad by the Gutaeans, the apparent evidence for a barbarian invasion of Egypt during the first 'intermediate period' of Pharaonic Egyptian history is not conclusive. However, there is no doubt about the success of the local nomarchs (prefects of departments) in transforming themselves from being Pharaoh's appointees and agents into becoming virtually sovereign princes. The evidence for this is not retrospective. After the political re-unification of Egypt at the beginning of the Age of the Middle Kingdom, the Pharaohs of the Twelfth Dynasty (1991–1786 B.C.), potent though they were, found that they had to edge their way very slowly and cautiously toward their objective of bringing the nomarchs to heel after these had been virtually independent for at least two hundred years.

[10]

THE ECUMENICAL HORIZON,

c. 2500—2000 B.C.

THE downfall of the Sargonid Empire of Sumer and Akkad and of the
Pharaonic Egyptian Old Kingdom is less surprising than the re-
establishment of each of these unitary political regimes after an interregnum which lasted in Sumer for more than a century (*c.* 2230–2120
B.C.) and in Egypt for nearly a century and a half (*c.* 2181–2040 B.C.).
These recuperations are remarkable; for, in both cases, the collapse of a
unitary political regime had brought with it an apparent disintegration
of the civilization itself. The sequel showed that both these regional
civilizations were tougher and more resilient than they had appeared to
be at the time of their first collapse. After their respective restorations,
the Sumero-Akkadian civilization survived for another 2,200 years, and
the Pharaonic Egyptian civilization for as long or even longer. However,
by the time of their rehabilitation, these had ceased to be the only two
regional civilizations in the Oikoumenê. Others had arisen side by side
with them. Already, as early as *c.* 2500 B.C., the commercial expansion
of the Sumero-Akkadian society north-westwards had called new
regional civilizations into life in Asia Minor and in Cyprus. The new
civilization that arose contemporaneously in Crete may have drawn its
inspiration not only from Sumer and Akkad but from Egypt as well.

The new civilization in Asia Minor was a satellite of the Sumero-
Akkadian civilization inasmuch as it had borrowed from it important
elements, including its script and some of its gods. But the borrowed
script was used, not only for writing in the Akkadian language, but also
for conveying the indigenous languages as well; and the indigenous
pantheon maintained itself side by side with the imported Akkadian
divinities.

The islands, as well as the continental perimeter, of the Mediterranean Sea had been colonized already, in the Neolithic Age. In the
colonization of the islands there had naturally been a time-lag; but,

when once the art of maritime navigation had been mastered, the
Levantine islands had become propitious sites for civilizations. The
copper mines on Cyprus, for example, became as important an element
in the economy of Egypt and Sumer as the forests on Mount Lebanon
and on Mount Amanus when, in the lower Tigris–Euphrates basin and
lower Nile valley, the Neolithic Age passed over into the Chalcolithic
Age, and then into the Copper and the Bronze Age. In Cyprus and
Crete and the Cyclades, the civilizations that arose in the course of the
second half of the third millennium B.C. were, no doubt, inspired by the
older civilizations of Sumer and Egypt, but the originality of the insular
civilizations was proportionate to their distance from the regions from
which the stimulus had come. Whereas Continental Asia Minor's
cultural indebtedness to Sumer and Akkad is clear, the indebtedness of
the Cretan civilization to Sumer and Akkad and to Egypt is less evident
than the distinctiveness of this civilization's features. The Cretan
civilization has been labelled 'Minoan' by the modern archaeologists
who have brought it back to light, in allusion to the legendary Cretan
sovereign of the Seas, King Minos. The 'Minoan' civilization created a
naturalistic art which had no contemporary counterpart except in the
art of the geographically remote Indus civilization. The Minoan civilization also distinguished itself in pursuing the art of navigation to
which it owed its birth.

In the pre-Metallic Age, a highly prized raw material for the making
of blades with sharp cutting-edges had been obsidian. This is a natural
glass that has been produced by volcanic action, and like tin—the indispensable alloy for transforming copper into bronze—obsidian is rare.
There are deposits in the island of Melos, which is within easy reach of
both Crete and the Cyclades. There are also deposits on the volcanic
Lipari Islands, in the Tyrrhene Sea, on the far side of the Straits of
Messina for mariners approaching from the Aegean. Cycladic mariners
—perhaps defeated by Cretan competitors for the command of the
obsidian on Melos—seem to have been the pioneers in the discovery and
exploitation of the obsidian on the Lipari Islands. The Minoans followed
their Cycladic neighbours into these western waters, and traded there on
a larger scale and in a greater variety of commodities. Thus, by the
close of the third millennium B.C., the coasts, nor only of continental
Greece, but also of south-eastern Italy and of Sicily, had been brought
within the ambit of the civilizations that were in existence by that date,
though Crete was still the farthest point westward at which a full-blown
regional civilization was, by then, already in being.

To the east of Sumer, the alluvium deposited by the Rivers Tigris and
Euphrates is adjoined by a smaller alluvial deposit of the Rivers
Karkhah, Diz, and Karun, and here, in Elam, a civilization had arisen

which can also be classified as a satellite of the Sumero-Akkadian civilization or alternatively as a veritable province of it. Like the Egyptians, the Elamites had created a script of their own, which resembled the Sumerian script in its structure but was composed of independently invented characters in a distinctive style. But, during the latter half of the third millennium B.C., the Elamites took, as the Akkadians had taken from the start, to writing their language in the Sumerian script, and, when Elam was incorporated in the Empire of Sumer and Akkad after this had been re-established by the Third Dynasty of Ur *c.* 2113 B.C., the Elamites even adopted the Akkadian language temporarily—and this for commercial as well as for political transactions. By the thirteenth century B.C., the Elamites had re-asserted their linguistic independence, but they never reverted to the use of their original non-Sumerian script.

The Elamite civilization—or Elamite province of the Sumero-Akkadian civilization—was in any case a minor society, though the Elamites impinged politically on the Sumero-Akkadian World in the second millennium B.C. and maintained their distinctive identity long enough for their language, still written in the Sumerian script, to be adopted in the last millennium B.C. as one of the official languages of the First Persian Empire.

Till recently, there was no archaeological evidence for the existence, in the third millennium B.C., of any civilization in the area between Elam and the Indus basin. Now, however, a city—dated between 2900 and 1900 by various scientific tests—is being excavated at Sharh-i-Sokhta, a site in present-day Iranian Seistan, just on the Iranian side of the Iran–Afghanistan frontier, which once adjoined the lowest reach of the Helmand River before this changed to its present course. The inhabitants practised agriculture and animal husbandry, metallurgy (copper), pottery-making, weaving, and dyeing. The excavators report that the Sharh-i-Sokhta civilization was independent of the Sumero-Akkadian civilization, but that there is evidence that it traded with Sumer and also with the regions that are now Afghanistan and Soviet Türkmenistan. Pending the further progress of the excavations and the publication of fuller reports, we remain in the dark. We do not know the Sharh-i-Sokhta civilization's origins or its affinities, if it had any.

Eventually the excavations at Sharh-i-Sokhta may perhaps throw light on a major new civilization that made its appearance in the Indus basin in the second half of the third millennium B.C., which is the date of the assimilation of the Elamite civilization to the Sumero-Akkadian and of the rise of a satellite of the Sumero-Akkadian civilization in Asia Minor.

The region in which the material remains of the Indus civilization have been disinterred is about twice as distant from Sumer, overland, as either Egypt or Asia Minor, and it is therefore not surprising that, to date, there is no evidence that the creators of the Indus civilization were inspired by any influences emanating from Sumer. The origin of the Indus civilization remains enigmatic, pending the decipherment and interpretation of its script. We do not know whether the Indus script resembles the Sumerian script in its structure, as does the Pharaonic Egyptian script.

However, in the Indus basin, as in the lower valley of the Nile, the regional civilization appears to have made its appearance suddenly, full-blown; and, if the influence of the Sumerian civilization radiated itself south-eastwards, by the sea, as well as north-westwards overland, the possibility that the Indus civilization may have been brought to birth by a cultural stimulus from Sumer cannot be ruled out of account, considering that the sea-passage from the head of the Persian Gulf to the Indus delta is less than half as long as the passage from the same starting-point to the Red-Sea coast of Upper Egypt. Moreover, we know that the Indus civilization made contact with the Sumerian, even if it was not originally inspired by it; for seals, engraved with inscriptions in the Indus script, have been found in Sumer in an archaeological stratum that is older than the Sargonid dynasty. This is evidence that the Indus civilization was already a going concern at least as early as 2500 B.C.

This dating of the presence of the Indus civilization in the Indus basin tells us that the language conveyed in the so far undeciphered script is not primary Sanskrit, since the invaders who brought this Indo-European language into the Indian subcontinent did not arrive there till at least a thousand years later than 2500 B.C. But we do not know whether the language of the Indus civilization's inscriptions was a member of the Dravidian family, which preceded primary Sanskrit in the subcontinent, or whether it was a language of the Austro-Asiatic family, which seems to have been an earlier arrival in the subcontinent than either primary Sanskrit or the Dravidian languages.

The Indus civilization's script was not its only distinctive feature. Its visual art was naturalistic by comparison with the more conventional art of Sumer and Akkad and of Egypt, as is revealed by the miniature works of Indus art that have been retrieved. The Indus civilization's architecture, both public and domestic, gives the impression of being the work of a utilitarian-minded society. The water-supply, drainage-system, baths, and quays are of an Imperial Roman and indeed almost Modern Western standard. The irrigation-agriculture that was the basis of the Indus civilization's economy was, of course, not peculiar to it; nor again were the practice of the techniques of spinning and weaving and dyeing, or the use of the potter's wheel. However, the cotton-bush, which provided the Indus people with the material for light textiles, may have been domesticated by them independently. They may also have been the original domesticators of the humped cattle (zebu).

Another feature that distinguishes the Indus civilization from its counterparts in the Tigris–Euphrates basin and in the lower Nile valley is the magnitude of its geographical scale. The two principal Indus cities so far discovered are Mohenjo-daro in Sind and Harappa in the Punjab, and these are 400 miles distant from each other. This is not far short of the distance between Aswan and Cairo; and the Indus civilization's domain was not confined to the Indus basin itself. It extended westwards into eastern Baluchistan and eastwards into Gujerat, while, farther to the north, it embraced at least the upper waters of the Jumna–Ganges basin. In this eastward direction the progress of archaeological exploration has been bringing more and more relics of the Indus civilization to light. We have not yet ascertained its eastern bounds.

While the number of the regional civilizations had thus been increasing, agriculture and animal husbandry had been spreading in the Old-World Oikoumenê from their place of origin in South-West Asia into areas far beyond the bounds of those regional civilizations that were already in existence by 2500 B.C., and agriculture, at any rate, may have been practised by that date in Meso-America too, though here it was almost certainly not disseminated from the Old World but was invented in the New World independently. Estimates of the age of the earliest specimens of domesticated maize that have been found in this region range from the first half of the fourth millennium B.C. to *c.* 2500 B.C. The wild plant from which domesticated maize has been bred may now have been found, if the maize-cobs, mentioned already, in a deposit, dated *c.* 4000 B.C., in Coxcatlán cave are really wild and are not even slightly domesticated. However, village-communities, supporting themselves by agriculture, had not appeared anywhere in the Americas by 2000 B.C. Meanwhile, in the Old-World Oikoumenê, the Neolithic culture, with its domesticated plants and animals, had spread westwards from South-West Asia along the continental and insular shores of the Mediterranean Sea into the Mediterranean's African and European hinterlands, till, by 2500 B.C., this way of life had become prevalent as far to the west as the eastern shore of the North-Atlantic Ocean, including the off-shore islands and southern Sweden, which was one of these offshore islands *de facto*, since it was accessible only across salt water.

The North-Atlantic fringe of the Old-World Oikoumenê is nearly twice as far away from South-West Asia as the Indus basin is; but the middle and lower sections of the basin of the Yellow River are still farther away from South-West Asia than the Atlantic coast of Europe. The oldest Neolithic culture of which relics have been found in the

Yellow River basin is the Yang-Shao culture. This has been labelled
with the name of a village in present-day Ho-nan which has been taken
as its type-site, but it seems to have started earlier and to have lasted
longer in what is now Kansu, the north-westernmost province of China
proper, and its painted pottery, which is its distinctive feature, resembles
the painted pottery of the Tripolje Neolithic culture that had established
itself in the western Ukraine before the close of the third millennium
B.C. This resemblance may not be fortuitous; it may be evidence of an
historical connexion; for Kansu and the Ukraine lie at opposite ends of
the Eurasian steppe—and the steppe, like the sea, is conductive. Neolithic pioneers from South-West Asia may have reached the southern
shore of the Eurasian steppe in Transcaspia, and may have travelled
across the steppe north-westwards to the Ukraine and north-eastwards
to Kansu simultaneously. The Yang-Shao Neolithic culture may have
established itself in the north-west of what is now China during the
second half of the third millennium B.C.

Thus the conductivity of the Eurasian steppe may have facilitated the
spread of agriculture and animal husbandry from South-West Asia to
China in the Neolithic Age. In the subsequent Chalcolithic Age the
steppe undoubtedly facilitated the dissemination of the languages of the
Indo-European family. The Indo-European languages, which may have
originated somewhere in eastern Europe, on the fringe of the Eurasian
steppe, have spread still more widely than the Semitic languages. Today,
Indo-European languages are spoken as far eastward as Bengal and
Eastern Siberia, and as far westward as the Pacific coast of the Americas,
as well as in Australia and New Zealand and also in Southern Africa,
though here they are spoken only by a small minority of the population.
It is no accident that the Indo-European-speakers, like the Semitic-
speakers, came out of, or over, a steppe in the first stage of their migrations. The conductivity of the steppes gave the first impetus to the
exceptionally wide dissemination of the languages of these two families.

Our oldest documentary records of any Indo-European language are
Indo-European Hittite documents. The name 'Hittite' is an English
rendering of the Hebrew rendering of 'Khatti', and the Kingdom of
Khatti in eastern Asia Minor was in existence, and was producing
documents in its rulers' Indo-European language, conveyed in an
adaptation of the Sumerian script, before the close of the seventeenth
century B.C. It is thought that the Indo-European language that had
established itself in Khatti by that date, and also the closely related
Luvian Indo-European language that had established itself in western
Asia Minor, had been introduced by immigrants as early as *c.* 2300 B.C.

Another Indo-European language, Greek, is thought to have been
introduced into continental Greece *c.* 1900 B.C. At about this date, a

distinctive new type of pottery, misleadingly labelled 'Minyan' ware, made its appearance in continental Greece and in the Troad, and in Greece there is evidence of contemporaneous destruction that was serious enough to give the regional culture a set-back. These pieces of archaeological evidence, taken together, seem to indicate the arrival in Greece of barbarian invaders, and, if the evidence is valid, these invaders must have been the bearers of the Greek language, since the decipherment of the documents in the 'Linear B' script shows that Greek was already being spoken in Greece before the next bout of barbarian invasions, which did not begin till *c.* 1200 B.C.

Both Greek and Luvian-Hittite are Indo-European languages of the so-called 'centum' set, in which an original K-sound survived, instead of changing in certain phonetic contexts into an S-sound, as it did in the languages of the set that has been given the label 'satem' because of this new departure. The languages of the 'centum' set are found at the two extremities of the Indo-European-speaking world. The Indo-European languages that established themselves in western Europe—Italic, Celtic, and Teutonic—are 'centum' languages, like Greek and like Luvian-Hittite, but a 'centum' Indo-European language was also spoken by the Tokharoi (called in Chinese Yüeh-chih), a people who, till the second century B.C., were living far away to the east, on the section of the Eurasian steppe that is adjoined nowadays by the western end of the Great Wall of China.

We have no information about the direction from which Asia Minor was reached by the intruders who introduced the Indo-European Hittite and Luvian languages there. They may have come out of the steppe at its western end and have reached Asia Minor via southeastern Europe and thence across the straits that link the Black Sea with the Aegean. This western route is their most likely route, and the Greek language was certainly brought from the steppe into Greece by a route running to the west of the Black Sea. Alternatively, it is possible, though less probable, that the Indo-European Hittite-speakers and the Luvian-speakers came out of the steppe on to its southern shore, in what is now Türkmenistan, and entered Asia Minor from the east, after crossing northern Iran.

It has also been suggested that the Indo-European Hittites at any rate, if not the Luvians, reached Asia Minor from the steppe by crossing the Caucasus Range. This suggestion is unrealistic; for, although a route across the Caucasus would have been relatively short, the Caucasus itself would have been an insuperable barrier for a migrating people. Armies have occasionally forced a passage between the south-eastern end of the Caucasus Range and the western shore of the Caspian Sea; yet, except for the Alans who have given their name to the Dar-i-Al Pass, across the mid point of the Caucasus Range, no Indo-European-speaking population has ever succeeded in lodging itself in the Caucasus or even in its foothills. At the present day, peoples speaking non-Indo-European languages still occupy the whole of the Caucasian highlands continuously from the western shore of the Caspian to the eastern shore of the Black Sea. There are now Turkish-speaking as well as Indo-European-speaking peoples on both sides of the Caucasus, but the Caucasian belt of non-Indo-European-speaking peoples and non-Turkish-speaking peoples still insulates the northern and southern Turkish-speaking and Indo-European-speaking peoples from each other.

What moved the Indo-European peoples to break out of the Eurasian steppe in a series of migrations that have eventually disseminated the languages of this family all round the globe? It is significant that Asia Minor is the region in which we have our earliest evidence of an Indo-European language's currency; for Asia Minor is the nearest region to the Eurasian steppe in which a civilization had established itself before the close of the third millennium B.C., and the latter part of that millennium is the date at which the Indo-European-speaking peoples are thought to have begun to migrate. It looks as if the lodestone that attracted them was the relative affluence of an adjacent civilization whose domain was accessible for barbarians to plunder. No doubt the civilization in Asia Minor radiated its influence beyond its own borders, and the barbarians who were dazzled by the glitter of a culture that was more productive than theirs were drawn towards this potential prize as a moth is drawn towards the flame of a candle.

The moth's self-inflicted doom is an apt simile for the nemesis that overtakes the barbarian invaders of more prosperous societies that lack the military strength to hold their aggressive barbarian neighbours at bay. The barbarian invaders' greed is self-defeating. If the intruders are not eventually exterminated by a counter-stroke, as the Gutaean conquerors of Sumer and Akkad were, they survive only to share in the impoverishment that they have inflicted on their victims. This was the ironical sequel to the conquest of Greece by the barbarians who probably introduced the Greek language there *c.* 1900 B.C.

[11]

THE OLD-WORLD OIKOUMENÊ,
c. 2140–1730 B.C.

THE Gutaean barbarian invaders of Sumer and Akkad had overthrown and replaced the Akkadian Sargonids, and it might have been expected that the native revolt by which the Gutaeans were exterminated or expelled after little more than a century of Gutaean domination (c. 2230–2120 B.C.) would have been led by the Gutaeans' Akkadian victims. Actually the liberator of Akkad, as well as Sumer, was not an Akkadian but a Sumerian. He was Utukegal of Uruk (ruled c. 2120–2113 B.C.). Neither Utukegal nor his city-state reaped the fruits of his victory, but the sceptre passed to the ruler of another Sumerian city-state, Ur. The Empire of Sumer and Akkad, which had been established originally by a Sumerian conqueror, Lugalzaggisi, and had then been wrested out of Lugalzaggisi's hands by the Akkadian Sargon of Agade, was now re-established by another Sumerian, Ur-Nammu of Ur (ruled c. 2113–2096 B.C.).

Since Sumer, not Akkad, was the cradle of the Sumero-Akkadian civilization, a Sumero-Akkadian empire, centred on a Sumerian city-state, might have been expected to be more firmly based than the semi-barbarian Akkadian regime of the Sargonids. Actually, Ur-Nammu's reconstituted Empire of Sumer and Akkad, and the Third Dynasty of Ur, of which he was the founder, lasted for little more than a century (c. 2113–2006 B.C.), and, during this spell of Sumerian political dominion, Akkad conquered Sumer linguistically. Sumer became first bilingual and then exclusively Akkadian-speaking; and, though the Sumerian language did not fall into oblivion in the Sumero-Akkadian World till the downfall and destruction of Assyria in 612–609 B.C., it survived only as a 'classical' language, in virtue of its being the vehicle of the Sumero-Akkadian civilization's traditional lore.

The Third Dynasty of Ur was overthrown by a revolt of its Elamite subjects. The city of Ur was sacked by them—a catastrophe from which

Ur never recovered—and the Empire was partitioned among a number of contending local successor-states. Elam not only recovered its independence; it imposed an Elamite dynasty on the Sumerian city-state Larsa. The Sumerian city-state Isin assumed the title of the Empire of Sumer and Akkad without being able to re-establish the Empire *de facto*. The other local successor-states of the fallen empire of the Third Dynasty of Ur were Eshnunna (east of the Tigris, north-west of Elam), Assyria (astride the Tigris, north-west of Eshnunna), Babylon (astride the Euphrates, in Akkad), Mari (astride the middle course of the Euphrates, north-west of Babylon), Carchemish (astride the westward elbow of the Euphrates), Yamkhad (Aleppo), and Qatna (south of Aleppo, in the Orontes valley). All these successor-states of the Empire of the Third Dynasty of Ur, except Qatna, Yamkhad, and Elam, were re-united politically by Hammurabi of Babylon (ruled 1792–1750 B.C.) in a series of nine successive annual campaigns, waged from the thirtieth to the thirty-eighth year of his reign; but this second re-establishment of the Empire of Sumer and Akkad by an Amorite empire-builder was still more ephemeral than the first re-establishment of it by the Sumerian Ur-Nammu.

Hammurabi's empire, like Naramsin's empire, half a millennium earlier, was menaced by highlanders in Gutium; like Naramsin before him, Hammurabi tried to avert this menace from Gutium by taking the offensive; and, once again, this strategy was ineffective. Only ten years after the completion of Hammurabi's conquests, in the eighth year of the reign of his immediate successor Samsu-iluna (i.e. in 1743 B.C.), the Kassite barbarians, descending from Gutium, made their first recorded encroachment on Babylonia (they seem to have dated the inauguration of the regime in Babylonia *c.* 1732 B.C.). During Samsu-iluna's reign Assyria, Mari, Carchemish, and even the 'Sealand'—in the swamps at the head of the Persian Gulf—seceded from Babylon. In 1595 B.C., Babylon, in its turn, suffered Ur's fate. It was sacked by raiders—in this case, not Elamites, but Hittites led by King Muršiliš I. The Hittites came and went; the Kassites reaped the harvest. The Hittite raiders had extinguished the First Dynasty of Babylon. The Kassites occupied Babylon and thus re-united all Sumer and Akkad, except the Sealand, under a barbarian domination that lasted till *c.* 1169 B.C.—that is to say, for nearly four times as long as the Gutaean barbarian domination which had followed the Sargonid regime.

The political re-unification of the Sargonid Empire of Sumer and Akkad had thus been abortive. Within a span of 370 years (2113–1743 B.C.) there had been effective unity for only about 130 years all told, as against about 240 years of disunion, strife, and political chaos. Yet, during this period of 370 years, two non-political developments had made steady progress. One of these developments was the spread of the Akkadian language. This had captivated not only the Sumerians but also the Amorites who had infiltrated into Akkad at about the same time as the Gutaeans and had founded the First Dynasty of Babylon *c.* 1894 B.C. (No doubt the Amorites were readily converted to speaking Akkadian, since their own mother-tongue was, like Akkadian, Semitic.) The second development was the north-westward expansion of Assyria's trading area. The records of an Assyrian settlement outside the wall of the native state of Kaneš, in eastern Asia Minor, show how active this trade was in the twentieth and nineteenth centuries B.C. Towards the close of this period, Assyrian merchants were also operating as far westward as the city of Khattušaš (Boğazkale).

In Egypt the sequel to the fall of the Old Kingdom had been different. In Egypt, there had not been a barbarian conquest and occupation of the whole country. There had been a domestic social revolution, and the United Kingdom had disintegrated into a litter of local principalities. This anarchy made it impossible to continue to regulate the flow of the Nile waters for the benefit of Egypt as a whole; and since, in Egypt, the people's subsistence, and even their survival, depends on obtaining water for irrigation, the local communities fought each other for the control of the water, as they had done in Sumer before Lugalzaggisi and his Sargonid successors had imposed political unity on Sumer and Akkad.

In Egypt, as in Sumer, this state of chaos was intolerable, and, as early as *c.* 2160 B.C., an attempt to re-establish the Pharaonic United Kingdom was made by a new dynasty based on Heracleopolis, a city in northern Upper Egypt, to the south of the Old Kingdom's capital, Memphis. The Heracleopolite regime was ineffective, and the urgently needed re-unification of Egypt was achieved by a dynasty—the Eleventh (*c.* 2113–1991 B.C.)—that was based on Thebes (Opet), a city in southern Upper Egypt, though not so far to the south as the twin cities Nekhen-Nekheb, from which the first unifiers of Egypt had come. In a country that depends on water-control for the population's subsistence, a power located upstream has an advantage over rivals that are downstream from it. It is not surprising that the Thebans overcame the Heracleopolitans. The Theban re-unifier of Egypt was Mentuhotpe II (*c.* 2060–2010 B.C.). He attained his objective of re-unification *c.* 2040 B.C., and the Middle Kingdom, which he thus founded, lasted for about three centuries.

This was three times as long as the time-span of Ur-Nammu's re-constituted Empire of Sumer and Akkad, but it was only one third of the length of the time-span of the Old Kingdom of Egypt; and, though, by comparison with the strife and penury of the first 'intermediate period' of Egyptian history (*c.* 2181–2040 B.C.), life under the regime of the Middle Kingdom was relatively peaceful and prosperous, the Pharaohs of this epoch had to be constantly struggling to assert and maintain their power. Amenemmes (Amenemhat) I (1991–1962 B.C.), the founder of the Twelfth Dynasty, appears to have been a minister before he became Pharaoh, and he also appears to have been assassinated. This can be read between the lines of his fictional admonition to his son and successor Sesostris (Senwosrat) I (1971–1928 B.C.).

The Middle-Kingdom Pharaohs had to bring the local princes to heel, and evidently this was a slow and arduous task. Moreover, unlike their predecessors in the Age of the Old Kingdom, they expanded their Empire, both up the Nile valley above the First Cataract into Nubia and north-eastwards into Palestine and perhaps as far north as Damascus. There is some archaeological evidence for Middle-Kingdom Egyptian influence even in northern Syria, and at Ugarit (Ras-ash-Shamrah) on the coast and at Alalakh in the interior. We do not know whether the Middle Kingdom's expansion into Asia was contested, but its expansion into Nubia certainly was. The characteristic monuments of the Twelfth Dynasty are not pyramids or temples; they are fortresses. Like the Fourth Dynasty's pyramids, the chain of eight barrier fortresses planted by Sesostris (Senwosrat) III (ruled 1878–1843 B.C.) between Wadi Halfah, below the Second Cataract, and Samnah, above it, are architectural masterpieces, but they are designed to serve a different purpose. A pyramid was built to secure immortality for a Pharaoh after his death; Sesostris III's fortresses were built to secure his hold, during his lifetime, on a hardly-won piece of territory.

It is instructive to compare the portrait-statues of Sesostris III with those of the Old-Kingdom Pharaohs Cheops and Chephren. These pyramid-builders' countenances are serene; Sesostris III's countenance is furrowed and grim. It is the face of a man who has paid a high personal price for his public achievements. The prize for which Sesostris III had been battling in Nubia was the command of the gold mines, or at least the command of the approaches to them. An Egyptian trading-post was established, in the Age of the Middle Kingdom, as far south in Nubia as Karmah, above the Third Cataract—far beyond the Middle Kingdom's military frontier.

The reign of Mentuhotpe II the re-unifier of Egypt was contemporaneous with the second half of the time-span of the Third Dynasty of Ur (c. 2113–2006 B.C.). The archives that have been disinterred at Mari cover the fifty-two years 1817–1765 B.C., and during that time Mari was in touch with all the local states of the Sumero-Akkadian World, including those to the west of the Euphrates. Yet there is no record in these archives of the presence of the Egyptians in Syria, and conversely there is no mention in the Middle-Kingdom Egyptian records of either

Ur-Nammu's or Hammurabi's resuscitation of the Empire of Sumer and Akkad. It is true that the Twelfth Dynasty, under which the Egyptian Middle Kingdom was at its apogee, did not come to the throne till fifteen years after the fall of Ur and came to an end only four years after the accession of Hammurabi and twenty-five years before the first of the nine annual campaigns in which Hammurabi re-established Ur-Nammu's empire. All the same, it is strange that these two worlds should have continued to ignore each other's existence when they had come within such close range of each other.

Meanwhile, during the three centuries *c.* 2140–1730 B.C., the Indus civilization was probably still in existence and the Minoan civilization in Crete was flourishing. It has been noted already that our only clue, so far, to the Indus civilization's chronology is the retrieval of seals, carved with legends in the Indus script, in datable strata of the Sumero-Akkadian civilization's material relics. The earliest of these strata containing Indus seals are pre-Sargonid, but the terminal date for the presence of Indus seals in Sumer and Akkad is uncertain. The archaeological evidence from the sites of the Indus civilization itself seems to indicate that this civilization came to a sudden violent end.

If this is so, its destroyers are likely to have been the barbarians who introduced into India the Indo-European language in which the Vedic scriptures are written and which came to be called Sanskrit retrospectively after it had been artificially revived to serve as a classical language. The Dravidian and the Austro-Asiatic languages must have been current in the Indian subcontinent before the date of the primary-Sanskrit-speakers' invasion, and it seems probable that the Dravidian languages, as well as primary Sanskrit, came in from the north-west. A language of the Dravidian family, Brahui, was still current in parts of Baluchistan in the twentieth century A.D. As for primary Sanskrit, the date of its arrival in India is as uncertain as the date of the destruction there of the Indus civilization. The Kassites who descended on Babylonia from the Iranian plateau in the eighteenth century B.C. seem to have included some primary-Sanskrit-speakers, to judge by the presence of the Vedic sun-god Suryash in the Kassite pantheon. There were also Vedic gods in the pantheon of the Kingdom of Mitanni in Mesopotamia (Jazirah) in the fifteenth century B.C.; but these traces of primary-Sanskrit-speakers in Babylonia and in Mesopotamia at these dates do not tell us the date of their kinsmen's destruction of the Indus civilization.

In the first quarter of the second millennium B.C. the Minoan civilization in Crete was in full flower. *Circa* 2000–1700 B.C. was the date of the first palaces at Knossos, Phaistos, Ayia Triadha, Mallia, and Palaikastro. These palaces were unfortified, and it may be inferred that they were not the capitals of so many mutually independent local sovereign powers. It may also be inferred that, in this age, the Cretans did not feel themselves to be in danger of being attacked from the sea. However, this first set of Minoan palaces was destroyed *c.* 1750–1700 B.C. There is no positive evidence that the disaster was man-made; it might have been caused by an earthquake; but the approximate coincidence of the date with the dates of the Kassite invasion of Babylonia and the Hyksos invasion of Egypt suggests that the destruction of the Cretan palaces, too, may have been the work of hostile invaders.

In the basin of the Yellow River during the first quarter of the second millennium B.C. the Yang-Shao phase of the regional Neolithic culture had been succeeded by the Lung-Shan phase. This was not merely a change in the style of pottery from painted ware to black. The Lung-Shan people had a wider range of domesticated animals, and at least one of their settlements was a city defended by walls made of stamped earth. However, this higher Neolithic culture in Eastern Asia had not yet been crowned by a civilization of the same species as those which were already in being farther west, from the Indus basin to the Aegean basin inclusive.

[12]

THE DOMESTICATION OF THE
HORSE AND THE INVENTION
OF PASTORAL NOMADISM ON THE
EURASIAN STEPPE

THE Kassite barbarians from the western rim of the Iranian plateau made their first descent on Babylonia in 1743 B.C. and they gradually extended their encroachments till they occupied the city of Babylon itself after Babylon had been sacked in 1595 B.C. by the Indo-European-speaking Hittites. The Egyptian Middle Kingdom seems to have been brought to an end by a similar gradual encroachment of barbarians, the so-called Hyksos, who infiltrated into the north-eastern corner of the Nile delta c. 1730 or 1720 B.C. and eventually occupied Memphis and extinguished the Twelfth Dynasty's feeble Thirteenth-Dynasty successors in 1674 B.C. To judge by their personal names, the Hyksos seem to have been Semitic-speaking; and, if a West-Semitic language was their mother-tongue, they were not the Kassites' kinsmen. But the contemporaneity of the Hyksos invasion of Egypt and the Kassite invasion of Babylonia and the devastation of the first set of palaces in Crete suggests that these movements may all have been put in motion by pressure from the rear.

Behind the movement of the Hyksos into Egypt there was certainly a massive movement intó Mesopotamia and Syria of Hurrians from the highlands in what is now eastern Turkey; but, as has been mentioned already, there is linguistic evidence for the presence of primary-Sanskrit-speakers among the invaders who, in the eighteenth century B.C., established the Kingdom of Mitanni in Mesopotamia (the Jazirah), as well as among those who imposed Kassite rule on Babylonia. This linguistic evidence suggests that, behind the local pressures, there may have been some single prime mover, and that this may have been an eruption of primary-Sanskrit-speaking people from the northern hinter-land of South-West Asia.

This hinterland is the Eurasian steppe. It is accessible from the Indo-European languages' probable place of origin somewhere in eastern

Europe, and its southern shore adjoins South-West Asia in Türkmeni-stan. If there was an eruption from the steppe, this may have followed the domestication of the horse, which made pastoral nomadism feasible there. At Troy, the bones of horses have been found in the lowest stratum of Troy VI, the date of which is *c*. 1800 B.C. On the other hand, horses were not yet possessed by the Sumero-Akkadians in the Age of the First Dynasty of Babylon or by the Egyptians in the Age of the Middle Kingdom. This indicates that the horse was domesticated on the Eurasian steppe not long before 1800 B.C. and that the invention and dissemination of a new military weapon—the horse-drawn chariot— accounts for the eighteenth-century-B.C. barbarian invasions of Sumer and Akkad and of Egypt, and also for the invaders' success.

Pastoral nomadism, like urbanism, is a non-agricultural way of life which is parasitic on agriculture and which could not have come into existence except within reach of, and in association with, agricultural populations who were already producing a surplus of food beyond their requirements for their own subsistence. Townspeople buy food from agriculturists in exchange for urban manufactures and services. Pastoral nomads likewise need to buy the products of sedentary societies by selling livestock and hides. Though the pastoral nomads themselves have abandoned agriculture, their novel way of life is not only post-agricul-tural but is practicable only in a symbiosis with neighbours who have continued to till the soil. Subject to this condition, pastoral nomadism is the most productive way of utilizing dry grassland without ruining it. The cultivation of land of this kind may yield greater returns in the short run; but there each year's harvest is precarious, and the penalty for ploughing up the grass-roots may be the transformation of a prairie into a desert. On a prairie the long-term alternative to using it for pasture is to use it as a hunting-ground, as the prairies of North America were used by the indigenous Americans till, in the nineteenth century A.D., settlers from Europe exterminated the wild herds of bison that had been the native people's game, and replaced the bison by a short-lived 'cattle kingdom'. On a prairie, pastoral nomadism is the most lucrative form of human usage that can exploit Nature without sterilizing her.

In order to make dry grasslands support the maximum head of stock the pastoral nomad has to be constantly moving his stock from one pasture-ground to another in a regular seasonal orbit. He cannot con-duct his flocks and herds on their recurrent trek without the aid of non-human auxiliaries such as horses and camels; and, since the trek has to be carefully planned and precisely executed if it is not to be overtaken by disaster, the nomadic pastoralist has to put himself and his animal auxiliaries, as well as his cattle, under a strict discipline. The logistics of a nomadic pastoral community's trek resemble those of a military campaign, and consequently pastoral nomadism automatically trains its practitioners for waging mobile warfare, though normally they make their annual round without coming into conflict either with other nomadic peoples or with the nomads' sedentary neighbours and trading-partners.

The domestication of the horse gave Man the non-human auxiliary that made pastoral nomadism practicable, but the original domesticated horse was a puny beast. He could not bear the weight of a human rider, and a team of four horses was required for drawing a two-wheeled chariot made of the lightest possible materials. A thousand years of horse-breeding were required for producing a horse that could carry even a lightly equipped cavalryman, and several centuries more were required for producing the 'great horse' that could carry armour of its own, as well as a rider armoured cap-à-pie. Yet, from the start, the pastoral nomad was militarily formidable on the exceptional occasions on which he broke out of the steppe that was his normal habitat. The invasions that were suffered by Babylonia and Egypt, and perhaps by Crete too, during the second half of the eighteenth century B.C. may have been the indirect effects of the first of a series of eruptions of nomad peoples that continued on the Eurasian steppe till the eighteenth century of the Christian Era, and on the North-Arabian steppe till after the First World War.

The inventors of pastoral nomadism on the Eurasian steppe seem likely to have been the primary-Sanskrit-speakers who, beyond the southern bounds of the steppe, made a temporary mark on Babylonia and on Mesopotamia and a permanent mark on India. But pastoral nomadism, once invented, did not remain the monopoly of any single people. The Eurasian steppe was occupied at different times by peoples speaking primary Sanskrit, Iranian, Turkish, Tungus, Mongol, and Finnish (the language of the Magyars). With the domestication of the one-humped camel on the Arabian steppe before the end of the second millennium B.C., and the acclimatization of the horse there before the beginning of the Christian Era, pastoral nomadism extended its domain to Arabia and, from Arabia, to North Africa. The pastoral nomads made history from the eighteenth century B.C. until a date that is still within living memory.

[13]

RELATIONS BETWEEN REGIONAL
CIVILIZATIONS, *c.* 1730–1250 B.C.

IN the preceding chapter it has been conjectured that the domestication of the horse had prepared the ground for the invention of the pastoral nomadic way of life at an early date in the second millennium B.C., and that in the eighteenth century B.C. there had been an eruption of primary-Sanskrit-speaking Eurasian nomads into South-West Asia. If this eruption did occur, it was brief, and the erupting Eurasian nomads themselves left only a slight mark on the sedentary populations on whose domain they had intruded. On the other hand, if a nomad eruption was the force that propelled the Hurrians into Mesopotamia and Syria and the Hyksos into Egypt, the indirect effect of this nomad eruption on the relations between the regional civilizations was prodigious. Indirectly, this *Völkerwanderung* impelled the regional civilizations of the Levant to enter into a relationship with each other that was unprecedentedly active and intimate.

The Sumerian civilization, the earliest specimen of the regional species, had not remained the solitary specimen for long. The Pharaonic civilization had arisen in Egypt at about the turn of the fourth and third millennia B.C., and, during the second half of the third millennium, other regional civilizations had arisen in Asia Minor, Crete, and the Indus basin. Yet, until the eighteenth century B.C., the only case of an intimate relation between two regional civilizations had been the cultural indebtedness of the civilization in Asia Minor to the Sumero-Akkadian civilization. The Asia Minor civilization was in fact the Sumero-Akkadian's satellite, but this degree of dependence was exceptional. The Sumerian influence on Egypt at the dawn of the Egyptian civilization was a stimulus that may partly account for the Pharaonic civilization's apparently sudden emergence; but here the Sumerian influence was short-lived, and, during the first twelve or thirteen centuries of its history, the Pharaonic civilization went its own way and developed on distinctive lines of its own.

It has been noted already that the Pharaonic and Sumero-Akkadian civilizations appear to have ignored each other's existence even during the first quarter of the second millennium B.C., when their respective domains were in contact with each other and possibly overlapped. The Sumero-Akkadian civilization's relations with the Indus civilization were still slighter. The Indus seals that have been found in strata of the material relics of the Sumero-Akkadian civilization indicate that these two societies were in commercial contact with each other as early as *c.* 2500 B.C., but the material remains of the Indus civilization itself have not yielded any trace of Sumerian influence. There is no counterpart in the Indus basin of the traces of Sumerian influence on pre-dynastic and proto-dynastic Egypt. This paucity of contacts between the regional civilizations in the Levant down to the eighteenth century B.C. contrasts strikingly with the multiplicity and the closeness of the contacts between them from the eighteenth to the thirteenth centuries B.C.

During these five centuries the civilization that played the leading military and political role in the Levant was the Egyptian, and the insulation of the Levantine regional civilizations from each other was brought to an end mainly by Egyptian action. This may seem surprising; for previously the Egyptian civilization had been less outward-looking and less expansive than the Sumero-Akkadian. However, we can recognize that the traditional introversion of Egyptian society generated a militant xenophobia when, for the first time in this society's history, barbarian invaders lodged themselves deep in its domain. Xenophobia stimulated the Egyptians first to expel the alien intruders and then to follow up their expulsion by a counter-attack on their original base of operations in Palestine and Syria. This region, however, had long since been drawn into the Sumero-Akkadian civilization's sphere of cultural influence. Consequently, the vehemence of the Egyptians' political and military reaction to an alien intrusion led the Egyptians to come into contact with the alien culture against which they were up in arms.

In the later decades of the eighteenth century B.C. the Babylonians submitted tamely to the imposition on them of a barbarian Kassite domination, and the Assyrians, who had seized the first opportunity to shake off the Babylonians' suzerainty, seem to have reconciled themselves to the overlordship of the barbarian Mitanni. The Kassite regime in Babylonia was tolerated for nearly six centuries, and the Mitanni Kingdom's suzerainty over Assyria for perhaps three centuries and a half, before it was liquidated by a reaction on the part of the subjugated people. The Hyksos infiltration into Egypt began *c.* 1730 or 1720 B.C. and reached its limit in 1674 B.C., when the Hyksos occupied Memphis. Now, for the second time since the union of the two crowns, Egypt had fallen apart politically into a northern and a southern kingdom; but, in this second 'intermediate period', the northern kingdom was of alien origin, whereas, in the first 'intermediate period', the Heracleopolite kingdom, as well as the Theban kingdom, had been indigenous. The Hyksos readily assimilated the higher civilization of their Egyptian subjects, but the Egyptians were not placated. In the sixteenth century B.C., as in the twenty-first century B.C., Egypt was re-united politically through the conquest of the northern kingdom by a southern kingdom with its capital at Thebes.

The Hyksos were expelled *c.* 1567 B.C. The Theban liberator and re-unifier was Amosis (Ahmose) (ruled *c.* 1575–1550 B.C.). The Eighteenth Dynasty, which Amosis founded, ruled *c.* 1575–*c.* 1308 B.C. The total time-span of the New Kingdom, from the inauguration of the Eighteenth to the Fall of the Twentieth Dynasty, was nearly five centuries (*c.* 1575–1087 B.C.). This was only half the time-span of the Old Kingdom, but it was nearly twice as long as the time-span of the Middle Kingdom. Moreover, the New Kingdom was a cosmopolitan empire. It has been mentioned that, in the Age of the Middle Kingdom, Sesostris III had carried the southern frontier of his dominions southward to Samnah, above the Second Cataract of the Nile, with an outlying trading-post at Karmah above the Third Cataract. After the establishment of the New Kingdom, Amosis' second successor, Thothmes (Tuthmose) I (ruled *c.* 1528–1510 B.C.), advanced his southern frontier to Napata, below the Fourth Cataract, and the whole stretch of the Nile valley from the First to the Fourth Cataract was now impregnated with the Pharaonic civilization. In an inscription dated in the second year of his reign, Thothmes I claimed that, north-eastward, his dominions extended to the Euphrates.

The population of the Nile valley above the First Cataract was barbarian; and, under Egyptian rule, its cultural relations with the Egyptians were one-sided. The Kushites received the Egyptian civilization without exerting any appreciable cultural counter-influence. On the political plane, Egyptian rule over what are now Nubia and the northern Nilotic Sudan was continuously effective till the break-up of the New Kingdom in 1087 B.C. By contrast, the extent and degree of Egyptian political authority in Palestine and Syria during the same period were fluctuating, but the cultural influence of the Egyptians and their Asian subjects on each other was reciprocal; its effect was cumulative; and the Egyptians received more cultural influence from the Asians than they imparted to them.

We do not know whether the Hyksos kingdom in the Delta included the Asian territory from which they had come, but it is clear that, after the overthrow of the Hyksos regime, the Egyptians, when they invaded Palestine and Syria, found this region split up politically into a large number of small principalities. The Egyptians posted some garrisons at strategic points, and appointed Egyptian residents whose control over the governments of the satellite states was effective if and when and in so far as it was supported vigorously by the Imperial Government at Thebes; but the Imperial Government does not appear to have imposed its direct rule over any part of its Asian domain, as it did over its dominions in the Nile valley above the First Cataract. The Asian cultural influence on Egyptian life in the Age of the New Kingdom was partly exerted by immigrants from the New Kingdom's Asian dominions into Egypt itself. Some of these immigrants were prisoners of war; others came voluntarily, in quest of profitable economic openings. Immigrants of both kinds brought with them their cults and their manners and customs, and the Egyptians found these attractive. The xenophobia that had been the Egyptians' retort to Asian military conquest was not aroused by the peaceful penetration of Egypt by Asians who were her subjects.

Egyptian political paramountcy was first imposed on Palestine and Syria in the reign of Thothmes I. During the reign of Queen Hatshepsut (1490–1469 B.C.) it seems to have been in abeyance; for her co-ruler Thothmes III, whom she had prevented, during her lifetime, from coming into power, conducted, immediately after her death, a series of twelve consecutive campaigns from the twenty-second to the thirty-third year of his own reign (i.e. from 1469 to 1458 B.C. inclusive). In the last of these campaigns he reached the Euphrates; found standing there a stele that had been set up by Thothmes I; set up a stele of his own beside it; and then made a raid across the river and compelled the Mesopotamian kingdom of Mitanni to acknowledge his suzerainty. Egyptian rule in Palestine and Syria was at its zenith from this year 1458 till the accession of Akhenaton. In the course of Akhenaton's reign (*c.* 1367–1350 B.C.) the Egyptian regime in the area was undermined, and it was never fully rehabilitated.

Akhenaton was a revolutionary. His revolution was not the first in Egypt's history. There had been a double revolution in the 'intermediate period' between the dissolution of the Old Kingdom and the establishment of the Middle Kingdom. In the time of the Sixth Dynasty, the nomarchs had made themselves into virtually independent hereditary local princes instead of continuing to be Pharaoh's appointees, and they had only gradually been resubjected to a reconstituted central government in the time of the Twelfth Dynasty. Meanwhile, immediately after the extinction of the Sixth Dynasty, there had been a twenty-year interregnum (*c.* 2181–2160 B.C.) during which there had been a violent social revolution. These two previous Egyptian revolutions had been different in kind. In the one case the 'establishment' had shaken off

Pharaoh's yoke; in the other case the masses had revolted against the 'establishment' itself; but the two revolutions in the first 'intermediate period' had had one feature in common. At different levels and in different degrees, they had both been revolutions from below upwards. Akhenaton's revolution was from above downwards.

Akhenaton's major conflict was with the ecclesiastical wing of the 'establishment'. Like his Fourth-Dynasty predecessor Cheops, Akhenaton quarrelled with the priesthood over a theological issue, and, by this time, the priesthood had become more formidable. Cheops' ecclesiastical opponents had been the priests of Re's holy city Heliopolis. Since Thebes had become the political capital of a re-united Egypt, Re, the head of the Egyptian pantheon, had been identified with Amun, who had been the local god of Thebes since at least as early as the reign of the founder of the Twelfth Dynasty, Amenemmes I, and Thothmes III had organized the priests of all the local gods of Egypt into a Pan-Egyptian corporation under the presidency of Amun-Re's high priest.

Akhenaton was putting Pharaoh's officially absolute authority to a practical test by challenging the greatest power in the Egyptian World other than Pharaoh himself. Akhenaton might have defeated the priesthood if he had won the people's support, and he might have won this if he had challenged the high priest of Amun-Re on behalf of the god Osiris; for Osiris was the giver of immortality, and immortality was the Egyptians' supreme objective. However, Akhenaton was contending, not for immortality, but for monotheism, and the ideal of monotheism left the people's hearts cold, besides being a menace to the priesthood's vested interests. Akhenaton's One God, the sun-disk (Aton), was only one man's god; and, though this one man was Pharaoh, even Pharaoh's power was not great enough to prevail over an ecclesiastical corporation serving a pantheon that was consecrated by tradition.

It is not surprising that Akhenaton failed to substitute the Aton for Amun-Re and the rest of the traditional pantheon, but it is remarkable that Akhenaton's revolution made a lasting mark nevertheless. Amun-Re was re-instated, but he was transfigured to the likeness of the One God whom Akhenaton had tried in vain to substitute for him. Akhenaton had composed a hymn to the Aton as the giver of life to all living creatures in the Universe; the post-Atonian hymns to Amun-Re present the old god in the abortive new god's guise.

Akhenaton had moved the site of the capital to a new city, and for this he had had precedents. The Old-Kingdom Pharaohs had migrated from Nekhen-Nekheb downstream, first to Thinis, and then to Memphis. The founder of the Twelfth Dynasty had migrated from Thebes to Iz-Taui, a new city not far upstream from Memphis. When the Theban founder of the Eighteenth Dynasty had re-unified Egypt once more,

Thebes became the capital again. Akhenaton had migrated to Akhetaton (the present-day Tall-al-Amarnah), which he had built at a point about half way between Thebes and Memphis. After Akhenaton's death, this new city was deserted, and the capital reverted to Thebes. Thebes was, indeed, no longer awkwardly close to the southern fringe of the Egyptian World now that the Empire extended as far up the Nile as Napata. However, Thebes did not retain for long her recaptured privilege of being the sole capital of the New Kingdom. The operational capital was pulled northwards, much farther to the north than the site of Akhetaton, by the pressure from the north-east that was making itself felt already in Akhenaton's reign. The ostentatiously orthodox soldier Horemheb (ruled *de facto c.* 1349–1319 B.C.) governed the Empire from Memphis; before the New Kingdom expired, its operational capital had shifted still farther north-eastward to Tanis, in the north-eastern corner of the Delta, on or near the site of the Hyksos capital, Avaris.

Akhenaton was a revolutionary in the fields of literature and visual arts, as well as in the fields of religion and politics, and in these fields, too, he left his mark. In literature he took to writing in the living language of his time, not in an obsolete language, and this innovation survived him till, in the course of ages, the living Egyptian language of the fourteenth century B.C. became a dead language in its turn. In art he stood for naturalism and for truth to life—including unflattering lifelike portraits of himself.

Akhenaton's taste for naturalism may have been caught from the Minoans. In the wall-paintings of New-Kingdom Egyptian tombs there are portrayals of Minoans carrying what appear to be Mycenaean, not Minoan, artefacts, and this is evidence of commercial and cultural relations between Egypt and the Aegean World in this age. Besides being prompted by his own genius, Akhenaton was inspired by his time and place. The empire whose throne he had inherited was ecumenical—not, of course, in the geographical sense of being literally co-extensive with the Oikoumenê, but in the cultural sense of comprising a fair sample of the diversity of human cultures. This was the first ecumenical empire in this sense, and it is not a mere coincidence that one of the rulers of this empire was the first recorded monotheist; for Akhenaton's monotheism is ecumenicalism expressed in religious symbolism. He conceived of the Aton as being, not a local god, but the lord of the whole Universe, and he signified the Aton's ubiquity by building temples for him in Syria and in Nubia, as well as in Egypt.

During the first two centuries of its existence the Egyptian ecumenical empire had no political peer in the Levant. Babylonia, under the barbarian Kassite regime, was politically impotent. Culturally, however, Babylonia was now in her prime. This was the age in which the epic

themes, bequeathed by the Sumerians, were put into their classical forms
in the Akkadian language: Gilgamesh's defeat in his quest for the Tree
of Life; Ishtar's (Inanna's) descent into the Underworld; the young god
Marduk's conquest of chaos and his accession to the headship of the
Sumero-Akkadian pantheon as his reward for having reduced the Universe to order. These Akkadian poems circulated wherever the Akkadian
language was spoken, and by this time it had become the language of
international relations throughout the Levant, including the Egyptian
Empire. One of the indispensable organs of the Egyptian Government in
this age was a chancery in which the clerks wrote in Akkadian in the
Sumerian characters on clay tablets. This was the medium in which the
Egyptian Government corresponded with the rulers of its satellite states
in Syria and Palestine. Egypt's military and political dominance was
matched by the cultural dominance of the Akkadian language.

Nor did the Egyptian Empire remain unchallenged on the military
and political plane. The Hittites had been quiescent since Muršiliš I's
raid on Babylon in 1595 B.C. In Akhenaton's time, they began to go on
the warpath again under the leadership of Suppiluliuma (ruled *c.* 1375–
1335 B.C.). Suppiluliuma subjugated Khatti's south-eastern neighbour
in Asia Minor, Kizzuwadna, crushed Mitanni, and cajoled or compelled
Egypt's client states in northern Syria to transfer their allegiance to him.
Towards the end of the fourteenth century B.C., Suppiluliuma's second
successor, Muršiliš III (*c.* 1334–1306) conquered and annexed the
Luvian empire of Arzawa in western Asia Minor, which, till then, had
been Khatti's equal. By the beginning of the thirteenth century B.C.,
Khatti had become a power of Egypt's calibre, and Ramses II (ruled
1290–1224 B.C.) and Suppiluliuma's grandson Muwatalliš (ruled *c.* 1306–
1282 B.C.) went to war for the control over Syria. The Hittite's victory
at the Battle of Kadesh, *c.* 1286/5 B.C., was inconclusive, and the two
belligerent powers recognized eventually that they could not afford to
remain at war with each other, since they were both threatened by the
increasing power of common enemies. They therefore concluded a compromise peace, partitioning Syria between them, in 1270 B.C. But they
had awakened to the realities too late. On the east the *tertius gaudens* was
Assyria; on the west the aggressors were the Mycenaeans and a host of
other restless and mobile maritime peoples.

In the twentieth and nineteenth centuries B.C. the Assyrians had been
enterprising long-distance traders before they had been submerged under
the flood of the Mitannian *Völkerwanderung*. In the reign of Asshur-
uballit I (ruled 1365–1330? or 1356–1320? B.C.) the Assyrians re-emerged
in the sinister new role of aggressive militarists. Adad-Nirari I (ruled
1307–1275) and Shalmaneser I (ruled 1274–1245) raided westwards
across Mesopotamia to Carchemish. Tukulti-Ninurta I (ruled 1244–

1208, or 1234–1197, or 1230–1198 B.C.) temporarily occupied Babylonia. However, the Assyrians had not yet crossed the westward arm of the Euphrates before they were overtaken, and were thrown back on to the defensive, by the new *Völkerwanderung* that started before the close of the thirteenth century B.C.

In the Aegean basin, the Minoan civilization not only recovered from the disaster that had wrecked the Cretan palaces *c.* 1750–1700 B.C.; it reached its zenith during the next quarter of a millennium—the periods labelled Middle Minoan III and Late Minoan I. Meanwhile, on the mainland of Greece, the barbarian invasion *c.* 1900 B.C., which probably introduced the Greek language, undoubtedly retarded the birth of a regional civilization there. Crete, which had escaped this invasion, shot so far ahead of the mainland in the course of the next three centuries that, in the late seventeenth or early sixteenth century B.C., there was a sudden reception, on the mainland, of the arts of the Minoan civilization.

This reception went to such lengths that the mainland might have seemed destined to be assimilated culturally by the Minoan World as thoroughly as, in the third millennium B.C., Akkad had been assimilated to Sumer. However, the mainland of Greece asserted a distinctive cultural individuality of its own, as Asia Minor had done after it had been impregnated with the cultural influence of Sumer and Akkad. The continental Mycenaean civilization—so labelled because Mycenae was its most brilliant site—developed side by side with the Minoan civilization of the Late Minoan I phase, and, *c.* 1480/1450 B.C., it overwhelmed it.

The Minoan civilization had recently survived a great natural disaster, the titanic eruption of the volcano-island Thera (Santorini) *c.* 1500 B.C. Before the eruption, Thera itself had been devastated by an earthquake. The effects of the eruption (not of the previous earthquake) were felt along the northern and eastern seaboards of Crete; but the disaster suffered by Crete later, *c.* 1480/1450 B.C., was far more severe, and the archaeological evidence indicates that this second disaster was man-made. On this occasion, Knossos, the principal palace in Crete, was spared, while the other palaces on the island were wrecked. At Knossos the immediate sequel was the emergence of a local culture, the so-called Late Minoan II, in which the rest of Crete did not share. This local Knossian culture was militaristic, to judge by the abundant finds of weapons, and its pottery was Mycenaean in style. This archaeological evidence suggests that, *c.* 1480/1450 B.C., Knossos was occupied by Mycenaean invaders who used it as a base of operations for attacking and devastating the other seats of the Minoan civilization.

This was only the first of a series of man-made disasters that were inflicted on the inhabitants of the Aegean basin in the course of the next three centuries. Soon after 1400 B.C. the palace at Knossos was destroyed —presumably by a second wave of continental Mycenaean invaders. The Mycenaean palace at Thebes was destroyed at about the same time or perhaps rather later—in a fratricidal war with Mycenae itself, if there is a grain of truth in the legend that survived into the Hellenic Age of Greek history. In spite of these disasters, the Mycenaean civilization flourished in the fourteenth century B.C. As a result, perhaps, of the occupation of Knossos *c.* 1480/1450 B.C., a syllabic phonetic script—the so-called Linear-B—was invented for conveying the Mycenaean-Age form of the Greek language, in imitation of Linear-A, which had previously been invented by the Minoans for conveying their own, not yet deciphered, language. The Mycenaean craftsmen drew level with their Minoan teachers. The Mycenaeans who built the 'bee-hive' tombs emulated their Egyptian counterparts' skill and precision in the use of masonry. In the fourteenth and thirteenth centuries B.C. the Mycenaeans traded as far eastward as Ugarit (Ras-ash-Shamrah) at the northern end of the coast of Syria, as far southward as Egypt, and as far westward as Sicily. They were equally ready to trade and to raid, whichever of those two activities promised to be the more profitable.

In the thirteenth century B.C., Mycenaean militarism became more grim. The Mycenaean palaces on the east side of Greece—for instance, Mycenae itself and Tiryns in the Argolid, and the acropolis of Athens— were now massively fortified, and pains were taken to make a water-supply accessible for the defenders if the fortress were to be besieged. During the same century there were man-made disasters on the eastern shore of the Aegean too: Troy VIIA was destroyed by human assailants *c.* 1260 B.C., and, farther south, the Hittite Empire was in trouble. The Hittites had found it easier to overthrow the rival empire of Arzawa than to bring its territory under effective Hittite control. Hittite rule over western Asia Minor was challenged by local rebellions and by Mycenaean incursions. Both the Hittite Empire and the Mycenaean principalities in continental Greece and in Crete were equipped with the elaborate administrative apparatus, in the Sumero-Akkadian and Egyptian style, which literacy made practicable. But we may guess, from the sequel, that, in Asia Minor and Greece, the literate class was a small minority and that the bureaucracy was too heavy a load for its economic foundations to carry without an excessive strain.

Thus trouble was brewing to the west of Egypt and of the Sumero-Akkadian World in the thirteenth century B.C. The contemporary situation in India is obscure. We have no archaeological evidence for dating the overthrow of the Indus civilization by primary-Sanskrit-speaking invaders. If these had erupted from the Eurasian steppe in the eighteenth century B.C., they may have reached India as rapidly as they reached

Babylonia and Mesopotamia, but it is also possible that it took them several centuries longer to find their way across the Hindu Kush from the Oxus–Jaxartes basin to the Indus basin.

In China, a regional civilization—labelled with the name of the Shang (*alias* Yin) dynasty—made its appearance *c.* 1500 B.C. Some of its elements were derived from the last phase (i.e. the Lung-Shan black pottery phase) of the regional Neolithic culture; and the emergence of civilization was not accompanied in China by a change of location, as it had been in the Fertile Crescent of South-West Asia and in Egypt. In China, as in the Levant, the regional Neolithic culture had depended on rainfall for watering its crops; its locus had been the belt of relatively high-lying wind-blown loess soil that had been deposited in Kansu and in the basin of the Wei tributary of the Yellow River and also farther east, along the watershed between the Yellow River and the Rivers Han and Hwai, and this was also the locus of the Lung-Shan Neolithic culture's successor the Shang civilization. The creators of this civilization did not open up the alluvial soil of the valley-bottoms for cultivation and settlement. Water-control on the Sumerian and Egyptian scale did not become a salient feature of the Chinese economy till about a thousand years after the appearance of the earliest civilization in China.

In this respect there was less of a break between this civilization and the antecedent Neolithic culture in the Yellow River basin than there had been between the Sumerian civilization and the antecedent Neolithic cultures in Mesopotamia and in western Iran. There was, however, one common and comparable new departure. In China, as in Sumer, the transition from a Neolithic culture to a civilization was accompanied by a sharp differentiation, in wealth and in privilege, between rulers and subjects. The royal tombs at Anyang, the last of the capital cities of the Shang dynasty, resemble the tombs of the First Dynasty of Ur, though these were more than a thousand years older. The Shang tombs, too, are grandiose, and the grave-goods, including human victims, are lavish. In Sumer, the increase in the community's aggregate wealth through the opening-up of the alluvium for cultivation enabled a dominant minority to live—and to die—luxuriously. In China the same invidious change was imposed on the community without any simultaneous increase in the community's total economic resources.

At the dawn of civilization in China, there were also innovations that recall those that accompanied the apparently sudden appearance of civilization in the Indus basin and in Egypt; and in China, likewise, the suddenness of the appearance of these innovations seems to indicate that, here too, civilization was brought to birth by a stimulus from abroad, in contrast to the apparently autonomous development of the Sumerian civilization.

One sudden innovation was the use of horse-drawn chariots, and this must have been introduced into Shang-Age China from the Eurasian steppe in or after the eighteenth century B.C. A second innovation was the use of a script, and the invention of the Shang-Age script of China, from which the classical Chinese characters are manifestly derived, must have been inspired, as the invention of the Egyptian hieroglyphic script must have been, by the influence of a Sumerian pattern. This influence may have been remote and indirect. The Chinese characters, like the Egyptian hieroglyphs, have a distinctive style of their own, but the structure of the script is Sumerian, and this structure—an illogical and clumsy use of ideograms and phonemes side by side with each other—is too peculiar for it to be credible that it was invented independently on three different occasions. A third sudden innovation in China at the dawn of civilization there was the use of bronze for casting tools, weapons, and sacrificial vessels, and this art, too, must have come to China from the west. The Shang bronzes, like the Shang script, have a style of their own which is already distinctively Chinese; the bronze vessels are elaborate, and the technique that they display is highly skilful. It is conceivable that they may have had Neolithic-Age wooden proto-types that have left no trace; but this hypothesis (and it is no more than that) would explain the apparently sudden appearance of the artistic style alone; the sudden acquisition of the metallurgical technique would still remain unexplained.

Shang bronze has a high content of tin—seventeen per cent—and the nearest sources of tin and copper to the Yellow River basin are Malaya and Yunnan; but the techniques of alloying copper with tin and of cast-ing the composite product cannot have been introduced into the Yellow River basin from the south. The earliest South-East Asian bronze cul-ture—labelled 'Dong Son', the name of a site in North Vietnam—is no older than the latter half of the last millennium B.C. However, the two metals may have been imported to the Yellow River basin from the south, even if the technique for working them came from elsewhere. The tropical zone of Asia may well have been Shang China's source of metals; for the Shang civilization had a component of tropical origin, besides the elements that it had inherited from the antecedent Neolithic culture of northern China and besides the other elements that had reached northern China from the west, via the Eurasian steppe. The Shang-Age Chinese cultivated rice as well as wheat and millet; they had the water-buffalo as well as ordinary cattle; and one of their two breeds of pig was of southern origin.

The water-buffalo and the rice-plant must have been domesticated originally in some tropical swampy region. The society that domesticated them must have been on a par culturally with the Neolithic precursors of the Shang civilization in northern China. But there does not seem to be any evidence for the existence of a pre-Shang-Age Neolithic culture of this calibre anywhere in the tropical zone of Asia to the south of the Yellow River basin. The regional civilization that was the least remote from the Yellow River basin geographically was the Indus civilization. But the Indus basin and the Yellow River basin are segregated from each other not only by sheer distance but also by a series of intervening mountain barriers. Moreover, there is no evidence that the Indus civilization spread eastwards and southwards into those parts of India in which, today, rice, not wheat, is the staple crop.

Thus the source of the tropical elements of the Shang civilization is a mystery. According to the Chinese tradition, the whole of what has now become China to the south of the Yellow River basin, and, *a fortiori*, what has now become Vietnam, received civilization only through being Sinified, partly by the assimilation of its native population and partly by the infiltration of Chinese settlers from the north. This tradition cannot be dismissed as being a mere reflection of Chinese cultural prejudice; it is confirmed by the survival, down to the nineteenth century A.D., of enclaves of culturally primitive unassimilated natives in some of the less accessible highland districts in the southern half of the Yangtse basin. There are other still surviving primitive peoples along the border between the southern frontier of present-day China and China's present South-East-Asian neighbours. The region in which the rice-plant and the water-buffalo were originally domesticated has still to be identified.

When, in the Yellow River basin in China, the Shang civilization was making its appearance, Meso-America was entering on the early 'Formative' phase of its culture. We can equate this with the Old-World Neolithic Age if we recognize that the invention of agriculture, not the invention of the technique for grinding stone tools, was the Neolithic Age's distinctive achievement. By *c.* 1500 B.C. the peoples of Meso-America had advanced from the 'Archaic Age', in which they had made their living by food-gathering and hunting, into a new age, labelled 'Formative', in which they were making their living by agriculture. The domestication of maize was almost certainly achieved independently by pre-Columbian American *homo sapiens*. Maize was unknown in the Old World till it was imported from the Americas by Europeans who had reached the New World by crossing the Atlantic. There seems, however, to have been a time-lag, which had no counterpart in Old-World economic history, between the domestication of a food-plant and the inauguration of an economic regime in which the cultivation of this plant was the staple means of subsistence. In the Old World the change-over from food-gathering to subsistence by means of agriculture seems to have followed promptly after the achievement of domestication. There is no indication of a time-lag there. In Meso-America the time lag was of the order of at least 1,000, and possibly even 2,500, years. This difference of pace at this stage, which accounts for the subsequent relative economic and technological backwardness of the pre-Columbian American civilizations, remains unexplained.

[14]

THE *VÖLKERWANDERUNG* IN THE OLD WORLD, *c.* 1250–950 B.C.

In the course of the three centuries 1250–950 B.C. all the regional civilizations of the Old World from the Minoan and Mycenaean in the Aegean basin to the Shang in the Yellow River basin were violently assaulted by relatively barbarous peoples, and these disturbances resulted in large shifts of population. Even assailants who had been successfully repulsed eventually won by 'peaceful penetration' the ground that they had previously failed to win by force of arms. The ultimate consequence was a sweeping change in the map of the Old World's regional civilizations. The oldest of them were enfeebled; some of the younger were destroyed; and several new civilizations arose in the geographical interstices between the ruins. This *Völkerwanderung* had a more revolutionary effect than the previous one in the eighteenth century B.C.

For the *Völkerwanderung c.* 1250–950 B.C. we have contemporary documentary evidence in Egypt. This evidence is unique, and it throws light on the course and outcome of the *Völkerwanderung* in other regions. The archaeological evidence from the Aegean area is consistent with the Egyptian documentary evidence; like the Egyptian evidence, it is contemporary, but unlike it, it is dumb. The Egyptian evidence gives information about the dates of the migrations of peoples, and about the names of the migrants, which cannot be deduced from the pottery sequences and the traces of man-made destruction in the Aegean area. Farther east, the light thrown on the history of the *Völkerwanderung* by the Egyptian documents is illuminating but is not so clear.

Circa 1220 B.C. the Libyans (Libu), accompanied by the Meshwesh and other Berber peoples and reinforced by five 'sea peoples', attacked Egypt from the west and reached the north-west corner of the Delta before they were defeated or repulsed by the Pharaoh Merneptah (ruled *c.* 1224–1214 B.C.). This was not just a raid, or even a military invasion;

it was an attempt at a migration, for the assailants brought with them their wives and children, their cattle, and their movable property. One of the five defeated peoples was the Luka, who certainly came from south-western Asia Minor; another was the Achaeans, who may have come either from continental Greece or from Crete, where, by this date, at least one band of Achaean intruders had already established itself. The other three defeated 'sea peoples' were the Sheklesh, Sherden, and Tursha. About five hundred years later, these three peoples reappear as the Sikels, Sardinians, and Tyrsenoi (Etruscans), while the Meshwesh reappear as the Maxyes in what is now Tunisia, but the western locations of these peoples in the last millennium B.C. may not have been the homes from which they were migrating in 1220 B.C.; their eventual locations may have been refuges to which the migrants repaired after their failure to establish themselves in Egypt.

In a retrospective inscription, rehearsing his military achievements, Merneptah not only mentions his crushing victory over the Libyans; he notes that 'Khatti is at peace', that Canaan had been looted and partly occupied, and that Israel had been devastated. These notices suggest that, in Merneptah's reign, the Hittite Empire had not yet been overthrown and also that it had not attempted to encroach beyond the boundary between its own and the Egyptian sphere in Syria that had been agreed in 1270 B.C. The mention of Israel indicates that the migration out of Arabia into the Fertile Crescent had already begun. This migration not only carried the tribes of Israel and Judah into Canaan; it also carried their fellow Semitic-speakers, the Chaldaeans, into the south-western fringe of Sumer, and another Semitic-speaking people, the Aramaeans, as far north as the northern end of the Great Rift Valley in what is now Turkey, as far east as the western border of Assyria, and as far south-east as the country between the east bank of the Tigris and the western brow of the Iranian plateau.

Circa 1194, and again *c.* 1188, the Pharaoh Ramses III (ruled *c.* 1198–1167 B.C.) repulsed further attacks on Egypt from the west. On these occasions the Berbers (Libyans, Maxyes, and other tribes) do not seem to have been reinforced by the 'sea peoples'. This time, the 'sea peoples' attacked Egypt independently from the north-east. Once again, they were engaged, not in a raid, but in a migration. Starting from a base of operations in the Aegean archipelago which may not have been their original home, they advanced, overland and by sea simultaneously, through Asia Minor and Syria and along their coasts. They overthrew the Hittite Empire, and ravaged not only its nuclear territory, Khatti itself, but also Arzawa in western Asia Minor, Kodi (? eastern Cilicia), and Carchemish, on the westward elbow of the Euphrates, as well as Alasya (Cyprus). They then set up a new base in Amor—a district (bearing the name of the Amorites, who had erupted out of Arabia *c.* 2000 B.C.) which was probably at the southern end of the defunct Hittite Empire's Syrian dominions. From here the 'sea peoples' advanced, as before, overland and by sea simultaneously.

Ramses III made only a show of defending Egypt's possessions in southern Syria and in Palestine. By this date the Israelite and Aramaean migrants may already have lodged themselves there. Ramses concentrated on opposing the 'sea peoples'' fleet, and he saved Egypt in the eighth year of his reign (i.e. *c.* 1191 B.C.) by winning a naval victory off the north-eastern corner of the Delta. But this naval disaster did not prevent the 'sea peoples' from moving south from Amor overland and settling permanently along the coast of what had been Egypt's Asian dominions. In 1191 B.C., as in 1220 B.C., the Sheklesh appear among the 'sea peoples', but the other members of the alliance were not the same on the two occasions. In 1191 the confederates of the Sheklesh were the Danu (Danaoi) the Tjeker (Teukroi), the Peleset (Philistines), and the Weshesh (not identified). The Danu seem to have settled in eastern Cilicia, and the Tjeker at Dor, just to the south of Mount Carmel, while the Peleset established five city-states along the southernmost strip of coastal Palestine.

The Egyptian records have preserved the names of the Libyan leader of the coalition of migrating peoples that was repulsed by Merneptah *c.* 1220 B.C., and of the other Libyan leader whose invading host was repulsed by Ramses III *c.* 1188 B.C. A far more famous name is Moses, who, according to the Israelite tradition, led the Israelites on a trek from Egypt to Transjordan which was the prelude to the Israelites' conquest of the Syrian territories that they eventually occupied; but the Egyptian records do not certify the historicity of Moses. At least two Egyptians named Mose do appear in thirteenth-century-B.C. Egyptian records. In this form the name seems to be an abbreviation of a compound theophonic name, ending in 'mose' or 'messe', in which the first of the two components is the name of a god. Ahmose (Amosis), Tuthmose (Thothmes), Remesse (Ramses) are familiar examples. According to the Israelite tradition, Moses was brought up in Egypt and was a monotheist. If there is any substance in this tradition, the most probable full form of Moses' name would be Aton-Mose, since Aton-worship is the only monotheistic cult of which there is a record in Pharaonic Egyptian history.

After the *damnatio memoriae* of the Pharaoh Akhenaton, a name compounded with the name of the Sun-disk could not have been given with impunity to any Egyptian subject. However, the Israelite tradition represents Moses as having lived for a time, before he led the Israelites out of Egypt, in territory beyond the Egyptian government's jurisdiction, and it is in non-Egyptian but ex-Egyptian territory, if anywhere, that

Akhenaton's religion might conceivably have survived. The Israelite tradition also represents Moses as having negotiated, after the Exodus, a pact between Israel and a god called Yahweh. His name is said to have been previously unknown to the Israelites. It has been interpreted tentatively as meaning 'live' or 'life-giving', and these had been attributes of the Aton.

These considerations suggest that Moses may have been a real person, like his well-attested Libyan counterparts and probable contemporaries Maraye and Mesher. Even if he did not lead the Israelites out of Egypt, he himself may have had an Egyptian cultural background. The historicity of Moses is not impugned by the obvious legendariness of some of the elements in the traditional account of his career. Some famous figures that are undoubtedly historical have come to be identified with legendary heroes of folklore. For instance, there is no doubt about the historicity of Cyrus II, the Persian founder of the Achaemenian Empire, yet the legendary story of the hero's miraculous escape in infancy from an exceptionally dangerous threat to his life has attached itself to the traditional accounts of Cyrus II's infancy and of Moses' infancy alike.

The Egyptians had saved their country from being conquered and forcibly occupied by barbarian migrants, but the cost had been too high. Egypt was exhausted. *Circa* 1087 B.C. the country fell apart into two states (a sure sign of weakness in Egypt), one still governed from Thebes and the other from Tanis, in the north-east corner of the Delta, which may have been the operational capital of Egypt since the beginning of Ramses II's reign *c.* 1290 B.C. Wen Amun, who, *c.* 1090 B.C., was sent by the Theban government to Byblos to buy timber, was treated with contempt, even in this city that had been Egypt's trading partner for 2,000 years. The King of Byblos refused to fell the timber on Mount Lebanon for Wen Amun till he had received payment in kind from the Egyptian government at Tanis. (The two Egyptian governments were in friendly relations with each other.)

However, the most remarkable sequel to the Egyptians' repulse of the Libyans' and the 'sea-peoples' ' military assaults was the eventual establishment of Libyan rule over Egypt by a gradual process of 'peaceful penetration'. *Circa* 945 B.C. the Double Crown was assumed by Pharaohs of a new dynasty (the Twenty-second) who styled themselves 'Chiefs of the Meshwesh'. We do not know whether these were descendants of the prisoners of war who had been captured in 1220 and 1194 and 1188 B.C., or whether they were descended from Libyans who had subsequently entered Egypt peacefully with the Egyptians' acquiescence. In any case, the 'take-over' of the Pharaonic government by Meshwesh *c.* 945 B.C. seems to have been peaceful and to have been carried out by agreement between the Libyan soldiery and the Egyptian priesthood. The Libyans respected the autonomy of four Egyptian temple-states—not only Thebes, which had been under the rule of the Chief priest of Amun-Re since *c.* 1087 B.C., but also Heliopolis, Memphis, and Letopolis, which were left respectively under the rule of the local priests of the gods Re, Ptah, and Horus.

Thus Egypt succumbed to the barbarian *Völkerwanderung* in the end. The Libyans, who had been signally defeated by the Egyptians, at least three times, when they had presented themselves under arms, eventually established themselves in Egypt as a military caste in partnership with the native Egyptian priesthood. In Egypt the history of the *Völkerwanderung* is recorded in contemporary documents. Elsewhere, except in so far as the Egyptian documentary information refers to regions outside Egypt itself, our contemporary evidence is archaeological, whereas our literary evidence is retrospective; it is derived from a tradition that in some cases had been transmitted orally for a number of generations before being committed to writing. In the Aegean region the tradition conflicts on a number of points with the archaeological evidence, and this discredits the tradition, but it does not give us the correct positive information. The history of the *Völkerwanderung* in the Aegean basin *c.* 1250–950 B.C. presents many puzzles which the archaeological evidence has, so far, failed to solve.

We have archaeological evidence that, at Mycenae itself, the suburbs outside the fortified palace were raided before the close of the thirteenth century B.C. *Circa* 1200 B.C. all the Mycenaean palaces except the acropolis of Athens were sacked, and Mycenae was sacked for the second time *c.* 1150 B.C. On the other hand, there is no archaeological evidence for comparable destruction at this date in either Crete or Thessaly, and eastern Attica and the Aegean islands escaped unscathed. So did the Ionian Islands, and the adjacent north-west corner of the Peloponnesos became an asylum for refugees who brought their ancestral Mycenaean culture with them. The archaeological evidence also indicates that successive waves of Mycenaean refugees occupied Cyprus in the course of the twelfth century B.C. There is no incompatibility between this Aegean archaeological evidence and the contemporary Egyptian documentary evidence; for Ramses III, in recording that the migration of the 'sea-peoples', which he brought to a halt, had started in the Aegean islands does not say that the islands themselves were devastated, but he does say that Cyprus was one of the countries that the migrants did devastate en route towards Egypt.

The Mycenaeans had already battered the Minoan civilization, and now the Mycenaeans' own civilization was crushed. After the catastrophe of *c.* 1200 B.C. literacy was lost in the Aegean basin. A syllabic script inspired by, if not directly derived from, one of the Aegean linear scripts was adopted in Cyprus for conveying the Greek language, which had presumably been introduced into Cyprus by the twelfth-century-B.C. Mycenaean Greek immigrants, and here this script survived the introduction of the Phoenician alphabet and continued to be used, side by side with this, till the third century B.C.; but, in Crete and continental Greece, the Aegean scripts fell into lasting oblivion. Texts were eventually disinterred, and the Linear-B texts were subsequently deciphered, in the twentieth century A.D. Nor was literacy the only cultural asset that was lost in Greece at the downfall of the Mycenaean civilization. The mason's craft also ceased to be practised. Lamps ceased to be manufactured. There was general impoverishment. Gold disappeared and the elaborate style of dress that the Mycenaeans had copied from the Minoans was abandoned. To judge by the number of sites known to have been inhabited in the thirteenth and in the twelfth centuries respectively, there was also a precipitous decline of population in the Mycenaean civilization's former domain as a whole, even though there were local increases in areas occupied by refugees.

There is no conclusive evidence that the devastated areas, from which the refugees had fled, were occupied by the devastators. If these were the 'sea peoples', they moved on to loot other regions farther east and south, according to the testimony of the Egyptian documents. During the twelfth and eleventh centuries B.C., the southern part of the Peloponnesos (Messenia and Laconia) seems to have been almost deserted; but, until *c*. 1050 B.C., the surviving inhabitants of the devastated areas retained the Mycenaean civilization in a degenerate form. It was then that a new civilization, with a distinctive style of its own, began to show itself in the defunct Mycenaean civilization's former domain.

There is archaeological evidence that the colonization of Ionia (the middle section of the west coast of Asia Minor) by settlers from Greece began in the tenth century B.C.; but there is no archaeological evidence for the arrival of the people, speaking the North-Western dialect of the Greek language, who came to be known retrospectively as the 'Dorians'. The evidence for their migration is the dialect-map of the Greek-speaking world in the last millennium B.C. On this map the zone occupied by North-West-Greek-speakers extends diagonally from Epirus in the north-west to the Dodecanese and to the south-west corner of continental Asia Minor in the south-east. A different dialect, the Arcado-Cypriot, was now spoken on either side of the Doric dialect's zone. This non-Doric dialect must have been brought to Cyprus by the Mycenaean Greek refugees who settled there, and it must have been retained in Arcadia because this heart of the Peloponnesos was a natural fastness. The Arcado-Cypriot Greek dialect of the last millennium B.C. is, in fact, closely akin to the Mycenaean-Age Greek dialect that is conveyed in the Linear-B script.

The south-eastward spread of the North-West-Greek-speakers can hardly have been later than the tenth century B.C., and the archaeological evidence for the survival of the Mycenaean style of material culture in the region that˙was devastated *c.* 1200 B.C. does not rule out the possibility that the so-called Dorian migration may have taken place as early as the twelfth century. Barbarian intruders may obliterate their tracks by adopting the material culture of their civilized victims.

In the Aegean basin, the destruction caused by the *Völkerwanderung* of *c.* 1250–950 B.C. went to extremes. There are a number of known cases in which a literate people has exchanged one script for another, but the loss of literacy itself in the Aegean basin *c.* 1200 B.C. is a unique event, and it gives the measure of the catastrophe that caused it. The civilization of Asia Minor fared better. Though the Hittite Empire, like the Mycenaean principalities, was overthrown, successor-states survived in northern Syria, which the Hittites had wrested out of Egyptian hands; and these refugee Hittites continued to use a Luvian hieroglyphic script which had been invented in Asia Minor before the *Völkerwanderung*, though they ceased to write the Indo-European Hittite and the Akkadian language in the Sumerian script.

The overthrow of the Hittite Empire had one abiding consequence that has come to be of world-wide importance. It ended the previous Hittite embargo on the dissemination of the knowledge of the technology for producing wrought-iron that was as hard as bronze. This technology seems to have been discovered in Asia Minor. When the Greeks made their way into the Black Sea, they attributed the invention to a legendary people, the Chalybes, whom they located on the north coast of Asia Minor. This had never been included in the Hittite Empire, but the Hittites managed to monopolize the invention and to keep it to themselves as a valuable state secret. The Hittite kings occasionally gave iron objects as choice presents to foreign rulers, and, outside the Hittite Empire until its fall, iron was treated as one of the precious metals.

Actually, the technology for making hard wrought-iron weapons and tools is more sophisticated, and proportionately more difficult to master, than the technology for making bronze implements of equal hardness. The incentive for using iron is that iron-ore is to be found close at hand almost everywhere (with, of course, such notable exceptions as the alluvial lower Tigris–Euphrates basin). Compared with iron-ore, copper-ore is rare, while tin is still rarer. Since bronze is a mixture of copper and tin, the enabling condition for the production of bronze is the possibility of transporting ingots of metal over long distances. There is therefore a premium on using iron instead of bronze at times and places at which communications have broken down.

This happened in the Aegean after the series of disasters there in the twelfth century B.C.; and, since the Aegean is next-door to Asia Minor, it is not surprising that, at Athens, iron began to be used for making tools and weapons as early as *c.* 1050 B.C. Here, iron continued to be the predominant industrial metal for the next two centuries, but then, as communications became better again, bronze came back into use, now side by side with iron, for some purposes. In Egypt, on the other hand, iron did not supersede copper as the material for tools till about the seventh century B.C. The Egyptians had fended off the 'sea-peoples'; their way of life had not been utterly disorganized; and, since the reaction against the revolution that had followed the fall of the Old Kingdom, the Egyptians had become conservative-minded. In Pharaonic Egypt more stone was cut than anywhere at any subsequent date. Yet the Egyptians did most of their stone-cutting with tools made of un-alloyed copper. They did not take kindly even to bronze. The Yellow River basin was remote from the Levantine seats of the earliest civiliza-tions, yet the Chinese had mastered the art of bronze-working by about the fifteenth century B.C. Their virtuosity as bronze-smiths became great, and sources of supply of both copper and tin were continuously accessible to them. This perhaps partly explains why it was that, in China, iron did not supersede bronze as the standard material for tools and weapons till about the fourth century B.C.

The dialect map of Asia Minor in the last millennium B.C. reveals an intrusive zone of Thraco-Phrygian language, running diagonally from north-west to south-east, like the 'Doric' Greek zone in the Aegean basin; and, here again, the previously prevalent languages, in this case Luvian and Hittite, survived on either side—Hittite in northern Syria and Luvian in western Asia Minor (i.e. in Lycia, Caria, and Lydia). The Phrygians were certainly not identical with the 'sea peoples'. They broke into Asia Minor, not from the Aegean archipelago, but from Thrace; they simply occupied a vacuum that the 'sea peoples' had created; but the date of their migration, like the date of the Doric-speaking Greeks' migration, is not revealed by the archaeological evidence.

The movement of the Chaldaeans and Israelites and Aramaeans out of Arabia into the Fertile Crescent seems to have been long-drawn-out. The Israelites were already in Palestine before the end of Pharaoh Merneptah's reign, i.e. before 1214 B.C. On the other hand the Ara-maeans' pressure on Mesopotamia and on northern Syria cannot have been heavy in the reign of King Tiglath-Pileser I of Assyria (ruled *c.* 1114–1076 B.C.), considering that he succeeded in marching westward as far as the shore of the Mediterranean. Assyria was not hit so hard by the *Völkerwanderung circa* 1250–950 B.C. as she had been by the previous *Völkerwanderung* in the eighteenth century B.C. On that occasion she had fallen under the suzerainty of Mitanni. During the years 1250–950 B.C. she retained her independence. The 'sea peoples' did not cross the Euphrates in their devastating migration that ended in 1291 B.C.; and the Euphrates, together with the Antitaurus and the Taurus Range, were obstacles in the Phrygians' path in the direction of Assyria.

India's history during the years 1250–950 B.C. is unknown. The primary-Sanskrit-speaking invaders may have entered the Indus basin and have destroyed the Indus civilization a quarter of a millennium earlier. Alternatively they may not have arrived in the Indus basin till *c.* 1250 B.C., and, if this was the date of their arrival, they may have been propelled into India by migrants who had broken out of the Eurasian steppe in their rear.

In the Yellow River basin, the Shang dynasty was overthrown and replaced by its former vassals, the Chou, in 1122 B.C. according to the canonical chronology, or in 1027 B.C. according to an alternative reckoning that may come nearer to the true date. The Chou invaded the North-China plain from the basin of the Yellow River's Wei tributary—that is to say from the direction from which, in previous ages, China may have received elements of culture from regions to the west, via the Eurasian steppe. But the archaeological evidence does not indicate that the Chou brought any further cultural innovations with them. The political change from Shang to Chou did not cause a breach of cultural continuity such as was caused in Greece by the overthrow of the Mycenaean principalities. The Chou seem to have been Chinese, or at any rate to have been thoroughly Sinified before they supplanted the Shang; and the arts of writing and of bronze-casting not only survived the change of regime; they continued to advance.

Moreover, the change of dynasty does not seem to have produced any immediate substantial change in the political structure of Chinese society. The archaeological evidence for the character of the Shang regime includes not only artefacts but also documents, namely, the inscriptions on the 'oracle bones'. The discoveries of Anyang, which, according to tradition, was the last of five successive capitals of the Shang dynasty, indicate that this dynasty was the dominant power in the Yellow River basin in the Anyang period. No comparable contemporary site, which might have been the seat of a rival power of the same calibre, has yet been found. The site at Cheng-Chou, about one hundred miles farther south, is thought to have been an earlier capital of the Shang power itself. However, the 'oracle bone' inscriptions show that the Shang lived in fear of enemies—a fear that was justified by the event.

The archaeological evidence does not reveal the extent of the Shang's direct dominions or of their sphere of political influence; but it is clear that the Shang polity was not an empire equipped with a provincial administration that was effectively controlled by the central government, as the Chinese Empire was, in its successive avatars, after the political unification of China in 221 B.C. by Ch'in Shih Hwang-ti. The title 'Shih Hwang-ti' ('First Emperor') that was then assumed by the unifier, King Chêng of the victorious local state Ch'in, was well coined, for, in China, there had never before been a centralized empire embracing the whole of the Chinese civilization's cultural domain. The Shang polity was not one of that kind. It was evidently much more like its own immediate successor, as the Chou regime is depicted retrospectively in the Chinese tradition.

Even in their early days, before they were irremediably and progressively enfeebled by a disaster that overtook them in 771 B.C., the Chou did not rule over more than a small territory directly. For the most part, their regime was merely a hegemony over perhaps as many as seventy or ninety autonomous local vassals. This Chou regime was weak, even at its prime, by comparison with the unitary regime that was imposed on the Chinese World, about eight hundred years later, by Shih Hwang-ti. On the other hand, the Chou regime was probably a strong one, measured by the standard of its Shang predecessor. The Chou did govern the Chinese World of their day, even if indirectly. The Shang, whom the Chou had replaced, had perhaps merely dominated their neighbours by raids that had not led to the establishment of any institutional relation between the dominant power and the semi-independent communities within its reach, whom it terrorized but also feared.

[15]

THE EMERGENCE OF THE 'OLMEC' CIVILIZATION IN MESO-AMERICA

The *Völkerwanderung* that, *c.* 1250–950 B.C., had such disturbing effects in the Old World from the Mediterranean basin at one end to the Yellow River basin at the other did not affect the Americas, but, within the same period, an historic event occurred in at least one district in Meso-America. *Circa* 1250 B.C. the 'Formative' phase of culture—which in its early and middle stages is the New-World counterpart of the Old-World 'Neolithic' phase—produced a civilization at a site in a piece of jungle-clad high ground now named San Lorenzo which over-hangs the valley of the Coalzacoalcos, the river that drains the northern side of the Tehuantepec Isthmus into the Gulf of Mexico. This is the oldest site yet discovered of the oldest known civilization in the Americas —a civilization that has been labelled 'Olmec' by its modern discoverers.

At San Lorenzo the Olmec civilization was not yet literate, but it produced massive works of architecture and sculpture. In the architecture a ceremonial centre was extended by the re-shaping of the land-scape on a vast scale. The distinctive Olmec works of sculpture both at San Lorenzo and at later sites are colossal human heads carved in the round in basalt hauled to San Lorenzo from a source about fifty miles away. These material remains are the outward visible signs of a human authority that must have been able to mobilize skill and labour on the grand scale for the achievement of a religious objective. The Olmecs' paramount god is portrayed in statues of a monster that is a cross be-tween a human being and a jaguar. The cult of this god was evidently the spiritual driving-force that produced the Olmecs' material achieve-ments, and we may guess that these achievements were partly the voluntary work of devotees. But we may also guess that they were partly produced by the forced labour of unbelievers who had been conquered in war; for Olmec San Lorenzo was wrecked with a violence that is evidence of the wreckers' resentment.

At San Lorenzo the Olmec civilization was at its height from *c.* 1150

to 900 B.C. before it was extirpated by violence at this site, but at other
sites, nearer to the coast of the Gulf of Mexico, the Olmec civilization
flourished from *c.* 800 to 400 B.C., and it did not die out there before it
had made its influence felt on the culture of a number of other parts of
Meso-America.

The later phases of the Olmec civilization, together with its Andean
counterpart, the 'Chavín' civilization, are dealt with in Chapter 21.
However, we may note here several surprising features of the relics of
the Olmec civilization that have been discovered at San Lorenzo. In the
first place, the emergence of a civilization only about 250 years after the
local culture had reached its 'Formative' phase is as surprising as the
time-lag of at least 1,000 years, and possibly nearly 2,500 years, between
the date of the domestication of maize in Meso-America and the date, *c.*
1500 B.C., at which the cultivation of this domesticated plant replaced
food-gathering and hunting as the staple source of food-supply in Meso-
America. In the second place, the site at San Lorenzo—in contrast to
later sites of the Olmec civilization in other places—appears to have
been not just a 'ceremonial centre' but a permanent settlement with
perhaps as many as a thousand inhabitants. In the third place, by *c.*
1150–900 B.C., the Olmec civilization at San Lorenzo had already
arrived at the artistic and technological zenith at which it continued to
stand at its later sites.

Meanwhile, the 'Formative' culture that had emerged in Meso-
America *c.* 1500 B.C. was spreading, particularly southwards. By *c.* 800
B.C., when the Olmec civilization was making its appearance in the lowlands along the shore of the Gulf of Mexico, and when the Chavín
civilization was emerging in Peru, the 'Formative' Meso-American
culture—including the art of pottery-making, as well as maize-cultiva-
tion—had spread throughout the whole of 'nuclear America', from
Meso-America to Peru inclusive. The cultivation of maize in 'nuclear
America' to the south of Meso-America, including Peru as well as
Central America and present-day Colombia and Ecuador, was almost
certainly derived from Meso-America; for the evidence indicates that
Meso-America was the region in which maize was originally domesticated. Yet, whatever may be the date at which maize was introduced
into northern coastal Peru from Meso-America, it is certain that the
Peruvians had, by then, already invented agriculture for themselves
independently of both Meso-America and the Old World. Two of the
numerous local plants that the Peruvians had domesticated—the potato
and quinoa—could be cultivated at the altitude of the Peruvian altiplano, and even as high up as the artificially terraced slopes of the
mountains that rise above the plateau. Agriculture has not been
carried to so high an altitude anywhere else in the Oikoumenê.

[16]

THE SUMERO-AKKADIAN WORLD
AND EGYPT, *c.* 950–745 B.C.

THE Sumero-Akkadian and Egyptian civilizations had accomplished most of their great creative achievements, in all fields of human activity, before the close of the third millennium B.C. By the year 2000 B.C., they had also lost their former distinction of being the only two civilizations in the Oikoumenê. Other regional civilizations had arisen alongside of them, and, meanwhile, the two oldest civilizations had each been over-taken by a disaster. However, both had rallied before the beginning of the third millennium, and this resilience revealed a toughness and a staying-power that enabled the Sumero-Akkadian civilization to survive till after the beginning of the Christian Era, and the Pharaonic Egyptian to survive till the fifth century A.D.

In Chapter 13 some account has been given of the roles played by these two senior civilizations in promoting relations between all the regional civilizations of the Levant. In the Age of the New Kingdom the Pharaonic civilization put together a cosmopolitan political empire that became a cultural melting-pot. In the same age the Akkadian language, conveyed in the Sumerian script, became a vehicle for giving a classical form to works of literature that were of Sumerian origin. In this form, these works became part of the cultural heritage of regions beyond the bounds of the Sumero-Akkadian World—for instance, Syria and Asia Minor. At the same time, Akkadian became the medium of diplomatic correspondence, not only between the sovereign powers in the Levant, including Egypt, but also between the Egyptian Government and its own client states in Palestine and Syria.

Politically, Sumer and Akkad had been enfeebled by the swift failure of Hammurabi's re-establishment, in 1761–1753 B.C., of an empire embracing the whole of the Sumero-Akkadian World, including Assyria and Mari and Carchemish; and Egypt, too, was eventually reduced to the same political impotence by the effort of repulsing the assaults of the

Libyans and the 'sea peoples' during the years 1220–1188 B.C. However, in each of these two ageing regional societies, there was an outlying province that retained its vitality. It has been noted already that Assyria, which had been submerged by the Mitannian *Völkerwanderung* in the eighteenth century B.C., had re-emerged in the fourteenth century B.C. as a militaristic power, and that, during the protracted *Völkerwanderung* c. 1250–950 B.C., Assyria, though thrown on the defensive once again, managed to preserve its political identity and independence. From c. 932 to 745 B.C., Assyria resumed her aggression against her neighbours, though not yet with the demonic ardour and brutal violence through which she condemned herself to be annihilated at the end of the last phase of her career, which opened at the accession of Tiglath-Pileser III in 745 B.C.

During the period c. 932–745 B.C. neither Egypt nor the Sumero-Akkadian civilization was any longer a principal source of cultural creativity or even an important agency of cultural intercourse. In this age, these roles were taken over by new regional civilizations that had emerged from the most recent of the *Völkerwanderungen*. These new civilizations were the Syrian, the Hellenic Greek, the Vedic Indian, and the Chinese—though in China there was a greater cultural continuity between the Chou Age and the preceding Shang Age than there was between the new civilizations to the west of China and these civilizations' respective predecessors. However, the two oldest of the regional civilizations had not yet wholly exhausted their cultural creativity. They were still sufficiently attractive to win cultural converts. After 950 B.C. the Egyptian civilization acquired a new cultural province far up the Nile valley, between the Third and the Fourth Cataract, and, in the same period, the Sumero-Akkadian civilization acquired one to the north of the mountain barrier that segregates the basin of Lake Van, and the two arms of the upper Euphrates, from the lowlands of Assyria and Mesopotamia and from the upper basin of the River Tigris.

In Egypt itself the Libyan regime of the Twenty-second Dynasty, c. 945–730 B.C., was as uneventful as the Kassite regime in Babylonia and the native Babylonian regime that replaced the Kassites c. 1169 B.C. The Libyan Pharaohs' only exploits were occasional raids into Palestine which led to nothing. Yet this was the age in which Napata, which had been the frontier fortress of the Egyptian New Kingdom, became the political and cultural capital of a state whose people were not Egyptians in nationality, but whose rulers were whole-hearted converts to the Pharaonic Egyptian religion and to the rest of the Pharaonic culture. Along the Nile for some distance up and down stream from Napata, there is a belt of fertile soil which still responds to irrigation by yielding rich crops. By 730 B.C. this agricultural basis had made the Kushite

Kingdom of Napata populous and potent enough to tempt its rulers into trying to re-unite the whole of the Egyptian World, right down to the Nile delta, under the sovereignty of Kushite wearers of the Double Crown.

The new cultural province that the Sumero-Akkadian World acquired after 950 B.C. was Urartu. Its geographical location has been noted already. This was the region from which the Hurrian migrants had descended upon the Fertile Crescent in the *Völkerwanderung* of the eighteenth century B.C., and the Urartians (Khaldi) of the last millennium B.C. were the descendants of Hurrians who had stayed at home. Early in the ninth century B.C. the local Urartian Hurrian cantons united to form a kingdom with its capital at Tušpa on the east shore of Lake Van. We may guess that the motive for this political unification was the fear of Assyrian aggression. Shalmaneser III did, in fact, invade Urartu in the first year of his reign (ruled *c.* 858–824 B.C.). Militarily, Assyria was the better organized and the better equipped of the two powers; yet Assyria never succeeded in conquering Urartu. In 612 B.C., the year in which Nineveh fell, Urartu was still surviving on the political map of South-West Asia.

Physical geography explains why Urartu did not succumb to a power that, before its collapse, had thrust south-westward as far as Egypt and south-eastward as far as Elam. Urartu is a natural fastness. As the plane flies, the distance to Tušpa even from Asshur, the oldest and southernmost of the capitals of Assyria, is slightly shorter than the distance from Asshur to Babylon; but, on the ground, it is possible to march from Asshur to Babylon along the shortest line between these two points, yet quite impossible to march straight from Asshur to Tušpa.

An Assyrian army whose objective was Tušpa could not ascend the upper valley of the Greater Zab River. This is as formidable a natural fastness as the basin of Lake Van itself. Nor could it cross the high range that is the Van basin's southern watershed. Assyrian invaders of Urartu had first to march, not north, but north-west, over less obstructive mountains, from Mesopotamia into the upper basin of the River Tigris. They then had to turn north-east and climb the long and steep pass that leads, past Bitlis, to the south-west corner of Lake Van. The road along the lake's southern shore would have been the shortest route from there to Tušpa. But this route is physically arduous even today, and it would have been prohibitively dangerous for an invader faced with military resistance. From the south-west corner of Lake Van, the practical choice for an Assyrian invader lay between skirting the northern and eastern shores of the lake and making a still longer detour through the rather more open country in the basin of the southern arm of the upper Euphrates (now called the Murat Su). This explains why Assyrian armies only rarely managed to reach Tušpa, and never managed to stay there. On the other hand, Urartian armies—screened by the intervening mountains and welcomed by neighbouring peoples who shared the Urartians' repugnance to being subjugated by Assyria—were able to oppose Assyria's attempts to advance over the mountains either north-eastward into Iran or north-westward into Asia Minor.

Thus, militarily, Urartu was the most effective, as well as the most resolute, of all Assyria's opponents in the last millennium B.C. On the other hand, in the ninth century B.C., at the very time when they began to suffer from Assyrian military aggression, the Urartians voluntarily received the Assyrian culture. They carved inscriptions in their own Hurrian language but in the Assyrian version of the Akkadian form of the Sumerian script. Assyria was the cultural heir of Sumer and Akkad, and this rich and ancient heritage made Assyria culturally attractive, repulsive though she was in herself. The Urartians, however, were not merely passive recipients of an alien culture. In at least one of the major arts—the craft of building in stone—the Urartian masons surpassed their Assyrian masters and attained almost an Egyptian standard—not in massiveness, but in precision.

For an Assyrian aggressor, the line of least resistance was not northward or eastward, but westward across Mesopotamia into Syria or southward into Babylonia. The relative military strengths of Babylonia and Assyria had been reversed since the eighteenth century B.C., when Hammurabi had reduced Assyria to submission. Since the fourteenth century B.C., Babylonia had not been a match for Assyria militarily; but, though Assyria now repeatedly went to war with Babylonia, and even occupied it temporarily, as, for instance in the reign of King Tukulti-Ninurta I of Assyria (see pp. 100–1 above), the Assyrians treated Babylonia with a certain amount of respect and consideration as the motherland of the two countries' common civilization, until Tiglath-Pileser III (*accessit* 745 B.C.) carried Assyrian militarism into its outrageous final phase.

During the years 932–745 B.C., Assyria found the main outlet for her aggression in the regions to the west of her. In the course of the years 932–859 B.C. she conquered the Aramaean communities that had established themselves to the east of the Euphrates, right up to the western threshold of Assyria's home territory. In 858–856 B.C. Shalmaneser III won for Assyria the entrée into Syria by conquering Bit Adini, an Aramaean state that bestrode the westward bulge of the Euphrates; but the common danger that now threatened the Syrian statelets induced them momentarily to suspend their local conflicts with each other. In 853 B.C. Shalmaneser III was defeated at Qarqar, on the River Orontes, to the north of Hamath (Hamah), by a Syrian coalition. He invaded

Syria again in 849 and 848 and 845 B.C., and the breakdown of the anti-Assyrian coalition enabled him in 841 B.C. to hit Damascus hard and to force Damascus's ex-allies to recognize Assyria's suzerainty. However, in 831 B.C. Shalmaneser III suffered a check in Urartu, and in 827 he was overtaken by a rebellion at home which immobilized him and his successor, Shamshi-Adad V, until 822 B.C. The Urartians, now united in a powerful rival state, competed successfully with Assyria, during the reign of their King Argištis I (785–753 B.C.) for command over northern Syria and eastern Cilicia. In 745 B.C. these strategically crucial regions were under the Urartians', not the Assyrians', control.

This spelled the failure of the attempt, initiated by Shalmaneser III, to make Assyria the dominant power in the Levant; yet, even so, the military power that Assyria was able to exert during the years 934–853 B.C. is impressive. Its economic basis was a belt of rich agricultural land in Assyria's home territory between the left bank of the Tigris and the south-western foot of the Zagros Range. This fertile heart of Assyria was larger than the agricultural land, round Napata, that was the economic basis of the military power of Kush, but it was far smaller than the cultivated area in Babylonia. Unlike both Babylonia and Kush, Assyria depended mainly, not on irrigation, but on rainfall for the supply of water for its crops. Some of the Neolithic-Age sites in which agriculture, fed by rainfall, had been invented in South-West Asia before the opening-up of the alluvium of the lower Tigris–Euphrates basin lay within what had subsequently become Assyria. This historical fact raises the question whether the migration of the seat of power in the Tigris–Euphrates basin upstream, first from Sumer to Akkad, and then from Akkad to Assyria, may have been due, at least in part, to a deterioration of the irrigation system which had conjured the fertile fields of Sumer and Akkad out of former swamps and deserts.

Irrigation systems can be damaged either by Man or by Nature. They can be put out of action by contests between local communities or by conquest from abroad. Alternatively, Nature may sterilize man-made fields by depositing the charge of salt carried in irrigation-water or by drawing up salt from the subsoil. This malignity of Nature has partly stultified some modern irrigation works—for instance, in the Punjab and in Mexico. As for the maleficent action of Man, records of this abound in Sumero-Akkadian history from the start.

In the Nile basin, Nature has been more provident than she has been in the Tigris–Euphrates basin. Till the completion in A.D. 1902 of the construction of the first barrage at Aswan, the Nile flood deposited on Egypt annually a fresh layer of fertilizing silt, and neither Nature nor Man had the power to cancel this gift. Does the artificiality, and the consequent vulnerability, of the irrigation of the lower Tigris–Euphrates basin account for Sumer's and Akkad's fall and for Assyria's rise? In Iraq the irrigation system was certainly put out of action at the time of the Mongol conquest in A.D. 1258, and the work of rehabilitating it was not begun till after the First World War. But had the sudden man-made disaster in A.D. 1258 been preceded by a gradual sterilization of the soil of Iraq through the action of natural forces? We do not have enough information to give a direct answer to this question, but surely it is answered indirectly by the fact that, after the downfall of Assyria, Babylonia continued to be fertile enough to provide the economic basis for a long series of empires, beginning with Assyria's Chaldaean successor-state and ending with the Abbasid Caliphate, which included less productive areas beyond Babylonia's own bounds.

[17]

THE SYRIAN CIVILIZATION,
c. 1191–745 B.C.

EVERY human culture that has ever been brought into existence has continued to influence the subsequent course of human affairs. The influence of cultures that have become extinct may still be potent. The continuing influence of the Sumero-Akkadian and the Pharaonic Egyptian civilizations illustrates this point. However, the influence of extinct cultures is indirect. Among the still surviving civilizations, one, the Chinese, made its appearance about half way through the second millennium B.C., and another, the Indian, may have destroyed and supplanted the foregoing Indus civilization at about the same date. Of the new civilizations that arose among the ruins left by the *Völkerwanderung c.* 1250–950 B.C., one, the Hellenic, is now extinct, but its contemporary, which arose in Syria in the broadest geographical meaning of the word, is still represented today by two communities, the Jews and the Samaritans.

The Jews have not only survived. Like the Chinese and the Indians, they have produced and preserved a literature. The earliest components of this literature are believed to have been put into writing in the tenth century B.C. The corpus of Jewish literature is by far the largest and the most famous of our sources for the religious and social and political history, not only of Judah and Israel, but of the Syrian civilization as a whole. Evidence independent of the Jewish scriptures (the Old Testament in Christian terminology) has only recently been brought to light by archaeology, but this evidence, illuminating though it is, is slight and fragmentary. The scriptures are relatively circumstantial and comprehensive. Without them, a student of the history of the Syrian civilization would still find himself groping almost in the dark. Yet this indispensable source would be misleading if it were to be taken at face value, and this for two reasons: the scriptures tell the story from the standpoint of only two of the constituent communities of the Syrian civilization, and they do not give even this tendentious version of the story in its original form. Since the date at which the oldest books of the Old Testament were written, the Jews' religion has undergone changes that, cumulatively, have been revolutionary, and the texts have been edited and re-edited, to make them conform to the thesis that the changes have not been innovations but have been reversions to a pristine faith and practice.

Thus the scriptures, in the form in which we now have them, give a picture of Judah and Israel themselves and, *a fortiori*, of their neighbours, that is not true to life. The picture can be corrected only partially by scrutinizing the 'internal evidence' of the Jewish scriptures and by confronting it with the small, though growing, body of evidence that is being produced by the progress of archaeological exploration. A party that has survived and has monopolized the telling of a controversial tale has an impregnable advantage over parties that have become extinct without having left any countervailing versions of the same story. Phoenician or Philistine scriptures, if they were extant, would no doubt differ dramatically from the Jewish.

These scriptures, as we now have them, maintain several theses that would not have been accepted by the contemporaries of Israel and Judah in Syria at and after the time at which these two communities established themselves there. Today, these Jewish theses are tenable only by orthodox adherents of the Jewish religion or of one of its two daughter religions, Christianity and Islam. The first thesis is that the Jews' god Yahweh exists and is the one true god, the omnipotent creator and master of the Universe. The second thesis is that Yahweh chose the Israelites to be, in a special sense, his own people. He confirmed his choice by making a covenant, or a series of covenants, with the Israelites. They and their forefathers, on their side, had been monotheistic devotees of Yahweh since the time of Abraham (perhaps the eighteenth century B.C.), though Yahweh did not reveal his name to them till the time of Moses (perhaps the thirteenth century B.C.).

Neither the history of the Syrian civilization nor the histories of Mankind and of the Universe can be interpreted in terms of these theses by an historian who is not an orthodox adherent of one or other of the Judaic religions. Yet the unorthodox historian, too, has to use the Old Testament as his principal source for the history of the Syrian civilization. Neither an unorthodox nor an orthodox version of this episode can escape being controversial—which is most unfortunate, because this chapter of the history of Syria has had a profound effect on the subsequent history of nearly one half of the human race.

This caveat is a necessary preface to an account of the Syrian civilization's history by an unorthodox historian. He cannot accept the traditional orthodox theses; he must do his best to look at the course of events objectively; he must also try to present his own version of the story unpolemically.

In the *Völkerwanderung c.* 1250–950 B.C., Syria suffered as severely as Asia Minor and the Aegean basin. The material destruction there and the change in the composition of the population were no less catastrophic. However, Syria recuperated more quickly than those other two regions from the common disaster that had overtaken them all. In Syria, before she was hit by this *Völkerwanderung*, civilization had struck deeper roots. By that time both the Sumero-Akkadian and the Egyptian civilizations had been infiltrating into Syria for nearly 2,000 years. These two foreign influences had been so overwhelming that they had inhibited Syria from creating an original civilization of her own till Egypt and Babylonia had lost much of their vitality. Yet, even before the beginning of the upheaval in the Levant *c.* 1250 B.C., Syria had begun to show her native capacity for creation. She had taken her first steps towards the invention of the Alphabet, and this, in various forms, has now become the script of all the World except for Eastern Asia.

Circa 1500 B.C., or even earlier, graffiti in the so-called 'Sinaitic' script were being scratched on rocks at the Egyptian mines on the west side of the Sinai peninsula, and some inscriptions in the same script have been found in southern Syria. Attempts have been made to decipher these texts on the hypothesis that the script is alphabetic and the language Semitic. None of these attempts at decipherment has yet won general acceptance, but, if this script did prove to be alphabetic, it might perhaps also prove to be the common ancestor of the Phoenician alphabet and the South-Semitic alphabet of the south-western corner of Arabia (the Yemen).

Some of the characters of the Sinaitic script look as if they had been inspired by Egyptian hieroglyphics. During the first third of the fourteenth century B.C., the Phoenicians at Ugarit (Ras-ash-Shamrah), towards the northern end of the coast of Syria, wrote works of literature in their own language in an alphabet composed of a few characters selected from the huge Sumero-Akkadian repertory of ideograms and phonemes. This first Phoenician essay at alphabetic writing did not survive the *Völkerwanderung c.* 1250–950 B.C. The earliest known inscriptions in the subsequently invented Phoenician alphabet, from which all present-day forms of alphabetic writing are derived, are probably not older than the eleventh century B.C. This successful second Phoenician alphabet was inspired by the Egyptian hieroglyphs, as is shown by the names and by the original shapes of a number of the letters. In their historic alphabet, as in their previous abortive one, the Phoenicians borrowed characters from a script that was a mixture of ideograms and syllabic phonemes, but, each time, they made the set of borrowed characters stand for a set of sounds that included all the consonantal sounds in the Phoenicians' own Canaanite Semitic language.

We can see why the inventors of the Alphabet were Semitic-speakers who had asserted their cultural independence of the two ancient civilizations of Sumer and Pharaonic Egypt, by which the Semitic-speaking peoples in the Fertile Crescent had previously been overwhelmed. The first Semitic-speaking people to become literate were the Akkadians, and their geographical location made it inevitable that they should adopt the Sumerian script and should use it in the Sumerian way. Yet a script composed of a mixture of ideograms and phonemes is not congenial to the structure of a Semitic language. The root of a Semitic word consists of a set of three consonants which retain their identity and their sequence through all modifications produced by the addition of prefixes and suffixes and by the insertion or omission of vowels. The structure of a Semitic language calls for the invention of a script in which the letters will represent each and all of the language's consonants, and in which the total set of letters will be limited to the small number required for denoting this limited set of sounds.

We do not know what language was spoken by the Palaeolithic cave-dwellers on Mount Carmel or by the Neolithic founders of Jericho. But no pre-Semitic language has left any trace in Syria, and influxes of non-Semitic-speaking peoples—Hurrians in the eighteenth century B.C., and Philistines and refugee Hittites in the twelfth century B.C.—were offset by the entry of fresh swarms of Semitic-speakers—as for instance, the Amorites towards the close of the third millennium B.C. and the Hebrews and Aramaeans in the thirteenth century B.C. Canaanite, which was the oldest Semitic language in Syria, was infectious. It was adopted by immigrants whose mother-tongue was non-Semitic—for instance, by the Philistines—as well as by peoples whose mother-tongue was some non-Canaanite Semitic language. The Amorites and, after them, the Hebrews (Moab, Ammon, Israel, Judah, Edom) all became Canaanite-speakers, though presumably the Hebrews had originally spoken a different Semitic language akin to that of the Aramaeans, who entered Syria in the same *Völkerwanderung*. Only the Aramaeans who settled in central and northern Syria and in Mesopotamia were allergic to the Canaanite language. They quickly adopted the Alphabet—the date of the earliest known Aramaic inscriptions is estimated to be *c.* 850 B.C.—but they did not use it for writing the Canaanite language which it had been invented to convey; they adapted the Alphabet to convey their native Aramaean Semitic language.

Thus one common feature of the civilization that emerged in Syria after the *Völkerwanderung c.* 1250–950 B.C. was the use of the Alphabet for conveying local Semitic languages; and among these the indigenous

Canaanite language still maintained its predominance during the period
c. 950–745 B.C. Another common feature of the Syrian civilization was
its religion. Long before the later centuries of the second millennium
B.C., Syria had become an agricultural country, and pastoral nomad
immigrants quickly became agriculturists when they settled on Syrian
ground. The festivals of the Jewish liturgical year are now deemed to
commemorate events (authentic or legendary) in the Israelites' history;
but these festivals bear the marks of having originally been celebrations
of the annually recurrent phases of an agricultural community's working
life.

Agriculture was originally a religious as well as an economic activity.
The main objective of agricultural religion was to foster the fertility of
domesticated plants and animals and of the human beings who won
their livelihood by living in a symbiosis with these other forms of life.
In most agricultural communities, all round the globe, one of the prescriptions for stimulating fertility has been sexual sympathetic magic,
and this was still being practised in Syria in the last millennium B.C.
Another expression of agricultural religion, which Syria shared with
other regions in the Levant, was the myth and ritual of the god who dies
at the harvest but comes to life again when the shoots of the next year's
crop appear above ground. The god who dies to rise again was called
Tammuz in Sumer and Akkad, Attis in Asia Minor, Osiris in Pharaonic
Egypt, and Adonai ('My Lord') in Syria, alias Baal (which also means
'Lord') at fourteenth-century-B.C. Ugarit. The myth and ritual of the
dying god must have had a common origin. The resemblances between
the several regional versions are too close to be fortuitous.

In all civilizations down to the present day, human sacrifice has been
practised in the form of war, and, since the invention of aviation, the
victims of military operations have no longer been confined to soldiers
killed in battle and to the civilian population of cities taken by storm.
But many of the peoples who have gloried in war have, illogically, been
shocked by the sacrifice of civilians in peace-time, whether the victims
are the servants of a king, sent to accompany him into the nether world
of the dead, or whether they are the first-born sons of a devotee who
hopes, in virtue of his having offered this supreme sacrifice, to constrain
a god to respond favourably to a prayer. There seems to be no evidence
for either of these non-military forms of human sacrifice in Pharaonic
Egypt, and the slaughter of a dead king's servants seems to have been
given up in Sumer after the First Dynasty of Ur. In the Old World in
the last millennium B.C. the practice of burning children alive seems to
have been peculiar to Syria and its overseas colonies. King Mesha of
Moab sacrificed a son when his capital city was being besieged by an
enemy coalition *c.* 850 B.C. King Ahaz of Judah, in similar circumstances,

c. 735 B.C., sacrificed his son to Yahweh by burning him alive, and so did one of his successors, Manasseh (ruled 687/6–642 B.C.).

A religious phenomenon that Syria shared, in that millennium, with some other Levantine regions was the prophet. (The Greek word *prophêtês*, which is used as the translation of the Canaanite word *nabi*, means 'proclaimer', not 'foreteller', though the prophet's message might be a presage as well as a directive.) Originally, a *nabi* spoke and acted in a state of ecstasy or frenzy. The earliest example recorded in Syria was witnessed by the Egyptian envoy Wen Amun at Byblos *c.* 1060 B.C. An attendant of the King of Byblos fell into a fit when the king was offering a sacrifice, and, while he was in this abnormal psychological state, he uttered a directive regarding Wen Amun that gave a new turn to Wen Amun's fortunes. Before the end of the eleventh century B.C., the Israelite Saul fell in with a band of ecstatic prophets on the first day of his political career, and he never got rid of the psychic infection that he caught on this occasion. Saul had fits of ecstatic frenzy from time to time throughout the rest of his life.

These Syrian phenomena had counterparts in the Hellenic World. The prophet in the entourage of the King of Byblos is a counterpart of the Pythia who uttered oracles at Delphi and of the sibyls who played similar roles in other Hellenic city-states. The band of prophets, roving and raving with a musical accompaniment, who infected Saul resembles an Hellenic band of bacchants. The common source of the Syrian and Aegean examples of these psychic phenomena may be central Asia Minor. Here, ecstatic congregational 'prophesying' to the accompaniment of music was practised in the pre-Christian Age by the devotees of the goddess Cybele, Attis' mother and wife; in the second century of the Christian Era by the Montanists; and in the Islamic Age by the Mevlevi dervishes, who performed at Konya from the thirteenth century of the Christian Era till A.D. 1925, when they were evicted from Turkey.

Politically, Syria was divided into a large number of small principalities when, in the fifteenth century B.C., it was incorporated in the Egyptian Empire. The first effect of the *Völkerwanderung c.* 1250–950 B.C. was to dissolve Syria's superficial political consolidation under the rule of an alien power. The Egyptian political control in the south and the Hittite control which latterly had replaced the Egyptian control in the north, now broke down; and Syria relapsed into a political disunity that went to further extremes than the fragmentation in the age before the reign of the Egyptian conqueror Thothmes III. The invaders who established themselves in Syria during the *Völkerwanderung* did not found any unitary national states there. The Philistines, for instance, set up five separate sovereign city-states at the southern end of the coastal lowlands; the Israelites who occupied the highlands consisted of tribes that were associated with each other in the worship of their national god Yahweh but were segregated geographically by unconquered enclaves of territory in which the Canaanites preserved their independence. Along the middle section of the coast, the ancient Phoenician city-states survived less precariously. They were sheltered from invaders by the Lebanon Range, which had not yet been denuded of all its forests. In northern Syria the refugee Hittites set up several separate local principalities; the Hittites' political unity did not survive the fall of the Hittite Empire in Asia Minor. Thus the Syrian civilisation started on its career in political disarray. In the eleventh and tenth centuries B.C., after the migrant peoples had begun to settle down, two successive attempts were made to unify Syria politically from the southern end, but both attempts ended in failure.

In the eleventh century B.C. the Philistines conquered the Israelite tribes in their hinterland. The Philistines were well equipped, and their five states acted in unison, but a shortage of man-power made it difficult for them to hold the conquered Israelites down, so they tried to disarm them both morally and materially. The symbol of the Israelites' common worship of Yahweh, and the physical container of the power which the god was believed to display, was a portable chest ('the Ark of the Covenant') which was a relic of the nomadic stage of the Israelites' history. The Philistines captured the Ark and deported it, but its presence appeared to work such havoc in the Philistine cities that the Philistines soon marooned it outside their home territory. The Philistines disarmed the Israelites materially by depriving them of smiths. They allowed them to keep metallic agricultural implements (if they had deprived them of effective means of cultivating their stony soil, they could not have levied from them taxes in the form of agricultural produce); but they compelled the Israelites to have their tools re-sharpened in Philistine smithies, to ensure that there should be no smith in Israel to re-forge tools into weapons. The Israelite tribes retorted by putting themselves under the unitary command of a king, Saul the Benjaminite. For the Israelites this was a controversial political innovation, and it did not bring them immediate liberation. Saul fell in battle. The Philistines were subsequently defeated and expelled from Israelite territory by David, the Judahite leader of a guerrilla band. The Philistines preserved their own independence till 734 B.C., when Philistia was overrun by King Tiglath-Pileser III of Assyria, but they had missed their opportunity of uniting Syria politically under Philistine rule.

The Judahites then temporarily succeeded, under David's leadership, in uniting under their rule the whole of southern Syria, except Philistia, as far northward, in the interior, as the northern end of the Antilebanon Range, to the north of Damascus. David's decisive victory over the

Philistines won him the allegiance of all the Israelite tribes (in accepting Saul as their king, the Israelites had already acquiesced in being politically united under a monarchy). David's victory over the Philistines also won him the friendship of Tyre. (The Phoenicians had no love for their immigrant southern neighbours the Philistines.) David conquered Judah's fellow Hebrews, the Edomites, Moabites, and Ammonites. He also conquered the two Aramaean principalities of Damascus and Zobah, and this won him the friendship of Hamath, the southernmost of the refugee Hittite principalities in northern Syria.

David was able to hand on his empire to his son Solomon. Their two reigns extended from *c.* 1000 B.C. to 922 B.C. But the Judahite empire, like the foregoing Philistine empire, was ephemeral. Judah was too small, too backward culturally, and too awkwardly located geographically to be able to hold what David had seized. Edom and Damascus revolted successfully during Solomon's lifetime, and, after Solomon's death, the non-Judahite Israelites, too, seceded from Judah and set up a separate kingdom of their own. Israel was stronger than Judah, but was not strong enough to prevent Ammon and Moab from recovering their independence. The only remnant of David's and Solomon's empire, outside Judah itself, that their successors on the throne of Judah retained was the southernmost strip of the territory of the tribe of Benjamin, together with the Canaanite city Jerusalem, which David had occupied and had made into his capital.

The important lasting consequence of David's empire-building was the political and cultural amalgamation with Judah and Israel of the Canaanite enclaves in the midst of the Israelite tribal territories that had preserved their political independence till then. Among these enclaves, the most important culturally was Judah's ex-Jebusite capital city of Jerusalem, while the most valuable economically was the plain of Esdraelon, which became the economic heart of the Kingdom of Israel. Those Canaanites who had survived in the interior of Syria may have made common cause with the Israelites against the Philistine invaders, or they may simply have been overwhelmed by the military power that David had built up. In any case, David's annexation of this Canaanite population, and his entente with the independent Phoenician Canaanite city-states, set the seal on the assimilation of the Judahites and Israelites. From the tenth century B.C. onwards, Israel and Judah were fully incorporated in the new post-*Völkerwanderung* society that was now taking a distinctive shape in Syria.

The Philistine and Judahite empires were transitory; the Canaanites' contemporary cultural and economic achievements were durable. While the Philistines and Judahites had been winning and losing their empires, the Phoenicians had been inventing the Alphabet. They had also been developing a hybrid commercial art, mainly Egyptian in its style, for the production of exportable artefacts. Hiram King of Tyre gave Solomon the artistic and technological aid that Solomon needed for building an ambitious temple for Yahweh in Jerusalem. The two kings also went into partnership for starting a maritime trade in the Indian Ocean based on Solomon's port at the head of the Gulf of Aqabah. By this time the Arabian camel had already been domesticated. The date of this historic achievement was later than the irruption into Syria of the Hebrews and Aramaeans, but a raid of camel-riding nomads out of Arabia into Syria is recorded at a date that must have been early in the eleventh century B.C. The domestication of the camel had made the nomads of the Arabian steppe more formidable to their sedentary neighbours than they had ever been before, but the same feat of domestication had also made the steppe itself more easily traversible. One effect of this had been to extend the domain of the Syrian civilization across Arabia to the fertile highlands in the southern corner of the peninsula.

The cultural annexation of the Yemen to Syria was confirmed by Hiram's and Solomon's joint enterprise of opening up a maritime route down the Red Sea into the Indian Ocean. We do not know whether the Queen of Sheba did in truth visit Solomon; but, even if the famous story is not authentic history, the tenth century B.C. is a likely date for the beginning of commercial relations between Syria and the Yemen. Evidently the Red Sea now became a Syrian lake, after having been an Egyptian lake for 2,000 years.

The break-up of Solomon's empire did not prevent the successor-states from trading with each other. The kingdoms of Israel and Damascus were a match for each other, and they were constantly at war over debatable territory in Transjordan. Their wars were inconclusive, but the prize of alternating temporary victories was the establishment of permanent commercial relations. When Damascus gained the upper hand, it compelled Israel to allot a quarter in its capital, Samaria, to Damascus merchants; when Israel subsequently defeated Damascus, it compelled Damascus to allot a quarter to Israelite merchants there. However, the break-up of Solomon's empire made Tyre's access to the head of the Gulf of Aqabah insecure, and this may have been one of the considerations that led the Phoenicians to seek a new outlet for maritime expansion in the western basin of the Mediterranean.

Before the close of the tenth century B.C. both the Israelites and the Judahites were beginning to compose a written literature in the Canaanite language conveyed in the Phoenician alphabet. The Jewish scriptures comprise writings in a number of different genres: myth, liturgy, secular poetry, history, law, proverbial wisdom, and records of the utterances of prophets. The historical accounts of the acts of David and Solomon appear to be based on official records that were almost contemporary with the events. A prophet's utterances may have been put in writing by his disciples, not by the prophet himself, and a book of this genre that won great prestige—for instance, Isaiah's—might be expanded by successive additions from the hands of anonymous later authors using the original prophet's name. The historical parts of the Torah (Pentateuch) and the books of the Prophets are original Israelite and Judahite works of literature; but even the authentic records of the utterances of the Prophets, which are in essence personal and individual, have been found to contain allusions to pre-Israelite literature, now that some of this has come to light.

Some of the myths in the Torah—for instance, the story of the Flood —are of Sumerian origin, transmitted via the Akkadians and the Canaanites. The so-called Mosaic Law is one version of a corpus of Sumero-Akkadian law of which Babylonian, Assyrian, and Hittite versions have now been discovered. The Babylonian version is the code compiled by Hammurabi. The discovery of the fourteenth-century-B.C. Phoenician literary texts in the Ugaritic script has shown that the psalms are in the style of an older Canaanite hymnology, and that chapters viii–ix of the Book of Proverbs are of Canaanite origin. Other proverbs in this book reproduce, almost verbatim, maxims contained in *The Instructions of Amenemope*, an Egyptian work, written probably in the fourteenth century B.C. under the influence of earlier Egyptian literature of the same kind. We may guess that these Egyptian proverbs reached the Israelites via the Phoenicians.

Thus there was literary as well as commercial intercourse between the Syrian states in the post-Solomonic Age, and the content of part of the literature that crossed the political frontiers was religious. This must have made for uniformity in the liturgies with which the local gods were worshipped. Each local community had its own god to whom its citizens felt that they owed a paramount allegiance. But this allegiance was not necessarily exclusive. Each community believed in the power of its neighbours' gods as well as in the power of its own god; and there was a general belief that each local god was more potent than all other gods within the limits of the local god's own domain. When, about half way through the ninth century B.C., King Mesha of Moab was being besieged in his capital city by the joint forces of Israel, Judah, and Edom, the allies decamped when Mesha sacrificed his eldest son on the city wall to the Moabites' god Chemosh. The invaders were not themselves worshippers of Chemosh, but they were trespassing on Chemosh's domain, and they did not believe that their own god could protect them if Chemosh were to be moved, by Mesha's act, to come to Mesha's rescue.

One means by which foreign gods could gain entry into a local god's domain was through royal marriages with foreign princesses. These diplomatic matrimonial alliances made for amicable relations between states. Solomon married a number of foreign wives in the hope of thereby shoring up an empire that was collapsing. Foreign wives had a customary right to bring with them their own gods, attended by a suite of these foreign gods' priests and prophets. Solomon's introduction of his foreign wives' gods brought upon him posthumous disapproval but no contemporary revolt on the part of the worshippers of Judah's and Israel's own Yahweh; but Ahab King of Israel (ruled *c.* 869–850 B.C.) ran into trouble when he introduced into Samaria his Sidonian wife Jezebel's god Baal ('the Lord'), together with Baal's prophets and priests. Though Ahab was following customary international practice, he was strenuously opposed, on Yahweh's behalf, by a Transjordanian Israelite prophet, Elijah. Elijah's chosen successor, Elisha, engineered an insurrection against Ahab's son King Jehoram in the Israelite army stationed in Gilead, on the frontier between Israel and Damascus. Elisha sent one of his disciples to anoint the local commander, Jehu, as king. Jehu, thus legitimized, drove to Jezreel, where Jehoram was recovering from wounds. Jehu massacred Jehoram himself, the Queen Mother Jezebel, all other members of the late King Ahab's family and entourage, some visiting members of the Davidic royal family of Judah, and all Israelite worshippers of the Sidonian Baal.

The 'liquidation' of the family of Ahab by Jehu, instigated by Elisha, is an example of the Syrian prophets' power. These prophets were formidable for kings. Their frenzy was taken as evidence that they were divinely inspired, so a king who defied a prophet risked arousing public opinion against himself. The prophets, on the other hand, were not afraid to take political action. Elisha had already engineered a revolution at Damascus before engineering one in Israel. The earliest recorded Syrian prophet—the one whom Wen Amun encountered at Byblos *c.* 1060 B.C.—intervened in Wen Amun's case. Ahab and Jezebel failed to tame the prophets of Yahweh and Baal by maintaining bands of them at public expense. A Syrian monarch could never ensure that every living prophet was under royal control.

The eleventh-century-B.C. Byblian prophet is the only non-Israelite and non-Judahite Syrian prophet, except for the Sidonians in Jezebel's suite, about whom we have any information, and this is a grievous gap in our knowledge of the Syrian civilization's history. Prophets must have continued to appear, after the eleventh century B.C., in other Syrian communities besides Israel and Judah. Prophets, like merchants, royal brides, and royal brides' gods, were able to cross political frontiers. Elijah operated in Sidonian territory, at Zarephath, though he objected to Sidonian prophets operating in Israel. Elisha had the entrée to Damascus. Amos was a Judahite who operated in Israel.

Ostensibly the issue between Elijah and Ahab was religious. In Israel, was Yahweh not merely to have precedence over foreign gods but to be worshipped exclusively? But the writings of the eighth-century-B.C. prophets indicate that an economic and social issue was being raised in these religious terms. One effect of the increasingly active relationship, on a number of different planes of activity, between the states of the Syrian World had been to produce stresses and strains in the domestic life of Syrian states that were economically and socially 'backward'. In such states—in the Kingdom of Israel, for instance—the local 'establishment' sought to emulate the Phoenician way of life, in which commerce predominated over agriculture and the power of wealth prevailed over customary rights. The result, in a country such as Israel, was an almost revolutionary change in the distribution of wealth to the disadvantage of the poor majority of the population. This comes out clearly in the writings of the prophet Amos, who was in action during the first half of the eighth century B.C.

By Amos' time, the social crisis in the Syrian World had been accentuated by the Phoenicians' second great achievement. In the eleventh century B.C. the Phoenicians had invented the Alphabet; during the temporary abatement of Assyrian aggression between the years 827 and 745 B.C., the Phoenicians opened up trade with Sardinia and North-West Africa and southern Spain, and began to plant colonies on the southern shores of the western basin of the Mediterranean. This economic achievement may have led to social trouble in the Phoenician states themselves. Amos' writings are evidence for the social repercussions in Israel. The social evils that Amos denounced may have already been part of Elijah's case against Ahab and Jezebel. It is perhaps significant that Elijah's home was in Transjordan—a region in which pastoral nomadism had not yet been entirely superseded by agriculture. In the ninth century B.C. a Tishbite might be shocked by Jezreel and Samaria, not to speak of Tyre and Sidon.

The prophets of Israel and Judah whose utterances have been preserved in writing were concerned with religion, with domestic social justice, and with international relations. These three concerns are so many aspects of a single underlying concern. *Tempora mutantur*. Ought we to resign ourselves to the painful fact that *nos mutamur in illis*?

[18]

THE HELLENIC CIVILIZATION,

c. 1050–750 B.C.

DURING the three centuries ending *c.* 750 B.C., the Syrians had invented the Alphabet, had explored and colonized the coasts of the western basin of the Mediterranean, and had produced notable works of literature, including the earliest written record of the utterances of a prophet. If the Hebrews and Aramaeans were illiterate at the time of their settlement in Syria, they quickly adopted the new script of the Canaanite population among whom they had settled, and there is no evidence that the Canaanites ceased to write in Akkadian in the Sumerian script before they started to write in their own language in a new script that they had invented for themselves. By contrast, the Greeks apparently ceased to write in the Linear-B script after the catastrophe *c.* 1200 B.C., and they did not adopt the Alphabet from the Phoenicians till *c.* 750 B.C. Thus the Greeks were perhaps two centuries later in adopting the Alphabet than the Hebrews and the Aramaeans. The Greeks were illiterate for almost 450 years.

In the history of the Aegean basin these 450 years are a dark age in two senses. No native written records were produced, and material culture was at a low ebb compared with its level both in the antecedent Minoan-Mycenaean Age and in the subsequent Hellenic Age. Yet, during those dark intervening centuries, the Greeks were feeling their way towards some of the Hellenic civilization's most remarkable eventual achievements. The development of the Protogeometric and Geometric styles of pottery was the prelude to Hellenic visual art of all genres; the development of oral Greek epic poetry was the prelude to the production of the whole corpus of Hellenic Greek literature and of the Latin literature that this inspired. The development of the city-state form of polity in the Aegean basin during this dark age was not a peculiar achievement of the Greeks. City-states had been created in Sumer 2,000 years earlier, and at least one of the Phoenician city-states, namely Byblos, was almost as old as Nippur and Uruk and Ur. However, the particular form of city-state that was evolved by the Greeks in the Aegean after the downfall of the principalities of the Mycenaean Age eventually became the standard pattern for the whole of the Mediterranean basin and also for regions to the east of the Euphrates.

The decipherment of Mycenaean-Age documents in the Linear-B script has revealed the gulf between the Mycenaean-Age and the Hellenic-Age Greek political regimes. The Mycenaean Greek principalities were miniature replicas of the Empires of Sumer and Akkad and of Pharaonic Egypt. They were administered bureaucratically by a professional literate 'establishment'. But they were neither large enough nor rich enough to carry this exotic administrative superstructure easily, and their top-heaviness was evidently one of the causes of their fall. The city-states that arose from their ruins were better adapted to the regional economic realities. The typical Hellenic city-state was—and continued to be throughout the course of Graeco-Roman history—a small agricultural community whose territory was limited to a radius of about half a day's walk from the market-place and citadel that were its nucleus. On the economic plane this community was almost self-contained. Its indispensable trade beyond its own border was minimal, and its domestic government was simple. Originally, public office was not remunerated, and consequently political power was monopolized by the more well-to-do landowners.

The difference between a Mycenaean principality and an archaic Hellenic city-state is striking, but, on the political plane, there is no evidence of any deliberate break with the past. Mycenaean-Age Greek public administration looks as if it had been a conscious imitation of Babylonian and Hittite and Pharaonic Egyptian administration; Hellenic-Age Greek public administration looks like an unselfconscious adaptation of the regional type of polity to the region's economic circumstances. On the other hand, the adoption of the Protogeometric style of pottery looks as if it had been an intentional new departure. Its adoption of abstract patterns of decoration was a sharp break with the Minoan-Mycenaean tradition, in which the dominant motif had been the depiction of plants and animals. The aniconic Protogeometric style started suddenly, *c.* 1050 B.C., at one place, Athens, and it spread from Athens rapidly, though there were parts of Greece in which a local variety of the Protogeometric and subsequent Geometric style was developed, apparently, independently. At Athens *c.* 1050 B.C. the sudden adoption of the Protogeometric style of pottery was accompanied by an equally sudden substitution of cremation for inhumation as the standard way of disposing of the dead. At the same date, iron replaced bronze as the standard metal for the manufacture of tools and weapons. The simultaneity of these sudden technological and artistic changes is striking. Does this indicate a change of population, or only a change of fashion? So far, the archaeological evidence has yielded no conclusive answer to this hotly debated question.

The creation of the new style—the Protogeometric style—of decorating pottery was made possible by a technological innovation, the use of multiple brushes attached to compasses; and this may not have been an Athenian invention; it may have been learnt by the Athenians from the Cypriots, at a moment when Cyprus and the Aegean basin were in contact again with each other. However, the technological aspect of the Protogeometric revolution in the potter's art is not the most significant one. There was a more important aesthetic revolution. Protogeometric Athenian vase-makers and vase-painters related the decoration of a vase to its shape; in the designing of a pattern, one of their main concerns was harmony; and they produced their artistic effects by giving exquisite expression to simple motifs. These three distinctive features of Protogeometric and Geometric Greek art continued to be characteristic of Hellenic art of all genres in all subsequent stages of Hellenic history except the last. The concern for harmony is illustrated by the artists' attitude towards the introduction of figures of human beings and horses into the decoration of Geometric vases in the last phase of the style. By that time, the influence of Syrian works of art, decorated with figures of men and animals, was challenging the abstract style which, by then, had been the rule in the Aegean basin for three centuries. Evidently the Geometric vase-painters were reluctant to jeopardize the harmony of their design by admitting figures of living beings in any form; and, when at last they did admit them, they 'geometrized' them to harmonize with the patterns in which they were set. The unlifelike presentation of the figures is evidence of the artists' concern for harmony; it is not evidence of incompetence.

In the visual art and in the political institutions of the post-Mycenaean dark age in the Aegean basin, there was a break with the Mycenaean past, and it looks as if the potter and his colleague the vase-painter broke with it deliberately. The dark-age oral poet, too, was conscious of the Mycenaean past; but his concern was, not to break with it, but to preserve it as his poetry's *mise en scène* in so far as he could do this without making the poetry incomprehensible to his audience in a society that was changing, slowly but continually, generation by generation. In each successive generation, the poet's audience demanded both archaism and intelligibility, and the poet had to meet both these two requirements. The world that he conjured up was a fictitious blend of a series of authentic worlds. The poet merged all the successive phases of Mycenaean life in a deceptively unitary picture, and he combined this partly misleading presentation of the Mycenaean past with features of the life of successive generations of the Mycenaeans' dark-age successors. The performance was a *tour de force*; and the performer had to have a gift for producing, out of his heterogeneous matter, a harmonious work of art that his audience would find both convincing and acceptable.

These demands on the poet's artistic and psychological powers were formidable, and his task was aggravated by the exacting technical problem of having to improvise his poetry in an elaborate metre. The poets solved this technical problem by creating and memorizing an immense store of metrical formulae. There was a formula for the name of each of the epic's heroes, coupled with each of a hero's numerous epithets, in each of the five cases of the Greek noun. This technical device enabled a poet to present his dramatis personae in correct hexameter verse in a great variety of situations. The verses were improvised at each performance, but most of the formulae of which the verses were composed were pre-fabricated. No doubt, a new formula was created from time to time in the course of a performance and was then added to the common stock of the fraternity of performers, but the improvisation of formulae must have been much rarer than the improvisation of oral poems composed of memorized pre-existing formulae that the poet strung together.

The gradual evolution of Hellenic Greek oral poetry, visual art, and political institutions in the course of the three centuries ending *c.* 750 B.C. looks insignificant by comparison with what was achieved during those same three centuries by the Hellenes' Syrian contemporaries. The importance of the Greeks' achievements during the post-Mycenaean dark age can be gauged only retrospectively by taking account of the sequel. Midway through the eighth century B.C. the Syrians, just before they were overwhelmed by the onset of the last and direst bout of Assyrian militarism, gave a sudden revolutionary stimulus to the Hellenes by transmitting to them the Phoenician alphabet. This gift was followed by the transmission of Phoenician commercial art—a base metal that the Hellenes and Etruscans transmuted into gold.

[19]

THE INDIAN (HINDU)
CIVILIZATION, *c.* 1000–600 B.C.

IT has been noted that, pending the decipherment of the Indus civilization's script, our knowledge of this civilization is derived solely from dumb artefacts, and that the dating of it depends on finds of Indus civilization artefacts in Iraq, in datable strata of the débris of the Sumero-Akkadian civilization. The latest date at which the Indus civilization is thus proved to have been still in existence may be *c.* 1500 B.C., but this terminal date is uncertain, and we have no means of ascertaining the initial date of the Indian (alias Hindu) civilization by which the Indus civilization was followed. The political history of India before the latter part of the sixth century B.C. is unrecorded, and the record of it during the lifetime of Siddhartha Gautama the Buddha (perhaps *c.* 567–487 B.C.) is incidental to the record—partly obscured by legend—of the Buddha's life. The period, perhaps a thousand years long, between the fall of the Indus civilization and the Buddha's enlightenment is only sparsely illustrated even by dumb artefacts. The archaeological evidence for this millennium of secular Indian history is virtually confined to a meagre sequence of potsherds.

By contrast, the evidence for the pre-Buddhaic period of the history of the Indian civilization is abundant and instructive in the field of religion; and religion is the most important of all human experiences and activities. The scriptures of Hinduism cannot be dated. They were composed and transmitted orally for an unascertainable length of time before they were committed to writing, but the oral transmission of them is likely to have been accurate, since the efficacy of a liturgy was believed to depend on its words being recited correctly. Moreover, we can discern the order in which the different genres of Hindu religious literature succeeded each other, though we cannot ascertain how long the development took, and therefore cannot guess the date at which the earliest of these genres was created.

The earliest genre is the Vedas: a collection of hymns and charms that were recited in liturgies which consisted of ritual acts and gestures as well as verbal formulae. The next genre is a collection of treatises on liturgical practice: the Brahmanas. These two earliest genres of Hindu literature are not distinctive; there are parallels to them in the religious literature, oral or written, of other archaic societies.

At this stage, the Hindus were mainly concerned to persuade or constrain the gods to fulfil their worshippers' wishes. The Hindu gods, like the Hittite and Greek and Scandinavian gods, were marshalled in a pantheon, and the pantheons of these Indo-European-speaking peoples were perhaps ultimately derived from a Sumerian model. The worship, according to correct ritual, of a team of gods has, for many peoples, been the end, as well as the beginning, of their religious history. But in the Aranyakas and Upanishads the Hindus went on to probe the mystery of the Universe in which a human being awakes to consciousness. They asked themselves what is the nature of the ultimate reality, what is the nature of a human soul, and what is the relation between the soul and the ultimate reality. They concluded that the soul (atman) is identical with the ultimate reality (brahman) in and behind the Universe, and that an intuition of this identity can be attained by introspection. This intuition is expressed in the three Sanskrit words *Tat tvam asi*: 'that is what thou art' or 'thou art that'—'thou' being a human soul, and 'that' being the ultimate reality.

This second phase of Hindu religion is a surprising sequel to the first phase. In the first phase the Hindus were concerned with the external side of religion; in the second phase they turned from ritual to meditation, and, in their exploration of the psychic dimension of the Universe, they went far.

We can follow the evolution of Hindu religion through its successive stages in the deposit of scriptures that each stage bequeathed to posterity. The evolution of the structure of Hindu society has to be inferred from non-contemporary evidence. The characteristic Hindu social institution is caste; and *varna*, the Sanskrit word that has been translated as 'caste' in modern Western languages, means 'colour'. This shows that caste originated in an attempt, on the primary-Sanskrit-speaking invaders' part, to keep themselves segregated racially from the conquered native population, who must have differed from the invaders in the colour of their skin, as well as in their manners and customs. The invaders' regime of apartheid was rigid, and we may guess that the reason for this was that the invaders were out-numbered by the 'natives' and were also outclassed by them in point of civilization. The 'natives' were heirs of the Indus civilization; the invading Aryas were barbarians.

This attempt to maintain a rigorous segregation of the conquerors from the conquered had an effect on the internal class-structure of the dominant Aryan community itself. The Aryas, like many other peoples in many different parts of the World, were divided into three classes: warriors, priests, and commoners. These classes were hereditary among the Aryas, as among other peoples, but, after the Aryas had established themselves as the ruling caste in India, their own internal class-divisions became as ultra-rigid as the division between Aryas and 'natives'. Gradually, too, the priests (brahmins) wrested from the warriors (kshatriyas) the status of being the highest class—a *tour de force*, considering that wealth and political power remained in the warrior class's hands. Thus the class-division within the dominant Aryan community became as hard-set as the caste-division between the dominant community and the 'natives'; and the result was a division of Hindu society into four castes, not just two, with the priests, not the warriors, at the summit. Each of the four castes eventually split into numerous sub-castes as Hindu society enlarged itself, partly by further conquests and partly by the assimilation of 'natives' through their incorporation into one or other of the four basic castes.

Since the Aryas had originally descended upon India from the Eurasian steppe, their first foothold in India must have been in the Indus basin, and the geographical evidence of the Vedas, such as it is, seems to indicate that this was the Aryas' habitat at the time the Vedas were being composed. By the Buddha's time, the geographical heart of the Hindu World had come to be the middle section of the Jumna–Ganges basin. By the second century of the Christian Era, the Hindu World had expanded southwards in the Indian peninsula and south-eastwards into what are now South Vietnam and Indonesia. The dates of this progressive expansion of the Hindu civilization are not recorded, but one thing is manifest: the farther this expansion went, the greater was the part played by assimilation, as opposed to conquest and colonization. The Aryas' Sanskrit language and its derivatives have never spread even over the whole of the Indian subcontinent. The Hindu civilization, with its specific institutions, such as caste and the use of Sanskrit as a sacred language, has spread far more widely. When the Buddha ignored caste and challenged the belief in a soul that is identical with the ultimate reality, the Hindu civilization gave birth to a missionary religion that has captivated the whole of Eastern Asia.

[20]

THE CHINESE CIVILIZATION,
1027–506 B.C.

DURING the first quarter of a millennium of the time-span of the Chou
dynasty, the Chinese World was probably more stable than it had been
in the preceding Shang Age, and it was certainly more stable than
during the five centuries that ended, in 221 B.C., in the effective political
unification of China by Ch'in Shih Hwang-ti. During the Chou
dynasty's first quarter of a millennium, its loose control over its seventy
or ninety vassals was probably effective as far as it went. About two-
thirds of the vassals were the Chou's kinsmen, and all branches of the
family probably felt a need to stand together in order to maintain their
ascendancy over the Shang and the other non-Chou communities whom
the Chou had conquered. These motives for loyalty to the Chou must
anyhow have grown weaker with the passage of time, and, after the
Chou's disaster in 771 B.C., their vassals quickly got out of hand.

By that date, the number of vassals had increased to about 300
through the practice of sub-infeudation. The effect of the Chou's loss of
power and prestige was to enable their now only nominal vassals to
behave as sovereigns *de facto* to the extent of going to war with each
other. These inter-state wars started before the close of the eighth
century B.C. and they continued throughout the next five hundred years.
The prevalence of warfare during this span of Chinese history distinguishes it from the relatively peaceful spans that immediately preceded
and immediately followed it, but the first half of the intervening period
of five centuries also differed markedly from the second half.

During the two centuries ending in 506 B.C. the wars were incessant
and, as a result of annexations of vanquished states by victors, the
number of local states in the Chinese World was reduced from about 300
to less than twenty, including the remnant of territory round Loyang
that remained under the direct rule of the still formally suzerain Chou
dynasty. Yet, for all except a small minority of the population, life

during this first bout of inter-state warfare continued to be stable. At this stage the warriors were aristocrats fighting from chariots; the chances and changes to which their calling exposed them were mitigated by the chivalry with which their wars were conducted; the peasantry, who were the only other social class besides the nobles, were not yet being conscripted for military service; and, while they had little opportunity of rising to the social level at which life was precarious, they were fairly secure in their tenure of the land from which they made a living for themselves as well as for their martial lords. The structure of Chinese society was based, down to this date, on traditional status. The only competition, so far, was the military competition among the nobles. There was not yet any economic competition. In particular, land had not yet become a marketable commodity.

In the course of the fifth and fourth centuries B.C., Chinese society became fluid and Chinese life became insecure, not only for the nobles, but for the whole people. Confucius (*c.* 551–479 B.C.) lived to see the beginning of this change. His philosophy, and the teaching in which he communicated it to a fraternity of disciples, were the earliest of the spiritual reactions that the social transformation of China evoked.

The most important difference between Shang China and the China of Confucius' generation was geographical. In the Shang Age the area of the Chinese World had been confined to the lower basin of the Yellow River in the North China plain, together with the basin of its right-bank tributary the Wei River in 'the Land beyond the Passes'. By 500 B.C. the Chinese World had expanded both southwards and northwards. On the south it had come to include the basins of the Hwai and Han Rivers, and the lowlands in the lower part of the basin of the Yangtse. The native peoples of this southern annex had not been original members of the Chinese society, but they were akin to the Chinese racially, their mother-tongues were closely related to the Chinese language, and they had been adopting the Chinese way of life as a result of their increasing implication in the Chinese World's power-politics. The simultaneous expansion of the Chinese World northwards and north-westwards had brought the Chinese into direct contact with the Eurasian pastoral nomads, and here the Chinese were confronted by unassimilable aliens. The nomads not only spoke non-Chinese languages; they had a non-Chinese way of life, and, by the time the Chinese peasants and the Eurasian nomads collided with each other, the two societies' incompatible ways of life had already become hard set.

THE MESO-AMERICAN AND ANDEAN CIVILIZATIONS,

c. 800–400 B.C.

THE history of the Olmec civilization of Meso-America at San Lorenzo, its oldest known site, has been touched upon in Chapter 15. When this civilization was extirpated by violence at San Lorenzo, it survived at two sites nearer to the shore of the Gulf of Mexico: at La Venta, an island in a marsh, and at Tres Zapotes, a clearing in a tropical rain-forest. At both these sites the monumental architecture and art of San Lorenzo reappears.

La Venta, like San Lorenzo before it, was destroyed by violence. Evidently the Olmecs were aggressive conquerors who provoked savage eventual counter-strokes. At La Venta and Tres Zapotes, unlike San Lorenzo, the ceremonial centre was not associated with a permanently inhabited urban settlement; but at Tres Zapotes, which outlived La Venta, the earliest known specimen of Meso-American writing has been found. It is a glyph of the kind that was carved, at later dates, by the Mayas in Guatemala and Yucatán. Some of these glyphs, including the one found at Tres Zapotes, were date-records, and the numerical values of these have been deciphered, but it is not certain that all Meso-American glyphs are calendrical. Some of them may have conveyed, not numerals, but ideograms or phonemes that still await decipherment.

The earliest known Andean civilization was approximately contemporary with the La Venta and Tres Zapotes phase of the Olmec civilization. This Andean civilization arose out of the Formative phase of nuclear American culture at Chavín, towards the north-western end of the central highlands of the Andean World. The Chavín civilization's outward visible signs are a monumental architecture and sculpture which, like their Olmec counterparts, are evidently the material manifestations of a religion. The distinctive symbolic motif of the Chavín civilization, like that of the Olmec civilization, is a monster that is a cross between a jaguar (or, in Peru, perhaps a puma) and a human being. The two civilizations have in common this feline artistic motif, and both emerged, apparently independently of each other, out of the Formative phase of culture in nuclear America which is common to Peru, Meso-America, and the intervening Central American and South American regions. However, these intervening regions produced no local civilizations of their own, and the Chavín and Olmec civilizations were not only geographically insulated from each other; their styles are different from each other, and so are their achievements.

The Olmecs invented a script which certainly conveyed dates, and perhaps also ideas and words as well, whereas there are no undisputed indications that even the rudiments of a script were invented anywhere at any date in the pre-Pizarran Andean World. On the other hand, in the Chavín Age, the Andean peoples had already mastered the use of at least one metal, gold, whereas the Meso-American peoples do not seem ever to have invented metallurgy independently. They learnt this art from the Andean World at a late stage of Meso-American history.

The Chavín and Olmec civilizations never made contact with each other, so far as we know, but each of them spread from its local home-land into other parts of its own 'world', though neither of them became world-wide, even within its own 'world's' limits. The Olmec civilization spread westwards on to the Mexican plateau and southwards into the Pacific coastal plain and the highlands of what is now Guatemala. The Chavín civilization spread south-westwards from the Andean highlands to the adjoining Pacific coastal plain, and from there south-eastwards from one Pacific coastal river-valley to another. The spread of the Olmec civilization was at least partly achieved by military conquest. The contemporary spread of the Chavín civilization appears to have been peaceful.

The dissemination of each of these civilizations, even within these limits, was a notable achievement—as, indeed, had been the earlier and wider dissemination of the nuclear American Formative culture. One cause of the rise of civilizations in the Meso-American and Andean regions of nuclear America was the co-existence, in nuclear America as a whole and in these two regions in particular, of landscapes, juxtaposed to each other, which differ from each other dramatically in configuration, altitude, and climate.

The climate of Meso-America is tropical in both the Atlantic and the Pacific coastal lowlands, whereas it is temperate in the highlands. On the Atlantic side, round the shore of the Gulf of Mexico and in the low-lands farther inland, the thirsty Yucatán Peninsula is adjoined by tropical rain-forests in northern Guatemala to the south and in the present-day Mexican states of Tabasco and Vera Cruz to the west and north-west, and this coastal strip of tropical rain-forest is adjoined, to the north, by a strip of desert that insulates it from the coastal green-belt in Texas. The Meso-American desert extends from coast to coast across the intervening highlands, except for a narrow belt of cultivable land under the westernmost mountain-range's eastern lee. The highland section of this desert adjoins the cultivable highlands that extend south-wards from southern Mexico into Central America.

In the Andean region the contrasts are still more extreme. The plateau, and the mountains that tower above it, are higher. The high-land basins are physically insulated from each other more sharply than their counterparts in Meso-America. The Peruvian coastal plain is made temperate, but also virtually rainless, by the cool Humboldt current, which flows northward, parallel to the shore. Consequently the coastal plain is a sand-desert interrupted at intervals by ribbons of vegetation along the courses of rivers—most of them short and with a limited volume of flow—that descend from the Andes to the coast. These river valleys can be cultivated intensively by irrigation. On the other hand, the uncultivable desert sections of the Pacific coast can provide a liveli-hood for shell-fish gatherers and for fishermen.

These diverse physical environments in close proximity to each other gave openings to human communities for finding different ways of turning non-human Nature to human account, and these different economies gave rise to different ways of life. This led to commercial and cultural relations between communities that were differentiated from each other without being out of reach of each other, and these relations were culturally stimulating. They were, however, also physically difficult, and consequently the history of pre-Columbian civilization in both Meso-America and the Andean World has been an alternation of periods in which the inhabitants of each of the region's natural divisions have lived in relative isolation with periods in which a civilization that has originated in one district has spread to others. The Olmec and Chavín civilizations are the earliest known examples of a cultural spread. In the Andean World the recurrent spreads extended farther than the corresponding spreads in Meso-America. This is remarkable, consider-ing that the physical obstacles to cultural uniformity and to political unification are more formidable in the Andean World.

[22]

THE FINAL BOUT OF ASSYRIAN
MILITARISM, 745–605 B.C., AND THE
CONTEMPORARY ERUPTION
FROM THE STEPPES

ASSYRIA had re-emerged, in the fourteenth century B.C., from her subjection to Mitanni as a militaristic power. For the next four centuries,
her militarism discharged itself in raids that neither aimed at, nor
achieved, permanent conquests, and, at least during the later stages of
the *Völkerwanderung c.* 1250–950 B.C., she was under pressure, on her
western flank, from Aramaean settlers in the former domain of Mitanni
in Mesopotamia. Assyria's wars for expansion did not begin till *c.* 932
B.C., and the Aramaean occupants of Mesopotamia were her first
victims. As has already been noted, Assyria conquered and incorporated
the Mesopotamian Aramaeans in the years 932–859 B.C., and then, in
Shalmaneser III's reign, she won a footing on the west bank of the
westward elbow of the Euphrates and set out to conquer and incorporate
Syria. This second stage of Assyrian empire-building ended in failure.
By 745 B.C., Assyria's western conquests were once again confined to
Mesopotamia. Northern Syria, which was one of the principal 'roundabouts' in the Old World's network of communications, was under the
control of Assyria's emulator, the Hurrian empire of Urartu.

The Assyrians' method of empire-building was more brutal and more
devastating than the Egyptians' method had been. Thothmes III and
his successors had been content to impose their suzerainty on the states
that they had conquered. They had left these states in existence under
Egyptian control. The Assyrians deported the élite of the population of
conquered states to some remote corner of the Assyrian dominions. The
deportees included the skilled artisans as well as the social and political
'establishment'. The illiterate peasantry was left *in situ*, but deportees
from elsewhere were quartered on them, and the former territories and
frontiers of the conquered states were obliterated. The annexed area was
re-mapped into a new mosaic of artificially delimited departments
(*pakhate*) administered direct by Assyrian officials. This combination of

drastic measures was designed to disintegrate the conquered communities and to eradicate their ex-citizens' memory of the days of their independence. This Assyrian policy was largely successful. For instance, Damascus, annexed in 732, and Israel, annexed in 722 B.C., were never resuscitated, although, before succumbing to Assyria, the peoples of each of these two Syrian states had had a lively national consciousness—as they had shown by the vigour with which they had waged war against each other.

However, the Assyrians themselves, as well as their alien subjects, became victims of Assyrian empire-building activities. The Assyrians' original homeland was depopulated by the drain of war casualties and of drafts on its man-power for planting Assyrian colonies and garrisons in the conquered countries (a form of deportation in reverse). The gap in Assyria's home territory was filled by the importation of alien deportees, till the population of nuclear Assyria became semi-Aramaean. Moreover, the social strain imposed on the Assyrian people by its perpetual mobilization for increasingly distant campaigns provoked domestic political disorders.

Shalmaneser III died in 824 B.C. during a rebellion that lasted from 827 to 822 B.C. In this upheaval the Assyrian cities Asshur, Nineveh, and Arbela rebelled, together with some of the provinces. In 746 B.C. the capital city at that date, Kalkhu (Calah), revolted, King Asshurnirari V was killed, and the throne was occupied in 745 by a man of unknown origin who assumed the name of Tiglath-Pileser III. Shalmaneser V, Tiglath-Pileser III's immediate successor, was succeeded in 722 by a king of a different family who bore, or assumed, the famous name Sargon —borne by the founder of the dynasty of Agade more than sixteen centuries earlier. There is no record of a violent revolution on this occasion; but it was recorded in Judah that Sennacherib (Sargon's son) was murdered by two of his sons, and it cost another of his sons, Esarhaddon, a civil war to secure the succession for himself. Two of Sargon's great-grandsons, Asshurbanipal and his brother Shamash-shum-ukin, who had been installed as King of Babylon, fought a fratricidal war (654–652 B.C.) in which Shamash-shum-ukin, a prince of Assyrian royal blood, headed a coalition of insurgent subject peoples. After Asshurbanipal's death in 626, the throne of Assyria repeatedly changed hands by violence until 605 B.C., when the last remnant of Assyria was wiped out.

In the final bout of Assyrian militarism, Tiglath-Pileser III and his successors, down to Asshurbanipal inclusive, tried to conquer and to incorporate in their empire as much of the Oikoumenê as came within their ken. They were foiled by the resistance of Urartu in the north and of the Chaldaean and Aramaean tribes in Babylonia. They could and did repeatedly defeat these antagonists, but they failed to put them permanently out of action. Meanwhile the struggle between Assyria and her regional adversaries was complicated by the simultaneous eruption of the Arabs from their peninsula and of two pastoral nomadic (probably Iranian-speaking) peoples, the Cimmerians and the Skyths, from the Eurasian steppe.

Tiglath-Pileser III's first move for re-habilitating and re-extending the Assyrian empire was to attack Urartu. He invaded Urartu's eastern dependencies in 744 B.C. and her western dependencies in 743, and in the second of these campaigns he signally defeated King Sarduris II. In 742–740 B.C. Tiglath-Pileser III subdued Arpad (near Aleppo), the strongest state in northern Syria, and its fall led to the temporary recognition of Assyria's suzerainty by a number of other states in Syria and in eastern Cilicia. In 735 Tiglath-Pileser III reached and besieged Tušpa, the capital of Urartu, but he failed to take it and was unable to occupy permanently any of Urartu's home territory. The Assyrian re-conquest of northern Syria was followed up—perhaps in Shalmaneser V's reign (727–722 B.C.)—by the imposition of Assyrian suzerainty on a tier of principalities in eastern Asia Minor, to the north of the Taurus Range and to the west of the upper Euphrates. This effectively insulated Urartu from Cilicia and Syria, but the strain of maintaining Assyrian control over such distant dependencies was severe. Moreover, it involved Assyria in hostilities with the Phrygians (Muski) to the west of her new north-west frontier, and led to a rapprochement between these new enemies of hers and Urartu.

In the opposite quarter, in 714 B.C., Sargon marched, unopposed, north-eastward over the Zagros Range and then round the east shore of Lake Urmiyah and the north shore of Lake Van. From this long circular march he returned home safely via the upper Tigris basin, but, like Tiglath-Pileser III, he failed to win any permanent foothold in Urartu, and he gave a wide berth to Tušpa. The Kingdom of Urartu was still in being in 605 B.C., when the extinction of Assyria was consummated at the Battle of Carchemish between the Babylonians and the Egyptians.

In 734 B.C. Tiglath-Pileser III sealed Syria off from Egypt by invading Philistia and taking Gaza. By 675 B.C. the only still independent states in Syria were two Phoenician islands, Arvad (Aradus) and Tyre, and three continental principalities: Byblos, Ascalon, and Judah. The Assyrians laid siege to Tyre in 673 B.C.; in 675 B.C. Esarhaddon had invaded Egypt (an enterprise that Sennacherib had had in mind in 700 B.C., when he had invaded, but had not annexed, Judah).

The Assyrians found it easy to defeat their Napatan (Kushite) competitors for the possession of Egypt. The Napatans had invaded Egypt in 730 B.C. and since *c.* 711 B.C. they had assumed the Double Crown. In 661 B.C. they gave up the struggle. Their regime had been unpopular in Egypt, and, when the Assyrians reinforced the resistance movement of the local princes in the Delta, the Napatans were not a match for this coalition. In 663 B.C. the Assyrians, chasing the Napatans southwards, sacked Thebes, but in the same year Asshurbanipal invested one of the Deltaic Egyptian princes, Psammetichus (Psamtek) I with the government of all of Egypt that was under Assyrian suzerainty. From the year 661/660 B.C. onwards, Psammetichus assumed the title of Pharaoh; by 655 B.C. he had established his authority over Thebes; between 658 and 651 B.C. he pushed the Assyrian garrisons out of Egypt, and Asshurbanipal tacitly acquiesced. Egypt was still more remote from Nineveh than it was from Napata. Experience had now convinced the Assyrians, as well as the Kushites, that a permanent occupation of Egypt with their own forces was too difficult a logistical problem for them to solve. The ultimate gainers from this collision in Egypt between two distant foreign powers were therefore the Egyptians themselves. For a century and a quarter, ending in 525 B.C., Egypt was once again politically independent.

The military occupation of Egypt had been, for Assyria, an unnecessary expenditure of her strength, and her subsequent evacuation of Egypt neither threatened her security nor damaged her prestige in South-West Asia. Here the acid test of Assyrian statesmanship was Assyria's relation with Babylonia.

Since the temporary conquest of Assyria by the Amorite Babylonian empire-builder Hammurabi, rather more than a thousand years before Tiglath-Pileser III's time, there had been a reversal of the relative strengths of the two principal powers in the Sumero-Akkadian World. From the fourteenth century B.C. onwards, Assyria had had the upper hand over Babylonia, but in the course of the *Völkerwanderung c.* 1250–950 B.C. the situation in Babylonia had been complicated by the lodgment there of the Chaldaean tribes in the south-west and of some Aramaean tribes in the north-east. These intruders on Babylonia's fringes had neither been expelled, as the Gutaeans had been, nor assimilated, as the Kassites had been. They had remained aliens, animated by a tribal *esprit de corps* and a martial spirit of their own.

The presence of these ex-pastoral nomads from Arabia was unwelcome to the old-established sedentary agricultural and urban population of Babylonia, and this might have been expected to facilitate a rapprochement between Babylonia and Assyria—a sedentary community that shared with Babylonia a civilization derived from a common Sumero-Akkadian source. Assyria was Babylonia's natural protector. She was the warden of the Sumero-Akkadian World's marches

against the highlanders in the Zagros mountains. However, if there was
to be an entente between Babylonia and Assyria, two conditions had to
be fulfilled: the Assyrians must be tactful towards the Babylonians, and
the tribesmen in Babylonia must not be allowed to get out of hand. If
the tribesmen were to gain control over the Babylonian cities—over
Babylon itself, above all—the Assyrians would find themselves in a
dilemma. They would have either to acquiesce in losing their own
control over Babylonia or to re-establish their control by force at the
risk of damaging Babylon materially and wounding Babylonian *amour
propre,* and then the Babylonians might be provoked into making common cause with the unruly tribesmen against the Assyrians' high-
handed re-imposition of law and order.

In 745 B.C., Tiglath-Pileser III spent the first campaigning season of
his reign on chastising the tribesmen in Babylonia with the blessing of
the Babylonian 'establishment'. But in 734 B.C. the Babylonian 'establishment' lost control, and then the chief of the Chaldaean tribe Bit-
Amukkani seized the throne. In 731 B.C.—the year after the fall of
Damascus—Tiglath-Pileser III harried the tribesmen in Babylonia, but
the political vacuum at Babylon remained unfilled. Tiglath-Pileser III
filled it himself by 'taking the hands of Bel'—i.e. assuming the sovereignty
over Babylon—in 729 and again in 728 B.C. But in 721 B.C.—the year
after the fall of Samaria—the chief of the Chaldaean tribe Bit-Yakin,
Merodach-Baladan (Marduk-apaliddinna) followed Tiglath-Pileser
III's example after having secured the support of the Aramaean tribes in
Babylonia and the Elamites. In 720 B.C. Sargon failed to overcome this
coalition, and Merodach-Baladan reigned at Babylon for twelve years.
Sargon evicted him at last in 710 B.C., and took the hands of Bel in his
turn in 709; but Sargon left Merodach-Baladan in possession of his
Chaldaean tribal territory.

So far, the Babylonians had been anti-Chaldaean and pro-Assyrian,
and so they still were when—once more with the Elamites' support—
Merodach-Baladan occupied Babylon again in 703 B.C. In the same year
the Assyrians once again evicted Merodach-Baladan. The Assyrians
could defeat the tribesmen, but they were unable to subdue them. In
694 B.C. Sennacherib brought Phoenician ships and crews overland to
Babylonian waters, but, with Elamite backing, Bit-Yakin survived two
campaigns on land and sea, and Babylon was now taken over by a pro-
Chaldaean Babylonian ruler. Sennacherib re-took Babylon in 689 B.C.
and sacked it, and this tactless brutality confirmed the Babylonians'
change of sides. It has been noted already that even an Assyrian king of
Babylon, Shamash-shum-ukin, waged war against his brother Asshurbanipal, King of Assyria, in 652–648 B.C. at the head of a coalition which included not only the Chaldaeans and the Babylonian

Aramaeans but the Elamites, Arabs, Egyptians, and some Syrian principalities. An apparently crushing defeat that Asshurbanipal had inflicted on Elam in 655 B.C. had not been conclusive after all. Asshurbanipal did destroy the Kingdom of Elam—though not the Elamite nation—between 646 and 639 B.C., but the gainers from Elam's fall were not the Assyrians; they were the Iranian peoples in Elam's hinterland.

Immediately after Asshurbanipal's death in 626 B.C., Babylon was occupied by a Chaldaean, Nabopolassar. An anti-Assyrian movement in Babylonia could not now look to Elam for support. Elam was prostrate; but Nabopolassar found a more potent—and more formidable—eastern ally in Media. The Assyrian menace had produced in Iran in the seventh century B.C. the same consolidating political effect that it had produced in Urartu in the ninth century B.C. The Median tribes had now established a united kingdom. Perhaps the spectacle of Elam's overthrow had prompted them to take this step. When Nabopolassar, who had taken the initiative in assaulting Assyria, was repulsed from an attack on the city of Asshur in 615 B.C., the King of Media, Cyaxares, intervened on the Babylonian side. Cyaxares took and destroyed Asshur in 614 B.C. The Medes and Babylonians, reinforced by the Skyths, took and destroyed Nineveh in 612 B.C. Thus the earliest and the latest capital of Assyria were both blotted out. The Assyrians then made a last stand at Harran—an ancient outpost of Sumero-Akkadian culture in Mesopotamia. Pharaoh Necho II, the son of Asshurbanipal's former protégé and supplanter in Egypt Psammetichus I, came to the Assyrians' rescue; but when, in 605 B.C., Nabopolassar's son Nebuchadnezzar defeated Necho II decisively at Carchemish, Assyria expired.

The true legatees of the Assyrian Empire were not the fallen empire's successor-states; they were the Aramaean version of the Phoenician alphabet and the Aramaean language, for which this alphabet was the vehicle. To write in the Aramaean alphabet and language on papyrus was easier and more expeditious than to inscribe a clay tablet in Akkadian in the Akkadian version of the Sumerian script. A bas-relief from Sennacherib's palace at Nineveh portrays two Assyrian clerks standing side by side. One is inscribing in Akkadian on a tablet with a stylus; the other is writing in Aramaic on a roll of papyrus with a pen. Penmanship was 'the wave of the future'.

Already before the close of the eighth century B.C., pastoral nomads from both Arabia and the Eurasian steppe were taking a hand in the contests between Assyria and her neighbours. In 732 B.C., the year in which the Assyrians took Damascus, they also fought the Arabs. In 710 B.C. the Assyrians took the offensive in Arabia, and, according to the Assyrian account, they penetrated the peninsula so deeply that the Sabaeans, in its south-western corner, sent them tribute. In 703 B.C.

there were Arabs in Merodach-Baladan's anti-Assyrian coalition. There was another Assyrian campaign in Arabia in 676 B.C. The Eurasian nomads make their first appearance in the Assyrian records in 707 B.C. when the Cimmerians are reported to have defeated King Argištis II of Urartu.

In their eruption out of the Eurasian steppe the nomads poured westward in two waves and also in two separate streams. The Cimmerians were chased by the Skyths, and both Cimmerians and Skyths migrated westwards, both north and south of the Caspian and the Black Sea. On the south the Cimmerians reached the west coast of Asia Minor; on the north the Odrysai (Athyrsoi) reached the Hungarian Alföld and the basin of the River Maríca in Thrace. The Cimmerians seem to have been no more successful than the Assyrians in making a permanent lodgment in Urartu; but they impressed their name on eastern Asia Minor—and on western Asia Minor, too, if the Sapardoi, who subsequently gave their name (Sparda) to the Persian satrapy there, were the Cimmerians' associates. The Skyths, being enemies of the Cimmerians, became Assyria's allies, and this alliance perhaps partly accounts both for the Assyrian Empire's survival into the seventh century B.C. and for its fall in the years 612–605 B.C. In 612 B.C. the Skyths joined forces with the Medes and Babylonians in the successful assault on Nineveh in that year.

In the *Völkerwanderung* during the eighth and seventh centuries B.C., the nomads from Arabia were camel-riders, as they had been already in the eleventh century B.C., in one of the final outbreaks of the *Völkerwanderung c.* 1250–950 B.C. In the previous *Völkerwanderung* in the eighteenth century B.C. the Eurasian nomad migrants had been, not riders, but charioteers; for their domesticated animals that could be used for transport had been, not camels, but horses, and, at that stage in the breeding of the horse, this animal had not been large enough or strong enough to bear the weight of a human rider. In the course of the next thousand years after the eighteenth century B.C., riding-horses had been bred. The Assyrian army included cavalry as well as chariotry during the final bout of Assyrian militarism (745–605 B.C.), and the Cimmerians and Skyths, too, were horse-riders. We do not know the date of the domestication of the Central Asian ('Bactrian') two-humped camel. Only the Arabian camel is portrayed on Assyrian monuments, and the earliest evidence that the Central Asian camel had been domesticated is the name of the north-eastern Iranian prophet Zarathustra, if his name means 'with Golden Camels'.

The evidence for the invasion of South-West Asia by the Eurasian nomads in the eighth and seventh centuries B.C. is contemporary, and it comes from Judahite and Greek, as well as Assyrian, sources. The evidence for the Eurasian nomads' migration in other directions is post-humous. Their presence to the north of the Caspian and the Black Sea is attested by Herodotus, who wrote in the fifth century B.C.; their presence in the Indus basin is attested by the descriptions and the names of some of the peoples whom Alexander the Great encountered there in the years 327–325 B.C. Did the Eurasian nomads invade China, too, in the eighth century B.C.?

It has already been noted that, in China, the Chou dynasty suffered a disaster in 771 B.C. In that year they were attacked by barbarians and were defeated so severely that they were constrained to move their capital eastwards from the basin of the Yellow River's tributary, the Wei, to Loyang on the eastern plain. The Wei basin is China's north-western march against barbarians beyond the pale. So long as the Chou were defending this march, they were performing a valuable service for the whole of the Chinese World. When they ceased to be marchmen, their prestige and power inevitably declined. They were followed in the Wei basin by the Ch'in, and, once again, the performance of the march-man's service was rewarded eventually with the gaining of a dominion over the Chinese World as a whole. However, we have no evidence that the barbarians who evicted the Chou from the Wei basin in 771 B.C. were Eurasian pastoral nomads. They may have been local sedentary barbarians. The earliest evidence of direct contact between China and the Eurasian nomads seems to be the record that, in the fourth century B.C., Yen, the north-easternmost of the local Chinese states in that age, imitated the nomads by creating a cavalry force equipped in the nomad style. We have no evidence that the barbarians who defeated the Chou in 771 B.C. were a wing of the nomad cavalry that invaded South-West Asia and south-eastern Europe before the eighth century was over.

The extant accounts of the eighth-century-B.C. and seventh-century-B.C. nomad invaders of South-West Asia present them as being merely savage and destructive, and this is not surprising, considering that these records have been made by the nomads' sedentary victims. However, it is possible that, on this occasion, the nomads may have imparted to some of the sedentary peoples on whom they impinged a distinctive set of beliefs and practices.

In both the Greek World and the Indian World in the sixth century B.C. there were people who believed that death was not the end of a living being's existence. Its soul, so they held, survived to be reincarnated in another living being which might be of the same or of a lower or higher species. Whether the next reincarnation would be a promotion or a demotion would depend on the character of this soul's moral perform-ance in previous incarnations. The number of re-births might be end-less, and this was a prospect that was felt to be far more formidable than any of the successive intervening deaths. For a believer in reincarnation, the objective, so far from being immortality, was to bring the series of rebirths to an end, and he believed that this could be done by living austerely as well as virtuously.

The resemblance between the Indian and the Greek form of the belief in reincarnation and its corollaries is so close that it can hardly have been fortuitous. It seems much more likely to be due to an historical connexion. The belief might have been transmitted from India to Greece or from Greece to India, or it might have been derived in both Greece and India from a source outside both regions. A possible medium of direct transmission in either direction was the Persian Empire, which was put together in the sixth century B.C. and which included both the western fringe of India and the eastern fringe of the Greek World. The establishment of the Persian Empire was accompanied by an improvement in the means of communication within the vast area that this empire covered. However, the belief in reincarnation was not shared with the Indians and the Greeks by the Iranian makers and masters of the Persian Empire whose homeland in the last millennium B.C. lay between the Greek and Indian worlds. We have therefore to consider an alternative possibility. The belief in transmigration may have been derived by both the Indians and the Greeks from the Eurasian nomads who invaded their respective domains in the seventh century B.C.

In northern Asia down to the present day, there is a belief that the soul can leave the body and re-enter it. The shaman's soul re-enters the body from which it has disengaged itself; it does not enter a different body that may be of a different species. Yet the shaman's belief is the essential enabling condition for a belief in transmigration. Thus it is possible, though it is not demonstrable, that the common belief of the Greek Pythagoreans and Orphics and their Indian contemporaries may be of Eurasian nomad origin.

23

THE AFTERMATH OF ASSYRIAN
MILITARISM, 605–522 B.C.

I F the Assyrian Empire had lasted, it might perhaps have welded together South-West Asia and Egypt into a political unity that would have brought with it a social and religious unification as well, and then, at a fearful price, empire-building might have secured peace over an area that was the hub of the Oikoumenê. However, the brutality of Assyrian militarism condemned the Assyrian Empire to an early death. It exhausted Assyria's own limited resources of man-power, and it provoked vehement resistance movements which, when they were concerted, became more than a match for Assyria's dwindling strength. The devastation caused by the imposition of Assyrian rule and by its subsequent overthrow was aggravated by the ravages of the Cimmerians and Skyths. This double scourge left some of the victims prostrate, and even the successful resisters were debilitated in varying degrees. The immediate result was an unstable balance of power among the Assyrian Empire's successor-states. The victorious allies fell apart after their annihilating joint victory over their common adversary. They quarrelled over the division of the spoils, and the weaker survivors feared that they, in their turn, might become the spoils of the stronger.

The derelict regions were Mesopotamia, the whole of Syria (except for Tyre and Judah), Urartu, and eastern and central Asia Minor. The surviving powers were Media, Babylonia, Egypt, and Lydia.

Of these four, Media was the most potent and the most self-confident —though even Media was not as healthy as she appeared to be, as was demonstrated by the ease with which the Median Empire was annexed, c. 550 B.C., by its outlying vassal, Persis (Fars). Meanwhile, during the sixty years beginning with the destruction of Nineveh in 612 B.C., Media was the most aggressive of Assyria's heirs. The Medes were economically and culturally backward by comparison with the Babylonians and Syrians and Egyptians, and their backwardness had been a prophylactic.

It had allowed them to recuperate rapidly, and in any case the damage that they had suffered from the Assyrians had been more than compensated for by the political unification into which their tribes had been driven by the Assyrian menace.

The Medes' first achievement after 612 B.C. was a common service to the whole of the sedentary world. They exterminated, evicted, or subdued the nomad invaders of South-West Asia—partly by means of adopting the nomads' military equipment and tactics. This led the Medes into annexing Urartu and eastern and central Asia Minor. Urartu, which had been raided by the Assyrians and then by the Cimmerians without being permanently conquered by them, now at last lost her independence to the Medes. This north-westward expansion of Media brought her into collision with Lydia, which was expanding into the derelict area in Asia Minor from the west. After a bout of violent warfare, Media and Lydia agreed, in 585 B.C., to make the lower course of the River Halys (Kizil Irmak) the frontier between their respective realms. This agreement was reached thanks to the mediation of Babylonia and of Cilicia, the Assyrian Empire's successor-state in south-eastern Asia Minor.

The lower course of the Halys ran through the former territory of the Kingdom of Phrygia. This had been the strongest power in Asia Minor before the Cimmerian invaders had overthrown it. Lydia had suffered too. *Circa* 663 B.C. she had defeated the Cimmerians—with Assyrian help, according to Asshurbanipal. But in 652 B.C. the Cimmerians temporarily occupied Lydia's capital city, Sardis, and *c.* 646 B.C. Sardis was again occupied, this time by the Trêres, a people from Thrace who had invaded Asia Minor, perhaps under pressure from the other stream of Cimmerians and Skyths that had been flowing westward to the north of the Caspian and the Black Sea. However, Lydia, unlike Phrygia, had recuperated, and she was able to play an active part in the struggle for the partition of the Assyrian Empire's former domain. Before Lydia came into conflict, in the sixth century B.C., with Media, she had sent troops to Egypt, at some date earlier than 652 B.C., in order to help King Psammetichus I expel the Assyrian garrisons.

The Chaldaean masters of Babylonia had been indomitable in their resistance to Assyria, and both the Egyptians and the Syrians found them as potent and as ruthless as the Assyrians had been when the Chaldaeans asserted, by force of arms, their claim to the Syrian portion of Assyria's former dominions. Facing westward, the Chaldaeans were raging lions, but, facing eastward and northward, towards Media, they were trembling lambs. The original home territory of Assyria had been partitioned between Media and Babylonia along the line of the River Tigris, while, farther south, Babylonia had not only regained her historic frontiers, including the Babylonian territory to the east of the Tigris; she had also obtained the lowland portion of Elam, including the city of Susa. In consequence of this partition, it had fallen to Babylonia to destroy the last remnant of the Assyrian army at Harran, in northern Mesopotamia, and she had accomplished this in the years 609–605 B.C., in spite of Egypt's military support of the Assyrians' last stand. Subsequently, however, Harran was occupied by the Medes, and they retained it till they were overthrown, *c.* 550 B.C., by the Persians.

This Median occupation of Harran was probably a breach of a previous understanding between the Medes and the Babylonians over the division of the Assyrian spoils. In any case, this was, for the Babylonians, both a grievance and a menace. Their inability to expel the Medes from Harran forced them to recognize that they were no match for their late ally, and the Median garrison at Harran was a threat, at close quarters, to the Babylonians' line of communications, up the course of the Euphrates, with their dominions in Syria.

Assyria's former provinces in Syria were the stake for which the Babylonians and the Egyptians contended with each other in the years 609–605 B.C. The defeat of the Egyptians at Carchemish in 605 B.C. decided Syria's fate. The northern adventure of Necho II (ruled 610–595 B.C.) had ended in failure. But this was an exceptionally unfortunate episode in Egypt's spell of re-gained independence. For Egypt, this was, on the whole, a period of achievement. The seventh century B.C. was probably the date at which the Egyptians at last took to making their tools of iron instead of copper. It was certainly the century in which Egypt entered into mutually profitable relations with the Greeks. The troops, sent by King Gyges of Lydia to help King Psammetichus I expel the Assyrians, were probably Greek and Carian mercenaries. Psammetichus posted these troops in two cantonments, one at each of the two northern corners of the Delta. The soldiers were followed by traders, and a Greek commercial settlement sprang up at Naucratis, on the Mareotic branch of the Nile, near Psammatichus' capital, Saïs.

At first the Greeks were left free to do business anywhere in Egypt. *Circa* 566–565 B.C. they were compulsorily concentrated in Naucratis by the Egyptian Government in deference to a popular explosion of xenophobia; but Egypt continued to employ Greek mercenary troops, while Greek traders continued to exchange Greek wine and olive-oil for Egyptian grain.

As for Necho II, he compensated for his military reverse in Asia by beginning to dig a canal from the easternmost arm of the Nile via the Wadi Tumilat to the head of the Gulf of Suez; and, from Egypt's Red Sea coast, he despatched a squadron of Phoenician ships which succeeded in circumnavigating Africa.

Between 651 B.C., when the last Assyrian garrison was expelled from Egypt, and 525 B.C., when Egypt was conquered by the Persian Emperor Cambyses, Egypt was exempt from foreign military occupation. Psammetichus I's Greek garrison at the north-eastern corner of the Delta fended off the Skyths. Necho II's defeat at Carchemish and loss of Syria was not followed by a Babylonian conquest of Egypt itself.

All the same, the Egyptians were not entirely sure of themselves dur-the years 651–525 B.C. Their confidence had been undermined by their previous adversity, and this rankled in their memory as a painful contrast to the grandeur of earlier periods of Egyptian history. In the age of the Saïte regime, the Egyptians harked back to the earliest and grandest of all periods, namely the Old Kingdom. There was an archaistic revival of the Old-Kingdom style of visual art and of protocol. It is noteworthy that in contemporary Babylonia the last king to reign during the spell of re-gained independence there, Nabonidus (Nabū-na'id) (ruled 556–539 B.C.) was likewise an archaist. Archaism is a symptom of diffidence, and, in the post-Assyrian Age, the Babylonians, like the Egyptians, were both proud of and disconcerted by the antiquity of their civilization. In the year 600 B.C. the Pharaonic Egyptian civilization still had ahead of it another millennium of survival, and the Sumero-Akkadian civilization six centuries more. But both civilizations were already feeling intimations of mortality, and indeed the future lay with other civilizations that were about 2,000 years younger than these two.

Nebuchadnezzar (ruled 605–562 B.C.), the son of Nabopolassar the founder of the neo-Babylonian Empire, does not seem to have invaded Egypt. On the other hand he not only took possession of all the former Assyrian provinces in Syria; he also subdued the two Syrian states that had escaped being conquered by the Chaldaeans' Assyrian predecessors. Nebuchadnezzar compelled Tyre to capitulate after a thirteen-year siege (586–573 B.C.). He besieged and captured Jerusalem in 597, 587, and 582 B.C., and each successive capture was followed by a deportation in the Assyrian manner. According to the contemporary Judahite prophet Jeremiah, Nebuchadnezzar deported 4,600 persons in all. This figure is compatible with the Assyrian official figure 27,290 for the number of persons who had been deported in 721 B.C. from the bigger and more populous Kingdom of Israel. Larger but less convincing figures than Jeremiah's are given in later sources for the numbers of Judahites deported in 597 and repatriated in 539 B.C.

The purpose of deporting a community's 'establishment' was to destroy that community's identity, and in most cases the policy was effective in achieving its aim. For instance, the deportation of 27,290 persons in 721 B.C. from the Kingdom of Israel had this effect. The Judahites were singular in discovering, and resorting to, ways and means for retaining their communal identity under this treatment. The years 597–582 B.C. saw the end of the Kingdom of Judah and the beginning of the history of the Jews and of Judaism. Judah, like Israel, had been one of a number of Syrian states that had enjoyed a spell of independence for a few centuries in the last millennium B.C. The Jews, unlike their predecessors the Judahites, have been in truth the singular people that they claim to be. To understand how they have achieved this, we have to take a retrospective view of the history of the Kingdom of Judah since the date, *c*. 922 B.C., when the Judahite war-lord David's empire over southern Syria fell apart. In later chapters, we shall be examining the Jews' reaction to the challenge of deportation.

Retrospectively we can discern several distinctive features in the history of the Kingdom of Judah from 922 to 587 B.C. In the first place, the House of David occupied the throne of Judah continuously for more than four centuries, reckoning from the date, *c*. 1000 B.C., of David's acquisition of the crown. This unbroken rule of a single dynasty contrasts with the instability, from 922 B.C. till their extinction, of the two neighbouring kingdoms of Israel and Damascus. In both of these states the crown was repeatedly seized by violence from its momentary wearers. These two kingdoms never shook off the subversive effects of their revolutionary origins. David's career had been the same as the Aramaean Rezon's and the Israelite Jeroboam's. David, too, had won his crown through a successful secession from the previous wearer; yet David's successors in Judah had retained the loyalty of the residue of their subjects, in spite of the humiliating collapse of David's short-lived empire.

The residue consisted of the Tribe of Judah, the ex-Canaanite city of Jerusalem, and the southern fringe of the territory of the tribe of Benjamin. It is surprising that, in these circumstances, both the Davidic dynasty and its capital city should have become sanctified in the Judahites' estimation.

It is also surprising that the Kingdom of Judah escaped conquest by Assyria, considering that King Hezekiah (ruled 715–687/6 B.C.) was a party to the Chaldaean Merodach-Baladan's anti-Assyrian coalition. The Kingdom of Judah survived 134 years longer than the Kingdom of Israel and 145 years longer than the Kingdom of Damascus, and, in the reign of King Josiah (ruled *c*. 637–609 B.C.), Judah was actually able to take part in the scramble for the dissolving Assyrian Empire's spoils. Momentarily Josiah re-established David's empire that had been broken up, three centuries earlier, by Rezon's *coup* at Damascus and by Jeroboam's *coup* in Israel. Josiah lost his life, and, no doubt his empire too, when, in 609 B.C., he rashly tried to halt the march of Pharaoh Necho II, the Assyrians' ally, from the Nile to the Euphrates. The Kingdom of Judah then became the vassal, first of Egypt and next, after 605 B.C., of

Babylon. Yet the Davidic monarchy survived this reverse also. It was not extinguished till 587 B.C.

This surprising duration of the Kingdom of Judah gave time for the appearance of a long series of Judahite prophets. Isaiah, King Hezekiah's counsellor, and Jeremiah, King Jehoiakim's opponent, were inevitably concerned largely with foreign policy. Both these prophets advised the crown not to challenge the imperial power of the day, and Jeremiah, who outlived the extinction of the kingdom, was justified by the event.

Prophets were not a peculiar Judahite phenomenon; as has been noted already, they were a feature of the life of the Syrian society as a whole. Nor was the rest of the religious life of Judah peculiar to this particular Syrian state. Judah, like Israel and all the other Syrian communities, had a national god of its own, but the cult of the national god co-existed with other religious practices. For Judah, the evidence for this has survived even in the edited version of the Jewish scriptures. The description of the temple at Jerusalem as Solomon equipped it and as Hezekiah and Josiah found it would probably have been applicable to Bethel in Israel and to the temples of Milcom in Ammon, of Chemosh in Moab, and of Rimmon at Damascus. When Kings Ahaz and Manasseh of Judah burned their sons alive in the hope of thus constraining Yahweh to fulfil their prayer, they were performing a common Syrian rite. When Hezekiah and Josiah asserted the prerogatives of the national god, they were doing what had previously been done in the Kingdom of Israel by Elijah and Elisha and Jehu. As for Josiah's destruction of Jeroboam's altar at Bethel, and his slaughter of all the priests of Yahweh at Bethel and at other places of worship in the former territory of the Kingdom of Israel, this was a belated political riposte to Jeroboam's secession from Josiah's Davidic ancestor Rehoboam.

Josiah's genuine innovation was the suppression of all local places of worship not only in the reconquered territories but also within the previous limits of the Kingdom of Judah. He decreed that, throughout his realm, Yahweh should be worshipped exclusively, and also that he should be worshipped nowhere except in the ex-Canaanite city of Jerusalem. Josiah was turning his kingdom into a city-state by an act that his Greek contemporaries would have called 'synoecism'—meaning, not a literal concentration of the whole of the population in one single place, but a proviso that only one single place should be the legitimate locus for acts of state, whether secular or religious. Josiah's liturgical revolution was reinforced by the production, in the eighteenth year of his reign, of a law-book which bore some relation to the present version of the Book of Deuteronomy. As a result of the long-drawn-out survival of the Kingdom of Judah, and of the actions of King Josiah in the seventh century B.C., the Judahites who were deported in 597, 587, and 582 B.C. went into exile better equipped psychologically than any previous deportees for preserving their communal identity under adverse conditions.

Before the sixth century B.C. was over, the fortunes of the Assyrian Empire's successors were changed through the rapid creation, by new empire-builders from an unexpected quarter, of an empire that dwarfed the defunct Assyrian Empire in scale and put the Assyrians to shame by its relative mildness. It has been noted already that the gainers from Asshurbanipal's destruction of the Kingdom of Elam were the Iranian highlanders in Elam's hinterland. The direct beneficiaries were the Persians in the districts known today as Fars and Luristan. Cyrus II, the scion of the House of Achaemenes who founded the First Persian Empire, styled himself 'King of Anshan', which seems to have been a city or a district somewhere in the valley of the River Karkhah (Choaspes), above the point at which this river emerges from the highlands of Luristan into the lowlands of Khuzistan.

Circa 550 B.C., Cyrus II supplanted the reigning King of Media, Astyages, and took over the whole Median Empire, no doubt with the co-operation of a faction of the Median 'establishment'. *Circa* 547 B.C. Cyrus conquered and annexed the Lydian Empire; in 539 he conquered and annexed the neo-Babylonian Empire, including its dominions to the west of the River Euphrates. It was probably after this that he conquered and annexed the territories to the north-east of Media (present-day Khorasan, Soviet Central Asia, and Afghanistan) that were inhabited by a sedentary Iranian-speaking population. Cyrus II was killed in an attempt to conquer the Massagetae, a horde of Iranian-speaking pastoral nomads to the east of the Caspian Sea, but this reverse did not bring the Persians' empire-building enterprise to an end. In 525 B.C. Cyrus II's son and successor Cambyses conquered and annexed Egypt.

Cambyses then died mysteriously and was succeeded by an emperor who claimed to be Cambyses' brother Smerdis (Bardiya). Smerdis, genuine or false, was then assassinated by Darius I, the representative of a different branch of the House of Achaemenes. This liquidation of the last emperor who purported to be a son of Cyrus II was the signal for a wide-spread revolt in the provinces to the east of the River Euphrates (both Egypt and Lydia lay low). The most resolute of the insurgents were the Babylonians, the Medes, the Armenians (recent occupants of the western part of the former Kingdom of Urartu), and also, surprisingly, the easternmost clans of the Persian people itself.

Darius, in his inscription on the cliff-face at Behistan, on the road from Babylon to the north-east, claims to have suppressed all these insurrections within a single year (522 B.C.). The re-subjugation of the insurgents probably took rather longer than twelve months, but it was authentic. Darius' remarkable victory was due only partly to his and his troops' demonic energy; it was largely due to an almost universal longing for peace and security among the peoples who had been afflicted by the Assyrians and by the nomads.

Darius I was the second founder of the First Persian Empire, and he also enlarged it. On the north-east he subjugated the Massagetae nomads, who had defeated and killed Cyrus II. On the east, he conquered and annexed the Indus basin. On the north-west he conquered and annexed a large bridgehead on the European side of the Dardanelles. This extended from the south bank of the lower course of the River Danube to as far to the south-west as Mount Olympus.

These European acquisitions were an incidental by-product of a rash campaign against the Skyth nomads on the steppe to the north of the Black Sea (here Darius I barely escaped Cyrus II's fate). In 490 B.C. an expeditionary force which Darius sent by sea to European Greece suffered a significant reverse. On the whole, however, Darius I was as successful an empire-builder as Cyrus II had been. At Darius I's death in 486 B.C. the First Persian Empire extended, east and west, from the Beas tributary of the Indus to the eastern foot of the Pindus Range; north and south, it extended from the southern foot of the Caucasus Range to the northern foot of the First Cataract of the River Nile. This was the biggest, and also the least oppressive, empire that had yet been built.

24

THE HELLENIC CIVILIZATION,

c. 750–507 B.C.

In the *Völkerwanderung c.* 1250–950 B.C., the Aegean basin had suffered more severely than any of the other regions that this *Völkerwanderung* had hit. In the twelfth century B.C. the Minoan and Mycenaean civilizations had foundered; their former domains had been depopulated; literacy had been lost; and the rise of a new civilization, the Hellenic, from the eleventh century onwards, had been so gradual that, even as late as *c.* 700 B.C., when the Hellenic civilization had already burst into flower, its blossoming was not perceived by the poet Hesiod, though his own poetry was one of Hellenism's notable early achievements.

Notwithstanding Hesiod's perhaps wilful blindness, the Greeks were as fortunate in the eighth and seventh centuries B.C. as they had been unfortunate in the twelfth century B.C. In these two centuries the Hellenic World, except for the Greek settlements along the west coast of continental Asia Minor, was just beyond the range of conquering Assyrian armies and raiding Eurasian nomad hordes. These scourges afflicted Syria, and blighted the promise of her precocious civilization, at the moment when the recuperation of the Greek World had been completed. In the eighth and seventh centuries B.C. the Hellenic civilization drew inspiration from the cultural advances that the Syrian civilization had been achieving since the twelfth century B.C., during the time when the Greek World had still, to all appearance, been dormant.

In the eighth century B.C. the Hellenic World's fortunate immunity from devastating assaults from abroad resulted in a population explosion that continued until the second century B.C. *Circa* 750 B.C. the Hellenes contracted their earliest debt to Syria. At about this date they borrowed the Phoenician alphabet. This was a far more efficient script for conveying the Greek or any other language than the Linear-B syllabary that had been invented, most probably in the fifteenth century B.C., in imitation of the Minoan Linear-A. When the Greeks adapted the Alphabet to the requirements of their own language by using some of the Phoenician consonantal letters to stand for vowels, they had at their disposal, for the first time, a script that was simple enough to be written and read by the common man, in contrast to the now long since forgotten Linear-B, which, like Linear-A and like the Sumero-Akkadian and Egyptian and Chinese scripts, had been an esoteric instrument that could be operated only by a small ring of specialists.

The Greeks' reception and adaptation of the Phoenician alphabet had momentous consequences for Hellenic literature and thought. During the four and a half centuries of illiteracy, each recital of epic poetry had been a fresh act of creation, extemporized by means of the artifice of coining a wealth of metrical formulae which the minstrel could memorize and reproduce. Are the *Iliad* and the *Odyssey* the last, besides being the longest and the grandest, improvisations of the pre-literary age, or are they the first-fruits of the acquisition of a new script? It seems certain that non-ritual texts of this length could not have become fixed if they had not been put into writing soon after the first recitals of them. Epic, unlike liturgy, is a genre of literature that is difficult to hand down, word-perfect, by memorization; for the efficacy of epic does not depend on the exact repetition of the whole of a form of words. So far from that, the appeal of oral epic to its audience lies in the use of a vast mental store of short metrical formulae to produce a fresh work of art at each performance.

The reproduction of an epic in writing ensures both the preservation of the poem and the death of the genre. Once the *Iliad* and the *Odyssey* had been written down, Greek authors invented a series of new genres: elegiac and lyric poetry, narrative prose, and dialogue; and these new genres were used for expressive and for didactic purposes as well as for entertainment. By the close of the sixth century, Greek writers were expressing their personal feelings and experiences, they were making religious and political propaganda, they were communicating scientific speculations, they were beginning to write plays—and the dramatic dialogue was eventually used as a medium for philosophical debate.

The Greeks' adoption, and adaptation, of the Phoenician alphabet, which had these literary consequences, was quickly followed by the reception of foreign motifs of visual art. By the close of the eighth century the Geometric style of decorating pots gave way to a new style, introduced from the Levant, in which abstract patterns were replaced by the delineation of the figures of living creatures—first animals, real or imaginary, and then human beings as well. The new style of decorating pots was inspired by contemporary Phoenician commercial art; the first Greek experiments in a three-dimensional representation of the human body were inspired by Egyptian models.

The reception of these artistic influences from the Levant in the seventh century B.C., and the previous reception, in the eighth century B.C., of the Phoenician alphabet, would not have been possible if the Greeks had not, by then, re-gained the contact with the Levant that had been interrupted since the twelfth century B.C. This contact must have been mainly maritime, and it must have taken the form of trade; for the Greeks cannot have imported Levantine wares gratis. A Euboean Greek trading-post was in fact established, perhaps as early as the ninth century B.C., at Al-Mina at the mouth of the River Orontes, towards the northern end of the coast of Syria. From the eighth century B.C. onwards the Greeks' paramount economic need was to obtain food for a now rapidly increasing number of Greek mouths. One way of increasing the food-supply of a region that was not rich in natural resources was to import cereals from beyond the borders of the Hellenic World in exchange for Greek products; but the line of least resistance was less sophisticated. It was to enlarge the area of the Hellenic World by the conquest and colonization of the territories of peoples who were too weak to be able to withstand Greek aggression.

In the later decades of the eighth century B.C. the Greeks started to expand overseas westwards, beyond the Straits of Otranto, along the south and west coasts of Italy and the east and south coasts of Sicily. In the seventh century B.C., they also began to expand northwards along the coasts of the narrow seas that connect the Aegean basin with the Black Sea. Greek traders may have preceded Greek settlers and have guided them to the sites that they seized; but the earliest Hellenic Greek colonies were replicas of the contemporary Greek communities which founded them. Like these, they were city-states whose staple means of livelihood was agriculture: producing crops for the growers' subsistence, not for sale abroad. In the maritime approaches to the Black Sea, the Greeks had no competitors. It has been noted already that the planting of Greek city-states along the west coast of Asia Minor and on the off-shore islands had turned the Aegean Sea into a Greek lake. On the other hand, in the western basin of the Mediterranean the Greeks met with formidable competitors, the Phoenicians and the Etruscans (a people who, like the Phoenicians and the Greeks, were probably, though so far not demonstrably, of East-Mediterranean origin).

In the competition for the command of the western basin of the Mediterranean, the Greeks had the advantage of numbers, whereas the Phoenicians were handicapped, not only demographically, but also by the Assyrians' assault upon them from their Asian hinterland. The final and most violent bout of Assyrian militarism started in 745 B.C., and this was only a few years after the date at which the Greeks began to plant colonies in the west. However, the colonial Phoenicians and the

Etruscans possessed some important advantages over the Greeks, and they took deliberate and effective measures to counteract the Greeks' superiority in numbers and their immunity from the Assyrian scourge.

The Phoenicians forestalled the Greeks in occupying strategic positions from which they could keep the Hellenic World's westward expansion within bounds. The Phoenicians held the shores of the Straits of Gibraltar, which command the access from the Mediterranean to the Atlantic. They also held both shores of the relatively narrow seas between the north-east corner of North-West Africa and the west end of Sicily, besides holding the south coast of Sardinia. The Etruscans held the mineral deposits on the island of Elba and on the adjacent Italian mainland. This was one of the chief economic prizes in the western basin of the Mediterranean, but the nearest point to it that the Greeks managed to seize was Cumae, farther southward on Italy's west coast. This was perhaps the earliest continental Greek colony in the West, but it was planted too late to forestall the establishment of an Etruscan mining community at Populonia, and, before the close of the sixth century, the Etruscans had occupied Cumae's Campanian hinterland.

The colonial Phoenicians and the Etruscans also countered Greek numbers by political consolidation. Towards the close of the sixth century B.C., all the Phoenician colonies in the western basin of the Mediterranean put themselves under the unitary command of the most powerful of them, Carthage, and, before that, the colonial Phoenicians and the Etruscan city-states had already made common cause with each other. Thus, when the Asian Greeks were seeking western asylums in order to escape from Lydian, and then from Persian, rule, they were frustrated. Before 500 B.C., Greek colonization in the western basin of the Mediterranean was brought to a halt, and at this date the only sections of the European shore of the western Mediterranean, to the north-west of Cumae, which the Greeks had succeeded in occupying, were the French Riviera and the Costa Brava. The Greek settlements here were under the unitary command of one of their number, Massilia (Marseilles), the location of which, near the mouth of the River Rhône, gave it access to the heart of continental Europe and also to the tin mines in Cornwall by a short cut that by-passed the Straits of Gibraltar, which the colonial Phoenicians under Carthage's leadership made impassable for Greek shipping. However, c. 500 B.C., the Massiliots' trade with their northern hinterland was interrupted by an upheaval among the native peoples.

In the seventh century B.C. the enlargement of the Hellenes' habitat by the plantation of overseas Greek city-states that still made their living by subsistence-agriculture came to be surpassed in economic importance by a more extensive enlargement of the Hellenic World's trading-area. The majority of the Hellenic city-states, both in nuclear Hellas and overseas, continued to consist of small, economically self-contained, agricultural communities, but a minority took to producing specialized products for export in exchange for foreign-grown cereals, and this enabled them to make a living by trade with peoples whose countries they could not conquer and colonize. One of these specialized exports was Greek mercenary soldiers. The import of these into Egypt in the seventh century B.C. has been noted already. In the sixth century B.C. a brother of the Mytilenaean Greek poet Alcaeus was a mercenary soldier in Nebuchadnezzar's service. Economically backward Greek communities could, and did, export mercenaries. A smaller number of economically advanced communities exported olive-oil and wine in attractively decorated containers that were valuable commodities in themselves and, though fragile, were more durable than the liquids that were conveyed in them.

By the seventh century B.C. the Greeks were tapping the surplus cereal production of two regions, Egypt and the Ukraine. Greek trade with Egypt has been noted already; Greek trade with the Ukraine became practicable when the *Völkerwanderung* of the Skyth pastoral nomads had come to a halt on the steppe to the north of the Black Sea. Among the Eurasian nomads, the Skyths were singular in having the economic good sense to levy a grain-tribute on the agricultural population of the Ukraine instead of wrecking this agriculture by making slave-raids. The Greek colonies along the western and northern shores of the Black Sea were numerous, but they were mostly small trading posts, not agricultural settlements like those round the narrow seas and in the west.

The subsequent development of Greek trade must have been stimulated by the invention of coinage, which is attributed to King Alyattes of Lydia (ruled *c.* 608–558 B.C.). Long before this—indeed, probably since the beginning of urban life in Sumer—ingots or bars or spits of gold, silver, and copper had been used as media of exchange. Alyattes' innovation was not the invention of a metallic currency but the stamping of pieces of metal with a monogram and the issuing of such stamped pieces by the government of a state. Coins were not only handier than ingots; if the issuing authority was of good economic repute, its coins could be taken on trust, without needing to be weighed each time they changed hands. Once invented, coinage spread rapidly. Soon there were mints in many Greek cities, and, when Darius I and his successors issued a gold coinage, the new invention was diffused throughout the Persian Empire. Yet, even in the Levant, the non-commercial majority of the population long continued to transact by barter its petty trade in the local market.

The expansion, first of the Greeks' habitat, and then of their trading-area, with the concomitant revolution in the economic activities of an

economically adventurous minority of the Greek city-states, had produced striking changes in the balance of power within the Hellenic
World. In the dark age in which the Hellenic civilization had been
brought to birth, the creative Hellenic city-state had been Athens—the
one Mycenaean citadel that had not been sacked in the twelfth century
B.C. Athens retained her pre-eminence throughout the Protogeometric
and Geometric Ages; but, from *c.* 750 B.C. till after the beginning of the
sixth century B.C. she temporarily lost her leading position. Athens took
no part in the colonization movement nor in the first stage of the subsequent economic revolution.

The makers of this revolution were the city-states along and off the
west coast of Asia Minor (e.g. Miletus and Chios) and round the Isthmus
of Corinth (e.g. Corinth herself, Sicyon, and Megara). Ionia was the
region in which the Greek epic culminated in the production of the *Iliad*
and the *Odyssey*. In the succeeding age, none of the eminent elegiac and
lyric Greek poets was an Athenian, and the new styles of vase-decoration
that superseded the geometric style were created, not at Athens, but at
Rhodes and Corinth and Sparta. Even in the sixth century B.C., when
Athens was coming to the fore again—first economically and then politically too—the fathers of Greek physical science were not Athenians;
they were two Milesians (Thales and Anaximander) and the Ephesian
Heracleitus (Heraklitos). These sixth-century-B.C. Asian Greeks performed the greatest of all Hellenic Greek intellectual feats. Their predecessors had thought of the process of physical Nature in the
anthropomorphic terms of procreation. The sixth-century-B.C. Ionian
physicists set themselves to explain impersonal phenomena in impersonal
terms. No native Athenian played a distinguished part in the development of Hellenic science either at the start or indeed at any later stage.

The quarter of a millennium beginning *c.* 750 B.C. witnessed an
immense outburst of Greek energy in a number of different fields, but
this outburst had its dark as well as its brilliant aspects. Much of this
energy was misspent on fratricidal strife between one city-state and
another, and, within each city-state, between contending social classes
and political factions. In the epoch of Greek history which began *c.* 750
B.C. and which continued till the Romans stopped the Greek states from
going to war with each other, the Greeks were as ruthless to each other
as they had been in the Mycenaean Age. In the Greek states that underwent economic revolutions in the seventh century B.C., domestic strife
became so acute that these states fell temporarily under dictatorial
regimes. These were the penalty for a failure to change over peacefully
from a monarchical or aristocratic form of government to one in which
wealth, not birth, was the qualification for exercising political power.

In this period, the outstanding case of ill-treatment of Greeks by

Greeks was the conquest of the southernmost two-fifths of the Peloponnesos, *c.* 750–715 B.C., by one of the local city-states, Sparta. This was a land-locked city-state, and its conquest of its neighbours in Greece was the counterpart of the conquest of non-Greek populations in Italy and Sicily by maritime Greek city-states such as Corinth and Chalcis.

The Spartans allowed some of the neighbouring city-states that they had conquered to keep their autonomy, subject to an obligation to perform military service for Sparta in war. These communities reconciled themselves to their loss of sovereignty on these terms; but in other conquered territories the Spartans reduced the population to serfdom, and the serfs were compelled to make payments in kind from the produce of their lands to Spartan citizens, in order that these might by exempted from agricultural labour and thus be enabled to spend all their time and energy on making war and on military training. By thus exploiting a subject Greek population that was many times larger than Sparta's own citizen-body, Sparta was able to give this privileged minority a democratic equality of political rights among themselves without abolishing her monarchy and her aristocratic council, and also without falling under a dictatorship. Sparta's democratic constitution—the earliest in the Hellenic World—was inaugurated at some date in the latter part of the seventh century B.C.

The Spartans' concentration on military training and discipline made them the most formidable soldiers in the Hellenic World. At first they tried to use their military power for conquering more Greek territory in order to reduce more Greeks to serfdom; but by *c.* 550 B.C. they recognized that their man-power, however valiant and well-drilled, was not numerous enough to hold down their present serfs and at the same time to add to their number by further conquests. The Spartans therefore abandoned the policy of conquest and replaced it by a policy of alliances. They promoted the overthrow of the dictatorships in the economically advanced states round the Isthmus of Corinth, and they allied themselves with the regimes, based on wealth, which followed the overthrow of the dictatorships there.

Circa 511 B.C. the Spartans sought to extend their network of alliances farther by overthrowing the dictatorship that was still in power at Athens, and, at the second attempt, they succeeded; but at Athens the sequel was not the same as at Megara, Corinth, and Sicyon. At Athens the oligarchy that had taken over the government from the evicted dictator failed to hold its own against a more radical movement, and, when the Spartans intervened at Athens for the third time in support of their conservative friends, they were defeated by a popular uprising.

Athens thus escaped from Sparta's control and the Athenians then (*c.* 507 B.C.) set up a democratic regime. In this they were following

Sparta's example, but at this stage there was a crucial difference between the Athenian state's social structure and the Spartan state's. In Sparta's territory the majority of the population were serfs. In Attica there were no serfs; there were some slaves and there was also an increasing number of unenfranchised freemen of alien origin, but the majority of the population consisted of enfranchised citizens. In 480 B.C., when Sparta and Athens momentarily co-operated to resist a Persian invasion, Athens had about 30,000 citizens and Sparta only about 8,000. Sparta's dominions contained a larger total population than Attica, but while the majority of the population of Sparta's dominions was an economic asset for Sparta, it was also a political and military liability, since it consisted of unreconciled serfs.

Sparta's dealings with Athens in the crucial years 511–507 B.C. had taken a turn that, for the Spartans, had been unexpected and disconcerting. The reason was that, during the sixth century B.C., Athens had been recovering from her temporary loss of the lead. At the beginning of that century, social tension in Attica had been as acute as it had been in the Kingdom of Israel in the eighth century B.C. It had looked as if Attica might become, as Sparta's dominions had already become, a country in which the majority of the population were serfs. Athens was saved from this fate by reforms introduced in 590 B.C. by a statesmanlike Athenian businessman, Solon; but Solon's voluntarily accepted reforms were not radical enough to save Athens from falling under a dictator, Peisistratus, who completed Solon's work; and, after that, it needed Sparta's intervention to relieve Athens of the dictatorship when it had carried out its mandate. However, Solon, rather than Peisistratus, must be credited with restoring Athens to prosperity. Solon initiated in Attica a policy of producing olive-oil for export and he promoted the development of manufacturing industries. He offered Athenian citizenship to any foreign technician whose intention to throw in his lot with his adopted country bona fide was guaranteed either by his bringing his family with him or by his having been exiled from his native city-state. The key industry that was thus fostered in Attica was the making and decoration of containers for oil and wine. By *c.* 550 B.C., Athenian pottery-wares had captured the international market, replacing the wares of Corinth and Sparta.

One of Sparta's allies, Aegina, was also hard hit by economic competition from Athens. This little island, which is within sight of Attica, lived by trade. Aeginetans played a leading part in the Panhellenic trading settlement at Naucratis in Egypt. The conflict between Aegina and Athens became so bitter that, on the eve of the Persians' invasion of European Greece, King Cleomenes I of Sparta had great difficulty in stopping Aegina from waging war on Athens.

Thus, during the period *c.* 750–500 B.C., strife, both international and domestic, had become intense in the world of Hellenic city-states. Yet, during the same period, the Greeks, in spite of their increasing economic and political discord, had become conscious of their cultural unity and solidarity, and this consciousness found expression in a number of Panhellenic institutions.

'Hellenes', which was the Greeks' new common name for themselves, means 'inhabitants of Hellas', and 'Hellas' was the name of a district in central Greece which contained the shrine of Artemis at Anthela near Thermopylae and of the goddess Earth and the gods Apollo and Dionysos at Delphi, the seat of a greatly revered and much consulted oracle. This pair of shrines had come to be administered by twelve adjacent (amphictyonic) Greek states, and this college of Amphictyons had won for itself such an important role in the Greek World as a whole that prominent states which had not been original members of this Amphictyony had managed to obtain representation on it. This enlargement of the Amphictyony carried with it an extension of the application of the names 'Hellas' and 'Hellenes', till these names came to signify respectively the whole of the area, and all of the adherents, of the new civilization which had arisen in the Aegean basin in the eleventh century B.C. and had been expanding from there since the eighth century B.C.

Other Panhellenic institutions, besides the Hellenic Amphictyony, were the four periodic festivals at Delphi, Corinth, Nemea in Corinth's Peloponnesian hinterland, and—oldest and most highly regarded of them all—the festival at Olympia on the western side of the Peloponnesos. Olympia, like contemporary Olmec La Venta and Tres Zapotes, was a ceremonial centre that was not accompanied by any permanent urban settlement. These festivals were the occasions for Panhellenic competitions, and these were not exclusively athletic; they included competitions in poetry and music as well.

Indeed, the Panhellenic institutions were the vehicles of the sense of cultural solidarity which the names 'Hellas' and 'Hellenes' expressed. However, the essence of this solidarity was not institutional; it was psychological. The psychological basis of 'Hellenism' was a common outlook, common aspirations and ideals, common concerns, and common manners and customs. For instance, the poetry that was composed in some particular Hellenic city-state in the local dialect quickly became the common possession of all Hellenes. The two Homeric epics, which took their final shape somewhere in Ionia, came to be recited throughout the Hellenic World, and poetry came to be composed in the Homeric dialect and metre by poets—for example the Boeotian Hesiod—whose mother-tongues were different dialects of Greek. Thus the Greek dialects became something more than local patois; they also became the media for particular genres of Panhellenic literature. The intellectual, emotional, and spiritual bonds of Hellenism were impalpable, but it was these bonds that held the Hellenes together by transcending their economic and political factiousness.

25

NEW DEPARTURES IN SPIRITUAL
LIFE, *c.* 600–480 B.C.

WITHIN a span of not more than about 120 years—that is to say, only about four or five generations—five great seers made their appearance in the Old-World Oikoumenê.

The earliest of the five was the Iranian seer Zarathustra. Both his date and his location are uncertain, but it seems probable that he did his work in the early years of the sixth century B.C. and that his field of activity was in the Oxus–Jaxartes basin, in lands that were inhabited by a sedentary population but were exposed to attack by the pastoral nomads of the Eurasian steppe. The second of these seers was 'Deutero-Isaiah'. He, or an editor of his writings, has concealed his name by attaching what he wrote to the book of the eighth-century-B.C. Judahite prophet Isaiah. But 'Deutero-Isaiah' testifies that he lived nearly two centuries later than the authentic Isaiah; for 'Deutero-Isaiah' hails, as Yahweh's anointed king, Cyrus II, the first founder of the First Persian Empire; and Cyrus II conquered the neo-Babylonian Empire, and gave the Jewish deportees in Babylonia permission to return to Judaea, in 539 B.C. There is no indication in 'Deutero-Isaiah's' writings of the place where they were written. Babylonia and Judaea are equally probable possibilities.

The Buddha's date is almost as uncertain as Zarathustra's. It may have been *c.* 567–487 B.C. It is, however, certain that Siddhartha Gautama the Buddha was born in Kapilavastu, a small city-state within the frontiers of the present-day Kingdom of Nepal, and that his field of activity was present-day Bihar. Confucius was a slightly younger contemporary of the Buddha, if his traditional date, 551–479 B.C., is approximately correct. His home country in China was the state of Lu, one of the smaller and weaker of the states into which the Chou dynasty's domain had fallen apart by Confucius' day. Pythagoras was an approximate contemporary of the Buddha. He was born on the Ionian off-shore island Samos, but his field of activity was the colonial Greek domain in southern Italy, and the city-state in which he settled was Croton.

With the possible exception of Pythagoras, these sixth-century-B.C. seers are today still influencing mankind, either directly or indirectly, more than any human being who is now alive. The Buddha is influencing directly more than half, and Confucius more than a third, of the living generation. The direct present-day influence of 'Deutero-Isaiah' extends to Christians, besides Jews. The direct present-day influence of Zarathustra is limited to Parsees, and today these are a numerically small community, though, like the Jews, they play a part in the present-day world that is more than proportionate to their numbers. However, indirectly, Zarathustra today is influencing Jews, Christians, and Muslims as well as his own adherents. As a result of the entente between Persians and Jews in the time of the First Persian Empire from its incorporation of the neo-Babylonian Empire in 539 B.C. till its extinction in 330 B.C., some of Zarathustra's most spiritually potent concepts— immortality, the Last Judgment, God's operation through the Holy Spirit—found their way into Judaism and thence into Judaism's two daughter religions.

There may have been some years in the sixth century B.C. during which all these five seers were alive simultaneously, but it is improbable that any two of them ever met, and it is even unlikely that any one of them was aware of the existence of any of the others. The beliefs and objectives and practices of two of them—the Buddha and Pythagoras— resemble each other so closely as to make it seem virtually certain that their inspiration was derived from a common source; but it seems no less sure that neither the Buddha in Bihar nor Pythagoras in Italy can have communicated this set of common elements to the geographically distant contemporary with whom he shared them.

On the strength of the contemporaneity of these five seers, the period spanned by their lifetimes has been called by Karl Jaspers the Axis Age, i.e. an age that is the hinge on which human history has turned. Their appearance has in truth been a turning-point in the sense that, as has been noted above, they have continued to influence mankind down to the present day and are likely to go on influencing posterity by their example, even if their precepts cease to be commandments and their doctrines cease to be articles of faith. However, if we are to think of human history in terms of an Axis Age—and this is, in itself, an illuminating concept—we must extend its time-span in both directions.

'Deutero-Isaiah' was a prophet of the Syrian school; and we have a record of a Syrian prophet who was encountered at Byblos by Wen Amun *c.* 1060 B.C.—that is to say, about five hundred years before 'Deutero-Isaiah'. We cannot understand 'Deutero-Isaiah' if we do not recognize that he was consciously following the Syrian tradition. He or his editor has indicated this by appending his writings to the book of the most famous of all the literate Judahite prophets. Zarathustra is clearly a prophet of the Syrian type, though in his case there is no evidence that he was influenced by any predecessor, either Syrian or Iranian. On the other hand, it is certain that Jesus and Muhammad were consciously following the Syrian prophetic tradition, and it would be misleading to set a chronological limit to the Axis Age that excluded these two mighty epigoni of Zarathustra and 'Deutero-Isaiah'. Thus the Axis Age expands from a period of about 120 years to one of about seventeen centuries running from *c.* 1060 B.C. down to A.D. 632, which is the date of the Prophet Muhammad's death. These seventeen centuries cover about one third of the time-span, to date, of the species of societies that we have labelled 'civilizations'; yet even a span of seventeen centuries is a twinkling of an eye, measured by the age, to date, of humanity and, *a fortiori*, of the pre-human hominids.

Though the five sixth-century-B.C. seers appeared independently of each other, we can discern some features that are common to the five, though not characteristic of these five exclusively.

The most momentous common feature is the attainment, by an individual human being, of a direct personal relation with the ultimate spiritual reality in and behind the Universe in which Man finds himself. Originally, Man's relation with the ultimate reality had been, not individual and personal, but collective and institutional. Pre-civilizational societies had approached ultimate reality through the medium of non-human natural forces which, at this stage, held Man at their mercy. After the achievement of civilization, Man had shifted his approach to ultimate reality. Instead of deifying non-human Nature, he had taken to deifying a human community's collective power. The organization of collective human power on the grand scale had inclined the balance appreciably to Man's advantage in Man's struggle with non-human Nature for the prize of mastery. In thus changing the object of his worship, Man had been consistent in always worshipping power, in whatever embodiment he found power to be most potent. Spiritually, however, the replacement of non-human Nature by collective human power as the object of worship had been a regression. Man had taken to aiming farther from, not nearer to, the mark when he had made this transfer of his spiritual allegiance.

Each of the five seers broke away from his heritage of spiritual subordination to the community in which he had been born and brought up. In defiance of tradition, he had rejected both Nature-worship and Man-worship and had broken through these obstructing and obscuring veils to win a direct vision of spiritual reality naked. This feat is manifest in the case of the prophets. A prophet believes, and maintains, that his utterances are inspired by his god direct, and not through any social medium. In a lower emotional key, Confucius believed and maintained that he was rehabilitating the ethical code of social conduct that 'Heaven' had made binding on the founding fathers of the Chinese civilization. 'Heaven' (*T'ien*) seems originally to have been conceived of as being a personal—that is to say, a human-like—god; by Confucius' day, this Chinese name for the ultimate spiritual reality may have ceased to carry the connotation of personality and may have come to be conceived of as being a supra-personal or impersonal spirit or law. The Buddha certainly did not conceive of ultimate spiritual reality as being human-like. He did not identify it either with all or with only one of the members of the traditional Hindu pantheon. For the Buddha, the ultimate reality that was the goal of his quest was a state of 'extinguishedness' (Nirvana), and he had to reach, and did reach, enlightenment by his own spiritual exertions, without any possibility of being aided by the non-human-like ultimate reality that was his objective.

The second common characteristic of the five seers is that they condemned, repudiated, and set out to change, the state in which they had found things. Their respective spiritual revolts differed from each other greatly in degree. The Buddha, who was the most sublime of the five, was also the most radical of them. What the Buddha set out to change was life itself as he had found it. He had found that every sentient being suffered pain; he had also found that every living being was greedy. He held that, if a living being were to succeed in purging itself of its greed, this would enable it to release itself from the painful state of life in which a greedy living being is implicated. Pythagoras, too, condemned life as we experience it, and he, too, set out to change life on the same lines as the Buddha, though he was not so whole-hearted as the Buddha in taking this formidable course. Zarathustra set out to subvert, and 'Deutero-Isaiah' to modify, the traditional form of his community's religion. Confucius set out to raise the standards of social conduct that were prevalent in China in his day.

Each of the five sought to lead his fellow human beings into the new way that the seer had found. Zarathustra and 'Deutero-Isaiah' published their messages in writing. (These messages were, in their belief, God's messages communicated to mankind through the prophet as God's human spokesman.) Zarathustra's Gathas (hymns) and 'Deutero-Isaiah's' additions to the original Isaiah's book appear to be authentic works of these two seers. There are also scriptures that purport to be records of discourses delivered by the Buddha and by Confucius and of conversations between each of them and some of his disciples. We do not know how closely these alleged records follow the master's original words, and we cannot be sure, either, of the authenticity of the sayings attributed to Pythagoras.

Four of the five, namely Zarathustra, the Buddha, Confucius, and Pythagoras, enlisted, or at any rate accepted, disciples, and this led to the creation of new societies, since relations between human beings have to be institutionalized if they are to be maintained for more than a single generation and to embrace more people than the small number that is the limit for a community based on personal acquaintance only. The Buddha founded a monastic order (*sangha*) supported by lay adherents; Confucius founded a school of philosophy; Pythagoras founded a society that was something more than a school, even if it was not a formal monastic order. 'Deutero-Isaiah' was content, we may guess, to deliver his message to the already existing Jewish community. On the other hand, Zarathustra became the founder of a new religion. The Buddha's concern to communicate his spiritual discovery likewise led to the foundation of a new religion; and this sequel to the Buddha's enlightenment is remarkable. The Buddha believed that everyone has to attain enlightenment by his own efforts, and that, if and when he attains it, he is free to make his exit into Nirvana. Yet the Buddha postponed his own exit, and thus voluntarily remained in the condition in which life involves pain, in order to show to other sentient beings the way out that he had found.

The Buddha kept himself aloof from politics and from social life outside the circle of his disciples. He was the heir apparent to a throne and he was also a husband and a father. He had renounced his inheritance of his father's throne and had parted from his wife and child in order to devote himself to his quest of a means of release from the painfulness of life. When, after his enlightenment, the Buddha became an itinerant teacher, he was recognized by the local kings as their social peer, and he did not eschew their company, but he did not seek it either. He was not concerned to promote the growth of his monastic order by securing a royal patron. Buddhism found its first royal patron, more than two hundred years after the Buddha's death, in the Emperor Ashoka. On the other hand, Zarathustra did look for a royal patron, and he found one. Confucius looked for a royal employer, and failed to find one—a personal rebuff that led this unemployed civil servant to create a novel career for himself as a teacher of ethics. 'Deutero-Isaiah' did not need a patron. All that he needed—and this he achieved—was that his message should be accepted by the Jewish community.

Among the five seers, the Buddha was exceptional in his aloofness from politics. Confucius would have welcomed a political career if he had been able to find an opening. The Confucians had to wait until nearly 350 years after their master's death for the Confucian philosophy to become a passport for appointment to public office. Zarathustra evidently felt that the patronage of a ruler was a necessary condition for the success of his mission. Pythagoras and his disciples could not avoid going into politics. In the sixth-century-B.C. Hellenic World, a fraternity of philosophers had to be master in some city-state if it was not to be victimized. The Pythagoreans played for mastery and met with disaster. As for 'Deutero-Isaiah', he gave rein to extravagant political expectations. He hailed Cyrus II as Yahweh's anointed king, because Cyrus was permitting the Jewish deportees in Babylonia to return to Judaea; but he expected the sequel to be the erection of a world-empire in which Yahweh, not Cyrus, would be the emperor and in which the Jews, not the Persians, would be the imperial people.

'Deutero-Isaiah's' creative new departures were on the spiritual, not on the political, plane. He was a monotheist, and he grappled with the problem of suffering. 'Deutero-Isaiah' is the earliest indubitable Jewish monotheist, and the earliest anywhere since Akhenaton's abortive monotheism eight centuries earlier. 'Deutero-Isaiah' did not merely believe that Yahweh was the sole legitimate object of worship for Jews, or that Yahweh was more righteous and more powerful than the gods of other nations. He believed that Yahweh was the only god, and that other gods were non-existent. 'Deutero-Isaiah's' attitude to suffering was the antithesis of the Buddha's. 'Deutero-Isaiah' did not seek a way of release from suffering; he accepted suffering as an experience that could bear positive spiritual fruit. We do not know whether 'the suffering servant' stands, as he does ostensibly, for an unnamed but historical individual, or whether he is a personification of the Jewish community. The second of these two possible interpretations of this enigmatic figure is the more convincing; it is more in line with the prophetic tradition to which 'Deutero-Isaiah' was attaching himself. In any case, it is clear that 'Deutero-Isaiah' believed that suffering, patiently borne, can be a creative experience for all concerned, including the sufferer himself in the denouement of his tragedy. 'Deutero-Isaiah's' writings are perhaps the earliest in which this attitude towards suffering is to be found.

Zarathustra saw the world as a battlefield between good and evil. Good is destined to win the battle eventually; meanwhile, it is Man's duty to be an active combatant on the side of the good god against this god's evil adversary. Zarathustra's vision and precept perhaps reflect the historical situation at the time and place in which this prophet lived. In the borderland between the Eurasian pastoral nomads and their sedentary neighbours, there was a perpetual border warfare in which the sedentary party hoped to win a definitive victory eventually, and, in this historical warfare, Zarathustra was certainly a militant opponent of the nomads.

Confucius was an ethical reformer who saw himself, no doubt sincerely, as a conscientious conservative. He was born into a society that had fallen out of its traditional framework and had lost its bearings. His intention was to rehabilitate precious ancestral institutions that were in danger of being discarded, but his remedies were actually innovations. For instance, he interpreted the word *chün tzu*, which meant 'nobleman' in the genealogical sense of 'son of a lord', as really meaning 'noble man', in the sense of a man who lives up to ethically noble standards of conduct. This interpretation was not the revival of an old meaning; it was the introduction of a new meaning. Confucius' 'rectification of names' endowed Chinese society with a new ideal.

The Buddha set out to eradicate the self-centredness and the greed that are innate in every living being. He had an intuition that the human spirit is capable of overcoming Nature; he had the courage to translate this intuition into action; and, when his own action had won for him his enlightenment, compassion led him to show the way to his fellow sentient beings. The Buddha attained his enlightenment when he recognized that the practice of extreme physical austerity was not the means by which enlightenment could be reached. Henceforth he followed a middle way that seems austere to ordinary people but seemed lax to unbridled contemporary ascetics. The Buddha's middle way has been vindicated by the contrast between the respective subsequent fortunes of Buddhism and Jainism—a religion founded by the Buddha's contemporary Vardhamana, known by his followers as 'the Jina' ('the victor') or 'the Mahavira' ('the Great Hero').

It has been noted already that the Buddha and Pythagoras shared both a belief and an objective. Their common belief was that death is not the end of life, but is normally followed by re-birth, and that the series of deaths and re-births will continue *ad infinitum* if strenuous measures are not taken for breaking this sorrowful circle. To break it was the two seers' common objective. The combination of this belief with this objective is peculiar; the belief, unassociated with the objective, is wide-spread. The idea that recurrence is the basic rhythm of the universe is suggested by familiar physical phenomena: the alternation of day and night; the annual recurrence of an identical series of seasons; the repeated replacement of one generation of living creatures by another. The belief that the generation-cycle is accounted for by re-birth is expressed in the practice of naming children after their grandparents.

In the Hellenic World the particular belief in re-birth, as distinct from the general belief in recurrence, started as a peculiar tenet of Pythagoras and his disciples but gradually gained a wider currency, notwithstanding the political disaster that the Pythagorean fraternity incurred. In India, the belief in re-birth seems to have been taken for granted by both the Buddha and his opponents. This common belief was at the root of their difference of opinion over the question whether there is or is not such a thing as a soul. The Buddha's opponents held not only that the soul is a reality but that this reality is identical with the ultimate reality (*Tat tvam asi*). The Buddha held that what is re-born is not a soul but is a mere tissue of disparate psychic states which are held together, from re-birth to re-birth, by nothing but the dynamic force of greed. If greed can be eradicated, this psychic cloud-wrack can be dissipated, so the Buddha held; and this opens the way for an exit into the state of 'extinguishedness' (Nirvana), in which there is a cessation of suffering.

Possibly the Buddha and his opponents were not so much at variance with each other as they were held to be by both parties to the controversy. The Buddha's opponents were making a statement: 'The soul is identical with ultimate reality'. The Buddha was giving a directive: 'Make your exit into "extinguishedness" by dissipating the psychic cloud-wrack that my opponents call "the soul".' It is possible that the Buddha's and his opponents' vision of the nature of ultimate spiritual reality did not differ from each other irreconcilably after all.

A confidence in the human spirit's capacity to overcome greed; a belief in the creative power of suffering endured patiently; a call to make an exit into 'extinguishedness'; a belief that there is only one God; a call to be a combatant on the side of Good against Evil: since these beliefs were declared, and these directives were given, by five great seers in the sixth century B.C., the vision of ultimate reality and the directives for human conduct have been transformed irrevocably.

The five sixth-century-B.C. seers were born and lived and worked in five different regional settings. It is perhaps significant that none of the five were children of the two oldest civilizations of all, namely the Sumero-Akkadian and the Pharaonic Egyptian. In the sixth century B.C. these two ancient civilizations were still in existence, but the new visions and the new directives came from regions whose civilizations were less venerable but were, at this date, more dynamic.

26

THE FIRST PERSIAN EMPIRE,

c. 550–330 B.C.

ASSYRIAN militarism, especially in its last and most demonic phase (745–605 B.C.), had been a tribulation for all its victims, including the Assyrians themselves. The devastation had been aggravated by a Eurasian nomad invasion. The immediate sequel to the fall of the Assyrian Empire had left the Levant politically divided and insecure. The measure of this tormented region's need for peace and order is given by the ease with which the Levant was united politically by Persian empire-builders within the quarter of a century *c.* 550–525 B.C. The Persian Empire gave the Levant a sorely-needed rest-cure. Its wars of conquest were less brutal than the Assyrians'; the administrative organization of the vast conquered territories was less oppressive. Unlike the Assyrians, the Persians were content to make their presence felt to the minimum degree required for making their sovereignty effective. They gave latitude to the existing local authorities; the Persian provincial governors' role was to supervise rather than take over local administration. Above all, the Persians made a point of respecting and patronizing their subjects' religions—an enlightened policy that did much to win acquiescence in Persian rule, except in the rare but embarrassing cases in which a subject community was torn by religious dissension in which it was difficult for the Persian authorities to preserve neutrality.

The Persian Imperial Government's toleration of alien religions is the more creditable and the more remarkable, considering that Darius I and at least his immediate successor Xerxes are shown, by their own inscriptions, to have embraced a religion which was akin to Zarathustra's —and militancy, not toleration, had been Zarathustra's spirit. In this spirit, Zarathustra had rejected the traditional religion of the Iranian-speaking peoples and had replaced it by a new one. Zarathustra believed that he had been commissioned to propagate this faith by the one good god, Ahura Mazda, to whom he had given his undivided allegiance. We do not know how far Darius I and Xerxes committed themselves to Zarathustra's religion. They do not avow themselves to be Zarathustra's followers; indeed they do not mention his name. The prophet himself must have been born about a century before Darius I, and his mission-field seems to have been the north-eastern part of the region inhabited by sedentary Iranian-speaking peoples (the present-day Khorasan, Soviet Central Asia, and Afghan Uzbekistan).

This region had been annexed to the Persian Empire by Cyrus II, probably at some date later than 539 B.C., and Darius' father was the Persian governor of Khorasan (Parthia) in 522 B.C., when Darius him-self assassinated and supplanted the false or authentic Smerdis. Darius' branch of the House of Achaemenes may not have become semi-con-verts to Zarathustra's religion till after 539 B.C., and we do not know whether, at this stage, even a diluted form of Zoroastrianism was adopted by the Persian and the Median people as well as by the Achae-menidae. Evidently Darius I was no friend of the Magi—the Median people's hereditary priesthood, who eventually took over Zarathustra's religion in a form that might not have been acceptable to the founder.

The Persian emperors' religious, as well as their political, liberalism reconciled to Persian rule the peoples of Syria, who had resisted so strenuously first their Assyrian and then their Babylonian conquerors. In the eyes of the Phoenicians, Samaritans, and Jews, the Persians were liberators.

The incorporation of the Phoenicians in the Persian Empire gave Phoenician traders a huge continental hinterland, while, in the Mediter-ranean, it won for them Persian support in their competition with their commercial rivals, the Greeks. The Asian Greeks had, like the Phoe-nicians, become Persian subjects; but they were recalcitrant subjects, whereas the Syrophoenicians played the Persians' game and won their favour. Three Syrophoenician city-states—Aradus, Tyre, and Sidon—were given miniature local empires of their own. The Phoenicians had no temptation to be disloyal to the Persians, and the Persians therefore had no fear that the colonial Phoenician city-states would try to meddle in Syria. The Persians did not try to incorporate the Libyphoenicians, as well as the Syrophoenicians, in their empire. On the contrary, they made an anti-Greek entente with Carthage when, towards the close of the sixth century B.C., the colonial Phoenician city-states formed a united front under Carthaginian command.

The Babylonian Jewish community was also the Persians' natural ally, since these expatriate Jews had not forgiven the Babylonians for having deported them. They were therefore a Persophile local minority and, as such, they were valuable to the Persians in a Babylonia in which the native majority of the population was irreconcilable, notwithstanding

Cyrus II's tactful gesture of signifying, by 'taking the hands of Bel', that he intended to respect the Babylonians' national *amour propre*. Cyrus II gave leave, to as many of the Jewish deportees as wished, to repatriate themselves in Judaea and to rebuild their temple at Jerusalem. Cyrus II's decree was traced in the archives at Ecbatana (Hamadan), and was then confirmed, by Darius I. Either Artaxerxes I in 445 B.C. or Artaxerxes II in 384 B.C. gave his Babylonian Jewish butler, Nehemiah, leave of absence from Susa, the Persian imperial capital, with a commission to go to Judaea and to refortify the city of Jerusalem. Both Darius I and Artaxerxes made a grant of imperial revenue and building-materials to the Jews for carrying out the public works at Jerusalem that they had authorized.

The Persian Empire was profitable for the Aramaeans as well as for the Jews and for the Phoenicians. The spread of the Aramaean script and language, which had begun under the Assyrian regime, made further progress under the Persian regime. In Syria the Canaanite (Hebrew) language was gradually supplanted by Aramaic. In Syria, Canaanite survived only as a liturgical language. As a language in everyday use it survived only in the colonial Phoenician World in the western basin of the Mediterranean. Eastward, the use of Aramaic continued to spread hand in hand with the Aramaic alphabet—a much more convenient script than the cuneiform. The Persians, like the Phoenicians at Ugarit seven or eight centuries earlier, invented an alphabet composed of characters selected from the Sumero-Akkadian repertory. Darius I, in his trilingual record of his acts on the cliff-face at Behistan, carved a Persian version in the Persian cuneiform alphabet side by side with Elamite and Akkadian versions in which the cuneiform characters were used in the traditional clumsy Sumerian way. However, the Persian cuneiform alphabet had the same fate as the Ugaritic. It failed to hold its own against an alphabet stemming from the one, composed of simpler and plainer letters, that had become current in Phoenicia at an early date in the last millennium B.C. By 330 B.C. most of the Persian Empire's official papers were being written in the Aramaic language and script; but these documents were probably being read in Persian—the group of letters composing an Aramaic word being pronounced as if it were the Aramaic word's Persian equivalent.

Thus the principal Syrian peoples were content to be Persian subjects. The Persians' kinsmen, the Medes, were less happy, as they showed by revolting in 522 B.C. They remembered that they themselves had formerly been an imperial people, and that the Persians had been their vassals. However, in spite of their revolt, the Persians re-admitted the Medes to partnership in a Medo-Persian Empire that was greater and grander than the former Median Empire. The Elamites were probably flattered by the promotion of their national capital, Susa, to the status of an imperial capital. The north-eastern Iranian-speaking peoples demonstrated their attachment to the Persian Empire when, after its fall, they maintained a three-year resistance-movement against the Persians' Macedonian Greek conquerors. The eastern nomad Skyths (the pointed-hood Sakas), who had resisted Cyrus II, seem to have become loyal to the Persian Empire after they had been subdued by Darius I. In Xerxes' campaign in European Greece in 480 B.C., they were given posts of trust, and in 330–328 B.C. they assisted their sedentary neighbours in their resistance to Alexander the Great.

Three subject peoples, however, proved irreconcilable to Persian rule, namely the Babylonians, the Egyptians, and the Asian Greeks. The Babylonians revolted not once, but twice, in the critical year 522 B.C. They revolted again in 484 B.C., but, this time, the Persians repressed the revolt so crushingly that, from then onwards, the Babylonians lay low till they were eventually liberated by Alexander. The Persians could not afford to let Babylonia escape from their control. Babylonia was the granary and the workshop of the Persian Empire, and it was also the central node of the Empire's internal network of overland communications. On the other hand, the occupation of Egypt was superfluous for the Persian Empire, as it had been for its Assyrian predecessor; Egypt was even farther from Fars than it was from Assyria; and, in revolting against a continental Asian master, Egypt could count on receiving support from the Greeks by sea. Though Egypt had lain low in 522 B.C., she revolted before the end of Darius I's reign; she was independent again from 464 to 455 B.C., and, once more, from 404 or 395 to 343 B.C. Egypt was then reconquered by the Persians only a dozen years before the Persian Empire itself was overthrown.

Even if all the subjects of the Persian Empire had been as loyal to it as were the Phoenicians and the Jews, its sheer size would have made communications a pressing problem for the Imperial Government. Overland communications were speeded up by the building of trunk roads and the provision of relays of horses for governmental despatch-riders, but Darius I saw that he must also try to link his empire's extremities by water. He sent a Carian seaman, Scylax, from the easternmost province of the Empire to the nearest navigable waterway in the Indus basin, with instructions to make for the Red Sea coast of Egypt via the Indus River and the Indian Ocean. When Scylax duly accomplished his mission, Darius annexed the Indus basin; and either after this, or in anticipation of it, he finished cutting the canal that Pharaoh Necho II had started to cut from the easternmost arm of the Nile delta to the head of the Gulf of Suez. Xerxes tried to repeat Necho II's feat of circumnavigating Africa. But Xerxes' squadron, which set out, not from the Red Sea, but from the Mediterranean, turned back, and Darius' and Xerxes' oceanic-mindedness was not inherited by their successors.

The First Persian Empire was short-lived, but its policy of religious toleration had an enduring effect. This policy confirmed the tendency towards syncretism that had already been stimulated by the Assyrian and Babylonian policy of deportation. A conqueror could deport a conquered country's human 'establishment', but not its gods. The remaining native peasantry would continue to worship them, and alien incomers would have to reckon with them. The cult of Yahweh at Bethel, the principal religious shrine of the extinct Kingdom of Israel, was carried eastward into Babylonia and southward to Elephantinê, the frontier fortress at the foot of the First Cataract of the Nile, where, in the fifth century B.C., the gods Eshem Bethel and Anath Bethel were worshipped, side by side with Yahweh, by a Jewish garrison in the Persian service, recruited from descendants of the Judahites who had taken refuge in Egypt to escape being deported to Babylonia by Nebuchadnezzar.

The Jewish community at Elephantinê was in friendly correspondence with Sanballat, the headman of the Samaria district, in which Jerusalem was included under the Persian regime before Nehemiah's mission. Sanballat was the descendant of a Babylonian deportee, to judge by his name (Sinuballit); but, to judge by his sons' names (Delaiah and Shelemaiah), he and they were Yahweh-worshippers, not Moon-worshippers. (The present-day Samaritans are strictly monotheistic Yahweh-worshippers who do not accept as canonical any of the written scriptures beyond the Pentateuch, and do not admit the existence of any unwritten scriptures.) However, Sanballat came into conflict with Nehemiah when this representative of the Babylonian Jewish community arrived at Jerusalem with a commission from the Persian Emperor.

The Persians were impartially well-disposed to the Babylonian, Elephantinian, and Samaritan Yahweh-worshippers, but, by Nehemiah's and Ezra's time, the Babylonian Jews had a programme of religious and social apartheid from all other communities, and they succeeded in imposing this programme on the Judaean *am ha-aretz* ('the people of the land', i.e. the peasantry who had not been uprooted). The intermingling of populations and religions had been followed by intermarriage—especially among the leading families, whose range of social relations was wider than the peasants' range. Intermarriage had been having the humanizing effect of breaking down the social barriers between communities, after these had paid for their traditional hostility to each other by forfeiting their independence. Nehemiah and Ezra forbade intermarriage, and they excommunicated those members of the Judaean Jewish community who had committed what, in Babylonian Jewish eyes, was a heinous offence.

By Nehemiah's and Ezra's time, the descendants of the Jewish deportees in Babylonia had succeeded in preserving their own communal identity for at least 150 years, and for 200 years if their patron Artaxerxes was the second, not the first, Achaemenian Persian Emperor who bore that name. This had been a remarkable *tour de force*; this one batch of deportees had succeeded in swimming against the tide that, in the Levant, had been setting so strongly towards a transcendence of traditional tribalism and a recognition of the brotherhood of Man. The Jewish deportees in Babylonia had successfully resisted this tendency among themselves, and they had now reversed it in Judaea too, but this at the cost of reviving the traditional hostility between the Judaean Jews and their neighbours—including those neighbours who, like the Judaean and the Babylonian Jews, were Yahweh-worshippers.

How had the Babylonian Jews managed to preserve their separate communal identity under the adverse conditions of exile? They had achieved this unique result by creating a unique institution, the synagogue. King Josiah had made it an article of Judahite faith that the liturgical worship of Yahweh could not be performed legitimately anywhere except in the temple at Jerusalem. The destruction of the temple there and the deportation to Babylonia of the Judahite 'establishment' had deprived the hereditary priests of their role, pending the rebuilding of the temple and the re-inauguration of the liturgy in it. The synagogue was the new institution that filled this vacuum, and, but for this new institution, the descendants of the 4,600 Judahite deportees in Babylonia might have lost their corporate identity as irretrievably as the descendants of the 27,290 Israelite deportees in Media. The synagogue was a weekly meeting—eventually held in a permanent meeting-house—in which the deportees' portable possessions (the books of the Law (Torah) and of the Prophets) were read and discussed. Hezekiah's and Josiah's innovations, which had been revolutionary before the deportation, became orthodox after the event. The Torah was now scrupulously observed, and the Prophets were posthumously honoured, by the deportees and their descendants, and this sovereign prescription for the preservation of the Babylonian Jewish community's corporate identity, which had worked wonders in Babylonia itself, was now imposed on the Jewish community in Judaea with the Persian Imperial Government's acquiescence.

In enabling Nehemiah and Ezra to do their decisive work, the Persian Imperial Government was unwittingly reversing its own general policy of toleration. This exceptional complaisance with a breach of one of the most important of the Persian Government's own rules was a negative act of state. It is one of the ironies of history that this negative act was fraught with more momentous consequences than any positive act to which the Persian Government ever committed itself.

27

THE CONFRONTATION BETWEEN THE FIRST PERSIAN EMPIRE AND THE HELLENIC WORLD, 499–330 B.C.

THE First Persian Empire's Medo-Persian 'establishment' and the contemporary citizenry of the Greek city-states were each enthralled by a political institution, and their enthralment was the more onerous because it was a voluntary self-dedication. The Medes' and Persians' political loyalty was focused on a person, the Achaemenian Emperor; the Greeks' loyalty was focused on deified abstractions, sovereign city-states. When these two loyalties came into conflict with each other, permanent peaceful co-existence between the two parties became impracticable. One party must eventually overthrow and supplant the other. In 499 B.C., when the Persian Empire's Asian Greek subjects revolted and received military support from two European Greek states, Athens and Eretria, it seemed as if the Persian Empire was now bound to conquer and annex the whole of the Hellenic World. The Persian Empire was the largest and most populous political structure that had ever been built; its Greek opponents were split up politically into hundreds of sovereign city-states, and many of these were perpetually at war with each other. Within the period of Graeco-Persian confrontation, 499–330 B.C., there were only two short spells—the two years 480–479 and the eight years 337–330—during which a certain number of Greek states formed a common front against the Persian Empire. On the first of these occasions the Greeks repulsed a formidable Persian invasion of European Greece; on the second occasion they themselves invaded and conquered the Persian Empire. During the interval between these two spells of Greek political co-operation, Greek political discord gave the First Persian Empire a reprieve, and thus gave it time to produce enduring effects on the religious and cultural planes.

By the date, c. 546 B.C., at which the continental Asian Greek city-states had been first subjugated by Persia, all of them except Miletus had already been subjugated by Lydia, which Persia had now annexed.

However, the Lydians had been the Greeks' familiar neighbours, and they had acquired a tincture of the Hellenic civilization. On the other hand, the Persians were, in Greek eyes, exotic strangers. The enlargement of the Asian Greeks' commercial hinterland through their incorporation in the Persian Empire did not reconcile them to their change of political masters.

The Asian Greeks' revolt took the Persians six years (499–494 B.C.) to suppress and taught the Persians that they had not yet secured a tenable north-west frontier. The Aegean Sea was a Greek lake; the Persians could not hold its east shore securely unless and until they conquered its west shore too; and this would commit them to annexing the rest of the Hellenic World. It has already been mentioned that, before the revolt of Darius I's Asian Greek subjects in 499 B.C., Darius had established a European bridgehead between the lower course of the River Danube and Mount Olympus. This included one Greek kingdom, Macedon, besides the Greek colonial trading-posts along the coast of Europe between the Danube delta and Mount Olympus. This Persian bridgehead was a greater threat to the rest of the European Greeks than it was to the Skyths. Darius had also already sent a naval squadron to reconnoitre the colonial annex of the Hellenic World to the west of the Straits of Otranto.

In 490 B.C. Darius sent a punitive expeditionary force by sea against Eretria and Athens. The Eretrians were overcome and were deported, but the Athenians then repulsed the Persians single-handed. In 480–479 B.C. Darius I's son and successor Xerxes invaded European Greece overland from the north. Almost all the European Greek city-states to the east of the Straits of Otranto, except Athens and Sparta together with Sparta's allies, had previously recognized the Persian Emperor's suzerainty. Argos, Sparta's defeated and embittered rival in the Peloponnesos, remained neutral. In 480 B.C., Attica was occupied and Athens was sacked. But the population had been evacuated and the navies of the belligerent Greek states were intact. In 480 B.C. they won a decisive victory over the Persian armada at Salamis, and this was followed in 479 B.C. by an equally decisive Greek victory on land at Plataea in Boeotia and by a second Greek naval victory off Mycale, on the west coast of Asia Minor. The Asian Greeks now revolted again, and the Persian Empire also lost its European possessions, including the Greek Kingdom of Macedon. When, in 449 B.C., Athens and the Persian Empire eventually made peace with each other, Persia had failed to reconquer the continental Asian Greeks, while Athens had failed to detach Cyprus and Egypt from the Persian Empire. However, in 386 B.C. Persia was able to re-impose her sovereignty over the continental Asian Greek states in collusion with Sparta. By that date the European

Greeks' resumption of their customary fratricidal warfare had played into the Persians' hands.

The European Greeks had been blind to the lesson of the years 480–479 B.C. In those two memorable years a minority of the still unsubjugated minority of the Greeks had defeated the Persian Empire by standing together. In 480 B.C. a momentarily united minority of the western colonial Greeks had likewise defeated the Carthaginian Empire. These two empires had been menaces to the Greek states' independence because of the large-scale political unification which each empire had achieved; the Greeks had defeated each of them by partially uniting with each other at the eleventh hour. The Greeks ought to have recognized the obvious truth that, in politics, union is strength. They ought to have made their own political union permanent and Panhellenic. The Hellenic World had already become an economic unity as a result of its commercial and industrial revolution in the seventh century B.C. Economic unity and political disunity cannot co-exist for long without disaster. Yet, as soon as the immediate danger from Persia and from Carthage was over, the Greeks fell apart again. The Siceliot Greek principality, centred since *c.* 484 B.C. on Syracuse, which, in alliance with Akragas, had defeated Carthage in 480 B.C., disintegrated in 466 B.C. Meanwhile, in 478 B.C., the continental European Greek alliance that had defeated Persia in 480–479 B.C. had split into two rival leagues, an old one, consisting of Sparta and her Peloponnesian allies, and a new one, the Delian league, consisting of Athens and the Greek city-states that had just been liberated from Persian rule.

In 459 B.C. Athens went to war with Sparta's allies in European Greece while she was still at war with Persia. In 460 B.C. she had committed herself more deeply and more hazardously to her war with Persia by sending a fleet to support an Egyptian insurrection, and in 454 B.C. the Athenian expeditionary force was destroyed after the Egyptian rebels had succumbed to a Persian counter-attack. Meanwhile, in 457 B.C. Athens had imposed her suzerainty on all the states in continental central Greece except Thebes. In 447 B.C. she lost her hold over them. The Athenians had egregiously overtaxed their strength, and, after making peace with Persia in 449 B.C., they had to make peace with Sparta and her allies in 445 B.C.

After 478 B.C. the Athenians had soon turned the Delian league into an Athenian Empire, and after 445 B.C. this empire survived for another forty years. It was a large-scale replica of Sparta's empire in the southern two-fifths of the Peloponnesos. Athens's serfs were the populations of the subject Greek city-states from whom she took tribute. In 461 B.C. the Athenian citizen-body had given itself a constitution that was as radically democratic as the Spartans'. Like the Spartan democracy, the Athenian democracy now lived off the tribute of a subject Greek population, far larger than the dominant minority. Though Athens had a larger citizen-body than any contemporary Greek city-state, the peace-settlements of 449 and 445 B.C. had demonstrated that Athens's weak point was the disparity between her man-power and her ambitions. Yet in 451 B.C. the Athenians actually voted to reduce their own numbers by disenfranchising every citizen who had even one non-Athenian-born parent. This Ezra-like act, which spelled the Athenian Empire's doom, was implemented in 445/4 B.C. This was a reversal of Solon's statesmanlike acts. In 590 B.C., Solon had enlarged Athens's citizen-body by repatriating Athenian insolvent debtors who had been sold into slavery abroad, and, as has been mentioned, he had given Athenian citizenship to immigrant alien artisans.

In 431 B.C. Athens and Sparta blundered into another war with each other that was disastrous for both. The Athenian Empire was overthrown in 405 B.C.; a Spartan empire that supplanted it was overthrown in 371 B.C.; between 359 and 338 B.C., all the city-states of continental European Greece, except Sparta, were dominated progressively by their northern neighbour, King Philip II of Macedon, and were finally compelled by him to join a new league, with its official headquarters at Corinth but with Philip as its president. The League of Corinth's agenda was to attack the Persian Empire with the League's united forces. An advance-guard of the Macedonian Army was already in Asia when, in 336 B.C., Philip was assassinated in the prime of life and at the peak of his career. Philip's son Alexander crossed the Dardanelles in 334 B.C.; by 330 B.C. he had overthrown the Persian Empire; by 323 B.C., he too was dead.

The Macedonians were Greeks, but they had not become Hellenes— that is to say, they had not become citizens of city-states, and had therefore remained strangers to the city-state way of life. The effect of the city-state system and mentality on international relations had been anarchic, and this had given Philip II his opportunity; the successive international failures of the city-states, Athens, Sparta, and Thebes, had worked together with Philip's personal genius to make Macedon's fortune. However, the city-state way of life, in spite of its international disruptiveness and its domestic factiousness, had had a stimulating cultural influence, which is the subject of the following chapter. The Macedonian Greeks had not been exposed to this civilizing influence; in their private lives, they were still undisciplined, and they were therefore not yet fit to assume the leadership that had been thrust upon them by the political bankruptcy of their Southern-Greek neighbours.

King Philip II, like his Macedonian countrymen, was undisciplined in his private life, but, in his public life, Philip was un-Macedonian. He was as patient and as astute as Themistocles, the Athenian whose fore-sight had saved Greece in 480–479 B.C., and as Pharaoh Psammetichus I, who had deftly pushed the Assyrians out of Egypt. If either Philip or his son Alexander had had as long a life as Psammetichus I, the subsequent history of the Hellenic World, and perhaps of the whole Oikoumenê, might have been less unhappy.

[28]

THE HELLENIC CIVILIZATION'S CULTURAL ACHIEVEMENTS, 478–338 B.C.

DURING the years 478–338 B.C., the Hellenic World sank to its political nadir and rose to its cultural zenith, and at least three famous fifth-century Athenians are implicated in Hellas's contemporary political disgrace, besides having contributed to her contemporary cultural glory. These three are the dramatic poet Sophocles (495–406 B.C.), the statesman Pericles (c. 490–429 B.C.), and the philosopher Socrates (469–399 B.C.).

Pericles' name is celebrated in virtue of its association with the Athenian acme of Hellenic architecture and visual art, and he did inspire his fellow-countrymen to adorn the acropolis of Athens with supremely beautiful works, after the conclusion of peace with Persia in 449 and with Sparta in 445 B.C. But it was also Pericles who prompted the Athenians to finance these works—and, in financing them, to provide remunerative employment for themselves—by diverting to this purpose the annual tribute exacted from Athens's Greek subjects. Common defence, not the adornment of Athens, had been the original purpose of these payments. The fund had been raised for paying Athenian naval crews, and when the restoration of peace had put an end to active Athenian naval operations the payments ought to have been remitted instead of being allocated to the same Athenians in their new civilian capacities as quarrymen, hauliers, and masons. This 'conversion' of the fund was dishonest; the sole sanction for it was Athenian armed force.

Sophocles and Socrates each raised the issue of conscience versus a morally unacceptable demand made on a citizen by a state. Sophocles raised this issue in a play; Socrates raised it by drawing upon himself a death-sentence for conscience' sake. Sophocles is said to have been rewarded for his play by being elected one of the generals who were commissioned to crush an attempt made in 440 B.C. by Athens's ally, Samos, to shake off the Athenian yoke. It is strange that this commission was accepted by the author of the *Antigone*. It is still more strange that Socrates willingly served in 432 B.C. in an Athenian expeditionary force that was operating against another insurgent ally of Athens, Poteidaia. Evidently, in both Socrates' and Sophocles' eyes, the state of which he was a citizen was a god that, in a conflict with other states, must be served, 'right or wrong', by its citizen-devotees, even though, in other situations, they might feel that their conscience had the paramount claim on their allegiance.

In an appeal to Sparta on the eve of the Second Atheno–Peloponnesian War, the Corinthians denounced Athens as a 'tyrant city', and, in the course of this war, an Athenian politician is reported to have told his countrymen that Athens must not shrink from committing atrocities if she wished to retain her empire. After the Athenian Empire's fall, her victorious opponents razed the 'Long Walls', connecting Athens with her harbours, which had made her impregnable to attacks by land, and this was greeted, throughout the Hellenic World, as an act of liberation. Yet the contemporary historian—the exiled Athenian naval officer Thucydides—makes another Athenian politician, Pericles himself, describe Athens as 'the education of Hellas'. Both these descriptions of fifth-century Athens are well warranted.

Fifth-century Athens was, in truth, 'the Hellas of Hellas' in the sense in which Athens had previously played this role in the Protogeometric and Geometric Ages of Hellenic history. Once again, the Hellenic World's cultural activity was focused at this particular geographical point. The Periclean Attic sculptor Pheidias was employed to make not only the statue of Athene for her new temple on the acropolis of Athens but also the statue of Zeus at Olympia. This was a remarkable recognition of the cultural pre-eminence of Athens; for, though Olympia was a Panhellenic ceremonial centre, it lay within the domain of the Peloponnesian alliance, headed by Sparta; and the adornment of Olympia to celebrate the repulse of the Persians in 480–479 B.C. was to some extent a Peloponnesian riposte to the contemporary adornment of Athens.

Of course, even in the fifth century B.C., there was no Athenian monopoly of Hellenic cultural achievements. The Parthenon at Athens was not only matched by the temple of Zeus at Olympia; it was surpassed in physical scale by temples built, rather earlier in the same age, in the Siceliot Greek city-states Akragas and Selinous. The most eminent composer of odes commissioned by the victors (including some Athenian victors) at the Panhellenic festivals was the Theban poet Pindar (*c*. 522–442 B.C.). The Italiot Greek city Elea was the seat of the uncompromisingly monist school of Greek philosophy represented by Parmenides (*c*. 515–445 B.C.) and Zeno (*c*. 490–420 B.C.); and the reversion to pluralism, associated with a Pythagorean belief in re-birth, was the work of the philosopher-medicine-man Empedocles of Akragas (*c.* 492–432 B.C.). At the time of the Second Atheno–Peloponnesian War (431–404 B.C.) the art of using language as an engine for producing practical effects, moral or immoral, was invented by adepts whom their opponents denigrated by calling them sophists ('cleverness-mongers'). One of the earliest of the sophists was Gorgias from the Siceliot Greek city-state Leontini (*c.* 480–395 B.C.). Sophists soon sprang up all over the Greek World, and many of them repaired to Athens because Athens was, at the time, the most powerful Hellenic city-state. Yet none of the eminent sophists was an Athenian born—unless we follow Aristophanes in his libellous misrepresentation of Socrates.

The distinctive major Athenian contributions to the Hellenic culture of the fifth century B.C. were in the fields of dramatic art, philosophy, and vase-painting.

Fifth-century Attic drama, both tragic and comic, differed from both the Homeric epic poetry and from the post-Homeric elegiac and lyric poetry in being a religious rite, but, unlike the Homeric poetry, it was also as personal and individual as the elegiac and lyric poetry had been. This was an astonishing outcrop from a ritual that had originally been crudely sexual and ecstatic and that never shed all traces of its origin. The purpose of this licentious ritual had not been pornographic; it had been designed to stimulate the fertility of human beings and domesticated plants and animals by sympathetic magic. However, other outcrops from it were the Bacchic orgies of the Hellenic World, the orgiastic worship of the goddess Cybele in Asia Minor, the effusions of the Montanist prophetesses, the hypnotic dance of the Mevlevi dervishes, and the frenzy of the band of prophets who had infected King Saul in Syria in the eleventh century B.C.

The Attic dramatists were performing an extraordinary feat of sublimation when they elicited from this unpromising primitive religious material a drama in which the problems and the pageant of human life were presented in an interplay between a chorus and a team of actors whose parts on the stage were as individual as those played in public life by the eighth-century-B.C. Israelite or Judahite prophets. The surviving works of four fifth-century-B.C. Athenian dramatists—the tragedy-writers Aeschylus (525–456 B.C.), Sophocles (495–406 B.C.), and Euripides (480–406 B.C.), and the comedy-writer Aristophanes (*c.* 449–380 B.C.) —reveal both the brilliance and the diversity of these dramatic poets' genius. They fashioned the genre of art which they worked into an instrument for commenting on controversial current political issues and for plumbing the spiritual depths of human nature.

Fifth-century Athens was not the mother of Hellenic philosophy. This had been brought to birth in sixth-century Ionia. But Socrates gave this

Ionian intellectual activity a new turn by deliberately shifting his field of inquiry from the physical universe to human nature. Socrates' life and death were the dominant inspiration of his pupil Plato (427–347 B.C.), though Plato was also a disciple of the ex-Samian Crotoniate philosopher Pythagoras, and found in the Syracusan dramatist Epicharmus a model for the dialogue form in which he cast his philosophical works. Plato's most original, and most controversial, contribution to Hellenic philosophical thought was a theory of knowledge which was also a theory of the structure of the Universe. Plato combined a Pythagorean confidence in a mathematical approach to metaphysics with a poet's intuition of the limits of logical thought and with the poet's ability to soar higher on the wings of myth.

Aristotle (384–322 B.C.) of Stageiros, a small colonial Greek city-state on the east coast of Chalcidicê, was Plato's pupil and subsequent critic, and was a temporary resident of Athens who could also make himself at home in Macedon, where he accepted an invitation from King Philip to serve for a time as tutor to Philip's son Alexander. Aristotle was neither a poet nor a mathematician; by Plato's standards he was pedestrian, and he would probably have plumed himself on keeping his feet on the ground. He was an intellectual giant of Plato's stature, and, in a lifetime that was shorter than Plato's by eighteen years, he carried out pioneer logical, epistemological, and metaphysical work which entered into all later Hellenic philosophy and dominated Western Christian thought from the twelfth to the seventeenth century of the Christian Era. Aristotle was also an original fact-finding researcher, and a skilful organizer of his pupils' research, in the fields of political and physical science. In the golden chain of Hellenic philosophers, Socrates and Plato and Aristotle outshine all their predecessors and successors, and Socrates shines the brightest of the three.

In the fifth century B.C. the Attic potters and vase-painters continued to hold the market, including the lucrative Etruscan market, that they had won in the sixth century B.C. from their Corinthian and Spartan competitors. It was not till the fourth century B.C. that the Attic ascendancy in the Italian market was threatened by the mass-production in Apulia of imitations of the current Attic style. Some of the best Attic vase-painters signed their works, and this indicates that these were regarded as works of art by the painters themselves and by their customers. The Attic vase-painters' surviving works are highly appreciated today. On the other hand, the vase-painters' Athenian contemporaries appear to have been less sensitive aesthetically to the beauty of this branch of Attic art, in spite, or perhaps because, of the importance of its vulgar economic role as an export that was profitable for Athens's balance of payments.

THE POLITICAL AFTERMATH OF ALEXANDER'S OVERTHROW OF THE FIRST PERSIAN EMPIRE,

329–221 B.C.

IN the course of the twenty-two years 359–338 B.C., King Philip II of Macedon had brought under his political control all the European Greek states to the east of the Straits of Otranto except Epirus, Sparta, and Byzantium. Within the ten years 334–325 B.C., Philip's son and successor Alexander had conquered the entire Persian Empire, including all the territory that it had ever held in the Indus basin, without losing control over the dominions that he had inherited from his father. For two years, 324–323 B.C., Alexander was in effective command of the whole of this central section of the Old-World Oikoumenê. In 324 B.C. he asserted his mastery over Greece by ordering all the city-states members of the League of Corinth to repatriate their exiled citizens. Alexander was planning to conquer the rest of the Oikoumenê, beginning with Arabia. (Neither he nor any of his contemporaries was aware of the extent of the inhabited part of the globe's land-surface.) But in 323 B.C. Alexander died prematurely, unexpectedly, and suddenly, and consequently his actual political achievement, though immense, was negative. He had lived just long enough to be able to destroy the Persian Empire, but not long enough to be able to establish the global empire that was his objective. He had vastly expanded the area of the Hellenic World by annexing to it the Persian Empire's domain bodily. But, at his death, this expanded Hellenic World relapsed into the anarchy in which the smaller pre-Alexandrine Hellenic World had been living before 338 B.C., the year in which Philip II had set up the League of Corinth.

Alexander's death gave the signal for a struggle to carve up his ephemeral realm. The states in Southern Greece, including Sparta, immediately took up arms against Macedon. In 322 B.C., all of them except Aetolia were compelled to capitulate, but in 321 B.C. the senior officers of the Macedonian army began to wage war against each other. The wars of Alexander's succession went on for forty years (321–281 B.C.),

and Philip II's, as well as Alexander's, unificatory work was soon undone. The rival heirs financed their contests with each other from the
bullion that the Persian Imperial Government had been exacting from
its subjects and hoarding for two centuries. They spent the hoard on
lavish competitive payments to the Macedonian troops, supplemented
by non-Macedonian Greek mercenaries, that each of the rivals managed
to enlist. The soldiers' pay was rapidly disseminated through the expanded Hellenic World, and the result was an inflation of the currency
that depressed the real wages of the civilian wage-earners in the seats of
Hellenic commerce and industry.

These wars between Alexander's successors were less brutal than the
wars that the Hellenic city-states had waged against each other before
peace had been imposed on them in 338 B.C. by Philip II. The citizens of
the deified city-states had fought each other with passionate hatred.
Alexander's successors, too, were deified by their subjects—or they
deified themselves—but they did not take their deification so seriously,
and in any case their paramount objective was plunder. The Hellenic
city-states, now *de facto* no longer sovereign, were the stakes in the successors' war-game, and the sinews of war were professional soldiers, not
the money with which the soldiers were paid. Therefore, instead of
slaughtering a defeated opponent's troops, the victor invited them to
change sides, and, instead of sacking cities, they 'liberated' them, which
was a euphemism for snatching from some rival war-lord the political
control over them. No Greek city was destroyed by Greek hands between
335 B.C., when Alexander sacked Thebes and sold its inhabitants into
slavery, and 223 B.C., when Mantinea was treated with the same barbarity by Antigonus Doson, the Regent of Macedon, and his allies.
(Within the same period, Akragas and other Greek cities to the west of
the Straits of Otranto were sacked, and their inhabitants enslaved, by
non-Greek hands.)

Even so, the wars of the successors, and the recurrent wars between
the successors' successors after that, kept the expanded Hellenic World
to the east of the Straits of Otranto in turmoil, and, for the majority of
the inhabitants of the territory of the former Persian Empire, the change
from Persian to Greek rule was a change for the worse. The Persian
regime had given its subjects the rest-cure that they had needed for
helping them to recuperate from the effects of the scourge of Assyrian
militarism. In contrast to the Assyrian Empire, the Persian Empire had
been loose-knit, and in its latter days it had been ramshackle and dis-
orderly. Egypt had seceded; provincial governors had revolted; highland
tribes had shaken off the Imperial Government's control. The Persian
yoke had been light by comparison with the Greek yoke by which it was
now replaced. In the post-Alexandrine, as in the pre-Alexandrine, Hel-

lenic World, the wars were chronic because they were inconclusive.

The country that suffered the most severely from the consequences of the vast Macedonian conquests was Macedon itself. The means by which Philip II had conquered Greece, and Alexander had then conquered the Persian Empire, had been the recruitment of an infantry from the Macedonian peasantry to supplement the aristocratic Macedonian cavalry. (The cavalry had continued to be the Macedonian Army's major arm; but it would not have been numerous enough to win and hold its conquests without the co-operation of the peasant phalanx.) When Alexander had invaded the Persian Empire, he had had to leave half the Macedonian Army behind in Europe to hold down the Southern Greeks and to hold off the northern barbarians. Macedon had then been drained of its last reserves of man-power to meet Alexander's constant demands for new drafts. After that, each of the successors kept at least a guards-corps of Macedonian troops to provide a nucleus for the private army with which he was conquering and holding his portion of the territorial spoils of Philip's and Alexander's realm. In 280–279 B.C., immediately after the end of the wars of Alexander's succession, Macedon was overrun by Celtic migrants from the Danube basin, and, when she had shaken off these barbarian invaders, she found herself, now with inadequate man-power, still having to fight on two fronts against northern barbarians who were still on the war-path and against Southern Greeks who had escaped from Macedon's control and were now taking the offensive against her.

Macedon's most effective Southern Greek opponent was the Aetolian Confederation. This was the only one of the insurgent Greek states that had not capitulated to Macedon in 322 B.C. *Circa* 300 B.C. the Aetolians established their political control over Delphi, a Panhellenic shrine which had retained its pre-Alexandrine importance. Aetolia then progressively incorporated the cantons to the north and to the east of her. By 235 B.C. she extended across continental Greece from coast to coast; in 226 B.C., at the brief high tide of her expansion, she advanced right up to Macedon's southern frontier. With Roman-like political large-mindedness, the Aetolians gave full Aetolian citizenship to the peoples whom they incorporated in their body politic.

Along the Peloponnesian shore of the Corinthian Gulf, the Achaean Confederation likewise started to expand in 251 B.C., but its acquisitions were less compact than Aetolia's, and it was no match for Aetolia in military strength. Moreover, the Achaean Confederation had a formidable competitor in Sparta, an older Peloponnesian power which remained indomitable, in spite of having been mulcted of territory by the Thebans in 369 B.C. and of more territory by Philip II in 338 B.C.

The two principal Greek successor-states of the Persian Empire were founded respectively by two of Alexander's officers, Ptolemy and Seleucus. Ptolemy acquired Egypt and the southern half of Syria; Seleucus acquired the major part, though much less than the whole, of the rest of the Persian Empire's Asian legacy. In north-western Asia Minor, Bithynia established its independence under a native dynasty; Pontic and Inland Cappadocia and North Media (Atropatênê; Azerbaijan) established theirs under Iranian dynasties. In 302 B.C., Seleucus had to cede the eastern fringe of Iran to an Indian empire-builder, Chandragupta Maurya, who, in 322 B.C., had been more successful than the Southern Greek states. Chandragupta had succeeded in expelling the Macedonian garrisons from the Indus basin and had then enlarged his realm to the magnitude of that of Seleucus by conquering the Empire of Magadha in the Ganges–Jumna basin.

The Seleucid Empire was too far-flung to be held together. In the last of the wars of succession, fought in 281 B.C., Seleucus had been the nominal victor; he had already re-crossed the Dardanelles, heading for Macedon, when he was assassinated; but the real victors had been a horde of migrant Celts who lodged themselves in the heart of Asia Minor and raided far and wide for the next half-century, till they were checked by a statelet that had been founded in 281 B.C. at Pergamon in western Asia Minor by a soldier of fortune who had taken possession of a substantial part of the ex-Persian treasure that had been lodged in the citadel there. About half way through the third century B.C., the extent of the Seleucid dominions was reduced drastically by the secession of the Greek governor of the province in the Oxus–Jaxartes basin and by the simultaneous occupation of Parthia, the next province to the west, by the Parni, a pastoral nomad people whose homeland was present-day Türkmenistan.

Inconclusiveness was the most disastrous feature of the wars that plagued Alexander's derelict heritage throughout the years 321–221 B.C. Macedon was unable to re-conquer Southern Greece, but the Southern Greeks were unable to prise off Macedon's hold on 'the three fetters' of Greece: Demetrias, Chalcis, and the acropolis of Corinth. The Achaeans liberated Corinth from Macedon in 243 B.C., but retroceded the acropolis of Corinth to Macedon in 225 B.C., as the price of Macedon's military intervention against Sparta on the Achaean Confederation's behalf. In 222 B.C. the Macedonians and Achaeans defeated the Spartans, and Sparta itself was occupied by a foreign army for the first time in its history; yet Sparta promptly recovered her independence and continued to count as a military power. Meanwhile, the naval command of the Aegean archipelago had been captured from Demetrius Poliorcetes by Ptolemy II and then from the Ptolemaic Empire by Macedon as a result of Macedonian naval victories off Cos *c.* 257 and off Andros *c.* 246

B.C. In 221 B.C. the fourth of the wars for the possession of southern Syria between the Ptolemaic and the Seleucid empires left this doggedly disputed territory still in the Ptolemaic Empire's hands.

The most important event of the year 221 B.C. in the Old-World Oikoumenê was the completion of the political unification of China through the Ch'in state's conquest and annexation in that year of the last of its six rivals. The unification of China was decisive and conclusive. It has never been undone more than partially and temporarily; in the 1970s a united China is playing a major part in world affairs. But in 221 B.C. the rest of the Old-World Oikoumenê, from India westward to the western basin of the Mediterranean, was on the eve of an Age of Agony from which the Mediterranean basin did not emerge till 31 B.C., and India not till A.D. 48.

[30]

THE DEVELOPMENT
AND DISSEMINATION OF
THE HELLENIC CIVILIZATION,
334–221 B.C.

THE year 334 B.C., in which Alexander crossed the Dardanelles, was not, of course, the starting-date of the Hellenic civilization's development and dissemination. By then, this civilization had been growing and spreading for more than four centuries. The process had begun in the eighth century B.C., when the Hellenic civilization had burst into flower after its long-drawn-out incubation. But, when the Greeks invaded the Persian Empire and overthrew it, they were disseminating their civilization on the grand scale self-consciously; they were confronting themselves with a choice between alternative policies for dealing with alien subject populations; and they were expanding the scale and transforming the conditions of their own life so suddenly and drastically that they needed to work out new philosophies to give them guidance and support in a social and ethical *terra incognita*.

In the course of the four centuries preceding Alexander's eastward expedition, earlier generations of Hellenes had prepared the way for him in this quarter. They had frequented Syria and Egypt as traders, had served in Egypt and Babylonia and in the Persian Empire as mercenary soldiers, and had been carried as deportees as far north-eastward as Soghd, beyond the River Oxus. The pre-Alexandrine coins of Greek city-states had circulated in the Persian Empire's markets in competition with the Imperial currency. In this direction, Greek settlements had been commercial, not agricultural, and they had been confined to Al-Mina (? Poseideïon) in Syria and to Naucratis in the Nile delta, but the Greeks had colonized in force the coasts of south-eastern Italy, Sicily, and Cyrenaïca, as well as the shores of the Straits leading into the Black Sea, and they had planted trading-posts along a large part of the Black Sea's perimeter. In Sicily by 334 B.C. the natives who had survived in the interior of the island had taken to speaking Greek and to living in city-states of the Hellenic type, while in Italy the Etruscans, Apulians, and other non-Greek peoples had adopted the Hellenic way of life in various degrees.

Now that the Persian Empire's vast domain had been conquered by Greek arms, the conquerors had to decide whether they should impose themselves as a master race on the conquered populations, or whether they should aim at living and inter-marrying on a footing of equality with their non-Hellenic fellow human beings. Alexander's former tutor Aristotle propounded the inhuman and unscientific racial thesis that Hellenes were born to be masters and non-Hellenes to be slaves; Alexander himself, however, and Aristotle's pupil Theophrastus opted for equality, and, before his premature death, Alexander had started to put this more generous-minded policy into effect, for the benefit of his Iranian subjects, at any rate. He had celebrated a festival of reconciliation and had promoted and rewarded Graeco–Iranian and other Graeco–Asiatic mixed marriages. Yet even Alexander seems to have taken it for granted that the cultural framework for the proposed racial fusion would be Hellenic, and this was the basis on which Alexander's policy was implemented by Seleucus I, the successor who secured for himself the largest slice of the Persian Empire's territorial spoils. Fusion between Greeks and Iranians seems to have been carried farthest in the Oxus–Jaxartes basin under the regime of the local Greek rulers who seceded from the Seleucid successor-state of the Persian Empire *c.* 250 B.C. On the other hand, in Egypt under the Ptolemaic regime this dynasty and its Greek agents behaved as if they were a master race. Here the Crown kept all except the most subordinate administrative posts in Greek hands, and all Greeks in Egypt co-operated with the Ptolemaic regime in exploiting the native Egyptians.

In 221 B.C. this illiberal Greek policy in Egypt was still working effectively, but the Egyptian majority of the population was not reconciled to being treated as an inferior race, and indeed the Egyptian civilization was superior to the Hellenic in at least two important points. Egyptian women had a better legal status than Greek women, and in Egypt slavery was rare. The exploited Egyptian peasants were freemen, and, though the well-to-do members of the Greek community in Egypt were slave-owners, the Ptolemaic Government took action to protect its own subjects from being enslaved.

Migrants can carry with them only moveable property, whether they migrate as conquerors, like the Greeks at Alexander's heels, or as deportees, like the Jews who had been carried away captive from Judah to Babylonia a quarter of a millennium earlier. If the migrants wish to preserve their social and cultural identity in new surroundings among aliens by whom they are outnumbered, the portable property that they take with them must be precious enough, in the migrants' own eyes, to give them an incentive to survive the traumatic experience of parting with those elements in their cultural heritage that are rooted inextricably in their ancestral soil. A Jewish deportee had to part with a liturgy that could not be performed validly anywhere except in the temple at Jerusalem; a Greek migrant had to part with the shrine of the tutelary goddess of his native city-state. Like the Jews in the sixth century B.C., the Greeks in and after the year 334 B.C. succeeded in solving this psychological problem. A migrant Greek's slaves were portable economic assets that were cultural liabilities. The Greeks could not have emulated the Jews' *tour de force* of surviving in diaspora if the Greeks had not also had, like the Jews, portable cultural assets of high psychological value.

Two Athenian Hellenic cultural assets that proved not to be transplantable from Athens were the writing of plays and the housing of fraternities of philosophers. Greek philosophy had originated in Ionia and had migrated to Italy before it had settled at Athens, but Socrates, Plato, and Aristotle had anchored it in an Athenian resting-place. In the writing of plays, Athens had almost won a monopoly, though there were also Siceliot and Italiot Greek schools of comedy and farce. But the playwrights and the philosophers who lived and worked at Athens did not have to be native Athenians.

The three most eminent fifth-century Athenian tragedy-writers and the fifth-century Athenian comedy-writer Aristophanes were all natives, but, among the four most eminent comedy-writers of the Athenian 'New' school, only one, Menander (*c.* 342–291 B.C.) was a native. Diphilus (*fl. c.* 318–274 B.C.) came to Athens from Sinope; Philemon (361–263 B.C.) came from Syracuse; Alexis (*fl. c.* 357–274 B.C.) came from Thurii in the 'toe' of Italy.

Among the founders of the four principal philosophical fraternities that were housed at Athens, only Plato was a fully native Athenian. Epicurus (341–270 B.C.) was the son of Athenian settlers who had been planted on Samos and had been evicted when Samos had been liberated in 322/1 B.C. The garden which housed the Epicurean fraternity at Athens had been bought for the founder in 306 B.C. by wealthy pupils of his at Lampsacus. Aristotle was a native of Stageiros who found Athens eventually too hot to hold him. Aristotle's fraternity was housed at Athens, in the Lyceum, after the founder's death, by his pupil Theophrastus (372/1–288/7 B.C.), a native of Eresus, on the island of Lesbos. As for Zeno (*c.* 326–264 B.C.), the founder of the Stoic fraternity, he came to Athens at some date between 320 and 314 B.C. from his native city Citium in Cyprus; and Citium was a Phoenician colony in which, during the fourth century B.C., more inscriptions were engraved in Canaanite (alias Hebrew) than in Greek. The successors of the four founders in the presidencies of their respective fraternities were drawn from all quarters of the expanded Hellenic World, and even from outside it. For instance, Hannibal-Cleitomachus, who was president of the Platonic Academy at Athens from 127/6 to 110/9 B.C., was, like Zeno, a colonial Phoenician. He came from Carthage.

Moreover, plays written at Athens could be performed elsewhere, and philosophical fraternities whose headquarters were at Athens could enlist adherents elsewhere. One of the institutions that held the expanded Hellenic World together was the Panhellenic union of itinerant actors (Dionysou Tekhnitai). Under the protectorate of Dionysos, the god whose cult at Athens had brought the Attic drama to birth, these strolling players staged Attic plays wherever there was a Greek city with a theatre. The tragedies of the fifth-century playwright Euripides held their own side by side with the younger Euripidean Attic comedy of manners.

The two pre-Alexandrine fraternities of philosophers that were housed at Athens were élitist and aloof; the foundation of the two post-Alexandrine schools was the response to current intellectual and social needs. Epicurus, like his Chinese contemporary the Taoist philosopher Chuang tzŭ, encouraged his followers to drop out of public life. Epicurus put his treasure in personal friendships. Zeno, like Confucius, taught his followers how to maintain a high personal standard of conduct in a new social milieu in which the individual could no longer rely on the moral support—and moral limitations—of his duties as a citizen of a sovereign city-state. These were missionary philosophies, and so, to a still greater degree, was the Cynic school. Its semi-Thracian Athenian founder Antisthenes (*c.* 445–366 B.C.) had been sedentary at Athens in the Cynosarges gymnasium. His disciple, Diogenes of Sinope, who probably died in the same year as Alexander, saw, as the Buddha had seen, that the price of spiritual freedom was the renunciation of material possessions. Post-Alexandrine Cynic philosophers were vagrants who directed their appeal to the masses. They propagated their austere doctrine by example, as well as by word of mouth.

The most readily portable of all post-Alexandrine Hellenic cultural assets was the international (*koinê*) form of the Attic dialect of the Greek language. Presumably the *koinê* began to take shape during the half-century life-time of the Athenian Empire (454–405 B.C.), but its fortune was made when King Philip II adopted it as the official language of the Kingdom of Macedon, in preference to the Macedonians' own local Greek dialect. From that time onwards the *koinê* served the Hellenic World as the language of government, of utilitarian literature, and of everyday life. It was a live language which continued to change in answer to Hellenic life's changing demands on it. Simultaneously, however, Attic Greek circulated in the 'precious' form into which it had been moulded for export by the Athenian littérateur Isocrates (436–338 B.C.).

The *koinê* Attic was a practical medium for conveying thoughts and feelings; Isocratean Attic was a linguistic artist's material for creating literary ornaments in which the mental content was subordinated to the verbal style. The *koinê* was the language of post-Alexandrine Hellenic science and scholarship, the focus of which was not Athens but Alexandria-on-Nile, and here the scientists made some fine discoveries. Eratosthenes of Cyrene (276–194 or 264–202 B.C.), who was the librarian of the Museum at Alexandria, calculated the length of the globe's circumference nearly correctly by ingenious observations and measurements; Aristarchus of Samos (*fl. c.* 280 B.C.) put the Sun, instead of the Earth, at the centre of the stellar cosmos. However, Hipparchus of Nicaea (*c.* 190–121 B.C.) put the Earth back into its traditional false position, and at Syracuse Archimedes (287–212 B.C.) apologized for the vulgarity of his application of scientific theory to civil and military technology.

Hellenism, moving in to occupy the derelict domain of the Persian Empire, also needed a portable social container, and Alexander and his successors found this in the pre-Alexandrine Hellenic civilization's master-institution, the city-state. Few pre-Alexandrine Greek city-states succeeded in retaining their sovereign independence. The outstandingly successful one was Rhodes. In 305–304 B.C. Rhodes, aided by Ptolemy I her 'saviour' (*soter*), warded off an attack by Demetrius Poliorcetes ('the city-taker'). The eastward expansion of the Hellenic World gave Rhodes a key position in the maritime network of communications. Rhodes commanded the sea-routes from the Aegean to the Ptolemaic capital, Alexandria, and to Seleucia-in-Pieria the port of Antioch-on-Orontes, which was the Seleucids' western capital. Though Philip and Alexander and their successors deprived most of the pre-existing Greek city-states of their sovereignty, they founded 329 new cities according to one modern count; and not only they, but also the Parnian Iranian nomad conquerors of Parthia and other Seleucid territories, usually treated Greek cities with respect and consideration. The destruction of Olynthus by Philip in 348 B.C., and of Thebes by Alexander in 335 B.C., were exceptional atrocities, and Thebes was refounded in 316 B.C. by Cassander, one of the two most murderous of Alexander's successors in the second generation. A number of other city-states made contributions to the restoration of Thebes, and when, in 227 B.C., the city of Rhodes was wrecked by an earthquake, kings and city-states in all parts of the Hellenic World sent generous gifts for her relief.

A non-sovereign city was a convenient instrument for the delegation of administrative authority, and, if it was a new foundation, not haunted by any glamorous memories of former sovereign independence, but confronted by a non-Greek rural subject population at its gates, it was likely to be loyal to its royal founder. The earliest royal foundation was Philip II's Philippi, which stood guard over his gold-mines; the most famous was Alexander's Alexandria-on-Nile (the first of the many new cities with this name). The most assiduous founders of new Greek cities among Alexander's successors were the Seleucids and the Greek rulers of the Oxus–Jaxartes basin who seceded from the Seleucids and eventually conquered north-western India. Every Greek city, old and new, had an agora, a theatre, and at least one gymnasium. The theatre and the agora were assembly-places for a great variety of purposes. The gymnasium was the diasporan Greek equivalent of a Jewish synagogue. As the cities became de-militarized, the gymnasium became an intellectual as well as an athletic club-house.

Full-blown cities were not the only containers in which Hellenism was propagated. There were also settlements of Macedonian veteran soldiers and their descendants which had rudimentary civic constitutions, and the diasporas of Greek and non-Greek soldiers, traders, and artisans were incorporated in non-territorial associations (*politeumata*).

Through the deployment of these various portable instruments, the Hellenic civilization had been disseminated, by 221 B.C., over the whole of the former domain of the Persian Empire except for Egypt, where the Ptolemies, having opted, like their contemporaries in Ch'in, for direct administration, founded only one new city, Ptolemaïs in the Thebaïd, in addition to the two, Alexandria and Naucratis, which they had inherited. In 334 B.C. the only Greek settlements within the Persian Empire's frontiers had been a fringe of city-states along the west coast of Asia Minor, a few patches of them on Asia Minor's south and north coasts, Cyrenaïca, Naucratis, and some plantations of Greek deportees in the far north-east. The coverage achieved within the next century was imposing, but it was also superficial. The new colonial Greek cities, numerous though they were, were only a scatter of Greek islands in a sea of non-Greek population. The peasantry in these cities' rural domains was non-Greek, and there were even some non-Greek quarters inside their walls. In Syria, the Aramaic *koinê* was more successful than the Greek *koinê* in superseding Canaanite (Hebrew) as the language of everyday life. The Greek *koinê* did temporarily supplant the Aramaic *koinê* everywhere as the language of administration, and in north-eastern Iran the Greek alphabet came to be used in some official inscriptions for conveying the local Iranian dialect. However, the Aramaic alphabet eventually prevailed over the Greek in most of the Persian Empire's former territories to the east of the River Euphrates.

[31]

THE WARRING STATES
OF CHINA, 506–221 B.C.

BETWEEN the years 771 and 506 B.C. the political configuration of China had been transformed as a result of two centuries of fratricidal warfare. It has been noted already that before the disaster that had overtaken the Chou dynasty in 771 B.C., China had consisted of about three hundred small fiefs under the Chou dynasty's suzerainty. In 506 B.C. there was an outer ring of seven large states surrounding a central group of small states, one of which was the tiny territory under the Chou's direct rule round Loyang, the city of refuge to which the Chou dynasty had migrated from the Wei valley after 771 B.C. Four of the seven large peripheral states—Yen at the mouth of the Yellow River and in the Pei Ho valley, and Ch'u, Wu, and Yüeh in the Hwai, Han, and Yangtse valleys—lay beyond the borders of the territory that had come under the Chou's suzerainty when, in the eleventh century B.C., the Chou had supplanted the Shang as the paramount power. A fifth large state, Ch'in, now occupied the Chou's original domain in the Wei valley; but Ch'in in 506 B.C., like Chou before the eleventh century B.C., was a culturally backward state. Among the seven peripheral great powers, Chin and Ch'i alone lay within the original domain of the Chinese civilization which the Chou had taken over from the Shang.

The seven peripheral great powers were all under threat from each other, and this gave the governments of each of them a strong incentive to be efficient militarily, and therefore administratively and economically as well. The key to efficiency was political absolutism. If a great power was to survive in the competition with its peers, its ruler must strive to save himself from falling into the impotence that had befallen the suzerain Chou dynasty. If possible, the local ruler must acquire an effective command over the persons of his subjects and over the resources of his territory. This, however, required a radical transformation of the traditional structure of Chinese society, in which the local rulers, even when they had become independent, *de facto*, of the suzerain Chou dynasty, were, in their own local domains, still only *primi inter pares* among the members of a hereditary aristocracy that competed with the members of the local ruling house for public office and for the produce of the land.

This domestic problem was the crux for the rulers of Ch'i and Chin, where the traditional aristocratic structure of Chinese society was fortified by long use and wont. It was also a crux for the southern power Ch'u, but, in the south towards the close of the sixth century B.C., the major problem was the relation of the local powers with each other. In the south the process of Sinification was spreading rapidly in formerly barbarian territories; the adoption of the Chinese way of life brought with it an increase in military and political strength; and consequently each southern state that entered the Chinese society was soon threatened from the rear by a state, more distant from the centre of the Chinese World, that was Sinifying itself in its turn.

In 506 B.C., Ch'u—an ex-barbarian state astride the middle course of the Yangtse which had been taking a leading part in Chinese power-politics since the Chou dynasty's decline—was attacked and overrun by Wu, a younger ex-barbarian state which had arisen in the lower basins of the Yangtse and the Hwai. Ch'u was aided by Yüeh, an inchoate state that was taking shape in the southern hinterland of Ch'u and Wu. Wu then imposed its suzerainty on Yüeh; but Wu overreached itself by going on, in 489–485 B.C., to attack Ch'i. Wu was making a bid for hegemony over the whole Chinese World, but its strength was not equal to its ambition; Wu's assault on Ch'i failed; this diversion of Wu's energies gave Ch'u the opportunity to re-establish itself in 488–481 B.C.; and in 473 B.C. Wu itself was conquered and annexed by Yüeh.

Ch'i not only repulsed Wu's assault; it also survived a domestic struggle between the hereditary nobility and the crown. In Ch'i the crown was the winner. On the other hand, in Chin the crown was crippled in 497–490 B.C. by a civil war between rival factions among the local nobility. In a second civil war, waged in 455–453 B.C., one of four competing noble houses was annihilated; the other three partitioned the Chin state between them *de facto*; and the three successor-states of Chin —Wei, Han, and Chao—were recognized *de jure* in 403 B.C. From 453 B.C. onwards, each of Chin's three successors attempted to play the part of a great power on its own account, but, like Wu in the years 489–473 B.C., they were attempting a feat that was beyond their strength. The weakness of Chin's successor-states was accentuated by the geographical intricacy of the partition. Parts of the territories that were inherited by Wei and Han were enclaves, insulated geographically from the main body of the state to which they had been assigned. The eventual beneficiary from the partition of Chin was its successor-states' eastern neighbour, Ch'in.

From 453 B.C. onwards there were eight competing great powers. How was the ruler of a great power to make the most of his state's military potentialities? One way of increasing a state's military efficiency was to replace hereditary office-holders by men who had proved their personal ability, even if these able men were not of royal or aristocratic blood. A second step, which presupposed the first, was to replace hereditary fiefs by commanderies (*chün*), subdivided into prefectures (*hsien*). These geographical departments were administered by employees of the crown whose tenure of their posts was terminable at the crown's pleasure.

After the partition of Chin, an enterprising and ambitious ruler of one of its three successor-states, Wei (Prince Wen of Wei, 446–397 B.C.), sought to compensate for the smallness of his state's territory, population, and resources by staffing his administration with able men of humble social origin. The consequent increase in Wei's military efficiency tempted Prince Wen in 419 B.C. to bid for hegemony. Wei state, like Wu state earlier in the century, failed to attain this ambitious objective. Wei was checked inconclusively in 419–370 B.C. and decisively in 354–340 B.C. The gainer from Wei's failure was its western neighbour, Ch'in.

After Prince Wen of Wei's death in 397 B.C., one of his able employees was hired by the King of Ch'u to do in Ch'u what had been done in Wei. In Ch'u, however, this radical reform was reversed after the death of the king who had initiated it. The hereditary aristocracy now re-established its hold on office in Ch'u's home territory. Yet Ch'u is believed to have been the first state to replace fiefs by commanderies and prefectures in annexed territories; and, between 479 and 445 B.C., Ch'u had annexed three of the small states in the centre of the Chinese World.

The most thorough-going of all these administrative reorganizations was carried out in Ch'in state during the reigns of Prince Hien (384–361 B.C.) and his son and successor Prince Hiao (361–338 B.C.). The effective reorganizer of Ch'in was Shang Yang, a cadet of the princely house of one of the petty central states who had found employment first in the Wei successor-state of Chin. Shang Yang transferred his services to Prince Hiao of Ch'in in 356 and he worked in Ch'in from that year till his patron Prince Hiao's death in 338 B.C. Shang Yang swept away, in Ch'in, the structure of society based on hereditary status; he opened careers to military talent; in order to strengthen Ch'in state's military power, he fostered agriculture; and, in order to foster agriculture, he made land a privately-owned marketable commodity. Shang Yang's innovations gave the Ch'in peasants an opportunity to rise to the highest posts in the state, but they also subjected the peasants to military conscription and to taxation, and exposed them, if they fell into economic difficulties, to the risk of having to sell their land. There were now two possible extreme alternative outcomes for a Ch'in peasant's career: he might make his fortune or he might be reduced to penury.

Prince Hiao's reign and Lord Shang Yang's work in Hiao's service in Ch'in state were contemporaneous with Philip II's reign in Macedon (359–336 B.C.). Ch'in was the counterpart in China of Macedon in Greece, and the policy of strengthening the state by militarizing the peasantry was pursued simultaneously by Philip and by Shang Yang. Ch'in's and Macedon's relations with the rest of the society to which they belonged respectively were similar both geographically and socially. Both states were next-door neighbours of their rivals, but were secluded physically by a ring of mountain barriers. Both peoples were socially backward, and were therefore malleable, when, in the fourth century B.C., their life was drastically transformed by a ruler's fiat.

Philip II lived to see his reforms bear fruit in the military and political unification of Greece under his hegemony. Prince Hiao died in 338 B.C., which was the year in which Philip triumphed. Ch'in did not succeed in unifying the Chinese World till the decade 230 221 B.C. But, unlike Macedon's unification of Greece, Ch'in's unification of China was conclusive. The Hellenic World was unified eventually neither by Macedon nor by any of Macedon's Greek successor-states and their rivals, but by a Hellenized non-Greek power, Rome. Ch'in had to compete with other Chinese powers, and, of these, first Wei and then Chao proved to be the most formidable; but eventually it was Ch'in that unified China, and Ch'in was a Chinese state, though not a state of the highest rank in terms of Chinese culture.

In the Chinese World in the fifth and fourth centuries B.C., the radical administrative changes were accompanied by economic and social changes and also by technological changes, both military and civil. Some of these changes on other planes of life were initiated by the administrative innovators; others were incidental consequences of their work; others again merely happened (so far as we know) to be contemporaneous. The cumulative effect of all these simultaneous changes was to dissolve the traditional structure of Chinese society. This had been weakened by the first round of fratricidal wars during the two centuries that had ended in 506 B.C.; it was shattered by the second round that ended in 221 B.C.

The principal economic change has been noted already apropos of the administrative innovations. Land was made alienable and marketable, and, while this had the intended effect of increasing agricultural production, it also widened the gulf between the rich and the poor and created a landless proletariat. The chief social change was the opening of administrative and military careers to talent, without regard to hereditary differences of class. This created a new class of professional administrators and military officers, and another new class of educators who offered a vocational training to aspirants for employment in governmental service. Confucius became a successful educator after he had failed to succeed as an administrator. He is the earliest recorded representative in China of a profession that had its counterpart in the Hellenic World in the fifth-century-B.C. sophists. Confucius was also the earliest founder, in China, of a school of philosophy.

The new autocratic rulers had not deliberately called the educators and philosophers into existence, but they tolerated their existence and treated them, on the whole, with respect. The rulers were inclined to frown upon the merchants—another new class that made its appearance spontaneously in the same age—but the merchants managed to survive and to prosper in spite of governmental disapproval. Evidently the merchants found their opportunity through meeting social needs. There was a need for trade in a society that was expanding geographically into regions producing a variety of natural products and manufactures and in which the warring governments were making increasing demands for supplies; and, though war made inter-state trade rather hazardous, efficient local government made domestic trade tolerably secure, particularly in the large states. Trade, manufactures, and the eviction of peasants from their ancestral holdings of land worked together to generate cities.

Among the principal civil technological innovations were the digging of canals and the issuing of metallic coinage. These two innovations were both introduced in the fifth century B.C., and both were acts of state. In the digging of canals the pioneer state was Wu, whose territory was traversed by the lower reaches of the Yangtse and the Hwai River. The Wu government's immediate purpose was to facilitate military transport, but the canals incidentally promoted the extension and intensification of agriculture by draining and irrigating potentially productive marsh-lands. The fourth century B.C. saw the introduction into the Chinese World of the ox-drawn plough and the replacement of bronze by iron as the material for agricultural implements, tools, and weapons. These fourth-century-B.C. technological innovations certainly served the purposes of the governments of the Chinese states of the day, but we do not know whether they, too, were introduced, as coinage and canals were, on governmental initiative; nor do we know the routes by which they reached China from the central region of the Old-World Oikoumenê, where both iron and the plough had long since been in use.

The principal military technological innovation was the adoption of the cavalry arms in Chao state in 307 B.C. Chao bordered on the Eurasian steppe, and its cavalry adopted the nomads' arms and dress, as the Median cavalry had done in Iran three centuries earlier. By the close of the fourth century B.C., chariotry, which had once been the major or perhaps even the only Chinese arm, had already been demoted in favour of massive infantry forces, raised by conscription. This change may have been started in the southern states, where waterways and marshes hindered the use of wheels, but the change had spread rapidly —for instance, to Ch'in state, at the opposite end of the Chinese World.

The second round of the wars that ended in the political unification of China started in 333 B.C. In that year Ch'u broke up Yüeh and incorporated Wu, which Yüeh had annexed in 473 B.C. In the same year 333 B.C. a defensive alliance against Ch'in was contracted by the other six surviving great powers. Thanks to Shang Yang's reforms, Ch'in had played a redoubtable part in the wars of 354–340 B.C., in which Wei's bid for hegemony had been definitively frustrated. In 318 B.C. Ch'in signally defeated the combined forces of all the other six powers, though these were reinforced by Eurasian nomad mercenaries. In 316 B.C. Ch'in expanded across the watershed between the Wei tributary of the Yellow River and the Yangtse basin in what is now Sse-Chwan province, and then attacked Ch'u from the west. In 278 B.C. Ch'in took Ch'u's capital city; by 272 B.C., Ch'in's encirclement of the remnant of Ch'u was completed. Simultaneously Ch'in was attacking the northern powers. She seemed to be on the point of unifying the whole Chinese World by conquest when in 270 B.C. she was defeated by Chao. Chao defeated Ch'in again in 258 B.C., and in 247 B.C. Ch'in had to accept an inconclusive peace. The wars of 333–247 B.C. had been savage and lethal, but they had not been decisive.

However, in the ten years 230–221 B.C. Ch'in attacked and conquered all her six surviving competitors, one after another. This time they did not combine to defend themselves, and Chao alone put up a stiff resistance.

The political unification of China in 221 B.C. was imposed by military force, yet it has proved to be durable. The first unifier's work has been undone a number of times in the course of nearly twenty-two centuries. It was undone for the first time in the year after this first unifier's death, but, so far, China's temporary lapses into political disunity have invariably been retrieved. The forcible political unification of China was feasible because her voluntary cultural unification was an accomplished fact already before Ch'in state set out on its career of military conquest. This is why Ch'in's achievement has outlasted Ch'in's own swift demise.

Indeed, the Chinese civilization had already spread, before 221 B.C., beyond the bounds of the area that was united politically by Ch'in Shih

Hwang-ti in and after 221 B.C. For instance, agriculture and metallurgy had been introduced into Korea perhaps as early as the fourth century B.C., and into Japan perhaps a century or so later—partly, perhaps, via Korea and partly perhaps direct from the Sinified basin of the Yangtse River. Previously the populations of Korea and Japan had remained in the food-gathering and mesolithic stage of culture, though, in both Korea and Japan, the art of pottery had been practised before the introduction of agriculture. The Korean and Japanese languages have no affinity with the languages of the Chinese–Thai and Tibetan–Burmese family, but the reception of Chinese civilization incorporated Korea and Japan in the Sinified World of Eastern Asia.

[32]

THE COMPETING PHILOSOPHIES
IN CHINA, 506–221 B.C.

In China the Age of the 'Warring States' was also the Age of the 'Hundred Schools' of philosophy. The competing Chinese philosophies were alternative emotional and intellectual responses to common contemporary experiences that were painful and disquieting. The social stimuli for philosophical reflections and precepts were the increasingly strenuous and savage political and military struggles between the surviving great powers; the effort of the local rulers to increase their power by getting rid of traditional restraints and, above all, by substituting ability for birth as the criterion for employment in public service; and the consequent extension to all classes of the opportunity and the insecurity which had previously been the peculiar fortune of an aristocratic minority.

Chinese philosophy of all schools differed from Hellenic philosophy in being concerned, from the beginning, primarily with practical life and only secondarily with science and metaphysics. Hellenic philosophy had been debating scientific and metaphysical problems for more than a century before Socrates oriented it decisively towards the study of human nature; and both Socrates himself and his successors in the different fraternities of Hellenic philosophers were interested in the study of the human intellect—for instance, in the theory of knowledge—besides being concerned with ethics. Confucius, who was Socrates' Chinese counterpart, did not re-orient Chinese philosophy; he inaugurated it; and Confucius was concerned with Man as a participant in society, rather than as an intellect or as a soul.

Reflection on human nature and human life does, of course, raise metaphysical questions. In India the Buddha's disciples were tempted to escape from the strenuous spiritual exercises that the Buddha prescribed by indulging in metaphysical speculations that he deprecated. Yet the Buddha himself held metaphysical tenets which provoked controversy.

Chinese minds were less prone than Indian minds to speculation; yet the Taoist school of Chinese philosophy plunged into metaphysics, and the Chinese theories of the rhythmic alternation of a static Yin-state with a dynamic Yang-activity and of the five elements in the structure of the physical cosmos were metaphysical and scientific speculations. However, even the Taoists' metaphysics were ancillary to their reaction to the social and political conditions in China in their time.

The reflections of most of the Chinese schools of philosophy were focused on the social and political plane of human affairs; and all schools agreed, implicitly, though not always overtly, that aristocratic birth could not, and also should not, continue to be the avenue to public office. The issue between the Confucianists and the Legalists was the question of what the alternative qualification for office should be. The Mohists and the Taoists did not take part in this controversy because they questioned the value of the two major current Chinese social institutions, namely states and families, and they challenged the legitimacy of the claims made on behalf of governmental and paternal authority.

The Legalist school of Chinese philosophy held that the kind of ability that ought to be the passport to public office in lieu of aristocratic birth was the administrative and military ability that would serve the purpose of the rulers of the warring states—and the purpose of each of those rulers was to maximize his own power. For the Legalists, 'Law' was tantamount to a ruler's fiat; and they held that a ruler was justified in imposing his fiat by force on his subjects and on his peers up to the limits of his power. His victims, so the Legalists held, had no legitimate grievance; for they also held that human nature is intrinsically bad, and that consequently a coercive regime is bound to be an improvement on the state of nature. Inevitably, Legalism was the philosophy which the governments of all the warring states put into practice *de facto* with various degrees of consistency and of ruthlessness.

So long as the Chinese World continued to be divided politically, the Legalists had a virtual monopoly of access to political power. Practical-minded Legalist philosophers were gladly employed by rulers to re-organize, and then to conduct, the administration of their states. Ch'in state put two famous Legalists in charge of its administration at crises, which consequently became turning-points, in Ch'in's and in the whole of China's history. Lord Shang Yang overhauled Ch'in state's administration in the course of the years 356–338 B.C. and also recorded in a book the theory that he had put into practice; Li Sse (280–208 B.C.) was the confidential adviser of the ruler who was King Chêng of Ch'in from 247 to 221 B.C. and who was then the first Emperor (Shih Hwang-ti) of a united China from 221 till his death in 210 B.C. Li Sse cut away the basis of the Legalist school's monopoly of power by enabling his master, King Chêng, to put an end to the political disunity that had made the Legalist school's fortune.

The practice and theory of Legalism evoked counter-theories. Thinkers who agreed with the Legalists that the qualification for public office could not and should not any longer be aristocratic birth did not agree that the right substitute for this was the ability to serve a ruler's will to power. They looked for a way (*tao*) that was ethically worthier and metaphysically better founded than subservience to an autocrat's self-interested decrees.

A way cannot be discerned and followed if it does not already exist. Confucius found a pre-existing way in the 'Way of Heaven' (*T'ien*), a term which seems to have stood originally for a human-like supreme god, but which, by Confucius' time, had perhaps already become depersonalized. As Confucius saw it, the 'Way of Heaven' was primeval, and therefore it must in some sense be identical with the traditional Chinese way of social and political life that was breaking down in Confucius' generation. One aspect of Confucius' policy for arresting the disintegration of Chinese society was to call for the rehabilitation of traditional ritual (*li*), which was the safeguard for propriety (*i*). But what was the criterion of propriety for rulers and their ministers? As Confucius saw it, true propriety was not the pursuit of unethical *raison d'état*; it was the cultivation of humaneness (*jen*). A ruler and his ministers and his subjects would be following the 'Way of Heaven' correctly in so far as they behaved towards each other with the kindness and the dutifulness that the members of a family were expected, traditionally, to display in their relations with each other.

It has been noted in Chapter 25 that the term *chün tzu*, which traditionally had meant 'nobleman'—'the son of a lord'—was reinterpreted by Confucius to mean a 'noble man', in an ethical sense. The new connotation was gradually substituted for the original one by Confucius' disciples. Mencius (371–289 B.C.) emphasized the Confucian virtue of humaneness. Hsün-tzu (perhaps *c.* 315–236 B.C.) emphasized the Confucian concern for the observance of traditional ritual. Living, as he did, during the last and most agonizing paroxysm of the struggle between the warring states, Hsün-tzu inclined towards the Legalist view that human nature is evil and that therefore it cannot dispense with some kind and degree of external control. Yet Hsün-tzu showed himself to be a genuine Confucian in his usage of the crucial term *chün tzu*. In his writings, this word is generally used in the imported ethical sense and only rarely in the original genealogical sense.

A more metaphysical conception of 'the Way' than the Confucian conception was developed by the school of Chinese philosophy that has been labelled Taoist *par excellence*. This conception is presented in two justly famous books: the *Tao tê Ching*, attributed to Lao-tzu, and the book named after its author Chuang-tzu, who lived *c*. 365–290 B.C. and was thus a contemporary of both Mencius and Shang Yang. For the Taoists, 'the Way' is the way of the ultimate reality in and behind and beyond the phenomenal universe. Reality's way is effortless, irresistible, and beneficial, and, in all these three characteristics, it is the antithesis of Man's way, in which Man frustrates himself through febrile activism, leading to violence that is aggravated by intellectual ingenuity. Taoism was the earliest philosophy, anywhere in the Oikoumenê, to surmise that Man, in achieving civilization, might have compromised his position in the Universe by putting himself out of harmony with the spirit of the ultimate reality in which Man lives and moves and has his being.

The Taoists deprecated the advances in technology and in the social technique of authoritarian administration which had been made in China by the fourth century B.C. (the century in which the *Tao tê Ching*, as well as the *Chuang-tzu*, were given something like their present shape). The practical corollary of the Taoists' metaphysics was a thorough-going policy of *laissez-faire*. The Taoists dismissed, as being superficial, the ideal of ethical sociality which was the Confucians' prescription for the Chinese civilization's malady. The Taoists' prescription for healing the wounds of the Age of the Warring States was to repudiate civilization and to revert to the way of human life that had been followed in a self-contained Neolithic-Age community. Passages of the *Tao tê Ching*, in which the Taoist *Weltanschauung* is expounded, have been quoted in Chapter 2. This fourth-century-B.C. Chinese philosophy is relevant not only to its own time and place but to all times and places and particularly to the global situation of mankind in the 1970s.

In fourth-century-B.C. China, Taoism could not have any practical contemporary effect; and it was open to criticism from the various standpoints of all the other competing philosophies of the Age of the Warring States on the ground that it was socially irresponsible; yet, just because it was visionary, Taoism had a future in China. There was room for it and need for it as a counterpoise to the predominantly practical bent of Chinese minds, since philosophies that expressed this prevalent Chinese attitude left some Chinese minds spiritually unsatisfied.

There was not, however, permanent room for the visionary philosophy of Mo-tzu (*c*. 479–388 B.C.). Mo-tzu held that love for fellow human beings ought not to be gradational but ought to be given equally to all alike. Mencius retorted that universal love was impracticable, and that Mo-tzu's insistence that nothing short of this was ethically adequate was tantamount to repudiating the practicable social virtues of filial piety and political loyalty. If Mencius had been acquainted with

Buddhism, no doubt he might have cited, in this context, the Buddha's desertion of his wife and child and of his father, to whose throne he was heir, and might have contrasted this positive violation of commonly accepted social obligations with the Buddha's aloof compassion for all his fellow sentient beings.

Mo-tzu did, in fact, offend against Confucian principles in the Taoists' company by rejecting authority, and in the Legalists' company by rejecting tradition. Mo-tzu differed from the Legalists in wishing to replace tradition by reason, not by coercion; and he differed from the Taoists in feeling concern and responsibility for his fellow men. In these points, Mo-tzu was more Confucian-minded than the adherents of those two other non-Confucian schools, but he was not sufficiently Confucian-minded to placate the Confucianists.

The rise of these diverse schools of Chinese philosophy and their controversies with each other give the measure of the emotional strain and the intellectual stimulus of the Age of the Warring States.

[33]

THE INDIAN CIVILIZATION,
c. 600–200 B.C.

OUR information about secular affairs in India for the four centuries ending *c.* 200 B.C. is less meagre than it is for the four immediately preceding centuries; yet in 600–200 B.C., as in 1000–600 B.C., the major events in Indian history occurred on the religious plane, and, in so far as our knowledge of Indian secular affairs during the period *c.* 600–200 B.C. is derived from Indian sources, it is incidental to the record of the religious events.

During the period *c.* 1000–600 B.C., the outstanding event on the religious plane had been the transfer of concern from ritual to meditation. This transfer had been made on the initiative of members of the Brahmin caste, and the Brahmins' leadership in giving Hinduism this spiritual turn is remarkable, considering that the Brahmins had a monopoly of the competence to perform rites efficaciously, and that this monopoly was the Brahmins' means of livelihood. It is also remarkable that, in an age in which Indian religion was becoming more spiritual, the Brahmins were successfully asserting against the Kshatriyas their claim to be the highest caste, in spite of the fact that military and political power was, and continued to be, in the Kshatriyas' hands.

During the period *c.* 600–200 B.C., the outstanding religious event was the foundation, by Siddhartha Gautama the Buddha and by Vard-hamana the Mahavira (*fl. c.* 500 B.C.), of the Buddhist and of the Jain monastic orders. Both these religious innovators were Kshatriyas, and both were aristocrats. The Buddha was the son and heir of the kinglet of Kapilavastu, a city-state within the frontiers of the present-day Kingdom of Nepal; the Mahavira (alias the Jina, meaning 'the victor') was the son of the head of a Kshatriya clan in the city of Vaisali, the capital of the Kingdom of Videha in northern Bihar. Neither of them disputed the Brahmins' monopoly of the performance of efficacious rites, but both of them ignored the rites, the gods, and the institution of caste itself.

They recruited their monks and nuns and their lay adherents from all castes indiscriminately, and the Brahmins were not given any special role in the Buddhist and Jain ways of life or in the constitutions of the Buddhist and Jain communities.

The Buddha and the Mahavira were each offering a way of winning release from 'the sorrowful round' of re-birth that, in the sixth century B.C., was believed to be potentially endless by most schools of thought in India and by the Pythagoreans and the Orphics in the Hellenic World. The common source of this belief may have been the religion of the Eurasian pastoral nomad peoples who had erupted out of the steppe in a number of different directions in the eighth and seventh centuries B.C. In their westward eruption in this age the nomads had advanced as near to Greece as the great western bay of the steppe and the basin of the River Hebrus (Marica), to the south of the lower course of the Danube. In India they had overrun the Indus basin.

This second invasion of the Indus basin by Indo-European-speaking migrant peoples is the political event that divides the period of Indian history *c.* 1000–600 from the period *c.* 600–200 B.C. The part of India in which these new arrivals had lodged themselves was the first part to have been occupied by the earlier, primary-Sanskrit-speaking invaders. It was, however, no more than the north-western fringe of the subcontinent. The Indus civilization and its successor the Hindu civilization of the primary-Sanskrit-speakers had, each in turn, expanded south-eastwards into the Jumna–Ganges basin. The Indus-basin seems to have been still the Sanskrit-speakers' habitat at the time when the Vedas were being composed, and the seventh-century-B.C. nomad settlers in the Indus basin eventually adopted the language and the way of life of this region's older-established Sanskrit-speaking inhabitants. We find the ex-nomad settlers here speaking local dialects derived from Sanskrit, and conforming to Hindu religion, and to the Hindu social structure that was associated with it, by the date of our earliest information about their manners and customs.

By the Buddha's and the Mahavira's generation, however, the Hindu civilization's centre of gravity had shifted south-eastwards from the Punjab to the region round the confluence of the Rivers Ganges, Gogra, and Son, and the orthodox Hindu majority of the population of this region now regarded their ancestors' home in the Indus basin with a disapproving and contemptuous eye, as a semi-barbarian country. This feeling must have been accentuated when, in the same generation, the Eurasian nomads' settlement in the Indus basin was followed up by the incorporation of the Indus basin in the First Persian Empire. Cyrus II annexed the basin of the Kabul River tributary of the Indus, probably at some date later than his conquest of the Babylonian Empire in 539

B.C.; Darius I annexed the rest of the Indus basin, right down to the river's delta, at some date later than his suppression of the great insurrection in 522 B.C. in the Empire's heartlands.

The state of political affairs in the Hindu World's new centre of gravity in the Ganges basin, in the lifetime of the Buddha and the Mahavira, resembled political conditions in the China of their contemporary, Confucius. Like China, the Ganges basin was partitioned politically among a number of local sovereign states of different sizes and strengths. The Buddha's native city-state, Kapilavastu, was small; the Mahavira's, Videha (the portion of present-day Bihar that lies to the north of the Ganges) was larger; the largest was Kapilavastu's southern neighbour Kosala (in present-day Uttar Pradesh); the strongest potentially was Magadha (the portion of present-day Bihar that lies to the south of the Ganges).

In the Buddha's and the Mahavira's generation, the competition among the states in this Indian constellation was becoming more intense, and like the competition among the warring states of China, the military struggle in the Ganges basin ended in political unification through the elimination of all the competitors save for a single victorious survivor. Kapilavastu was an early victim. The Buddha lived to see its conquest by Kosala and the massacre there of the Buddha's Sakya kinsmen and fellow-countrymen. In India, as in China, the eventual victor was a dark horse. In India the victor was not the relatively large and populous state Kosala; it was Magadha.

In India, too, the struggle for existence between the governments of the states did not disrupt the society's social and cultural unity. Gaya, where the Buddha won his Enlightenment, was in Magadha; the sacred deer-park at Sarnath, which was the principal scene of the Buddha's subsequent preaching, was in Kasi. The park adjoined the holy city of Benares, which was already a pilgrimage-resort, and the attraction of the park for the Buddha was presumably the possibility of finding there an audience drawn from all parts of the Indian World. Neither Gaya nor Sarnath was in the Buddha's home state; and, though the Buddha spent much of his time in the well-frequented park at Sarnath, he and his disciples were itinerant, except during the season of the monsoon rains, when travelling was difficult. The political frontiers were barriers for armies and were obstacles for spies, but they did not impede the movements of religious preachers and ascetics. The Buddha's royal birth gave him the entrée to the entourages of the local kings, but there is no indication that in this he was specially privileged. Indian preachers and ascetics crossed the frontiers of the warring states as freely as contemporary Chinese sophists and philosophers.

The political unification of present-day Bihar and Uttar Pradesh under the Saisunaga dynasty of Magadha state was probably accomplished *c.* 500–450 B.C. It might have been expected that this unification of a large part of north-eastern India beyond the Persian Empire's frontiers would have been followed by a collision between the Persian Empire and the new Indian empire. No such collision has been recorded, and, if in truth it did not occur, the reason may have been that, by the date at which Magadha state united Bihar and Uttar Pradesh, the Persian Imperial Government had already lost its hold over its dominions to the east of the River Indus. The 'highland Indians' who fought in the Emperor Darius III's army at the Battle of Gaugamela (331 B.C.) were probably the inhabitants of the Indian territories to the west of the river.

When Alexander made his raid through the Indus basin in 327–325 B.C., he found this region divided politically among a large number of independent kingdoms and tribal republics. Alexander's raid was brief, and the regime that he set up was ephemeral. It collapsed when the news arrived of the conqueror's death; but, by depriving the states in the Indus basin of their independence, Alexander had opened the way for an Indian empire-builder. *Circa* 322 B.C. an Indian of unknown antecedents, Chandragupta Maurya, expelled the Macedonian garrisons from the Indus basin, made himself master of this part of Alexander's heritage, and then conquered and annexed the Empire of Magadha. This had been taken over from the Saisunagas by the Nanda dynasty *c.* 362 B.C., and the Nandas may have enlarged the Empire by annexing the Deccan. Thus, for the first time, so far as we know, the Indus basin, the Jumna–Ganges basin, and perhaps also the Deccan were united with each other politically.

Circa 305 B.C. Chandragupta collided with one of Alexander's Macedonian successors, Seleucus I, who, from a base in Babylonia, was uniting under his own rule the eastern provinces of the defunct Persian Empire. Seleucus still had to settle accounts with another Macedonian successor of Alexander's, Antigonus I, who held Syria and Asia Minor in Seleucus' rear. In 303 B.C. Seleucus bought from Chandragupta 500 war-elephants for use in his coming trial of strength with Antigonus I. The price was the cession to Chandragupta of an eastern fringe of the former Persian dominions. The ceded zone must have included Lamghan on the Kabul River near Jalalabad and Kandahar in the Helmand valley; for in both these places there are inscriptions engraved by Chandragupta's grandson and second successor Ashoka, and there is no evidence that the frontier between the Mauryan and the Seleucid Empires was ever moved farther westward than the line agreed between Chandragupta and Seleucus I in 303 B.C. The other frontiers attained by the Mauryan Empire in Chandragupta's reign (322–298 B.C.), or at any rate in the reign of his first successor Bindusara, are also indicated by the locations of Ashoka's inscriptions. These inscriptions are found as far eastward as the angle of territory to the north of the confluence of the Ganges and the Brahmaputra in Bangladesh, and as far south as the latitude of the present-day city of Madras. We know that Ashoka conquered and annexed Kalinga (present-day Orissa), and that he made no subsequent military conquests. We may infer that, when Ashoka came to the throne, Kalinga was still an independent enclave in a Mauryan Empire whose southern frontier was a line running, approximately along the latitude of Madras City, from coast to coast of the peninsula. This southern frontier may have been attained already in the fourth century B.C. by the Mauryas' predecessors the Nandas.

Our relatively copious information about Ashoka's reign comes partly from Ashoka's own inscriptions and partly from chronicles of a later age, written in Ceylon. Neither source is objective. The chronicles, written from the southern (Theravadin) Buddhist standpoint, maximize the effect on Ashoka of his conversion to Buddhism by stressing both his previous wickedness and his subsequent piety. This source is semi-legendary, and Ashoka is not a disinterested witness about himself. However, his own record (in his Thirteenth Major Rock Edict) of the slaughter, devastation, and suffering that he had caused in the war in which, in 260 B.C., he had conquered Kalinga is surely veracious, and his expression of his remorse for this is surely sincere. It is also probably true (though this information comes from the chronicles, not from Ashoka himself) that he had originally won his throne by waging a fratricidal war in which he had put some of his brothers to death. On the other side of Ashoka's ethical account, we can take as being true a number of things, stated by him, or about him, that are to his credit.

For instance, Ashoka's conversion to Buddhism was a consequence of his remorse for the evil that he had done in conquering Kalinga. He never went to war again. He did not round off his dominion by conquering the Cholas and Pandyas and Kerelaputras on the southern tip of the peninsula, or the people of the adjacent island Ceylon. He reassured his independent neighbours that he had no aggressive intentions (Second Separate Edict). He diverted his action in regions beyond his empire's frontiers from conquest to the propagation of the Buddhist *dhamma*, the equivalent, in the living dialect of Ashoka's own day, of the Sanskrit word *dharma* (Thirteenth Major Rock Edict). He sent missions, between the years 258 and 255 B.C., to five Greek rulers: the Seleucid Antiochus II (Seleucus I's grandson), Ptolemy II, Magas the ruler of Cyrenaïca, Antigonus II King of Macedon, and Alexander King of Epirus (Second and Thirteenth Major Rock Edicts). He sent a mission to Ceylon *c.* 250 B.C. (Second and Thirteenth Major Rock Edicts). He also sent missions to the independent peoples at the southern extremity of continental India.

In contrast to the enigma of Darius I's relation to Zoroastrianism, Ashoka's adherence to Buddhism was explicit. In his Bhabra and his Rumindei inscriptions he mentions the Buddha by name, and in the 'Schism Edict' he intervenes in the affairs of the Buddhist monastic order (*sangha*). He feels himself to be under an obligation to safeguard the preservation of the order's unity. On the other hand, his description of the *dhamma* (Ninth and Eleventh Major Rock Edicts; Second Pillar Edict), which he is concerned to foster and to propagate, resembles Confucius' description of the *Tao* rather than the Buddha's precise prescriptions for his followers' spiritual exercises and the likewise precise formulations of the tenets on which the Buddha's injunctions for action were based; and, though Ashoka, like Darius I and Xerxes, has a religion of his own, he is as scrupulous as these Persian emperors and their predecessor Cyrus II in providing for the toleration of all the religions that are practised by his subjects (Twelfth Major Rock Edict; Sixth and Seventh Pillar Edicts). He is particularly concerned to ensure that his subjects shall show respect for Brahmins and for Jain monks, who represented the two religions that were the principal contemporary rivals of Ashoka's own religion, Buddhism (Third, Fourth, Ninth, Eleventh Major Rock Edicts; Seventh Pillar Edict).

The sincerity of Ashoka's zeal for propagating his conception of the *dhamma* is demonstrated by the number and the geographical range of his inscriptions. The inscription at Kandahar is bilingual. It is written in both Greek and Aramaic, Greek being the official language of the Persian Empire's Macedonian successor-states, and Aramaic the official language of the defunct Persian Empire itself. The two north-western-most of Ashoka's inscriptions are conveyed in the Kharosthi alphabet, which is derived from the Aramaic (the territory in which these two inscriptions lie may have remained under Persian rule until the over-throw of the Persian Empire by Alexander). All the rest are conveyed in the Brahmi script.

This was the script in which the Brahmins had recorded their liturgies. The language which the Brahmins had employed had been primary Sanskrit, but Ashoka used the Brahmi script for conveying living local dialects (prakrits), derived from primary Sanskrit. He inscribed in Prakrit even in the south, though here his subjects' mother-tongues were Dravidian, not Indo-European. Presumably the Dravidian languages had not been given literary form by Ashoka's time, and perhaps an educated minority among Ashoka's Dravidian-speaking subjects could read the living form of their northern fellow-subjects' Indo-European mother-tongue.

To what extent did Ashoka succeed in implementing his new departures in Mauryan imperial policy? It seems to be certain that, after his conquest and annexation of Kalinga, he did not wage any more wars. It is quite certain (his inscriptions are conclusive evidence) that he propagated, both at home and abroad, the *dhamma* as an ethical standard of conduct. But we have no means of ascertaining whether or not he was justified in claiming (Fourth Major Rock Edict) that his measures had had a signal effect in raising his subjects' level of ethical performance. Nor do we know whether or not his attempts to make the Empire's administration more humane were efficacious.

He charged his officials to take to heart their responsibility towards the huge numbers of people under their rule, and to treat them as gently as nurses treat children (Seventh Pillar Edict; First Separate Edict). He instituted, or at any rate revived and maintained, the practice of sending out touring inspectors (Third Major Rock Edict); he went on tour himself (Eighth Major Rock Edict; Minor Rock Edict), and he instituted a new class of officials to superintend the administration of philanthropic foundations, religious denominations, and welfare work such as the planting of trees, the digging of wells, the establishment of hospitals for animals as well as for human beings (Fifth Major Rock Edict and Seventh Pillar Edict), and restrictions on the killing of animals (First, Second, and Eleventh Major Rock Edicts; Fifth and Seventh Pillar Edicts; Kandahar Inscription). But we do not know whether these measures were as effective as he claims (Fourth Major Rock Edict; Kandahar Inscription) in humanizing the administrative machine that he had inherited. As the Pharaoh Akhenaton had found, organizations that are going concerns have a toughness and a momentum that may defeat the best-laid and most sincerely cherished schemes of a ruler whose powers are officially absolute. There are at least two indications (Sixth Major Rock Edict; First Separate Edict) that Ashoka did not find it easy to keep himself informed promptly and to control his subordinates' actions effectively.

Most of our information about the Mauryan regime is derived from an extant handbook, the *Arthashastra*, which purports to be the work of Kautalya, an expert on public administration who is said to have been the founder, Chandragupta's, adviser and aide. But we do not know how much of this book as it has come down to us—or, indeed, whether any portion of it—is in truth Kautalya's own work. Much of it may consist of later revisions and additions. Moreover, even if we surmise that parts are authentic, we cannot tell whether the authentic *Arthashastra* is a description of actual practice. It might be only an academic counter-utopia, presenting an unachieved ideal of *Realpolitik*. However, if even part of the *Arthashastra* is authentic and represents actual Mauryan practice, it shows that the Mauryan Empire was an authoritarian bureaucratic police-state, which exercised a meticulous and oppressive control over its subjects' lives, including their economic activities. This picture of the Mauryan regime that is presented in the *Arthashastra* is borne out to some extent by the surviving fragments of a book written by Megasthenes, the Seleucid Government's ambassador at the Mauryan court at Pataliputra (the present-day Patna). If the picture is true to life, the Mauryan regime was unlike the easy-going regime of the First Persian Empire and of its Asian Macedonian successor-state the Seleucid Empire. The Mauryan regime will have been as efficient as the contemporary Ptolemaic regime in Egypt, but it will also have been more sinister, though not more sinister than Ch'in state in China.

If that is the truth, it is improbable that Ashoka had much success in his attempts to make life more tolerable for his human subjects. He and the Jains, between them, did succeed in permanently raising the standard of respect for non-human forms of life, to judge by the remarkable temerity of animals and birds, wild as well as domesticated, in present-day India. They are confident that they have nothing to fear from their human fellow-creatures, and their present-day confidence is founded on more than twenty-two centuries of reassuring experience. Ashoka's human subjects probably gained less benefit from his humanitarianism. The Mauryan bureaucratic regime probably could, and did, largely defeat the Emperor's intentions. If so, this would go far towards explaining the shortness of the Mauryan Empire's life.

The Mauryan Empire was a going concern during the ninety years 322–232 B.C. It was one of the great powers in the constellation of local sovereign states, extending from the east coast of India to the Straits of Gibraltar, that occupied the political vacuum created by Alexander's success in overthrowing the Persian Empire and his failure to establish the greater empire, embracing the whole of the Old-World Oikoumenê, which he had planned to build. This ninety-year spell of political unity and domestic peace was unprecedented in India, at any rate since the destruction of the Indus civilization. During at least the last thirty years of the Emperor Ashoka's reign, the suffering of sentient beings, including non-human animals, was mitigated to some extent by a ruler who had taken to heart the Buddha's concern for the alleviation of suffering and who was also sympathetic to the Jains' particular tenderness towards all non-human forms of life. But, even before Ashoka's death in 232 B.C., the Mauryan Empire was beginning to show signs of disintegration. After his death it appears to have broken up. It was extinguished in 183 B.C.

[34]

THE STRUGGLE FOR THE
MASTERY OF THE WESTERN BASIN
OF THE MEDITERRANEAN

c. 600–221 B.C.

IN the western basin of the Mediterranean the eighth and seventh centuries B.C. had been auspicious for the Greeks. They had established themselves along the coast of Italy from Taras (Tarentum), on the south-west side of the 'heel', right round the 'toe' and as far up the west coast as Pithecusa (Ischia) Island and Cumae (the two earliest, as well as the most distant, except for Massilia, of all the Greek colonies that were planted to the west of the Straits of Otranto). The Greeks had also occupied the east and south coasts of Sicily. They had thus secured control of the passage through the Straits of Messina from the eastern basin of the Mediterranean into the Tyrrhene Sea, and *c.* 600 B.C. they had planted a colony at Massilia (Marseilles), the starting-point of a route up the Rhône valley into northern continental Europe and also across the Channel to the tin-mines in Cornwall. However, Akragas (Agrigentum), planted on the south coast of Sicily in 580 B.C., was the last important Greek colonial foundation in the west. By 500 B.C. the Greeks had tried and failed to wrest the north-west corner of Sicily from the Carthaginians and from the Carthaginians' local allies the Elymi; the Carthaginians had mastered the Straits of Gibraltar and had closed them to Greek shipping; and the Carthaginians and the rest of the colonial Phoenicians had co-operated successfully with the Etruscans in preventing the Greeks from linking up their Sicilian and Italian settlements with Massilia by gaining control over Sardinia and Corsica.

Already, in the seventh century B.C., the Asian Greek participants in the Greeks' expansion into the western basin of the Mediterranean had suffered the misfortune that had dogged the Greeks' Phoenician competitors in Syria since 745 B.C. The Syrophoenicians were attacked from the rear by aggressive land-powers, first the Assyrian Empire and then Assyria's Babylonian successor-state. From about 660 B.C., the Asian

Greeks were attacked and conquered progressively, first by the Lydians and then by the Lydians' conquerors, the Persians; and the advent of the Persians, which had aggravated the Asian Greeks' plight, had brought relief to the Phoenicians in and after 539 B.C. Yet, in the west by that time, the Greeks had secured two advantages over their opponents: superiority of numbers and the geographical advantage of holding the interior lines. The Carthaginians were separated geographically from their Etruscan allies by the Greeks' hold on the coasts of Sicily and southern Italy. Nevertheless, the western Greeks had been thrown on the defensive by 500 B.C. One reason for their weakness was their fratricidal strife with each other. *Circa* 550 B.C. the Greek colonial city-state Siris, and then in 511–510 B.C., Sybaris, was wiped out by the hands of other Italiot Greeks. Sybaris was replaced by Thurii in 444/3 B.C.; Siris was replaced later by Heraclea; but the damage that the western Greeks had inflicted on themselves during the critical sixth century B.C. was never fully repaired, and they continued to be each other's most destructive enemies till their common subjection to Rome compelled them at last to co-exist with each other in peace.

The western Greeks might have been subjected two centuries earlier —not, at that date, by the Romans but by the Carthaginian-Etruscan alliance—if the Siceliot Greeks had not succeeded, just in time, in building political structures on a supra-city-state scale. This was achieved by despots who employed the Assyrian device of deportation to bend their subjects' wills. Between 505 and 491 B.C., one Siceliot Greek principality was built in south-eastern Sicily, with its capital at Syracuse, by methods as brutal as those that had been employed in the Peloponnesos by the Spartans in the eighth century B.C. Between 488 and 483 B.C., a second Siceliot Greek principality expanded across Sicily from the south to the north coast by annexing Himera to Akragas.

In 480 B.C. the Carthaginians retorted to this second Siceliot Greek move by invading Sicily in force. There is no positive evidence that this Carthaginian invasion of the Greek part of Sicily was timed to be simultaneous with the Persian invasion of continental European Greece in the same year, but it is improbable that the two invasions were not concerted. The colonial Phoenicians were in close touch with the Syrophoenicians, and these were not only Persian subjects; they, as well as their colonists, were the Greeks' commercial rivals, and they therefore stood to gain if the Greeks were crushed. However, in 480 B.C., the Syracusan-Agrigentine alliance won as sensational a victory over the Carthaginians as the Spartan-Athenian alliance won over the Persians in the same year. Both victories were remarkable, considering that in the west, as in continental European Greece, a majority of the local Greek states failed to take up arms against the invaders. Indeed,

the Carthaginian invasion of the Greek part of Sicily was prompted by
the evicted despot of Himera, and Selinous and Rhegion (the Italiot
Greek state that commanded the Straits of Messina) were 'non-belligerent' in the Carthaginians' favour.

For the next two centuries the western Greek states continued to wage
war against each other—Syracuse against Rhegion and Croton, and
these two against Epizephyrian Locri, which was wedged in between
them. Western Greek states had always had eastern Greek trading
partners, and the partners became involved in each others' political
feuds on both sides of the Straits of Otranto. At some date before 450
B.C. some anti-Syracusan Siceliot Greek and Elymian states allied themselves with Athens, and consequently the western Greeks became
involved in the Atheno–Peloponnesian War of 431–404 B.C. This en-
tanglement culminated in an Athenian assault on Syracuse in 415–413
B.C. The adventure ended disastrously for Athens, but also for the
victorious Siceliots. Their exhaustion gave the Carthaginians an opening
for taking the offensive again in Sicily in 409 B.C., and, from then
onwards till 275 B.C., Carthage and Syracuse were repeatedly at war
with each other, with fluctuating fortunes, but with no conclusive result.
For instance, in the war of 312–306 B.C., the Carthaginians besieged
Syracuse unsuccessfully in 311–310 and again in 309; and in 310–307
the Syracusans invaded Carthage's home territory in Africa—a daring
move by the despot of Syracuse, Agathocles, but likewise a failure. The
Siceliot Greeks just failed, under the leadership of an earlier despot of
Syracuse, Dionysius I, to expel the Carthaginians from the north-west
corner of Sicily in 398 B.C. They just failed, for the second time, under
Pyrrhus' leadership, in 278–276 B.C.

The Siceliot Greeks had to choose between political unity under a
despotic regime and domestic democracy or oligarchy at the price of
political fragmentation. They submitted to despots whenever they were
in danger of succumbing to the Carthaginians; they overthrew their
despots whenever the Carthaginian menace receded. Sicily was well
placed for serving as a base for a naval domination over the waters of
both basins of the Mediterranean; but, even if Syracuse had succeeded
in uniting the whole of Sicily under its rule, a united Sicily, by itself,
would not have been strong enough to dominate the whole of the
Mediterranean and its perimeter. This could be accomplished only by
a power that succeeded in combining the strategic asset of holding Sicily
with a command over the demographic and economic resources of
either Italy or North-West Africa.

The Greek settlers in Sicily did succeed in uniting Sicily on the
cultural plane by Hellenizing the whole of it, including non-Greek
Sicilian communities that were anti-Greek politically. Before the close

of the fifth century B.C. the whole population of Sicily had not only become Greek-speaking; it had adopted the Greek institution of city-states, and originally non-Greek Sicilian city-states were now issuing coinages and building temples in the Hellenic style. On the other hand, in Italy the Greek language never gained ground in the hinterland of the Greek settlements, and these settlements themselves were eventually overwhelmed by the natives. This had happened to Cumae and to Poseidonia (Paestum) before the end of the fifth century B.C. In 289 B.C., native Italian ex-mercenaries of the defunct despot of Syracuse, Aga-thocles, seized Messina, on the Sicilian side of the Straits.

The institution of city-states was adopted in the north-west of Peninsular Italy, in Etruria and in Umbria, and down the west coast, as far south as Campania inclusive. The institution was also adopted in the south-eastern lowlands, from the 'heel' to as far north-westwards as the 'spur'. But, in the highlands in between, the natives were still in the stage of tribal organization, though they were not impervious to Hellenic culture (they adopted the West-Greek version of the Phoenician alpha-bet). During the period *c.* 600–221 B.C., Italy continued to be far more diverse than Sicily on all planes of life; yet, as it turned out, Peninsular Italy was united politically by Rome between *c.* 340 and 264 B.C., and Rome's success in uniting Italy enabled her to go on eventually to unite the whole perimeter of the Mediterranean basin. However, Rome was not the first power to attempt to unite Italy politically, and, though Rome succeeded in an enterprise in which her precursors had failed, she did not succeed easily.

The first attempt to unify Italy politically was made by the Etruscans *c.* 550–423 B.C. In the sixth century B.C. the Etruscans seized two bridge-heads, Fidenae and Rome, on the right bank of the lower Tiber, and they then occupied the lowlands, south-eastward, as far as the hinterland of Cumae. In the opposite direction they seized from the Ligurian high-landers the pass leading from Faesulae (Fiesole) to Felsina (Bologna). They began to develop the potential agricultural wealth of the Po-basin by starting to drain it, and they co-operated with the Greeks in establish-ing a commercial port at Spina, in the marshes round the mouth of the River Po. Fortune favoured the Etruscans here, since, *c.* 500 B.C., as has already been mentioned, upheavals in the interior of continental Europe diverted trade from the Rhône valley to the Po-basin via the passes through the Alps.

By about 525 B.C. it looked as if the Etruscans might be going to unite under their rule not only Peninsular Italy but the Po-basin as well. However, in 524 they tried and failed to take Cumae; between *c.* 509 and 474 B.C. they lost their hold on Latium and on Rome; in 474 B.C. they were defeated in a naval battle off Cumae by the Syracusans;

between *c.* 450 and 350 B.C., most of their settlements in the Po-basin were overrun by Celtic barbarians (Gauls) from the far side of the Alps. In 423 B.C. the Oscan highlanders from the hinterland of Campania took Capua from the Etruscans and then, in 421 B.C., took Cumae from the Greeks. The Etruscans failed politically for the same reason as the Greeks. Unlike the colonial Phoenicians, the Etruscans were unwilling to put themselves under a unitary command. Their expansion was the work of single city-states or even of single leaders of bands of military adventurers. Eventually the Etruscan states allowed themselves to be subdued, one by one, by Rome.

The Etruscans had been well placed for uniting the whole of Italy politically from the Alps to the 'toe', and if they had operated in unison they might have succeeded. The Italiot Greeks had no serious prospect of uniting even Peninsular Italy. They were too few in numbers, too far from the centre, and, above all, too destructive of each other. (The Etruscan states failed to work in unison, but at least they did not destroy each other, as the Italiot Greek states did.) The Italiot Greek state that was the least awkwardly placed for embarking on a career of expansion was the Spartan colony Taras (Tarentum), which had been founded *c.* 707 B.C. But in 473 B.C. the Tarentines were defeated crushingly by the native peoples of the south-eastern lowlands.

The Greeks came nearest to uniting both Sicily and Peninsular Italy under Syracusan rule in the reign of the despot of Syracuse Dionysius I (405–367 B.C.). Dionysius started by fortifying the city of Syracuse itself with a ring-wall, crowning the escarpment of the plateau to the west of the built-up area, which made Syracuse the largest and strongest walled city in the Mediterranean basin. In his first war with Carthage (398–392 B.C.) Dionysius cooped up the Carthaginians and their Elymian allies in the north-west corner of Sicily. He then made an entente with the Italiot Greek states Locri and Taras, with the Lucanian tribesmen in the hinterland of the 'toe' of Italy, and with the Celtic tribesmen who were overwhelming the Etruscan settlements in the Po-basin. Dionysius I's main target in Italy was Caere, the southernmost Etruscan city with a seaboard. We may guess that the sack of Caere's ally Rome by the Senones Celts in 386 B.C. had been instigated by Dionysius, and that this was the opening move in his operations against Caere. The Celtic sackers of Rome were subsequently defeated by the Caeritans, and both Caere and Massilia helped Rome to recover from her disaster. *Circa* 384 B.C. Dionysius turned the Adriatic Sea into a Syracusan lake by planting naval stations at strategic points round its coasts and in the Dalmatian archipelago. This enabled him to get into direct touch with the Celts to the north-east of the Appennines and to threaten the Etruscans from the Adriatic side. Simultaneously, also *c.* 384 B.C., Dionysius' navy in the

Tyrrhene Sea sacked Pyrgi, Caere's principal port, which was also used by Rome. By this date, Dionysius was well on the way towards building a Sicilian-Italian empire, but he failed to follow up his raid on Pyrgi by taking the cities Caere and Rome.

Dionysius had made two mistakes. In 390 B.C. he had attacked the Italiot Greek city-states that were hostile to him, and, though he succeeded in taking Rhegion in 387 and Croton in 379 B.C., this stubbornly and bitterly waged fratricidal war was exhausting for both Syracuse and its Italiot Greek victims. Dionysius' second mistake was to go to war with Carthage again in 383 B.C. This time he was defeated, and in 378 B.C. he had to make peace at the cost of ceding territory. These two mistakes of Dionysius I left the field in Italy open for other competitors. Dionysius I's son and successor Dionysius II (at Syracuse 367–356, at Locri 356–347, at Syracuse again 347–344 B.C.) was not equal to the task that he had inherited, and the decline of Syracuse under his regime was not arrested by Plato's second and third visits to Syracuse in 367 and 361 B.C. and was not counterbalanced by the regime at Taras, from 367 to 360 B.C., of a 'philosopher-king', Archytas, who here temporarily put Plato's political ideal into practice.

By 344 B.C. the western Greeks had fallen into such a desperate plight that they began to call for help from their kinsmen to the east of the Straits of Otranto. The first of the six East-Greek 'saviours' who responded to West-Greek appeals between 344 and 280 B.C. was the most estimable and the most successful. Timoleon, a citizen of Syracuse's mother-state Corinth, succeeded, with slender resources, in overthrowing Dionysius II and all the other Siceliot Greek local despots. He then defeated the Carthaginians at the head of the united Siceliot Greek forces. Between his arrival in 344 and his voluntary retirement in 337 B.C., he had set up moderate democratic regimes in Syracuse and in the other Siceliot Greek states; he had federated these with each other; and he had united some of the native Siceliot city-states with Syracuse by giving their citizens Syracusan citizenship in addition to the citizenship of their own states, which were not deprived of their local autonomy. Timoleon also persuaded the eastern Greeks to send, and the Siceliot Greeks to receive, large numbers of new Greek settlers. (The population explosion in the Hellenic World, which had started in the eighth century B.C., was still vigorous enough in the fourth and third centuries B.C. to provide these settlers for Timoleon in Sicily and a still more numerous contingent for Alexander and his successors in Asia.) Unhappily, Timoleon's enlightened constructive work in Sicily did not long outlive him.

The other five East-Greek 'saviours' of the western Greeks all failed more swiftly. They came from two states: Sparta, which was the mother-state of Taras, and Epirus, which was the nearest East-Greek state to the Straits of Otranto. The resources of Sparta and Epirus were almost as inadequate as Corinth's for salvaging the western Greeks; and Timoleon's Spartan and Epirot successors did not succeed, as Timoleon had succeeded, in inspiring the western Greeks to work together for their own salvation. King Archidamus III of Sparta, who arrived in 343 B.C. to help Taras against the Samnite confederacy in its hinterland, was killed in battle in 338 B.C. The next 'saviour', King Alexander I of Epirus, arrived *c.* 334 and was killed in 331 B.C. The expeditions of two Spartan princes—Acrotatus to Syracuse in 315 and his brother Cleonymus to Italy in 303 B.C.—were fiascos.

The latest and least ineffective 'saviour' was King Pyrrhus of Epirus, who campaigned in Italy against the Romans at the Tarentines' invitation, and in Sicily against the Carthaginians at the Siceliot Greeks' invitation, from 380 to 375 B.C. Pyrrhus was helped by the failure of the Carthaginians and the Romans to give each other military and naval aid against their formidable common enemy. Pyrrhus nearly succeeded in building an Epirot empire that would have included the whole of Sicily and also south-eastern Italy, perhaps as far north-westward as Terracina. His failure was due partly to the inadequacy of Epirus's resources and partly to his own personal volatility—a weakness which made Pyrrhus no match for the pertinacity of the Roman empire-builders whom he was attempting to contain. Pyrrhus came too late in the day. In 272 B.C. not only Taras but the native South-Italian Samnite, Lucanian, and Bruttian confederacies all capitulated to Rome. The political unification of Peninsular Italy under Roman rule was completed in 264 B.C.

Rome was well placed for uniting Peninsular Italy. She held the lowest bridge over the Tiber, Peninsular Italy's greatest river, and the Tiber reached the Tyrrhene Sea at the midpoint of the Peninsula's north-western lowlands. Yet Rome's inland Etruscan neighbour Veii, which Rome took and destroyed in 391 B.C., and her maritime Etruscan neighbour and ally Caere, which she annexed in 274 B.C., were both almost equally well-placed for empire-building. Rome owed her success to the political ability of her nobles, who kept the government in their own hands, but this native ability might not have borne fruit if it had not been ripened by an Hellenic education. The Romans were Hellenized first indirectly, by Etruscan rulers and residents, and later directly, by an intercourse with Cumae which was extended progressively to the rest of the Hellenic World.

Rome was created by Etruscans who established themselves there *c.* 550 B.C. They found a cluster of Latin pastoral village communities; they turned this into an Etruscoid city-state with a dense agricultural population in its rural domain. In the last millennium B.C., city-states and associations of city-states were the only acceptable forms of polity in the Mediterranean basin. This originally Sumerian institution was common to the Phoenicians, the Etruscans, and the Greeks. Any polity in this reign that did not conform to the city-state pattern was severely handicapped. This was one of the reasons for the failures of Macedon, Aetolia, and Samnium, and for Rome's success. Rome's city-state constitution and culture were impressive and attractive for peoples that were still in the pre-city-state stage of political development. This was a Roman gift that helped to reconcile more backward peoples to being incorporated in the Roman body politic. In particular, Rome's city-state constitution was an asset for Rome in her contest with the Samnite Confederacy, since most members of this were still in the pre-city-state stage during the years 343–272 B.C., in which the Romano–Samnite wars were waged.

From *c.* 550 B.C. onwards, Rome's fortunes were affected intimately by events in the surrounding non-Roman World. Rome's subjection to Etruscan despots from *c.* 550 till 509 B.C., or perhaps till *c.* 474 B.C., made Rome a city-state and gave her a miniature empire over her fellow Latins. The price, for Rome, of getting rid of Etruscan rule was the Latins' liberation from Roman rule. They became a federation of city-states that was associated with the Roman republican city-state on a footing of equality. However, the liquidation of the Etruscan regime at Rome did not sever relations between Rome and Carthage. We do not know whether the Romano–Carthaginian treaty of *c.* 506–501 B.C. was the first of the series, or whether it was concluded after or before the inauguration of the republican regime at Rome, but there may have been as many as four subsequent Romano–Carthaginian treaties before the breach between the two powers in 264 B.C.; and these treaties were advantageous for both parties.

The doubling of Rome's power through her capture and destruction of Veii and annexation of the Veientine territory *c.* 393–388 B.C. alarmed the Latins and evoked Dionysius I's counter-measures against Rome and against Rome's ally Caere. The sack of Rome by the Senones Celts in 386 B.C. enabled the Latin federation to dissociate itself from Rome. From 386 to 356 B.C., while the two Dionysii successively held Syracuse, a series of further Gallic raids on Roman territory, launched by the Dionysii from a base in Apulia, prevented Rome from constraining the Latins to re-associate themselves with her, and a Gallic raid, accompanied by a fresh break-away on the part of the Latins, occurred in 346 B.C., the year after Dionysius II's temporary re-establishment at Syracuse. Archidamus III's presence in southern Italy from 343 to 338 B.C. induced the Samnites to make a peace-settlement with Rome on terms which left the Campanian city-states under Rome's hegemony. Pyrrhus' campaigns in the west from 280 to 275 B.C. obviously affected Rome's fortunes directly and vitally.

Like most other states at most other times and places, Rome expanded her domain whenever and wherever she found an opportunity. An early case in point is her persistently sustained assault on Veii ending in the conquest of Veii *c.* 393–388 B.C. Rome's conquest of the rest of Peninsular Italy and her subsequent conquest of Sicily were initiated by two Roman acts of aggression, each of which was deliberate, though the implications were perhaps not perceived by the Roman Government, and the consequences were probably not foreseen by it, in either case. In 340 or 339 B.C. Rome challenged Samnium by taking the Campanian city-states under her protection in contravention of a Romano–Samnite treaty that had been concluded in 350 B.C. In 264 B.C. Rome challenged Carthage by taking under her protection the Mamertine Italian occupants of Messina (Agathocles' former mercenaries) in contravention of a Romano–Carthaginian treaty or understanding.

By 264 B.C. Rome had succeeded in an enterprise in which first the Etruscans and then the despot of Syracuse, Dionysius I, had failed. Rome had now united the whole of Peninsular Italy under her rule. What were the means by which she had achieved this?

One of Rome's assets has been mentioned already. She had been organized effectively as a city-state by her transitory Etruscan despots. In the second place Rome had managed to achieve and maintain domestic political harmony after the overthrow of a despotic regime. In Greek city-states the usual sequel was a struggle for power between factions whose interests were conflicting. This was, for instance, the sequel at Athens, where the Peisistratidae were overthrown at about the same date as the Tarquins at Rome. At Rome, too, the inauguration of a republican regime was followed by domestic strife, but in 364 B.C. the Roman aristocrats struck a bargain with the leaders of the unprivileged majority of the citizen body at the expense of these turncoats' followers, and this unholy alliance survived till 133 B.C. with only occasional popular upheavals (e.g. in 339 and 287 B.C.). This entrenchment of social and political injustice at home enabled Rome to present a united front to her neighbours.

The reinforced Roman oligarchs' policy in conducting Rome's foreign affairs was to support their own counterparts in other states, and this Roman policy tempted foreign oligarchs, whose monopoly of power at home was insecure, to sacrifice their state's independence for the sake of winning the firmly established Roman oligarchy's support. The collusion of the Capuan oligarchs with the Roman 'establishment' is the classic example of this particular Roman manoeuvre for drawing a foreign state into Rome's toils.

The Roman 'establishment's' ententes with foreign oligarchies were underpinned by family friendships and by mixed marriages. Conversely, the citizens of communities that had been forced by Rome to become her allies on terms dictated by Rome were hindered in some cases from making common cause with each other against Rome by vetos on mixed marriages and on inter-state trade. Rome's allies, like Sparta's, had to supply contingents of troops for Rome's armies, and, unlike Sparta's allies, they did not have a say in the political decisions that involved them in participating in Rome's wars. However, like Sparta's allies, and unlike Athens's allies in the fifth century B.C., Rome's allies did not have to pay any monetary tribute to the paramount power. They were exploited without being humiliated.

After the defeat, in 335 B.C., of the Latin and Campanian federations, which had seceded from Rome in 337, both federations were dissolved, and in 334 B.C. a number of Latin and Campanian city-states were incorporated in the Roman body politic without being deprived of their autonomous municipal self-government. In some cases their citizens were given the full rights of Roman citizenship, besides having the concomitant duties imposed on them; in other cases, they were subjected to all the duties without being granted all the rights. This Roman institution of 'dual citizenship' may have been modelled on the relation which Timoleon had established between Syracuse and some of the Siceliot city-states in 344–337 B.C. Syracuse had harassed Rome so severely from 386 to 346 B.C. that the Roman Government must have kept a close watch on Syracusan affairs.

In 333 B.C. Rome made a further experiment in 'dual citizenship'. She planted a small coastguard colony of Roman citizens at Antium and gave them an autonomous municipal constitution without depriving them of their Roman citizenship. This and subsequent Roman coastguard colonies were modelled on the Latin colonies that had been founded by the now dissolved federation of Latin city-states. Rome preserved the already existing Latin colonies. She gave them the status of first-class allies, and she added to their number as she extended her hold farther over Italy. She planted new Latin colonies in skilfully chosen strategic positions to serve as garrisons for holding down conquered territories.

The Roman Government's exploration and exploitation of the strategic geography of Peninsular Italy was masterly. Between 318 and 313 B.C., Rome encircled Samnium by finding a route across the central Appennines and securing a foothold in Apulia. Between 304 and 289 B.C. she insulated the southern from the northern independent Peninsular

Italian states by crushing some highland peoples and planting a string of Latin colonies, Roman coastguard colonies, and non-autonomous settlements of Roman citizens on expropriated territory.

Rome's policy was to stalk her intended victims one by one. After the expulsion of Dionysius II from Syracuse in 356 B.C., Rome's only remaining formidable competitor for the domination of Peninsular Italy was the Samnite Confederacy. Accordingly, from 350 till after Pyrrhus' withdrawal from Italy in 274 B.C., Rome concentrated her energies on expansion southward and kept the Etruscan states quiet by concluding truces (not permanent treaties) with them. Rome even cajoled the Senones Celts, who had sacked Rome in 386 B.C. and had settled on the Adriatic coast of Peninsular Italy just to the north of the Syracusan colony Ancona. In 330 B.C. Rome induced the Senones to make a truce with her, to hold good for thirty years, and the Senones conveniently kept faith. Thus Rome had her northern neighbours at her mercy when the departure of Pyrrhus and the capitulation of the Samnites set Rome's hands free for subduing the last surviving independent states in the peninsula.

In the Romano–Carthaginian war of 264–241 B.C. fleets and armies were mobilized, and casualties were suffered, on a scale that had no precedent in the history of warfare in the Mediterranean basin. This great war left Rome in possession of the whole of Sicily except Syracuse's domain, as well as the whole of Peninsular Italy. Syracuse's domain had been at peace while the rest of Sicily had been a grievously devastated war-zone. This portion of Sicily had owed its immunity to the sagacity of Hiero II, the most benign of Syracuse's series of despots. In 263 B.C. Hiero had presciently changed sides, and during the last forty-eight years of his reign, down to his death in 215 B.C., he was Rome's loyal client. The years 263–215 B.C. were as happy an interlude in the turbulent history of Syracuse as the years 344–337 B.C.; and the Pax Hieronica lasted seven times as long as Timoleon's regime.

As for Rome, the outcome of her first war with Carthage left her navally predominant in the western basin of the Mediterranean. In 238 B.C., while Carthage was paralysed by a revolt in Africa of the mercenary troops whom she had had to evacuate from Sicily and had been trying to pay off cheaply, Rome seized Sardinia and compelled Carthage to cede it to her. However, in 237 B.C. the mercenaries' revolt was suppressed by Hamilcar Barca ('the lightning'), the hero of the recent war with Rome. In the same year Hamilcar took an expeditionary force to Spain. By 221 B.C., he and his son-in-law and successor Hasdrubal had built up in the Iberian Peninsula a new Carthaginian land-empire that was far larger and more valuable than Carthage's lost beach-heads at the north-western tip of Sicily. In 221 B.C., Hasdrubal was succeeded in the

Spanish command by Hannibal, Hamilcar's son. Hannibal had long since determined to retrieve Carthage's defeat by Rome in the war of 264–241 B.C., and he was now in a position to make the attempt. Thus in 221 B.C. the situation in the western Mediterranean was as inconclusive as it was in the eastern Mediterranean. In the next phase of the history of the western end of the Old-World Oikoumenê, these two regions were going to coalesce into a single war-zone.

[35]

THE CH'IN AND WESTERN HAN
IMPERIAL REGIMES IN CHINA,

221 B.C.–A.D. 9

IN the regions of the Old-World Oikoumenê to the west of China, from the Indian subcontinent to the Straits of Gibraltar, the year 221 B.C. was not marked by any conclusive event. By contrast, this year was an epoch-making one for China. This was the year in which the political unification of China was completed, and the date of its completion does mark a dividing line in Chinese history. Before 221 B.C., China had been a cultural but never yet a political unity. Since then China has sometimes fallen apart politically, but, to date, she has always come together again politically after a short or long interlude of disunity and disorder.

There was continuity between pre-221-B.C. China and post-221-B.C. China in one respect. Since the dawn of Chinese history the Chinese World has been constantly expanding geographically. By 221 B.C. it had expanded southwards, into the Yangtse basin, from its nuclear domain in the lower basin of the Yellow River and in the valley of the Yellow River's tributary the Wei. King Chêng of Ch'in state, who became the First Emperor (Shih Hwang-ti) of a united China in 221 B.C., incorporated in his empire, before his death, the territory covered by present-day Kwangtung, Kwangsi, and Northern Vietnam. In 111 B.C. the Emperor Han Wu-ti re-conquered this southern territory, which had recovered its independence after the fall of the Ch'in Empire. In 108 B.C. Han Wu-ti overthrew an independent Chinese state in Korea that had been established by Chinese settlers, annexed northern Korea, and made it into four Chinese commanderies.

Korea and the South could be incorporated in the Chinese Empire because they were cultivable. On the Chinese World's northern border there was a fringe of territory, the present-day Inner Mongolia, that can make either poor cultivated land or good pasture, but the Eurasian steppe itself was baffling terrain for Chinese peasants, armies, and administrators. Here the pastoral nomad economy, institutions, and method of warfare had been worked out to fit the physical environment, and the nomads on their own ground were formidable for their sedentary neighbours. The Hsiung-nu (Hun) nomads defeated the re-founder of the Chinese Empire, Han Liu P'ang (Kao-tsu) in 200 B.C. The Emperor himself only just escaped suffering Cyrus II's fate. The Chinese Imperial Government had to cede territory to the Hsiung-nu and to pay them tribute, and they invaded China in 177 B.C. and again in 158 B.C. A Chinese counter-offensive was started in 128 B.C., but the Hsiung-nu were as elusive as the Skyths, at the western end of the steppe, had been when their pastures had been invaded by Darius I. Like the Skyths, the Hsiung-nu could not be exterminated; nor could they be subjugated or evicted effectively.

As a prelude to the Chinese counter-offensive, Han Wu-ti had sent an envoy, Chang Ch'ien, in 139 B.C., to get into touch with the Yüeh-chih (*alias* Tokharoi) a nomad people who, in 174 B.C., had been driven westward out of Kansu by the Hsiung-nu. Chang Ch'ien's mission was to persuade the Yüeh-chih to co-operate with the Chinese in catching their common enemy, the Hsiung-nu, between them, in a pincers' grip. In 128 B.C. Chang Ch'ien found the Yüeh-chih in Transoxania. He failed to persuade them to try conclusions with the Hsiung-nu again, but he made his way back to China in 126/5 B.C. In 115 B.C. he started on a second mission, this time to Farghanah in the Jaxartes basin and to Soghd, between the Jaxartes and the Oxus. The Chinese occupied Farghanah in 104, 102, and 42 B.C. Chang Ch'ien's missions made the Chinese aware of the existence and the cultural eminence of the civilizations to the west of China. China had, of course, been receiving stimulus and knowledge from the west and from other quarters, beyond China's own borders, since at least as early as the Neolithic Age. From the last quarter of the second century B.C. onwards, China began to be conscious of her links with the rest of the Old-World Oikoumenê.

The momentum of the Chinese World's expansion had not been arrested in 221 B.C., but, in a number of other respects, Ch'in state's career had made a clean sweep of China's past since 356 B.C., the year in which the Legalist philosopher-statesman Shang Yang had started work on his revolutionary reorganization of Ch'in institutions. In 256–249 B.C., Ch'in Shih Hwang-ti's grandfather had extinguished the House of Chou, which had preserved for the Chinese society a vestige of unity on the plane of ritual. By 221 B.C., Shih Hwang-ti himself had extinguished all the six local states that had been Ch'in's rivals. But Ch'in Shih Hwang-ti also doomed his own ancestral kingdom to extinction. This result of his work was the exact opposite of his intentions, and no doubt he was unaware of what he was doing. Like Assyria four hundred years earlier and Macedon a hundred years earlier, Ch'in died of empire-building. Her native population was depleted by military casualties and by expatriation in garrisons posted abroad, and the vacuum in Ch'in's home territory was filled, like the vacuum in Assyria's, with deportees. After 221 B.C. the 'establishments' of all the six conquered local states were deported to 'the land beyond the passes', but the deadliest of the means by which Ch'in state committed suicide was by making her regime intolerable for her victims.

Political unification in Ch'in Shih Hwang-ti's style was, in fact, so intolerable that the Ch'in Empire was overthrown and was broken up within three years of the grim founder's death in 210 B.C., but political unification itself proved to be irreversible. After the liquidation of the Ch'in Empire in 207 B.C., the Han Empire was founded in 202 B.C. Ch'in Shih Hwang-ti's imperial acts had made both the liquidation and the re-foundation inevitable.

Shih Hwang-ti not only destroyed the structure of the conquered states by deporting their 'establishments'; he effaced their frontiers by re-mapping the whole Chinese World into commanderies. These were administered by Ch'in officials in the Legalist spirit. The peasantry was oppressed with corvées and taxes. Li Sse (*c.* 280–208 B.C.), Shih Hwang-ti's Legalist minister, tried to suppress the non-Legalist schools of philosophy. In 213 B.C. he instigated 'the burning of the books', and he proposed to follow this up by burying alive about four hundred obnoxious scholars the next year. At the same time, Shih Hwang-ti satisfied some of the Chinese society's most pressing needs.

The greatest of these needs—political unification—has been mentioned already; the next greatest need was standardization. Shih Hwang-ti standardized scripts and axle-gauges by making the whole of China conform to the Ch'in pattern. (On the soft loess soil of nuclear China, wheels must run in ruts, and local differences of axle-gauge had limited the range of carts, as the range of locomotives and rolling-stock is limited by differences of rail-gauge in the Modern Age.) Shih Hwang-ti's greatest feat of standardization and unification was to consolidate the anti-nomad walls of his own state Ch'in and of Ch'in's northern neighbours Chao and Yen into a single continuous Great Wall. Shih Hwang-ti's Great Wall ran to the north of the Yellow River's north-west loop. It thus embraced what is today the Ordos district of Mongolia, and its effect was partly counter-productive. Its construction moved the Hsiung-nu to retort to this ocular evidence of China's political unification by uniting among themselves, with consequences for China that have been noted already.

The objective of the general insurrection in 209 B.C. was to restore the *ancien régime*. The consequence of the insurgents' success in liquidating the Ch'in regime was a struggle with each other for the spoils. The most imposing of the pretenders was Hsiang Yü, an aristocrat from the former Ch'u state. Hsiang Yü proposed to instal a scion of Ch'u state's royal family as nominal emperor of the whole of China, with Hsiang Yü as the power behind the imperial throne, but the winner in the civil war of 205–202 B.C. was Liu P'ang (Kao-tsu), a soldier of fortune from the lower basin of the Hwai River.

Liu P'ang had to reward his confederates by giving them fiefs, and had also to placate public sentiment by reviving some of the liquidated kingdoms, but he kept the former territory of Ch'in state 'within the passes' under his own direct rule, and he sited his capital at Ching-chao, adjoining the future site of Ch'ang-an, and close to the site of the latest capital of the Western Chou, but on the opposite side of the Wei River from Ch'in state's latest capital, Hsien-yang. Liu P'ang had learned the lesson of both Shih Hwang-ti's and Hsiang Yü's failures. He and his successors saw that they must unite China more effectively than Hsiang Yü but less provocatively than Shih Hwang-ti; so, in restoring Shih Hwang-ti's effective unification, they hastened slowly.

The fiefs were first made innocuous by rapid transfers and depositions of the incumbents, and they were then shredded into fragments by the operation of a decree, promulgated in 144 B.C., that in future they should be divided among all the sons of a defunct fief-holder and should no longer be kept intact through being inherited by the eldest son only. The progressive fragmentation of local political and administrative units of all kinds was the Han dynasty's sovereign device for tightening the Imperial Government's control over them. The Han Empire started as a bundle of fifteen commanderies administered by Imperial officials and ten officially autonomous kingdoms. By the year A.D. 1/2 there were eighty-three commanderies and twenty kingdoms. The proportion between the two kinds of local unit had been changed, and the units of both kinds had been drastically reduced in size. All newly conquered territories had been made into commanderies. A concerted revolt of seven local kings in 154 B.C. had moved the Imperial Government to consummate the process of reducing the kingdoms to impotence by decreeing, in 127 B.C., that, when a king died, his eldest son must cede half of his father's kingdom to his youngest brother.

The Imperial Government's progressive re-assumption of direct control over the local administration of a vast territory raised the question of how the Imperial administrative service was to be recruited. To re-create a corps of local administrators in the Ch'in style was out of the question. Ch'in Shih Hwang-ti's Legalist agents had provoked the insurrection of 209 B.C., and they had been massacred by the enraged insurgents. The reaction against Shih Hwang-ti's autocracy had been so

vehement and the nostalgia for the *ancien régime* was so strong that Liu
P'ang's first impulse after becoming Emperor in 202 B.C. was to adopt in
practice (Liu P'ang was no theorist) the Taoist policy of deliberate
laissez-faire. However, a Confucian scholar is said to have convinced
Liu P'ang that this antithesis of the Ch'in policy was impracticable. In
196 B.C. Liu P'ang ordered the authorities in each of the commanderies
and kingdoms to send promising candidates for posts in an Imperial
administrative service to Ching-chao for a selection of them to be made
there after an informal examination. After 191 B.C. Confucian scholars
reconstructed five classical books, which were held to have been edited
and canonized by Confucius. The Emperor Han Wu-ti (ruled 140–87
B.C.) decreed that the qualification for appointment should be proficiency
in writing in the style of the Confucian classics, and in interpreting the
Confucian philosophy, to the satisfaction of the Confucian scholars of
the day.

In theory, Wu-ti was throwing the public service open to intellectual
talent; but at this stage the Chinese civil service examination system was
not yet cut-and-dried; academic distinction was not, and never became,
the sole avenue to appointment and to promotion; personal influence did
not cease to count; and in any case it was hard for a poor family to pay
for a boy's long preparatory education in a difficult subject. Moreover,
the adoption and study of the Confucian philosophy was now *de rigueur*,
and this philosophy had become very different from what it had been in
Confucius' day. The virtually non-theistic rationalism of Confucius had
been diluted with religiosity and superstition as a result of the mixture
of many local traditions, which were also of many different cultural
levels, in the melting-pot of a Chinese Empire which now included a
number of culturally backward populations on its fringes.

Confucius had sought to obtain an administrative appointment in one
of the local warring states, and his aim in his eventual career as a teacher
had been to preserve the traditional structure of Chinese society. He
had not foreseen the political unification of China, and possibly he would
have disapproved of it. The statesmen who brought it about were not
Confucians; they were Legalists. It is also possible that Confucius would
not have recognized his paternity of the Confucianism of the second
century B.C. Yet the Emperor Wu-ti's act of 'establishing' the adulterated
Confucianism of his day was a posthumous victory for the Confucian re-
interpretation of the meaning of the term *chün tzu*. Officially at least, the
Chinese Empire was to be administered henceforth by men who held
their posts, not by right of birth, but as the reward of personal merit.

The sequel, however, was ironical. An official who had obtained his
appointment in virtue of being a *chün tzu* in the Confucian sense had, and
often took, the opportunity, given to him by office, of making himself a

chün tzu in the original sense. He could make himself a landowner and could bequeath his estate to his son, whom he could then afford to educate for becoming a Confucian civil servant in his turn. The Confucian officials soon came to feel a loyalty to their families and to their class, and these loyalties might and did conflict with their loyalty to the Emperor and with their duty to the non-privileged mass of the Emperor's subjects, whom the Confucian officials governed on the Emperor's behalf.

Nor was this division of loyalties reprehensible in Confucians; for the arch-Confucian Mencius had maintained, as against Mo-tzu, that a virtuous man's love for his fellow human beings ought to be gradational. A man's nearest ought also to be his dearest, and an official's family and class were nearer to him than either the Emperor or the common herd. In an empire in which the central government had re-asserted its direct authority over its subjects, an official's duty to the Emperor was to apply the harsh Legalist system that had been introduced in Ch'in state in the fourth century B.C. and had been imposed on the rest of China by Ch'in Shih Hwang-ti after 221 B.C.; and in truth, under the re-centralized Han regime, there was a hard core of Legalism beneath the Confucian veneer. The inhabitants of a politically unified China felt that the Chinese Empire was virtually conterminous with the civilized world, and the Chinese philosophy that might have inspired ecumenical civil servants to perform their duty to mankind benevolently was Mo-tzu's; for Mo-tzu had maintained that a virtuous man ought to feel an equal concern for all his fellow human beings. However, it was not Mo-tzu, but Confucius as interpreted by Mencius, who won the posthumous prize of having his philosophy made official on an ecumenical scale.

For the Confucian official the Han regime was vastly preferable to the Ch'in regime. He was the political master of the Emperor's subjects whom he governed; he was the economic master, as well, of the peasants on the land which he had acquired; he and his colleagues were even potentially the masters of the reigning Imperial dynasty. The Emperor Wu-ti's Confucian adviser Tung Chung-shu established the doctrine that a dynasty reigned in virtue of having received a mandate from Heaven; that this mandate could be withdrawn; and that its withdrawal was signified by the onset of social disorders and natural disasters. A tacit corollary of the doctrine was that the Confucian civil service was to be the judge of whether these signs of the times declared that a dynasty's mandate had been exhausted. For the unprivileged mass of the population, the difference between the Ch'in and Han Imperial regimes became less and less perceptible as the Confucian scholar-administrator-landlords added field to field. From first to last, the Chinese peasantry was near the limits of its powers of endurance. For the peasantry, the rise of a new class of private landlords armed with public authority was the last straw.

Under any regime the maintenance of the Empire was bound to impose heavy burdens on those of its inhabitants—and they were the great majority—who were not the regime's privileged beneficiaries. Under the Han regime a Chinese peasant had to perform one month's labour service every year, and he might be conscripted to serve for two years in the army. In the huge area of a united China, a conscript's service might take him much farther from his home than his ancestors had been taken when they had been conscripted by the local governments of the warring states. The risk of death was, no doubt, less. Military service now meant doing garrison duty along the Great Wall instead of being engaged in deadly pitched battles in the heart of the Chinese World. But the absentee's risk of economic ruin was now greater, and the peasant's distress was the acquisitive landowner's opportunity. This opportunity was increased when the conscript peasant soldiers were carried off not only to the Wall but far out into the steppe beyond the Wall during the Chinese Empire's Hundred Years War with the Hsiung-nu (128–36 B.C.).

Forced labour service might take the form of working in the Imperial iron and salt mines, building roads, digging canals, keeping existing roads and canals in repair, and hauling loads of grain along canals, or up rivers against the current, to supply the court and government at the Han dynasty's capital, Ching-chao, in 'the land beyond the passes', or to supply the garrisons along the Great Wall, which was still farther away than Ching-chao was from the eastern and southern fields in which the wheat and the rice were grown. The garrisons' needs could not be met from the produce of fields in their neighbourhood; for the country through which the Wall ran was arid.

The Chinese World had a strikingly different geographical structure from the Hellenic World. It was not the perimeter of a chain of inland seas; it was a solid land-mass; and this made for greater uniformity of culture and for greater durability of political unity in so far as the problem of transport could be solved. The greater part of the Hellenic World was within easy reach of the sea shore, and, except in the hinterlands of the Black Sea, navigable rivers did not have an important role there. The Chinese, like the Hellenic, World was dependent for its communications on waterways, and it was well supplied with rivers, but no great Chinese river runs either from south to north or from east to west— and the food-producing districts of the Han Empire lay to the south of the Great Wall and to the south-east of the capital.

The rivers therefore needed to be supplemented by canals; on the usable reaches of the rivers, freight had to be hauled upstream; and the water-route up the course of the Yellow River is particularly difficult to negotiate at the point where the river, turning at an acute angle from southward to north-eastward, breaks through the mountain-chain that is the western boundary of the North-China plain. Freight bound for Ching-chao had to run the gauntlet of the natural obstacles in this defile; freight bound for the Great Wall had to be carried overland to those sectors of the Wall that were not adjacent to the Yellow River. The hauling of food-supplies was not profitable for private enterprise; so conscript labour had to be drawn upon for the performance of this indispensable public work.

Thus the Han Empire had no unemployed reserves of economic energy. It had to exert itself up to the limit of its economic power in order to keep itself in being, and, in these circumstances, the Confucian bureaucracy's conversion of itself into a new class of landlords was too heavy a burden for the Imperial economy to bear. The Han regime was successful in progressively reducing the size and the autonomy of the political and administrative subdivisions of the Empire; it failed to prevent the number and the size of large private estates from increasing. Already, in Han Wu-ti's reign, the danger of this for society and for the Empire had been perceived by Tung Chung-shu, the Emperor's Confucian adviser who had formulated the doctrine of 'the mandate of Heaven'. In the year 6 B.C. an Imperial decree was promulgated which set a limit to the amount of land that an individual might hold. But the implementation of this decree rested with the administrator-landlords whose private interests conflicted with their public duty. Accordingly, the decree remained a dead letter, and in A.D. 9 the Western Han dynasty fell.

It was replaced by an Emperor, Wang Mang, who conceived of his mandate from Heaven as being a mission to solve the agrarian problem which the Confucian bureaucracy had prevented the Western Han dynasty from doing. The bureaucracy frustrated Wang Mang too. In A.D. 18, before Wang Mang's death in A.D. 23, a peasant revolt in Shan-tung had proclaimed the failure of Wang Mang's attempt to do the peasants justice and to alleviate their lot. But the peasant insurgents did not inherit the Empire and its problems. In A.D. 25 a branch of the House of Han, the Eastern Han dynasty, set itself up with its capital at Loyang, the former seat of the Eastern Chou. By A.D. 36 the founder of the Eastern Han dynasty, Kwang-wu, had suppressed the peasant revolt and had re-instated the fallen Western Han dynasty's Confucian bureaucratic regime.

Both the Western Han dynasty and the peasantry had been victims of the Confucian bureaucrat-landowners. This new social class was the Empire's cement, but it was also 'China's sorrow'. The mandarinate was the true culprit from whom 'the mandate of Heaven' ought to have been withdrawn. Confucians in office had become Legalists in spirit, and the interests that they served with a Legalist ruthlessness were their own, not the Crown's. But by this time the new privileged class had become firmly entrenched. It was the one element in the society of Imperial China that survived the wrath of Heaven which this master-class itself had called down upon China during the tragic years A.D. 9–36.

[36]

THE MEDITERRANEAN BASIN, SOUTH-WEST ASIA, AND INDIA,

221 B.C.–A.D. 48

FROM 221 B.C. to A.D. 36 the Chinese peasants suffered severely. The first political unifier's draconian regime lasted for only twelve years (221–210 B.C.), and it was followed by eight years of chaos and civil war (209–202 B.C.). The subsequent Western Han regime was followed by an unsuccessful peasant revolt (A.D. 18–36). Yet the Chinese peasants' lot during this period was not so hard as it had been during the preceding period of Chinese history—the Age of the Warring States; nor was it so hard as the peasants' lot in the regions between China and the Atlantic during the years 221 B.C.–A.D. 48.

At the centre and at the western end of the Old-World Oikoumenê, this quarter of a millennium saw the extinction of five great powers: the Mauryan, Seleucid, Ptolemaic, and Carthaginian Empires, and the Kingdom of Macedon. Of the great powers that had been in existence to the west of China in 221 B.C., only one, the Roman Empire, was still in being in A.D. 48. By 31 B.C. this empire, which in 221 B.C. had been confined to Italy and the adjacent islands, had expanded to embrace the whole perimeter of the Mediterranean, but not the whole of the power-vacuum to the west of China. To the east of the River Euphrates, a region comprising Mesopotamia, Babylonia, and Iran was now occupied by the war-band of Parthian nomads from the Eurasian steppe who in 221 B.C. had not yet encroached on the sedentary world farther westward than Parthia (the present-day Khorasan). To the east of the Parthian Empire, another war-band of Eurasian nomads, the Kushan section of the Yüeh-chih (*alias* Tokharoi), established in A.D. 48 an empire that straddled the Hindu Kush and united the upper basins of the Oxus and Jaxartes rivers with north-western India.

These changes in the political map of the Old-World Oikoumenê to the west of China had been the product of catastrophic wars, revolutions, and *Völkerwanderungen*. The Roman revolution had engulfed all the countries that had fallen into Roman hands; the migration of the Yüeh-chih from what is today the Chinese province of Kansu had set in motion all the Eurasian pastoral nomad peoples farther to the west and had driven southwards those of them that, during the preceding five centuries, had ranged over the steppe to the east of the Caspian Sea. Meanwhile, on the cultural plane, the development and dissemination of Hellenism had continued during the ethnic, military, political, and economic turmoil.

Not one of the three empires that were in being, to the west of China, in A.D. 48 was ruled by Greeks; each of them was founded on the ruins of previous Greek states. Yet all three empires were consciously and proudly 'philhellenic'. Each, in its own dominions, had adopted the Hellenic civilization and was propagating it. Greek was now the language of civilization from the upper course of the River Jumna, in north-western India, as far westward as the western tip of Sicily. Hellenism in Roman dress was being propagated through the medium of the Latin language from Peninsular Italy into continental Europe up to the line of the Rhine and the Danube, and into North-West Africa up to the northern edge of the Sahara. By A.D. 48 Hellenism had been expanding for eight centuries, and the farther it had spread, the more intimately it had come to be interfused with the diverse non-Hellenic cultures on whose domains it had intruded; yet, in this gradually maturing cultural compost, the Hellenic component was still everywhere the dominant element.

The earliest symptoms of the upheaval which was thus accompanied by the progress of Hellenization manifested themselves in India. Here the structure of the Mauryan Empire began to show signs of weakening already before the Emperor Ashoka's death in 232 B.C.; but the tornado that devastated three-quarters of the Old-World Oikoumenê was generated at its opposite extremity. In 219 B.C. Hannibal attacked and took Saguntum, a town on the Mediterranean coast of Spain which was a Roman protectorate, though it lay to the south of the line of the River Ebro, which, in 226 B.C., had been accepted as the boundary between the Roman and the Carthaginian spheres of influence in an agreement between the Roman Government and Hasdrubal, Hannibal's brother-in-law and immediate predecessor in the command of the new Carthaginian Empire in Spain that had been founded by Hannibal's father Hamilcar. In 218 B.C. Hannibal marched (with elephants) from the Ebro across the Pyrenees and the Rhône and the Alps into the Po-basin, which Rome was then in the act of incorporating in her dominions. Hannibal defeated a Roman army there, crossed the Appennines, destroyed another Roman army at Lake Trasimene, in Etruria, in 217 B.C., and then destroyed a third Roman army, the largest of the three, at Cannae in Apulia in 216 B.C.

Hannibal's crowning victory at Cannae put his strategy to the test. In the first Romano–Carthaginian War (264–241 B.C.) Rome had wrested from Carthage the naval command over the western basin of the Mediterranean, and the military man-power that Rome had acquired through the political unification of Peninsular Italy far outnumbered that of Carthage's citizens, her Libyphoenician allies, and her Libyan and Spanish subjects. Carthage's inferiority in numbers was offset by the expertise and *esprit de corps* of the small professional army that Hannibal had inherited from his father and his brother-in-law; Carthage's loss of her former sea-power had been circumvented by Hannibal's logistical *tour de force* of invading Italy from Spain overland. Hannibal knew that Rome's domination was unpopular among the non-Roman majority of Italians, and especially among those who had had the onerous obligations of Roman citizenship imposed on them without having been given the first-class Roman citizens' prerogatives. Hannibal had reckoned that, if he achieved what he actually achieved at Cannae in 216 B.C., Rome's Peninsular Italian allies and second-class citizens would secede, that Rome's superiority in man-power would then be lost, and that Rome would have to capitulate on terms that would reduce her territory and man-power to the modest dimensions within which they had been confined before Rome's first 'great leap forward' in 340 B.C.

After Rome's third and worst defeat by Hannibal at Cannae, most of Rome's south-eastern Italian allies did secede, and so did Rome's Campanian second-class citizens; but the Roman Government continued to hold central and northern Peninsular Italy, and Hannibal's invincible professional army was too small to follow up its sensational series of victories by taking the offensive against the heart of Rome's power. This anti-climax spelled the failure of Hannibal's strategy. After Rome's survival of her disaster at Cannae, Hannibal's eventual defeat was only a matter of time. From now onwards the Roman Government gave Hannibal no further opportunities of defeating Roman armies in pitched battles. The Roman Government mobilized its still abundant man-power to the full for holding the front in south-eastern Italy and for garrisoning massively the still intact portion of Rome's Peninsular Italian domain.

Rome's command of the sea was also intact, and this enabled Rome to prevent reinforcements for Hannibal from reaching Italy except in ineffective driblets, and it also enabled Rome to take the offensive against the Carthaginian dominions in Spain. By 206 B.C. the whole of Carthaginian Spain was in Roman hands. In 205 B.C. the Roman victor in Spain, Publius Cornelius Scipio, invaded Carthage's home territory in North-West Africa, and, unlike the previous expeditions of Agathocles in 310–306 B.C. and of Scipio's Roman predecessor Marcus Atilius

Regulus, in 256–225 B.C., Scipio's expedition was successful. Hannibal was recalled from Italy to Africa in 203 B.C. In 202 B.C. he was decisively defeated there at Naraggara by Scipio.

Before this conclusive ending, the Hannibalic War had spread from Italy not only to Spain and Africa, but also to Sicily and Greece. In 220 B.C. war had broken out between Aetolia and an alliance of other states in Greece, headed by Macedon. The Aetolians had been getting the worst of it, and in 217 B.C. the news from Italy enabled them to induce their Greek opponents to make peace. In 215 B.C., King Philip V of Macedon made an alliance with Hannibal; his envoys, accompanied on their way home by Carthaginian commissioners, were intercepted by the Romans; Rome went to war with Macedon; in 212 B.C. Aetolia made an alliance with Rome and thus involved herself again in war with Macedon and her allies in Greece. In this war Aetolia lost so much territory to Macedon in Thessaly that in 206 B.C. she made a separate peace with Macedon, and this constrained Rome too to make peace with Macedon in 205 B.C. Both these peace-treaties were advantageous for Macedon in the short run, but the price was the certainty of an imminent war of revenge; for by 205 B.C. it was already clear that Rome was going to win a decisive victory over Carthage.

Carthage's war of revenge against Rome had failed. So far from having succeeded in reversing the result of the war of 264–241 B.C., Carthage had now ceased to be a great power and was henceforth at Rome's mercy. Materially, however, Carthage had suffered less than Rome in the Hannibalic War. Carthage had fought on her home territory for only three years (205–202 B.C.), whereas Hannibal had been devastating Peninsular Italy for fifteen years (217–203 B.C.). The devastation of south-eastern Italy and Sicily was not repaired, and it had economic, social, and political consequences that were tantamount to a posthumous victory for Hannibal which was more fatal for Rome than Hannibal's barren military victory at Cannae in 216 B.C.

The hardest hit of all the victims of the Hannibalic War were the Italiot and Siceliot Greeks. King Hiero II of Syracuse had remained faithful to his alliance with Rome, but, after his death in 215 B.C., Syracuse, Taras (Tarentum), and Akragas (Agrigentum) had successively seceded from Rome and had consequently been taken by storm and been sacked, together with Leuntini, the next greatest Greek city, after Syracuse, in the Hieronic Kingdom. In Greece, Macedon's allies had suffered from the terms of the alliance between Aetolia and Rome. It had been agreed that, when an enemy city was captured by the allies, the Aetolians should take the land and the buildings, and the Romans the moveable property, including the survivors of the population, whom the Romans might, and did, sell into slavery.

King Philip V of Macedon was short-sighted; his Seleucid contemporary, the Emperor Antiochus III, was blind. After having provoked Rome and humiliated Aetolia, Philip marched eastwards in 202 B.C., when Rome was on the point of defeating Carthage and thus regaining her freedom of action. In 202 B.C., Philip, without provocation, attacked and took five Greek cities, and he followed the Romans' atrocious example by selling the inhabitants of three of these five unoffending cities into slavery. As for Antiochus, he had waged the fourth Seleucid–Ptolemaic war for the possession of southern Syria in 221 B.C., and the fifth in 219–217 B.C. In 217 B.C.—the year of the battle of Lake Trasimene—Antiochus III had been defeated by Ptolemy IV at Raphia (the present-day Rafa). During the years 216–213 B.C., Antiochus had been busy in western Asia Minor, liquidating his cousin Achaeus, who had recaptured for Antiochus, from King Attalus I of Pergamon, the Seleucid Empire's possessions to the north-west of the Taurus Range and had then seceded from Antiochus. From 212 to 205 B.C. Antiochus was campaigning to the east of the Euphrates. In 206 B.C. he was in the Kabul River valley (a corner of the tottering Mauryan Empire's dominions). Before the end of the same year, he was campaigning in the Persian Gulf.

Antiochus III's mileage was comparable to Alexander's, but the political results were ephemeral. Antiochus obtained a nominal recognition of his suzerainty over Armenia, North Media (present-day Azerbaijan), Parthia, and Bactria, but the local rulers recovered their independence *de facto* as soon as his back was turned. In 202 B.C., Antiochus III started the sixth Seleucid–Ptolemaic war, and, this time, southern Syria remained in his hands when peace was made in 198 B.C. By that time, however, Philip V of Macedon was already losing his second war with Rome and Aetolia.

Between 200 and 168 B.C., Rome imposed her domination on the whole perimeter of the eastern basin of the Mediterranean. In 197 B.C. she defeated Macedon decisively at Cynoscephalae in Thessaly and evicted the Macedonians from all their possessions in Greece to the south of Mount Olympus and in south-western Asia Minor. In 195 B.C. the Roman expeditionary force in Greece paralysed Sparta by detaching from her the whole of her seaboard. Sparta was now, once again, the land-locked petty state that she had been before she had expanded her territory during the second half of the eighth century B.C. In 192 B.C., Antiochus III and Aetolia together went to war with Rome. Antiochus was forced to capitulate in 190 B.C., and Aetolia in 189 B.C. Antiochus had to cede all Seleucid territory to the north-west of the Taurus Range, and to pay a big war indemnity. In a third Romano–Macedonian war (171–168 B.C.) Rome liquidated the Kingdom of Macedon and partitioned its former territory into four republican cantons under Roman suzerainty.

Antiochus III could have avoided his collision with Rome. In the negotiations before the outbreak of war, Rome offered him two alternative sets of conditions for peaceful co-existence; both alternatives were moderate; Antiochus could have accepted either of them without difficulty; and peaceful co-existence would have been possible; for there was room for both powers in the now vastly expanded Hellenic World, and their constitutional structures were developing on parallel lines. The Seleucid Empire and the Roman Empire were each beginning to turn into an association of autonomous city-states. But the humiliating defeat that Antiochus III brought upon himself at Magnesia-under-Sipylus in 190 B.C. doomed the Seleucid Empire to be partitioned eventually between Rome and Parthia.

The Romans over-estimated the Seleucid Empire's strength because of its size, because of Antiochus III's deceptively spectacular previous successes, and because Hannibal had taken service with Antiochus in 195 B.C. The Romans gauged Macedon's strength correctly in 215–208 B.C. and in 200–197 B.C., and consequently they under-estimated it in 171–168 B.C. Macedon was foredoomed to succumb to Rome, because she had not succeeded permanently in uniting Greece politically under her suzerainty, as Rome had succeeded in uniting Italy, and because of the consequent disparity between the two powers in military man-power. In the third war, Macedon was able to put all her man-power into the field, since Rome had previously deprived her of the fortresses abroad in which a large part of Macedon's forces had been locked up during the two previous Romano–Macedonian wars. This time, the Romans had to exert themselves in order to defeat the Macedonians; for these, though inferior to the Romans in equipment and tactics, as well as in numbers, were valiant and were also bent on living up to the illustriousness of their national military record. However, this was the only serious exertion that Rome had to make in order to impose her domination on the Levant. A word from a Roman envoy, bringing the news of the decisive Roman victory over Macedon at Pydna, sufficed in 168 B.C. to make Antiochus III's son and second successor Antiochus IV evacuate Egypt, which he had conquered while the Romans had been preoccupied with the most taxing of their wars in Greece.

The Roman 'establishment' employed diplomacy as a supplement to war, and they used the same diplomatic arts in mastering the Levant that they had already used with signal success in mastering Peninsular Italy. They recruited 'fifth columns' in hostile states by ensuring the dominance there of the rich minority of the population over the poor majority. They recruited allies among the weaker neighbours of great powers that were Rome's rivals, and then 'astonished these allies by their ingratitude' as soon as the overthrow of a rival power, with the allies' help, had made the allies' services superfluous. Thus Rome jilted Aetolia after defeating Macedon in 197 B.C. with Aetolia's aid. She jilted Macedon after Macedon had helped her, in 190–189 B.C., to defeat the Aetolians. She jilted Pergamon and Rhodes and the Achaean Confederation after she had liquidated the Kingdom of Macedon in 168 B.C., though Pergamon and Rhodes had helped Rome to defeat Antiochus III in 192–190 B.C., and though the Achaeans had been Rome's faithful allies ever since they had deserted their previous ally, Macedon, in 198 B.C. Rome jilted Numidia after she had defeated Carthage in the war of 218–201 B.C., and had annihilated her in the war of 150–146 B.C., with Numidia's aid. After her conclusive victory in 168 B.C. in Greece, Rome did what Ch'in Shih Hwang-ti had done after his conclusive victory in China in 221 B.C. The Romans deported to their own home territory eminent members of the 'establishments' of Macedon, the Achaean Confederation, and other continental Greek states. The Molossian Epirots, who had been non-belligerent in Macedon's favour, and the Aetolians, who had been Rome's reluctant allies in the Romano–Macedonian War of 171–168 B.C., were hit still harder. The Molossians were looted and enslaved; the Aetolians were mulcted of territory, besides being made to deliver their quota of deportees.

The years 221–168 B.C. had been painful for the inhabitants of the Mediterranean basin; the years 167–31 B.C. were agonizing for them. The ordeal of the Hannibalic War had implanted in the Romans a phobia of great powers within striking distance of Italy. Only the distant Seleucid Empire might perhaps have been allowed by the Roman 'establishment' to continue to co-exist with the Roman Empire if Antiochus III had been less unwise in the fateful years 196–192 B.C. From 190 B.C. onwards, the Roman 'establishment' neglected no opportunity of reducing the Seleucid Empire's power, though the outcome of the war of 192–190 B.C. had already revealed this geographically enormous empire's military impotence. Carthage, which had been impotent since 201 B.C., was nevertheless wantonly attacked by Rome in 150 B.C. and was destroyed in 146 B.C. Corinth was destroyed in the same year, just fifty years after the Romans had relieved her of the Macedonian garrison of her acropolis. The Roman 'establishment's' aim was negative. It wanted merely to strike down any state that showed any sign of still having the wish to assert its independence, even if the offending state was utterly incapable of repeating Hannibal's performance.

The Roman 'establishment's' unwillingness to fill the political vacuum that it had deliberately created contrasts strikingly with Ch'in Shih

Hwang-ti's action after his destruction in 221 B.C. of the last surviving independent power in the Chinese World. So far from leaving any political vacuum, Ch'in Shih Hwang-ti had immediately annexed the territories of the rival states that he had destroyed, and he had embodied the entire Chinese World politically in a highly centralized and autocratically administered empire. After 168 B.C., the year in which Rome destroyed the only remaining great power that was within range of her, the Roman 'establishment' made the shattered Mediterranean World wait for a century before it took the first step towards reconstructing it. In 67 B.C. a Roman war-lord, Gnaeus Pompeius (Pompey) was given dictatorial powers to re-establish law and order in the Levant, and between 67 and 62 B.C. he carried out his commission efficiently; but it was not till 46 B.C. that a single Roman war-lord, Pompey's successful rival, Gaius Julius Caesar, had the whole of the Mediterranean World in his power. Julius Caesar then set out to do in the Mediterranean what Ch'in Shih Hwang-ti had done in China. Caesar started to build a centralized, autocratically administered empire on the waste land which his republican Roman predecessors had left derelict, and he was on the point of setting out to expand his empire into the Transeuphratean regions of the Hellenic World when, in 44 B.C., his work was cut short by his assassination.

Caesar had only two years of autocratic power in which he was free to concentrate on re-shaping his world, as compared with Shih Hwang-ti's twelve years, and Caesar's work of reconstruction during his two years was interrupted by a fresh military challenge to his dictatorship. By comparison with Shih Hwang-ti, Caesar was merciful to his defeated opponents, and his assassination was the price of his relative clemency. (Shih Hwang-ti had survived an attempt, by an agent of Yen state, to assassinate him in 224 B.C., when he was still no more than King Chêng of Ch'in state, and had not yet completed his work of forcibly unifying the whole of China.) However, the sequel in China to Shih Hwang-ti's death indicates that Caesar's work, like his Chinese counterpart's, would not have long outlived him, even if he had had Shih Hwang-ti's spell of twelve years for carrying it out; for, though Caesar was unlike Shih Hwang-ti in being clement to opponents, he resembled him in being impatient and tactless. The Mediterranean World needed, and duly found in Augustus, a successor to Caesar who would re-build Caesar's empire, as Liu P'ang had re-built Shih Hwang-ti's, in a less provocative and therefore more durable form.

Meanwhile, the military defeat of the Carthaginian Empire, Macedon, and the Seleucid Empire by Rome between the years 218 and 190 B.C., and the simultaneous decline of the Ptolemaic and the Mauryan Empires, followed up by Roman depredations at the expense of Rome's defeated antagonists, had opened the way for the resurgence of native Asian and African peoples.

Even before Rome had intervened in the Levant the Egyptians had begun to react against the exploitative Ptolemaic Greek regime. In the fifth Seleucid–Ptolemaic war (219–217 B.C.) the Ptolemaic Government had trained and armed, in the Macedonian style, a corps of native Egyptian infantry, and, at the Battle of Raphia, these Egyptian troops had defeated Seleucid troops of Greek race. This military victory of Egyptians over soldiers of the same breed as the Egyptians' Macedonian Greek masters gave the Egyptian peasantry a new confidence. From 217 B.C. onwards, they became more and more difficult for the Greek 'ascendancy' to control, and the Egyptian priesthood—a powerful corporation—took the opportunity to exact more and more concessions and privileges from an alien government that was now visibly weakening. The priesthood would have been the natural leader of an Egyptian anti-Greek nationalist movement, but the peasants' revolts were primarily social—they were revolts of the poor against the rich. The Egyptian ecclesiastical establishment, as well as the Greek political establishment, was their target, and the priesthood's position was equivocal.

After 201 B.C., Rome's North-West African ally, Numidia, persistently encroached on Carthage's territory. After 190 B.C., the Seleucid Government had to wring from its subjects the means for paying the war-indemnity to Rome, and the government's pressure evoked resistance, now that its defeat by the Romans had exposed the Empire's military weakness. The biggest hoards of bullion in the Seleucid dominions were those that had been accumulating in the treasuries of temples. Antiochus III lost his life in 187 B.C., and Antiochus IV lost his in 163 B.C., in attempts to pillage temples in Elymais (Elam).

The temple that gave the Seleucids the greatest trouble, with the greatest effect on the course of history, was the Jewish temple of Yahweh at Jerusalem. Under the Persian and the subsequent Ptolemaic regimes, the Jewish community in Judaea had not come into conflict with the imperial government and had also lived in peace, though, since Ezra's day, not in amity, with its local fellow-subjects. But the Judaean Jewish community, like the Egyptian people, was split internally by a tension between a rich minority and a poor majority. The rich owned the land and controlled the treasure accumulated in the temple at Jerusalem. They included the most powerful families of the priests. The poor were the peasants, the urban artisans, and the interpreters of the Jewish Law, which was recognized by the Seleucid Government, as it had been recognized previously by the Ptolemaic Government, as being valid for the Jewish community in Judaea. Within the Judaean Jewish community, the rich minority was split by a rivalry between two families of nobles, the Tobiads and the Oniads, and between rival representatives of each of these houses; during the sixth Seleucid–Ptolemaic war, which ended in the transfer of the sovereignty over southern Syria, including Judaea, from the Ptolemaic to the Seleucid Government, this domestic Jewish feud became entangled with a new domestic Jewish quarrel between a pro-Ptolemaic and a pro-Seleucid faction; and this quarrel became entangled, in its turn, with a more bitter quarrel between a rich Hellenizing and a poor anti-Hellenist Judaean Jewish party. The Judaean Hellenizers proposed to go to greater lengths than the Jewish community that had grown up in Alexandria-on-Nile during the century for which Judaea had been under Ptolemaic rule. The Jewish migrants from Judaea to Alexandria had taken to speaking Greek instead of Aramaic, but they had not given up their ancestral religion. The Jewish Hellenizers in Judaea under the Seleucid regime that had super-seded the Ptolemaic regime were attracted by the Hellenic way of life in its entirety.

After the accession of Antiochus IV in 175 B.C., the Hellenizing Judaean Jewish party took the initiative in asking the new Seleucid Emperor for his assistance, and, with his support, the Jewish temple-state was transformed into a city-state of the Hellenic style, re-named Antioch. This was not an exceptional measure. From the start it had been the policy of the Seleucid dynasty to turn the Empire, bit by bit, into an association of Hellenic or Hellenized city-states, linked with each other by a common allegiance to the imperial crown. After the Empire's defeat by the Romans in 190 B.C., its traditional policy of Hellenization was pursued with increased vigour. The imperial government saw in Hellenism a cultural cement that might serve to arrest the disintegration with which the Seleucid Empire was now threatened as a result of its humiliating reverse in a major war.

Competing Judaean Jewish Hellenizers had outbid each other for Antiochus IV's support with bribes paid by each successive Hellenizing incumbent of the high priesthood who gained temporary control over the temple treasure. In 169 B.C. Antiochus, on his way back from his first campaign in Egypt, pillaged the temple at Jerusalem with the acquiescence of the momentary incumbent. In 168 B.C., after he had evacuated Egypt at a Roman envoy's word of command, Antiochus was confronted by an insurrection among the anti-Hellenist majority of the Judaean Jews. This revolt was directed against the Hellenizing minority of the Judaean Jewish community, but Antiochus took it as being an act of rebellion against himself, and he retorted militantly. He built a fort at Jerusalem and planted a garrison there, and in December 167 B.C. he Hellenized the cult in the temple of Yahweh and banned, in Judaea, the practice of Judaism in its traditional form. Apparently Yahweh was now identified with Olympian Zeus, and he was perhaps represented in the temple by a statue that may have been a portrait of Antiochus himself as 'the God Manifest' ('Epiphanes').

All this was done by Antiochus in concert with the Judaean Jewish Hellenizers, and, since these appeared still to be dominant in Judaea, Antiochus must have been taken by surprise when, in 166 B.C., the traditionalist Judaean Jews' resistance movement took an effective military form under the leadership of the Hasmonaean family. The insurgents overcame the Hellenizers; they captured Jerusalem, except for the fort, and in December 164 B.C. they de-Hellenized the temple. The Roman Government concluded a treaty with the anti-Seleucid insurgent regime in Judaea in 161 B.C. The Seleucid garrison of the fort at Jerusalem capitulated in 141 B.C., and in the same year the Parni (conventionally, though inaccurately, called 'the Parthians') conquered from the Seleucid Empire not only Media but also the Empire's economic power-house, Babylonia.

In 139 B.C. the Seleucid Emperor Demetrius II tried and failed to regain the lost territories; he was defeated by the Parthians and was taken prisoner. His brother, Antiochus VII Sidetes, forced Jerusalem to capitulate *c.* 133 B.C.; he made the Hasmonaean Government recognize his suzerainty; and in 130 B.C. he compelled the reigning representative of the house, John Hyrcanus, to accompany him, at the head of a Jewish contingent, in a campaign in which Antiochus hoped to retrieve his captive brother's failure. Antiochus VII did reconquer Babylonia and Media in 130 B.C., but in 129 B.C. his army, dispersed in winter-quarters in Media, was destroyed piecemeal by the Parthians. Antiochus VII was killed, but the Parthians let John Hyrcanus lead his Jewish contingent back to Judaea unscathed.

From 129 to 63 B.C., Judaea was an independent state under Hasmonaean sovereignty, and it conquered and annexed some adjoining districts of southern Syria, including most of the Greek or Hellenized cities along the coast and in the interior. In 64–63 B.C., however, Pompey liberated the conquered cities and imposed Rome's suzerainty on Judaea itself.

The Jewish, like the Egyptian, nationalist movement had been directed politically against a Greek imperial government, and the Kingdom of Numidia had been enlarged at the political expense of Carthage. But it is easier to overthrow a political regime than to resist the attraction of a civilization. Even after Carthage had been blotted out, the Syrian civilization of the surviving Libyphoenician cities along the coast of North-West Africa continued to make headway in Numidia; and, as soon as the Hasmonaeans had stepped into the Seleucids' shoes

in Judaea and in the adjoining districts of southern Syria, they succumbed to Hellenization like their counterparts in other native successor-
states of the Seleucid Empire, such as Commagênê.

The Hasmonaeans had won their crown as champions of the traditional form of Judaism, and their subsequent compromise with Hellenism
caused a breach between them and the Hasidim—the representatives of
traditional Judaism who, under the Hasmonaeans' leadership, had
waged and won the war against the Jewish Hellenizers and against the
Seleucid Government. The Hasidim included the interpreters of the Law
('the scribes'), and these had taken up arms with mixed motives. For
them, the re-instatement of the Law meant not only the re-establishment
of the Jewish religion in its traditional form; it also meant the recovery
of the scribes' former status and emoluments. But power in Judaea had
now passed, not to the scribes, but to the Hasmonaean dynasty—Jewish
successors of the Macedonian Greeks who reigned, like them, as absolute
monarchs. During the reign of the Hasmonaean King Alexander
Jannaeus (102–76/5 B.C.) there was a civil war between the Hasmonaean
'establishment' and the Pharisees ('separators'), as the Hasidim had now
come to be called, and 6,000 of these are said to have been massacred in
Jerusalem, within the precincts of the temple, by the king's guard, who
were non-Jewish mercenaries.

Even the ex-nomad Parthians, or at any rate their rulers, the Arsacid
dynasty, acquired a tincture of Hellenism when, after their annexation
of Babylonia, they moved their capital to Ctesiphon, the east-bank
suburb of Seleucia-on-Tigris; but, within the years 221–30 B.C., in which
the Greek successor-states of the First Persian Empire all foundered,
Hellenism enjoyed a triumph to the east of Parthia, in the upper basins
of the Oxus and Jaxartes Rivers (Bactria and Soghd) and in north-
western India. Here, as elsewhere, the cultural influence of Hellenism
long outlasted its political submergence.

In Bactria and Soghd the military resistance to Alexander the Great
had been more vigorous than in any other part of the Persian Empire's
former dominions; yet it was here that the most amicable symbiosis of
Iranians and Greeks was subsequently achieved, and this local Graeco-
Iranian entente survived the secession of the Greek governor of Bactria
and Soghd from the Seleucid Empire *c.* 250 B.C. (the date was approximately the same as that of the occupation of Parthia by the nomad
Parni). The ineffectiveness of the Seleucid Emperor Antiochus III's
eastern expedition (212–205 B.C.), his resounding subsequent defeat in
190 B.C. at the hands of the Romans, and the decline of the Mauryan
Empire after Ashoka's death in 232 B.C., worked together to tempt the
Bactrian Greeks to occupy the political vacuum to the south of the
Hindu Kush.

One of two Bactrian princes named Demetrius may have conquered, soon after 200 B.C., the territory, in what is now south-western Afghanistan, that had been ceded to Chandragupta Maurya by Seleucus I. The Greek King Menander reigned, *c.* 160–130 B.C., in India as far south-eastward as the mouths of the Rivers Indus and Narbada. It may have been in Menander's reign that the Greeks who had established themselves in India momentarily occupied Pataliputra, the former capital of the defunct Mauryan dynasty. Coins of thirty-nine Bactrian and Indian Greek kings and of two Greek queens have been found. They are as beautiful as the fifth-century-B.C. Syracusan coins, and many of the portraits on them are superb; but the very number of the Greeks who reigned in this region within a period of less than two centuries confirms the literary evidence about them. They were rulers of bits and pieces who ruined each other by fratricidal warfare, the Greeks' inveterate political vice. Like the Greek city-states before Philip II's day and like the successors of Alexander, these Bactrian and Indian Greek kings were perpetually contending with each other—in their case for morsels of territory on both sides of the Hindu Kush—and they never attempted to form a united front for staving off the *Völkerwanderung* that descended on them from the Eurasian steppe.

Bactria's and Parthia's immediate neighbours to the north were two Saka (Skyth) peoples: one in what is now Kazakhstan, to the east of the Caspian Sea, and the other in Farghanah, in the upper basin of the River Jaxartes. Both these peoples had been under Persian suzerainty before the First Persian Empire's decline and fall. *Circa* 140 B.C. they were driven southwards by the impact of the Yüeh-chih, who were migrating south-westwards to get out of range of the Hsiung-nu. The Sakas overwhelmed the Greeks in Bactria; but Parthia—strengthened by its acquisition of Babylonia—fended the Sakas off from *c.* 138 to 124 B.C. and diverted them into the lower basin of the Helmand River (known, since then, as 'the Sakas' country', Seistan). From there the Sakas entered the Indus valley and conquered the Greek principalities in India, one by one. A detachment of the Parthians followed at the Sakas' heels and imposed its rule on them. Meanwhile, *c.* 100 B.C., the Yüeh-chih had crossed the Oxus into Bactria and had overrun their Saka subjects who had occupied Bactria previously. It has been mentioned already that Chang-ch'ien, the Chinese Emperor Han Wu-ti's envoy, found the Yüeh-chih established in Transoxania by *c.* 128 B.C. In A.D. 48 the dominant section of the Yüeh-chih, the Kushans, crossed the Hindu Kush into the Indus basin and imposed their rule on the Partho-Sakas there and on the independent Sakas whom the Partho-Sakas had driven farther south-eastwards and southwards. The Kushans thus united Bactria with north-western India in an empire that straddled the Hindu Kush.

The Parni ('Parthians'), the Sakas, and the Yüeh-chih (Tokharoi) were, all of them, Eurasian pastoral nomads by origin. The Parni and the Sakas were Iranian-speaking peoples who had been in contact first with the Persians and then with the Greeks before they had moved out of the steppe into regions inhabited by sedentary agricultural populations. As for the Yüeh-chih, they had come from the back of beyond, out of range of the Persian and Greek and Chinese civilizations, and their ancestral Indo-European language, Tokharian, is non-Iranian. Yet all these three ex-nomad migrant peoples, and not least the Kushan branch of the Yüeh-chih, adopted the Hellenic civilization of the region they had conquered. Their coins, for instance, are imitations, or even over-strikes, of the coins of their Greek predecessors. The Arsacidae and the Kushans succumbed to Hellenization as readily as the Hasmonaeans and the Romans.

Hermaeus, the last Greek king in what is now Afghanistan, and Hermaeus' wife, Queen Calliope, died, perhaps at the Partho-Sakas' hands, *c.* 30 B.C., the date of the suicide of the last Greek queen of Egypt, Cleopatra VII. The last serious Greek military resistance to Rome had been the Macedonian insurrection of 149–148 B.C. The Achaean Confederation's war with Rome in 146 B.C., after the Macedonian insurrection had been crushed, had been a forlorn hope in the face of fearful odds. After that, the challenges to Rome were delivered, not by any established Greek governments, but by Greek or Hellenized slaves and by Iranian, not Greek, rulers of some successor-states of the First Persian Empire.

The House of Seleucus had weakened itself by fratricidal wars between rival heirs since 241 B.C. From 129 B.C., the date of the defeat and death of the Emperor Antiochus VII Sidetes in Media, till the extinction of the last remnant of the Seleucid Empire in 64 B.C., civil war within its dwindling domain was chronic. This made Syria a happy hunting ground for slave-traders. Before 168 B.C., the Rhodian navy had policed the Levant; but, after the liquidation of the Kingdom of Macedon, Rome ruined Rhodes by giving the island of Delos to Athens on condition that it should be a free port. Rhodes could not now afford any longer to maintain her navy, and, for a century, the naval command of Levantine waters was held by pirates based on Western ('Rough') Cilicia and on Crete. The pirates co-operated with Italian and Syrian businessmen, working from Delos, in kidnapping the victims of civil war in Syria and selling them into slavery, to be bought on Delos for stocking the Italian and Sicilian plantations and ranches. These were operated with slave-labour after the ground had been cleared for the most lucrative possible methods of economic exploitation of these countries after the devastation that they had suffered during the Hannibalic War.

The new slave-populations of Peninsular Italy and Sicily included representatives of all ranks of society. Anyone of any rank might become a victim of the chances and changes of civil war. Some of the leaders of the eventual insurrections of slaves in Sicily were well-educated and statesmanlike. As early as 198 B.C. there was an abortive insurrection of plantation-slaves at Setia, a Latin colony to the south-east of Rome; but plantation-slave insurgents started under a handicap; they worked in chain-gangs, and they were imprisoned at night. The initiative lay with the slave-shepherds. These had to be armed, to enable them to protect their flocks against predators, both non-human and human, and, in their summer pastures up in the mountains, these armed slave-shepherds were virtually beyond control. The slave-shepherds had weapons and freedom of manoeuvre, the slave-plantation-hands had numbers. When the slave-shepherds took up arms and liberated the plantation-hands, the united slave-insurgents could find effective leaders and could raise armies capable of facing Roman troops in the field. This is why the Sicilian slave-wars of 135–132 and 104–*c.* 100 B.C. were as successful as they were, and why they lasted as long as they did.

In 135 B.C., the opening year of the first Sicilian slave-war, there were also insurrections of slaves on Delos and in Attica. There is no evidence that these simultaneous slave-revolts at different points in the Mediterranean World were concerted, or that the news of one of them was the stimulus that evoked the others; but it is probable that their simultaneity was not fortuitous. In 135 B.C. Delos was linked politically with Athens and commercially with Sicily and Italy. In 132 B.C. Aristonicus, a claimant to the throne of Pergamon, took up arms in the former territory of the kingdom, which, in 133 B.C. had been bequeathed to the Roman people by the last king of the Pergamene dynasty. The Roman Government had turned the kingdom into the province of Asia and had farmed out the collection of the provincial taxes to Roman businessmen. Aristonicus appealed to the slaves for support, and he proclaimed the foundation of a 'Commonwealth of the Sun'. He was making explicit the idea that inspired the leaders of the Sicilian slave-insurgents. The Sun is the divine embodiment of justice. It gives light and warmth impartially to slaves and to freemen, to the poor and to the rich. The Roman 'establishment' stood for the rich and for the slave-owners and slave-traders. The insurgents were attempting to set up not merely a counter-state to replace the Roman state but a counter-society to replace the Hellenic society now that this was treating its proletariat inhumanely. This was also the objective of the Thracian gladiator Spartacus, who broke out of prison, raised an army of insurgent Italian slaves, and dominated the Italian countryside from 73 to 71 B.C.

The first Iranian ruler to challenge Rome was king Mithradates VI of

Pontic Cappadocia in north-eastern Asia Minor. In 88 B.C. Mithradates overran the Roman province of Asia, occupied Delos, and won the support of Athens. He presented himself as a liberator of the Greeks from Roman oppression, and in the liberated territories there was a massacre of Italian tax-farmers and other Italian businessmen. In 88–86 B.C., Mithradates' army advanced as far into Greece as Xerxes' army in 480–479 B.C. Mithradates, like Xerxes, was defeated, and in 85 B.C. he had to make peace, but he took up arms against Rome twice more before his death in 63 B.C.

Mithradates' unsuccessful challenge to Rome had been more formidable than any the Romans had met with since the unsuccessful Macedonian insurrection in 149–148 B.C. Another Iranian power, Parthia, inflicted on Rome in 53 B.C., at Carrhae (Harran) in Mesopotamia, the most disastrous military defeat that Rome had suffered since Hannibal's victory at Cannae in 216 B.C. The battlefield of Carrhae was a plain. Its distance from the nearest Mediterranean port created a difficult logistical problem for a Roman army that had marched that far into the interior of the continent, and the terrain nullified the invincibility of the numbers, equipment, and tactics of the Roman infantry. At Carrhae Crassus' army found itself helpless against a numerically inferior force of Parthian horse-archers supported by a camel-train carrying a copious supply of arrows. Crassus' army was annihilated.

This was the first irreversible defeat that the Romans had suffered. The Carthaginians, the Greek powers, the insurgent slaves, and Mithradates had all succumbed, each in their turn. But the Romans' direst enemies and most hapless victims in the post-Hannibalic Age were not the Parthians; they were the Romans themselves.

Rome's post-Hannibalic wars with the Levantine Greek powers had been short, and in the Levant Rome had been able to hamstring her adversaries without immediately incurring permanent local military and political commitments. On the other hand, Rome's victory in the Hannibalic War had bequeathed to Rome an immediate legacy of permanent commitments in continental Italy to the north of the Appennines, and overseas in Spain; and, for the Roman peasant-soldiers, long-term military service in these distant fields was as disastrous economically, and, conversely, as opportune for acquisitive Roman large-scale landowners, as service along the Great Wall and beyond it was for the corresponding classes among the Romans' Chinese contemporaries and counterparts. The last independent tribesmen in the Po-basin were not exterminated till 25 B.C., and the last in Spain were not subdued till 19 B.C. By those dates the Roman Empire's military frontiers had been pushed forward in western continental Europe to the line of the Rhine and in continental Asia to the line of the Euphrates, while in south-eastern Europe, where Rome had been constrained by the formidable Macedonian insurrection in 149–148 B.C. to annex Macedon outright and to take over the defence of Macedon's northern frontier, the local Roman frontier, thus created, was pushed forward to the line of the Danube in 27 B.C.

Meanwhile, the devastation of south-eastern Italy and Sicily in the Hannibalic War, and the Roman 'establishment's' subsequent policy of wrecking the rest of the Mediterranean World and then leaving it derelict, had opened up an opportunity for exploitation on the grand scale, and this opportunity had called into existence a new social class of predators in the Roman body politic. In Peninsular Italy while it was being conquered and unified by Rome, as in China during the Age of the Warring States, businessmen had accumulated liquid capital. These Roman capitalists and the landowning members of the Roman 'establishment' possessed, between them, the lion's share of the wealth of the Roman community. The majority of the Roman citizen body was poor, and so was the Roman state.

In 215 B.C., the fourth year of the Hannibalic War, the Roman Treasury went bankrupt, but the contractors who were supplying the Roman armies in Italy and overseas with food, clothing, and arms then undertook to continue to provide these indispensable supplies on credit for the duration of the war, and they proved to have enough liquid capital at their command to go on doing this from 215 to 201 B.C. Moreover, in 205 B.C., a number of city-states in the undevastated area of north-western Peninsular Italy—some of them being Roman municipalities and others being Rome's allies—fitted out with copious voluntary gifts the expeditionary force that Scipio was assembling for his invasion of Carthaginian Africa. In the same year the bankrupt Roman Treasury offered for sale slices of the valuable land that had been expropriated from the Roman municipalities in Campania that had seceded in 215 B.C. and had been re-subjugated in 211 B.C., and purchasers presented themselves who could pay in ready money.

From 215 B.C. onwards, the Roman Government was at its private Roman creditors' mercy; it had to grant them terms that gave them golden opportunities for fraud; and, when their frauds became flagrant, the public authorities prosecuted the fraudulent contractors only reluctantly; they feared that the offenders might cut off supplies, and this would have condemned Rome to suffer swift military defeat. In 204 and 202 B.C., before the war was over, the Treasury had to start re-imbursing its creditors by instalments, and in 200 B.C. it had to commute the final instalment, most advantageously for its creditors, by making a payment in kind in the form of public land within a radius of fifty miles of Rome, a location in which land-values were certain to rise. Besides raising credit on unfavourable terms, the Treasury had financed the cost of the Hannibalic War partly by imposing an annual capital levy on its tax-payers. In 187 B.C. twenty-five and a half out of thirty-four annual levies at the rate of one per mille were refunded to the tax-payers from funds that the Treasury had acquired from the Government's share of the loot brought back to Rome by a Roman expeditionary force that had plundered Asia Minor in 188 B.C.

The Roman Government's share of the loot brought home by Roman armies was not the only source from which the Roman Treasury replenished its funds between the years 201 and 168 B.C. There were also war-indemnities—for instance, those imposed on Carthage in 201 B.C. and on the Seleucid Empire in 190 B.C.—and there were permanent revenue-producing capital assets: for instance, land expropriated from re-subjugated secessionist communities in south-eastern Italy, the entire territories of Carthage and Corinth, mines and forests in Macedon that had been the property of the Crown, and mines in Spain that had been the property of the Carthaginian Government or of conquered native Spanish communities. After the conquest of Macedon in 168 B.C. direct taxation was abolished for Roman citizens domiciled in Italy or in Roman municipal communities outside Italy that had been granted Italian fiscal status.

Thus, from 215 B.C. onwards, the rich minority of the Roman citizen body had been growing richer while the poor majority had been growing poorer. The *nouveaux riches* businessmen were not economically productive. They were not industrial entrepreneurs; they were not even traders except in supplies for the army and in slaves; they made their fortunes mainly as farmers of customs revenues and of taxes payable by Rome's provincial subjects. The members of the 'establishment', who monopolized the holding of public office and who were therefore in duty bound to protect Rome's subjects from being fleeced by the Roman tax-farmers, were more concerned to make illegitimate gains for themselves. They did this partly by investing in the tax-farming business covertly, but mainly by lucrative rentings and purchases of land in the Roman state's expanded territory in Italy.

In south-eastern Italy, large tracts of land had become Roman territory and at the same time Roman public property as a result of expropriations of land from Italian states that had seceded during the Hannibalic War, and land in Roman territory that was private property was also coming into the market through the ruining of peasant-proprietors who were having to perform military service for years on end on distant fronts. There were now large profits to be made from renting public land and from buying up bankrupt peasant-soldiers' holdings.

A large part of the total area of Peninsular Italy consists of rugged highlands that are unrewarding for agriculture but make valuable summer pastures for sheep and cattle if complementary winter pastures can be found in the lowlands and if there are secure rights of way for moving the flocks and herds twice a year. Ever since the completion of the political unification of Peninsular Italy in 264 B.C., it had been possible to develop the country's pastoral capacity on the grand scale. The large expropriations and sales of land in Roman territory in Italy after the Hannibalic War made this lucrative economic development practicable for a minority of the Roman citizen-body that had enough money to rent public land and to buy private land and livestock. Human livestock, in the shape of slave-herdsmen, was as necessary as the herds themselves for making the land yield a profit from animal husbandry. Renters or purchasers of land in the lowlands had a choice between two uses of it. An alternative to changing lowland arable into winter pasture was to plant it with vines and olives. There was a lucrative market for oil and wine in the city of Rome and in other Italian towns, and also in European regions, to the north of Italy, in which the production of oil and wine was ruled out either by the local climate or, in territories that were in Rome's power, by the Roman Government's veto. But, during the period 221–31 B.C., vineyards and olive-orchards, like flocks and herds, yielded a profit only if they were serviced by slave-labour.

It is true that slave-labour was relatively expensive. Slaves had to be bought, and then they had to be fed and housed all the year round, and worn-out slaves who could not be sold off were wholly on the debit side of the commercial planter's or cattleman's account, whereas he could employ casual free labour in busy seasons without incurring any permanent responsibility towards his temporary employees. But, for staffing his permanent labour-force, slaves had a point in their favour that was decisive. A slave's labour was wholly at his master's disposal so long as the slave remained able-bodied; a hired freeman might be conscripted by the Government for military service at any moment and be retained, as a virtual public slave, for years on end, and his private employer had no security against this risk.

Consequently, from the close of the Hannibalic War onwards, both the rural economy and the population of Peninsular Italy began to undergo a revolutionary transformation. Small freeholds, owned by free peasants and producing mainly cereals for the owners' subsistence, were replaced progressively by ranches, composed of linked summer and winter pastures, and, in the lowlands, also by olive-orchards and vineyards; and both these new methods of using the land were operated with slave-labour. The transformation was never carried through to completion. Freeholds survived in considerable numbers, and not all the cereals needed for feeding the population of the City of Rome were

provided by the tribute-grain shipped from Sicily and Sardinia. Yet, by
135 B.C., the date of the outbreak of the first Sicilian slave-war, the
economic and demographic revolution had already gone far enough to
cause a shortage of the Italian man-power that was legally subject to
military conscription.

The members of the Roman 'establishment' were indifferent to the
gross injustice and cruelty of the institution of slavery and to the impoverishment of the politically impotent majority of the oligarchs'
fellow-citizens. But they were alarmed by the increasing difficulty of
raising armies of the strengths required for meeting Rome's military
commitments. They were also finding that reluctant conscripts were
making poor soldiers. In 133 B.C. this concern for the maintenance of
Rome's military efficiency, perhaps even more than a concern for social
justice for freemen who were Roman citizens, led a member of the
Roman 'establishment', Tiberius Sempronius Gracchus, to propose, and
to carry the enactment of, a law that precipitated a revolution in the
Roman body politic. Gracchus' law limited the amount of public land
that a citizen might hold, and it provided for the distribution of the
remainder in allotments of a size that would make the recipients subject
to conscription for military service. This law raised a storm at the western
end of the Old-World Oikoumenê that raged destructively for a hundred
years—the century during which the eastern end of the Old-World
Oikoumenê was blighted by the protracted war between the Chinese
Empire and the Hsiung-nu.

The Gracchan law cost Tiberius Gracchus himself his life in 133 B.C.
(he was lynched by his fellow-aristocrats). It then cost Tiberius' brother
Gaius his life in 121 B.C. This law infuriated not only the Roman
'establishment' but also the citizens of the ex-secessionist states, many of
whom were still squatting, hitherto undisturbed, on part of the land that
had been expropriated from their respective states by Rome. By 111 B.C.,
all recoverable Roman public land had been re-allocated, and neither
the military nor the social problem that had evoked the Gracchan
legislation had been solved. From 108 B.C. onwards, it began to be
solved on lines that were inimical to the survival of constitutional
government in the Roman body politic.

In 107 B.C. Gaius Marius, a Roman citizen who was not a member of
the hereditary 'establishment', was elected consul (a pair of annually
elected consuls were the supreme public officers of the Roman state).
Marius raised an army by the unconstitutional innovation of enlisting
pauper Roman citizens. These took service willingly; they had nothing
to lose, and they had much to gain; for there was a tacit bargain between
them and Marius that he would not discharge them without providing
for them, and that he and they would co-operate in applying the

political pressure of organized military force to impose on the Roman 'establishment' terms that would satisfy both the soldiers' demands and their commander's ambitions. Marius was the first of Rome's revolutionary war-lords. From 108 B.C. onwards, Rome was virtually governed by war-lords—but never avowedly, except for Julius Caesar's overt, and therefore quickly and violently terminated, monarchical reign.

This new unconstitutional, autocratic, and militaristic form of Roman government was not veiled by a transparent pretence of rehabilitated legality till after 31 B.C. Before that date, the new order (or, rather, disorder) cost the inhabitants of Italy two bouts of civil war—the first in 90–80 B.C. and the second in 49–31 B.C. The most ironical feature of the Roman revolution was that, from the lynching of Tiberius Gracchus in 133 B.C. to the suicide of Marcus Antonius in 30 B.C., the thunderbolts of an outraged Jupiter Optimus Maximus blasted one after another of the tallest trees in a dwindling grove. Jupiter's targets were the players of the Roman power-game. The two Gracchi, Cinna, Sertorius, Catiline, Pompey, Crassus, Julius Caesar, Sextus Pompeius, Marcus Antonius—all these players of this lethal game died violent deaths. Marius just escaped this fate after having experienced extreme vicissitudes of fortune. Two other war-lords in this series also died in their beds. The first of these adroit political acrobats was Lucius Cornelius Sulla, the grimmest war-lord of them all. The second was the craftiest of them. He was Gaius Julius Caesar Octavianus (Augustus), Julius Caesar's nephew and adopted son.

Octavian well earned his quiet death. He had succeeded in bringing the hundred-year-long Roman revolution to a halt, but not before a series of defeated and desperate Roman statesmen had taken the revolutionary road on which they had been preceded by the forlorn leaders of the proletariat. Marius himself, and his comrades Cinna and Sertorius, are Roman counterparts of the Pergamene egalitarian prince Aristonicus and the Sicilian slave-kings Eunous and Salvius. Sextus Pompeius made common cause with the pirates whom Sextus' father, the murdered Pompey, had once swept off the seas.

The Roman revolution was Hannibal's posthumous revenge on Rome; but, in scarifying the sinister Roman state—Ch'in state's western counterpart—the deadly Carthaginian shirt of Nessus enveloped the whole of the tormented Mediterranean World.

[37]

THE CHINESE, KUSHAN, PARTHIAN, AND ROMAN EMPIRES, 31 B.C.–A.D. 220

FROM the year A.D. 48 till after the beginning of the third century A.D. nearly the whole of the area occupied by the regional civilizations of the Old-World Oikoumenê was encapsulated politically in four big empires. Their domains extended, in a continuous belt, all the way across the continent from its Pacific to its Atlantic coast.

Thus, during this period of the Old World's history, political unification on a gigantic scale was the general rule. There was, however, a conspicuous local breach of this rule in the Indian subcontinent. The establishment of the Kushan Empire in A.D. 48 gave political unity to north-western India and also united this quarter of India politically with Bactria. This was a striking change from the political chaos that had afflicted India since the early years of the second century B.C.; yet the India of the first century A.D. was still politically fractured by comparison with the India of the third century B.C., when the whole of the subcontinent except for its southern tip had been politically under the regime of the Mauryan dynasty.

In the first century A.D. the heartland of the former Mauryan Empire in the present-day states of Bihar and Uttar Pradesh was under the rule of the Sunga dynasty, which had superseded the Mauryas here in 183 B.C. The Mauryas' former capital, Pataliputra, was now the Sungas' capital; and, though a Greek king had occupied Pataliputra at some date in the second century B.C., the Kushan Empire never expanded that far south-eastward. Moreover, the greater part of the Mauryas' former dominions in the Deccan was now under the rule of another successor-dynasty, the Andhras (*alias* Satavahanas) (*c.* 230 B.C.–A.D. 225), who were a power of the same calibre as the Sungas, while the southern tip of the subcontinent was, as before, divided politically among a number of small states. Between *c.* A.D. 40 and *c.* A.D. 150, the Sakas, whom the Partho-Sakas had driven south-eastwards out of the

Indus basin, were establishing themselves at Ujjain, and were gaining ground in Maharashtra at the Andhras' expense. The Saka principalities at Ujjain and in Maharashtra were autonomous satrapies of the Kushan Empire, but the major part of the subcontinent was still outside the Kushan Empire's bounds.

Another portion of the Old-World Oikoumenê that was not included in any of the four empires was the upper basin of the River Nile. It has been mentioned already that the southern political frontier of Pharaonic Egypt had been pushed forward to a point on the Nile just above the Second Cataract in the Age of the Middle Kingdom and, to Napata, just below the Fourth Cataract, in the Age of the New Kingdom. After the New Kingdom's collapse in the eleventh century B.C., Napata had become the capital of one of its successor-states (Kush), and this state had survived its failure, in the eighth and seventh centuries B.C., to re-unite the Egyptian World politically by bringing Egypt itself under the Kushite Kingdom's rule. At an unknown date the Kingdom of Kush expanded up the Nile valley, beyond Napata, to Meroe, on the right bank, between the confluence of the Atbara River and the Sixth Cataract, and the capital was moved from Napata to Meroe, perhaps in the sixth century B.C.

Meroe had three advantages over Napata. At Meroe there is some rainfall, whereas at Napata agriculture is entirely dependent on irrigation. At Meroe there are rich deposits of iron-ore, which made possible the development there of a metallurgical industry. In the third place, a state with its capital at Meroe has access to the belt of traversible and habitable country (devastated by drought in A.D. 1973) that stretches westwards, between the desert in the north and the tropical rain-forest in the south, all the way from the west bank of the White Nile to the Atlantic coast of Africa.

Though the Kingdom of Kush failed to incorporate Egypt, it succeeded in maintaining its independence from the First Persian Empire, the Ptolemaic Empire, and the Roman Empire in succession. The Kushite Kingdom seems to have been destroyed by African barbarians, the Noba (Nubians), in the third century A.D.

Meanwhile, since perhaps as early as the seventh century B.C., the northern end of the Abyssinian plateau had been colonized by settlers from the Yemen (the southern corner of the Arabian Peninsula), and both the Yemen and its colony in Africa remained outside the frontiers of the four empires.

Thus the four empires did not embrace quite the whole of the civilized part of the Old-World Oikoumenê; yet they did cover, between them, a remarkably large part of it.

The four major empires' political relations with each other were largely governed by the configuration of the political map. The Roman and Parthian Empires had no common frontiers with the Chinese Empire; the Kushan Empire had no common frontier with the Roman Empire. Since the Chinese and the Roman Empires lay at opposite ends of the Continent, direct relations between them were infrequent. Indeed, the inhabitants of each of these two outlying empires were only dimly aware of the other's existence. On the other hand, the Kushan and the Parthian Empires were each in comparatively close touch with all the other three empires, including the outlying empire that was not its direct neighbour. These two were the central powers, and their businessmen were the middlemen in the indirect transcontinental trade between the Chinese and Roman Empires. The Roman and Kushan Empires had commercial and cultural relations with each other without ever going to war with each other; the relations between the Chinese Empire and the Parthian Empire were equally happy. On the other hand, there were wars between Romans and Parthians, between Parthians and Kushans, and between Kushans and Chinese. But these wars were neither chronic nor devastating, nor did they result in any important permanent changes in the political map.

The Western Han dynasty's fitful occupations of Farghanah between 102 and 40 B.C. were repeated by the Eastern Han dynasty between A.D. 73 and 102, and in the second century A.D. both Farghanah and the Tarim basin were debatable areas between the Chinese and Kushan Empires. Seistan was a debatable area between the Kushan and Parthian Empires, and Armenia between the Parthian Empire and the Roman Empire. In A.D. 63–6 it was arranged that the crown of Armenia should be a perquisite of the Parthian Arsacid dynasty, but that an Arsacid candidate for the Armenian crown should have to make his title good by visiting Rome and receiving his investiture there at the Roman Emperor's hands.

Between the Parthian Empire and the Roman Empire there was no considerable permanent alteration of the frontier, along the course of the Euphrates and its westward elbow, which had been established between the two empires when, in 64 B.C., Pompey had made Syria into a Roman province. The Parthians invaded Syria, but did not succeed in making any permanent lodgment there, after their sensational victory over Crassus' army at Carrhae in 53 B.C. In 36 and 34–33 B.C. Marcus Antonius invaded the region to the east of the Euphrates as far north-eastward as North Media (Azerbaijan); in A.D. 114–17 the Emperor Trajan tried to incorporate Armenia, Mesopotamia, and Babylonia in the Roman Empire. Each of these two ambitious Roman military adventures ended disastrously. In A.D. 117 Trajan's successor Hadrian drew the Roman Empire's eastern frontier back to the line of the

Euphrates, but he retained for the Roman Empire the access to the head of the Persian Gulf which Trajan had won momentarily by making untenable military conquests. Hadrian granted autonomy to the oasis-state Palmyra and encouraged the Palmyrenes to set up unobtrusive trading-posts on the Parthian Empire's south-western fringe. The only lasting extension of direct Roman rule beyond the Euphrates was the annexation of north-western Mesopotamia between A.D. 194 and 199.

The four empires were linked with each other by three routes—though travellers along these routes, whether they were armed forces, diplomatic envoys, traders, or missionaries, seldom made the through-passage between the Chinese and Roman Empires; these two outlying empires were kept in touch with each other mainly by middlemen, who passed goods and messages and information in relays from hand to hand and from mouth to mouth.

The northernmost route ran across the Eurasian steppe from the garrisons along the Great Wall of China to the Greek colonies along the northern shore of the Black Sea, which had now become Roman protectorates. A shorter but physically more arduous overland route was 'the Silk Road'. This ran from Loyang, the Eastern Han dynasty's capital on the North China plain, through the Tarim basin and over the T'ien Shan, to Soghd in the Zarafshan valley between the upper courses of the Jaxartes and the Oxus. From Soghd westward, this route bifurcated. Travellers who wished to avoid setting foot on Parthian territory could reach the eastern shore of the Black Sea via Khwarizm, the Caspian, and the trough between the Caucasus Range and the Armenian plateau. Travellers who were willing to run the gauntlet of the Parthian customs officials and police could make for any of the ports along the Syrian shore of the Mediterranean. The shortest way was across the Syrian desert via one or other of two 'caravan cities', Palmyra and Petra. Palmyra was the junction of the route from Parthia to the Mediterranean with a route from the ports along the Arabian shore of the Persian Gulf; Petra was the junction of the route from Parthia with the overland route from the Yemen.

The sea-route was the most hazardous but was also the most profitable for commerce. The canal linking the Red-Sea port, Suez, with the easternmost arm of the Nile delta via the Wadi Tumilat may have been completed, or perhaps merely reconditioned, by Ptolemy II (282–245 B.C.), and this provided a through-route by water between the Mediterranean and the Red Sea. So long as the Ptolemaic Empire had been a naval and military power, it had commanded the Red Sea and had held beach-heads on what is now the coast of Eritrea. Its object there had been to capture African elephants to pit against the Indian elephants of its rival the Seleucid Empire; but, at this stage, the Greeks domiciled in Egypt had been content to leave the maritime trade between Egypt and India in the hands of the Sabaean Yemenite mariners. Towards the close of the second century B.C. the Ptolemaic Government set itself to by-pass the Sabaeans by initiating direct voyages from Egypt's Red-Sea ports to the delta of the Indus. At an unascertained date a nebulous Greek navigator of the South Seas learnt the seasons and the directions of the monsoon winds. ('Hippalos' may be, not the personal name of an historical Greek mariner, but a poetic epithet of the wind on which anonymous Greek skippers learned to ride.)

The Egyptian Greeks' discovery of the habits of the monsoons enabled them to shorten the length of time required for the 'round trip' between Egypt and the Indus delta; it also enabled them to sail straight across the open sea between the Straits of Bab al-Mandab and the southern tip of India, and even to circumnavigate Ceylon and to establish an entrepôt at Arikamedu, on the east coast of India, just to the south of present-day Pondichery, which offered easier access to the interior than any west-coast port could provide.

The Greek maritime traffic between Egypt and India seems to have reached its peak about half way through the first century A.D.—that is to say, at the moment when the interior of north-western India was being made safer for trade by the imposition of a *pax Kushanica* which united north-western India politically with Bactria. In the same century the Greeks' feat of sailing to India straight across the Arabian Sea was emulated by Indian navigators. These now reached the Malay Peninsula by sailing, from ports along the east coast of India, straight across the Bay of Bengal. Some of them headed for the Isthmus of Kra, made the portage, and took ship again on the waters of the Gulf of Siam and of the China Sea. Others made a continuous but circuitous voyage from the Bay of Bengal to the China Sea by finding their way through the Straits of Malacca. Like the Greek voyages across the Arabian Sea and beyond, the Indian voyages across the Bay of Bengal and beyond were peaceful. The ships were not warships, they were merchantmen; the mariners were not conquerors, they were traders.

International trade has to be conducted through the media of international languages and scripts. In the period 31 B.C. to A.D. 225, three international languages, each conveyed in a script of its own, were current in the western half of the Old-World Oikoumenê, from the domain of the Kushan Empire to the eastern shore of the Atlantic.

The first in the field was the Aramaic language, written in an alphabet derived, like the Greek alphabet, from the Phoenician. This had become the most widely used medium for official communications in the First Persian Empire. In the Persian Empire's Greek successor-states, Aramaic had forfeited its official role to the Greek *koinê*; yet in three

Iranian successor-states of the Persian Empire's Seleucid Greek successor-state—namely Parthia, Fars, and Soghd—Aramaic came back into official use, and became a medium for literature as well, in the forms of three varieties of Pehlevi: a contrivance in which Aramaic words, written in the Aramaic alphabet, were treated, apparently, as ideograms and were then read as if they were the Iranian words of the same meaning. Meanwhile, by the close of the last century B.C., Aramaic had almost completely supplanted both Canaanite and Akkadian as the language of everyday life for the Semitic-speaking population of 'the Fertile Crescent'. Akkadian, which in the second millennium B.C. had been the international language of Asia Minor and Egypt, as well as of 'the Fertile Crescent', was now almost extinct. Even in Babylonia, few scholars could now read Akkadian written in its cuneiform characters. In Syria, Canaanite ('Hebrew') survived only as a liturgical language (for instance, in the liturgy of the Palestinian Jewish community). Canaanite was still a language of everyday life only in the surviving Phoenician colonial city-states in the western basin of the Mediterranean.

The official use of the Greek language outlived Greek rule. The Parthian, Partho-Saka, and Saka rulers who supplanted the Greeks politically to the east of the Euphrates followed the Bactrian Greek and Indian Greek rulers' precedent of issuing bilingual coins on which one of the inscriptions was in Greek. The inscriptions on the Kushan Emperors' coins are conveyed in the Greek alphabet, though the language is not Greek but a variety of Saka Iranian. In Bactria, an Iranian country in which the relations between the native Iranians and the intrusive Greeks had been particularly friendly, the Greek alphabet was used for conveying the local Iranian language—for instance, in an inscription in the temple built by the Kushan Emperor Kanishka (ruled *c.* A.D. 120–44) at the site that has been named Sirkh Kotal by the modern archaeologists who have discovered it.

West of the Euphrates, in territories in which Greek rule had been supplanted by Roman, Latin, written in the West-Greek ('Roman') alphabet, was the official language; but the Imperial Government and its local representatives and agents communicated in Greek with Roman citizens and subjects whose mother-tongue was Greek or for whom Greek was the language of their cultural life. As the language of everyday life, Greek held its own against Latin except in south-eastern Italy, and in Asia Minor Greek continued to gain ground at the expense of the local non-Greek languages. On the other hand, Latin was the medium in which the Hellenic culture was disseminated in territories under Roman rule round the perimeter of the western Mediterranean (except for Greek-speaking Sicily and Naples) and in Transappennine continental Europe up to the line of the Danube and the Rhine.

Trade and language carried with them other elements of culture—for instance, religion and the visual art that was one of the media in which religion expressed itself. The history of religion in the Old-World Oikoumenê from *c*. 334 B.C. to A.D. 220 is the subject of the next chapter. In the present context, it may be noted that Hellenic visual art, and also Hindu visual art and social institutions, won new ground during the first and second centuries A.D. This period saw the first wave of Indian-ization in present-day Cambodia and South Vietnam; it also saw Hel-lenic visual art win a new field for itself in the Kushan Empire, especially at this empire's capital Taxila (Takshasila) in Gandhara on the road between Bactria and Bihar. Taxila was Hellenized from two directions—from Bactria across the Hindu Kush and from Alexandria across the Arabian Sea. The relative strengths of the respective Hellenic influences from these two sources, and the date at which this double stream of influence began to flow, are at present open questions.

The infiltration of Indian culture into South-East Asia and of Hellenic culture into Gandhara were instances of 'peaceful penetration'. There is a close resemblance between the styles of Hellenic visual art in Gandhara and in the Roman Empire; but, in the provinces of the Roman Empire in which Hellenism was propagated in a Latin dress, Hellenization followed in the wake of Roman military conquest.

The four empires that, from A.D. 48 to the early years of the third century A.D., embraced, between them, most of the Old-World Oikou-menê, differed from each other in their antecedents, and consequently also in their structures.

The Eastern Han Empire in China (A.D. 25–220) and the Parthian Empire during the two centuries ending in A.D. 224, were reproductions, respectively, of the Western Han Empire and of the Parthian Empire of 141–*c*. 31 B.C. In both areas, there had been an intervening period of relative turbulence, but this had not resulted, in either area, in any constructive institutional changes. In both cases, the previous regime, after a temporary breakdown, had been re-established. It had been enfeebled, not rejuvenated, by the interregnum. On the other hand, the foundation of the Kushan Empire in A.D. 48, and the previous termina-tion of the Mediterranean World's century of revolution and civil war by Octavian's (Augustus') victory over Antony and Cleopatra at Actium in 31 B.C., had been genuine new departures, comparable to the new departure in China when the warring states had been replaced first by the Ch'in and then by the Western Han imperial regimes.

In structure there was a close affinity between the Kushan and Parthian Empires, and a fainter resemblance between the Eastern Han and the Roman Empires. In each of the two central empires there was a high degree of political devolution. A large proportion of the imperial dominions was in the hands of autonomous local satraps or sub-kings whose recognition of the Imperial Government's suzerainty was sometimes only nominal. Moreover, the authority of both the Imperial Government and its feudatories was limited in practice by the power of barons who exercised the immediate control over the peasantry—that is to say, over the source of all rents and taxes.

The Eastern Han regime was, in theory, centralized and bureaucratic, but in practice the bureaucrats were also landowners; their duties as civil servants and their interests as private men of property conflicted, and they subordinated their duties to their interests. This had been the reason why previously the Western Han dynasty and its successor Wang Mang had each failed in turn to carry out the agrarian reforms that were required for saving Chinese society from breaking down. The only agents at the emperors' disposal for putting the needed reforms into effect were the bureaucrat-landowners who had a strong private interest in ensuring that the reforms should remain a dead letter.

After the installation of the Eastern Han dynasty in A.D. 25 and their suppression of the peasant revolt in A.D. 36, the bureaucrat-landowners were all-powerful, and they abused their power outrageously. Appointments to office were now made by patronage, not by merit. The entrance examinations for the civil service were no longer conducted honestly. The rents paid to the landowners by their peasant-tenants were raised out of proportion to the scale of the taxes that the landowners themselves had to pay. In northern China, which was the cradle of the Chinese civilization and was also now the immediate hinterland of the Great Wall, the number of registered tax-payers declined and there was a consequent increase in the incidence per head of taxation, corvée-service, and conscript-service in the army. The decline in the number of registered tax-payers is not wholly accounted for by depopulation after the bout of anarchy and civil war (A.D. 9–36). Northern free peasants absconded in large numbers. Some took refuge on the big landowners' estates, where, as the landlords' clients, they were under less heavy economic pressure than when, as freeholders, they had been at the Imperial Government's mercy. Others migrated to the South, where the Imperial Government's control was laxer and where there was still good virgin land to be brought under cultivation.

After the mid-point of the second century A.D., the Chinese bureaucrat-landowners' power was challenged first by the eunuchs at the Imperial Court and then, in and after A.D. 184, by the Taoist leaders of two more peasant revolts. However, the victors were neither the eunuchs nor the peasants, but war-lords, most of whom were also big landowners. In China in the latter part of the second century A.D. there happened what had happened in the Roman commonwealth after the Hannibalic War.

The supply of peasant-conscripts for military service fell off; professional armies, recruited from paupers, took their place; and these became the private armies of the generals who commanded them, since the soldiers looked to the generals to recompense their service. In the years A.D. 220–2, the Eastern Han Empire broke up overtly into three kingdoms, ruled by three generals who had already divided the Empire between them *de facto*.

In principle, the Roman Empire in the period 31 B.C.–A.D. 235 had less in common with the Eastern Han Empire than with the contemporary Parthian and Kushan Empires. The Eastern Han Empire was in theory a centralized bureaucratically administered state, though its theoretical constitution was not effective in practice. The Roman Empire resembled the two central empires in being addicted to devolution. The Roman 'establishment' had always fought shy of taking direct responsibility for the administration of territories that it had turned into political vacuums by destroying their previous governments, and Augustus adhered to this Roman tradition as closely as was compatible with the restoration of order in a Mediterranean World which the previous republican Roman regime had reduced to anarchy. From 31 B.C. onwards, Augustus and his successors, following the precedents set in the Levant by the Seleucids and then, in 67–62 B.C., by Pompey, sought to organize the Roman Empire as an association of autonomous city-states. The Imperial Government tried to confine its own responsibilities to preventing the Empire's constituent city-states from continuing to go to war with each other and to shielding them all against attacks by enemies from beyond the Empire's frontiers.

The Roman Empire, like the Eastern Han Empire, was short of manpower. The population explosion that had started in the Hellenic World in the eighth century B.C. had died down in the third century B.C. in Macedon, in the second century B.C. in other Greek-speaking countries, and in the last century B.C. in Italy. During the first phase of the Roman Empire's history (31 B.C.–A.D. 235), only one people within the Empire's frontiers, namely the Jewish people, was increasing conspicuously in numbers. The population of Judah must have been tiny in 586 B.C., the year in which the Kingdom of Judah had been liquidated by Nebuchadnezzar, but, since then, the Jews had populated a large part of the former Kingdom of Israel, which was Judaea's next-door neighbour, while a Jewish diaspora ('dispersion') had spread far and wide: first into Babylonia, next into Egypt, and eventually throughout the Hellenic World. In Babylonia and, from 63 B.C., in Rome, the pioneers of the Jewish diaspora had been deportees, but most of the Jewish dispersion had been voluntary; the Jews had settled abroad as mercenary soldiers and as traders. The constant increase in the Jewish people's numerical strength is the more remarkable, considering the magnitude of the casualties that they suffered (and also inflicted on their non-Jewish neighbours) in their insurrections against the Roman Imperial Government in Palestine in A.D. 66–70 and A.D. 132–5, and in Cyprus and Cyrenaïca *c.* A.D. 115–17. In this last-mentioned insurrection, the local Jewish community not only gained temporary command over Cyrenaïca itself; it also used Cyrenaïca as a base for an invasion of Egypt.

Augustus stabilized the frontiers of the Roman Empire along lines which could be held by a professional army of volunteers that was small enough to make it possible for the Empire's diminishing population to keep this army up to strength, and was also small enough to be a bearable burden for the tax-payers. Augustus reduced the huge armies that had been mobilized by Augustus himself and by his now eliminated competitors to the minimum strength that the holding of the new frontiers required. No provision was made either for reserves or for defence in depth. If a mobile force had to be assembled for suppressing some local revolt of the Empire's subjects or for waging a civil war, the troops had to be found by depleting the garrisons along whatever section of the Empire's frontier seemed, at the time, to be not in danger of being attacked. Serious demands for mobile Roman armies were made by the three Jewish insurrections that have been mentioned, and by the two civil wars of A.D. 69 and 193–7.

On the south, the Roman Empire found 'natural frontiers' along the northern edges of the Sahara and the Arabian Desert. The narrow passage, between deserts, down the course of the River Nile was not difficult to block in Lower Nubia. In continental Europe, Augustus' adoptive father, Julius Caesar, had carried the Roman frontier to the Rhine; Augustus carried it to the Danube as well; his successors closed the gap between the upper waters of the Rhine and of the Danube between *c.* A.D. 70 and 138 by building an artificial rampart between the Rhine above Coblenz and the Danube above Regensburg. After the conquest and incorporation in the Empire of the greater part of the island of Britain, similar artificial ramparts, here running from sea to sea, were built from Tyne to Solway by the Emperor Hadrian in and after A.D. 122 and between the Firth of Forth and the River Clyde by the Emperor Titus Antoninus Pius in and after A.D. 142. These artificial Roman ramparts were short and frail, measured by the standards of the Chinese Great Wall's length and massiveness. The Roman ramparts were merely supplements to the natural frontiers provided by the sea in Britain and by the two great rivers on the Continent; but the 'naturalness' of the river-frontiers was delusive. Though, during the seasons in which these two rivers were open for navigation, they were patrolled by Roman flotillas, they were easy to cross at all seasons, and particularly in the winter if the weather was severe enough for either river to be bridged by a coating of ice. Moreover, the Rhine–Danube line is the longest of any that can be drawn between the North Sea and the Black Sea.

Augustus tried to shorten the Roman Empire's continental European river-frontier by carrying this forward from the Rhine to the Elbe, but the Empire's man-power—diminished by the economic and political revolutions of the preceding two centuries—was not equal to completing a task that, if successfully performed, would have reduced considerably the amount of requisite military man-power. This project of Augustus was defeated by the revolt, in A.D. 6–9, of the recently subjugated Pannonians between the Adriatic Sea and the Danube and by the annihilation, in A.D. 9, of three Roman legions between the Rhine and the Elbe by the recently subjugated Germans. The impossibility of going on with the Elbe frontier project after these reverses revealed the narrowness of the Roman Empire's resources of man-power at this date (a striking contrast to their abundance before and during the Hannibalic War). This demographic weakness continued to make itself felt. The Roman Empire embarked on the conquest and incorporation of Britain but failed to carry this to completion. The Emperor Trajan, the Roman counterpart of Han Wu-ti, succeeded in conquering and annexing Dacia (Transylvania) in A.D. 101–6, but failed in A.D. 114–17 to carry the Empire's eastern frontier forward, more than momentarily, to the shores of the Caspian Sea and the Persian Gulf.

The Roman Empire's greatest political achievement was the progressive conversion of its subjects into Roman citizens. This policy had been inaugurated in the fourth century B.C., and it had been one of the causes of the Romans' success in incorporating into their commonwealth first Peninsular Italy and eventually the whole perimeter of the Mediterranean. The implementation of the policy had not been continuous. There had been hesitations and pauses. However, the process was consummated in A.D. 212, when Roman citizenship was conferred—or imposed—on all but a small residual minority of the Empire's previously unenfranchised population.

Rome's liberality in enfranchising conquered aliens contrasts strikingly with Athens's narrow-heartedness in the fifth century B.C. The contrast partly explains why it was that Rome, not Athens, achieved the political unification of the Mediterranean basin. However, equality of political status does not compensate for economic and social injustice. Rome's other effective policy for promoting her territorial expansion had been to guarantee the vested interests of the rich against the demands of the poor. In the Roman Empire during the period 31 B.C.–A.D. 235, the progressive extension of political enfranchisement was accompanied by a progressive widening of the gap between the rich and the poor. Inequality before the law increased, besides inequality in possessions, in income, and in the standard of living, spiritual as well as material. In this period, social injustice was being aggravated in each of the two empires that lay at opposite ends of the Old-World Oikoumenê.

It has been mentioned that, in the Han Empire, the Confucian bureaucrat-landowners failed to subordinate their private interests to their public duty, and that, under the Eastern Han regime, the moral shortcomings of this strongly-entrenched 'establishment' became more crude and more shameless than they had been when they had brought the preceding Western Han regime to grief. All the same, the Han Confucian civil service was the least bad of any that had been created anywhere so far. It was as superior to the Roman civil service, instituted by Augustus, as the Great Wall was to the little Roman ramparts in Germany and in Britain.

The Roman city-state had started on its career of expansion with an utterly inadequate administrative staff. Like most other city-states—Etruscan, Greek, and Phoenician—in the Mediterranean basin in the last millennium B.C., Rome had been governed by a small team of annually elected non-professional public officers, and the administrative demands made by Rome's progressive expansion were not met to any appreciable extent by increasing the number of the elective offices and the length of their tenure by their temporary incumbents. The Roman Government's main recourse for remedying its administrative deficiencies had been to farm out the provisioning of its armies and the collection of its taxes to companies of private citizens. These companies had acquired all the administrative expertise of the Hellenic World of the day. They had employed task-forces of educated slaves and freedmen.

Augustus, taking his cue from his adoptive father Julius Caesar, reduced the companies' opportunities for making undue private profits at the expense of Rome's government, her citizens, and her subjects, but Augustus copied their organization. He built up a 'Caesar's household' of slaves and freedmen on the grand scale to serve as his personal administrative staff, and he compensated the former aristocratic Roman 'establishment' and its parasites who had battened on public contracts by recruiting from among them the two highest grades of a well-paid civil service. This Roman bureaucracy did not have the cohesiveness of its Chinese counterpart. In particular, it was not held together by adherence, *ex officio*, to an hereditary philosophy. Still, this Augustan Imperial Roman civil service, staffed with wolf-cubs transfigured into sheep-dogs, was much better than the rudimentary imperial administrative improvisations of the two central powers, the Parthian and the Kushan Empires.

The Imperial Roman civil service eventually had to take on a task for which Augustus had not designed it. His intention had been, not to conduct, but merely to supervise, the local administration of the city-states that were the cells composing the imperial body politic. The personnel of the imperial service had therefore originally been kept small in numbers. The inaugurator of the Augustan Peace had failed to foresee that the citizens of the Empire's component city-states would lose interest in the local government of their communities when these had been deprived of their historic sovereign prerogative of going to war with their neighbours. By an early date in the second century A.D.—a deceptively apparent golden age in the Mediterranean World—local government was beginning to fall into disorder and the central government of the Empire was finding itself compelled, reluctantly, to intervene directly in this vast field of administrative work.

In the third century A.D. a disaster overtook each of the empires that, during the preceding two centuries, had divided between them the greater part of the Old-World Oikoumenê.

The Roman Empire endured, and surprisingly survived, half a century of chaos (A.D. 235–84) which was itself a surprising sequel to a preceding pseudo-golden age (A.D. 96–180). During this desperate Roman half-century, the imperial coinage was debased to zero value; the Empire's territory was overrun and was devastated by raiders from beyond the frontiers; in A.D. 250 the Emperor Decius was defeated and killed by the Goths; in A.D. 260 the Emperor Valerian was defeated and captured by the Persians, and he ended his life in captivity. The Empire itself broke up temporarily, like the Chinese Empire in A.D. 220–2, into three mutually independent fragments. The Roman financial collapse went to such extremes that, for a time, payments were made in kind and trade was conducted by barter. This was a portentous economic retrogression in a Mediterranean World in which coinage had been invented in the seventh century B.C. and which, long before that date, had been using bullion as a measure and medium of exchange.

In Iran in A.D. 224 there was a sudden capture of imperial power by a sub-king in Fars which was a repetition of a similar *coup c.* 550 B.C. About half way through the sixth century B.C., the Median Emperor Astyages had been overthrown and supplanted suddenly by his Persian vassal Cyrus. In A.D. 224 the Parthian Emperor Artabanus V was overthrown and supplanted by his Persian vassal Ardeshir (Artaxerxes). The new imperial masters of Iran and Iraq denigrated their deposed predecessors by styling them 'kings of bits and pieces'; yet actually the Parthian Empire's loose-knit structure was taken over, without any essential change, by the Second (the Sasanian) Persian Empire. The Sasanids behaved more aggressively towards their neighbours than the Arsacids had been able to behave in the Parthian Empire's decrepit last phase; but the Sasanids were not notably more successful than the Arsacids in imposing the central government's authority on the local barons.

The Sasanids' aggression against the Roman Empire provoked a backlash after the Roman Empire's rehabilitation in A.D. 284. In A.D. 298 the Roman Government compelled the Sasanian Emperor Narseh to retrocede all formerly Roman territories that had been annexed by Shahpuhr I (ruled A.D. 242–73) and to agree to the annexation to the Roman Empire of five Armenian provinces on the left bank of the upper course of the River Tigris. The Sasanids' successful aggression was in the opposite quarter. The founder, Ardeshir himself, enlarged the Empire that he had captured from the Arsacid Emperor Artabanus V by conquering the Kushan Empire as well. However, he may have merely imposed his suzerainty on it without liquidating it, for a remnant of the Kushan Empire survived, or re-emerged, in the Kabul valley. This remnant weathered the storm of the Hun *Völkerwanderung* in the fifth and sixth centuries A.D., and was not extinguished finally till the eleventh century.

After the break-up of the Eastern Han Empire into three warring fragments in A.D. 220–2, China remained disunited politically from A.D. 220 to 589, save for a brief spell of re-unification from A.D. 280 to 304. The political interregnum that began in A.D. 220 is the longest that there has ever been in the Chinese World since its first political unification in 221 B.C.

On the political plane the encapsulation of the greater part of the Old-World Oikoumenê in no more than four huge empires for nearly two centuries, beginning in A.D. 48, foreshadowed the possibility of a future political unification of the entire Oikoumenê, all round the globe. The four empires themselves were ephemeral, though each of them afterwards reappeared on the map in a series of avatars. (The avatars of the Chinese Empire were the most substantial.) Religion, however, was the plane on which the four empires, in their short lives, made the greatest mark on Mankind's history.

[38]

THE INTERPLAY OF RELIGIONS
AND PHILOSOPHIES IN THE
OLD-WORLD OIKOUMENÊ,

334 B.C.–*c.* A.D. 220

'SUFFERING is the price of learning.' This dictum was uttered in a play written by the Athenian dramatic poet Aeschylus and produced in 458 B.C.—a year in which Athens was waging a reckless war on two fronts. This recklessness foreboded a 'time of troubles', and an agonizing but enlightening time of this kind was the prelude to the establishment of each of the four empires that co-existed in the Old-World Oikoumenê between A.D. 48 and 220. The Hellenic World's 'time of troubles' ran from 431 B.C. to 31 B.C.; South-West Asia's and Egypt's ran from 745 B.C. to 522 B.C. and recurred, after a breathing-space, from 334 B.C. to 31 B.C.; India's 'time of troubles' ran from *c.* 500 B.C. to 322 B.C. and recurred, after a breathing-space, from *c.* 200 B.C. to A.D. 48; China's 'time of troubles' ran from 506 B.C. to 221 B.C.

In Chapter 25, some account has been given of five great souls who responded individually to the common experience of suffering as early as the sixth century B.C.

Each of the five made a break with his society's traditional religion. In some cases the break was violent and in other cases it was more discreet, but in every case the break was revolutionary. 'Deutero-Isaiah' declared, as uncompromisingly as Akhenaton seven centuries earlier, that one god alone existed. (King Josiah of Judah had prepared the way for 'Deutero-Isaiah's' stand by abolishing all holy places in Judah except the temple at Jerusalem, and evicting from the temple all the gods and goddesses who had previously shared it with Yahweh.) Zarathustra degraded all the gods of the traditional Iranian pantheon save one—'the great spirit' Ahura Mazda—to the status of devils. Pythagoras tried to reform the Hellenic way of life so high-handedly that he provoked a counter-revolution. In India, both the Buddha and the Mahavira (the founder of the Jain religion) ignored both the gods of the traditional Indian Aryan pantheon and the institution of caste. Confucius professed

—and perhaps believed—that he was restoring the original essence of traditional Chinese institutions; yet, in interpreting 'nobility' as being a moral quality and not a hereditary privilege, he was actually initiating an ethical revolution.

All five seers broke out of the social framework of traditional religion and made direct personal contact with the ultimate spiritual reality behind the phenomena, though only two of the five, namely Zarathustra and 'Deutero-Isaiah', conceived of this ultimate reality as being a human-like personality which differed from its demoted or discarded fellow gods and goddesses solely in the two points of being unique and being omnipotent—and, in Zarathustra's theology, even these two attributes of Ahura Mazda were only potential, pending his eventual victory in his current war with the not yet conquered powers of evil.

As Old-World mankind's suffering continued and became progressively more acute, it generated the need for a relation with the ultimate reality that would not merely be direct but would also be emotionally satisfying, and this demand required the preservation or revival of a conception of the nature of the ultimate spiritual reality that would be human-like in the sense of being a personality, or at least of having a personal facet. The worshipper longed to be a devotee, and to have faith in the ultimate spiritual reality's benevolence and power, and this longing was matched by a yearning for a spiritual reality that would manifestly feel concern for the human worshipper's welfare and would unquestionably have the power to deliver him from evil. These emotional requirements could be met only by the establishment of a relation between two personalities, one human and the other divine.

In China and India and the Hellenic World, where the human-like conception of the nature of ultimate reality had sunk below the philosophers' horizon, the emotional reaction to suffering now called for the revival of the traditional human-like personal aspect of ultimate reality which had been retained in the theology of Zoroastrianism and Judaism. In India and China the new religions that were begotten, incongruously, by the regional philosophies, rehabilitated theism and inclined tentatively towards monotheism, without becoming uncompromisingly monotheistic in the Jewish style. In the Mediterranean basin, theism was revived in the tentatively monotheistic but tolerant Indian and Chinese spirit in all the competing regional religions except for the eventual victor. Victorious Christianity inherited the intolerant monotheism of its parent religion, Judaism; but Christianity defected from Jewish monotheism in so far as it devoured and assimilated the defeated rival religions, all of which were of non-Jewish origin.

The third century A.D. saw the breakdown of each of the four empires that, for nearly two centuries, had stretched across the Old World in a geographically continuous line; but by the third century, Old-World mankind's long-drawn-out spiritual travail, which had preceded the brief respite, had produced historic results. In each of the four empires the regional religions and philosophies had given birth to new religions of a distinctive type. The new had been elicited from the old by a process of selection, dissemination, and syncretism. The agents of the propagation of the new religions had been diasporas ('dispersions'). The earliest recruits of these diasporas were deportees; they were followed by garrisons posted by empire-builders in conquered countries; these were followed by traders. The permanently or temporarily uprooted and transplanted people carried with them as much of their ancestral way of life as was portable, and they became, automatically, disseminators of this among the alien majorities in the migrants' new domiciles. The migrants might also become conscious and deliberate disseminators of the spiritual treasure that they had brought with them. Eventually the new religions were served, *in partibus infidelium*, by priests, and were carried farther afield by missionaries. These priests and missionaries were professionals, though their religious vocation was not necessarily a full-time occupation.

The dissemination and adaptation of foreign religions, and their fusion with the existing local religions, were at a premium in regions in which the local religions were conspicuously inadequate for meeting mankind's common need for some religion that would help human souls to cope with a time of troubles. The spiritually starved and hungry regions were the two outlying areas, namely the Hellenic World and China.

The dissemination of the new religions to meet regional demands was facilitated by the new means of communication that were the positive products of war, deracination, imperialism, and ecumenical trade. There were long-distance sea-routes and land-routes linking together the Old-World Oikoumenê's extremities. There were 'lingue franche': for instance, the Attic Greek *koinê*, Aramaic, the three varieties of Pehlevi, the Indian prakrits, the neo-Sanskrit that prevailed over the prakrits in the second century A.D. in northern India and in the third century in the Deccan, and a Chinese *koinê* (standardized forms of both the characters and the spoken language) that became current throughout China, among civil servants and merchants, after the political unification of the Chinese World in 221 B.C. A third medium of communication was visual art. These media of various kinds were particularly effective while the four empires were co-existing in geographical contact with each other. In this brief period of relative political consolidation and relative peace, the Old-World Oikoumenê was in an unusually conductive state.

In the process of selection, diffusion, adaptation, and syncretism out of which the new, emotionally satisfying, religions arose, the Hellenic media were particularly efficacious. The Greek language, Greek visual art, and Greek philosophy worked together in the Mediterranean basin to 'process' both the various religions that competed there with Christianity and their eventual conqueror and devourer, Christianity itself. Hellenism did not make itself felt direct in any form anywhere farther to the east than India; but in north-western India Hellenic visual art provided a vehicle for Mahayana Buddhism, as, in the Mediterranean basin, it provided one for Christianity, as well as for Christianity's unsuccessful competitors. When the Mahayana was transmitted, via the Oxus–Jaxartes basin and the Tarim basin, from north-western India to Eastern Asia, its artistic vehicle travelled with it, and, in this visual form, Hellenism influenced Eastern Asia indirectly. In the opposite direction, Hellenic art, and Hellenic philosophy as well, continued their penetration of western Europe and North-West Africa as adjuncts of Christianity. Thus Hellenism, alone among the regional civilizations of the pre-modern age, made itself felt in some degree throughout the Old-World Oikoumenê from coast to coast.

The time of troubles and its sequel knit together, for the first time, not only the nuclear regions of the Old-World Oikoumenê but its outlying regions too. Before that, the regional civilizations had arisen separately from each other and each had developed its own way of life, and religion had been an integral part of this. Yet, though the general style of each of the regional civilizations had been distinctive, on the plane of religion they had all inherited from the pre-civilizational stage of mankind's history a number of common 'primordial images'. This common mental heritage made it possible for the religious element in one regional civilization, when disengaged from the rest of that civilization's components, to be adapted to, and to be adopted into, the religion of another regional civilization. Unlike some of the secular elements in a regional civilization, the religious elements were not wholly alien to other regional civilizations.

Of these common religious 'primordial images', probably the oldest, and certainly the most potent, was the Mother. She is the subject of the oldest visual representations of the human form; and since, in this image, motherhood is not seen to be incompatible with virginity, this mother-image must have taken shape before the discovery of paternity—that is to say, before it had been recognized that a woman cannot become pregnant without having had sexual intercourse with a male. It must have been recognized, since the dawn of consciousness, that motherhood implied the birth of a Child, but the recognition that the Mother must have had a male consort, and that the Child must have had a Father, is not primordial. Originally, the Mother overshadowed the Child, and the Father was either non-existent or, at most, a shadowy figure. The

Mother's potency is formidable for any male that is associated with her, and consequently, some strong-minded male gods have chosen to remain celibate. The Aton, Asshur, Yahweh, and Mithras are cases in point.

The relative potency of Mother, Child, and Father has varied as between one regional civilization and another and, within any single civilization, as between different stages of its history. These variations have made each of the diverse portrayals of the Holy Family attractive to people whose own ancestral portrayal of it was different. One regional civilization could supply features of the common picture that were lacking in other regional civilizations.

The image of the Mother is protean. She may be the mother of a human child or of the progeny of any species of living creature. At the same time she may be the Earth, who is the common Mother of all life. In each of these aspects the Mother is usually expected to foster and cherish her offspring, but, though she is invariably fertile, she is not invariably benign. The Meso-American earth-goddess Coatlícue, mother of gods and men, the Hellenic mother-goddess Hecate, and the Indian mother-goddess Kali can and do use their powers destructively and malignantly, as well as creatively and benignly. In Asia Minor the mother-goddess Cybele blighted Attis, her child or her consort or perhaps both child and consort combined in a single male companion.

If even the Mother can sometimes turn savage, it is no wonder that the Weather is a morally ambivalent power; for the Weather is capriciously inconstant, and its caprice can either devastate the crops by flood or drought or can make them yield a harvest by giving and withholding rain in due season ('due', that is to say, for serving the human husbandman's purpose). The weather-god is apt to be male, and it is easy to identify him with the Father; for, in contrast to the Mother's normal tenderness towards her child, the Father's mood, like the Weather's, can veer unpredictably, because irrationally, from benevolence to wrath and then back again from wrath to benevolence.

By contrast, the Sun's daily and yearly course is predictably regular, and the Sun himself is just. He gives his light and warmth to all living beings impartially; we can count on him with greater assurance than we can count on Mother Earth, not to speak of Father Weather; but, since the Sun sees and hears everything that is done on Earth, he keeps an account of every human being's moral credits and debits.

The other Stars are not so reassuring as the Sun. The planets are as erratic as the Weather; the fixed stars are inexorable; Man's fate is determined by the Stars' influence; and this influence may be malign.

The Seed dies for a season in order that it may come to life again as a crop which the human sower will harvest. This vegetative power's human devotees live by eating its flesh and drinking its blood. Surely the food-begetting power is a self-sacrificing benefactor of mankind, and the guilt for its voluntary death is on the heads of its human beneficiaries. The mystery of this power's annual death and resurrection gives its human devotees a hope that their death, too, will be followed by a resurrection. But is not this self-sacrificing power also criminal? Does it not afflict its human devotees with a frenzy in which they tear living beings —including human beings—to pieces and devour their flesh raw?

Another primordial image is the Saviour—needed by us poor human beings at all times, but most of all in a time of troubles. Another one is the God Incarnate in a human being. Pharaoh was a god incarnate. From at least as early as the beginning of the Fifth Pharaonic Dynasty, every Pharaoh was deemed to have been begotten on his human mother, without the intervention of a human father and without any divine sexual act, by the divine utterance of a commanding word. Who knows how far back in the history of the evolution of *homo sapiens* and of the pre-human hominids the primordial image of the God Incarnate took shape?

The primordial images are not mutually exclusive. The God Incarnate and the Saviour and the Seed and the Son may be identical with each other. The Mother may be a virgin whose fertility requires no human consort, and whose child may consequently have no father. Alternatively the Mother may be a wife who is as utterly devoted to her husband as she is to her child. There is also no certainty about the sex of any image save one. The Mother, of course, cannot be male, and the Weather is rarely female, yet, in the religion of Pharaonic Egypt, the Earth was male and the Sky was female. In most religions the Sun is male; but the Sun is regular and just, and an uncapricious male is a paradox. There is better logic in the feminine gender of the Sun-goddess of the Hittite city of Arinna, and of Amaterasu the Sun-goddess who is the ancestress of the Japanese Imperial Family, and of the Sun—*die Sonne*—in the German language.

We have now surveyed the potential materials for new religions that might satisfy mankind's spiritual needs in a time of troubles. We can pass on to a survey of the actual products, and it will make for clarity if we conduct our survey region by region.

In China the ancestral religion of the 'establishment' had become virtually extinct before the need for a devotional religion made itself felt. 'Heaven' (*T'ien*) had probably lost its original connotation of personality before Confucius' day. 'The mandate of Heaven', which gave an imperial dynasty its credentials according to the Confucian scholar-administrator-landlords who came into power in Han Wu-ti's reign, was, in truth, a human mandate, conferred and withdrawn by this new dominant class. The only materials at hand in China for a devotional religion were culturally primitive local popular cults. The political unification of the Chinese World in 221 B.C. had opened the way for these cults to fuse with each other and with the philosophies of the 'establishment'.

The Confucianism that was made the qualification for public office by Wu-ti was no longer the philosophy of Confucius and Mencius. This had been adulterated by an incongruous infusion of popular religion. The corresponding adulteration of Taoism went to great lengths. The Taoist philosophy—standing, as it did stand, for a withdrawal from participation in public affairs—was apt to flourish when Confucianism was at a discount. For instance, Taoism was in the ascendant at the beginning of Han Liu P'ang's reign, and it enjoyed another *floruit* in the second century A.D., when three centuries of melancholy experience had demonstrated that Confucianism had abused its monopoly of administrative power. But, simultaneously with this revival of Taoism as a sophisticated philosophy, Taoism had also generated a popular religion, and this religion had been organized effectively enough to provide inspiration and leadership for the two abortive peasant revolts that challenged the Eastern Han regime in A.D. 184.

Was this metamorphosis of an indigenous Chinese philosophy into a religion a spontaneous Chinese development, or was it inspired by the example of the Mahayana—a devotional religion of Indian origin which had been evolved out of the Theravadin Buddhist philosophy? This latter possibility cannot be ruled out, considering that, in the second century A.D., the Mahayana was already seeping into China. It is certain that later on, when the influx of the Mahayana into China was in full flood, the Taoist religion—which had survived the failure of the peasant revolts that it had sponsored—did copy the Mahayana's doctrine and organization in order to provide a professedly indigenous Chinese equivalent for this intrusive Indian religion.

The evolution of the Mahayana in India was a gradual process, and, on the social and institutional plane, there was no breach of continuity. The Buddhist monastic order (*sangha*) was transmitted from Theravadin Buddhism to the Mahayana, and this continued to be the institutional basis for Buddhism of all varieties. On the other hand, on the doctrinal plane the cumulative effect of the evolution amounted to a metamorphosis.

The Theravadin Buddhist monk must strive to make his individual exit into Nirvana by his own exertions; for, though he is inspired by the Buddha's instructions and example, he cannot call upon the Buddha himself for spiritual aid, since the Buddha, when once he had made his own exit into Nirvana, ceased to be accessible. Nirvana is still the ultimate goal of the Mahayanian monk, but this monk's prior aim is to become a bodhisattva, and he can look for help in this endeavour to a pantheon of bodhisattvas who already exist and are within call. With a bodhisattva's help, the Mahayanian Buddhist can hope to reach his immediate goal, which is, not an exit into Nirvana, but a sojourn in Heaven.

A bodhisattva is an adept in the spiritual practice which the Buddha has prescribed. He has reached the threshold of Nirvana and could now make his exit into Nirvana if he chose; but he has chosen instead (as the Buddha himself chose) voluntarily to postpone his exit in order to help his fellow sentient beings. In terms of 'primordial images', the bodhisattva is the Saviour. One bodhisattva, Avalokita, changed his sex in China in order to become Kwan Yin, the feminine spirit of mercy. In China after the collapse of the Eastern Han regime, there was a crying need for the Mother, and Kwan Yin stepped in to play this timely part. A bodhisattva's unselfish compassion evokes in the Mahayanian Buddhist a responsive devotion and an impulse to try to follow the bodhisattva's example. The Mahayana is, in fact, a devotional religion of the kind that is demanded by a time of troubles.

The Mahayana seems to have taken shape in the course of the first two centuries A.D. and to have crystallized in north-western India, where the local Sarvastivadin school of Buddhist philosophy was readier than the Theravadins in the South to move in the Mahayanian direction. Contemporaneously, Hinduism was undergoing a corresponding change, and this too, though gradual, resulted in a metamorphosis. Here, likewise, there was no breach of continuity on the institutional plane. The institutional link in this case was the Brahmin caste. The Brahmins retained their command over Hinduism in spite of this religion's protean transformations.

In Vedic Hinduism, as in the original religion of the Romans, the relation between the gods and their worshippers had been prosaic. If the ritual was performed correctly, the gods were virtually bound to make the appropriate response, and, on both sides, the governing consideration was self-interest. In the new form of Hinduism, which was really a new religion, the gods Shiva and Vishnu were the counterparts of the Mahayanian Buddhist bodhisattvas. Probably these two Hindu gods were already being worshipped, though perhaps under other names, long before the beginning of the Christian Era. The new feature, which transformed their worship, was the introduction of an emotional relation between them and their devotees. Vishnu, like the bodhisattva Amitabha, is the Saviour, and he is also the god who becomes incarnate. His most popular incarnations were, and are, Rama and Krishna, but he had been incarnate in the Buddha as well. Shiva has the moral ambivalence of the primordial images of the Weather and the Vegetation and the Mother. He can be destructive as well as creative; he has never become incarnate; and his human devotees are at the mercy of his caprice. Shiva is the spiritual reality ander pow behind the totality of Nature. He is not particularly concerned for Man's welfare; but Man has to take Shiva as he finds him, since Man himself is a part of the Nature that Shiva represents.

In Iran Zarathustra's militant monotheism had missed fire. His revolutionary religion had been captured by the hereditary Iranian priesthood, the Magi, as in India the devotional worships of Vishnu and Shiva were captured by the Brahmins. In Iran after Zarathustra's death, as in Pharaonic Egypt after Akhenaton's death, polytheism revived in response to a continuing hunger for it. Ahura Mazda's spiritual attributes became so many goddesses in their own right. Moreover, Anahita, a cherished pre-Zoroastrian water-goddess, succeeded in re-instating herself. These were steps towards the transformation of Zoroastrianism into an emotional religion; but these first steps were not followed up, and even the adulterated Zoroastrianism of the Magi never fully won the Iranians' hearts.

The Levant, even including the Tigris–Euphrates basin, is no larger in area than either India or China, but, in the age before this area was united politically in the Persian, and eventually in the Roman, Empire, the Levant was far less homogeneous on the cultural plane than either the Indian or the Chinese subcontinent. This relatively small region to the west of Iran housed no fewer than five civilizations: the Sumero-Akkadian, the Pharaonic Egyptian, the Syrian, the Anatolian, the Hellenic. Moreover, these five civilizations, in spite of the closeness of their juxtaposition to each other, were not merely separate; they were strikingly different from each other both in their outward style and in their inner spirit. Their interplay was therefore lively when the experience of a time of troubles created the demand for a religion that would be emotionally satisfying. The interplay was stimulated by the conspicuous spiritual poverty of one of the five regional civilizations, namely the Hellenic. It is true that the post-Alexandrine Hellenic World was not so poor in indigenous spiritual resources as contemporary China. In the new age that was inaugurated in the Levant by Alexander's invasion of the Persian Empire in 334 B.C., at least two major Hellenic religions still retained their vitality: the Eleusinian mysteries and the worship of Dionysos. The Eleusinian Demeter was Mother Earth; her daughter the Girl (Korê) was the Seed that dies and is buried and comes to life again. Initiation into the mysteries guaranteed everlasting bliss, after death, in a paradisiacal Other World. Dionysos was the Hellenic counterpart of Shiva. He was the capricious moral ambivalence of Nature. In the post-Alexandrine Age of Hellenic history, the Eleusinian mysteries survived, and the worship of Dionysos achieved a positive revival.

At the same time, private life asserted its claims against the demands of public service, and both the Eleusinian mysteries and the worship of Dionysos catered for the spiritual needs of human beings, regardless of whether their customers happened to be citizens or aliens, free persons or slaves, males or females. There was, of course, a public cult of Dionysos at Athens; the Attic drama was one part of this. The Eleusinian mysteries, too, were under the Athenian city-states' wing; but Eleusis itself was not, like Athens, a sovereign city-state. It was a holy city that happened to lie in the Athenian state's territory; and, as a non-political holy city, Eleusis was accessible to any human being. As for the worship of Dionysos, its revival in the post-Alexandrine Age was an achievement of private religious enterprise, catering for personal spiritual needs. The agents of the Dionysiac revival that spread through the vastly expanded post-Alexandrine Hellenic World were not governments; they were private congregations (*thiasoi*); and the popularity of this wild religion when it became a private affair put some governments in a quandary. Ptolemy IV (ruled 221–203 B.C.), the most eminent politically of the post-Alexandrine Bacchants, required the Bacchic *thiasoi* in his dominions to register. The Roman Government crushed the Bacchic *thiasoi* in Italy in 185–181 B.C.

In the Levant after Alexander's overthrow of the Persian Empire, and round the whole perimeter of the Mediterranean after its political unification in the Roman Empire, there was a competition between rival religions for the prize of becoming the universal religion of the region as a whole. This competition was won by Christianity by a method that had been foreshadowed in Pharaonic Egyptian theology. The Egyptians believed that, when a Pharaoh died, one of his souls, his detachable soul, ascended into Heaven and there devoured the other gods whom the newcomer found in occupation. By devouring these rival gods, Pharaoh appropriated their powers. Christianity appropriated the powers of its competitors by emulating an ascending Pharaoh's mythical performance. Christianity devoured Syrian, Egyptian, Anatolian, and Hellenic gods and goddesses and thereby made their powers her own.

In the competition for capturing the role of the Mother, at least five candidates presented themselves. These were Egyptian Isis, Phrygian Cybele, Ephesian Artemis, Eleusinian Demeter, and a goddess incarnate in Mary, the wife of a Galilaean Jewish carpenter. Mary won by assuming the character, image, and attributes of a Hellenized Isis. In 204 B.C. the Roman Government had relieved the anguish of the Hannibalic War by importing Cybele from Pessinus, or perhaps from Pergamon, in her native form of a black stone served by eunuch priests. When the anguish abated, this rashly invited Phrygian guest was insulated at Rome as far as was practicable. On the other hand, Isis had been Hellenized as a radiant counterpart of Demeter before she had become sea-borne (*pelagia*), and in this guise Isis had made a triumphant conquest of the Roman Empire.

At home in Egypt, Isis had been the devoted wife of the dead and mummified god Osiris, but the goddess's indigenous husband was not exportable. The Egyptian priest Manetho and the Eleusinian Greek priest Timotheos, who were Ptolemy I's co-consultants on religious affairs, devised an exportable consort for Isis in Sarapis—a conflation of Osiris with Apis the Egyptian god incarnate in a calf. The spiritual vacuum left by the effacement of Zeus (he had suffered the same fate as *T'ien*) left room for Sarapis to gain an entry into the Hellenic pantheon; but, in his gracious Hellenized form, Sarapis was a superfluous replica of Asclepius, the Hellenic god of healing, and Sarapis had no chance of replacing Zeus as the Hellenic World's Father figure. This role was seized by Yahweh, the masterful national god of the Jews.

Isis was not only the faithful wife; she was also the tender Mother; and she nursed her son Horus to become the resuscitated Osiris' champion and saviour. In the competition for the role of the Son in the Levant beyond the limits of Egypt, Horus had no chance against Mary's son Jesus.

The oldest surviving accounts of Jesus are works written by devotees who had already come to believe that, like the Pharaohs, Jesus had had no human father but had been begotten on his Mother by a god—in Jesus's case, not Re but Yahweh. (Yahweh's agent was his Spirit; for Yahweh's attributes, like Ahura Mazda's, had become divinities in their own right, to relieve the spiritual austerity of monotheism.) On the evidence of the Christian scriptures, Jesus himself repudiated the suggestion that he was divine in any sense. In at least two utterances of his that are there recorded, Jesus implies that he and God are not identical with each other. Yet he may have been God in the Hindu sense of being a man who had annihilated his ego and has thus stripped away the veil that, in most men, hides the underlying ultimate spiritual reality. According to the non-dualist school of Hindu thought, this ultimate reality underlies all phenomena, and it shines through where and when the obstructive veil of individual self-centredness has been removed. This direct vision, through Jesus, of ultimate spiritual reality may have been the experience that moved Jesus's non-Jewish devotees to deify him; but, if Jesus himself had lived to be hailed as God, he would no doubt have disclaimed a status that, as a Jew, he could not accept. Like other Jewish rabbis of his time, he may have called himself Yahweh's son, but in Jewish parlance this sonship of Yahweh was a figurative expression for indicating a relation of mutual intimacy and trust. Jesus was an orthodox Jew, and his geographical and ethnic horizon was limited to Palestinian Jewry. When he sent his disciples out on a missionary expedition, he instructed them to address themselves to Jews only.

Jesus's fellow Jews did not accuse him of being unorthodox. Jesus and the Pharisees fell out with each other because Jesus interpreted the Jewish Law on his own authority, without waiting to obtain a previous rabbinical consensus. Most of Jesus's unconventionally individual interpretations were identical with those of his fellow rabbis who followed the conventional procedure. The Sadducees concurred when the local Roman authorities sentenced Jesus to death for having allowed the Jewish population of Jerusalem to hail him as the Messiah (i.e. as a human royal liberator of the Jewish people). The Sadducees reasonably held that the execution of a single incautious Jew was a legitimate insurance against the risk of a Jewish *émeute* that would be suppressed at the cost of many Jewish lives. We may guess that Jesus himself did not dissent; for Jesus had much in common with the Pharisees, and the Pharisees, in contrast to the Hasmonaeans and to their heirs the Zealots, refused to take up arms against governments, native or foreign, that allowed their Jewish subjects to practise the Jewish religion in accordance with the requirements of Jewish orthodoxy.

Mary's son Jesus, and Jesus's father Yahweh, overshadow Mary herself according to the Christian Church's official theology. At first sight, it might look as if Isis had lost by being transfigured into Mary; for Isis had left both her husband and her son behind in Egypt when she had set out on her progress through the Hellenic World. Yet, in the non-Protestant major part of Christendom, Mary the 'Mother of God' (the Theotókos) is a goddess in all but name. In this Christian avatar, Isis has retained her pre-Christian potency.

Yahweh, like Zeus, had started as a Weather-god, and, since Zeus was out of the running, Yahweh's only competitor for this role was Jupiter Dolichenus, a Romanization of the Weather-god of the strategically-sited town Dolichê (Dulukh) in northern Syria. At Dolichê the south-north route between Egypt and Asia Minor crosses the east-west route between the westward elbow of the River Euphrates and the eastern shore of the Mediterranean. Consequently Dolichê was an unavoidable *étape* for Roman troops on the move to, from, or along the Roman Empire's eastern frontier, and, as a further consequence, Jupiter Dolichenus became popular in the Roman army. His local Hittite worshippers had stood him on the back of a steer, brandishing the Weather's thunderbolt and double axe. His Roman military devotees put him into Roman uniform, and in this guise he travelled, with the troops, up the Danube and down the Rhine and over the sea to the Hadrianic rampart in Britain.

Dolichenus had one advantage over his competitor Yahweh. Dolichenus had a female consort who faced him as an equal, standing on the back of a hind. Soldiers' wives played a part, alongside of their husbands, in Dolichenus' cult. Yet Dolichenus' captivation of the Roman Army was short-lived. It began only in the second century A.D. and it ended in the third. Jupiter Dolichenus had more vitality than Sarapis, but Dolichenus, too, was no match for Yahweh.

In the competition for the role of the Seed that dies and comes to life again, Egyptian Osiris was disqualified by his mummification, and Anatolian Attis by his self-castration; Sumero-Akkadian Tammuz had sunk below the horizon together with all but the stellar components of the Sumero-Akkadian pantheon; Syrian Adonis was in the running, neck and neck with Dionysos and with Eleusinian Korê and Iakkhos; but, in this race too, Jesus was the winner. Some of his followers believed that they had seen him alive again on the third day after the day on which he had been crucified and also in a number of further apparitions. By the time St. Paul wrote his First Epistle to the Corinthians, the distinctive rite of the Christian community had already come to be the eating of Jesus's body and the drinking of his blood in vegetarian surrogates, bread and wine. The verbal formulae of the ritual had already become fixed. Jesus, not Dionysos or Adonis, had won the Dying and Reviving God's role in addition to all his other victories.

Jesus had more formidable competitors for the role of the Saviour, and his hardest struggle of all was to capture the role of being the God Incarnate.

The rival Saviours were Horus, the conqueror of his fratricide uncle Seth, and Mithras: an Iranian god whom Zarathustra had degraded to the ranks of the devils, but who, as a migrant from Iran to Asia Minor, had reasserted his divinity in alliance with the Sun and with the fateful Stars. Mithras' fortune, like that of Dolichenus, was made by the Roman Army. The troops carried Mithras from Euphrates to Tyne and Solway; but his fortune was short-lived. It started in the first century A.D., and by the fourth century Mithras was fighting a losing battle with Jesus.

Mithras vied with Jesus in the exactingness of the ethical demands that he made on his devotees, but Mithras was at a disadvantage in at least two decisive points. Instead of being a self-sacrificing innocent victim, Mithras was an invidious slayer (unless, perchance, the bull that Mithras slays is a double of Mithras himself). In the second place, Mithras was a misogynist. He was not only motherless and celibate himself; his cult, unlike that of Dolichenus and unlike Christianity, was open to males only. Jesus, like Mithras, was celibate, but Jesus had an Isis-like mother, and there were holy women in the innermost circle of his followers. Consequently there was a field for women in the life of the Christian Church.

Jesus, not Mithras, became the Saviour for the Mediterranean peoples. They wanted the Saviour to be a fellow human being, and they also wanted this human saviour to be a representative of the unprivileged majority of mankind who had participated to an extreme degree in the suffering that is the common lot. The human winner of this role was an apparently powerless carpenter, not an apparently puissant monarch. When King Ptolemy I accepted the title 'Saviour' that had been conferred on him by the Rhodians, he would assuredly have been astonished if it had been foretold to him that this title would be inherited by an artisan who would be a descendant of some of Ptolemy's Asian subjects —and this at a date when the Ptolemaic dynasty would be extinct.

The competition for the role of God Incarnate was the fiercest of all. The prototype of the God Incarnate was Pharaoh. A Roman Emperor was Pharaoh, besides being the Roman Senate's and people's *princeps*. Thus each successive Roman Emperor was the Egyptian God Incarnate's legitimate heir (until Aurelian repudiated this Egyptian legacy), and the worship of the imperial human god was the cement that held the Roman Empire together, as, for more than three millennia, it had held together the Egyptian Dual Monarchy. In so far as the Roman Imperial Government tolerated a refusal, on the part of any of its subjects, to worship the Emperor as a god, the Government would be jeopardizing the precious political unity—and, with it, the inestimably precious peace—that Rome had conferred on the Hellenic World.

The Roman Government did tolerate its Jewish subjects' refusal to pay to the Emperor the requisite divine honours; but the incidence of this exceptional indulgence to the Jews was limited by the fact that the Jews were an ethnic community. It would have been far more perilous for the Empire to extend this indulgence to the Christians; for the Christian Church had no ethnic limits; its avowed aim was to convert the whole of mankind. Conversely, it was impossible for the Christians to perform the ritual act of emperor-worship without implicitly conceding that the Christians' own triune godhead was not, after all, the sole True God, and this would have been tantamount to a renunciation of the essence of Christianity. A head-on collision between the Roman Government and the Christian Church was unavoidable. Christianity's victory in this battle is amazing.

The one rival religion that Christianity was unwilling to absorb and was also unable to destroy was Babylonian astrology.

The years 334 B.C.–A.D. 220 saw the rise, in the Old-World Oikoumenê, of three major devotional religions: theistic Hinduism, Mahayanian Buddhism, and Christianity. The Mahayana and Christianity were missionary religions whose devotees aspired to convert all mankind. On the other hand, theistic Hinduism, like Zoroastrianism and Judaism, was the religion of one particular society, and was bound up with the rest of this society's native institutions and structure, though, in the case of Hinduism, the social matrix of the religion was so vast that it was the equivalent of a whole world in itself.

Christianity started as one among a number of sects within Judaism. The Judaeo-Christians, who were the original Christians, believed, no doubt, that Jesus had come to life again after having been put to death. Whatever may have been the experiences that gave rise to this belief among Jesus's followers, the belief itself was unquestionably sincere, and being sincere, it was exhilarating. This accounts for Christianity's recovery from the disillusionment that had been the Christians' first reaction to Jesus's crucifixion. The Judaeo-Christians can hardly have believed that the man—their fellow Jew—who had risen from the dead was the son of God in any but a figurative sense; for, if they had believed this, they could not have stayed within the Jewish fold, and they did stay within it till they died out.

An astonishing feat—performed by a Judaeo-Christian, Paul—is the extrication from Judaism of a non-Jewish Christianity to which non-Jews were free to adhere without having to commit themselves to the observance of the Jewish law. It is equally astonishing that this ex-Jewish Christianity succeeded eventually in converting all the inhabitants of the Roman Empire except the Jews themselves and the Jews' strict fellow-Yahwists the Samaritans.

Pauline Christianity had got the better of rival regional religions of non-Jewish origin by absorbing them, at the price of diluting the mono-theism that Christianity had inherited from Judaism. In Pauline Christianity, as in Magian Zoroastrianism, the attributes of a Sole True God—in this case, Yahweh's Word and Yahweh's Spirit—were raised to the status of co-equal facets of the godhead. Jesus became God Incarnate in the same sense as Pharaoh and Caesar and Rama and Krishna. As the 'Mother of God', Jesus's human mother became in effect a goddess.

The Christian Church also derived strength from the efficiency of its organization. The rival Levantine religions, like the Buddhist monastic order, had no central organization. The local congregations that adhered to these other religions were administratively independent of each other; all that they had in common was an identical doctrine and ritual. Christianity, too, had its local congregations. These coincided geographically with the Roman Empire's city-state cells. But Christi-anity copied the Roman Empire to the further extent of subordinating its local cells to an ecclesiastical hierarchy on an imperial scale; and this organizational achievement was unique. The extinct secular empires of Alexander's successors Ptolemy, Seleucus, and Lysimachus were re-suscitated in the form of Christian ecclesiastical patriarchates, and the Patriarch of Rome ('the Pope') was recognized by his eastern colleagues as being *primus inter pares*, though they did not accept the Pope's claim to have been invested with a supremacy and an autocratic authority over the whole of the Catholic Christian Church outside the Roman-Patriarchate's geographical limits.

The metamorphosis of a Jewish sect into the ecumenical Christian Church is indeed astonishing; but so, too, is the metamorphosis of the Indian Theravadin Buddhist philosophy into the ecumenical Mahayanian Buddhist religion. The strength of the Mahayana as a missionary religion lay in its devotees' willingness to come to terms with the pre existing religions of the areas that the Mahayanian missionaries evangelized. The Mahayana was not inhibited by anything in its Theravadin Buddhist past from being frankly tolerant and from overtly aiming, not at conquest, but at symbiosis. On the other hand, Christianity's Jewish past was a handicap for Christian theologians and missionaries. Christianity could not bring itself to live and let live; it had either to destroy its rivals or to absorb them; and it would absorb them only in so far as it could do this covertly. Yet Christianity absorbed far more than it destroyed. In fact, its method of propagating itself was more Mahayana-like than its official representatives could afford to admit.

The rise and spread of the Mahayana and of Christianity gave a new turn to mankind's history. The Old-World Oikoumenê was the theatre of these dramatic events, but the eventual effect of them has been global.

[39]

THE MESO-AMERICAN
AND ANDEAN CIVILIZATIONS,

c. 400 B.C.–A.D. 300

THE rise of culture in Meso-America and in the Andean World to the level of civilization has been recorded in Chapter 21. The creators of civilization in Meso-America were the Olmecs; in the Andean World they were the inventors and disseminators of the Chavín style of art. At one site, at least, in Meso-America, namely San Lorenzo on the Isthmus of Tehuantepec, radiocarbon tests have dated the first appearance of a recognizably Olmec style of civilization as early as c. 1250 B.C.; but at La Venta and Tres Zapotes, nearer to the Atlantic coast, the Olmec civilization was flourishing c. 800–400 B.C., and was coeval there with the Chavín 'horizon' in the Andean World. In the course of the immediately following age, c. 400 B.C.–A.D. 300, civilization climbed to its zenith in both regions simultaneously if we adopt one of two alternative computations of Andean chronology. There is, however, another computation which dates the Andean civilization's arrival at its zenith about six hundred years earlier, that is to say c. 300 B.C.

The chronology of the Meso-American civilization is well established. There was a Meso-American system of continuous dating which was probably invented by the Olmecs and was certainly perfected by the Maya in the 'Classic' age of Meso-American history (c. A.D. 300–900). This system, known by modern archaeologists as the 'Long Count', has been correlated with an absolute chronology, in terms of years B.C. and A.D., by the ascertainment, through radiocarbon tests, of the age of numerous samples of wood from the lintels of Maya temple doorways that are associated with datings in terms of the 'Long Count' inscribed on Maya monuments.

The Andean peoples are not known to have had any dating-system of their own. The only evidence for Andean chronology, other than the evidence of radiocarbon tests, is the stratification of the deposits of arte-facts (e.g. buildings and potsherds) on the sites of the Andean civilization. Archaeologists have interpreted these strata in chronological terms by taking account of the thickness of the deposits, the number of the successive styles preserved in the stratified débris, and the degree of the differences between the styles in a sequence. But, where it has been possible to test this conjectural chronology by taking radiocarbon tests of sample contents of the strata, the dates given by these radiocarbon tests have turned out, for the period *c.* 400 B.C. to A.D. 1438, to differ widely from the archaeologists' estimates. For instance, the so-called 'Classic' or 'Florescent' period of Andean history, at which the Andean civilization was at its zenith, is dated *c.* 300 B.C. to A.D. 500 by the radio-carbon tests, whereas the reckonings based on stratification date this period *c.* A.D. 400–1000.

This discrepancy is baffling, and, in the present state of our knowledge, it is not possible to judge, with assurance, which of the two conflicting chronologies is the right one. The conjectural conversion of strata into dates is subjective, and the result may be erroneous. On the other hand, the samples on which the radiocarbon datings for Andean chronology are based are not yet numerous, and isolated radiocarbon datings may be no less misleading than conjectural datings based on stratification. A radiocarbon dating cannot be used with confidence unless we know the tested object's history. For instance, a beam found in a building may have been taken from an older building, and, if it has been, it will not yield the right date for the building in which it has been found. For the use of radiocarbon datings there is safety only in numbers, and, to date, the number of tests at our disposal for the clarification of Andean chronology is hazardously small. Accordingly, for the eighteen centuries and a half of Andean history ending *c.* A.D. 1438, the best that we can do at present is to accept the existing radiocarbon datings provisionally, with the mental reservation that, when the number of the tests has been increased, the result may possibly come nearer to the calculations based on stratigraphy than to the precarious indications of the few radiocarbon tests that have been made so far.

The Andean and the Meso-American civilizations arose independently of the other; and, though they influenced each other reciprocally (the Andean World was indebted to Meso-America for maize, and Meso-America to the Andean World for metallurgy), there is no cogent reason why the successive phases of the two civilizations should correspond, or, if they do correspond, why the corresponding phases should be coeval. However, the Olmec phase of Meso-American history and the Chavín phase of Andean history are in fact approximate counterparts of each other and are also approximately contemporary with each other. Again, in the last phase of the pre-Columbian history of the Americas, the expansion of the Aztec state in Meso-America started at nearly the same date as the expansion of the Inca state in the Andean World. The starting dates are A.D. 1428 and 1438 respectively. The Andean chronology that is based, not on radiocarbon tests, but on stratification, makes the 'Florescent' phase of Andean history likewise coeval with the corresponding 'Classic' phase of Meso-American history. Of course there is no cogent reason why all the corresponding phases of the two civilizations should be coeval with each other, and in the present chapter it is assumed that the right dating of the 'Florescent' phase of the Andean culture is *c*. 300 B.C. to A.D. 500, not *c*. A.D. 400–1000.

In Meso-America the Olmec civilization made its first appearance on the Isthmus of Tehuantepec and along an adjacent strip of the Atlantic coast, but it spread from there north-westwards to the Mexican plateau and south-eastwards along the Pacific coast. There is some archaeological evidence that the Olmecs expanded by force of arms, and the vehemence of the successive destructions of the Olmec sites at San Lorenzo and at La Venta suggests that the Olmecs employed the forced labour of resentful conquered peoples for transporting the massive materials of their gigantic works of art. Yet, if the Olmecs were hated, they were also imitated. Tres Zapotes, the north-westernmost Olmec site along the Atlantic coast, survived till about the beginning of the Christian Era, and is the location of the earliest dating, so far known, in the 'Long Count'. The date is the equivalent of the year 31 B.C. To the east of the Isthmus of Tehuantepec, at Chiapa de Corzo, there is a dating equivalent to 36 B.C.; at El Baúl, in highland (i.e. southern) Guatemala, there is one that is equivalent to A.D. 36. Thus the Olmecs' most important invention was diffused in Meso-America beyond the probable limits of the territory that the Olmecs conquered.

Between *c*. 100 B.C. and A.D. 150, monumental architecture began in the two lowland areas of the Maya region. The central Maya area, Petén, is now covered with dense tropical rain-forest; the northern area, Yucatán, is comparatively dry and bare. The date of the earliest dated stela at Tikál, the principal ceremonial centre in the central Maya area, is A.D. 292. Thus the Meso-American civilization reached the central and northern Maya areas later than it reached the southern area (the highlands of Guatemala), but, once established in the central Maya area, it developed several distinctive features. One is the corbel vault surmounted by a roof-comb; another is the combination of an altar with a stela. To date, the only Meso-American glyphs that have been deciphered are the dating glyphs (both those that give dates in the continuous 'Long Count', and those that give them only in a recurrent fifty-two-year cycle). It is guessed that the still undeciphered glyphs are a script, and that, if they are, the script is a Sumerian-like combination of ideograms with phonemes. The Meso-American hieroglyphs and the

'Long Count' were not Maya inventions, but, when the Maya adopted them in the Petén area, they elaborated and refined them.

This notable development of the Meso-American civilization in the Maya lowlands was matched by a contemporary development on the Mexican plateau. Teotihuacán, in a side-valley opening on to the lakes-basin, was not merely a ceremonial centre, though its pyramids of the Sun and the Moon are the two largest Meso-American monuments except for the man-made mountain at Cholula; Teotihuacán, like San Lorenzo about 1,500 years earlier, was a true city. Teotihuacán was laid out on a rectangular grid plan; it was densely populated; and it subsisted partly by the intensive cultivation of an adjacent rural area and partly by manufacturing wares for sale to the peoples of the tropical lowlands along the Atlantic coast.

The 'Classic' phase of the Meso-American civilization began, both at Teotihuacán and in the Maya lowlands, *c.* A.D. 300. The corresponding 'Florescent' phase of the Andean civilization also falls within the scope of the present chapter, since we are accepting provisionally the dating of it—*c.* 300 B.C. to A.D. 500—which is indicated by the small number of radiocarbon tests that have been made so far.

The expansion of the Chavín style did not extend to the limits of the Andean World. It did not reach either the south-eastern section of the coast or the south-eastern highlands, and, even in the areas it did reach, its prevalence was followed by a high degree of local re-diversification. This was culturally fruitful. It was in this post-Chavín phase that the Andean civilization reached its apogee. Its outstanding technical and artistic achievements were its pottery and its textiles. The two foremost areas in this phase were both in the coastal lowlands. They were the Moche valley in the north-west and the Parácas peninsula and the Nazca valley in the south-east. Mochica pottery can bear comparison with the Attic pottery of the 'classical' phase of Hellenic history; the woollen textiles of the Parácas peninsula and the Nazca valley are finer than any modern counterparts; the cotton textiles of this region have barely been surpassed in modern Bangladesh and Lancashire. Metallurgy was already being practised in the Andean World in the Chavín phase, and it continued in the subsequent 'Experimental' and 'Florescent' phases, but the material was still limited to gold, and the products were ornaments, not tools or weapons. The gold was worked by beating, not by casting, and neither silver nor copper was worked as yet. However, in metallurgy, the Andean civilization was in advance of the Meso-American. In Meso-America, metallurgy was never invented independently. It was not practised there before the post-Classic age, and even then it was a product of stimulus-diffusion from Ecuador and Peru.

[40]

THE WESTERN END OF THE OLD-WORLD OIKOUMENÊ,

A.D. 220–395

In Chapter 37, some account has been given of the four empires that, from A.D. 48 to 220, spanned, between them, the whole breadth of the Old-World Oikoumenê. Chapter 38 concerned the competition, *c.* 334 B.C.–A.D. 220, between regional religions for the conquest of hearts and minds in the vast area that was opened up for religious missionary enterprise by the area's eventual political consolidation in no more than four gigantic states. The outcome was the rise of three new religions: theistic Hinduism, Mahayanian (as opposed to Theravadin) Buddhism, and Pauline (as opposed to Jewish) Christianity. These three religions resembled each other in being devotional. The theistic Hindus were devotees of the gods Shiva and Vishnu; the Mahayana Buddhists were devotees of bodhisattvas who officially were, not gods, but potential Buddhas; the Christians were devotees of the god Yahweh, of Jesus (for non-Jewish Christians, also divine), and of Jesus's mother, who had become virtually a goddess by the time she was styled 'Mother of God' (Theotókos). The objects of devotion differed; the spirit was identical.

The rise of these devotional religions, and the deification of the bodhisattvas and of Jesus and Mary, were symptoms of a need for superhuman help; and this need was felt because people had become aware that they were not masters of the situation in which they found themselves. There had been times and places in which the people and their rulers had felt confident enough to put their trust in living gods incarnate —in, for instance, the Pharaohs of the first four dynasties, in Alexander and the first few generations of his successors, in Julius Caesar and Augustus and Augustus' successors down to A.D. 274. In that year, a living god incarnate, the Emperor Aurelian, made a change in his own status which signified his and his subjects' recognition that a god of this kind was no longer equal to the occasion. In this fortieth year of the Roman Empire's crisis, Aurelian substituted for himself the 'Unconquered Sun' (Sol Invictus) as the tutelary God of the Empire, and he reigned thenceforward, not as a god, but as a supreme god's terrestrial vice-gerent.

In the next phase, *c.* A.D. 220–395, of the Old-World Oikoumenê's history the four empires had different fortunes. It has been noted in Chapter 37 that the Arsacid Parthian Empire in Iran and Iraq was conquered and was taken over in A.D. 224 by the Sasanid Persian dynasty, and that the Kushan Empire was conquered by, and was incorporated in, the Sasanian Empire (though a remnant of the Kushan Empire re-emerged from the Sasanian Empire and outlived it). The Chinese Empire and the Roman Empire each broke up and fell into anarchy temporarily—the Chinese Empire for 370 years (A.D. 220–589), the Roman Empire for fifty years (A.D. 235–84). Thus, in the middle decades of the third century A.D., the Iranian Empire was faring the best. It had survived a change of dynasty; it had then expanded eastwards; and the second Sasanid Emperor, Shahpuhr I won three victories over the Romans, in the third of which (A.D. 260) he captured a whole Roman army, including the Emperor Valerian; but Shahpuhr was then defeated in a counter-attack delivered, on the Roman Empire's behalf, by Odenath, the prince of the semi-autonomous commercial oasis-state Palmyra, in the desert between Syria and Mesopotamia.

Palmyra's economic heyday had been the years A.D. 117–224, after Trajan's failure to incorporate Babylonia (Iraq) in the Roman Empire and before the take-over of Iraq and Iran from the Arsacids by the Sasanids in A.D. 224. After Odenath's victory over Shahpuhr I, he, and then his widow Zenobia, tried to make Palmyra into a successor-state of the Roman Empire in the Levant. Zenobia was neither the first nor the last ambitious queen of an Arabian oasis; but Palmyra was conquered and destroyed by Aurelian in A.D. 274. Another intermediate kingdom, Armenia, was more successful. Armenia saved herself, first with Palmyrene and then with Roman help, from being incorporated in the Sasanian Persian Empire, and from A.D. 298 to 387 she maintained her independence under the rule of the branch line of the Arsacid dynasty which had occupied the Armenian throne, under Roman suzerainty, since A.D. 66.

The re-unification and rehabilitation of the Roman Empire was the work of a series of soldier-emperors from the martial but culturally backward Illyrian provinces between the north-east shore of the Adriatic and the south bank of the Danube. Aurelian (ruled A.D. 270–5) was one of these. The two greatest of them were Diocletian, who reigned for twenty-one years (A.D. 284–305), and Constantine I, who reigned for thirty-one years (A.D. 306–37). From A.D. 235 to 284, all reigns but one had been short, and most emperors had met with tragic deaths.

Diocletian and Constantine died in their beds. Between them, they re-established the Roman Empire by transforming it. Constantine completed what Diocletian had begun, and he also retrieved Diocletian's failure to impose religious unity on the Empire by reversing the policy of Diocletian and of Diocletian's junior colleague Galerius towards the Christian Church.

Between A.D. 284 and 337, Diocletian and Constantine created a mobile field-army for the defence of the Empire in depth (and also for Constantine's use in civil wars against rivals). They re-stabilized the currency (the gold coin in which the troops were paid; not the poor man's copper small change). They re-surveyed the land and re-assessed the tax on agricultural production. They conscripted a number of professions for the compulsory performance of public services. They filled with a hierarchically organized bureaucracy the administrative vacuum left by the breakdown of municipal self-government in the city-states, the cells of the Roman imperial body politic. They also shifted the site of the Empire's capital.

Rome, the city-state that had built up the Empire, is well-placed for serving as a capital for Peninsular Italy or for a circum-Mediterranean empire based on sea-power. It is not well-placed for defending frontiers drawn along the lines of the Euphrates, the Danube, and the Rhine; and it lies far from the Levant, which was the Empire's economic centre of gravity. Diocletian sited the new capital at Nicomedia (Ismit) near the north-west corner of Asia Minor. Constantine moved it a short distance westward to Byzantium, a site at the tip of an easily fortified peninsula, with a splendid natural harbour, at the southern end of the European shore of the Bosphorus. At Byzantium (Constantinople, now Istanbul), the waterway between the Mediterranean and the head of the Sea of Azov is crossed by the overland route between Singidunum (Belgrade), at the confluence of the Sava with the Danube, and Jupiter Dolichenus' home-town Dulukh, to the west of the westward elbow of the Euphrates.

The nadir of the Roman Empire in the middle decades of the third century A.D. was the reign of Valerian's son Gallienus (A.D. 260–8). The contemporary zenith of the Sasanian Persian Empire was the reign of Shahpuhr I (A.D. 242–73). The two greatest men at the western end of the Old-World Oikoumenê in this turbulent age were Gallienus' protégé the Egyptian Neoplatonist philosopher Plotinus (A.D. 205–70) and Shahpuhr I's protégé the Iraqi-born Iranian founder of a new missionary religion, Mani (*c.* A.D. 216–77 or 276).

Each of these seers once adventurously accompanied an army as a civilian in quest of foreign wisdom. If they both found this opportunity in the same Romano–Persian war, this will have been the war of A.D. 243–4, and they will have confronted each other, unknown to each other, on opposite sides of no-man's-land. Both men wrestled with the perennial problem that had once exercised Zarathustra and Plato: what is the relation between this imperfect world in which mankind finds itself living and the ultimate reality in and behind and beyond the phenomena? Is the ultimate reality good, and, if it is, what is the origin of the evil which is a tragic fact of human experience and also of human performance?

Christianity was part of both men's backgrounds. Plotinus was a Hellenist, but his teacher, Ammonius, was an ex-Christian. Mani's father had become a convert, in Iraq, to a sect called 'Baptists', but the family had migrated to Iraq from Hamadan in Media, where the Magian version of Zoroastrianism was the chief regional religion, and Mani himself claimed to be the successor of Zarathustra, of the Buddha, and of Jesus. Plotinus was a Platonist who rejected Gnosticism, but Plotinus' disciple, Iamblichus, the founder of a Neoplatonic anti-church, plunged as deep into Gnosticism as Mani, who combined Gnosticism with a dualism which, in contrast to Zoroastrian dualism, was absolute. According to Zoroastrian doctrine, the current war between light and darkness (between good and evil) is temporary, and is going to end in the permanent victory of the good god Ahura Mazda over his evil adversary Angra Mainyush. According to Mani, light is going eventually to be almost completely re-extricated from darkness, with which it has been partially entangled, but the two opposing principles, light and darkness, are both eternal, and they are also light and darkness in the literal physical sense, whereas for Plotinus, as for Zarathustra, light and darkness were mental images, standing respectively for good and evil; and, for Plotinus, evil, in contrast to good, was not a positive spiritual power; it was something that was merely negative: an absence of the good, not an 'anti-good'.

At the western end of the Old-World Oikoumenê *c.* A.D. 220–395, the two most momentous events occurred on the religious, not on the political, plane. One event was the defeat of Mani by Kartir, a militant Zoroastrian ecclesiastic who succeeded in establishing the Magian version of Zoroastrianism as the official religion of the Sasanian Persian Empire. The other momentous event was the victory of Christianity over all pre-Christian religions except astrology, first in Armenia *c.* A.D. 285–90, and then in the Roman Empire between A.D. 312 and 395.

The Sasanids' family history is not unlike the Hasmonaeans'. Before they had been princes, they had been priests. The Sasanids had been the hereditary priests of a temple of the goddess Anahita at Stakr, a city in Fars which had taken the place of the First Persian Empire's ceremonial centre Persepolis. The pre-Zoroastrian Iranian water-goddess Anahita had been associated, incongruously, with Ahura Mazda in the Magian version of Zoroastrianism, and thus the Sasanids were committed to Zoroastrianism more definitely than any previous Iranian rulers except Zarathustra's own patron Hystaspes (not the Hystaspes who was Darius I's father, but a king of the same name, about two generations earlier, whose realm probably lay in the Oxus–Jaxartes basin).

The Achaemenid rulers of the First Persian Empire had proclaimed their allegiance to Ahura Mazda, who, for Zarathustra, was the one true god, but they had refrained from declaring themselves to be adherents of the religion that Zarathustra had founded. The Arsacids had been professing Magian Zoroastrians, but, like the Achaemenids and the Achaemenids' Macedonian Greek successors, the Arsacids had been tolerant of all the diverse religions that had adherents among their subjects. Shahpuhr I endowed Zoroastrian fire-altars for the benefit of the souls of eminent persons in his entourage, but he did not seek to impose his family's ancestral religion on non-Zoroastrians. So far from that, Shahpuhr gave Mani permission to propagate his new religion in Shahpuhr's dominions.

Mani had been in India—perhaps in A.D. 241, the year in which Shahpuhr, then still crown prince, had conquered the Indus basin from the Kushans. It has been mentioned already that Mani accompanied a Persian army that later invaded the Roman Empire. These expeditions gave Mani some first-hand acquaintance with Buddhism and with Christianity respectively. He declared that he was the successor of Zarathustra, the Buddha, and Jesus, 'the Seal of the Prophets', the recipient of a complete and definitive revelation, and 'the messenger of the God of Truth in Babylonia', and that he himself was an incarnation of the Holy Spirit; and he aspired to convert, not only the inhabitants of the Sasanian Persian Empire, but the whole human race. Mani won the personal devotion of his adherents, he had a genius for organization, and his doctrine proved to be attractive. Babylonia (Iraq) was in truth the heart of the Old-World Oikoumenê; the local language, Syriac, the contemporary form of Aramaic, was current all round the Fertile Crescent; Babylonia was thus a central base of operations; and from Babylonia Mani sent out missionaries not only to the north-eastern and north-western borders of the Sasanian Empire, but to Egypt. Manichaeism spread far more rapidly than Christianity had done in the course of the preceding two centuries.

However, Mani's design for founding a world-religion centred on Iraq was incompatible with Kartir's intention, which was to make Zoroastrianism the established religion of the Sasanian Empire, or at least of the Iranian part of it, and to stamp out the practice there of any other religion. Kartir, the Zoroastrian ecclesiastic, had risen to the summit of the hierarchy in the reign (A.D. 277–93) of Shahpuhr I's third successor

Vahram II. Kartir was now made priest of the Sasanids' ancestral temple of Anahita at Stakr and also of the fire-altar there. Kartir already had the ear of Shahpuhr I's second successor, Vahram I (ruled A.D. 274–7). At Kartir's instigation, Vahram I arrested and imprisoned Mani, and Mani died a martyr. The progress of Manichaeism in Egypt also drew a savage repressive decree from the Roman Emperor Diocletian in 297, six years before Diocletian's declaration of war against Christianity. Diocletian denounced Mani's converts as a Persian 'fifth column', ignoring the fact that the Persian Government had put Mani to death and that by A.D. 297 it had been persecuting its own Manichaean subjects for twenty years. Persecution had the same effect on Manichaeism as on Christianity. So far from discouraging it, it stimulated it.

In the Roman Empire, Decius in A.D. 250, Valerian in A.D. 257–60, and, finally and most ferociously, Diocletian and Galerius in A.D. 303–11, attempted to stamp Christianity out. The attempt was a tacit confession that the only alternative was a capture of the Empire by the Christian Church. In the Great Persecution of A.D. 303–11, Galerius, not Diocletian himself, was the moving spirit. Diocletian was reluctant; yet he, too, under-estimated the strength of the Christian Church. Both these emperors were Illyrian soldiers, and, in Illyricum and among soldiers of Illyrian origin, Christianity had hardly risen above the horizon. The Illyrian soldiers' gods were Aurelian's 'Unconquered Sun', Jupiter Dolichenus, Mithras, and the original Roman pantheon.

The Christian Church's strength was better appreciated by anti-Christians in the Levant, where Christians were most numerous (though, even there, they were still in a minority). Plotinus' disciple Iamblichus tried to organize an anti-Church, based on a Gnostic version of Neoplatonism, in which all the non-Christian gods and goddesses of the Mediterranean World were mobilized, under the leadership of the 'Unconquered Sun', against the Christian pantheon. This Mediterranean counterpart of the Taoist Church in China was patronized by two emperors, Maximinus Daia (ruled A.D. 310–13) and Constantine's ex-Christian nephew Julian (ruled A.D. 361–3), but it was foredoomed to failure. The Christian Church had anticipated the Neoplatonic anti-Church in assimilating the Mediterranean deities. Jesus had already become Orpheus, Sarapis, and the 'Unconquered Sun'; Mary had already become Isis the 'Mother of God'. As for the Neoplatonic philosophy, Iamblichus' abortive polemical misapplication of it would have been more distasteful to Plotinus than its eventual effective incorporation in the theology of the Christian Church.

In A.D. 311 Galerius, on his death-bed, grudgingly revoked his and Diocletian's edicts against Christianity and granted freedom of worship to all inhabitants of the Roman Empire, Christians and non-Christians alike. In A.D. 312 Constantine I became a convert to Christianity. His conversion was sudden and surprising—perhaps even to Constantine himself; for in A.D. 306 Constantine had inherited from his father, the Emperor Constantius I, not only a regional rule over Gaul and Britain but a devotion to the 'Unconquered Sun'. In A.D. 312 Constantine was invading Italy, which, together with North-West Africa, was then in the hands of Constantine's brother-in-law Maxentius. On the eve of a battle on the north-western outskirts of Rome, in which Maxentius was defeated and killed, Constantine dreamed that he saw a monogram composed of the first two letters of the name 'Khristós' in the Greek alphabet, together with four shining words in Latin: 'with this sign you will be victorious' (*hoc signo victor eris*). Christ, so Constantine dreamed, instructed Constantine to affix the monogram to his helmet and to have it painted on his soldiers' shields. Constantine did what he had been told to do in his dream, and he then won the decisive battle in the first of three civil wars, in each of which he was the winner.

Constantine's conversion was overt and sincere, but he did not renounce his devotion to Aurelian's and Constantius I's god the 'Unconquered Sun', though eventually he identified *Sol* with Christ—an identification that had already been made implicitly by the Christian Church. Constantine also did not renounce his role of Pontifex Maximus, a non-Christian high priesthood that he held *ex officio* as the political head of the Roman state. Holding the supreme pontificate was technically incompatible with being a Christian, but Constantine's protégés the Christian ecclesiastical authorities did not raise this issue, and Constantine himself did not become a member of the Christian Church formally till he was baptized on his death-bed in A.D. 337. Moreover, Constantine was most imperfectly acquainted with Christian doctrine— and this not only at the time of his conversion to Christianity in A.D. 312 but throughout the rest of his life. His interventions in Christian ecclesiastical politics made it manifest that in these waters Constantine was out of his depth, though in secular affairs he was a shrewd politician.

Constantine has sometimes been accused of being a sceptic, cynic, and hypocrite, whose motive for professing Christianity was a calculation of political expediency. This interpretation of his conversion is an anachronism. There were no sceptics in the Mediterranean World after the breakdown of society there in A.D. 235. No inhabitant of the Roman Empire believed that he could survive without divine aid in this terrible age. Constantine was sincerely and fervently religious, and in this he was a typical representative of his time and place. Plotinus, Mani, Iamblichus, Diocletian, Galerius, Maximinus Daia, and Julian were all likewise sincerely and fervently religious in their various ways. Constantine's religiosity was no less genuine than that of Plotinus, but it differed in being crude. The God of the Christians won and held Constantine's allegiance by manifesting his power. This God brought disaster on Roman emperors who persecuted the Christian Church. The fates of Galerius, Maximinus Daia, and Licinius were cases in point. This same God gave Constantine military victory in three civil wars. Within the twelve years A.D. 312–24, the God of the Christians carried Constantine forward from the Tiber to the Bosphorus and made him the sole ruler of the entire Roman Empire, though Constantine had started at York in 306 as ruler only of the remote and backward provinces beyond the Alps and the Pyrenees.

Constantine was profoundly grateful to the God of the Christians for having rewarded his allegiance by making his fortune, but this manifestation of the God's mighty power inspired Constantine with fear as well as with gratitude. He feared that he might draw on himself the fate of Galerius and Maximinus Daia and Licinius if he were to fail to carry out his duty to his divine patron—for example, if he were to fail to heal the contemporary schisms in the Christian body ecclesiastic. A corresponding fear of the displeasure of the non-Christian gods had animated the emperors who had persecuted the Christians.

Constantine's motive for becoming a convert to Christianity was ethically much inferior to Ashoka's motive for becoming a convert to Buddhism. Ashoka's motive had been repentance for his crime of having waged an aggressive war, and he had never gone to war again. Constantine's motive was gratitude for his victories in three successive civil wars.

Constantine followed up Galerius' edict of toleration by putting Maximinus Daia under pressure to suspend the persecution of Christianity in the Levant and by inducing Licinius to join with Constantine himself in confirming the toleration of Christianity in their respective dominions. Constantine never persecuted his non-Christian subjects, but he did confer valuable privileges on the Christian Church, and his ex-Christian and anti-Christian nephew Julian showed similar favour to the Neoplatonic anti-Church. The Roman Emperors' grudging toleration, after A.D. 311, of religions other than their own contrasts unfavourably with Ashoka's benevolence towards his non-Buddhist subjects and neighbours and with Kanishka's even-handed treatment of Brahminical Hindus and Buddhists of diverse sects.

In the Roman Empire, even the precarious toleration inaugurated in A.D. 311 was short-lived. The Emperor Gratian (ruled A.D. 367–83) refused to assume the office of Pontifex Maximus and started to liquidate the non-Christian religions of the Roman Empire by closing their temples and expropriating their revenues. The liquidation was virtually completed by Theodosius I (ruled in the East, A.D. 379–95: in the West, A.D. 392–5).

Meanwhile, the Roman and Persian Empires continued to co-exist, side by side. A long Romano–Persian war (A.D. 337–60) ended inconclusively. Julian's invasion of the Persian Empire in A.D. 362 ended in Julian's death and in a Roman disaster in A.D. 363. Julian's successor Jovian extricated the Roman expeditionary force at the price of ceding to the Persians Nisibis, the Roman frontier fortress in north-eastern Mesopotamia, together with five Armenian border provinces that had been annexed to the Roman Empire in A.D. 298. These cessions left the Kingdom of Armenia at the Persians' mercy. In A.D. 378 a Roman army suffered, at Adrianople, at the Visigoths' hands, a defeat that was as crushing as the historic previous Roman defeats at the Allia and Cannae and Carrhae. The Romans now had to devote what remained of their military strength to fighting a losing battle to salvage their dominions in Europe, and they had to purchase peace on their Asian front by making a further concession to the Persian Empire. In A.D. 387 the Kingdom of Armenia was partitioned by agreement between the two empires along a line that gave about four-fifths of the country to the Persians. This was part of the price that the Roman Empire paid for its survival in the Levant.

The fluctuations in the relations between the two empires were reflected in the fortunes of the growing Christian community in the Persian Empire. The Zoroastrian Church made no converts in the Roman Empire, and no voluntary converts in Armenia. Unlike the Christian and Manichaean churches, the Zoroastrian Church did not seek to convert all mankind. Its objective continued to be Kartir's, namely to make Zoroastrianism not merely the 'established' religion of the Persian Empire, but the exclusive religion of at least the Iranian provinces. However, even among the Empire's Iranian subjects, the Magian version of Zoroastrianism proved to be less attractive than either Manichaeism or Christianity; and, so long as the two empires were hostile to each other, the spread of Christianity in the Persian Empire was doubly obnoxious to both the Sasanian Imperial Government and the Zoroastrian ecclesiastical authorities. It was not only an offence against the exclusive-mindedness of the Zoroastrian Church; the progressive adoption of Christianity, in and after 312, as the 'established' religion of the Roman Empire made the Christian subjects of the Persian Empire suspect of being a Roman 'fifth column', as the converts to Manichaeism in Egypt had been suspected, with less reason, by Diocletian of being a Persian 'fifth column' in the Roman Empire. In the original territories of the Sasanian Persian Empire, the Christians were only a diaspora, though a growing one; but at Nisibis and in the five

Armenian border provinces that were ceded by Jovian to Shahpuhr II in 363, the local population was Christian *en bloc*.

For these reasons, the Sasanian Emperor Shahpuhr II (ruled A.D. 309–79) started to persecute his Christian subjects in 339/40 and continued to persecute them till his death. But his second successor, Shahpuhr III (ruled A.D. 383–8) made friends with the Roman Emperor Theodosius I, and this détente in the relations between the two powers made possible, not only the partition, by agreement, of the Kingdom of Armenia in 387, but the grant of toleration to the Christians in the Persian Empire as a result of Romano-Persian negotiations. The persecution of the Christians in the Persian Empire was suspended; the administration of the Persian Christian Church was unified; and, after the holding of a council of the Persian Christian Church at Seleucia-on-Tigris in 410, the Emperor Yazdigerd I (ruled A.D. 399–420) confirmed an edict of toleration which he had previously promulgated.

THE INDIAN CIVILIZATION,

c. A.D. 224–490

THE overthrow of the Kushan Empire in A.D. 241, in the reign (A.D. 224–42) of the first Sasanid Persian Emperor Ardeshir I had been preceded by the break-up of the Satavahana (Andhra) Kingdom in the Deccan. The effect of these two successive political débâcles was to produce a political vacuum in the Indian subcontinent which lasted for more than a century. Since the annexation of the Deccan to the Empire of Magadha in the fourth century B.C., the Deccan had been a political unity for about six hundred years, first in association with northern India and then as a separate political unit when the Empire of Magadha had disintegrated after Ashoka's death in 232 B.C. The most stable area during this widespread political interregnum was the southern tip of the peninsula. Here the local kingdoms that Ashoka had refrained from conquering still survived. So did at least one of the two Saka satrapies in western India that had been established, under the suzerainty of the Kushan emperors, in the first century A.D. The more southerly of these two Saka principalities had occupied Maharashtra, and this one may have succumbed in a struggle with the Satavahanas, on whose domain it had trespassed. The more northerly satrapy, which occupied Malwa, round Ujjain, outlived the Kushan Empire and thus became an independent state *de facto.*

There was greater continuity on the non-political planes of activity. The Gandharan style of visual art survived to give visual expression to the development of Mahayana Buddhism in north-western India; and Mathura, on the upper course of the River Jumna, which had lain just within the Kushan dominions, continued to be the home of a school of art in which the indigenous Indian style was tempered, without being dominated, by Greek influence. On the plane of language and literature, the first three centuries A.D. saw the living dialects (prakrits) that had developed out of primary Sanskrit gradually give way to a neo-Sanskrit as the language used for inscriptions. The same centuries saw the beginning of a South-Indian literature in the Tamil language.

Ashoka's inscriptions, except those in the ex-Achaemenian territory ceded to Chandragupta by Selenaus I, are all in prakrit, and no doubt the administration of the Maurya Empire was also conducted in the living language. The Pali language of the Theravadin Buddhist scriptures is one of the prakrits of the Mauryan age. In that age, primary Sanskrit, which had been the living language of the original Indo-European speaking invaders of the subcontinent, must have ceased to be spoken except in the Brahmins' ritual, and have also ceased to be read except in so far as the Vedas and the Upanishads, which had originally been learnt by heart and transmitted orally, had been reduced to writing. Neo-Sanskrit was as artificial a language as the neo-Attic Greek which was devised at the same date. Neo-Sanskrit was adopted as the language for the scriptures of Saivism, Vaishnavism, and Mahayana Buddhism, and it is the language of the two Indian epic poems, the *Ramayana* and the *Mahabharata,* in their eventual form. They are believed to have taken this form between *c.* 200 B.C. and A.D. 200, though the original theme of the *Mahabharata* shows that this poem, at any rate, must have begun to take shape not later than the early centuries of the last millennium B.C. The vigour of the revival of Sanskrit is illustrated by its influence on the nascent Tamil literature. In the Deccan the living languages were, and still are, Dravidian. Ashoka's inscriptions in the Deccan are nevertheless all in prakrits, i.e. in dialects derived from primary Sanskrit. But the Indo-European language that has made its mark on Tamil literature is not one of the prakrits; it is neo-Sanskrit.

In the third and fourth centuries A.D. the Indian civilization continued to expand its range beyond the limits of the subcontinent. Its expansion overseas south-eastward into South-East Asia had started in the first century A.D. In the fourth century the impetus of its expansion in this direction increased. The whole of continental South-East Asia now became part of the Indian civilization's domain, except for the portion that is now North Vietnam, which had been incorporated in the Chinese Empire since 140 B.C. Trade and religion, not military conquest, were the agencies of Indianization, and the peoples of South-East Asia were not passive recipients of Indian culture. They made of it something which, though not un-Indian, was distinctively South-East Asian. Contemporaneously, Buddhism was spreading from north-western India into China overland via the Oxus–Jaxartes basin and the Tarim basin. Here the Mahayana eclipsed the Sarvastivadin version of Theravadin Buddhism; neo-Sanskrit was the language of the Mahayana scriptures that were translated into Chinese; and the Gandharan Graeco-Indian style of art, which was the Mahayana's visual medium, had a revolutionary effect on the visual art of China and hence of Korea and Japan, too, eventually.

The physiography of the Indian subcontinent has made it natural for Indian empires to be based on the areas of the present-day states of Bihar and Uttar Pradesh in the Jumna–Ganges basin. This had been the nucleus of the Empire of Magadha from the date of its establishment in the fifth century B.C. till its break-up in the second century B.C. From the second century B.C. onwards, however, till the overthrow of the Kushan Empire in the third century A.D., the Indus basin, not the Jumna–Ganges basin, had been northern India's political centre of gravity. In the fourth century A.D. the political configuration of northern India suddenly returned to normal. Now once again, as in the fifth century B.C., southern and northern Bihar coalesced politically—this time, not by conquest, but by a royal marriage—and, again, a united Bihar had the strength to expand from its strategically advantageous location.

The founder of the Gupta dynasty bore the same name as his fourth-century-B.C. Maurya predecessor Chandragupta. The fourth-century-A.D. Chandragupta took the equivalent of the year A.D. 320 as the starting-date for a Gupta dynastic era, but the true creator of the Gupta Empire was the founder's son Samudragupta (ruled *c.* A.D. 330–80). Samudragupta made his presence felt in the Deccan in a spectacular raid, but his enduring achievement was the enlargement of the Gupta dynasty's domain in the Jumna–Ganges basin. The decisive step in the construction of the Gupta Empire was taken by Chandragupta II (ruled A.D. 380–418). *Circa* A.D. 395 he conquered the Saka satrapy whose capital was Ujjain. He then pushed on westwards to the coast, and thus opened for the Gupta Empire a window on the Arabian Sea.

The Gupta Empire did not expand, either southwards or north-westwards, as far as the Maurya Empire had done. Southwards the Gupta Empire's limit was the Vindhya Range or the Narbada River; north-westwards, the limits of its direct rule were the River Chambal and the upper course of the Jumna, and only the south-eastern half of the Punjab was ever under its suzerainty. There is no record of a collision between the Guptas and the Sasanids. A remnant of the Kushan Empire may have re-emerged precariously to serve as a buffer-state.

The Guptas themselves were Brahminical Hindus, but they were as tolerant of all religions as the Mauryas and the Imperial Kushans had been. Under the Gupta regime in the fourth and fifth centuries A.D., the Indian civilization reached its zenith in the fields of sculpture, neo-Sanskrit secular literature (particularly drama), and astronomy. Some light from the Graeco-Roman World's sunset reached the Gupta Empire through its western window, but this was only a gleam; the brilliance of the Indian civilization in the Gupta Age was indigenous.

The Gupta Empire was shattered, and the 'Golden Age' of the Indian civilization was cut short, by the irruption into India of the Hun pastoral nomads from the Eurasian steppe. The first of the Huns' assaults on India was delivered in A.D. 455; it was followed up by others, and, though the Huns were repulsed in A.D. 528, they were not expelled.

[42]

THE ERUPTION OF THE HUNS FROM THE EURASIAN STEPPE IN THE FOURTH AND FIFTH CENTURIES A.D.

THE Turkish-speaking pastoral nomads known as the Hsiung-nu by the Chinese and as the Huns by their other sedentary victims, farther to the west, are the earliest recorded occupants of the eastern end of the Eurasian steppe. They were in occupation there when, in the course of the fourth century B.C., the southern edge of the steppe was reached by the northernmost of the Chinese contending states—Ch'in, Chao, and Yen. In 307 B.C. the ruler of Chao state raised a cavalry force equipped in the nomad style. By the close of the fourth century B.C. the three Chinese border states were building walls along their steppe-frontiers to keep the nomads out.

The pastoral nomad way of life schools its practitioners not only for raiding and plundering but also for organizing and governing. Without planning and discipline, life on the steppe would not be practicable for Man and his domesticated animals. It is therefore not surprising that when, in 221 B.C., Ch'in Shih Hwang-ti unified China politically and consolidated the local frontier-walls into a continuous line of defence, the Hsiung-nu retorted by organizing a counter-empire on their side of the fence. The short but sharp bout of anarchy through which China passed in 209–203 B.C. gave the Hsiung-nu the opportunity for taking the offensive against China; c. 174 B.C. they also expanded westward; and they thus set in motion a migration of their nomad western neighbours that carried the Yüeh-chih into the Oxus–Jaxartes basin and the Sakas into India. In 128 B.C. the Chinese Emperor Han Wu-ti launched a counter-offensive against the Hsiung-nu. The Chinese objective was to exterminate the Hsiung-nu or at least to subjugate them permanently, but the Sino-Hun Hundred Years War (128–36 B.C.) was inconclusive. In 52 B.C. the nearest section of the Hsiung-nu recognized the Chinese Empire's suzerainty; but this Chinese success was superficial and temporary, and meanwhile the rest of the Hsiung-nu escaped Chinese control altogether by trekking still farther westwards, beyond the reach of Chinese armies based on the Great Wall.

So far, the Hsiung-nu had not made any impact on other sedentary societies besides the Chinese, but in the fourth and fifth centuries A.D. they not only re-invaded China but invaded the Oxus–Jaxartes basin, India, Iran, and Europe as well. This was the fifth eruption of nomads out of the Eurasian steppe, but the Hun eruption differed from all its predecessors in breaking out in all directions.

In A.D. 304 one horde of Hsiung-nu invaded China; sacked Loyang in A.D. 311 and Ching-chao, the first capital of the defunct Han dynasty, in A.D. 312; and extinguished in A.D. 316 the Western Chin dynasty, which had succeeded in A.D. 280 in reunifying China politically. This Hsiung-nu horde's successful re-invasion of China opened the way for a swarm of other barbarian invaders, some of them Hsiung-nu, others Tibetan or Tungus or Mongol. The whole of northern China was partitioned into barbarian successor-states of the ephemeral Western Chin Empire.

At the opposite end of the steppe *c*. A.D. 375, another horde of Huns hit the Iranian-speaking Alan Sarmatian nomads between the Volga and the Don, overthrew the empire that the Teutonic-speaking Ostrogoths from Scandinavia had established on the Dnepr, and drove the Visigoths to seek asylum in Roman territory to the south of the lower course of the Danube. The eruption of these westernmost Huns was thus the ultimate cause of the conflict between the Visigoths and the Romans in which the Romans suffered their disastrous defeat at Adrianople in A.D. 378. The Huns themselves continued their westward advance, carrying the subjugated Alans and Ostrogoths along with them and driving other Teutonic-speaking barbarian peoples ahead of them.

The Huns pitched their camp on the Hungarian Alföld—an enclave of the Eurasian steppe, in the heart of the continent's European peninsula. Since A.D. 395 the Roman Empire had been partitioned, and the eastern part was proving to have more vitality than the western part. The western Hun war-lord Attila therefore concentrated on attacking the West Roman Empire, which was the less lucrative but the more vulnerable of his two possible Roman targets. In A.D. 451 he invaded Gaul and was defeated at Orleans by the West Roman army together with the Visigoths, who had expected the West Roman Government's permission to settle in south-western Gaul and were concerned to prevent the Huns from appropriating the Visigoths' Roman territorial spoils. In A.D. 452 Attila invaded northern Italy, but withdrew without marching on Rome. In 453 he died; his reluctant German and Sarmatian subjects revolted; and the western horde of the Huns ebbed back eastwards from the Hungarian Alföld on to the western bay of the Eurasian steppe to the north of the Black Sea.

The West Roman Empire then became the prize, not of the Huns, but of the Teutonic-speaking barbarians who had escaped being subjugated by the Huns or who had been subjugated by them but had revolted after Attila's death. In A.D. 406 a host of Suevi, Vandals, Alans, and Burgundians crossed the Rhine into West Roman territory. In 410 the West Roman Government had confessed its inability to provide for the defence of Britain, and had failed to save Rome itself from being taken and sacked in the same year by the Visigoth refugees from the Huns. Thus the western Huns had made fortunes, at the expense of the West Roman Empire, for other barbarians. The Huns' eventual share of the territorial spoils of the Roman Empire was modest. In A.D. 681 a Bulgar horde that was part of the progeny of Attila's Huns won for itself a permanent foothold on East Roman territory between the lower course of the Danube and the southern slopes of the Haemus (Balkan) Range.

The horde of Huns that defeated and killed the Sasanian Persian Emperor Peroz in A.D. 484 made its first appearance in history as the Persians' ally in a campaign in A.D. 359 that ended in the Persians' capture of the Roman fortress Amida (Diarbekr). By 484 this horde, the Ephthalites (Abdalis), had occupied the upper part of the Oxus–Jaxartes basin. Soghd and Bactria had been part of the Kushan Empire, and had presumably been incorporated in the Sasanian Persian Empire when the Kushan Empire had been conquered by the Persians in 241, in the reign of the first Sasanian Emperor, Ardeshir I. We do not know whether these provinces had escaped from the Persians' control before the Ephthalite Huns occupied them, or whether the Ephthalites had conquered them direct from the Persian Empire before the trial of strength that had ended in the Persian disaster in 484.

After this disaster, the Persian Empire had to pay tribute to the Ephthalites, and it may have remained tributary to them till the reign of Khusro (Chosroes) I Anosharvan (531–79). In Khusro I's reign, at a date *c.* 558 or 563–7, the Persian Empire took its revenge on the Ephthalites. Khusro now found allies in the Turks, a nomad horde that had made itself master of the steppe in the Huns' rear. The Persians and Turks, in concert, overthrew the Ephthalite Empire and partitioned its former territory along the line of the River Oxus. The Persian Empire thus acquired the part of Bactria to the south of the Oxus (Tokharistan, now Afghan Uzbekistan). But a remnant of the Ephthalites survived in Zabulistan (Arachosia), to the south of the Hindu Kush Range.

The Ephthalites were the rearguard of the Hun horde that had broken out of the steppe across the section of the steppe's southern border between the Pamir plateau and the Caspian Sea. It has been mentioned that this vanguard invaded India in A.D. 455 and that, though the Huns were repulsed eventually in 528, they had shattered the Gupta Empire and had made havoc of the Indian civilization which had been enjoying a 'Golden Age' under the Gupta Empire's aegis.

The impact of the Huns was an ordeal that put the Huns' victims to the test. The East Roman Empire and the Sasanian Persian Empire responded to the challenge the most successfully. Though the East Roman Empire failed to ward off Attila's raids, and though the Persian Empire was signally defeated by the Ephthalites, neither of these two empires was conquered; they survived at the price of paying tribute. The survival of the Persian Empire is surprising, for the Mazdakite revolution in the sequel to the military disaster of 484 revealed the gravity of the social sickness from which the Persian Empire was suffering in the fifth century A.D. The West Roman Empire was suffering from the same sickness in the same century, and, unlike the Persian Empire, the West Roman Empire collapsed and dissolved.

The disintegration of the West Roman Empire left the East Roman Empire unscathed. Indeed, it relieved the East Roman Empire of a liability; for, in the western basin of the Mediterranean and its African and European hinterlands, the Graeco-Roman civilization had never recovered from the débâcle in the third century A.D.; the socially sound part of the Graeco-Roman World in its last phase was the Levant.

In India and China the effects of the Hun invasions were not so catastrophic as in the West Roman Empire, but they were more serious than in the East Roman and Persian Empires. In India and China the Hun invasions were not just passing storms; the invaders lodged themselves permanently in the two subcontinents. In north-western India the Huns are still represented today by the Rajputs. These were soon converted to Hinduism and were incorporated in the Kshatriya caste, like previous Eurasian nomad invaders of India (e.g. the Sakas and the Pahlavas). In China, too, the barbarian invaders were eventually assimilated, but China had been hit exceptionally hard by the Huns. The part of the Chinese World that was occupied by the Huns and other barbarians in and after the fourth century A.D. was the basin of the Wei River and the lower basin of the Yellow River, and this region had been the birthplace of the Chinese civilization. By contrast, the region that the Graeco-Roman civilization lost when the West Roman Empire collapsed was only an expendable colonial annex. However, the Chinese and Indian subcontinents were saved by their size. In both, there was an asylum in the south for refugees from invaders entering from the north. Southern China was protected by the works of Man as well as by nature. The lower courses of the Hwai and Yangtse rivers had been supplemented by man-made canals, and this network of waterways was a serious obstacle for Eurasian nomad horsemen who were more at home on the North-China plain.

43

THE ROMAN AND PERSIAN
EMPIRES, A.D. 395–628

IN A.D. 395 the Roman Empire, which had been re-united, not for the first time, in A.D. 388 by the Emperor Theodosius I, was partitioned, likewise not for the first time, between Theodosius' two sons Arcadius and Honorius. Since the disastrous defeat and capture of the Roman Emperor Valerian by the Persian Emperor Shahpuhr I in A.D. 260, there had been frequent partitions—some of them voluntary, others imposed—and, after each of them, the Empire had eventually been re-united. In A.D. 395 there was no reason to expect that the voluntary partition in that year would be permanent; yet, this time, the fortunes of the eastern and the western sections were dramatically different.

In and after A.D. 406, the West Roman Empire was progressively overrun and overwhelmed by Teutonic-speaking and Iranian-speaking peoples fleeing westward from the Huns. Rome itself was sacked by the Visigoths in 410 and by the Vandals in 455. The West Roman Imperial Government had become impotent long before the year 476, in which the last Roman Emperor at Ravenna (the Western Empire's fifth-century refuge-capital) was dismissed by his Rugian *magister peditum in praesenti*, Odovacer. This dismissal nominally re-united the Empire under the sovereignty of the reigning emperor at Constantinople, Zeno (ruled 474–91). By contrast with the Western Empire's extinction, the East Roman Empire survived, though its frontier along the lower course of the Danube was under greater pressure from the north than any other section of the Empire's continental European frontier between the Black Sea and the North Sea. Moreover, along the eastern frontier the Roman Empire's next-door neighbour was not any barbarian war-band; it was the Persian Empire, which was a state of the Roman Empire's own kind and calibre.

Evidently the difference between the fortunes of the two parts of the Roman Empire after 395 was not due to any difference in the degree of pressure on their respective frontiers. The fundamental causes were the social and economic disparity between them and the Constantinopolitan Roman Government's relative success in saving its own situation by timely statesmanship.

The Constantinopolitan Government quickly perceived that the West Roman Empire was both unsalvageable and expendable. The East Roman Empire's only energetic intervention on the foundering Western Empire's behalf was a disastrously defeated naval expedition in 468 against the Vandal conquerors of North-West Africa. The Constantinopolitan Government recognized the accomplished fact of the West Roman Government's final extinction in 476; and in 488 it got rid of the Ostrogoth war-lord Theodoric, whose war-band had been pillaging the Eastern Empire's north-western provinces, by acquiescing in Theodoric's invasion of Italy and liquidation of Odovacer. Theodoric installed himself at Ravenna as the Constantinopolitan Government's vice-gerent there. This fiction was convenient for both parties. In 508 the Emperor Anastasius I decorated the Frankish war-lord Clovis as a reward for his having defeated the Visigoths, though the first feat in Clovis' career of conquest had been the liquidation of the last remnant of Roman rule in Gaul. Until 518, the East Roman Government gave the retention of Syria and Egypt precedence over the acquisition of Italy. Its foreign policy was reflected in its ecclesiastical policy, which is dealt with in the next chapter.

One of the West Roman Government's fatal mistakes was that it gave the chief posts in its civil service to the big landowners, thus enabling them to convert their economically self-contained estates into virtually independent principalities. These West Roman landlords were willing to save some part of their property by betraying the Imperial Government that had taken them into its service. They readily came to terms with the barbarian war-lords who were carving out successor-states for themselves at the Western Empire's expense. The East Roman Government kept the politically dangerous landowners out of office and staffed its civil service, from the praetorian prefects downwards, with middle-class professionals, many of them jurists. These professionals might be corrupt, but they were patriotic in the sense that they recognized that their private interests demanded the preservation of the East Roman state.

At least two East Roman Emperors, Marcian (450–7) and Anastasius I (491–518), reduced the amount of official corruption by imposing stricter control over the administration of the Imperial finances, and about half-way through the fifth century the power of the praetorian prefects in the Eastern Empire was curbed by taking out of their hands the appointment of their subordinates. Marcian's and Anastasius I's administrative strictness rehabilitated the East Roman Government's finances, which had been crippled by the disastrous naval adventure in 468. The soldiers, as well as the Treasury, benefited by the checking of the malpractices of the Army's financial officers. The tax-payers may not have benefited so much by Anastasius I's exemption of the members of the municipal councils from their collective responsibility for the payment of their fellow-tax-payers' taxes. He appointed Imperial officials to collect the tax direct from the individual tax-payers, but his purpose was largely defeated by the practice of auctioning these posts and thereby turning salaried officials into speculative tax-farmers.

In the Western Empire the *magister peditum in praesenti* had acquired dictatorial powers by subordinating his colleagues to himself. In the Eastern Empire the two *magistri in praesenti* were kept co-equal in power with each other and with their three regional colleagues, and in 528 the Emperor Justinian I created a fourth regional *magister, per Armeniam*. The administrative staffs of the East Roman *magistri* were also placed under the control of civil servants, and their private guards (*bucellarii*), though not abolished, were reduced in numbers.

Moreover, the East Roman Army, from the high command downwards, was taken out of the hands of barbarian mercenaries and was recruited instead from citizens of the Eastern Empire. At Constantinople, Gainas the Goth was liquidated in 400 and Aspar the Alan in 471. The Emperor Leo I (ruled 457–74) was a Thracian-speaking Bessian; his successor Zeno, *né* Tarasicodissa, was an Isaurian highlander from the Taurus. Justin I (ruled 518–27) came from the southern fringe of the Latinized northern zone of the Balkan Peninsula.

The transformation of the Isaurians from wolves into sheep-dogs in the course of the fifth century was a remarkable achievement. In 404 and 405 the Isaurians were still raiding their more law-abiding fellow-subjects. The Bessian Leo suppressed the Alan Aspar by making the fortune of the Isaurian Tarasicodissa. When the Isaurians tried to follow the example of the foreign barbarians by abusing their power, Isauria itself was brought under the Imperial Government's effective control by Anastasius I in 491–6. In the sixth century the Isaurians, the Bessians, and the Latinized peoples (Vlakhs) in the north of the Balkan Peninsula provided Justinian I with the troops with which he reconquered parts of the former West Roman Empire's domain in the western basin of the Mediterranean.

The land-wall of Constantinople, built in the reign of Theodosius II (408–50), had replaced Constantine I's original land-wall, and it was supplemented by Anastasius I's Long Wall, running from coast to coast in Constantinople's European hinterland. Anastasius made the Empire's frontier with the Persian Empire secure. He built at Dara a better fortress than Nisibis, which Jovian had had to cede to the Persian Empire in 363. Anastasius also fortified Theodosiopolis (Erzurum) to defend the Roman slice of the former Kingdom of Armenia.

In the fifth century the West Roman Empire was so weak that even an able and energetic Emperor (e.g. Majorian, ruled 457–61) was power-less to avert the Western Empire's doom. The contemporary Eastern Empire was healthy enough to give ability, energy, and statesmanship a chance of being effective and, from 414 to 518, the East Roman Empire was fortunate in its rulers. Theodosius I's son and successor in the East, Arcadius (395–408), had shone only by contrast with his brother and Western colleague Honorius (ruled 395–423). Arcadius' son Theodosius II was a nonentity and he reigned for forty-two years (408–50). However, he reigned without governing, and his elder sister Pulcheria, who took command in 414 and continued to be the effective power behind the throne for most of the time till her death in 453, was the equal of Hatshepsut and Zenobia in strength of character, while she surpassed them both in statesmanship. Pulcheria's husband Marcian and Marcian's successors Leo and Zeno were equal to their task. Anastasius I can challenge comparison with the greatest of the other incumbents of the Roman Imperial throne in the series running from Augustus' victory at Actium in 31 B.C. to Constantine XI's death at Constantinople in A.D. 1453 at the Gate of St. Romanus.

Anastasius I has been eclipsed, in the eyes of posterity, by Justinian I. Justinian was the well-educated and sophisticated nephew of the simple soldier Justin I, the Vlakh peasant-recruit who had risen from the ranks. Justinian was probably managing Justin's affairs even before Justin's accession in 518. Justinian I himself reigned from 527 to 565, so he was in power *de facto* for forty-seven years, and the reversal of the East Roman Government's foreign policy and ecclesiastical policy in 518 was prob-ably Justinian's, more than Justin's, doing. Justinian was proud of being a member of the Latin-speaking minority in the population of an East Roman Empire in which the lingua franca was Greek, and he aspired to re-unite with the Eastern Empire the Western Empire's former domain, except perhaps for Gaul.

In 533–4, North-West Africa was conquered, and the Western Em-pire's Vandal successor-state there was extinguished by Justinian I's brilliant Thracian general Belisarius. The African campaign was easy and short, but the subsequent pacification of this reconquered territory was laborious and slow. The conquest of the Ostrogoths' dominions in Italy and Illyricum took twenty-six years (535–61), and this Romano–Ostrogothic war devastated Italy, used up Anastasius I's reserves of treasure, and ruined the hitherto economically prosperous Levantine provinces by imposing on them crushingly heavy taxation. Undeterred by the lesson of his war with the Ostrogoths, Justinian I attacked the Visigothic dominions in Spain in 550 and conquered a beach-head there before being brought to a halt in 554.

Justinian I's conquests gave the Constantinopolitan Roman Empire the naval command of the whole Mediterranean basin and its backwaters, from the mouths of the rivers Don and Orontes and Nile to the Straits of Gibraltar, but the consequences for the East Roman Empire were disastrous, as the consequences of the single naval campaign in 468 had been in a lesser degree. The sequel to Justinian I's reign vindicated retrospectively the prudence of his predecessors at Constantinople in refraining from committing themselves, except just once, to western adventures.

Justinian I's western conquests were ephemeral. The Lombards invaded Italy in 568, only seven years after the fall of the last Ostrogoth fortress there. Justinian's lasting achievements were in the fields of law and architecture. Between 529 and 533 Justinian I's jurists reduced to manageable compass (though not to rational order) not only the Roman laws that had been enacted, but also the far greater mass of legal opinions that had been rendered, in the course of the previous millennium. In architecture Justinian did not make a revolution, but he confirmed and consecrated one by commissioning two men of genius, the mathematician-engineers Anthemius of Tralles and Isidore of Miletus, to design and build a masterpiece, the Church of the Ayia Sophia (**Holy Wisdom**) in Constantinople.

The original standard shape for a building in the Hellenic World had been the megaron, an oblong rectangular house with a gable roof. Embellished with external columns, either at the front end only or on all sides, this had served as the design for the temples of pre-Christian Greek, Etruscan, and Roman gods and goddesses. With the columns transferred from the exterior to the interior, the megaron had become the basilica in the post-Alexandrine Age, and the basilica had been designed for secular uses before it had become the standard model for a Christian Church. But, in the second century A.D. in Italy, the invention of a new kind of cement had provided the technical means for constructing a round building surmounted by a shallow dome. The pioneer building in this style is the Emperor Hadrian's Pantheon in Rome. In the Church of St. Vitalis at Ravenna, which was completed by Justinian I and his consort Theodora, and in the Church of SS. Sergius and Bacchus at Constantinople, which was built by them, a dome is superposed on an octagonal base—a plan that sets the architect a difficult problem. In the Church of the Ayia Sophia the dome is supported on four piers, delimiting a square.

The Ayia Sophia at Constantinople can confront the Parthenon at

Athens with confidence. Ictinus' art is less subtle than that of Anthemius and Isidore. In the megaron the predominant features are perfectly vertical and horizontal lines, and perfectly even surfaces, and the columns are perfect cylinders. But there are no perfect geometrical figures in Nature; such figures (either genuine or apparent) are devised and constructed by human minds and are imposed by human hands on Man's non-human environment. In a Byzantine church in the style of the Ayia Sophia, the predominant features are domes and semi-domes that reproduce the curves of living bodies. They seek, not to dominate Nature, but to achieve a harmony with her. A Byzantine church would be more pleasing than an Hellenic temple to a Taoist Chinese philosopher's eye.

The Hellenic Greeks did not disdain natural curves. They were supreme masters of the naturalistic representation of the human body, and the curve is the beauty of Hellenic vases in all their successive styles, from the Protogeometric style onwards. The Hellenic Greeks also knew how to introduce nicely calculated curves into their buildings, but here the curves were designed to give the optical illusion of perfect straightness. The Byzantine architects put their treasure, not in apparently straight lines, but in curves akin to those that were congenial to Hellenic sculptors and potters, but not to Hellenic architects.

Justinian I's Ayia Sophia still stands, and his *Corpus Iuris* has inspired codes of law that are still in force; but his ephemeral western conquests brought to the ground, only thirty-seven years after his death, the Empire that his prudent predecessors had carried safely through the storms of the fifth century. In 550, before the end of Justinian's long-drawn-out war of attrition with the Ostrogoths, troops levied in his native Vlakh country for service in Italy had, en route, to repulse raiders from the north bank of the Danube. When, during the Romano–Persian war of 572–91, the East Roman Army was concentrated in Asia on the Empire's eastern front, Avars and Slavs raided the Empire's Balkan provinces unopposed. During the still more agonizing Romano–Persian war of 604–28, the Slavs returned and, this time, they stayed.

The East Roman Empire's Sasanian Persian counterpart was afflicted with the evils that the East Roman Empire avoided or combated, while the same evils had been the death of the West Roman Empire in the fifth century. In the Sasanian Empire, as in its predecessor the Arsacid Empire, high office was not merely monopolized by the grandees; particular offices were the hereditary perquisites of particular noble families. Moreover, the Zoroastrian Church was as powerful in the Sasanian Persian Empire as the Christian Church was in the Constantinian and Theodosian Roman Empire, and, in the Sasanian Age, in contrast to the preceding Arsacid Age, the Zoroastrian Church was also as strongly imbued with Iranian nationalism as the Orthodox Christian Church in the Levant came to be imbued with Greek nationalism when, in the fifth century, Egyptian, Syrian, and Armenian nationalism began to find theological expression in the rejection of the Acts of the Council of Chalcedon (451).

In 440 the Sasanid Emperor Yazdigerd II called upon all his non-Zoroastrian subjects to adopt the Empire's established religion, and he persecuted non-conformists till his death in 457. The opposition was most militant in Persarmenia. (The Armenian national consciousness had been heightened by the invention, *c.* 400, of an alphabet for conveying the Armenian language, and by the consequent outburst of an Armenian literature.) The Armenian insurgents were crushed in 451, but they revolted again in 481, after the Persians had begun to suffer military reverses at the hands of the Ephthalite Huns; and the Sasanian Imperial Government had to grant complete toleration to the Armenian Christian Church after the Emperor Peroz's defeat and death in 484. An Armenian grandee was now appointed governor of Persarmenia.

Meanwhile, the Syriac-speaking Christians in Iraq had profited by the outlawing of the Nestorian version of Christology in the Roman Empire in 431. The Nestorians took refuge at Nisibis, a Syriac-speaking city which, since 363, had lain on the Persian side of the Romano–Persian frontier. As refugees from persecution by the Roman Imperial Government, the Nestorians were welcome on Persian soil. In 482–6 the Christian Church in the Syriac-speaking territories of the Sasanian Empire retorted to the Roman Emperor Zeno's philo-monophysite *Enotikón* ('Unifying') pronouncement of 482 by adopting the Nestorian form of Christianity. Thenceforward, the Persian Empire had a national Christian Church, committed to a theology that was anathema to both the Monophysite and the Orthodox Christian subjects of the Roman Empire, to match the national Zoroastrian Church in the Persian Empire's Iranian-speaking territories. The adoption of Nestorianism did not save the Persian Empire's Christian subjects from all further persecution, but it did make their position more secure by clearing them of the suspicion that they were a Roman 'fifth column'.

The Persian military disaster of 484 not only won toleration for the Sasanids' non-Iranian Christian subjects; it also opened the way for a violent social revolution in Iran itself, where there was a great and growing gulf between the wealth of the grandees and the poverty of the masses. The social crisis was brought to a head by a famine at an early date in the reign of Peroz's second successor Kavadh I (*accessit* 488). The opportunity was seized by Mazdak, the contemporary head of a sect of Manichaeism which had been founded as far back as the next generation to Mani's own. This sect, the Drist-Den, differed from orthodox

Manichaeism on some points of doctrine, but, by Mazdak's time at any rate, the Drist-Den's distinctive feature had come to be a demand for social justice. Property was to be shared, including wives (an invidious point, which was made much of by Mazdak's adversaries).

Mazdak's version of the Drist-Den won popular support; the Emperor Kavadh I became a convert, and the social revolution was put into effect at the grandees' expense. Mazdakism was socially obnoxious to the Iranian nobility; it was both socially and doctrinally obnoxious to the Zoroastrian clergy; a Sasanian emperor was not a match for the clergy and the nobility when these combined against him; and Kavadh I was deposed and imprisoned in 496; but he escaped to the Ephthalites and was re-instated on the Persian Imperial throne by an Ephthalite army in 498 or 499. Meanwhile, Mazdak retained his ascendancy, and his communism continued to be put into effect; but in 528 or 529 Kavadh I disavowed Mazdakism at the instigation of one of his sons, Khusro (Chosroes), whom he had chosen to be his successor. In concert with the heads of the Zoroastrian and Nestorian churches, who made common cause on this occasion, Khusro crushed Mazdakism. He massacred large numbers of the sect's adherents, including Mazdak himself.

Khusro I, surnamed 'Anosharvan' ('the Immortal'), was astute, and he had a freer hand than any of his predecessors. He was in the good graces of the Zoroastrian clergy, since he had been the moving spirit in the suppression of Mazdakism towards the end of his father's reign. Therefore he did not have to fear an alliance against him between the Zoroastrian Church and the grandees, over whom he succeeded in asserting his authority. By the time Khusro put an end to Mazdak's ascendancy, the Mazdakite revolution had been in train for about forty years, and the grandees had emerged from it ruined and discredited.

Though Khusro I had put down Mazdakism, and had gone on, after his accession, to curb the power of the grandees, he recognized that he must take positive steps to alleviate the social injustice that had provoked the Mazdakite revolution, and that he must reform the institutions that had given the grandees their hold over the Crown. Khusro seems to have taken his cues from post-Diocletianic Roman history. He reassessed both the land-tax and the poll-tax. He taxed land in proportion to its productivity, and persons in proportion to their means. Under the post-Sasanian regime of the Arab Caliphate in Iran, the country squires (*dehkans*) were responsible for the collection of the rural taxes. Perhaps Khusro I had given the *dehkans* this role. In his struggle to quell the grandees, the *dehkans* were the Emperor's natural allies. Khusro also abolished the office of commander-in-chief and replaced it by four regional commands. It looks as if he was aware of one of the causes of the East and the West Roman Empires' respective fortunes.

In 572 Khusro I fell into a war with the East Roman Empire which dragged on till 590 and ended in the deposition and murder of Khusro I's son and successor Hormizd IV. The unpopularity of the war had given the grandees a chance to reassert themselves. A rebel grandee now seized the throne, and Hormizd IV's son, Khusro II, was re-instated by the East Roman Emperor Maurice. In return, Khusro II made peace with Maurice in 591 and ceded to him the western half of Persarmenia. Maurice could now at last transfer the East Roman Army to Europe and launch a counter-offensive against the Avars and the Slavs. His counter-offensive was so successful that, by 602, the Romans were once again on the north bank of the lower Danube, for the first time since their evacuation of Dacia in the third century. But Maurice's orders to the Army to go into winter quarters beyond the Danube provoked a mutiny which cost Maurice his throne and his life and plunged the Empire into anarchy.

In 604 Khusro II invaded the East Roman Empire on the pretext of avenging his benefactor Maurice's death. The consequent war was the most desperate of any that had been waged between the Romans and their Iranian neighbours since their first encounter with each other in 53 B.C. The Persians advanced, at least twice, to the Asian shore of the Bosphorus. In 626 they were barely prevented by the East Roman navy from joining hands with the Avars, who were besieging Constantinople from the European side of the Straits. Persian armies occupied Syria, Palestine, Egypt, and Cyrenaïca. The Persians had not been seen so far westward at any date since 331 B.C.; and the East Romans, in their eventual counter-attack, advanced farther eastward than any Roman army since A.D. 117. In 628 the East Roman Emperor Heraclius (*accessit* 610) was almost within sight of Ctesiphon, and then the war ended, like the war of 572–91, in the deposition and death of the reigning Sasanid Emperor.

In 628 the two powers made peace on the basis of the territorial *status quo ante bellum*. The Persian Empire now fell into as extreme an anarchy as that through which the East Roman Empire had passed during the years 602–10, but, unlike the East Roman Empire, the Persian Empire failed to recover.

In 628 both powers were exhausted. The *tertius gaudens* was the Islamic Arab state founded by the Prophet Muhammad at Medina in 622. The rise of Muhammad had been as swift as the rise of the Prince of Palmyra, Odenath, after Shahpuhr I's victory over Valerian in A.D. 260. In 633 Muhammad's first successor, Abu Bakr, attacked both of his exhausted northern neighbours simultaneously. The Persian Empire fell; the East Roman Empire once again survived, but its territory was now reduced progressively to Asia Minor and Constantinople, together with some islands and some continental beach-heads along the north shore of the Mediterranean.

44

WESTERN CHRISTENDOM, 395–634

AMONG all the states of the Old-World Oikoumenê that were hit by the eruption of the Huns from the Eurasian steppe, the West Roman Empire failed the most signally to stand up to the test. The Sarmatian nomadic and the East German sedentary peoples who were driven westwards by the impact of the Huns in this direction broke through the West Roman Empire's frontiers in and after 406, and by 476 even the now merely nominal Imperial regime in the West was liquidated. The fall of the West Roman Empire was due not so much to the barbarian invaders' strength as to the Empire's internal weakness. This weakness was both social and administrative. The West Roman Empire's maladies were the same as those that were the death of the Han Empire. The Imperial Government was defeated in struggles for power with the large land-owners and with the army's high command. The landlords diverted the peasantry's 'surplus' product from the Government's treasury to their own pockets. The high command succeeded in turning itself into a political dictatorship by concentrating military power in a single pair of hands.

On the eve of the Western Empire's collapse, two great men of two different generations, St. Ambrose and St. Augustine, made a mark on Western Christendom which outlasted the extinction of the Empire within which they lived and worked. St. Ambrose, who was bishop of Milan from 372 to 397, died only seven years before the West Roman Empire's capital was moved in 404 from Milan to Ravenna—a natural fortress made impregnable by its swamps—and only nine years before 406, when the East German refugees from the Huns broke through the Western Empire's frontier on the Rhine. Augustine, who was bishop of Hippo Regius in North-West Africa from 395 to 430, died in the year following the Vandals' invasion of Africa. The Vandals crossed from Spain to Africa in 429, only twenty-three years after their crossing of the

Rhine. In 430 they were already besieging the African city that was Augustine's episcopal see.

These two Western clerics came from very different social milieux, and they had followed different secular professions before they were ordained as Christian priests. Ambrose was the son of a civil servant who had risen to the highest rank, and Ambrose himself began as a civil servant and would, no doubt, have repeated his father's career if he had not been diverted to a field of action in which he could, and did, exert power more effectively. Augustine was the son of middle-class parents at Thagaste, a small town in the interior of North-West Africa. Augustine started as a professor of rhetoric in his home-town, and, in this intel-lectually and socially arid profession, he distinguished himself. He was promoted from Thagaste to Carthage and from Carthage to Rome and then to Milan. At Milan in 388 he was converted from Manichaeism to Christianity and thus found a way to employ his gifts in an ecclesiastical career in his own country.

Ambrose had courage and strength of will, and he used these qualities to dominate another forceful personality, the Emperor Theodosius I. Ambrose exerted his pressure on Theodosius by refusing him com-munion unless and until he did what Ambrose demanded. Theodosius was amenable because he was a believing Christian and also because he had to reckon with Christian public opinion (Ambrose had been made bishop of Milan at the insistence of the local Christians). Ambrose used his power over Theodosius well in making the Emperor do penance for having perpetrated two massacres. He used his power over the Emperor evilly by preventing him from punishing a Christian bishop for having destroyed a Jewish synagogue, and also by moving him in 384 to reject a petition from Symmachus, the President of the Senate at Rome, to replace in the Senate-House the altar of Victory, which had been re-moved by Theodosius' Western predecessor Gratian in 382. Symmachus, in his petition, had written: 'So great a mystery cannot be approached by a single road only'. The mystery that Symmachus had in mind was the ultimate reality behind the phenomena and the question of the relation between this ultimate reality and Man. Ambrose did not answer Symmachus' plea for toleration. Ambrose's objective was to suppress the practice of all non-Christian religions within the frontiers of the Roman Empire by prevailing upon the Imperial Government to use its power to this effect. Theodosius carried out Ambrose's policy in 391–2. The only non-Christian religions that ultimately survived in the Empire were astrology and the Jews' and the Samaritans' worship of Yahweh.

Augustine was also intolerant, and he spent much time and energy in controversy with the Donatists and the Pelagians. The Donatists had already been proved to have no case on the ethical issue of their intransigence towards fellow-Christians who had compromised themselves during the years 303–11. Nevertheless they were irrepressible because they had identified themselves with a local African movement that was not religious but social and political. Pelagius held that the human will is at least partially free, and that Man is in duty bound to use his freedom to work on the side of good against evil. This British theologian's Iranian-like insistence on Man's moral responsibility is salutary at all times and places, and never more so than in the West in Pelagius' and Augustine's generation, when, in the West Roman Empire, society was collapsing. St. Augustine held that Man's merit could never be great enough to enable him to win salvation by his own unaided exertions. For Man's salvation, God's 'grace' was indispensable. In the non-theological usage of everyday life, the Latin word *gratia* meant a powerful human being's 'favour' in the sense of favouritism. Augustine's controversy with the Pelagians led Augustine on to propounding the doctrine that God's sovereign arbitrariness has gone to the length of predestining some human being to salvation and others to damnation. Augustine was picturing God in the likeness of a Roman Emperor who abuses his power because he has been intoxicated by the plenitude of it.

Augustine's most valuable literary legacies to posterity are two non-theological books. In his *Confessions* he used his mastery of the Latin language to write a psychological autobiography. In his *City of God* (*De Civitate Dei*) Augustine broadened and deepened a work that had started as a controversial pamphlet, making it into an investigation of the 'great mystery' along one of the alternative possible roads by which human minds can approach it. The controversy that was the germ of Augustine's *De Civitate Dei* was a sequel to the capture and sack of the City of Rome by the Visigoths in 410. Constantine had believed and declared that his military victories were rewards given to him by the God of the Christians for his conversion to Christianity. After 410 the adherents of the non-Christian religions retorted that the fall of Rome in 410 was a punishment inflicted by the non-Christian gods for the suppression of the worship of them in 391–2. Augustine set out to refute this contention and was led on to explore the relation between Man's mundane life and his simultaneous participation in the Kingdom of Heaven.

While Augustine was writing, the northern barbarians were invading. Some of these invasions were sudden—for instance, the descents upon Rome of the Visigoths in 410 and of the Vandals in 455, and the Vandals' previous advance, in company with the Alans and the Suevi, from the east bank of the Rhine to the south side of the Pyrenees, within the three years 406–8. By contrast, the partial occupation of Britain by the Angles, Saxons, and Jutes and of Italy by the Lombards were gradual piecemeal processes, as had been the partial occupation of Canaan by the Israelites and Judahites in the course of the last two or three centuries of the second millennium B.C. In Britain, Hadrian's rampart may have ceased to be held effectively as early as A.D. 383, but there may have been Roman garrisons at some points in Britain forty years later. The permanent lodgment of Teutonic-speaking invaders on British soil may not have begun before *c.* 420–40, and here the process took about two centuries.

The country that suffered worst from barbarian occupation and Roman counter-attack was Italy, which had been the nucleus of the whole Roman Empire and had been the most highly civilized of the Empire's western territories. The exhaustion of the East Roman Empire by the Romano–Gothic war of 535–61 has been noted already; in this war the Ostrogoth occupants of Italy were exterminated, but the worst sufferers were the native Italians. The Visigoths' and Vandals' invasions of Italy in the fifth century, though sensational, had been sporadic and transitory. The extinction of the West Roman Imperial Government in 476 had been peaceful, and the Ostrogoths' invasion, like so much of the fighting during the German *Völkerwanderung*, had been between one barbarian war-band and another. Till 535 Italy remained politically united and economically and socially more or less intact. The war of 535–61 was a turning-point in Italy's history. The Lombards broke into Italy in 568, only seven years after the re-unification of the country under East Roman rule had at last been achieved. From 568 onwards Italy was broken up politically for the first time since 264 B.C., the year in which the original Roman conquest and unification of Peninsular Italy had been completed. The Lombards were more barbarous than the Ostrogoths, and Italy, already devastated by the war of 535–61, suffered still more grievously from the slow conquest of portions of the country in the teeth of the East Roman garrisons' stubborn resistance in those portions that they managed still to hold.

Meanwhile, in 486, two years before the Ostrogoth war-lord Theodoric had marched on Italy from Illyricum, a local Frankish war-lord, Clovis (Chlodovech) the Merovingian, had started to build up an empire in Gaul. The Franks had not yet been converted to any form of Christianity, and Clovis, at some stage in his career, was baptized as a Catholic. He chose the Catholic form of Christianity partly, no doubt, because this was the religion of his Roman subjects, and perhaps also because the rival German empire-builders in his neighbourhood were Arian Christians. In 486 Clovis became the Visigoths' neighbour along the line of the River Loire, and he became the Ostrogoths' neighbour too when, in 496, he conquered the Alamanni in the upper part of the basin of the Rhine.

The adoption of the Arian form of Christianity by the East Germans had been an incidental consequence of the date of their conversion; but, after they had occupied West Roman territory and had set up successor-states of the Empire there, the conquerors were glad to have a national religion of their own which distinguished them from their Catholic Roman subjects. However, the price of this distinctiveness was alienation, and this became a serious handicap for the Arian Germans after the emergence of the Franks as a Catholic Christian power. Moreover, the Arian Germans themselves were gradually captivated by the religion of their subjects, who were their superiors in civilization as well as in numbers. Catholicism did not have time to exert its spell on the Vandals (who were exceptional in being bigoted Arians) or on the Ostrogoths. These two peoples were exterminated by the East Roman counter-offensive before the question of a change of religion had arisen. But in 586 the Visigoth King Reccared in Spain abandoned Arianism for Catholicism voluntarily, and the Lombards made the same change more reluctantly and more gradually in Italy in the course of the seventh century.

By 586 the Visigoths had been confined to Spain for eighty years. In 507 Clovis had defeated them at Vouglé (Vouillé) and had expelled them from all their domain to the north of the Pyrenees except for a coastal strip between the eastern end of the Pyrenees and the mouth of the Rhône. Thus Clovis, by the time of his death in 511, had united under his rule the whole of the rest of Gaul except Provence, which had been taken over from the Visigoths by the Ostrogoths. Clovis had previously established his sovereignty over all sections of the Frankish people. In 531–4 his successors annexed Thuringia and Burgundy. In 552 they imposed their suzerainty on Bavaria. The Merovingians were building up a new empire, centred on northern Gaul, to fill the political vacuum that had been left in Western Europe by the dissolution of the West Roman Empire. A Frankish Empire might have replaced the West Roman Empire before the close of the sixth century if the descendants of Clovis had not treated the dominions of the Merovingian dynasty as private property to be divided and re-divided in successive generations. These partitions, and the consequent civil wars, devastated Gaul and reduced its disunited Frankish masters to impotence.

At the turn of the sixth and seventh centuries, the East Roman Empire still retained its naval command over the western as well as the eastern basin of the Mediterranean, and it still held all the Mediterranean islands, including not only Sicily but also North-West Africa, which is the biggest island of them all and is truly an island, since it is insulated from the rest of Africa by a sea of sand, the Sahara. The East Roman Empire also still held a beach-head in north-eastern Italy, based on

Ravenna, together with the islets in the lagoon of Venice. As for the enclave of East Roman territory round the City of Rome itself, the Constantinopolitan Government left it to the Pope to defend and provision this outlying piece of East Roman territory as best he could. The Ducatus Romanus that survived the Lombards' irruption into Italy was not much larger than the Ager Romanus had been in the fifth century B.C.

In the fifth and sixth centuries A.D., all the fragments of Western Christendom were in an apparently desperate plight. Yet, even at the darkest hours, some of the western representatives of the Catholic Christian Church showed spirit. Pope Leo I (440–61) produced a decisive effect on the decisions of the Ecumenical Council held at Chalcedon in 451, and in 452 he played the leading role in a Roman embassy that induced the Hun war-lord Attila to break off his invasion of northern Italy. Leo I's pontificate was contemporary with St. Patrick's mission to Ireland. Patrick was a British Roman of the same social class as the African Roman St. Augustine. Patrick had been captured and enslaved by Irish raiders. He escaped from slavery in Ireland to return there voluntarily as a Christian missionary (*c.* 432–61). Christianity struck root in Ireland, and in the sixth century the Irish Christians adopted monasticism both in its solitary and in its communal form.

Contemporaneously St. Benedict was founding his monastic order at Monte Cassino. Benedict began his work *c.* 529, when Italy was still at peace; he died *c.* 547, when Italy was in the throes of the Romano–Gothic war. Yet Benedictine monasticism not only survived; it spread. Benedict's work was carried on by Pope Gregory I (590–604). Gregory had turned his own house in Rome into a Benedictine monastery and had become a monk there before he was made, first papal envoy at Constantinople, and then Pope.

As Pope, Gregory had to feed the population of Rome from the produce of the papal estates in Sicily; he had also to negotiate with the aggressive Lombards on the East Roman Government's behalf. Yet in 597, when the Lombards were at the gates of Rome, Gregory had the spirit to send a mission to convert the distant Jutish Kingdom of Kent, and this mission was followed up, after Gregory's death, by one to the Anglian Kingdom of Northumbria. The Roman missionary Paulinus officiated at York from 627 to 632, but in 634 his place was taken by the Irish missionary Aidan from Iona, an islet off the west coast of Scotland. Aidan planted a monastery on the islet of Lindisfarne (Holy Island) off the Northumbrian coast.

In Ireland the introduction of monasticism had generated an explosive missionary movement. The Irish monastery on the islet of Iona had been founded *c.* 563 by St. Columba. St. Columba died on Iona in 597, the year in which Pope Gregory sent his mission from Rome to Kent. *Circa* 590 another Irish missionary, St. Columbanus, had crossed from Ireland to Britain and from Britain to the Continent. Columbanus founded a monastery in Burgundy at Luxeuil, a key point in the communication-network of the Frankish dominions. By 610 he had reached Lake Constance. In 613 he crossed the Alps and founded a monastery at Bobbio in north-western Italy. He died there in 615.

In Northumbria the installation, in 634, of the Irish missionary Aidan filled the vacancy left by the Roman missionary Paulinus, who had become a refugee in 632. In Northumbria the Roman and the Irish mission-fields met and overlapped. A confrontation between the Roman and the Irish Christian churches then became inevitable.

[45]

THE ESTABLISHMENT AND DISRUPTION OF THE CHRISTIAN CHURCH, 312–657

In the years 311–12, the Christian Church experienced a sudden and extreme change of fortune. After having endured for eight years the worst persecution of any that it had suffered at the Roman Imperial Government's hands, the Church was first grudgingly tolerated by the dying Emperor Galerius, and then, within eighteen months, it was positively favoured by the victorious Emperor Constantine I, who had already made himself master of half the Empire. This experience would have put the Church's character to the test at any stage of its history, but in the third century its character had deteriorated as a consequence of its growth in numbers, wealth, and power. This turned the Church's highest offices into tempting prizes for careerists. In the year 217 there was a sordid contest for the post of bishop of Rome. The Church also became in the years 250, 257–60, and 303–11 the target for persecutions that were more systematic than the short and sharp local persecutions at dates in the first two centuries of the Christian Era, and Callistus I's unedifying episcopate at Rome (217–22) was offset in 258 by the martyrdom of Cyprian, the bishop of Carthage.

Galerius' motive for persecuting the Church was the same as Constantine's motive for favouring it. Both emperors were concerned to maintain the Empire's unity. Since Aurelian had put the Empire under the aegis of the 'Unconquered Sun' as the supreme god in the Empire's non-Christian pantheon, it had been recognized that the unity, and indeed the existence, of the Roman Empire could not be preserved without the support of an established religion. Before the close of the third century, the Sasanian Persian Empire had chosen the Zoroastrian Church, and the Kingdom of Armenia the Christian Church, to serve as its ecclesiastical establishment. After Galerius had admitted that the Christian Church was stronger than he was, and after this demonstration of the Christian Church's strength had been confirmed, for Constantine, by his victory with the monogram that he had seen in a dream, Constantine was bound to identify Christ with the 'Unconquered Sun', and to establish Christianity as the Roman Empire's unifying religion.

It was reasonable to expect that an established Christian Church would promote the unity of the Roman Empire effectively, considering that, down to the year 311, the Church had been remarkably successful in preserving its own unity. Since the foundation of the Church soon after Jesus's death, its survival had constantly been jeopardized by domestic dissensions, but these had constantly been overcome. The dissentients had either been reconciled or else the weaker party in a dispute had been suppressed or expelled. In the year 311 the Catholic non-Jewish Church was a unity, from Osrhoene and Armenia on the east to Britain on the west. Now, however, the Church was suddenly released from a pressure that had been particularly severe in its final phase; the Church's historic unity failed to survive this test; the previous schism in the population of the Roman Empire between non-Christians and Christians was now replaced by schism within the bosom of the Church itself; and the Roman Imperial Government, which, since Constantine's conversion, had been counting on the Church's unity to underpin the Empire's, found itself impotent to induce the contending Christian parties to make peace with each other. The Church's domestic dissensions baffled Constantine I from his conversion in 312 to his death in 337; they were still baffling Constans II (ruled 641–68). The quarrel in Constans II's reign between the Constantinopolitan Imperial Government and the Papacy was solved for the two disputants by the Muslim Arabs, who relieved the Empire of all its Monophysite Christian subjects and thus absolved the Imperial Government from its impracticable obligation to satisfy simultaneously two irreconcilable Christian factions.

Though the uncontrollable disruption of the Christian Church after the years 311–12 was disconcerting for Constantine I and his successors, it was virtually inevitable. When Christianity became the Roman Empire's established religion, and when consequently the Christians became a majority in the Empire's population, the Roman Imperial Government was no more able to control the Church than it had been able to control it in the previous situation, in which the Christians in the Empire had been an unpopular minority. This is not surprising. Christianity was an offshoot of Judaism, and it had inherited Judaism's traditional dislike of compromise.

Moreover, in the new situation, ecclesiastical issues became identified with social and political issues. The conflict between Catholic and Donatist Christians became also a conflict between Numidia and Carthage and between peasants and landlords. The theology of Arius, which was eventually defeated within the Empire, became the distinctive badge of barbarian invaders of the Empire who had previously been converted to Christianity at a time when, within the Empire, Arianism had been temporarily in the ascendant. The debate over the constitution of the Trinity became also a struggle for ecclesiastical power between Alexandria—the former political capital of the Ptolemies—and Antioch —the former political capital of the Seleucids. The subsequent debate over the relation between the human and the divine aspect of the second member of the Trinity became also a struggle between the Roman Imperial Government and its Syriac-speaking and Coptic-speaking subjects. These now challenged the Greek ascendancy imposed on them by Alexander the Great and maintained by Roman power, while the Imperial Government sought to preserve its sovereignty over them. Incidentally, the second and the fourth ecumenical councils of the Christian Church gave the See of Constantinople opportunities for asserting itself. The second council (381) recognized that the Constantinopolitan See ranked next after the Roman. The fourth council (451) gave the Patriarch of Constantinople the ecclesiastical jurisdiction over Asia Minor to the north-west of the Taurus Range and over the easternmost part of the Balkan Peninsula.

The ecclesiastical controversies of the fourth and fifth centuries were not mere camouflage for the secular disputes with which they came to be identified. The ethical, theological, and jurisdictional issues that divided the Christians were genuine, and the feelings that these issues aroused were sincere and widespread. There was a practical reason why, at this stage, Christian ecclesiastical affairs and Imperial secular affairs merged with each other. The Christian Church had become the dominant institution in the Roman Empire, and therefore all peoples, regions, classes, and parties in the Empire were implicated in the Church's concerns.

The ethical issue was the first to arise. During the persecution of 303–11, as during the two third-century persecutions, a number of Christians had lapsed, while others had held out—some of them at the cost of martyrdom. Were the lapsed Christians to be received back into communion with their more steadfast co-religionists? Or were they to be permanently stigmatized? For the most part, the survivors among the members of the Church who had not given way took the more generous-minded, humane, and statesmanlike line. They were in favour of pardoning the weaklings, and in most regions the unforgiving members of the Christian community were a minority who were eventually overruled. In North-West Africa, however, these opponents of reconciliation were intransigent. They were as hostile to peace-makers whose own record was unblemished as they were to the lapsed Christians whose bad record the peacemakers wished to condone. This quarrel in North-West Africa rapidly became so fierce that Constantine felt himself called upon to intervene in 313, the year after his conversion. Constantine believed that dissension within the Christian Church was displeasing to God and that, if the Emperor failed to put an end to it, he as well as the Church risked forfeiting God's favour. Constantine tried to bring the African dissentients together, first by conciliation and then by coercion, but he was baffled.

The theological issues that were debated from 317 to 657 had been implicit already in the beliefs about Jesus that are expressed in the prologues to the first, third, and fourth Gospels. These issues had, of course, been raised before the year 312, and since the second century there had been Christians who could and did discuss theology in terms of Hellenic philosophy—for instance, Irenaeus in a work *Against the Heresies*, written *c*. 185. But the 'establishment' of the Christian Church as first the favoured, and then the obligatory, religion for Roman subjects turned Christian theological controversies into Imperial public affairs. Moreover, the Hellenically educated minority in the Empire remained, on the whole, allergic to Christian doctrine until this was presented to them in Hellenic philosophical terms. For these two reasons, an explicit and exhaustive discussion of Christian theological issues was inevitable after 312, and Christianity's dislike of compromise made these discussions stubborn and acrimonious.

When the first, third, and fourth Gospels were written, some non-Jewish Christians already believed that Jesus was God. According to the first and the third Gospel, Jesus had no human father; he had been begotten on his human mother by God's spirit. According to the fourth Gospel, Jesus was God's word incarnate. By this time Judaism had come to attribute to God's word and to God's spirit a semi-independent status, comparable to the status that Zoroastrianism attributed to various aspects of Ahura Mazda; but this was the limit of the derogation from God's unity and uniqueness that Judaism was willing to make. Christians would not and could not disavow the monotheism that they had inherited from Judaism, but how were they to reconcile monotheism with their belief that Jesus, as well as Yahweh, was God?

Jesus was recorded to have spoken of himself as being 'the Son of God'. This claim to sonship could be interpreted in the metaphorical sense in which some other orthodox Jewish rabbis, besides Jesus, had called themselves sons of God. The second Gospel could be read as meaning that God had declared to Jesus that he had made him his son by adoption. But the other three gospels implied that Jesus was a son of God in the literal sense in which God's fatherhood had been attributed to the Pharaohs since the Fifth Dynasty. Whether or not Jesus was God in one or other of the possible senses, it was unquestionable that he had been a human being; so, if he was held to be literally the Son of God, this fact raised not only the question of the Son's relation to the Father but the further question of the relation between the Son's divine and human aspects. It also raised the question of the status of Jesus's mother, Mary. She was a human being, not a goddess. Was it permissible to style her the 'Mother of God' (Theotókos) in virtue of her son's divine aspect?

In asking themselves these questions, Christian theologians were carrying words beyond the range of human experience. They went to this length because they were talking and writing in Greek, and, as early as before the close of the fifth century B.C., Greek-speakers had taken to playing with words as if words were realities even when the words were counters that had no equivalent in thought or in phenomena. In 324, Constantine I, already frustrated in his attempt to settle the dispute in North-West Africa over the status of lapsed Christians there, found that he had also to intervene in a dispute over the relation of the Son to the Father between Alexander, bishop of Alexandria, and Arius, who had been one of Alexander's parish priests. Constantine wrote to the two disputants that the issue in dispute between them ought never to have been raised. In 648 Constans II positively forbade any farther discussion of the current Christological issue, which was whether there were two wills and operations in Christ or only one will and operation.

The words in dispute in 324 and in 648 and in intervening years may or may not have been meaningless, but they certainly excited strong feelings; these feelings boiled over into physical violence; intimidation was practised by Egyptian monks and ecclesiastical 'orderlies' (*parabolani*) and sailors at the councils held at Ephesus in 431 and 449; on the second of these occasions, the Egyptians inflicted mortal physical injuries on the Patriarch of Constantinople, Flavian. All emperors in turn, from Constantine I to Constans II, proved unable to silence the theologians. In 325 Constantine I had to convene at Nicaea the First Ecumenical Council. He presided over it, and he coined for it the Greek word *homoousios* ('same in essence')—a word of the kind that he had originally deplored. Arius' opponent Athanasius, who succeeded Alexander in 328 as bishop of Alexandria, appeared to have won; yet, in 381, Theodosius I had to convene the Second Ecumenical Council at Constantinople, and, even then, the issue raised by Arius was not given its quietus. The Gothic missionary Ulphilas (*c.* 311–83) exported Christianity to the East German peoples in its Arian form. The Emperors Constantius II and Valens were Arians, and, since Ulphilas was their contemporary, presumably he supposed that he was transmitting Christianity in its permanent standard formulation. When the East Germans invaded the Empire, they brought their Arian Christianity with them. As for

Constans II's injunction to keep silence, this evoked a vociferous protest from Pope Martin I. The Pope was silenced only by being arrested, physically assaulted, and deported to the Crimea.

Arius had not denied that the Son was God. By his lifetime (*c*. 250–336) the belief in the divinity of Jesus prevailed in the non-Jewish Christian Church. Adoptionists survived only in natural fastnesses at the extremities of Christendom: in the mountains between the two arms of the upper course of the Euphrates, and in the Pyrenees and in Asturias. But Arius did maintain that the Son had been created by the Father and that therefore he was not coeval with the Father and was not his equal. The Council of Nicaea put the three members of the Trinity on an absolute par with each other. At the same time it was reaffirmed that the three persons constituted one God. This combination of monotheism with trinitarianism was merely verbal. The actual result of the Council of Nicaea was to raise the Son to the status of being a second supreme god. Christianity was now monotheistic only nominally.

This enhancement of the divinity of the Son was a victory for the Egyptian point of view. (Though Arius was a cleric of the Alexandrian Church his theology was Antiochene.) At Ephesus in 431 and 449 the Egyptians went farther. In 431 they secured the condemnation of the Patriarch of Constantinople, Nestorius, who had re-emphasized the human aspect of the Son by objecting to the practice of styling Mary the 'Mother of God'. Nestorian Christians were stigmatized as being 'Diophysites' (i.e. believers that the Son had two un-unified natures). The defeat of Nestorius was a final defeat for the Antiochene school of theology within the bounds of the Roman Empire. The philomonophysite Emperor Anastasius I closed the Nestorian-minded school of theology at Edessa in 489, but the Nestorian theologians found asylum at Nisibis, which, since 363, had lain just outside the Roman Empire's eastern frontier. Thus Nestorianism, like its more radical congener Arianism, survived—outside the Roman Empire.

In 449 the Egyptians went still farther than in 431. They imposed the doctrine that the Son had only one nature, namely his divine nature, while he was incarnate in a human body. But at Chalcedon in 451 the acts of the council held at Ephesus in 449 were annulled. The Son was now declared to have two natures, the divine nature and the human, united in a single person. The Egyptians now suffered the fate of the Nestorians. They were stigmatized as being schismatics.

The Egyptians were stigmatized, but they could not be expelled or suppressed. In Egypt, the theological tendency that had culminated in Monophysitism was a mass-movement, and this movement won to its side Syria, which had originally been the home of a theology that emphasized the Son's human aspect. Monophysitism also captivated

Armenia. The Armenian Church adopted Monophysitism in 491, and it did not follow the Roman Imperial Government when, in 518, the Imperial Government reverted from Monophysitism to Chalcedonianism. The Armenians relished a version of Christianity that differed from both the Roman and the Persian versions. The Monophysites stigmatized the Chalcedonians as being Diophysites, crypto-Nestorians, and Melchites ('running dogs of the Roman Imperial regime'). From 451 onwards the Imperial Government had to try to satisfy both its Chalcedonian and its Monophysite subjects, and it could ill afford to alienate the Monophysites, since, on the economic plane, Monophysite Egypt and Syria were the East Roman Empire's mainstays.

The Emperor Zeno's 'Unifying Act', promulgated in 482, led to a breach between the Eastern Empire and the Papacy in 484. When, in 518, Zeno's and Anastasius I's philomonophysite policy was reversed by Justin I, no doubt at the instance of his nephew and future successor Justinian, the Monophysites became politically disaffected, and Justinian himself was constrained, *c.* 543, to make an ineffective gesture of appeasement by stigmatizing retrospectively, as being Nestorian, the doctrines of three fifth-century theologians.

From 518 until 633–41 (the years in which Syria, Palestine, and Egypt were conquered by the Muslim Arabs), the East Roman Empire's Monophysite subjects were in adversity. Fortunately for them, they found three redoubtable champions: the Pisidian Severus, who was Patriarch of Antioch from 512 to 518; Justinian's consort the Empress Theodora (Justinian had married her before his accession in 527, and she died, about fifty years old, in 548); and James Baradaeus, who was one of Theodora's Monophysite protégés. At the instance of Harith, the Monophysite Arab warden of the Roman Empire's eastern marches, James Baradaeus was appointed bishop of Edessa in 543, and for the rest of his life he 'went on the run' and kept the Monophysite Church alive by ordaining Monophysite clergy at all levels of the hierarchy.

Theodora also won for Monophysitism a new domain beyond the Roman Empire's frontiers. *Circa* 540 she forestalled her husband by converting Nubia to her form of Christianity instead of his. To the southeast of Nubia, the Kingdom of Aksum, in the northern part of present-day Ethiopia, had been converted to Christianity about half way through the fourth century. In the sixth century, Aksum, like Nubia, adopted Monophysitism, and the East Roman Imperial Government had to acquiesce. Aksum commanded the sea-route between Egypt and India, and its ruler was in a position to intervene in the Yemen in the Roman Empire's interest. Constantinople could not afford politically to quarrel with Aksum over a theological issue.

One effect of the change in the Christian Church's fortunes in the

Roman Empire in 311–12 was to transfer from the martyrs to the ascetics the beau role of the Christian community's heroes. Within the Empire, it was now no longer possible for a Christian to be martyred by non-Christians. Christian heroes of some new kind were needed, and the ascetics met this psychological demand. The Egyptian anchorite ('withdrawer') St. Antony (251?–356) was more widely famous and more highly revered than any Pharaonic-Age Egyptian had ever been; but the future lay, not with Antony the anchorite, but with another Egyptian, Pachom (290–345), who founded at Tobennisi, in Upper Egypt, the first Christian fraternity of ascetics living together as a disciplined community. Buddhist communities of this kind had been in existence in India since the Buddha had founded his *sangha* about eight centuries before Pachom's generation, but Pachom's cluster of monasteries was a novelty at the western end of the Old-World Oikoumenê.

In creating this institution, Pachom produced an enduring effect on the life of the whole of Christendom. A fourth-century Cappadocian, St. Basil (*c.* 320–79), worked out, for the Greek-speaking World, a milder form of communal monasticism than the Pachomian form, from which Basil took his cue. *Circa* 529 St. Benedict, taking his cue at least partly from St. Basil, organized a monastery at Monte Cassino, to the southeast of Rome, and drew up a rule which became the standard for the Latin-speaking World. In the course of the sixth century, monasticism struck root, beyond the western bounds of the Latin-speaking World, in Ireland. The Basilian and the Benedictine rules both bear the impress of the Pachomian rule. They derive from their Egyptian exemplar their insistence on communal life, on discipline, and on work.

Basil's and Benedict's spiritual history resembled the Buddha's. Each started on his ascetic career as an anchorite before he became the founder of a monastic order. Basil's and Benedict's change-over from St. Antony's form of asceticism to Pachom's was their response to their own spiritual experience, and it was also a testimony to Pachom's wisdom. Pachom's creation of the institution of communal monasticism was an extraordinary feat; for, in general, the Egyptians, like the Irish, were attracted more strongly by the anchorite's way of life, and indeed this way has attractions which the communal way does not offer. The anchorite is a law unto himself, and his freedom gives him opportunities for genuine spiritual prowess, though it also exposes him to the risk of lapsing into sterile self-mortification or into egotistic exhibitionism. At all times and places in which asceticism has been practised, an ascetic's fame has usually been proportionate to the degree of his austerity. The communal form of monastic life is less spectacular, and, though the Pachomian monasteries in Upper Egypt rapidly became famous throughout Christendom, the anchorites in the western desert became more famous still. St. Antony was the most celebrated man of his generation at the western end of the Old-World Oikoumenê, and so, in turn, was St. Symeon 'Stylites'—so named because he lived for forty-seven years (412–59) on the top of a pillar. A stylite could excite mass-emotion; but the communal monks' effect on society was deeper and more fruitful.

THE INDIAN CIVILIZATION, 490–647

In most periods of the history of the Indian subcontinent the Indians have felt more concern about religion than about politics and economics. The indigenous Indian record of the subcontinent's history is the copious Indian religious literature. This, however, is difficult to date; even the chronological order of the various genres cannot in all cases be ascertained; and the light thrown by this literature on secular affairs is only incidental and fitful. Our knowledge of secular Indian history is largely dependent on records made by foreign observers: Greeks, Chinese, Muslims, Westerners. It is only within the last century that India has produced a school of Hindu historians who research and write in the modern Western style. Even for the age of the Gupta dynasty, the Chinese Buddhist pilgrim Fa-hsien, who was in India from 401 to 410, is an important source; so, likewise, for the reign of the Emperor Harsha (606–47), is another Chinese Buddhist pilgrim, Hsüan-tsang, who was in India from 635 to 643, though there is also an account of Harsha's reign by an Indian author who, like Hsüan-tsang, was Harsha's contemporary and was also Harsha's subject.

The governing factor in the history of the subcontinent from 455 onwards was the *Völkerwanderung* of the Huns and other Eurasian nomad peoples, for instance the Gurjaras. The first Hun invasion was in 455. This was repulsed by the Gupta Emperor Skandagupta, who had recently come to the throne, but Hun invasions continued, and, under their impact, the Gupta Empire broke up after Skandagupta's death in 480.

In the struggle between the invaders and the peoples previously in possession of the subcontinent there were fluctuations. In 528 the Huns were driven off into Kashmir. But *c.* 558 or 563–7 the Ephthalite Hun Kingdom in the Oxus–Jaxartes basin was overthrown by the concerted action of the Persians and the Turks. The victors partitioned the

Ephthalites' former dominions, and we may guess that the Huns who had already won a footing in India were now reinforced by Ephthalite refugees. At any rate, the sequel makes it clear that the Eurasian nomad invaders of the subcontinent in this *Völkerwanderung* were numerous; for, by at least as early a date as the Muslim Arab conquest of Sind and Multan in 711, northern India was under the rule of a new secular governing class, the Rajputs ('sons of kings'), who appear to have been the nomad invaders' Hinduized descendants.

The invaders had been checked again by the Emperor Harsha's father, who was king of Sthanesvara (Thanesar) on the upper course of the River Jumna. Harsha himself succeeded in re-uniting northern India politically in 606–12. This feat gave northern India a spell of peace during the rest of Harsha's lifetime, but Harsha's Empire was only a simulacrum of the Gupta Empire. Harsha's chief merit was his religious tolerance. He himself was a Saiva, a Sun-worshipper, and a Buddhist.

During the bout of political disunity in northern India after the Emperor Ashoka Maurya's death in 232 B.C., the Deccan had been united politically under the Satavahana (Andhra) dynasty. After the break-up of the Gupta Empire *c.* A.D. 490, it looked as if history were going to repeat itself. *Circa* 543 the Deccan was united politically under the Chalukya dynasty, and in 620 Harsha was defeated by Pulakeshin II Chalukya when Harsha was trying to extend his empire southwards beyond the River Narbada. However, in 642 the Chalukyas themselves were defeated by a rival South-Indian dynasty, the Pallavas, who had established themselves at Kanchi (Conjeeveram) on the east coast of the peninsula. (The Pallavas may have been descended from the Pahlavas, i.e. the Partho-Sakas who had held the Indus basin in the early years of the first century A.D.) For two hundred years after 642, the Deccan continued to be divided between local states whose warfare with each other was inconclusive and chronic.

In southern India during the period *c.* 490–647, the one point of political stability was the Pandya kingdom, which continued to survive in its relatively secluded domain at the peninsula's southern extremity. The one stable cultural feature in the South during the same period was the continued development of literature in the Tamil language, which had originated at an early date in the Christian Era.

The political adversity into which the Indian subcontinent fell after the beginning of the Hun invasions in 455 did not prevent the Indian civilization from continuing to expand beyond its native subcontinent's bounds. The establishment of the Gupta Empire had been accompanied by an intensification of the Indianization of continental South-East Asia and Indonesia. There was a fresh spurt of emigration to these regions from India in the fifth century, and we may guess that the Huns' pressure on India was one of the causes of this. In continental South-East Asia, the Chinese civilization's domain remained confined to what is now North Vietnam. In Tibet in the course of the first half of the seventh century, there was a competition between the Chinese and the Indian civilizations for influence, and the Indian civilization prevailed.

Though Tibet lies close to the original heartland of both the Chinese and the Indian civilizations, it is insulated from them by such formidable physical barriers that it remained almost impervious to influences from either quarter till the early years of the seventh century A.D. Tibet was unified politically for the first time in 607, perhaps in emulation of the political re-unification of China in 589, and in 641 its king, Srong-tan Gampo, married simultaneously a Chinese princess and a Nepalese princess. At that date China was politically in the ascendant. In 639/40 the second emperor of the T'ang dynasty, T'ai Tsung, had embarked on the conquest of the Tarim basin, the country that lies immediately to the north of Tibet. There was a Chinese envoy at Harsha's court at the time of Harsha's death in 647. A usurper seized Harsha's throne and maltreated the envoy and his suite. Thereupon, the Chinese envoy escaped to Nepal, which was then under the suzerainty of Tibet, and, at the envoy's instances, King Srong-tan Gampo of Tibet invaded India, defeated and captured the usurper, and sent him as a prisoner to China. However, the Indian civilization captivated Tibet by creating for the Tibetan language a script in an Indian style. This script, not the Chinese characters, was then employed for translating Sanskrit texts of the Mahayana Buddhist scriptures into Tibetan, and these translations anchored Tibet to India culturally. Thenceforward, Chinese cultural influence, though never absent in Tibet, was never paramount there.

[47]

THE POLITICAL DISRUPTION OF CHINA AND HER RECEPTION OF BUDDHISM, 220–589

WHEN the Emperor Han Wu-ti (ruled 140–87 B.C.) gave a monopoly of posts in the Chinese imperial public service to Confucian scholars selected by competitive examination, he had intended, as has been noted in Chapter 35, to throw the public service open to intellectual talent. The consequence, however, had been to enable the Confucian scholar-administrators to misuse their power by acquiring extensive private property in land. The founder of the Chinese Empire, Ch'in Shih Hwang-ti, and its second founder, Han Liu P'ang (Kao-tsu), had liquidated the feudal aristocracy of the Age of the Warring States because they had recognized that, if large landowners were allowed to survive, they would compete with the newly established unitary government of China for appropriating the 'surplus' product of the Chinese peasantry, which was the main source of revenue in China so long as her economy was predominantly agricultural. In making themselves into large-scale landowners, Han Wu-ti's scholar-administrators had re-created a social class of subjects who were powerful enough to challenge the ruler even of a unified Chinese state.

The administrator-landlords' combination of powers was formidable. They were able to divert the major part of the peasantry's surplus into their own pockets as rent, instead of collecting for the Government its proper share of this fund in the form of taxes and corvées. The administrator-landlords' pursuit of their private interests at the expense of their public duty had brought the Western Han Dynasty to grief in A.D. 9. Wang Mang had tried and failed to vindicate the rights of the Imperial Government and the peasantry, whose interests, in opposition to the administrator-landlords' interests, were identical. The Eastern Han dynasty had merely re-established the regime that had been the ruin of the Western Han. This regime had been given a respite by the depopulation of China during the civil disorders of A.D. 18–36, but eventually the

Empire's continuing social malady had brought the Eastern Han dynasty to grief in its turn.

The break-up of the Empire in 220–2 into three successor-states of the Eastern Han aggravated China's social sickness. Her still unsolved agrarian problem was now made even more intractable by chronic civil war. In 265–80 China was re-unified. One of the three warring local states conquered the other two. But the new Imperial dynasty, which had taken the name Chin, failed, as signally as its predecessors, to solve the agrarian problem. Consequently it fell to pieces in 290, and, in and after 304, northern China was invaded and conquered by war-bands of pastoral nomad barbarians from the eastern end of the Eurasian steppe. It is surprising that this catastrophe did not overtake China sooner.

The condition of China in the third century A.D. resembled the contemporary condition of the Graeco-Roman World. In China, as in the Mediterranean basin, there was a spiritual vacuum. Confucianism had been discredited by the Confucian civil servants' misuse of power. Their self-seeking had twice condemned the Imperial Government to break down. In the closing years of the second century, when the Eastern Han regime had been in its death-agonies, a sophisticated minority had turned away from Confucianism to the rival Taoist philosophy, while the masses had looked for salvation to a nominally Taoist popular religion. But the peasant revolts inspired and led by popular Taoism had been crushed by war-lords, commanding private professional armies, who became the founders of 'the Three Kingdoms', and the philosophical Taoists had discredited themselves, not, like their Confucian rivals, by abusing power, but by shirking the responsibility of assuming power. They preferred to withdraw into a frivolous enjoyment of private life. In taking this negative line, they were being true to the Taoist tradition. At its origin in the Age of the Warring States, Taoism had deprecated practical economic and political activity. Its ideal had been the social simplicity of the Pre-Civilizational Age.

This negative philosophy did not meet the Chinese intellectuals' spiritual needs either in the fourth century B.C. or in the third century A.D. What China needed in the third century A.D. was a solution of her agrarian problem or, failing this, a more satisfying spiritual asylum than Taoism could provide for defeatists. In the fifth century the agrarian problem was at last tackled effectively by the T'o-pa, one of the war-bands of barbarian invaders who had founded a state in northern China in the name of the Wei dynasty. Meanwhile, in and after the third century, the spiritual vacuum in China was being filled by Mahayana Buddhism, as it was contemporaneously being filled in the Graeco-Roman World by Christianity.

Since the second century the Mahayana had been seeping into

north-western China from the Oxus–Jaxartes basin via the Tarim basin. The Eastern Han had re-occupied both the Tarim basin and Farghanah in the upper basin of the Jaxartes in A.D. 73; their control over these Central Asian territories had been disputed by the Kushans, who in A.D. 48 had established an empire that straddled the Hindu Kush. The Kushan and Eastern Han Empires were in direct contact with each other for at least a century till, in the latter part of the second century, both empires lost their grip. The century of contact included the reign (A.D. 120–44) of the Kushan Emperor Kanishka, who was a patron of the Mahayana, and the contact was not continuously hostile. The Sino-Kushan war-path was also the silk-road from Loyang to Soghd and the Mahayana's road in the reverse direction from Soghd to Loyang. China and Transoxania had, indeed, been in touch with each other inter-mittently ever since 128 B.C., the year in which Han Wu-ti's envoy, Chang Ch'ien, had tracked down in Transoxania the Kushans' Yüeh-chih ancestors.

In the second and third centuries A.D. the physical road for the Mahayana's entry into China lay open. The Buddhist missionaries were zealous; their prospective Chinese converts were spiritually hungry and were therefore receptive. The limiting factor was not physical; it was mental. The Chinese and the Indian minds, languages, and scripts were poles apart; and, in each of these two worlds, the civilization's distinc-tive mentality, language, and script were closely interrelated. By this date, Chinese had already become an uninflected monosyllabic langu-age, and the 'characters' in which this language was conveyed were something more than just a script; they were the apt expression of the Chinese attitude to life. Anything presented in the 'characters' comes out in them terse and concrete; but Indian thought is abstract and diffuse, and the neo-Sanskrit language, which was the original vehicle of the Mahayana Buddhist scriptures, is polysyllabic and highly inflected.

The earliest translators of these scriptures are said to have gone to such lengths in transposing the Sanskrit texts into Chinese terms that the product ceased to be recognizably Buddhist without becoming intelli-gible to Chinese readers. One translator who worked at Loyang during the latter part of the second century was a Parthian prince who is known to us only by his Chinese name An Shih-kao. One of the best qualified translators was Kumarajiva (344–413). His father was an Indian and his mother a native of Kucha in the Tarim basin, where at that date the local language was, like Sanskrit, Indo-European. Kumarajiva had studied Sarvastivadin Buddhism in Kashmir, as well as Mahayanian Buddhism in Kashghar and in his native city Kucha, before being taken prisoner by a Chinese raiding party *c.* 382. From Kansu, where he was first held, Kumarajiva reached Ch'ang-an in 401, and there, within the next eight years, he translated a huge corpus of scripture with the aid of a large staff of specialists.

Some of the translators were Chinese. In the course of the fifth, sixth, and seventh centuries, a number of Chinese Buddhist pilgrims made their way, overland or by sea, to India, learned Sanskrit there, acquired manuscripts of the Mahayana scriptures, and translated these from Sanskrit into Chinese after coming back home. Two famous Chinese pilgrim-translators were Fa-hsien, who was abroad from 399 to 414, and Hsüan-tsang, who was abroad from 629 to 645. Their visits to India have been mentioned in the previous chapter.

Thanks to the translators, Chinese Buddhists gradually acquired Chinese texts of the Mahayana scriptures which reproduced the sense of the Sanskrit originals. Yet the forms of the Mahayana that struck root in China at the popular level were virtually new creations of a distinctively Chinese kind. One of these was the 'Pure hand' school that offered salvation by faith in the bodhisattva Amitabha. Another was the Ch'an school (in Sanskrit Dhyana, in Japanese Zen), which offered enlightenment through meditation. These two schools were founded by Chinese contemporaries of Kumarajiva. The Sinifiers of the Mahayana made a greater mark than the conscientious translators.

For the Chinese, Buddhist practice was at least as exotic as Buddhist thought. Monasteries and, *a fortiori*, hermits were unknown in China before the introduction of Buddhism. The Taoist philosophy was the nearest indigenous Chinese approach to Buddhism. The Taoists deprecated the rise of civilization and stayed aloof from public affairs, but their ideal was not otherworldly; what they prescribed was merely a reversion from a technologically sophisticated society to the relatively simple life of a self-contained Neolithic village. Yet the first translators of Buddhist scriptures into Chinese drew largely on Taoist terminology for want of any other that would have come nearer to expressing Buddhist ideas in Chinese language. The Taoists (both philosophical and popular), on their side, began to borrow ideas and institutions from Buddhism in order to hold their own against it now that it had established itself in China. The relation between the two religions—or the two philosophies—was ambivalent. Their respective adherents were in competition with each other because they were conscious of their affinity with each other.

Evidently Buddhism would have had little prospect of gaining an entry into China if, at the time, China had not happened to be at the climax of a long period of failure to solve the agrarian problem that was crucial for Chinese society and government. The penalties for this failure had been political disruption followed by barbarian invasion. For three hundred years, beginning in A.D. 185, the Chinese of all classes were in a chastened mood in which they were readier than they usually were to look to a foreign religion for salvation. But in northern China the popular Taoists and the Confucians joined forces in campaigns for curbing Buddhism whenever there was a turn for the better in the social and political situation. At their instance, Buddhist institutions were placed under governmental surveillance through the agency of a clerical bureaucracy modelled on the Confucian secular civil service, and attempts to curtail Buddhist activities were made in 438, 446–52, and 574–8.

The political fragmentation, fratricidal warfare, economic collapse, and social chaos went to greater extremes in northern China in the fourth century than in the western provinces of the Roman Empire in the fifth century. Yet the barbarian successor-states of the Western Chin, like those of the West Roman Empire, prospered only in so far as the conquerors succeeded in assimilating the civilization of their subjects; and, in northern China, both the Chinese peasantry and the Chinese large landowners were tenacious. They held on to the agricultural land and kept it under cultivation, in spite of their subjugation by pastoral nomads, and the Confucian tradition survived the impact of Buddhism, in spite of being discredited by the misconduct of the deposed Confucian administrator-landlords.

Northern China was re-unified by the T'o-pa, a perhaps Mongol people who, in 338, had established a local successor-state of the Western Chin dynasty to the north-west of the great northern bend of the Yellow River. In 386 the T'o-pa royal family assumed the dynastic name Northern Wei. By 439 the T'o-pa (Wei) had extinguished all other barbarian states in northern China. At least five times in the course of the first half of the fifth century they even managed to invade the Tarim basin. In 493–4 the T'o-pa (Northern Wei) Emperor Hsiao Wen-ti (ruled 471–99) moved his capital from its original location in northern Shansi to Loyang. At about the same date he systematically Sinified his tribesmen, and assimilated the status of the tribal chiefs to that of the major Chinese landowners in the Wei dynasty's dominions. This forcible Sinification of the T'o-pa by their own ruling house, followed by the final failure of the Wei dynasty's successive attempts to conquer southern China, led to the overthrow of the dynasty and the disruption of its Empire, but northern China was reunited again in 377, and in 381 it was taken over by the founder of the Sui dynasty, the Emperor Sui Wen-ti (ruled 581–604), who did succeed in 589 in re-uniting the whole of China by conquering the South.

Though the Wei dynasty had failed to re-unify China, they bequeathed to the Sui and the T'ang a solution of the agrarian problem. In 485 the remarkable Hsiao Wen-ti undertook to provide a land-holding of a minimum size for every able-bodied adult peasant. He also made associations of peasants collectively responsible for the payment of taxes. Hsiao Wen-ti did not venture to take the further step of setting a maximum for the size of the large landowners' estates; but at least he checked the expansion of the large estates at the expense of the peasants' holdings and of the Imperial Government's revenues. Between 535 and 581 the Northern Wei dynasty's successors also strengthened both the peasantry and the government by organizing a trained peasant militia. This rehabilitation of the peasantry in northern China was the prelude to the political re-unification of North and South and to the rejuvenation of the Chinese civilization.

The China that was re-united politically in 589 differed greatly in the geographical distribution of both its population and its resources from the united China that had been invaded by the northern barbarians in and after 304. The original nucleus of the Chinese civilization was the lower basin of the Yellow River and the valley of its right-bank tributary the Wei. In the Age of the Shang and the Western Chou dynasties, China had included only the northern fringe of the basin of the Hwai River and no part at all of the huge basin of the Yangtse. However, in the course of the ensuing Age of the Warring States, the peoples in-habiting the Hwai basin, the lower Yangtse basin, and the highlands to the south-east of the lower Yangtse basin had, one after another, become Sinified and, concomitantly, had come to play an active part in Chinese international politics. The first political unifier of China, Ch'in Shih Hwang-ti, had annexed the whole of the South of present-day China, and also present-day North Vietnam, and the annexation of North Vietnam to China had been confirmed in 111 B.C. by Han Wu-ti. Only a coastal enclave of Yüeh had remained politically independent. How-ever, even the former territories of Ch'u and Wu states had remained culturally backward, and the vast territories to the south and south-west of these had remained sparsely populated and agriculturally un-developed.

The barbarian invasions of northern China that started in 304 set in motion a movement, on an unprecedentedly large scale, to colonize the South and to open it up economically. Though, in the North, the Chinese peasants and large landowners held their ground in sufficient strength to be able to Sinify their barbarian conquerors and re-unify the whole of China eventually, there was a massive migration from North to South in the course of the years 304–589. In 317 a refugee branch of the Chin dynasty (the 'Eastern Chin') re-established the Chin Empire in the South, behind the protective swamps and waterways in the lower basins of the Hwai and the Yangtse, which baffled the barbarians still more effectively than the miniature swamp round Ravenna and the lagoon round the Venetian islands at the opposite end of the Old-World Oikoumenê.

The lower basins of the Rivers Hwai and Yangtse make highly productive rice-paddies when drained and irrigated. Much of the country on either side of the watershed between the Yangtse basin and the south-eastern and southern coasts of present-day China is hilly; some of it is mountainous; but the whole of the south receives ample rainfall, and therefore its inhabitants do not live under threat of famine produced by drought—in contrast to the inhabitants of even the fertile loess country in northern China. Moreover, the native population of the South was, for the most part, easy to subdue and to assimilate—in contrast to northern China's pastoral nomad neighbours. The Roman Empire had, in its north-western provinces, an economic equivalent of the Chinese Empire's southern provinces. North-Western Europe offered to the Levant large reserves of fertile well-watered land, but this region had been hard for the Romans to conquer, and it proved still harder for them to defend eventually against barbarian invaders. The East Roman Emperor Justinian I had tried, from 533 to 561, to re-unite the Roman Empire from a Levantine base of operations; but his success had been only partial and ephemeral, and the price had been ruinous for the Levant and still more for Italy.

From 317 to 589 southern China was held by five imperial dynasties in succession. They fended off the northern barbarians and they maintained their hold over the whole of the South, including even present-day North Vietnam. In 589 the Chinese Empire was re-united at a comparatively low cost, and in this re-united China there was a southward shift of both the demographic and the agricultural centres of gravity. The rice-paddies of the South now began to replace the millet-fields and wheat-fields of the North as the principal source of food supply for the imperial capital of a re-united China and indeed for the whole of China's population.

The long period of disorder and disunity in China had not discredited the Chinese civilization, nor had it checked its spread beyond China's own borders. The barbarian invasion of northern China in and after A.D. 304 gave the Koreans the opportunity of destroying, in 313, the Chinese colonial outpost that the Emperor Han Wu-ti had planted in Korea after his conquests there in 109–108 B.C. In the north-western corner of Korea, this outpost had survived throughout the intervening four centuries. Korea was now divided among three indigenous states, apart from a beach-head on the south coast that was held by the Japanese. However, the northernmost of the three Korean states, Koguryo, adopted Buddhism in its Chinese form in 372, and also Sinified its administrative system at about the same date.

The Japanese Empire, with its centre in Yamato (in the south-western corner of the main island, Honshu), was in existence and was already expanding by the third century A.D. Chinese cultural influences had been seeping into Japan since perhaps as early as the third century B.C., and in the fifth and sixth centuries A.D. this influence was intensified by an extensive immigration into Japan of Koreans who claimed to be of Chinese descent. Whether or not these were truly descended from the Han-Age Chinese settlers in Korea, they certainly brought Chinese civilization with them. The Japanese were acquainted with the Chinese characters as early as the fifth century A.D. By that date the Chinese civilization introduced via Korea into Japan included Buddhism, and the Japanese adopted the Chinese version of the Mahayana in its Korean form in the course of the half century ending in A.D. 587. They did not begin to borrow Chinese political institutions till after 589, when the political re-unification of China had been followed by the rehabilitation of the administrative regime that had been inaugurated in China by Han Wu-ti.

[48]

THE MESO-AMERICAN AND
ANDEAN CIVILIZATIONS, *c.* 300–900

FOR this period, as for the period from *c.* 400 B.C. to A.D. 300, Meso-American chronology is more or less convincingly established; at any rate there is a consensus about it among archaeologists. There is likewise a consensus about the relative chronological order of the various phases of the Andean civilization, but the absolute dating is in dispute for the eighteen centuries and a half of Andean history running from the end of the Chavín horizon *c.* 400 B.C. to the establishment of the Inca Empire *c.* A.D. 1438. Radiocarbon tests (to date, perhaps too few to be trustworthy) date the 'Florescent' phase of the Andean civilization *c.* 300 B.C. to A.D. 500 and the ensuing Tiahuanáco horizon *c.* A.D. 500 to 1000. A reckoning based on stratigraphy dates the 'Florescent' phase *c.* A.D. 400 to 1000 and the Tiahuanáco horizon *c.* A.D. 1000 to *c.* 1300. In the present chapter, as in Chapter 39, it is assumed that the dating indicated by the radiocarbon tests is approximately correct; that, *c.* A.D. 300, the 'Florescent' phase of Andean history was nearing its close; and that the greater part of the time-span of the Tiahuanáco horizon falls within the years A.D. 500–900.

In the Meso-American World, the 'Classic' phase was at its zenith *c.* A.D. 300–600. During those three centuries, Teotihuacán city was still flourishing, and the Mayan variety of the Meso-American civilization had already established itself not only in the central Maya area but in Yucatán as well. Teotihuacán was so dominant culturally, during these three centuries, over all three Maya areas—Yucatán, the central area, and the highlands—that it has been inferred that Teotihuacán must also have exercised some political control over the whole Maya region. One of the 'Classic' Maya ceremonial centres that had been established in Yucatán before 600 is Oxkintok in western Yucatán, and the style of the monuments there is Teotihuacán, not Maya. On the other hand, the ceremonial centre at Cobá, in eastern Yucatán, which was also founded before 600, is directly inspired by the 'Classic' monuments of the central Maya area.

Circa 600, Teotihuacán was suddenly destroyed by violence. (There is no archaeological evidence for the identity of the destroyers, but we may guess that, like later destroyers of civilization in southern Mexico, they were barbarian invaders from the deserts of northern Mexico.) At Cholúla the influence of Teotihuacán can be detected in the earliest of the four successive layers of the man-made mountain, but the later layers have an independent style of their own. Cholúla is relatively close to Teotihuacán; farther afield in the Meso-American World, the influence of Teotihuacán likewise ceases *c.* 600. Cholúla, in its turn, was overwhelmed *c.* 800, and its conquerors are known to have been northern barbarians.

The Maya were not involved in the catastrophes that, farther north, overtook Teotihuacán and Cholúla successively; but in the ninth century the 'Classic' sites in the central Maya area were abandoned, one after another. The cause of this is undiscovered, and it is the greatest enigma of Meso-American history. Whereas there is evidence that Teotihuacán was destroyed violently by unknown hands, there is no clue to the cause of the abandonment of Tikál, Uaxactún, and the numerous other magnificent ceremonial centres of the 'Classic' period in the central Maya area. Among the most striking works of 'Classic' Maya art are the brilliant, though gruesome, murals at the site to the west of the Usumacinta River, about half way down its course, that the archaeologists have labelled 'Bonampák'. These murals were painted in the early ninth century, i.e. just before the abandonment of the central Maya area began.

Since the scenes painted at 'Bonampák' represent the Assyrian-like atrocities committed against prisoners of war by the victor, these murals, taken by themselves, would suggest that the 'Classic' Maya communities in the central area ruined themselves by indulging in venomous fratricidal warfare. Yet the deserted 'Classic' sites in this area show no signs of the deliberate destruction for which we have archaeological evidence at San Lorenzo, La Venta, Teotihuacán, and Cholúla. In the central Maya area, the evidence for the abandonment of sites in the course of the ninth century is negative. The key is the discontinuation, at one site after another, of the 'Classic' practice of erecting a series of dating-stelae. The most convincing alternative guess (and it is no more than that) is that the peasants lost faith in the ability of the 'establishment' to make the Universe work—in particular, by inducing the rain-god to bring sufficient rain to produce satisfactory harvests. A disillusioned peasantry may have cut off the 'establishment's' supplies of food and may have refused to go on performing the arduous corvée labour needed for maintaining the great monuments and adding to them. Yet, if this is the explanation of the abandonment of the 'Classic' sites in the central Maya area, it does not explain why the Maya version of the Meso-American civilization survived—as it did, in a degenerate and eventually hybrid form—in parched and stony Yucatán.

According to both the alternative chronologies of Andean history, the 'Florescent' Age outlived the year 500. According to the chronology based on stratigraphy, not on radiocarbon tests, it ran from *c.* 400 to 1000 and was thus approximately contemporary with the 'Classic' Age of the Meso-American civilization. Since the chronology indicated by radiocarbon tests is being adopted provisionally in this book, a sketch of the Andean civilization's 'Florescent' phase has been included already in Chapter 39, and a sketch of the Tiahuanáco-Huári horizon must now be given here, though it is possible that the whole of this phase of Andean history may be later than the present chapter's lower chronological limit.

The Tiahuanáco-Huári horizon resembles the ancient Chavín horizon in originating in the highlands (in the later of the two cases, in two different highland localities). The later horizon, too, spread from its highland starting-point to other parts of the highlands and also to parts of the coastal plain. Another common feature of these two Andean horizons is that each of them is identifiable by a distinctive motif in its visual art which looks like the emblem of a missionary religion. However, there is evidence, lacking for the Chavín culture, that the Tiahuanáco culture was imposed on coastal Peru by violence.

Tiahuanáco itself stands about thirteen miles to the south-east of the south-eastern end of Lake Titicáca. It seems to have been a non-urban ceremonial centre. Its massive masonry is grander than that of contemporary Huári and of ancient Chavín. The Tiahuanáco style seems to have been created at Tiahuanáco itself during the 'Florescent' Age, though it did not spread to other parts of Peru till after the close of the 'Florescent' Age. If the spread of the Tiahuanáco culture to the coast was achieved by conquest, this may have been one of the events that brought the 'Florescent' Age to an end.

THE PROPHET AND STATESMAN
MUHAMMAD, *c.* 570–632

ISLAM was created by the genius of the Prophet Muhammad in conjunction with the history of Arabia. Since the domestication of the
Arabian camel, nearly 2,000 years before Muhammad's day, Arabia
had been traversible, and ideas and institutions had been seeping into
the peninsula from the Fertile Crescent that adjoins it on the north. The
effect of this infiltration had been cumulative, and, by Muhammad's
time, the accumulated charge of spiritual force in Arabia was ready to
explode. Yet it might not have found vent if Muhammad had not arisen
to direct it. Conversely, if Muhammad had been born before the time
had become ripe in Arabia, even his vision, determination, and sagacity
might have been defeated.

The Arabian Peninsula is a subcontinent. Its area is of the same order
of magnitude as that of the continent's Indian and European peninsulas.
But, unlike these two, the Arabian Peninsula is arid, except for the highlands in its south-western corner (the Yemen and Asir), which catch the
monsoons, and are replicas of the Eritrean-Abyssinian highlands in
present-day Ethiopia, on the African side of the Red Sea. Muhammad's
home-town, Mecca, stands at a relatively low altitude in the highlands
overhanging the Red-Sea coast of Arabia, just out of range of the monsoons. Mecca is not rainless; it is made habitable by a perennial spring;
but its water-supply is too scanty to allow an urban population to make
its living by agriculture or even by animal husbandry, which, until
within living memory, was the sole source of livelihood for the population of the greater part of the habitable three-quarters of Arabia. An
urban community round the spring at Mecca must live by trade, and
this trade must be protected by some religious sanction against the
pastoral nomads' temptation to take an excessive toll from the urban
merchants' caravans.

Since the domestication of the camel, the Yemen had been linked

with Palestine and Syria by an overland route. This route runs through
Mecca; and, when a sanctuary (the Ka'bah) had been founded near the
spring at Mecca and had gained prestige, the Meccans could make
profits by holding an annual fair to which traders who were also pilgrims could resort during a truce that could be relied upon because it
would be sacrilege to break it.

Though the population of Arabia was, and is, sparse, it has always
been numerous in the aggregate, because of the vastness of the peninsula
and the healthiness of the steppe that slopes down gradually from the
western highlands to the Arabian shore of the Persian Gulf and to
the Euphrates valley. In Arabia, Nature was niggardly to Man till, in the
twentieth century, Man tapped the mineral oil beneath the surface. Till
then, Arabia's inhabitants, outside the Yemen, were always hungry, and
the gradual seepage of civilization into Arabia on camel-back has been
accompanied by eruptions of population out of Arabia.

All the Semitic languages have originated in Arabia and have been
propagated, outside Arabia, by *Völkerwanderungen* of emigrants from the
peninsula. A Yemenite Semitic language was introduced into the
Eritrean-Abyssinian highlands at an unknown date. The Akkadian
language was introduced into the Tigris–Euphrates basin, the Canaanite
language into Palestine and Syria, and then successively the Amorite
and Aramaic languages into both horns of the Fertile Crescent before
Arabic-speaking migrants began to follow in the tracks of earlier Semitic-
speakers. In the eighth century B.C. the first recorded eruption of Arabs
from Arabia was repulsed by the Assyrians. In the second century B.C.
the Seleucid monarchy failed to repulse a second eruption of Arabs, and
this time the Arab migrants made permanent lodgments in Syria and
Mesopotamia. The titanic eruption that followed Muhammad's death
in A.D. 632, and a subsequent eruption in the eleventh century, have
swamped the Fertile Crescent and northern Africa. Today, Aramaic's
derivative, Syriac, the Arabic language's immediate predecessor in the
Fertile Crescent, is almost extinct there; Coptic, which is descended
from the Pharaonic Egyptian language, is extinct in Egypt, except for
its liturgical use; in North-West Africa, the native Berber language is
being confined, by the advance of Arabic, to natural fastnesses in the
highlands and the desert.

The counter-movement of institutions and ideas into the peninsula
had also become intensive by Muhammad's time. A trinity of goddesses
that had been worshipped in the second and third centuries A.D. at
Hatra in north-eastern Mesopotamia and in the oasis of Palmyra, at the
northern extremity of the Arabian desert, had also found its way into the
Hejaz (the north-west Arabian highlands). Judaism, perhaps first
introduced by refugees from the Romano–Jewish wars of A.D. 66–70 and

132–5, had won converts in the Hejaz in the oases of Tayma', Khaybar, and Yathrib (Medina, 'the city' of the Prophet Muhammad) and also in the Yemen. Christianity had also won converts in the Yemen. In the sixth century A.D. the Yemen had also been drawn into the commercial and political competition between the East Roman and the Persian Empire. From some date before 523 and again from *c.* 528 to *c.* 571 the Yemen was under the rule of the Kingdom of Aksum, which was Christian and was consequently the East Roman Empire's satellite; from *c.* 571 to 630 the Yemen was under Persian rule. At some date in the third quarter of the sixth century an Aksumite viceroy of the Yemen tried to march on Mecca.

Muhammad's lifetime, *c.* 570–632, covered the time-span of the two last and most exhausting of the Romano–Persian Wars, waged in 572–91 and 604–28. Each empire had already enlisted Arabs to serve as wardens of its marches confronting the rival empire. The capital of the Persian Empire's Arab march was Hirah, near the future site of the Muslim Arab cantonment at Kufah. The Ghassanid Arab dynasty guarded the East Roman Empire's marches in Syria. In the Romano–Persian wars, Arabs served both belligerents as mercenaries. These gained not only pay but also military training and experience, and they spent part of their pay on equipment—for instance, on buying cuirasses and on breeding war-horses. The excellent Arab breed was a *tour de force*; in Arabia it was, and is, a parasite on the domesticated camel; beyond the bounds of Arabia after Muhammad's death, the Arab horse carried Arab conquerors to the Loire and the Volga and the Jaxartes.

Thus, by Muhammad's time, the civilizations of the Levant and Iran were closing in on Mecca from all directions, and Muhammad himself went out to meet the civilization of the East Roman Empire. When the Arabs were not serving the East Romans and the Persians as mercenary soldiers, they did business with them as traders. Muhammad himself conducted caravans from Mecca to Damascus and back as the employee of his future wife, a Meccan businesswoman, Khadijah. The most probable dates of his journeys are the peace-years between 591 and 604. After the Persian Emperor Khusro II had started to invade and occupy successively Mesopotamia and Syria and Palestine and Egypt, Meccan trade with the East Roman Empire must have become precarious. The date of Muhammad's first experience of receiving a message from God is *c.* 610. By then he was married to Khadijah and was a householder in Mecca.

Muhammad's religious experience took the form of epiphanies of the Archangel Gabriel. Muhammad heard Gabriel dictate words to him and heard him command him to transmit these words to his Meccan fellow-townsmen. At first Muhammad was unsure of the authoritativeness of these experiences and was shy of acting on them, but, since the experiences were persistent and the commands imperative, Muhammad eventually believed and complied. The heart of the message transmitted by Muhammad was that there was only one true God, *the* God (Allah, an equivalent of the Syriac-speaking Christians' word for God, Alaha). Monotheism was in the air in Arabia at this date, as it had been in the Roman Empire during the century that had ended in Constantine I's conversion to Christianity in 312. According to Muhammad's message, God's first and foremost demand from Man was self-surrender (Islam). One of his particular commandments was that the rich and powerful should practise charity towards the poor and the weak—for instance, widows and orphans. When Muhammad became convinced of the authenticity of his mission, he spoke, as Jesus had spoken, 'as one having authority'.

The message was as unwelcome at Mecca as it had been at Nazareth. Mecca was an oligarchically-governed oasis-state whose oligarchs, the Banu Quraysh, made their living by trade, like the Palmyrene oligarchs in the second and third centuries A.D. They were efficient and ruthless practitioners of economic private enterprise; they were aware that the success of their business was dependent on the prestige of their sanctuary; they feared that, if Muhammad's call for monotheism were to prevail, the Ka'bah, which housed a pantheon, would forfeit its prestige and that then Meccan trade would suffer from the discrediting of its indispensable religious sanction. The Quraysh may have been further offended by Muhammad's authoritative tone; for, though he was a Qurayshite, he was not a member of the inner circle of the Qurayshite 'establishment'.

For twelve years Muhammad preached at Mecca at his peril. He made a few converts, and these too were in such peril that at last Muhammad authorized them to take refuge in the Christian kingdom of Aksum. In 622 Muhammad's fortunes took a dramatic turn for the better. Envoys from the agricultural oasis-state Yathrib had surprisingly invited him to emigrate to Yathrib and to take over its government. Yathrib was being torn by political dissensions which the Yathribites themselves had failed to overcome. In 622 Muhammad escaped from Mecca with one companion, Abu Bakr. The fugitives eluded pursuit, and, at Yathrib, Muhammad carried out his political mission brilliantly. The Yathribites had diagnosed his ability correctly. Though, so far, his administrative experience had been limited to the management of a small persecuted religious sect, he proved fully equal to the new occasion. In his larger field for administration as the ruler of Yathrib by invitation, Muhammad reconciled the Yathribite factions with each other and with the Meccan converts to Islam who came to join him at Yathrib.

The non-Jewish majority of the Yathribites seem to have become Muslims readily, and their common new religion was an effective bond between the natives and the refugees.

Sovereign states go to war, and Muhammad, now that he had become a ruler, did not hesitate to make war on his Meccan kinsmen. Muhammad's political situation was different from that of Jesus when Jesus had submitted to being arrested. Jesus was a subject of the Roman Empire, and if he had become a rebel his revolt would have cost many Jewish lives, without having any prospect of achieving a military victory. Muhammad did have a possibility of winning, and he won; but his success as a ruler and a belligerent had the same consequences for Islam that Constantine I's conversion had for Christianity. It implicated the religion in politics and in war.

At Yathrib Muhammad was well placed strategically for making war on Mecca, since Yathrib lies on the overland route between Mecca and Syria. Muhammad looted Meccan caravans, even in the annual truce-months. In 630 Mecca capitulated. Muhammad gave his Qurayshite tribesmen lenient terms, and he made the fortune of the Ka'bah and the pilgrimage by incorporating them in the institutions of Islam. By 632, the year of his death, his government's sovereignty was acknowledged throughout Arabia, up to the southern bounds of the pasturelands of those Arab tribes that paid allegiance to either the East Roman or the Persian Empire. One of the conditions of political submission to Muhammad's state was conversion to Islam, but this was in most cases perfunctory—not least at Mecca. Muhammad's wars between 622 and 632 were minute compared to the contemporaneous Romano–Persian war of 604–28, but the combined effect of the great war in the north and the little wars in Arabia was immense in the sequel.

The provision of opportunities for winning loot was one of the means by which Muhammad kept his heterogeneous body politic united and loyal. The Meccans were the first victims of the Muslim community's appetite for loot; the spoliation of the Jewish clans at Yathrib, and later of the Khaybar Jews as well, was still more lucrative.

Muhammad knew that the Jews and the Christians were 'People of the Book', i.e. that they had scriptures containing information and commandments which, so they believed and as Muhammad took on trust from them, were revelations made by God. Muhammad believed that the Koran which was being dictated to him was God's latest revelation—a definitive revelation addressed particularly to the Arabs, and therefore in Arabic. Since monotheism was the fundamental truth revealed in the Koran, as well as in the Jewish scriptures and the Gospel, it was reasonable for Muhammad to expect to receive the sympathy and support of those Arab clans at Yathrib that had embraced Judaism.

Muhammad was being naive, however, if he expected the Jews of Yathrib to abandon their Judaism for Islam on the ground that the Koran was the book in which God was giving his revelation to Arabic-speakers. Muhammad cannot have been unaware that the Jews had persistently declined to abandon Judaism for Christianity.

The Yathribite Jews did not respond, as the Yathribite pagans did, to Muhammad's call to them to become Muslims, but the Jews were needlessly and recklessly tactless. They pointed out that the Koran made a number of mistakes in its references to information given in the Torah. These mistakes were gross but they were innocuous, and, for Muhammad, the rebuff was wounding and damaging. His retort was savage, out of all proportion to the measure of the Jews' offence, and it was also unprincipled. The Yathribite Jews were a minority and they were rich. Muhammad gave the Muslim majority of the Yathribite community a free hand to despoil the Yathribite Jews and to evict them. The last batch of Muhammad's Yathribite victims were not even allowed to depart beggared but in peace. They were not only robbed; the men were massacred and the women and children were enslaved.

Thus robbery, war, and massacre were among the means by which Muhammad won his victory for Islam. The same crimes have been committed by Christians and, less frequently, also by Buddhists, and in the Jewish scriptures they are attributed to Moses and to Joshua. But at least the founders of Buddhism and Christianity did not set their followers these bad examples.

[50]

THE EXPANSION OF THE
ISLAMIC STATE, 633–750

WHEN Muhammad died it seemed doubtful whether either Islam or the Islamic state would survive. The Arabs' conclusion from Muhammad's success had been the same as Muhammad's own, and this had been identical with Constantine I's conclusion from his victory in 312. The God who had given this success to a human adherent of his had demonstrated that no other god was a match for him in power. In the Old-World Oikoumenê to the west of India there were no atheists either in the fourth or in the seventh century A.D., though there were also perhaps few theists there in that age whose conception of God's, or the gods', nature and behaviour was not crude. Muhammad's converts and subjects were convinced that Muhammad's god Allah was almighty, but they were irked by the duties—for instance, prayer and alms-giving (i.e. taxation)—that were laid upon them by Islam. In Arabia outside Yathrib and Mecca, the reaction to the news of Muhammad's death was a widespread revolt under the leadership of local prophets and prophetesses who claimed to have won Allah's favour for their own people.

This revolt was successfully overcome by Yathrib's and Mecca's combined forces. The Yathribites fought to retain for their oasis the privilege of being the capital of an empire—a privilege that Yathrib had acquired in virtue of its having become 'the city' (of the Prophet). Those Meccans who had not emigrated to Medina fought to preserve Mecca's economically valuable sanctuary and pilgrimage which Muhammad had incorporated in the institutions of Islam. The insurgents were defeated by the ability of the Quraysh. In 633 the Quraysh proved, like their Palmyrene forerunners in 260, to be as able in unfamiliar fields—government, generalship, and diplomacy—as they were in their ancestral commercial business. Some of the Quraysh who saved the situation for Islam and for the Islamic state in 633 had been late and reluctant converts: Khalid b. al-Walid, the most dynamic of the infant

Islamic state's military captains and Mu'awiyah b. Abu Sufyan, Muhammad's fifth successor in the headship of the Islamic state, are examples. Even so, the combined power of Medina and Mecca might not have been strong enough to re-subdue the rest of Arabia if the dead Prophet's Khalifah (Caliph, 'successor'), Abu Bakr, had not opened up for the insurgents an attractive alternative to rebellion.

Either on his own initiative or at the suggestion of the Islamic state's informal steering committee by which he had been elected, Abu Bakr invited the insurgents to turn their arms, under the Islamic state's leadership, against the two empires that adjoined Arabia on the north. Both empires had emerged exhausted from the deadly Romano–Persian war of 604–28; they would be an easy prey for an assault delivered by the united forces of the whole of Arabia; and, though both empires were now economically ruined in the eyes of their own subjects, they were still a rich prize in Arab eyes. Abu Bakr was here taking his cue from Muhammad himself. He was soliciting loyalty by rewarding it with opportunities for acquiring loot—for which the poverty-stricken Arabs had an insatiable appetite. This combination of allurement with coercion succeeded in deflecting the Arab insurgents from rebellion to foreign conquest.

The speed and range of the Islamic state's conquests are amazing. From the East Roman Empire the Muslim Arabs had conquered Syria, Mesopotamia (the Jazirah), Palestine, and Egypt by 641. From the Persian Empire they had conquered Iraq by 637 and the whole of Iran, as far north-eastward as Merv inclusive, by 651. In 651 the Sasanian Persian Empire was extinguished. In 653 the Armenians and Georgians (both ex-Roman and ex-Persian Armenian and Georgian subjects) capitulated to the Islamic state on favourable terms. Between 647 and 698 the Arabs conquered North-West Africa from the East Romans, and in 710–12 they went on to extinguish the Visigothic Kingdom. Except for the north-western corner of Spain, they conquered all the Visigoths' dominions, including the remnant of Visigothic territory in south-western Gaul. Simultaneously in 711 the Arabs were conquering Sind and the southern Punjab, up to, and including, Multan.

In 661–71 the Arabs conquered Tokharistan (present-day Afghan Uzbekistan), which had been the Persian Empire's share of the territorial spoils of the Ephthalite Hun Empire. This conquest was strategically important. It put the Islamic state astride the overland route between India and China via the Oxus–Jaxartes basin. In 706–15 the Arabs went on to conquer Transoxania, which had been the Turkish steppe-empire's share of the Ephthalite Empire's spoils. Here the Arabs suffered a set-back, but in Transoxania they returned to the attack. They were as persistent there as they had been in North-West Africa, and in 739–41 they conquered the whole of Transoxania definitively. On four other fronts, however, they met with checks that they failed to overcome.

The Arabs failed to follow up their conquest of Syria by conquering Asia Minor. In 741 they were brought to a halt along the line of the Amanus Range. The 'Mardaites' of the Amanus were 'insurgents' from the Arab standpoint, but, for the East Roman Empire they were loyalists. In 677 they gained a temporary foothold in the Lebanon. The Arabs did eventually carry their frontier beyond the Amanus to the Taurus, but they never won a permanent foothold beyond that line. The fifth Caliph, Mu'awiyah I (ruled 661–80) recognized that, in order to conquer Asia Minor and to extinguish the East Roman Empire, the Arabs must take Constantinople, and that, to take it, they must wrest from East Roman hands the naval command of the Mediterranean. In 669 Mu'awiyah built a fleet, and in 674–8 his forces besieged Constantinople by both sea and land; but this siege turned into a disaster for the Arabs. The East Roman fleet had been armed with napalm ('Greek fire'), and with apparatus for discharging it, by a refugee Syrian technician. A second Arab siege of Constantinople in 717–18 was an equally disastrous failure. In 732 the Arabs failed to conquer Gaul. Before reaching the Loire, they were checked at Poitiers. In 737/8 they failed to conquer the empire of the Khazar nomads, between the Volga and the Don.

The Muslim Arabs' conquests thus found their limits, but these conquests had been swift and wide-ranging for the same reason as the Vandals' conquests and Alexander the Great's conquests had been. Each of these invaders was attacking an empire that had become militarily weak but that had kept its network of communications intact for the invaders' benefit. The Arab conquests in the seventh century undid the effects of Alexander's conquests in the same area in the fourth century B.C. The Arabs put an end to a Greek ascendancy in the Levant that, by 633, had been maintained for 963 years.

The Arabs were aided by the attitude of the East Roman Empire's Monophysite Christian subjects. These did not regret their change of rulers; nor did the Sasanian Persian Empire's Nestorian subjects feel any active loyalty towards their former Iranian masters. The Zoroastrian Iranians themselves soon abandoned the struggle to preserve their political independence, though they were the Persian Empire's imperial people and Zoroastrianism was their national religion. In North-West Africa the Berbers fraternized with the Arab conquerors of the East Roman dominions there. The Berbers had been the mainstay of the Donatists, who had not been reconciled to the Roman Imperial regime by Constantine I's conversion to Christianity.

On the other hand, in Asia Minor, where the population was loyal to the East Roman Empire and to the Chalcedonian form of Christianity, the Arabs were strenuously resisted and were permanently checked. They were also checked—though here only temporarily—in Transoxania, whose inhabitants at that date were Mahayana Buddhists. Alexander likewise had met with strenuous resistance in Transoxania. In Khorasan and Tokharistan (the former Parthia and Bactria), the local Iranian inhabitants fraternized with the Arabs, as in Bactria their ancestors had fraternized with the Greeks after the Achaemenian Persian Empire had been conquered by Alexander. At all times, all inhabitants of the sedentary world's borderlands adjoining the Eurasian steppe have had a common interest in fending off the pastoral nomads.

The Arab conquests were also facilitated by the directive, in the Koran, that 'People of the Book' were to be tolerated and protected if they submitted to the Islamic Government and agreed to pay a surtax. The benefit of this directive was extended from Jews and Christians to Zoroastrians, and eventually to Hindus as well. The Arabs left the collection of the taxes payable by their non-Muslim subjects in the hands of the existing native fiscal officers. In the former Sasanian dominions, these were the *dehkans* (the country squires). These officers continued to keep their books in Greek or Pahlavi till the reign (685–705) of the Caliph Abd-al-Malik. Abd-al-Malik made them change over to Arabic, and his successor Walid I put an end in Egypt to the official use of Coptic, which had formerly been used there side by side with Greek. But the native fiscal authorities, though now compelled to do their work in Arabic, were allowed to remain in office; they were not replaced by Arabs.

The Arab garrisons that held the Islamic state's subject territories were stationed in cantonments. Some of these were on the frontiers; others were on the border between Arabia and the southern fringes of the Fertile Crescent. Most of them were on new sites, not in or near the existing cities; and, though the Arab cantonments attracted non-Arab settlers, the social contact between the conquerors and the conquered was minimal during the first phase of the Islamic Empire's history, and the spread of Islam lagged far behind the expansion of the Islamic state's dominions. In Arabia, Islam was obligatory, but in the subject territories conversion, so far from being imposed, was positively discouraged.

The Muslim Arab garrisons in the subject territories were not missionary-minded. Their attitude towards their religion resembled that of the former Arian Christian masters of the German successor-states of the West Roman Empire. They wore their religion as a national badge that served to distinguish them from the Christian and Zoroastrian subject population. For the Islamic Empire's subjects, conversion to

Islam was attractive financially as a possible means of acquiring the Muslim 'establishment's' relatively favourable fiscal status; but, just because this status was less onerous, the Islamic Treasury opposed conversions and sought, when conversions occurred, to nullify their fiscal effect. The civil war of 747–50, in which the Umayyad dynasty of Caliphs was replaced by the Abbasid dynasty everywhere except at the western extremity of North-West Africa and in Spain, was a forcible assertion, by the converts, of their right to enjoy juridical parity with Muslims who were Arabs by descent. This revolution was engineered in, and was directed from, the Arab cantonment at Kufah in Iraq, but the insurrection was launched from Khorasan, where the converts were exceptionally numerous and where their social amalgamation with the local Arab soldier-settlers had gone to unusual lengths. However, the first Khorasanis to respond to the incitement to rebel were not local Iranians; they were a group of Arab settlers who were aggrieved at the depression of their status under the Umayyad regime.

The change of dynasty which was the superficial issue in the civil war of 747–50 was an incident in a dispute over the succession to Muhammad in his political capacity as the head of the Islamic state. Muhammad himself had not left any sons and had not designated any successor. His cousin and son-in-law Ali claimed that he was the lawful successor because he and his wife, Muhammad's daughter Fatimah, were Muhammad's next of kin. If Ali had succeeded in making his claim good, the Islamic Caliphate would have become the perquisite of Muhammad's family, as the headship of the Jewish Christian community became a family affair when, after Jesus's death, it was taken over by Jesus's brother James, not by Jesus's senior apostle Peter. However, the management of the Arab Muslim state was taken over, after Muhammad's death, by an informal steering committee; in electing Muhammad's political successors, this committee disappointed Ali three times by passing him over; when, at the third vacancy, Ali did obtain the appointment, he proved to be politically incompetent; and, after the assassination of Ali in 661, Muhammad's political heritage was captured by Mu'awiyah I, the son of one of Muhammad's most bitter and implacable Qurayshite opponents.

Mu'awiyah I's mother was Hind, who, like Muhammad's first wife (previously his employer), Khadijah, was a Meccan businesswoman. Hind and her son Mu'awiyah were not Muhammad's kinsfolk, unless all Qurayshites were to be reckoned as being akin to each other. Mu'awiyah I was the most able Qurayshite of his generation. Ali was no match for him politically and Ali and his son Hussein, Muhammad's grandson, met with tragic deaths by violence. Mu'awiyah founded a dynasty which reigned from 601 to 750 at Damascus and from 756 to 1031 in

Spain. But this Umayyad dynasty never succeeded in winning un-contested recognition of its legitimacy.

Thus, in the political structure of the Islamic state, a breach opened immediately after Muhammad's death, and this breach was never closed. The greatest enthusiasts for the anti-Umayyad revolution of 747–50 were devotees of Ali and of his heirs, but, on this occasion, the Alids were frustrated, as Ali himself had been during his short and unhappy tenure of the Caliphate (656–61). Abu'l-Abbas 'the Butcher', who, at Kufah in 749, succeeded in securing acceptance as Caliph in place of the last Syrian Umayyad Caliph Marwan II, was, unlike the Umayyads, a member of the family of Ali and of Ali's cousin the Prophet Muhammad, but Abu'l-Abbas was not a descendant of Ali himself and of his wife, Fatimah; he was a descendant of Ali's and Muhammad's uncle Abbas, who, like the Umayyads Abu Sufyan and Abu Sufyan's son Mu'awiyah I, had been one of the eleventh-hour Meccan converts to Islam.

51

THE REJUVENATION OF THE EAST ROMAN EMPIRE, 628–726

WHEN the Muslim Arabs challenged the East Roman Empire and the Persian Empire simultaneously, they evoked two very different responses. The East Roman Empire resisted and survived, truncated; the Persian Empire succumbed and disintegrated. Yet the Persians and the East Romans were both rejuvenated, though this in different ways, by their common harrowing experience.

The Arabs' subject Zoroastrians were readier and quicker to accept Islam than their subject Christians of any denomination. In Iran the Zoroastrian community was eventually reduced to a small minority confined to a few secluded enclaves. Zoroastrianism was kept alive by a diaspora of refugees in western India. Pahlavi (the Middle-Persian language) was conveyed in words written in the Syriac alphabet but used as ideograms for the equivalent Persian words. This clumsy way of writing the Persian language was retained for the Zoroastrian liturgy and scriptures, but the Persian converts to Islam took to writing Persian in the Arabic alphabet, used alphabetically, with a strong infusion of Arabic words into its vocabulary. The converts were creating a New-Persian language for future administrators and poets.

The East Roman Empire maintained itself in Asia Minor to the north-west of the Taurus Range, with a bridgehead on the far side of the Straits at Constantinople. Cyprus was neutralized by agreement after the failure of the Arab siege of Constantinople in 674–8, but other Mediterranean islands, from Crete to the Balearic islands inclusive, remained in East Roman hands, and, though the East Roman Government failed to hold its virtually insular dominion in North-West Africa, it did not yet lose either Sicily or the islets in the Venetian lagoon, and in Europe, to the west of Constantinople, it also retained a chain of continental beach-heads stretching westwards from Thessalonica to Ravenna and to Rome.

The Greek language had completely supplanted the local pre-Greek language in Sicily in the fifth century B.C., and in Asia Minor before the close of the sixth century A.D. The East Roman Empire's former Latin-speaking population between the Haemus (Balkan) Range and the lower Danube had first been decimated by drafts on it for the East Roman Army and had then been overwhelmed by invasions of Trans-danubian barbarians. These invasions had started in the third century A.D. They culminated in the seventh century in the permanent occupation of the whole interior of the Balkan Peninsula by Slav settlers. These even occupied the greater part of the Peloponnesos. In the north the surviving Latin-speakers were reduced to a diaspora of shepherds (the Vlakhs) who had found shelter in the mountains.

The Slav settlers displaced large numbers of East Roman citizens, but they were not a military menace to the Empire itself. The walls of Constantinople, Thessalonica, and other maritime cities kept the Slavs at bay, and these cities' new Slav rural neighbours were not united politically. They formed numerous small separate 'Sklavinias', and these were at the East Roman Empire's mercy; it could subjugate them when-ever it had the necessary military force to spare. The situation changed to the Empire's disadvantage when, in 680–1, a war-band of Turkish-speaking Bulgars (ex-Huns), driven westward by the Turkish steppe-empire's Khazar ex-subjects, lodged themselves permanently in the angle between the lower course of the Danube and the western shore of the Black Sea. The Bulgars, being Eurasian pastoral nomads, proved adept at shepherding human as well as non-human flocks. They subju-gated the nearest of the 'Sklavinias' and founded a state in which the Bulgars were the ruling class. The Bulgars' arrival in the Balkan Peninsula started a race between the Bulgarian and the East Roman state for the political control over the 'Sklavinias' in the interior, which were waiting helplessly to be taken over by any state that had the power.

One result of these shifts of population and changes of sovereignty was that Greek became the national language of the East Roman Empire: modern Greek as the living language of everyday life; the Attic *koinê* as the language of public administration and of the liturgy of the Chalce-donian (alias Orthodox or Catholic) Christian Church everywhere except in the surviving fragments of the Empire's Latin-speaking territories. Rome had been a bilingual city from the second century B.C. to the third century A.D., and so had Constantinople for the first two centuries after its foundation in A.D. 330. But in the sixth century Constantinople became Greek-speaking exclusively. Byzantine Christen-dom and Western Christendom still professed an identical doctrine, but a linguistic barrier was beginning to arise between them.

The Hellenization of the East Roman Empire was promoted by the work of the fourth-century Cappadocian Christian Fathers. St. Basil of Caesarea's introduction of a version of Pachomian communal monasticism into the Greek-speaking world has been mentioned in Chapter 45. St. Basil, his brother St. Gregory of Nyssa, and their friend St. Gregory Nazianzene were sons of well-to-do upper-class parents in an outlying part of Asia Minor, where, in the fourth century, a local non-Greek language was probably still spoken in everyday life. Basil and Gregory Nazianzene went as students to the University of Athens, and there they met the future Emperor Julian (like them, Julian had been brought up in the interior of Asia Minor). The three Cappadocian Fathers produced voluminous literary works written in the neo-Attic Greek of the second-century non-Christian 'high-brow' lecturers. The Cappadocian Christian Fathers' Greek style was more elegant than Julian's, and their matter, unlike Julian's, was impeccable. The Cappadocian Fathers were taken as models by later writers in Greek for works on secular as well as religious subjects. The admiration and imitation of the Cappadocian Fathers' works was an impediment to the literary use of the modern Greek language, though, by the seventh century, this had already become the living language of the Greek-speaking world.

Syria was severed politically from the East Roman Empire by the Arab conquest in the course of the years 633–41, but, since the progressive conversion of the population of the Levant to Christianity, the Syriac civilization had been influencing the Greek civilization. Greek-speaking Christians did not feel culturally superior to their Syriac-speaking co-religionists, and they had received some lasting cultural gifts from these before the Christological issue had begun to alienate Greeks and Syrians from each other theologically and politically. The creator of the Byzantine style of music and liturgical poetry that became the common possession of all the Eastern Orthodox Christian peoples was a Syrian Jewish convert to Chalcedonian Christianity, Romanus the Composer (*c.* 480–550). Romanus wrote his hymns in the dead Attic *koiné*, but his metres and melodies were Syrian, and, for Greek poetry and music, this was an inspiring new departure.

Mention has already been made of the Syrian technician who saved the East Roman Empire from extinction in 674–8 by arming it with a fearful new weapon. Leo III (ruled 717–41) was also a Syrian by descent. Leo became emperor just in time to save Constantinople from succumbing to the second Arab siege (717–18). The truncated East Roman Empire had become Greek-speaking, but it had been given a new vitality by eminent recruits of non-Greek origin. A Syrian imperial dynasty was founded by Leo III. Heraclius (ruled 610–41) was the son of an Armenian father who had become viceroy of the East Roman dominion in North-West Africa; and, after the inroads of the Arab

Islamic state on the Empire's territories to the south of the Taurus Range, the Empire's diminished population was recruited by an influx of Armenian, as well as Syrian, refugees who preferred living under East Roman Christian rule as Chalcedonians to living under Arab Muslim rule as Monophysites.

For the East Roman Empire, the seventh century was a time of almost continuous troubles. The mutiny in 602 and the murder of the Emperor Maurice plunged the Empire into anarchy. In 604 the Persians started to invade the Empire's Asian provinces, while the Slav *Völkerwanderung* from the north bank of the lower course of the Danube swamped the whole of the interior of the Balkan Peninsula. The Empire had hardly begun to recover from the last and worst Romano–Persian war of 604–28, when the Arabs launched their assault in 633. The climax of this assault was the Arab siege of Constantinople in 674–8, and this peril had only just been surmounted when, in 680–1, the Eurasian nomad Bulgars established a permanent foothold on the south bank of the Danube. Paradoxically, the depopulation of the Empire through this series of calamities cleared the ground for an economic recovery.

This recovery took the same form as the recovery of northern China in the fifth century. The peasants were now holding their own against both the large landowners and the Imperial tax-collectors. For fifth-century China, we have the record of measures taken, for the protection of the peasants, by the Wei Emperor Hsiao Wen-ti. For the seventh-century East Roman Empire, our evidence is the text of a 'farmers' law' which is thought to have been promulgated towards the close of the century. This law shows the peasants bringing waste land under cultivation and installing water-mills. We can infer that taxation was not so heavy as to discourage the peasants from increasing the size and the productivity of their holdings. We can also infer that, at this date in the East Roman Empire, the large landowners were not powerful enough to be able to appropriate all unoccupied land. No doubt in the East Roman Empire, as in China, large estates had not disappeared, but, here too, their expansion at the expense of small holdings must at least have been checked.

In northern China in the sixth century the peasantry had been armed and trained to serve as a militia. In the East Roman Empire before the close of the seventh century a peasant militia, maintained principally from the produce of allotments of land, had come to be the mainstay of the Imperial Army. We find this militia organized in four army-corps, and the names of these corps show that they were the corps which, before the Arabs' onslaught, had been stationed along the upper Euphrates and the lower Danube. They had then been concentrated in Asia Minor in order to hold this core of the Empire even at the cost of leaving the defence of outlying Imperial territories to be provided for by local self-help. The settlement of these corps on the land in Asia Minor must have been the first step towards the re-peopling of this area. Each corps-commander gradually became also the civil administrator of the district in which his troops were stationed. The Diocletianic-Constantinian provinces fell into abeyance for secular purposes; they survived only on the Empire's ecclesiastical map. Both the corps themselves and the corresponding administrative districts came to be known as themata (a word that probably means 'booking' or 'entries' in the East Roman bureaucrats' ledgers).

From 642 onwards Asia Minor was plagued by Arab raids, but, on balance, this state of insecurity was to the advantage of an armed and trained peasantry. The peasant could defend his land-allotment; the enemy raids kept the Imperial tax-collectors away and made large rural estates an unattractive investment for the rich. For the East Roman peasant, the Arab raider was a lesser evil than either the tax-collector or the investor who might have found it profitable to add field to field. In Asia Minor, as in China, the rejuvenation of society lasted so long as the peasantry continued to be able to hold its own.

52

WESTERN CHRISTENDOM, 634-756

THE salient feature of the history of Western Christendom during the years 634-756 was the continuance of the tendency for its geographical centre of gravity to shift north-westwards. This tendency had already declared itself on the political plane in the building up of the kingdom of the Franks in Gaul, and on the ecclesiastical plane in the conversion of the Frankish empire-builder Clovis to Christianity in its Nicene and Chalcedonian form and in territorial gains for the Roman See in Britain. These years saw a revival of the Frankish kingdom's vitality under the rule of the Arnulfing (known retrospectively as the Carolingian) family in the role of majordomos (chief administrative officers of the royal palace) for the Merovingian dynasty. The same years also saw the confirmation and the geographical extension of the Papacy's ecclesiastical authority in the British Isles, and also in continental north-western Europe through the agency of English missionaries. In the same period the centre of gravity of Western Christendom's agriculture (here, as everywhere at this date, the principal form of economic activity) moved northwards from the shores of the western basin of the Mediterranean.

The region in which the climate is of the Mediterranean type is not so propitious for agriculture, apart from a few exceptionally fertile patches, such as the alluvial valleys of the Nile, Tigris and Euphrates, and the Indus or as the northern hinterlands of the Mediterranean and of its backwater the Black Sea. Carthaginian, followed up by Roman, agronomists had made the most of the Mediterranean region's agricultural potentialities by the application of science, and their work was not undone in either North-West Africa or southern Spain by the Arab conquest of these countries. On the other hand, the more accessible of the forests in the Mediterranean region had been depleted by the continual depredations of architects, shipwrights, and purveyors of fuel for heating baths, and this widespread deforestation had not only created a scarcity of timber in this region; it had led to a denudation of hills and mountains that had reduced the area utilizable for agriculture and even for pasture as well. Northern Europe, however, still possessed abundant forests, and, even if these had been felled, the local climate and physiography would have been safeguards against denudation here.

The annexation to the Roman Empire, first of the basin of the River Po, and then of extensive territories in Transalpine Europe, had brought within the ambit of the Graeco-Roman civilization tracts of the potentially productive heavy soils in the northern hinterland of the western basin of the Mediterranean; and, before the collapse of the Roman Empire in the West, a beginning had been made in developing the agricultural technique for bringing these soils under cultivation. The key to this was the invention of a more powerful and effective build of plough than the type that had been adequate for the cultivation of lighter soils. This development had not yet gone far enough to make agriculture more remunerative in northern Europe than it was in the Mediterranean region. The yield of the Mediterranean wheat-fields, vineyards, and olive orchards had been the economic lure that had drawn the northern barbarians, who were being pushed from behind by the Huns, to overrun Spain and North-West Africa after they had broken through the Roman frontier along the Rhine. No doubt they would have occupied, as well, the far richer irrigated lands of Egypt and Iraq if these had been within their reach. But the East Roman Empire and the Persian Empire retained their hold over Egypt and Iraq respectively till, in the seventh century, both these economic power-houses were captured by the expanding Islamic Arab state.

Meanwhile, Gaul to the south of the River Loire was so attractive to the Franks that, in the successive partitions of the Frankish kingdom between members of the Merovingian family in the course of the sixth and seventh centuries, each claimant stipulated that he should be given a slice of the Midi in addition to his slice of northern Gaul, which had been the principal area of Frankish settlement and was consequently the seat of Frankish power. At the same time, the winning, for agriculture, of the heavy soils of northern Gaul and south-eastern and central Britain, which had been started by the Romans, was being continued by the Teutonic-speaking barbarian settlers in these ex-Roman territories. If the German and Arab conquests of ex-Roman and ex-Persian territories caused any set-back for agriculture, this was temporary. The continuance of the opening-up of the northern soils had not yet produced any spectacular results; yet it was significant, because this was new ground of wide extent and high potential productivity.

The centre of gravity of the ecclesiastical domain and the sphere of moral and political influence of the episcopal See of Rome likewise shifted north-westwards in the course of the years 634–756. The Muslim Arabs' conquest of North-West Africa, of most of the Iberian Peninsula, and of the Mediterranean coast of Gaul between the Pyrenees and the mouth of the Rhône did not deprive the Papacy of its jurisdiction over its ecclesiastical subjects in these regions, but, under the Islamic regime, Christianity in North-West Africa, like Zoroastrianism in Iran, lost adherents, through conversions to Islam, more rapidly than it lost them either in the former Visigothic kingdom or in the Levantine Fertile Crescent. However, the adversity which the Christian Church in North-West Africa had been suffering since the Donatists had broken with the Catholics removed an obstacle to the assertion of the Papacy's authority in Western Christendom. Christianity had struck root in North-West Africa more widely, at an earlier date, than to the north of the western basin of the Mediterranean, and, so long as the North-West African Church had been united and vigorous, it had been reluctant to admit Rome's ecclesiastical supremacy.

On the other hand, the East Roman Imperial Government dealt a heavy blow to the See of Rome when, *c.* 732/3, it transferred the 'toe' of Italy, Sicily, and the whole of the Eastern Illyricum from the Roman See's jurisdiction to that of the Constantinopolitan See, and diverted from the Papal to the Imperial Treasury the revenues from estates in Sicily that had belonged to the patrimony of St. Peter. From the East Roman Imperial Government's point of view, this penalization of the Papacy did not compensate for the Government's inability to chastise Popes Gregory II and III in person, as it had chastised Pope Martin I. Gregory II had defied the Emperor Leo III by supporting the Emperor's western subjects, first in their resistance to the imposition of additional taxes to pay for the costs of the defence of Constantinople against the Arabs in 717–18, and then in their resistance to the ban laid by Leo in 726 on the harbouring of images in churches. Pope Greogry II (715–31) and his successor Gregory III (731–41) each in turn excommunicated the amenable Patriarch whom Leo III had installed at Constantinople. These two Popes had thus demonstrated their ecclesiastical and political independence, but the cost to the Papacy in terms of lost ecclesiastical territory and revenues had been high. Though the interior of the Eastern Illyricum was now in the hands of non-Christian Slavs and Bulgars who were beyond both the Pope's and the Emperor's control, the Eastern Illyricum also included Thessalonica, the Cyclades, and Crete.

Before it suffered this territorial loss in the south-east, the See of Rome had made territorial gains in the north-west. In 634 the Kingdom of Northumbria, the northernmost of the Roman Empire's English successor-states in Britain, had been captured from the Roman See by the Irish missionary church. It was recaptured for Rome in 664, and this victory of the Roman See in England was followed, in the course of the eighth century, by the submission to it of the Celtic churches in Scotland, Wales, Brittany, and Ireland. In England, the Roman Church was reformed and reorganized in 669–90 by a refugee Greek monk, Theodore of Tarsos, who had been appointed Archbishop of Canterbury by the Pope. Benedictine monasticism struck root in England in the seventh century, and Bede, a monk in the Benedictine monastery at Jarrow in Northumbria, published his famous *Historia Ecclesiastica Gentis Anglorum* in 731.

In 690 a Northumbrian English monk, Willibrord-Clement, went to the Continent as a missionary to the Frisians. He was followed, in and after 716, by a West Saxon English monk, Wynfrid-Boniface, who, under Papal auspices, worked as a missionary in Thuringia, Hesse, and Bavaria. Willibrord and Boniface were under the political aegis of the Carolingian majordomos of the Merovingian Frankish kingdom. In 741–7, at the instance of Carloman, the majordomo of Austrasia (Eastern Frankland), Boniface reformed and reorganized the Frankish church on Roman lines. But Carloman and his successors in the government of Frankland took care, like the East Roman Emperors, to have the last word in the government of the Christian Church within their dominions.

However, the Carolingian House and the Papacy found that each needed the other's support. The Carolingians had been rulers of the Frankish kingdom *de facto* since 687. They wanted to become its rulers *de jure*. In 750 Pippin III ('the Short') asked for the Pope's ruling on this issue. In 751 or 752, when he had in his pocket a Papal response in his favour, he convened an assembly of the Frankish people which elected Pippin to be its king after deposing the nominal Merovingian king. Pippin's election was clinched by his being anointed king by Boniface. (This rite was copied from the Israelite practice recorded in the Old Testament.) Meanwhile, in 751, while Pope Zacharias's favourable answer to Pippin's inquiry was on its way, the Lombards had taken Ravenna, the East Roman Empire's principal beach-head in Italy.

The East Romans could not re-conquer Ravenna, and did not try. The first call on their armed forces was for the defence of their Empire's main body against the Arabs and the Bulgars. It was evident that the Lombards now had it in their power to take Rome as well, unless the Papacy could find a substitute in some other quarter for the military aid that Constantinople could no longer give. So far the Papacy had not sought to detach itself from the East Roman Empire politically, but in 753–4 Pope Stephen II/III crossed the Alps to ask for Pippin's military intervention in Italy. In 754 he himself anointed Pippin, together with his sons Charles (the future Charlemagne) and Carloman. In 755 and again in 756 Pippin crossed the Alps, defeated the Lombards, and, besides preventing them from taking Rome, compelled them finally to cede the ex-East Roman territory round Ravenna. Pippin did not comply with a request from the Emperor Constantine V to give back this territory; he gave it instead to the Pope.

53

EASTERN ASIA, 589–763

FOR more than a century and a half, beginning in 589, China enjoyed a spell of unity, power, and prosperity which contrasts strikingly with the disunity and adversity of the preceding period which had begun with the disintegration of the Eastern Han regime in 185. In 589 the North and South of China were re-united, for the first time since the barbarian invasion of the North in 304, and this re-unification was followed by the re-introduction of Han Wu-ti's system of recruiting the Imperial civil service by examination in the Confucian classics. The re-united China also now expanded again beyond the bounds of China proper.

The cause of these successes was the Wei Emperor Hsiao Wen-ti's undertaking to provide a land-holding of a minimum size for every peasant. His successors had followed up this epoch-making reform by organizing a peasant militia. This was the instrument with which the founder of the Sui dynasty, Sui Wen-ti, conquered southern China and re-annexed it to the North in 589. The peasant militia also enabled the second Emperor of the T'ang dynasty, T'ai Tsung (ruled 626–49), to make his conquests in Central Asia. The Wei and their successors in the North had not ventured to limit the estates of the large landowners. This was done by the Sui after 589. They fixed maxima for the large land-holdings, on scales that differed in accordance with the holder's rank. Neither the Sui nor their successors the T'ang went so far as to expropriate the large estates, and no doubt the limitation of the size of these, and the guarantee of a minimum size for a peasant holding, were ideals that were never fully realized in practice. All the same, it is recorded that, in the early days of the T'ang dynasty, nearly four-fifths of the Imperial revenue was obtained from taxes levied on the peasantry per capita, and it is clear that the disasters that overtook the Empire half way through the eighth century were consequences of the Imperial Government's failure, during the first half of that century, to continue to provide the peasants with holdings of the regulation minimum size.

This failure had several causes. One cause was the increase in the numbers of the peasantry as a result of the re-establishment of domestic law and order in 628. Though the opening-up of the South and the migration to the South from the North continued, the growth of the population shot ahead of the means of providing even minimum-size land-holdings for it. A second cause was the Sui dynasty's revival of the system of recruiting the civil service by examination. The new crop of Confucian civil servants behaved like their predecessors in the Age of the Western Han dynasty in and after the reign of Han Wu-ti. Once again the civil servants took advantage of their official position in order to acquire land. This reduced the amount of land distributable in minimum-size peasant freeholds. It also caused a conflict between the revived class of Confucian administrator-landlords, who now established themselves mostly in the South and East, and the older and larger landowners in the North-West, who were derived from intermarriages between descendants of the administrator-landlords of the Han Age and descendants of the barbarian invaders who had overrun the North in and after 304. The T'ang Emperor Hsüan Tsing (ruled 712–56) fought vigorously but un-successfully to arrest and reverse these untoward developments. Disasters began to descend on the Empire in 751.

The Sui dynasty, which re-unified China in 589, was almost as short-lived as the Ch'in dynasty had been after its achievement, in 221 B.C., of unifying China for the first time. The second Sui Emperor Yang-ti (ruled 604–18) was as demonically active as the first ruler of a united China, Ch'in Shih Hwang-ti, had been, and his demands, too, on his subjects were so intolerably heavy that they provoked a general revolt that brought the dynasty to the ground. This cost China twelve years of civil war and anarchy (617–28) before unity and order were re-established by a new dynasty, the T'ang. Like the Han, the T'ang were the bene-ficiaries from their fallen predecessors' achievements. They rehabilitated the fallen regime in substance, but in a milder and more tactful form which did not provoke the violently hostile reaction that had cost the preceding dynasty its throne.

The Sui dynasty's most onerous and unpopular public works were canals, dug by forced labour conscripted on a vast scale. The Sui created the Grand Canal. This started from Hangchow, on the east coast to the south of the Yangtse, and, in its original alignment, it linked the Yangtse with the Yellow River near Loyang. Sui Yang-ti added a branch run-ning northwards, along the later alignment of the northern section of the Grand Canal, to carry troops and supplies towards his war-zone in northern Korea. In the pre-railway and pre-aircraft age, the digging of artificial waterways on the grand scale was indispensable for welding southern China on to northern China. The great Chinese rivers flow from west to east; canals were needed to make water-borne traffic possible from south to north. Eventually, when the T'ang dynasty's court and central civil service became top-heavy, their Sui predecessors' Grand Canal served them well for bringing rice from the South to their capital, Ch'ang-an, in the valley of the Wei tributary of the Yellow River, which had been founded by the Sui on a site adjoining the Western Han's capital Ching-chao.

Sui Yang-ti's northward branch of the Grand Canal did not enable him to conquer Koguryo, the northernmost of the three indigenous states in Korea. The T'ang did succeed in overthrowing Paekche in 660 and Koguryo in 668 with the aid of Silla, but Silla then expelled the T'ang forces from Korea and united the whole of Korea under his own rule. This united Korea accepted Chinese suzerainty only nominally. On the other hand, political unification gave fresh impetus in Korea to Sinification and to the progress of Buddhism.

The re-unification of China had been anticipated by a re-unification of the pastoral peoples on the Eurasian steppe. In 552 the Turks (T'u-chüeh) established a steppe-empire on the scale of the empire that had been built by the Hsiung-nu (Huns) in the second century B.C. (both the Huns and the Turks spoke dialects of the Turkish language). The Turkish steppe-empire broke in two in 581; T'ang T'ai Tsung conquered the Eastern Turks in 630; and in 637 the Western Turks were pulverized by the Chinese in concert with the Uighurs (also a Turkish-speaking pastoral nomad people). However, by this date the Chinese had to reckon with the Tibetans, and the Arabs were already on the war-path.

In 607 Tibet had been unified politically, and the Chinese civilization had been less successful than the Indian in the competition between them for drawing Tibet into the one or the other cultural orbit. Tibet now disputed China's control over the Tarim basin. In 661–71 the Arabs annexed Tokharistan. Thus in the T'ang Age, as in the Eastern Han Age, China's advance overland towards India and south-western Asia was challenged and was restricted; yet, once again, an ephemeral Chinese military drive westwards opened the way for the entry of western cultural influences into China. Chinese Buddhists were still in touch with Indian Buddhists overland as well as by sea. Zoroastrianism had gained a foothold in China *c.* 525; there is a record of a Nestorian Christian missionary working at Ch'ang-an in 635; and Manichaeism seems to have reached China before the close of the seventh century. The eastward dissemination of the three principal religions of the Sasanian Persian Empire must have been facilitated by Khusro I's annexation of Tokharistan about half way through the sixth century, and it must then have been stimulated by the Arab conquest of the Sasanian Empire, which no doubt started a flow of refugees in an eastward direction.

The Sui and T'ang emperors were addicted to Buddhism and were tolerant of other religions of foreign origin. However, the revival of Confucian studies for the practical purpose of re-constituting an Imperial administrative service gradually built up a Confucian reaction against all foreign religions, Buddhism included.

Meanwhile, under the early T'ang, Ch'ang-an was the most cosmopolitan of all the cities in the Old-World Oikoumenê. In this respect, Ch'ang-an surpassed contemporary Constantinople. But the Chinese visual art and poetry of the early T'ang Age are distinctively Chinese. Terracotta figurines provide vivid glimpses of everyday life. The poets Li Po (701–62) and Tu Fu (712–70) were contemporaries of the ill-starred Emperor Hsüan Tsing. The T'ang Empire and the Chinese civilization were admired and imitated not only in Korea but also, farther afield, in Japan. The Japanese Empire had sent embassies to one of the South-China dynasties in the fifth century. From 607 onwards, frequent embassies were sent to Ch'ang-an, and in 608 an ambassador from the Sui accompanied the Japanese mission on its return home. In 646 the Japanese Imperial Government introduced, at least on paper, an administrative system, including allotments of land to peasants, that was a replica of the Chinese. In 710 it laid out at Nara a miniature replica of Ch'ang-an.

The Japanese and Korean imitation of China gives the measure of China's prestige, but, midway through the eighth century, China met with a series of calamities. In 751 the Arabs defeated the Chinese on the Talas River in present-day Soviet Central Asia, to the north of Farghanah, and this was the end of Chinese military activity and political influence anywhere to the west of the Tarim basin. In the same year the Thai state Nan-chao, in the present-day Chinese province of Yunnan, repulsed a Chinese attack. The Thais, like the Koreans and the Japanese, had copied the T'ang Empire's institutions, and this had enabled them to build a state that could hold its own even against a united China and could eventually take the offensive. This was a portent; for, previously, the barbarians to the south of the Yangtse had proved easy for the Chinese to conquer and to assimilate. In 755 An Lu-shan, a general of Soghdian Turkish parentage, led a revolt. This rebellion was not put down till 763. Its effect was devastating. According to the official census figures, the population of China in 764 was less than one third of what it had been in 754.

[54]

THE ISLAMIC WORLD, 750–945

THE revolution in 750 changed the character of the Islamic state. From 633 to 750 this state had been the prey of a privileged Muslim Arab 'ascendancy', dominating vast numbers of non-Muslim subjects and a small but increasing number of non-Arab converts to Islam. The Muslim Arab 'ascendancy' was now replaced by a Muslim 'ascendancy' that was still a minority and was still privileged, but was a community of Muslims of any nationality. Potentially, this Islamic community (*ummah*) was ecumenical. It might come to embrace all the inhabitants of the Islamic state and indeed the whole of mankind. The deposition of the Arab 'ascendancy' in 750 was confirmed in 813, when Ma'mun, the son of the fifth Abbasid Caliph, Harun-ar-Rashid, who had been given the Iranian portion of the empire as his heritage, annexed his brother Amin's portion, which contained most of the Empire's Arab population.

For the Islamic state, the price of putting an end to the identification of the Islamic community with the Arab nation was the transformation of the government into an autocracy of the Sasanian Persian type. The Arabs were anarchic-minded, and this was true not only of the Arab pastoral nomads but also of the settled Arab population in the oases in Arabia itself and in the cantonments in which the victorious Arab tribesmen had been stationed. The Greek chronicler Theophanes (writing c. 810–13) calls the head of the Islamic state 'President of the Council'. This is an accurate description of the status of the first four Caliphs; and their Umayyad successors, too, were not autocrats in their relation to their fellow Arabs. Their political and military power was dependent on the Arabs' support. The Arabs were factious and were quick to take offence. They had to be humoured and coaxed by the Umayyad Mu'awiyah I and his successors. The deposition of the Arabs relieved the Abbasids of this restraint on their exercise of authority. The non-Arab Muslims now won equality with the Arabs as against non-Muslims, but they did not inherit the privilege—which the Arabs themselves had now lost—of taking liberties with the Government.

The Arabic language was not involved in the Arab people's demotion. Under the Abbasids, Arabic continued to be the Islamic state's administrative language, and also, of course, to be the language of Arabic poetry, though neither Arab poets nor students of Arabic grammar were now necessarily Arabs by descent. Ma'mun who was Caliph from 813 to 833 relied on Iranian military and political support, but he promoted the translation of Greek works of philosophy and science into Arabic, some direct from the original Greek, and others from existing translations from the Greek into Syriac. The non-Arab officials of the Islamic state had been compelled to become bilingual before the close of the seventh century. This was the class from which the ninth-century translators were recruited. One channel of transmission was Harran, a city in Mesopotamia in which a Hellenized form of pre-Christian and pre-Islamic Babylonian religion survived into the ninth century. Another was Jund-i-Shahpuhr in Khuzistan (the ancient Elam). Jund-i-Shahpuhr had been founded by the Sasanid Emperor Shahpuhr I to house the prisoners that he had carried away captive from Syria. It had become the seat of a Nestorian school of medicine.

The spate of translations from Greek and Syriac into Arabic in the ninth century indicates that by then there was already an intellectually lively Arabic-reading public. The focus of this nascent Arabic culture was Baghdad, on the left bank of the River Tigris, a short distance above Ctesiphon, the former capital of the Sasanian Persian Empire and of its Arsacid Parthian predecessor. Baghdad had been founded in 762 to serve as the capital of the Abbasid Caliphate. Baghdad became a cosmopolitan city such as Ch'ang-an had been during the preceding century and a half. The refinement of the Arabic language through the intellectual ferment in Baghdad in the ninth century qualified Arabic for becoming a cultural lingua franca for the entire Islamic World, from the Oxus–Jaxartes basin to the Atlantic.

Arabic now also began to supplant some of the other languages current in the Islamic Empire as the language of everyday life. At this level, Arabic failed to gain ground against Persian. The Persians retained their ancestral language, though they took to writing it in the Arabic alphabet and enriched their vocabulary with Arabic loan-words. This New Persian (Farsi) was to become the vehicle for a great literature. It was easier for Arabic to supersede its sister Semitic language, Syriac, which was the mother-tongue of the peasantry all round the Fertile Crescent at the time of the Arab conquest. Arabic also gradually spread at the expense of Coptic in Egypt, and more rapidly in North-West Africa at the expense of the Berber dialects. The Berbers were culturally backward, and they readily accepted both the Arabic language and Islam. On the other hand, the peasantry in the Fertile Crescent and in Egypt remained faithful to Christianity throughout the period covered by this chapter, and, at this stage, the adoption of Arabic made little headway among them.

The ninth-century intellectual ferment in Islamic society was stimulated by the need to equip Islam with the intellectual apparatus that was already possessed by the religions of the Islamic Empire's non-Muslim subject population. Islam manifestly needed systems of law and of theology that would be adequate for the dominant community in an empire that included the homes of several ancient and mature civilizations. The ambition to make the Arabs into 'People of the Book' had been one of Muhammad's motives.

Islamic law had to be founded on Muhammad's *dicta*, and the raw materials were inadequate. The Koran consisted of spiritual admonitions intermingled with *ad hoc* administrative rulings given by Muhammad in his capacity as political head of the Islamic community at Medina. The legal material in the Koran had to be sorted out and then to be supplemented by traditional reports of Muhammad's sayings. These reports had to be verified, and the still remaining gaps had to be filled by analogy and by the application of local custom, which, in ex-Roman territories, might mean provincial versions of Roman law. Between 750 and 900, classified collections of traditions were compiled, and four schools of Islamic law were founded. For Sunni ('beaten-path', i.e. orthodox) Muslims as distinguished from Shi'is (sectarians, i.e. partisans of the House of Ali), all four schools of law were eventually held to be valid. A local Muslim community was then left free to choose to follow whichever school it preferred.

Islamic theology was influenced by Christianity, partly because an elaborate Christian theology was already in existence, and partly because the belief in the uniqueness and unity of God created identical problems for the two religions. The doctrine that the Koran was created, not uncreated, was an Islamic counterpart of the Arian conception of the relations between the First and the Second Persons of the Christian Trinity. This doctrine was imposed in 827 by the Caliph Ma'mun and was abrogated in 847 by the Caliph Mutawakkil. In making these theological pronouncements, the two Caliphs were acting *ultra vires*; for a Caliph was Muhammad's successor in the political field only. Open questions in the field of theology are settled for Muslims, as they are for Jews, by a consensus of the doctors of the law. The unadulterated monotheism of Judaism and Islam does not require creeds drafted in terms of Greek philosophy. However, the Muslims' access, in translation, to works of Greek philosophy stimulated a series of Muslim thinkers to synthesize Greek philosophy with Islam. Within the hundred years end-ing in 945 the Basran philosopher Kindi (d. 873) had been followed by a Muslim philosopher of Turkish extraction, Farabi (d. 950).

The revolution in 750 was the end of the Islamic Empire's expansion and was also the beginning of the end of its unity. Considering the Arabs' chronic indulgence in civil war while they were the Islamic state's privileged masters, it is amazing that they managed not only to make and to retain their vast conquests but to go on extending them until the eve of the Umayyad regime's fall. The Abbasids did not succeed in tak-ing over the domain of the Islamic Empire intact. In 756 a refugee survivor of the Umayyad House won the allegiance of the Sunni Muslim community in the Iberian Peninsula. Between 757 and 786, three Kharijite states were founded in Berber territory in Algeria and on the southern flank of the Atlas Mountains. (The Kharijis, i.e. 'separatists', were a faction that had broken with Ali because he had compromised with Mu'awiyah.) In 788 an Alid principality was founded in Northern Morocco. In Ifriqiyah (Tunisia) the Sunni Arab Aghlabid dynasty, established in 800, which had paid a nominal allegiance to the Abbasids, was supplanted in 909 by a 'Fatimid' dynasty, supported by one of the Berber tribes, which denied the Abbasids' legitimacy and aspired to bring the whole Islamic World under its own rule.

For the Abbasids, defections—religious and political—in their Iranian dominions were more serious, since Iran had been the source of their power. As the Iranians had not found the Sasanian Empire's Zoroastrian established church spiritually satisfying, they had readily embraced Manichaeism and its offshoot Mazdakism. The Iranians did not find Islam satisfying either, though they were less reluctant than their Christian fellow-subjects to embrace it. Abu Muslim, the agent of the House of Ali, who had engineered the overthrow of the Umayyad dynasty, had raised hopes in Iran that the sequel would be a congenial Shi'i Muslim, or perhaps even a Mazdakite or a Zoroastrian, regime. When in 749 the Caliphate was captured by the Abbasids, and when in 754 the second Abbasid Caliph Mansur (ruled 754–75) put to death Abu Muslim, the man to whom the Abbasids owed their throne, Iranian resentment boiled over in a series of insurrections. Sinbadh the Magian led a revolt in 755/6, Ustadhsis another in 766–8, Muqanna, 'the veiled prophet', another in 777–783/4. Indeed, non-Islamic religions and un-orthodox forms of Islam pullulated in Iran, and also in Iraq, in the Abbasid Age.

It was tempting, but dangerous, for a Muslim to be a mystic. Al-Hallaj was put to death in 922 for having proclaimed his identity with God. A Mazdakite, Babak, maintained an insurrection in western Iran from 816 to 838. From 869 to 883, black slaves, imported to reclaim land in the lower Tigris–Euphrates basin, were in revolt under Kharijite leadership. The Iranian country between the Elburz Range and the south coast of the Caspian Sea had remained unconquered by the Arabs, but it was eventually converted to Islam, not in the Sunni but in the Zaydi Shi'i form. This country was under Zaydi Shi'i rule from 864 to 928. In and after 932 the Buwayhids, who were Shi'is of a different sect from the Zaydis, and who came from the north-west corner of the independent territory along the Caspian shore, overran western Iran. In 945 they occupied Baghdad and turned the Abbasid Caliphs into their puppets.

Since the reign of the Caliph Mu'tasim (833–42), the Abbasids had been the puppets of their Turkish slave-guards, successors of those Iranian Khorasanis who had originally placed the Abbasid dynasty on the throne. (Though the Turkish steppe-empire had been split in 581 and liquidated in 630–7, the Turks themselves had survived, and numerous tribes of them had continued to occupy the greater part of the Eurasian steppe.) The Abbasid Caliphs' Turkish slave-guards were at least nominally converts to Sunni Islam. The Iranian Samanids, who ruled Tokharistan, the Oxus–Jaxartes basin, and Khorasan from 874 to 995, were descendants of a Zoroastrian convert to Sunni Islam, and they were as careful as the Aghlabids in North-West Africa to pay lip-service to the Abbasid Caliphs' nominal sovereignty. The occupation of Baghdad itself in 945 by the Shi'i Iranian Buwayhids exposed the fiction of the Abbasids' sovereignty over the Sunni Muslim community.

The fiction had, in fact, already been made untenable when, in 929, the title 'Caliph' had been assumed by Abd-ar-Rahman III, the reigning representative of the refugee branch of the Umayyad dynasty in the Iberian Peninsula. When the domain of the Sunni Islamic community was thus divided between two rulers, each of whom claimed to be Muhammad's legitimate political successor, it became manifest that there was now no longer an Islamic state that included among its subjects even the members of the Sunni Muslim community, not to speak of politically independent dissenters from orthodox Islam.

In the course of the years 750–945, the only Muslim victories were, with one signal exception, achieved by western Muslim governments or private adventurers. On land the refugee Umayyad state in the Iberian Peninsula receded. By 803 it had lost not only the last of its holdings to the north of the Pyrenees, but also Catalonia to the south of them. But in 826 or 827 Muslim insurgents, evicted from Umayyad Spain, conquered Crete from the East Roman Empire, and in 827–902 the Aghlabids conquered from the East Roman Empire the whole of Sicily except one stronghold. The disintegration of Charlemagne's Empire in the ninth century gave the Sicilian and the Spanish Muslims an opening for naval assaults on Italy. They almost succeeded in insulating Italy from the Transalpine portion of Western Christendom by occupying the Alpine passes, and they were on the verge of making contact, via Apulia and Dalmatia, with Bulgaria when the East Roman Empire intervened in 868–76.

The Abbasids' one historic victory was over the Chinese on the Talas River in 751, the year after the Abbasids had overthrown the Umayyads. If the Chinese had won this battle, they might have recaptured the Oxus–Jaxartes basin for China and for Buddhism, and in that event the descendants of the hereditary abbot (*parmak*, Sanskrit *pramukha*) of the Buddhist 'New Monastery' at Balkh would not have become the 'Barmakids' who administered the Abbasid Empire for forty years ending in 803. If the Muslims had been defeated in 751, these ambitious Tokharistanis would never have become converts to Islam, and we may guess that they would have reverted from Zoroastrianism to Buddhism in order to play a leading part in the rehabilitation of the Chinese T'ang dynasty's finances after China's catastrophe in 755–63.

Actually, in Central Asia, Islam did not recede; it spread. In the reign of the Abbasid Caliph Muqtadir (908–32), when the Abbasid dynasty had sunk politically to its nadir, the Volga Bulgars, a Turkish-speaking people living round the confluence of the Volga and the Kama, on the far side of the Eurasian steppe, asked Muqtadir to send them a mission. These Bulgars must by then have been converted to Islam. The mission arrived at their capital, Bulghar, in 922. In 960 the Qarluq ('Snowmen') Turks, who then occupied the section of the steppe, to the north of Farghanah, which the Abbasids had compelled the Chinese to evacuate in 751, were converted to the Sunni Islam of their Muslim neighbours in Transoxania. These neighbours were no longer the Abbasids themselves; they were the virtually independent Samanids. The Qarluqs expanded into the Tarim basin and carried Islam with them. Thus, while the once unitary Islamic state was splitting up into fragments, Islam itself was winning converts beyond the bounds that the unitary Islamic state had attained at the height of its power.

55

THE BYZANTINE CIVILIZATION, 726–927/8

THE East Roman Empire that survived the Arab sieges of Constantinople in 674–8 and 717–18 was small by comparison with its southern neighbour the Islamic Empire and also by comparison with the Frankish Empire that was built up by Charlemagne (ruled 768–814). The Carolingian Empire was the East Roman Empire's north-western neighbour till the Carolingian Empire disintegrated in the course of the ninth century. The East Roman Imperial Government's foreign policy was therefore cautious during the years 719–925. The Empress Irene's unsuccessful attempt in 788 to evict the Franks from Lombardy by supporting a Lombard claimant to the throne at Pavia was an uncharacteristic adventure.

During this period the East Roman Government normally confined itself to pursuing two objectives: the retention of the territories that it still possessed, and the incorporation of as many of the 'Sklavinias' in the interior of the Balkan Peninsula as it could salvage from the encroachments of Bulgaria. Wars with Bulgaria for the possession of the interior of the Balkan Peninsula were, during this period, the first charge on the East Roman Government's military resources. After the Muslim conquest of Crete in 826 or 827, the East Roman Government did make repeated attempts to reconquer this island; for the Muslim stronghold at Candia commanded the waters of the Aegean Sea; it was a dagger pointed at the Empire's heart. The East Roman Government also contested, stubbornly though unsuccessfully, the gradual conquest of Sicily by the Muslims of Ifriqiyah (827–902). When the Sicilian Muslims occupied Apulia and besieged Ragusa on the far side of the Adriatic, the Emperor Basil I (ruled 867–86) intervened energetically in 868–76, and annexed Apulia to the Empire.

This was not a departure from the policy of remaining on the defensive. After the loss of Sicily, the East Roman Empire needed to provide itself with an alternative insulator in order to prevent the North-West African and Sicilian Muslims from joining hands with the Bulgars across the Adriatic. The cautiousness of East Roman policy was manifested after the annihilation, in 863, of the Emir of Malatiyah's expeditionary force in north-eastern Asia Minor. This was the turn of the tide on the Romano–Arab front along the line of the Taurus and Antitaurus Ranges; but the East Romans waited for sixty-three years before launching their counter-offensive in 926. Meanwhile, their only offensive action in Asia Minor was against the non-Orthodox Paulician Christians, who, with the Malatiyah Muslims' support, had established a stronghold at Tephrikê (Divriği), just inside the East Roman Empire's north-eastern frontier. The Romano–Paulician war dragged on from *c.* 843 to *c.* 878.

The Romano–Bulgarian wars were more serious. The Emperor Constantine V just failed to destroy Bulgaria in a twenty-one-year war (755–75). This trial of strength was followed in the ninth century by a race between the two powers for the control of the Sklavinias. In 804/5 or 805/6 the Empire subjugated most of the Slavs in the Peloponnesos. In 809 Bulgaria destroyed the Empire's north-western outpost Serdica. The Emperor Nicephorus I (ruled 802–11) tried to check the Bulgars' advance by planting Asian Greek, and also Turkish, settlements between the Aegean and the Adriatic, but he lost his life in a military disaster, and, when the frontier was stabilized in 904, it skirted the hinterland of Thessalonica at a distance of only twenty-two kilometres from this vitally important East Roman city.

From 726 to 843 the East Roman Empire was paralysed by an acute domestic conflict over the exhibition and veneration of images in Christian churches. This practice was a contravention of the second of the Ten Commandments that Christianity had inherited from Judaism; it made Christians easy targets for Jewish and Muslim strictures; but the practice was almost coeval with the creation of the non-Jewish offshoot of the Christian Church, and, if it had not been adopted, Christianity might have found it difficult to win non-Jewish converts.

The Umayyad Caliph Yazid II (ruled 720–4) is said to have ordered the destruction, in his dominions, of pictures in Christian churches and in public places, but it is not known whether Yazid's act was one of the considerations that moved the East Roman Emperor Leo III to issue a decree to the same effect in 726. Leo's action was demanded by the troops cantoned in Asia Minor, but it was strongly opposed by the ecclesiastical subjects of the See of Rome, which, at that date, included the Cyclades Islands and Crete and the surviving enclaves of the Greek-speaking Christian population of continental Greece. The East Roman Imperial Government retorted to this opposition *c.* 732/3 by transferring from the Roman to the Constantinopolitan See all the Roman See's Greek-speaking ecclesiastical subjects.

In 843 the domestic conflict within the East Roman Empire was ended by a compromise that was favourable to the devotees of images. It was agreed that three-dimensional images should continue to be banned, but that two-dimensional images should be sanctioned—not as objects of worship in themselves, but as symbols of the persons—human, angelic, or divine—that they represented. This compromise in the East Roman Empire removed the cause of the rupture between the Patriarchates of Constantinople and Rome. The Pope's ecclesiastical subjects had not been unanimous in supporting the Pope's stand. In 787 the devotees of images in the East Roman Empire had won a momentary victory at the Seventh Ecumenical Council, held at Nicaea. The decisions of this Council had been approved by the Pope, but in 794 they had been condemned by a council of bishops of the Carolingian Empire, held at Frankfurt. Logically, in 787 and again in 843, the Patriarch of Constantinople ought to have retroceded to the Pope the territories that had been transferred *c.* 732/3. But restitution was not made on either occasion.

The ending of the domestic strife in Eastern Orthodox Christendom was followed there by a cultural renaissance, in which the moving spirit was Photius (Patriarch of Constantinople 858–67 and 877–86). The radiation of Byzantine culture was extended by the work of a pair of Thessalonian scholar-missionaries, Constantine-Cyril and his brother Methodius. Constantine's first mission was to the Khazars, Turkish-speaking ex-subjects of the defunct Turkish steppe-empire who, at the western end of the Eurasian steppe, had created the most civilized empire that this region had seen since the collapse of the Skyth Empire there in the third century B.C. The Khazars were old allies of the East Roman Empire against the Persians and the Arabs, and in 860—the year of Constantine-Cyril's mission to Khazaria—the allies had a new common enemy in the Swedes. In 860 a Swedish pirate flotilla from Russia came within an ace of taking Constantinople. Yet Constantine-Cyril's mission to the Khazars was unsuccessful. By 860 the family of the Khazar Khaqans was already too deeply committed to Judaism (a religion which the Khazars could embrace without the political complications in which they would have involved themselves if they had adopted the established religion of either the East Roman Empire or the Islamic Caliphate). In 863, however, on the invitation of the ruler of the Slav principality of Great Moravia (in present-day Czechoslovakia and Hungary), Constantine-Cyril and Methodius went to this relatively distant Slavonic-speaking country, bringing with them the Glagolitic alphabet that Constantine-Cyril had invented for conveying the dialect of the Slav settlers in the hinterland of Thessalonica.

Great Moravia lay in, and to the north of, the Western Illyricum; this territory was indisputedly within the Roman See's domain; Constantine-Cyril and Methodius were as loyal to the Papacy as Theodore of Tarsos had been two centuries earlier; and the Papacy approved of their work; but this work was opposed by the Frankish Church, which interpreted it, in political terms, as an attempt, by the East Roman Empire, to poach on the Frankish Empire's preserves. By this date the Frankish Empire was disintegrating, but the Frankish Church was not, and on this occasion, as in 794, it pursued a policy of its own which conflicted with the policy of the Roman See. In 885 the Frankish Church succeeded in destroying the Slavophone Moravian mission. Its surviving clergy (Constantine-Cyril had died in 869 and Methodius in 885) became refugees. Some of these refugees made their way to Bulgaria. Here they found a new mission-field that was fruitful because here they were welcomed.

The turn of the tide in 863 in the Romano–Arab border-warfare in Asia Minor had been followed in 864 by the conversion of Bulgaria to Eastern Orthodox Christianity, and in 870 the Bulgar Khan Boris-Michael had confirmed his allegiance to the See of Constantinople after having tested whether allegiance to the See of Rome would be less compromising for Bulgaria's political independence. Since the Patriarch of Constantinople was the East Roman Emperor's political subject, the acceptance of this Patriarch's ecclesiastical supremacy might be taken to imply an acceptance of the Empire's political suzerainty. Boris's reception in 885 of the refugee Slavophone clergy enabled him to build up a Bulgarian national church without having to harbour foreign clergy, either Greek-speaking or Latin-speaking.

The Slavonic language had become the national language of Bulgaria now that Bulgaria's south-westward expansion had increased the numerical strength of the Slavonic-speaking population under the rule of the originally Turkish-speaking founders of the Bulgarian state. In Bulgaria after 885 a new alphabet—known, misleadingly, as the 'Cyrillic'—had been invented as a simpler alternative to Constantine-Cyril's own invention, the Glagolitic alphabet. The Slavonic dialect spoken in the hinterland of Thessalonica became the liturgical language not only for the Bulgars but also for all subsequent Slav converts to Eastern Orthodox Christianity and also for some of the Slav converts to Roman Christianity in Dalmatia.

The conversion of Bulgaria put a temporary strain on the relations between Constantinople and Rome. The nucleus of Bulgaria lay within the Constantinopolitan See's domain, but the territory into which Bulgaria had expanded since 809 lay in the disputed prefecture of the Eastern Illyricum. However, the arrival of the Great-Moravian Slavophone clergy in Bulgaria in 885 clinched Bulgaria's adherence to the Eastern Orthodox form of Chalcedonian Christianity.

The *annus mirabilis*, 863, in which the Emperor Michael III had annihilated the Emir of Malatiyah's expeditionary force and in which Constantine-Cyril and Methodius had reached Great Moravia, had also seen the rehabilitation of the University of Constantinople. Khan Boris's second son and second successor Khan Symeon was educated at Constantinople; he was captivated by Byzantine Greek culture; and, when in 913 the Imperial crown was inherited by a child, Constantine VII Porphyrogenitus, Symeon planned to unite the East Roman Empire with Bulgaria by edging his way on to the Imperial throne as Constantine VII's senior colleague. Symeon's plan miscarried. He was forestalled by Romanus I Lecapenus, the admiral of the East Roman fleet; and Symeon proved unable to impose his will by force of arms in a war that lasted from 913 till Symeon's death in 927. Symeon had no navy, and he failed to obtain the co-operation of the Muslim naval powers. Thus Asia Minor remained beyond his reach, and therefore he could neither starve out nor take by storm Constantinople and the other coastal walled cities in the East Roman Empire's south-east-European dominions.

After Symeon's death Romanus I came to terms with Symeon's successor Peter. He gazetted Peter as Emperor, and one of his archbishops as Patriarch, and he gave Peter his granddaughter Maria to be Peter's Empress (with an annual stipend). Already in 926 Romanus I had launched the long-delayed East Roman counter-offensive against the Eastern Muslims. The abnormally severe winter of 927/8 upset the domestic balance of power, within the East Roman Empire, between the peasantry, the large landowners, and the Imperial Government. For the Byzantine World, the events of the years 926–9 were as momentous as those of 860–4.

56

WESTERN CHRISTENDOM, 756–911

In 756 the future looked promising for the Frankish Kingdom under Carolingian rule. The reigning representative, Pippin III, had secured recognition as the legitimate King of the Franks in place of the last representative of the deposed Merovingian dynasty. In 756 Pippin had, for the second year running, successfully invaded Lombardy and forced its king to accept his peace-terms. In the same year the Islamic dominion in the Iberian Peninsula, which, till 750, had been part of a vast Islamic empire extending from the Atlantic to the Oxus–Jaxartes basin, had become a separate local principality under the rule of a refugee member of the Umayyad dynasty, which had been supplanted in 747–50 by the Abbasid dynasty in the rest of the now no longer unitary Islamic state. When Pippin's sons Charles II and Carloman II succeeded Pippin in 768, and when, in 771, Charles (Charlemagne), became sole king as a result of Carloman's premature death, Charlemagne had a free hand.

In 773–4 Charlemagne annexed the Lombard Kingdom to his dominions, taking thenceforward the double title of King of the Franks and of the Lombards. As 'Patrician of the Romans', he also annexed *de facto* the former East Roman territories in Italy that he and his father had officially preserved or recovered for the Papacy. The Papacy lacked the material power to take effective possession of the ex-East Roman beach-head round Ravenna to which it had been given title by the Franks, though not by the East Roman Imperial Government. As a result of having enlisted the Franks' aid for acquiring the Ravenna beach-head, which had never been under Papal rule, the Papacy had now forfeited to the Franks even the local sovereignty over the Ducatus Romanus, which the Popes had exercised *de facto*, on the East Roman Imperial Government's behalf, ever since 568, when the Lombards' irruption into Italy had shattered the East Roman dominion there into a residue of isolated fragments.

The political union of northern Italy with Gaul in 773–4 was accepted by the northern Italians. The Lombards were the Franks' kinsmen, and they had become their co-religionists when, in the course of the seventh century, they had abandoned Arianism for Catholicism. The Lombards' ex-Roman subjects were kinsmen of the Franks' ex-Roman subjects in Gaul, and, in both regions, the ex-conquered majority of the population was now coalescing with the ex-conquerors. On the Franks' northern frontier the still pagan Saxons put up a far more active resistance to being conquered by the Franks, though the Saxons, like the Lombards, were the Franks' kinsmen. It took Charlemagne thirty-two years (772–804) to conquer continental Saxony, and this war developed like Justinian I's war with the Ostrogoths. A delusively rapid and easy initial victory was reversed abruptly by violent counter-attacks which were costly for the victor. In 778, the year of the first Saxon counter-attack, Charlemagne had rashly opened a second front in Spain, and, during his withdrawal from Spain to cope with the Saxons, his rear-guard, commanded by Roland, the warden of the Frankish frontier-province over against Brittany, was annihilated by the Basques. The Basques and the Bretons (refugees from the English conquerors of Britain) were small peoples, but they were intractable. The Franks' Avar neighbours on the enclave of steppe-country in Hungary were a fugitive band of the former nomad overlords of the Turks. In exterminating the Avars on the Hungarian Alföld between 791 and 805, Charlemagne was aided by the Bulgars. All the same, these campaigns in four different quarters imposed an unbearable cumulative strain on Charlemagne's resources. Charlemagne's successors, like Justinian I's, paid the price for a too ambitious policy of territorial expansion.

Charlemagne's opening campaign, in 772, for the conquest of the region between the rivers Rhine and Elbe was launched 784 years after Augustus had embarked on the same enterprise, and 758 years after Augustus had abandoned it. Charlemagne carried his repetition of Augustus' enterprise to completion. He clinched his conquest of the Saxons by converting them forcibly to Catholic Christianity; and this incorporation of the continental Saxons in Western Christendom was not reversed. But, in subduing one barbarian neighbour, Charlemagne aroused another. When Charlemagne carried the northern frontier of a revived and expanded Roman Empire up to the southern border of Denmark, the Danes retorted by launching naval raids on the Empire's coasts. This was the beginning of the eruption of the Scandinavian peoples that is dealt with in the next chapter.

On Christmas Day 800, in St. Peter's, Rome, Pope Leo III crowned Charlemagne Emperor of the Romans. It is not clear whether or not Leo did this with Charlemagne's foreknowledge and at Charlemagne's desire, but it is certain that Charlemagne's assumption of the Imperial title was a diplomatic liability for him. His prestige was in jeopardy so long as he was not recognized as an emperor by the Roman Emperor at Constantinople, whose right to the title was unquestionable. The Constantinopolitan Government's price for recognition was a comprehensive settlement of outstanding territorial disputes on terms that were favourable to the East Roman Empire. This settlement was negotiated in 811–12 and was ratified in 814, after Charlemagne's death.

The name of the defunct West Roman Empire was less difficult to revive than the reality. Charlemagne did not have at his command sufficient educated and experienced personnel to administer the extent of territory that he had amassed. His institution of itinerant inspectors (*missi dominici*) enabled him to keep some control over his local administrative officers so long as the Empire remained under the undivided command of a single energetic and respected ruler. Charlemagne also recruited from Northumbria a talented ecclesiastical and cultural adviser, Alcuin. Charlemagne himself had the advantage of being the successor of an able father and grandfather, Pippin III and Charles I Martel; and Charlemagne's brother Carloman's early death was a piece of political good fortune for the survivor. But Charlemagne's son and successor Louis the Pious lost control. The Carolingians had inherited from the Merovingians the politically disastrous practice of dividing up Frankland among rival heirs as if it were a private estate. In 843 the Carolingian Empire was partitioned between Louis the Pious's three sons, and its re-union under Charles the Fat (881–8) was not effective. In West Francia, i.e. France, the Carolingian dynasty survived till 987, but these epigoni of the Carolingians were as ineffective as the Merovingian *rois fainéants* had been.

Before the end of the ninth century, the local administrative officers who had once been supervised by Charlemagne's itinerant inspectors had become virtually independent hereditary rulers *de facto*, and the Pope re-emerged as the ruler, *de facto*, of the Ducatus Romanus. Neither the local rulers nor their Carolingian nominal overlords were able to cope with the Scandinavian naval raids that had baffled Charlemagne himself. In the ninth century the Scandinavian naval raiders competed with Spanish and North-West-African naval raiders in attacking the Mediterranean coasts of the disintegrating Carolingian Empire. In 846, and again in 849, African Muslim raiders only just failed to repeat the Vandals' exploit, in 455, of capturing Rome by an attack from across the sea. Rome was included in the slice of the Carolingian Empire that had been assigned in 843 to the nominal Emperor Lothaire I, but it was Pope Leo IV, not Lothaire, who saved Rome by fortifying, in 849, the suburbs on the right bank of the Tiber, which contained St. Peter's.

After 896, the Scandinavian and Western Muslim naval raids were emulated overland by Magyar cavalry raids. (The Magyar Eurasian nomads, driven westward by the still fiercer Pechenegs, had occupied in 896 the vacuum created by the extermination of the Avars in the enclave of steppe-country in present-day Hungary.)

The barbarian invasions in the ninth and tenth centuries were perhaps more grievous for Western Christendom than those in the fifth and sixth centuries. Charlemagne's attempt to revive the West Roman Empire seemed to have been counter-productive. Yet, once again, a West European society that looked down-at-heel when viewed from within looked glamorous to the barbarians who had descended upon it. In 911 Charles the Simple, the Carolingian King of West Francia, acquiesced, perforce, in the permanent settlement of a band of Scandinavian sea-rovers in what is now Normandy, on condition that they should become converts to Christianity. It then became apparent that Charlemagne's cultural work had been more substantial than his empire-building. The Normans were captivated by the civilization into whose domain they had made a forcible entry. They adopted enthusiastically the language and the manners and customs, as well as the religion, of the piece of Carolingian country that they had made their own.

In 910, the year before the date of the Scandinavian settlement in Normandy, one of the local successors of the Carolingians founded an abbey at Cluny in Burgundy—a region that was the geographical node of early Western Christendom's network of communications, and in which the Irish monastery at Luxeuil had been founded, more than three centuries earlier, by St. Columbanus.

Both Normandy and Cluny were slow in bearing fruit. At the date of their establishment it would have been hard to discern that, for Western Christendom, this marked a turn of the tide. During the first half of the tenth century, Western Christendom was at its nadir. Within the next hundred years, the Normans and the Cluniacs were demonstrating that Western Christendom was recovering from the prostration that had been the price of the strain imposed on it by the prematurely ambitious policy of Charlemagne.

57

THE ERUPTION OF THE
SCANDINAVIANS, 793–1000

T HE Scandinavians' eruption in and after 793 was as sudden, as violent, and as unexpected as the Arabs' eruption in and after 633, and, like the Arabs' eruption, the Scandinavians' had causes that are discernible. Once again, the immediate occasion was a great war, just beyond the volatile barbarians' borders, which had left the belligerents exhausted and which therefore made them a tempting prey, while the underlying cause was the stimulus of an age-old interplay between barbarism and civilization.

Scandinavia had been under human occupation since the latter end of the Ice Age. Upper Palaeolithic hunters had followed up the progressive retreat of the ice-cap till they had gained a footing on Scandinavian ground. Before the close of the third millennium B.C. the north-western pioneers of the agricultural revolution had begun to cultivate fertile soils in Denmark and in southern Sweden. Thus, by the date of the eruption of the Vikings, southern Scandinavia had been occupied by a sedentary agricultural population for at least 3,000 years, and, though there had been southward migrations out of Scandinavia in the course of the last two centuries B.C., this previous eruption, like that of 793–1066, had been an exceptional episode in Scandinavian history. Meanwhile, the stimulus of the seepage of successive phases of higher culture into Scandinavia from the south had been cumulative; the vicissitudes in the Scandinavian peoples' relations with the southern civilizations had been unsettling for the Scandinavians psychologically; and this malaise had been brought to a head by Charlemagne's conquest of the continental Saxons; for this had brought the northern frontier of Western Christendom into immediate contact with Scandinavia.

Though in A.D. 14 Augustus had abandoned his attempt to carry the frontier of the Roman Empire up to the line of the River Elbe, Graeco-Roman civilization had played upon Scandinavia vigorously during the first three centuries A.D. This cultural contact had been interrupted when, in the fifth century, the West Roman Empire had been over-whelmed by the *Völkerwanderung* of the East German peoples and the Franks. The Scandinavians had then been insulated, and consequently sheltered from the West Roman Empire's Christian German successor-states, by the Saxons. Now that the Saxons had been conquered and been forcibly converted to Christianity by the Franks, the Scandinavians suddenly found themselves in touch again with a southern civilization, and this at closer quarters than ever before. The impression that Charlemagne's figure made on Scandinavian minds is indicated by the popularity of the name Magnus in Scandinavia as a personal name, not as a title.

The Scandinavians' reaction to this disturbing experience was aggres-sive, and their aggression ranged over a vast field. In 880, Swedish raiders reached Abaskun at the south-eastern corner of the Caspian Sea, after having crossed the Baltic Sea, ascended the River Neva, negotiated the portage over the watershed, and then descended the Volga. In the opposite direction, from *c.* 987 to *c.* 1025, Scandinavian settlers held a beach-head at some point on the north-east coast of continental North America. They had reached this 'Vinland' from Greenland; they had occupied the west coast of Greenland in 985–6, coming from Iceland; and Iceland had been occupied by Norse settlers *c.* 874. The Scandi-navian settlers in Greenland and Vinland are the first human beings who are known for certain to have reached the Americas from the Old World by crossing the Atlantic Ocean.

The Scandinavian rovers in the Viking Age had diverse destinies. There were raiders who made no permanent settlements. The effect of these raiders on their victims was negative, but the raiders themselves were influenced by the experience of their adventures and by the economic and cultural value of the loot that they brought home. The raiders' earliest victims were Christian monasteries that had been planted on off-shore islands along the coasts of the Carolingian Empire and of Britain (Lindisfarne, for instance, was sacked in 893 and Iona in 895). There were settlers on Western Christian ground, who had won acceptance in return for their consent to being converted. The settlement in Normandy in 911 has been mentioned already. This had been antici-pated in England in 878 by the settlement in the 'Danelaw', negotiated by King Alfred. The Scandinavian settlers round the coasts of Ireland imposed themselves unconditionally but became converts to Christi-anity eventually. Other Scandinavians settled in territoiy that was already populated but whose native inhabitants were still pagans. The most important settlers of this class were the Rhos, who bequeathed their name to Russia. These were assimilated linguistically by their

Slavonic-speaking subjects and were converted to Eastern Orthodox Christianity by their East Roman victims. Finally there were settlers in previously uninhabited countries—for instance the settlers in Greenland. In Iceland the Scandinavians had been preceded by Irish Christian anchorites. In Vinland they encountered a native population, and here they were perhaps forcibly evicted.

The Vikings' Christian and Muslim victims in the Old World were no match for their assailants militarily. The heroic and versatile King Alfred had to allow the invaders to settle on the terms agreed, thirty-three years later, by Charles the Simple. The Christians' policy was to tame the Scandinavians by converting them, and the Christian missionaries were prompt, brave, and enterprising. The date of the earliest recorded Viking raid on the coast of the Carolingian Empire is 799. King Harald—a claimant to the Danish crown—was baptized at Louis the Pious's residence at Ingelheim in 826 and took home with him a Frankish missionary, St. Anskar, who worked in Denmark for two years, till his patron Harald was finally evicted. St. Anskar then went on a two years' mission to Sweden. In 831 an archbishopric was founded, with St. Anskar as incumbent, at Hamburg. When Hamburg was sacked by Vikings in 845, the seat of the see was moved to Bremen. The See of Hamburg-Bremen was given the whole of Scandinavia for its diocese.

The East Roman ecclesiastical counter-offensive was as adventurous as the Frankish. The raid on Constantinople by the Rhos in 860 was answered by the installation of an Eastern Orthodox bishop by 867, and an archbishop *c.* 874, at Kiev, the raiders' base of operations in the Ukraine on the River Dnepr. In 957 Princess Olga, the ruler of Kiev, visited the East Roman Emperor Constantine VII Porphyrogenitus at Constantinople. She had probably been baptized at Kiev already. Her son Sviatoslav rejected the new religion, but the Christian community at Kiev survived, and Sviatoslav's successor, Vladimir, was converted to Eastern Orthodox Christianity in 989. In return for this, he was given an Imperial bride, Basil II's sister Anna.

Harald Gormsson, King of Denmark, was converted to Roman Catholic Christianity in 974, as part of the price of the peace that he had to purchase from the Saxon Emperor Otto II, whose territory Harald had invaded. King Olaf Tryggvason (ruled 995–1000) imposed Roman Catholic Christianity on Norway. Here, as at Kiev during Sviatoslav's reign, the resistance to conversion was violent, and it was violent in Sweden too, where, as in Norway, Christianity was imposed, *circa* 1008, by a king's, King Olaf Skotkonung's, fiat. Yet in 1000, the year in which Olaf Tryggvason died in battle with another Scandinavian Christian king, Sveinn of Denmark, the Icelanders decided voluntarily to adopt Roman Catholic Christianity *en masse*. Their motive was political. They feared that, if they remained divided between a Christian and a non-Christian faction, their frail republican institutions might break down.

Among the Scandinavian communities that established themselves abroad during the Viking Age, the Icelandic community was the most articulate. It was in Iceland that the corpus of pre-Christian Scandinavian poetry was preserved, and the heroes and heroines of the Icelandic sagas are Icelanders of the pre-Christian Age, down to, and inclusive of, the generation that adopted Christianity. However, this pre-Christian Icelandic literature has survived only in the form in which it was edited by twelfth-century and thirteenth-century Icelandic Christians. In Norway a new style of poetry was introduced in the ninth century. Culturally, Iceland and Norway were the foremost countries in the Viking-Age Scandinavian World. Politically, Viking-Age Sweden left a deeper and more enduring mark on the World's history. The Rhos Swedish settlers at Novgorod and Kiev were the creators of Russia, and, when Russia was converted to Eastern Orthodox Christianity in 989, Western Christendom, penned up in the European peninsula of the Old-World continent, was outflanked by Eastern Orthodox Christendom. This was outflanked, in its turn, by Islam, which had won the allegiance of the Volga Bulgars at some date before 922. But Volga Bulgaria was no match for Russia in scale. Thus the conversion of Russia in 989 opened the way for Eastern Orthodox Christendom to expand eventually northwards to the shore of the Arctic Ocean and eastwards to the shore of the North Pacific.

[58]

INDIA AND SOUTH-EAST
ASIA, 647–1202

By 647, which is the date of the Emperor Harsha's death, the Indian civilization had shown a remarkable capacity for assimilating outsiders. The Aryan invaders themselves, who had imposed themselves and their language on the North, and had disseminated their institutions throughout the subcontinent since the second millennium B.C. had not escaped cultural captivation by their pre-Aryan victims, and the same fate had overtaken successive conquerors of India from the north-west—for example, the supercilious Greeks who had overrun the derelict domain of the Maurya Empire, and the fierce Huns who had shattered the Gupta Empire. There had been Greek converts to both Buddhism and Hindu theism; the Huns had been incorporated in the Indian body social by being admitted to membership of the Kshatriya caste. In the race between the Indian and the Chinese civilizations for the cultural conquest of continental south-eastern Asia and Indonesia, the Indian civilization had captured the whole of this vast region except for what is now North Vietnam. In the competition between the same two civilizations for the cultural conquest of Tibet during the first half of the seventh century A.D., the Indian civilization had been the winner once again. The Indian civilization's greatest cultural triumph had been the propagation of an Indian religion, Mahayana Buddhism, in China itself, and, via China, in Korea and in Japan.

The Muslims were the first of India's invaders whom the Indian civilization proved unable to assimilate. There were Buddhist and Hindu converts to Islam, but there were no Muslim converts to Buddhism or to Hinduism. Islam established itself in the subcontinent as a politically dominant element that remained alien because it was unassimilable culturally. This novel sequel to a foreign invasion broke the religious and cultural unity of Indian life, and the break changed the course of Indian history. It is true that Hinduism showed greater survival-power under

Muslim rule than either Zoroastrianism or Christianity. Mass-conversions to Islam were confined to regions in which a majority of the local Hindu population were outcasts, and the Muslim conquerors found that they must treat unconverted Hindus as if they were 'People of the Book', though Hindus are polytheists, or, if they are not polytheists, they are monists. Hindus are therefore not entitled to toleration on a strict interpretation of Islamic law; yet in this case the application of the law was impracticable, since the conquered Hindu population was numerous, civilized, and indispensable.

The Muslim conquest of the Jumna–Ganges basin and Bengal was completed in, at most, ten years (1192–1202), or perhaps in seven (1192–9). The pace of Muslim conquest was even more rapid in India during those years than it had been in south-western Asia in the seventh century. Yet the military and political catastrophe that overtook India at the close of the twelfth century is not surprising. It is more remarkable that the greater part of the subcontinent had escaped being conquered by the Muslims for so long. It has been mentioned already that, in the sequel to Harsha's death, a Chinese envoy had routed a usurper of Harsha's throne by raising a punitive expeditionary force in Tibet. India's military weakness had thus been revealed, yet, from 647 to 1192, India —and the Indianized major part of continental south-eastern Asia and Indonesia too—continued to be divided among a large number of ephemeral local states, which squandered their energies in waging inconclusive wars with each other that merely aggravated the Indian World's political disunity and chaos. The warring Hindu states of northern India did join forces against the Muslim aggressors in 991 and in 1001, and again in 1191–2, but, on each occasion, this concerted action at the eleventh hour came too late to avert defeat. The Hindu states never responded to the Muslim's successive encroachments on Indian ground by forming a permanent political union even within regional limits. Yet the Muslim encroachments, like the Chinese envoy's punitive expedition after Harsha's death, had been ominously facile.

In 711 the lower Indus valley, as far north as Multan inclusive, had been conquered and annexed to the Umayyads' unitary Islamic state. This isolated enclave of Islamic territory on Indian soil would have been difficult to hold against a serious Indian counter-attack; yet the Muslims were never evicted from it. The Turkish Muslim Emir of Ghazni, Subuktegin, gained a foothold at Peshawar beyond the eastern exit from the Khyber Pass, as the result of his victory in 991 over a momentary coalition of Hindu kings. Subuktegin's successor Mahmud carried the Ghaznavid principality's eastern frontier forward to Lahore as a result of his victory in 1001. Mahmud also annexed the already existing enclave of Islamic territory in the Indus basin from Multan southwards to the coast, and beyond the eastern limit of his permanent conquests, he raided far afield in the Jumna–Ganges basin and in Gujerat during the years 1001–24. These were the preludes to the conquest of the rest of northern India in 1192–1202 by the Ghaznavids' supplanters the Ghoris —barbarians from the highlands of what is now central Afghanistan, whom Mahmud of Ghazni had conquered and had converted to Islam as recently as the year 1010.

The Muslims' progressive conquest of Indian territory was facilitated by the strife among their Indian opponents. In the North, Harsha's immediate political successors were various clans of Rajputs ('kings' sons' whose royal ancestors were the Huns who had descended on India in the fifth century). From *circa* 750 onwards, the Jumna–Ganges basin was disputed territory between the Rajputs and the Pala dynasty based on Bengal, till both Rajputs and Palas were overthrown by the Muslim Ghoris. In the Deccan, the Chalukya dynasty, which in 620 had checked Harsha's advance southwards, had then contended with the Pallavas, whose domain was the Tamil country in the South-East of the peninsula, till the Chalukyas were supplanted temporarily by the Rashtrakutas in 757 and the Pallavas permanently by Cholas in 897.

The Cholas, at their acme in 983–1035, came nearer to uniting the Indian World politically than any other power between the years 647 and 1202. During their half-century of potency, the Cholas did unite under their rule the whole of continental south-eastern India up to the line of the River Tungrabhadra and the lower course of the Godaveri. Still farther north-eastward, they annexed Kalinga and even raided the Pala dominions in Bengal. The Cholas also expanded overseas. They annexed Ceylon and the Maldive, Andeman, and Nicobar Islands, and they raided the Kingdom of Srivijaya on Sumatra in 1025 and the Malay Peninsula in 1068–9. However, in 973 the Chalukyas overthrew their own temporary overthrowers the Rashtrakutas, and they contended with the Cholas, as the first Chalukya dynasty had contended with the Pallavas, till both these competitors for the command over southern India were exhausted. The Chalukya Empire collapsed in 1190, the Chola in 1216. The Cholas at their zenith had organized an effective system of administration, but this did not outlive the Chola Empire itself. After 1216, southern India lay open to invasion by the Muslims who, from 1202 onwards, were masters of the whole of the North.

In Sumatra the Empire of Srivijaya, which had been founded towards the close of the seventh century, won the command over both shores of the Straits of Malacca. Srivijaya's power stood at its zenith from the close of the ninth century till it was crippled by the Cholas' raid in 1025. In Java, the Shailendra Empire, founded in the course of the latter half of the eighth century, dominated Cambodia, raided Champa, and won the throne of Srivijaya for a branch of the Shailendra dynasty. The Shailendras were in decline before the close of the ninth century, but this Javanese power and its local successors prevented the Sumatran Empire of Srivijaya from unifying Indonesia politically, notwithstanding Srivijaya's command over both the Malacca Straits and the Sunda Straits—a command which had given Srivijaya the two keys to the naval control over the passage between the Indian Ocean and the China Sea.

In continental South-East Asia the earliest known stratum of the population spoke (and still speaks in Cambodia and in parts of Burma) languages of the Mon-Khmer branch of the Austric family, to which the Munda languages in India also belong. In Champa (present-day central Vietnam) the Chams spoke a language of the kindred Austronesian (Malay) family. But, since the second century A.D., which is the earliest age of South-East-Asian history for which we have a record, continental South-East Asia has been invaded culturally by religious and artistic influences from the west and ethnically by immigrants from the north. India and Ceylon have been the sources of the cultural influences (Hindu, Buddhist, and eventually Muslim) from the west. The immigrants from the north have been speakers of languages of the continental East-Asian monosyllabic family. These immigrants, like the speakers of the Austric and Austronesian languages whom they have submerged or have driven southwards, have been captivated culturally by the influences from India—except for the Vietnamese, who have adopted the Chinese culture and the Chinese form of Mahayana Buddhism, in spite of their successful resistance, on the political plane, to becoming incorporated in China permanently. After having been annexed to China for the second time in 111 B.C., the Vietnamese regained their political independence in A.D. 939.

The Vietnamese were already established in what is now North Vietnam before the first annexation of that country to China *c.* 214 B.C. The Vietnamese language belongs to the Chinese-Thai branch of the monosyllabic family. The Burmans, whose language belongs to the Burmese-Tibetan branch of the family, descended on present-day Burma from the north-west at some date between *c.* 850 and 1050. In the reign (1044–7) of Anawrata, the Burmese King of Pagan in present-day Upper Burma, the Burmans conquered the rest of present-day Burma. The inhabitants were Mons; and the Mon language and the Mon version of Indian religion and culture were current till 1167–73 in the northern part of the country in which a Burmese-speaking population had already installed itself.

Champa was in a chronic state of war with Vietnam from 975 onwards, and with Cambodia, too, from 1145 onwards. This warfare in continental South-East Asia was a counterpart of the contention between

Srivijaya and the Shailendra Empire in Indonesia and between the Cholas and the Chalukyas and between the Palas and the Rajputs in India. In continental South-East Asia, as in India, the inconclusive contests between indigenous local states were terminated by military intervention from outside. In the thirteenth century South-East Asia was invaded by the Mongols, while part of it was occupied by the Thais from Nan-chao (the present-day Chinese province Yunnan).

The military and political history of the Indian civilization from the second half of the seventh century to the early years of the thirteenth century reads like a tale told by an idiot. The same verdict is deserved by the history of warfare and politics at most times and places; but the vanity of these activities is conspicuously manifest in the Indian World, and in this period above all. The significant fields of activity were religion and visual art, and, in Hindu society, religion includes social organization and customary law, as well as ritual practice and spiritual experience.

When we move from the military and political plane to the religious plane, we find that the history of the Indian civilization during this period makes sense. On this plane the outstanding event is the gradual recession of Buddhism within the subcontinent. Here Buddhism's last stronghold was the Pala Kingdom in Bengal, and Buddhism was given its *coup de grâce* in India when Bengal was conquered by Ghori Muslim invaders in 1199 or in 1202. Here the Buddhist monasteries were singled out for destruction; yet Buddhism in India might perhaps have survived even this attack if, in India, it had not been in decline already for the past six or seven centuries. Jainism's fortunes were the inverse of Buddhism's. Jainism never found its way into either East or South-East Asia. On the other hand, Jainism never became extinct in India itself, though in India it never became more than a minoritarian sect.

Theravada Buddhism fared like Jainism. Though it competed with the Mahayana in the Tarim basin, it fell out of the race when the Mahayana advanced into China. On the other hand, the Theravadins kept a foothold in the subcontinent—not on the mainland, but in Ceylon—and in 1190 some Mon and Khmer Theravadin Buddhist monks who had visited Ceylon planted the Sinhalese form of the Theravada in Burma. For South-East Asia, this was as significant an event as the Muslim military conquest was for northern India in the following decade. The dominant Muslim minority of foreign invaders reinforced by native converts brought India, for the first time, under the rule of masters whom she was unable to assimilate culturally.

On the religious and artistic planes, the rulers and subjects of the warring local states of India and South-East Asia achieved results of enduring importance and value.

The Pala Kingdom disseminated the Mahayana not only in Tibet in the seventh century but also, in the eighth century, in distant Java. In Java the Mahayana is no longer alive, but it has left an abiding monument of its presence at Borobudur in one of the most lovely of all human works of art. Here in 772 the founder of the Shailendra dynasty encased a hill in a stupa, and the bas-reliefs that adorn the encircling tiers of terraces give a visual presentation of the whole world of Mahayanian mythology and metaphysics. The natural setting of this exquisite work of art is as lovely as the architecture and the sculpture. The sheer mountain that rises on one side is balanced by the green paddies that spread out on the other side. Borobudur has immortalized the ephemeral Shailendra Empire that created this monument.

The Kingdom of Cambodia was founded in the sixth century A.D. and it survived into the 1970s. At Angkor it had time to bequeath to posterity a number of magnificent works of architecture. The *chef d'oeuvre* is Angkor Wat, a temple, built by King Suryavarman II (1113–*c*. 1145), which can challenge comparison with the Parthenon on the acropolis of Athens, whether our criterion is the symmetry of the architectural design or the vitality of the figures that animate the frieze.

At Sravana Belgola in southern India, the Jains have done what the Buddhists have done in central Java, at Borobudur. They have made Nature minister to the creation of a human work of art. At Borobudur, Nature has been coaxed; at Sravana Belgola she has been overpowered. In 983 the summit of one of the twin mountains beneath which the Jain monastery nestles was shorn away to disengage the colossal statue of a spiritual hero. The statue is all of a piece with the mountain that has been cut away round it. The rock is hard and steep and hot. Its surface scorches the soles of the climber's feet. This Jain monument is not a thing of beauty, but it has an awe-inspiring grandeur with which neither Angkor Wat nor Borobudur can vie.

The Cholas failed to found an enduring empire, but they have left enduring monuments. At the Chola dynasty's acme, the southern style of Indian temple-architecture reached its zenith.

The two most influential men among all the human beings that lived and died in India between the years 647 and 1202 were not soldiers or rulers; they were not even architects or sculptors; they were philosophers: Šankara (*c*. 788–838) and Ramanuja (born *c*. 1028 and lived on into the twelfth century). Both these great teachers were southerners. Šankara's home was Kerala, in the extreme south-east of the peninsula; Ramanuja's home was the Tamil country; but the whole subcontinent was their mission-field. In India in their time there were social barriers between castes, but there were no geographical barriers for sages and saints. These were not confined within political or linguistic frontiers.

Šankara and Ramanuja were both concerned with a question that was being debated in northern India already in the sixth century B.C.: What is the nature of the ultimate spiritual reality in and behind the phenomena? And what is the relation between this reality and a human being? Šankara was an uncompromising monist. He held that a human being is identical with the ultimate reality and that the phenomenal world is illusory. If the truth is as the monist sees it, individuality, and therefore personality, must be numbered among the illusory phenomena. In a wholly unitary reality there is no room for either a personal god or for a personal god's personal human devotee. Ramanuja criticized Šankara's philosophy. Ramanuja stood for a 'modified monism' which would allow the human being Ramanuja to feel a personal devotion to the god Vishnu.

Ramanuja accused Šankara of being a crypto-Buddhist, and he was right. Šankara's philosophy pre-supposes the metaphysics which the Mahayana Buddhists had thought out in defiance of the Buddha's disapproval of metaphysical speculation. Ramanuja's criticism of Šankara pre-supposes Šankara's thesis. Ramanuja and Šankara were in agreement with each other in standing for a Hindu reaction against Buddhism. Yet neither of these neo-Hindu philosophers could have made their war on Buddhism if Buddhism itself had not supplied them with their intellectual weapons.

[59]

EASTERN ASIA, 763–1126

THE Chinese civilization, and even the T'ang dynasty, survived the devastating bout of anarchy through which China passed during the years 755–63. One of the components of contemporary Chinese society that enabled it to survive was the professional civil service recruited by competitive examination in the Confucian classics. The civil service had had time to re-establish its hold by this date. This institution had been rehabilitated by the Sui dynasty, and the civil servants' *esprit de corps* and personal ambition had been stimulated by the foundation of the Han-lin Academy on the eve of the catastrophe. The civil service fortified the fabric of Chinese society at the price of making it resistant to reform, as well as to disintegration.

In 780 the basis of taxation was changed. One major cause of the temporary collapse of the T'ang regime had been the breakdown of the system, in force since the later decades of the fifth century, under which the Imperial Government had assigned allotments of land to the peasantry and had exacted, in return, personal tax-payments and corvée-services. From 780 onwards the tax was levied, no longer on the person, but on the land. The Government failed to save the peasants' land from being acquired by landlords. The peasants became tenants, and their economic position deteriorated, but the Government did not lose revenue.

The Government was able to compel the landlords to pay the new land-tax because the average size of the land-holdings of this new class of landowners was not large enough to enable these to live as unemployed rentiers. The landowning class was now approximately identical with the revived Confucian bureaucracy, and it depended for its livelihood partly on the salaries that its members received as officials in the Government's service. This gave the Government a leverage for keeping these administrator-landowners under control.

The Confucian civil servants and the Taoists, both philosophical and popular, had a common interest in working for a reduction of the power and wealth that had been won in China by Buddhist monasteries and convents since the period of barbarian invasion and political disunity (304–589). The Confucianism of the pre-Buddhist Age of Chinese civilization was no match for Mahayana Buddhism intellectually, but, in the generation immediately following the catastrophe of 755–63, there appeared the first representatives of a neo-Confucian school of philosophy, Han Yü (768–824) and his contemporary Li Ao (d. *c.* 844). These neo-Confucians, like their Indian contemporary the Hindu neo-monist Šankara, were actually crypto-Buddhists. They were rejuvenating Confucianism by infusing into it the spirit of the Mahayana and by concentrating attention on Confucian works that lent themselves to this Buddhist-like interpretation, namely the book of Mencius and a chapter called 'The Great Learning' from one of the five classics, *The Book of Rites*. This transfiguration of Confucianism was making China spiritually independent of the presence of Buddhist institutions, and in the years 842–5 the Imperial Government gave practical effect to the Confucians' and the Taoists' persistent criticism of Buddhism on economic and social grounds. Buddhist monks and nuns were now defrocked in large numbers and reduced to the status of tax-paying laymen, and much of the property of Buddhist monasteries and convents was expropriated. By Jewish–Christian–Muslim standards at the western end of the Old-World Oikoumenê, the persecution of Buddhism in China in 842–5 was mild, but by East Asian standards it was severe.

Buddhism in China was not extirpated by this persecution. Buddhism had become inextricably intertwined with Confucianism and Taoism, not only at the sophisticated level but also at the popular level—and at this level to a still greater degree. In Confucian and Taoist disguise, Buddhism continued to be a major influence in Chinese spiritual and intellectual life. However, the persecution in 842–5 was not confined to Buddhism. It was extended to other religions which, unlike Buddhism, were recent alien importations at this date. Manichaeism, Zoroastrianism, and Nestorian Christianity in China did not survive this ordeal. Yet the persecution of these religions did not have the same economic and social justification as the persecution of Buddhism. The number of their adherents and the value of their assets were relatively small.

Manichaeism had been privileged in China because the Uighur Turks, who had been China's allies since an early date in the T'ang era, and who had helped the T'ang dynasty to surmount the crisis of 755–63, had adopted Manichaeism as their national religion in the latter year. But in 840 the Uighurs had been evicted by the Kirghiz from their domain on the Eurasian steppe in what is now Mongolia, and had been driven into China and into the Tarim basin. The Chinese Imperial Government started to suppress Manichaeism in China in 842.

The T'ang regime's reprieve lasted from 763 to 874. We have first-hand contemporary evidence for the state of affairs in China during that century in the poems of the Chinese poet Po Chü-i (772–846) and in the diary of the Japanese Buddhist monk Ennin, who was a pilgrim in China during the years 838–47. Both these writers were witnesses of the persecution in China of Buddhism and of other non-indigenous religions in 842–5; yet both give the impression that China in this age was governed both effectively and humanely. However, the reforms that had been the regime's response to the catastrophe of 755–63 failed to avert an eventual breakdown. The T'ang dynasty expired in 909; the Sung dynasty, which was the next to rule over a united China, was not inaugurated till 960. *De facto* the interregnum lasted from 874 to 979, and the Empire was not re-united intact. It lost fringes of territory in all quarters.

The state of P'o-hai in eastern Manchuria, which had been founded in 713 and, like the Korean state Silla, had acknowledged the T'ang dynasty's suzerainty, was conquered in 926 by the Khitan, a Eurasian nomad people whose mother-tongue was perhaps Mongol. In 946 the Khitan proclaimed themselves rulers of China under the dynastic name Liao; and, though they were unable to make this claim good, they did compel the Sung dynasty in 1004 to recognize their title to sixteen border districts to the south of the eastern end of the Great Wall and also to undertake to pay them tribute. In 1038 the Tanguts, a Tibetan people whom the T'ang had allowed to settle in north-western China, followed the Khitans' example. They took the dynastic title 'Western Hsia' (Hsia was the name of the legendary first dynasty of China). In 1044 the Sung had to purchase peace from the Tanguts too at the price of agreeing to pay them tribute. In the South, which was the direction in which Chinese expansion had met with the least resistance originally, China's territory was diminished permanently in 939 by the secession of North Vietnam, which had been an integral part of China continuously since 111 B.C.

The Sung re-unifiers of China were caught in a dilemma. Their first concern was to save the Empire from being broken up again by the rise of local war-lords, and they succeeded in avoiding this, but the price was a sacrifice of military efficiency which put the Sung at a disadvantage in their relations with their aggressive barbarian neighbours. Once again, the regime needed a thorough-going reform, and it found a clear-sighted, energetic, and courageous reformer in a civil servant, Wang An-shih (1021–86). Between the years 1069 and 1076 Wang An-shih carried out a number of fundamental reforms, and these remained in force throughout the reign (1067–85) of the Emperor Shen Tsung. Wang An-shih was able to put these reforms into effect because he had the Emperor's confidence, but, after Shen Tsung's death, Wang An-shih's measures were all rescinded in 1085–6, though they were the right remedies for Sung China's social sickness.

Wang An-shih failed for the same reason as Akhenaton in fourteenth-century-B.C. Pharaonic Egypt and as the Gracchi in second-century-B.C. Roman Italy. Wang An-shih had to work with an utterly conservative-minded 'establishment'; he was singular in being free from the mental shackles of tradition, and his free thought offended and perturbed his mentally hide-bound colleagues. No doubt his radical measures would have alienated the conservatives in any case, but their opposition was exacerbated by a provocativeness that was inherent in Wang An-shih's temperament. The enemies that he made included some upright and distinguished men whose support he ought to have wooed. The minister who repealed Wang An-shih's acts was the eminent historian Ssu-ma Kuang.

Wang An-shih perceived, and proclaimed, that an academic education in the Confucian classics, in which the student's aim was to placate pedantic-minded official examiners, was not the right preparation for the performance of a civil servant's practical task. Wang An-shih's remedy was to introduce a new official interpretation of the classics and to reform the public examination system. If the Emperor Shen Tsung had lived longer these educational reforms might have produced a new generation of open-minded civil servants. Meanwhile, Wang An-shih had to work through colleagues who were products of the old school. In spite of this handicap he succeeded in putting his plans into effect. He arranged for the government to make loans to peasants at a lower rate of interest than the rate charged by private money-lenders. He replaced the corvée by paid labour, and he financed the cost of this by assessing the land-tax on productivity, not on area, and by imposing most of this burden on those landowners who could best afford to bear it. These fiscal measures of Wang An-shih's were revivals of reforms that had been made under the T'ang regime after 755–63. Wang An-shih's re-establishment of a peasant militia was a revival of a measure that had been the prelude to the rejuvenation and re-unification of China by the Sui dynasty.

Wang An-shih's reforms were timely; their repeal was prompted by personal animus; and within forty years it brought its nemesis. In 1114–25 the Jurchen (Jürched), a Tungus-speaking people on the north-eastern borders of the Khitans' dominions beyond the former state of P'o-hai, overthrew the Khitan. In 1126 the Jürched, who had taken the dynastic title Kin (Chin) in 1115, conquered the Sung dynasty's capital Kaifeng on the Yellow River, to the east of Loyang, and took prisoner the reigning emperor and his predecessor. At this one stroke, the Sung

Empire lost all its territory to the north of the Yangtse basin. Wang An-shih's opponents blamed him retrospectively for this disaster. A juster verdict on the disaster of 1126 is that it might have been averted if Wang An-shih's reforms had been given time to bear fruit.

On the military and political planes, China's history from 755 to 1126 is a story of disaster that was not averted by the reforms in 780 and 1069–76. On the cultural plane, however, China's history in this age is a story of achievement. Like the barbarians who had overrun northern China in and after 304, their successors in the tenth, eleventh, and twelfth centuries were captivated by the Chinese civilization and, besides adopting it themselves, they propagated it in territories under their rule that had never been embraced within the Chinese Empire's frontiers. Thus the contraction of the Chinese Empire was offset by an expansion of the Chinese civilization—and this not only in the Chinese Empire's peripheral successor-states, but also in Korea and Japan.

In this age Chinese civilization made itself still more attractive than it had been in past ages. Its current achievements were many-sided. The working-out of the neo-Confucian philosophy was carried forward by two brothers, Ch'eng Hao (1032–85) and Ch'eng Yi (1033–1108) who were Wang An-shih's contemporaries. (Ch'eng Hao co-operated with Wang An-shih at first, but opposed some of his measures later.) The Ch'engs carried to completion a change that their predecessor Han Yü had inaugurated. Ch'eng Yi virtually deposed the five classics that had been canonized in the Han Age, except for two chapters of *The Book of Rites*, namely 'The Great Learning' and 'The Doctrine of the Mean'. He established a new canon of four books, by adding to these two the book of Mencius and the *Analects*, which purports to be a collection of Confucius' answers to questions. Ch'eng Yi's school of neo-Confucianism became the standard version for the education of civil servants, and its metaphysical component gave Confucianism a new dimension, but this did not inspire Confucian students, examiners, and administrators to think for themselves.

In the arts the Chinese of the T'ang and Sung Age were not prisoners of their past. The Chinese had readily accepted the Graeco-Indian visual art that had entered China with the Mahayana. They turned it into something distinctively Chinese, and they developed particular genres of their own. Chinese landscape-painting reached its zenith in the Sung Age, and so did Chinese painted and glazed pottery, the making of which was an indigenous Chinese craft. The T'ang Age achieved the block-printing of books. The poet Po Chü-i's works were perhaps printed in 800–10, in the poet's own life-time, and his poems were circulating in Japan before his death. The stimulus for book-printing was given by a demand for the mass-production of the Mahayana Buddhist scriptures—

for laymen as well as for monks—and of the texts of the Confucian classics for examinees. The Han-lin Academy produced a printed edition of the Confucian classics, with a commentary, in 130 volumes during the years 932–53, i.e. at a time when, politically, China was in turmoil. The scriptures of the Mahayana, and of Taoism, in editions that ran to several thousand volumes or rolls, were printed within the first sixty years of the Sung Age. Sets of these were exported to Korea and to Japan.

Gunpowder, invented in the sixth century for use in fire-crackers, was being used in war by the twelfth century. In navigation and maritime trade the initiative was taken by the Indians and the Muslims. When, in 879, Canton was sacked by Chinese rebels, there was a large community there of foreign businessmen, and they suffered severely. Yet commercial relations with the Indian and Islamic worlds were interrupted only temporarily. The Chinese took an increasingly active part in this trade, and the south coast of China, which had been, in Chinese eyes, the end of the Earth at the time when it had first been incorporated in the Chinese Empire, now began to replace Kansu as China's front door. The conductive Eurasian steppe was being replaced by the still more conductive Ocean as China's principal medium of communication with other parts of the Old-World Oikoumenê.

In Korea, T'ang China's satellite Silla lapsed into anarchy towards the end of the ninth century, contemporaneously with the collapse in China itself, but in Korea the interregnum was shorter. It lasted only from 889 to 936, when Korea was re-united by the Koryo dynasty, which had been founded in 918.

In Japan the ambitious attempt to produce there a replica of T'ang China gradually went awry. The T'ang Empire's capital, Ch'ang-an, was reproduced in the physical sense, though on a smaller scale, at Nara in 710 and then at Kyoto in 794. In theory the whole of the Japanese Empire was now administered and taxed on the Chinese pattern. But Japan could not muster a Chinese-educated personnel in the numbers required for translating theory into practice. The Chinese institution of recruiting civil servants by competitive literary examination was never acclimatized in Japan, and the governors of the provinces who ruled in the emperor's name became virtually independent hereditary princes, like the contemporary descendants of Charlemagne's provincial governors at the opposite end of the Old World.

However, the period of peace in Japan that had been inaugurated in 646 by the official adoption of a T'ang-style constitution lasted for more than a quarter of a millennium. In the course of those 250 years Chinese civilization, including the Chinese version of Mahayana Buddhism, struck such deep roots in Japan that it became ineradicable there; and, though the Japanese were unable to maintain this exotic import in its original form, they could, and did, transmute it into something Japanese, as the Chinese had transmuted into something Chinese the Buddhism that they had imported from India.

Three histories of Japan, in chronicle form, were produced between 712 and 791, while the capital of the Empire was at Nara. These histories were written in Chinese characters, and, while most of the characters were used in the Chinese way as ideograms, to express their Chinese meanings, some were used as phonemes, to convey the sounds of syllabic components of Japanese words. In the ninth century two syllabaries for writing Japanese phonetically were created out of the Chinese characters that had been given phonetic values. This invention would have made it possible to write Japanese without using any other Chinese characters phonetically or any at all ideographically, but the characters continued to be used ideographically, in combination with the syllabaries, for writing Japanese, partly because of the characters' prestige and partly because of their clarity for the conveyance of the Chinese words with which the Japanese had enriched their own vocabulary. Many of these borrowed Chinese words are indistinguishable from each other in their Japanese pronunciation and were therefore also indistinguishable in the phonetic conveyance of this pronunciation in one of the Japanese syllabaries, but the same words, written ideographically in the original Chinese characters, cannot be mistaken for each other. For these reasons, the use of Chinese ideograms, employed ideographically, persisted in the writing of Japanese.

This mixture of Chinese ideograms with Japanese syllabic phonemes was as complicated as the Pahlavi script in which Aramaic words, written in the Aramaic alphabet, were used as ideograms for representing Iranian words pronounced in the Iranian way; yet this awkward script provided the vehicle for a sophisticated Japanese literature which flowered early in the eleventh century. The *chef d'oeuvre* is the Lady Murasaki Shikibu's *The Tale of Genji*.

Thus, by 1126, China, whose people had once believed that theirs was the only civilization in the World, had become 'the Middle Kingdom' of half the World, surrounded by cultural satellites that had each adopted the Chinese civilization to some degree but had fashioned it into a distinctive variety of Eastern Asia's common Sinic culture. Moreover, Eastern Asia as a whole was now interacting with other parts of the Old-World Oikoumenê. A religion of Indian origin, the Mahayana form of Buddhism, had been disseminated, via China, to Japan, Korea, and the country that is known today as North Vietnam, and all East Asian countries were now in touch, both by sea and overland, not only with South-East Asia and with India, but also with the Islamic World on the far side of the Indian subcontinent.

[60]

THE MESO-AMERICAN AND
ANDEAN CIVILIZATIONS, *c.* 900–1428

F or this period, as for the preceding periods, there is a consensus among archaeologists over the dating of Meso-American events in terms of years of the Christian Era, but, for this period also, there is disagreement over the dating of Andean events. It has been mentioned already that the relative chronological order of the phases of Andean history is not in doubt; but that, from *c.* 400 B.C. to *c.* A.D. 1438, the absolute datings, in terms of years B.C. and A.D., that are indicated by radio-carbon tests differ widely from the reckonings based on stratigraphy. According to the radio-carbon-test chronology, which has been adopted provisionally in this book, the 'Florescent' phase of Andean history ended *c.* A.D. 500, and in A.D. 900 the Tiahuanáco horizon was approaching its terminal date. These two phases of Andean history have therefore been dealt with in Chapter 48, though, according to the stratigraphical chronology, the 'Florescent' phase was not over by the year 900, and the whole of the Tiahuanáco horizon falls within the years 1000–1300.

In the Meso-American World the 'Classic' Age (*c.* 300–900) had ended in downfall. On the Mexican plateau, first Teotihuacán *c.* 600, and then Cholúla *c.* 800, had been taken and sacked by barbarian invaders from the desert to the north of the region that had been brought under cultivation. In the Maya region, the central area, in which the Maya form of the Meso-American civilization had risen to its zenith, had been abandoned progressively in the course of the ninth century. Early in the tenth century, another band of northern barbarians, the Toltecs, had invaded the cultivated country to the south of the desert, and these differed from their predecessors in being something more than mere destroyers. They acquired enough of the Meso-American civilization to enable them to create their own distinctive version of it. Their capital, Tula, to the north of the Mexican lakes, cannot compare with Teoti-huacán; yet its architecture and sculpture are impressive.

The Toltecs and their successors in the post-'Classic' phase of Meso-American history were militarists. These were not the first militarists in the Meso-American World. The Olmecs had been militarists, and so, in the ninth century A.D., had been the Maya in the Usumacinta valley, to judge by the evidence of the brutal murals at 'Bonampák'. In the post-'Classic' Age, however, Meso-American militarism was accentuated to a degree at which it became the dominant feature of Meso-American life.

The beginning of the post-'Classic' Age of Meso-American history also saw the introduction of metallurgy from the Andean World. This technique reached the west coast of Mexico by sea, probably from coastal Ecuador. In the contemporary Andean World, copper, and eventually also bronze, was used for making tools and weapons, but, with the exception of the Tarascans in the hinterland of the Pacific coast, the Meso-American pupils of the Andean metallurgists did not follow their teachers in this. They became exquisitely skilful in making gold and silver ornaments, but, when the Aztecs encountered the Spaniards in the sixteenth century, the Aztecs were still using weapons made of stone and wood. It is remarkable that a people who had become as obsessively militaristic as the Aztecs had never set their smiths to work on making metal sword-blades and spear-heads in emulation of their neighbours and adversaries the Tarascans.

Tula, like Cholúla and Teotihuacán and La Venta and San Lorenzo, was destroyed by violence. This fate overtook Tula at some date in the second half of the twelfth century. Meanwhile, the Toltec founder of the city of Tula, Topíltzin, had been expelled by a hostile faction of the Toltecs and was known to have taken to the sea. A prophecy that, one day, he would return from the sea was handed down to the Toltecs' successors, the Aztecs. Topíltzin seems to have travelled by sea to the west coast of Yucatán and to have conquered for himself a miniature empire there, with its capital at Chichén. According to the records of the Yucatec Maya, a conqueror named Kukulkán arrived in Yucatán by sea from the west in or shortly before 987. In the Maya language, 'Kukulkán' means 'feathered serpent', and this is also the meaning of the exiled Toltec King Topíltzin's surname 'Quetzalcoatl'—the name of a Mexican god in the form of a feathered serpent with whom Topíltzin was identified. (Topíltzin's offence, in the eyes of one faction of the Toltecs, may have been his devotion to this god, who demanded penitential discipline, but disapproved of human sacrifice.)

The state founded by Kukulkán–Quetzalcoatl in north-western Yucatán lasted from *c.* 987 to *c.* 1224. Here there was a blend of Toltec and Maya architecture, visual art, religion, and manners and customs. The Toltec spirit asserted itself in an obsessive addiction to human sacrifice. Topíltzin, if he is truly identical with Kukulkán, may not have been bloodthirsty enough to satisfy the more ferocious faction of his fellow Toltecs, but the hybrid Toltec-Maya civilization that he inaugurated in Yucatán was more bloodthirsty than the Maya had been before their Toltec conquerors arrived. The bloodthirstiness of western Yucatán's Toltec rulers is commemorated at Chichén in a platform decorated with a frieze of human skulls; it is also betrayed by the human skeletons that have been dredged up from the bottom of the Chenóte at Chichén. (The Chenóte is a pool, in a cavity, into which human victims were flung.)

After the Toltec makers and masters of Chichén had faded away, Chichén was occupied by a wandering band of Maya, the Itzá, and, *c.* 1283, the Itzá's leader, who styled himself Kukulkán in imitation of Chichén's Toltec founder, built, about half way between Chichén and the west coast of Yucatán, the city of Mayapán. This was the earliest walled city in the Maya region, and it was the capital of north-western Yucatán from *c.* 1283 to *c.* 1461, when Mayapán was abandoned after having been destroyed in a civil war.

In the Itzá phase, as in the preceding Toltec phase, of the history of Yucatán the local Maya form of the Meso-American civilization was blended with elements introduced from the Mexican plateau, and one Itzá clan in the series that bore rule successively at Mayapán seized power there with the help of a company of expatriate Mexican mercenaries.

Though Mayapán was encased in a wall, it was not laid out on a plan, as the unwalled city Teotihuacán had been. By contrast, the city of Chanchán in north-western coastal Peru was laid out, on a rectangular grid, on the scale of Babylon and of Alexandria-on-Nile.

According to both of the discrepant datings of the phase of Andean history that followed the fading-out of the Tiahuanáco horizon, this post-Tiahuanáco phase falls within the time-span 1000–1430. In this phase the Andean World was neither a political nor a cultural unity, but, at least in the coastal lowlands, it was divided politically between not more than three states—Chimú, Cuizmanco, Chincha—and these dwarfed the states of the pre-Tiahuanáco Age of 'Florescence', when the lowland section of each river valley had constituted a separate political unit.

If we take a synoptic view of Andean history and Hellenic history, we shall find ourselves equating the 'Florescent' period of Andean history with the four centuries of Hellenic history, ending in 334 B.C., in which the standard political units in the Hellenic World were city-states. In the 'Florescent' period of Andean history, as in the 'classical' period of Hellenic history, the arts rose to their zenith. The Andean coastal states of the post-Tiahuanáco Age were counterparts of the successor-states of the Persian Empire that were founded by the Persians' Macedonian Greek conquerors.

The Andean coastal cities in this phase of Andean history were the capitals of empires in which a number of valleys were welded together. In each state the population was concentrated in the capital, and the irrigation-system was reorganized. Water drawn from several valleys was diverted to irrigate land in the neighbourhood of the populous capital city. The scale of Chanchán, the capital of Chimú, in particular, is so impressive that archaeologists have labelled this period of Andean history the 'Urbanizing' or 'City-building' Age. The great size of the cities is, in truth, characteristic. In the 'Florescent' Age there had been no city in the Moche valley on the scale of Chanchán; but, in quality, the pottery of the 'Urbanizing' Age in the Moche valley cannot compare with the Mochica pottery of the 'Florescent' Age. The 'Urbanizing' Age was prosaic. It excelled, not in decorating vases, but in making metal tools.

Chanchán is a row of vast rectangular compounds enclosed within massive mud-brick walls. The purpose of these walls does not appear to have been defence. The Chimú state's defences were on its frontiers—for instance, at Paramonga, overhanging the lowland section of the Fortaléza valley, which was probably the south-easternmost of the valleys that were included in Chimú state.

Chanchán was the largest city in the Andean World in the 'Urbanizing' Age—and indeed in any age, before or after this, till the growth in the size of Lima within living memory. But the most highly revered shrine in the Andean World in the 'Urbanizing' Age lay in the territory of Cuizmanco, at Pachacámac—so named after the god who was worshipped there. Pachacámac was an ecumenical god. His shrine was visited by pilgrims from all quarters.

[61]

THE ISLAMIC WORLD, 945–1110

THE occupation of Baghdad in 945 by the Buwayhid rulers of one of the Abbasid Caliphate's successor-states made it manifest that the disintegration of the Abbasid Empire, which had started in the ninth century, was irreversible. The Buwayhid dynasty was not the first that had made itself master of Abbasid territory *de facto* without asking the Caliph's leave, but it was the first that had occupied the Abbasids' metropolitan province Iraq and that had established a direct control over the Caliphate itself. The Buwayhids were Iranians from Gilan, and their domination of the Abbasid Caliphate was the culmination of the Iranians' progressive gains in political power in the Islamic state at the Arabs' expense. This tendency had already declared itself in the revolution in 747–50 that had enabled the Abbasids to capture the Caliphate, and then in the Caliph Ma'mun's victory over his brother Amin in 813. However, the Buwayhids, besides being Iranians, were Shi'is, and their arrival at Baghdad in 945 therefore seemed to portend a reversal rather than a completion of the revolution of 747–50 in its religious aspect. In working for the revolution the Shi'is had hoped that it would result in the Umayyads being replaced by the Alids. On that occasion, they had been disappointed. Now, two centuries later, their long-deferred hopes seemed at last to be on the way towards being realized.

In North-West Africa in 909 the Aghlabids had been overthrown by the representative of a family that claimed descent from Ali and Fatimah. The Aghlabids were Arabs and Sunnis who had nominally recognized the Abbasids as their suzerains. The Fatimids, too, were Arabs, but their troops were Kutamah Berbers. The Fatimids aspired to supplant the Abbasids, and their victories were victories for the Berber race and for the Isma'ili (Seven-Imam) denomination of the Shi'ah sect. In 914 they tried, but failed, to conquer Egypt, but they succeeded in 969. Meanwhile in 890 the Qarmathians, a community of Shi'is of the same

Seven-Imam denomination as the Fatimids, had tried to establish a state in Iraq. The Abbasids had succeeded in evicting the Qarmathians from the Fertile Crescent in 903-6, but the Qarmathians had found a secure base of operations in north-eastern Arabia, in Hasa and on the Bahrain Islands. From here they raided not only Iraq but Mecca. They carried off the Black Stone from the Ka'bah in 930. Shi'is of a different denomination, the Zaydis, who had ruled the Caspian coast of Iran from 864 to 928, had founded in 897 a second state in the Yemen. Isma'ili Shi'is gained control of Multan in 977 and of part of Sind in 985. By this latter date, the only considerable parts of the Islamic World that were still effectively under Sunni rule were the Samanid Iranian successor-state of the Abbasids in Transoxania and Khorasan and the refugee Umayyad Caliphate in the Iberian Peninsula; and the Umayyads were as hostile to the Abbasids politically as were the Shi'is. In 985 it looked as if the Islamic World were going to be partitioned between the Iranians and the Berbers and that, if it were to be re-united, the re-unifiers would be the Isma'ili Shi'i Fatimids.

Moreover, the Isma'ili Shi'is and the Iranians were now in the ascendant on the cultural as well as on the political plane. The epic poet Firdawsi (934-1020), the philosopher Ibn Sina (Avicenna) (980-1037), and the scientific observer Biruni (973-1048) were Iranians. From *circa* 970 onwards, the 'Pure Brethren' (Ikhwan-as-Safa), an Isma'ili community at Basrah, were producing an encyclopaedia, and in 973 the Fatimid Isma'ilis founded a theological college at the Mosque of Al-Azhar in their new capital, Cairo. In general, the political break-up of the Abbasid Empire was beneficial for literature and art. The multiplication of local courts multiplied the number of potential patrons.

The Iranian version of the Islamic civilization had come to stay; it immortalized itself in a New-Persian (Farsi) literature; but, before the close of the eleventh century, other expectations that had been reasonable *c.* 985 had been disappointed. By 1085 Sunni governments were once again in power in all parts of the Islamic World except Egypt, and, though Egypt was still under Shi'i Fatimid rule, the Fatimids' Egyptian Sunni Muslim subjects had not adopted their rulers' version of Islam. In 1085 the Abbasid dynasty was still on the throne at Baghdad and was still under tutelage, but, since 1055, its masters had been no longer the Shi'i Iranian Buwayhids; they were now the Sunni Turkish Saljuqs. The Turks had replaced the Iranians as the masters of the Asian part of the Islamic World almost everywhere except in the Arabian Peninsula.

The Shi'ah had failed to seize opportunities in 656-61 and in 747-50. In 969-1055 it failed again. The Fatimids and the Qarmathians did not co-operate with each other. Though both parties were Shi'is of the Isma'ili denomination, the Qarmathians felt a concern for social justice, whereas the Fatimids' main concern was to vindicate their own hereditary divine right. The Fatimids and the Qarmathians were not congenial to each other. As for the Buwayhids, they held aloof from them both. The Buwayhids were Shi'is of some non-Isma'ili denomination. They preferred being the Abbasids' masters to becoming the Fatimids' subjects, and, for the Buwayhids, this would have been the only alternative. The various non-Isma'ili denominations of the Shi'ah agreed with each other and with the Sunni majority of the Muslim community in being reluctant to fall under Isma'ili rule. The Isma'ilis, resenting their consequent failure to make themselves masters of the Islamic World, retorted by organizing *c.* 1090 a secret society, the Assassins. An early eminent victim of theirs was the Nizam-al-Mulk, the Iranian minister of the Saljuq Turkish Sunni supplanters of the Buwayhids.

For the population of the Islamic World, the tenth and eleventh centuries were a time of tribulation. The break-up of the unitary Islamic state brought with it a breakdown of domestic law and order. The Buwayhid regime at Baghdad, and the Saljuq regime that replaced it, brought some alleviation, but this was only local and temporary. The Islamic World was now afflicted with Christian invaders, and still more grievously, with migratory pastoral nomad barbarians who were nominal converts to Islam.

The East Romans took Crete in 961, Tarsos in 965, and Antioch in 969, the year in which the Fatimids occupied Egypt. For the next hundred years the Fatimids and the East Romans competed with each other inconclusively for the possession of Syria till they were both ousted, first by the Saljuq Turks, and then, in 1098-9, by the Western Christian Crusaders. The Normans conquered Sicily between 1060 and 1090. The Castilians took Toledo in 1085.

More widespread suffering and devastation was inflicted by the nomads—Turkish, Arab, and Berber—who were now let loose. In 999 the Abbasids' Samanid Iranian successor-state was partitioned, along the line of the River Oxus, between a Turkish dynasty, founded in 962 at Ghazni in present-day Afghanistan, and the Qarluq Turks, who had been converted to Islam in 960. Since an early date in the ninth century, Turks had been imported into the Islamic World individually as soldier-slaves, and had learned how to turn the tables on their masters. In 999 a whole horde of free Turkish nomads, the Qarluqs, settled *en masse* in Islamic territory for the first time. The Qarluqs were soon followed by the Ghuzz, who were being driven westward by the Qipchaq. One band of Ghuzz, converted to Sunni Islam and led by members of the House of Saljuq, defeated their fellow Turks the Ghaznavids in 1040 and occupied Khorasan. The Saljuqs' ambition was to win an empire for themselves, and in this they succeeded temporarily when they supplanted the

Buwayhids as the masters of the Abbasids at Baghdad in 1055. The Saljuqs' nomad followers wanted pastures and loot. The Saljuqs conspired with their newly acquired Iranian and Arab sedentary subjects to pass the nomad Türkmens on. They let them loose on Armenia in 1046 and on Asia Minor after 1071. But, before these mobile nomads started to devastate these Christian countries, they had devastated Iran *en passage*.

Two tribes of Arab pastoral nomads were let loose on North-West Africa by the Fatimids as a reprisal for the secession, in 1047, of the Fatimids' viceroys there. In North-West Africa the olive-orchards, which had made this region prosperous in the Carthaginian and the Roman Age, had survived both the Vandal conquest and the first Arab conquest. The devastation caused by the second Arab conquest was not repaired. This was not a military operation; it was a mass-migration of nomads. These westward-trekking Arab nomads did not reach the Atlantic. Their way was blocked by Berber nomads from the Sahara, led by a religious fraternity, the Murabits. These were puritan Sunnis. When, in 1086 and 1090, they crossed into Spain and deposed the successors of the Spanish Umayyads who had failed to arrest the Castilians' advance, the Spanish Muslims discovered, too late, that their Christian fellow-Spaniards' domination was the lesser evil.

In the western basin of the Mediterranean and in Syria, the political frontier of Islam was being pushed back by Western Christian invaders. Contemporaneously, however, the frontier was being pushed forward in India and in Asia Minor. The Ghaznavid Turkish dynasty conquered non-Islamic territory that had never been under Samanid or Abbasid rule. Mahmud of Ghazni brought the whole of the Indus basin under Sunni Muslim rule (he liquidated the Isma'ili Shi'i Muslim regime in Multan and Sind, besides making war on the Hindus). The Saljuqs, whose rule over Iran and Iraq was ephemeral, founded, in the heart of what had been East Roman Asia Minor, a Sunni Muslim state that lasted for 231 years (1077–1308).

The Turks had entered the Islamic World via Iran, and they did not come in *en masse* till the Iranians had created a brilliant Iranian version of the Islamic civilization. The Turks retained their ancestral language, but they embraced the Islamic civilization in its Iranian form. This was the form in which Islam was propagated south-eastwards into India and north-westwards into Eastern Orthodox Christendom. The expansion of Islam at the expense of these two neighbouring civilizations in and after the eleventh century was far more extensive than its permanent contraction in the West and than its temporary contraction in Syria.

Islam's domain was thus expanding conspicuously at a time when the unitary Islamic state was disintegrating. In theory the unitary state is an obligatory political framework for the religion; but theory was refuted by experience. This demonstrated that Islam could survive and spread without requiring the support of a unitary government. The experience had two momentous effects. It produced a change in the Muslims' conception of the character of God and the character of the Muslim worshipper's relation to God, and it generated the first wave of mass-conversions among the non-Muslim subjects of the defunct unitary Islamic state's successor-states.

The political motive for these mass-conversions is manifest. The non-Muslim majority of the once unitary Islamic state's subjects had been sheltered by the *Pax Islamica* that had been imposed on them. When the Islamic unitary state disintegrated, its subjects—Muslims and non-Muslims alike—looked for some alternative shelter. They perceived that the Islamic religion had greater survival-power than the Islamic state, and this moved the disintegrating state's non-Muslim subjects to adopt the religion of their former rulers. To be a Muslim now offered greater security to the individual than to be the ex-subject of a state that had failed to ride the storm in an age of tribulation. The incentive for conversion was now something more than a quest for fiscal and political parity; it was an agonizing concern for survival.

The form of Islam that promised survival was Sunni orthodoxy. The Shi'i Buwayhids had recognized the Sunnah's mass-appeal when they had refrained from liquidating the Abbasid Caliphate; for, though this Caliphate had ceased to be the effective government of a unitary Sunni Muslim state, it had continued to be the institutional symbol of the psychological and social solidarity of the Sunni Muslim community. Moreover, the Sunnah, in contrast to the Isma'ili version of the Shi'ah, was becoming more responsive to human needs. God, as experienced by Muhammad, had been the Israelite God of the Pentateuch. He had been unapproachable and unaccountable; and therefore, for orthodox Sunni Muslims, the mystic's attempt to bridge the gulf between God and Man had been suspect. This had seemed like an impious encroachment on God's transcendence. Unsophisticated eleventh-century Muslims were, no doubt, unaware that the God of the Pentateuch had been transfigured into God the Father by the Prophets of Israel and Judah and by their successors the Pharisees and the Christians. But this loving and lovable God was the God for which the ex-subjects of the unitary Islamic state were yearning in the age in which this state was falling to pieces, and, in their hour of need, their need was met by a Khorasani Iranian scholar-mystic, Ghazzali (1058–1111).

Ghazzali was, like Augustine, a successful professor who voluntarily relinquished his chair; but, unlike Augustine, Ghazzali did not go into controversial ecclesiastical politics. He went into retreat for eleven years

(1095–1106), in order to follow up his study of mysticism by a direct experience of the mystic's relation with God. Ghazzali did not reject Sunni orthodoxy, but he humanized it by infusing mysticism into it, and, when the Sunni community eventually followed Ghazzali's lead, Sunni Islam took a new turn that gave it a fresh lease of life. Ghazzali won his co-religionists' confidence by rejecting and combating two unpopular movements: Isma'ili Shi'ism and rationalist philosophy. The Isma'ilis were unpopular because they were secretive and violent revolutionaries. The philosophers were unpopular because free thought was felt to be too expensive a luxury for a dangerous age. At the price of jettisoning these two bugbears, Ghazzali salvaged mysticism for Sunni Islam; and, if mysticism, too, had been jettisoned, the Sunnah might have failed to gain a hold on human hearts.

[62]

THE BYZANTINE WORLD, 927/8–1071

THE two outstanding events in this period of Byzantine history are the conversion of Russia to the Eastern Orthodox form of Chalcedonian Christianity in 989 and the military collapse of the East Roman Empire in 1071. The Empire's collapse was disastrous for the Greeks. In the seventh century the Empire had become Greek *de facto*, in spite of the maintenance of its Roman name, and the Empire's reverses in and after 1071 were therefore also reverses for the Greek people. However, by 1071 the fortunes of Byzantine civilization were no longer wholly dependent on those of the Greek people and of the East Roman Empire. By that date Byzantine society had come to include, besides the Greeks, three Slavonic-speaking peoples—the Bulgars, the Serbs, and the Russians—as well as the Georgians and the Alans in Caucasia.

The vicissitudes in the military history of the East Roman Empire in this age seem paradoxical if they are viewed in isolation, but they are intelligible in the light of their economic and social setting. From 926 to 1045, East Roman military history is a record of continuous, though not always facile, success. The turn of the tide in the fifth decade of the eleventh century, and the Empire's sensational defeats in the year 1071 on both its Armenian and its Apulian fronts, are explained by the previous failure of the series of Imperial agrarian enactments which started in 929, or possibly in 922, and ended in an acknowledgment, in 1028, of the Government's failure. The insurrections of members of the East Roman rural aristocracy in Asia Minor, in 963, 970, 976–9, 987–9, and 1057 can be seen in retrospect to have been the prelude to the occupation by Saljuq and Danishmend Turkish war-lords, and by their nomad followers, of the region in the interior of Asia Minor which had been occupied previously by the estates of the East Roman aristocrats—estates which had expanded at the expense of the freeholds of the members of the East Roman peasant militia.

This peasant militia had held Asia Minor successfully against Arab assaults so long as the East Roman Empire had continued to stand on the defensive. An armed peasantry was, indeed, an effective instrument for defensive warfare. It was defending productive land that was its own property, and it therefore had a strong motive for performing its military duty efficiently. The cost to the Imperial Treasury was small, since the peasants made their living mainly from their land, and they paid more in taxes than they received as military pay. But this peasant militia was not an equally suitable instrument for offensive warfare in which the objective was the conquest and the permanent occupation of territory beyond the Empire's borders.

Even during the three centuries, ending in 926, in which East Roman military operations had been defensive and in which the peasant militia had been defending its own property, it had been difficult to induce the militiamen to devote sufficient time to active service and to training. A militiaman's first concern had been to cultivate his land and to tend his livestock in order to produce enough to cover the payment of his taxes besides providing military equipment for himself and subsistence for his family. The rate of taxation was high, and, in dealing with the peasantry, the taxation-officers were always harsh and frequently dishonest. Their behaviour alienated the peasantry from the Imperial Government. In the seventh century, one cause of the Arabs' failure to conquer Asia Minor had been the local population's readiness to fight for their country. In and after 1071 the peasantry in Asia Minor were as ready to tolerate, and in some cases even to welcome, a foreign invader as the peasantry in Syria and Egypt had been in and after 633.

The relations between the peasantry and the resurgent landowning aristocracy in eastern Asia Minor were paradoxical. The peasants' military prowess had made the large landowners' fortune. Though Muslim raids, overland and by sea, on East Roman territory did not cease till the East Roman Empire's reconquest of Crete in 961 and of Tarsos in 965, the tide had turned in the Empire's favour in 863; from that date onwards, security in Asia Minor had improved progressively; consequently, land there had become a more attractive investment, and the peasants' financial straits had been the investors' opportunity. The pressure of taxation had constrained the peasants to sell, though any land that they held as the *quid pro quo* for their military service was legally inalienable. The famine caused by the exceptionally severe winter of 927/8 had enabled the rich to buy up poor men's holdings at derisorily low prices; but this temporary crisis could not have been exploited to that degree if the peasantry had not already been hard pressed financially by onerous taxation.

The scandal of the exploitation of the crisis in 927/8 was so flagrant that it evoked the Imperial agrarian legislation which was finally defeated in 1028. This had been a struggle between the East Roman Imperial Government and the large landowners in eastern Asia Minor for the appropriation of the peasantry's 'surplus' product. Most of the East Roman Empire's gross national product was provided by the peasantry's produce. The issue was whether the peasantry's annual 'surplus' should be taken by the Government in taxes or be taken by the large landowners in rents, and, for the peasant, this was a choice of evils. As a 'freeholder' the peasant was taxed mercilessly; as the tenant of a large landowner he transferred to the landlord the onus of dealing with the Imperial taxation-officers, but he did this at the price of putting himself at his landlord's mercy.

The Government's objective was to make the big landowners disgorge the land that they had acquired unjustly, and in some cases also illegally, since 927/8. The struggle reached its climax in the reign (976–1025) of Basil II. Asian nobles made armed insurrections against him in 976–9 and again in 987–9. Basil's retaliation was vehement. In 1003/4 he decreed that the collective responsibility for the payment of the total amount of tax assessed on a taxation-district was to be confined to the rich tax-payers, and that the poor were to be relieved of this liability. In 1028 this enactment was repealed, under pressure from the large land-owners, by Basil II's brother, *fainéant* colleague, and survivor, Constantine VIII. Basil's posthumous defeat was due to the same cause as the defeat, in China, of Wang An-shih in 1085–6. In the East Roman Empire, as in the Chinese Empire, the only agents at the disposal of a would-be reformer were disloyal and dishonest officials whose personal interest lay in sabotaging the measures of reform which it was their duty to execute.

Basil II was at daggers drawn with both his civil servants and his rebellious aristocratic subjects in eastern Asia Minor. He sought to defend the peasantry against both flocks of harpies, though his ulterior object was to promote, not the peasantry's interests, but the state's. The civil servants were at daggers drawn with the Asian aristocrats; for normally, when the Imperial throne was not occupied by an emperor of Basil II's calibre, the civil servants governed in the reigning emperor's name, and the aristocrats' objective was either to capture the Imperial Government or to secede from it. The aristocrats' and the peasants' feelings about each other were ambivalent. They agreed in detesting the Imperial taxation-officers; for, though the aristocrats could evade their own tax-obligations, they saw that the pressure of taxation reduced the peasant militia's military efficiency; and an aristocrat's power depended on his holding the command of one of the provincial militia-corps—a post that carried with it the governorship of the province itself.

The peasants' feelings about the aristocrats were mixed. They resented the aristocrats' land-grabbing, but they were grateful to them for their support against the taxation-officers and they admired their military prowess. This admiration moved the peasants to follow the aristocrats' lead not only in wars for the Empire but also in insurrections against it. The five insurrections in Asia Minor between 963 and 1057 could not have been as formidable as they actually were if they had not had the peasantry's support. These insurrections commended themselves to the peasantry as revolts against the taxation-officers. The insurrection in 963 put one aristocrat, Nicephorus II Phocas, on the Imperial throne; the insurrection in 1057 won the same prize for another aristocrat, Isaac I Comnenus. The other three insurrections were eventually unsuccessful, but Basil II only suppressed the two in his reign with the aid of foreign mercenaries—Iberians (i.e. Georgians) in 979 and Russians in 988–9.

The substitution of mercenaries, foreign or native, for the peasant militia was one of the causes of the Empire's collapse in 1071. The East Roman Army had always included a component of professionals who gave full-time service and were paid a living wage, but this expensive arm had been small in numbers down to the reigns of the three successive ambitious conquerors Nicephorus II Phocas (963–9), John Tzimisces (969–76), and Basil II. There was a consensus in favour of reducing the peasant-militiamen from being part-time soldiers to being whole-time agriculturists and full-scale tax-payers. Basil II and the civil servants were in agreement in wishing to demilitarize the Asian peasants, because they recognized that the peasant militia was the source of the contumacious aristocrats' military power. Nicephorus II was torn between several conflicting considerations. He genuinely wished to protect the peasant militiamen, who were his soldiers and his fellow-provincials. On the other hand, he hankered after a professional army for achieving conquests for which the militia was unfit, and he was also reluctant to restrain his fellow-aristocrats from adding field to field. In 1071 the unfortunate Emperor Romanus IV Diogenes had to confront the Saljuqs with mercenary troops whose only interest in serving was to draw their pay.

Nicephorus II's conquest of the Muslims' raiding-bases in Crete and Cilicia was worth its cost for the East Roman Empire. John Tzimisces's and Basil II's conquest of Bulgaria in a war that lasted (with one short break) from 971 to 1018 was a military triumph. It achieved what Constantine V had failed to achieve in the Romano–Bulgarian war of 755–75; but the consequences of the war of 971–1018 were calamitous for the conquerors, as well as for the conquered. Bulgaria lost her political independence for 167 years (1018–1185); the East Roman Empire suffered a financial, economic, and social strain from which it never recovered. A symptom of the financial strain was the debasement of the nomisma, the East Roman gold coin that had retained its intrinsic value since its rehabilitation by Diocletian and by Constantine I. Nicephorus II Phocas perhaps issued a debased gold coin for domestic circulation; the nomisma itself was debased in Constantine IX's reign (1042–55).

The years 1040–6 marked a turning-point in East Roman history as significant as the turning points in 860–5 and in 926–8. In 1040 the East Romans re-occupied Syracuse, which had been lost in 878, but in 1041 Norman adventurers occupied Melfi, a key position in the East Roman domain in Apulia. In 1045 the East Romans completed their annexation of Armenia, except for the small principality of Qars; but in 1046 the Saljuqs began to harry Armenia, which was now no longer defended by Armenian arms.

In 1071 the Normans completed their conquest of the East Roman possessions in Apulia and Calabria by taking Bari. In the same year the Saljuq war-lord Alp Arslan took the East Roman Emperor Romanus IV Diogenes prisoner at Manzikert (Melazgerd), and, after that, the Saljuqs occupied the interior of Asia Minor, which had been the heart of the East Roman Empire since the seventh century.

After 1071, for the first time since the seventh century, the East Roman Empire's dominions in south-eastern Europe were more extensive than its dominions in Asia. The Bulgars had rebelled in 1041, but they had been subdued. After 1071 the Bulgars continued to be the East Roman Empire's subjects and the Serbs to be under East Roman suzerainty. But in Europe the Greeks were only a dominant minority, whereas the whole population of Asia Minor had been Greek-speaking since the sixth century. In south-eastern Europe the East Roman regime was precarious.

Thus, during the century and a half that ended in 1071, Byzantine history, looked at from the Greek and from the East Roman standpoints, was a story of failure, but, looked at from the Slav and from the Eastern Orthodox Christian standpoints, it was a story of success.

When, in 989, Prince Vladimir of Kiev was baptized, Eastern Orthodox Christianity, which had been the religion of a minority in Russia since *c.* 867, became the established religion of the Russian state. Vladimir's baptism was followed by his marriage to a Greek princess, Basil II's sister Anna, but the Byzantine civilization flowed into Russia through a Bulgarian, as well as through a Greek, channel. The East Roman Empire was the Byzantine civilization's fountain-head, but, in the propagation of this civilization in Russia, Bulgaria had a linguistic advantage. Though the Bulgarian and the Russian states had been founded respectively by Turkish-speaking Huns and by Teutonic-speaking Swedes, the majority of the population in both countries was Slavonic-speaking, and, by the time each of them was converted to Christianity, the language of the majority prevailed. When Russia was converted, her princes brought in Greek artists and architects, but the Russians adopted, for their liturgy and for their literature, the Macedonian Slavonic dialect conveyed in the 'Cyrillic' alphabet that had been invented in Bulgaria as an alternative to Constantine-Cyril's more complicated Glagolitic alphabet. Through this medium, much that had originally been written in Greek was introduced into Russia in a Bulgarian form. By 1071 Russia was breaking up politically, but she was expanding geographically, and her expansion was carrying the Byzantine civilization towards the shores of the White Sea.

Russia made Eastern Orthodox Christianity's fortune by adopting it through both a Greek and a Bulgarian channel, and there is no evidence of any simultaneous entry into Russia of either Paulicianism (apparently an heretical form of Christianity) or Bogomilism (an anti-Christian religion), which had challenged Eastern Orthodox Christianity in both the East Roman Empire and Bulgaria. The Paulicians had originated in Armenia and had made conquests in the north-eastern corner of East Roman Asia Minor. Paulicians (probably Armenian Paulicians) had been planted in Thrace, first by Constantine V *c.* 755–7, and then by John Tzimisces in 972 in re-conquered territory that had been captured from the East Roman Empire by Bulgaria at some date after 809. The Bogomil religion had been founded in Bulgaria by an Eastern Orthodox Christian priest named Bogomil (his name means either 'Dear to God' or 'Deserving of God's pity') between 927 and 954.

Bogomilism was the Bulgarian peasantry's reaction to a sharp turn of the screw after the Bulgarian 'establishment's' reception of Eastern Orthodox Christianity. The peasantry was now fleeced by a greedy and disreputable Christian clergy in addition to the original Bulgarian lay aristocracy. The Bogomils rejected Christianity but took over the asceticism and celibacy of Christian monasticism as a protest against the Christian Church's betrayal of its own nominal ideals. The original Bogomils held that the World had been created by Satan. However, they also held that Satan was the elder son of God the Father; that the Father himself was good; and that he had sent his younger son, Jesus, to depose Satan and to rescue mankind.

In contrast to the Thracian Paulicians, the Bogomils were eager missionaries. Bogomilism spread into the East Roman Empire after the incorporation of Bulgaria in the Empire in 1018, while, in the opposite direction, it struck root in Bosnia, a debatable territory between Eastern Orthodox and Western Christendom, and it spread from there to Lombardy, Tuscany, and Languedoc. In all Chalcedonian Christian countries except, apparently, Russia, Bogomilism profited by the ill-fame and unpopularity of the Christian ecclesiastical 'establishment'.

At some date before 1167, the Bogomils in a Dragovichian district of Bulgaria founded a radical sect. These Dragovichian Bogomils held that the principles of evil and good were on a par with each other, and this eternally. This radical Bogomilism may have been a reaction to a further turn of the screw on the Bulgarian peasantry. The annexation of Bulgaria and of the rest of the interior of the Balkan Peninsula by the East Roman Empire in 1018 had widened the field for Bogomil missionary work, while the Romano–Bulgarian war of 971–1018 and the savage repression of a Bulgarian insurrection in 1041 had aggravated the Bulgarian peasants' misery.

During the century and a half that ended in the two disasters of 1071, the East Roman Empire's economic and social structure was going awry. This is indicated by the failure of the Imperial Government's agrarian legislation. But, during the same age, there was a revival of mysticism and a florescence of the visual arts in the Empire. Basil II's contemporary St. Symeon 'the New Theologian' (949–1022) had a more enduring influence than Basil on Byzantine life. The blossoming visual arts were not blighted by the military disasters of 1071. Byzantine artists excelled in work on a miniature scale: mosaics, for instance, and bas-reliefs on ivory or metal plaques. The style was reminiscent of the Hellenic style by which Greek minds were haunted in the Byzantine Age; but tenth-century and eleventh-century Byzantine visual art was not a mere imitation of an Hellenic prototype. Hellenic art inspired Byzantine artists to create something that was distinctively their own; and, when this Byzantine art was transplanted from Constantinople to Kiev and Novgorod, it began to develop on novel lines on this new ground. By 1071 Russia had become the land of promise for both the Byzantine civilization and the Eastern Orthodox Church.

WESTERN CHRISTENDOM, 911–1099

On the military plane the vicissitudes of Western Christendom's fortunes in this age were the inverse of the East Roman Empire's contemporaneous experiences. Western Christendom was being assaulted by Scandinavian sea-raiders already before Charlemagne's death in 814; it remained on the defensive till Otto I's victory over the Magyars in 955; and in the years 896–955 its sufferings at the hands of alien assailants reached their climax; for, during those sixty years, the Magyar horsemen's raids on Western Christendom hit the inland regions which had suffered the least severely from the Scandinavian and Muslim sea-raiders. The tide turned in Western Christendom's favour in the course of the second half of the eleventh century, which was the half-century in which the tide turned against the East Roman Empire.

In both cases the sudden change on the military plane becomes intelligible when account is taken of antecedent social and cultural changes that were gradual—for instance, the reception of the Western Christian civilization by the Scandinavian settlers in the Danelaw in England and in Normandy in France, and the spread of the influence of the Abbey of Cluny's way of observing the Benedictine monastic rule. The assimilation of the Scandinavian settlers indicates that the Western Christian way of life had become attractive to local barbarians who were not already committed to Eastern Orthodox Christianity, Islam, or Judaism. The Cluniac reform of Western monasticism indicates why the Western Christian civilization had become attractive. This reform was a symptom, on the religious plane, of a vitality that Western Christian society was now displaying in other fields of activity as well.

Christianity had won a footing in Bohemia at the time of the mission (863–85) of Constantine-Cyril and Methodius in a neighbouring Slav country, Great Moravia. For perhaps two centuries, a Slavophone rite co-existed in Bohemia with the Latin rite that eventually prevailed there, and the Slavonic liturgy facilitated the dissemination of Christianity in Poland, as it did in Russia. Poland was converted to Western Christianity in 966, eleven years after the Saxon Emperor Otto I's decisive victory over the Magyars. The Magyars were converted to Western Christianity between the years 970 and 1000. Denmark was converted in 974 and the other Scandinavian countries at the turn of the tenth and eleventh centuries. In some of these countries—for instance, in Norway, Sweden, and Hungary—conversion met with resistance. But the resistance was unsuccessful because, among Western Christendom's pagan neighbours by this date, the Western Christian civilization's prestige had become invincible.

Western Christendom also made conquests during the second half of the eleventh century at the expense of Eastern Christendom and Islam. Between 1041 and 1071 Norman adventurers conquered the East Roman Empire's possessions in Apulia and Calabria; between 1060 and 1090 they conquered Sicily from the Muslims. The Apulians were Italian-speaking Lombard ecclesiastical subjects of the Papacy, and, for them, the Norman conquest was not altogether uncongenial, but for the Eastern Orthodox Greeks in Calabria and Sicily, and for the Sicilian Muslims, the Norman conquest spelled subjugation by aliens. In 1085 the independent Christians in north-western Spain conquered Toledo— a centrally-situated city which, before the Muslim conquest, had been the capital of the Roman Empire's Visigothic successor-state in the Iberian Peninsula. In 1098–9 a Western Christian expeditionary force conquered Antioch and Edessa from the Saljuqs and Jerusalem from the Fatimids.

This expedition—the First Crusade—was a remarkable financial, logistical, and strategic exploit. A band of Western Christian adventurers achieved what the Emperors Nicephorus II Phocas and John Tzimisces had failed to achieve, in spite of their having had at their command the East Roman Empire's resources. The Norman conquest of England in 1066 was a military exploit of comparable impressiveness, though, unlike the Western Christian conquests in the basin of the Mediterranean, this did not extend the area of Western Christendom, to which pre-Norman England already belonged. However, the Norman conquest of England did demonstrate that, by 1066, West Francia, i.e. France, had forged ahead of the outlying regions of the Western Christian World. Military prowess was only one aspect of a general French superiority.

The second half of the eleventh century A.D. in the history of Western Christendom resembles the second half of the eighth century B.C. in the history of the Hellenic civilization. After a long incubation, a civilization suddenly burst into flower. In this age the Western Christian civilization revealed its vigour in its eagerness to borrow from more precocious contemporary civilizations and to revive its own Graeco-Roman past.

In and after 1088, Justinian's corpus of Roman law was re-discovered and was enthusiastically studied at Bologna, an Italian city that had been under East Roman rule till 751. Before the close of the tenth century, Boethius's Latin translations of Aristotle's works on logic were being studied and expounded in the West, after having lain dormant there for 450 years, by the French scholar Gerbert of Aurillac. Water-mills, invented in the Fertile Crescent, were being installed on the running streams of Transalpine Western Europe. An efficient method of harnessing a draft-horse, which appears to have been invented either in China or on the Eurasian steppe, may have been adopted in Western Christendom as early as the tenth century. The equipment of the Western Christians in the First Crusade included the cross-bow, with which the Chinese had been armed already in the Age of the Warring States (506–221 B.C.).

In the eleventh century the Roman military equipment which had been taken over by the West Roman Empire's barbarian conquerors was suddenly discarded in the West in favour of the more efficient Sarmatian equipment that the Alans had brought with them into Gaul in the fifth century. The Norman knights depicted on the Bayeux Tapestry have their prototypes in paintings of Sarmatian-style cavalry-men in tombs of the first and second century A.D. in the Crimea and the Taman Peninsula, but the eleventh-century Westerners made one change (the first of many) in these borrowed accoutrements. They replaced the small round Sarmatian shield with a kite-shaped shield that gave maximum cover with minimum surface-area and weight. These eleventh-century 'Knights' (*milites*) were so conscious of their value that, about half way through the century, novices began to be inducted by older hands into a kind of secular fraternity.

Since the fall of the West Roman Empire, Latin verse had continued to be written in the West in the classical Greek metres in which the prosody was based on a distinction between long and short syllables. For the Latin language, in which there is a stress accent, this classical Greek prosody had been an irksome strait-jacket. Latin was liberated from this servitude by Christian hymn-writers. They created an accentual Latin poetry, and at about the turn of the eleventh and twelfth centuries an epic poem in one of the living Romance languages of the day, the *Chanson de Roland*, broke its way out from beneath the Latin crust that had hitherto masked the evolution of languages that were Latin's progeny.

On the plane of politics the tenth century saw a partial re-establishment of Charlemagne's Empire, with Saxony now, instead of Frankland, as its nucleus. The Saxon king of East Francia, Otto I, who defeated the Magyars in 955, was crowned emperor at Rome in 962. He added

Burgundy as well as Italy to his German dominions, but West Francia (France) retained her independence. Here in the tenth century the no longer effective Carolingians were replaced by a new dynasty that commanded more support, as, in the eighth century, the Carolingians had replaced the Merovingians. In the eleventh century the Normans introduced efficient monarchical government in states on a smaller scale than the kingdoms of France and Germany. The Normans' feat of conquering England, Apulia, Sicily, and Antioch was surpassed by their subsequent feat of organizing the administration of their new dominions.

The Norman Kingdom of Sicily was an autocratically governed successor-state of the East Roman Empire and of the Islamic Caliphate. Its 'establishment' blighted the nascent city-states in southern Italy, but in northern Italy Venice had made herself independent of the East Roman Empire *de facto* before the end of the eleventh century, and the cities of Lombardy, which at the beginning of the century had still been under the rule of the hereditary successors of Charlemagne's provincial governors, or else of the local bishops, became autonomous in the course of the next hundred years. The governments of these city-states were oligarchical, but they were republican. Two maritime Lombard city-states, Pisa and Genoa, participated, as virtually independent powers, in the Western Christian offensive in the Mediterranean basin in the second half of the eleventh century.

Thus, in the course of the eleventh century, two competing forms of political structure had arisen in the West: a republican form on the city-state scale and a monarchical form on the kingdom-state scale. By 1100 both forms of contemporary Western political organization had become more efficient than any political regime that had made its appearance in this region since the decline and fall of the Roman Empire.

The city-state form of political structure, which appeared in northern Italy in the eleventh century, also appeared in eleventh-century Flanders. In both areas there was a contemporaneous population explosion, and this was accompanied by a growth of trade and industry. As early as 992 Basil II paid for Venetian naval services by giving the Venetians commercial privileges throughout the East Roman Empire. The Venetians then began to capture trade from the Greeks in the Greeks' home waters, and, after the establishment of the Crusader principalities along the coast of Syria, the maritime North-Italian city-states won privileges there too. These Western Christian beach-heads 'beyond the sea' depended on Genoese and Pisan and Venetian shipping for their communications with Western Europe. The West as a whole was now making gains at Islam's and at Eastern Orthodox Christendom's expense, but, among the Westerners themselves, the chief gainers were the northern Italians.

On the plane of religion the awakening of Western Christendom in the course of the years 910–1099 was revealed in a series of efforts to inaugurate reforms, beginning with the foundation in 910 of a new-model Benedictine abbey at Cluny in Burgundy. The Cluniac reforming movement spread throughout Western Christendom, and the monasteries that adopted the Cluniac form of observance of the Benedictine rule entered into an association with Cluny under Cluny's hegemony; but, by the close of the eleventh century, the Cluniac observance was no longer giving satisfaction, and in 1098 another new-model abbey was founded in Burgundy at Cîteaux. St. Benedict himself, like Pachom, the Egyptian inaugurator of Christian monasticism, had aimed at a balance between liturgical and economic activities for his monks. The Cluniac movement had elaborated the liturgical side of a Benedictine monastery's life, and the monasteries that adopted the Cluniac observance were as heavy a burden on their peasant tenantry as their neighbours and social counterparts the secular landlords. The Cistercians aimed at achieving both greater spiritual austerity and greater material productivity. They reclaimed the wilderness, but, unlike the original Pachomian monks in the Thebaid, the Cistercian monks employed workers who were lay brothers, i.e. second-class members of the order. The Cistercians made the wilderness produce iron and wool. In achieving this economic success they sowed the seeds of the capitalist system of production.

In the eleventh century the religious reformers in Western Christendom introduced three innovations. They imposed celibacy on the secular clergy (i.e. on clerics who were not monks) and they attempted to ban the purchase of ecclesiastical offices and the investiture of ecclesiastical office-holders by lay authorities. The movement for non-monastic clerical celibacy was eventually successful, but it met with strong opposition; for there was no precedent for it in the practice of the Western Church or of any other of the regional churches. The conflict over investiture ended in 1122 in a compromise, and this was reasonable, since secular as well as ecclesiastical offices were normally held by ecclesiastical dignitaries. The purchase of ecclesiastical offices from local lay patrons was curbed for the benefit of the Papacy, which assumed the prerogative of making clerical appointments and did not make them gratis. The aggregate effect of these ecclesiastical reforms was to turn the clergy into a privileged corporation within Western Christian society at the price of subjecting them to the Papacy instead of leaving them subject to the lay aristocracy.

In the eleventh-century movements for clerical celibacy and for the banning of 'simony' and of the investiture of clerics by laymen, the lead was taken by a reformed Papacy. The Papacy was the most important institution in Western Christendom. Its reform, half way through the eleventh century, was sudden and sensational. The consequences were controversial and disruptive.

Geographically, the city of Rome lay on the south-eastern fringe of Western Christendom since the detachment of North-West Africa from the Roman patriarchate by the Muslims and of the Eastern Illyricum by the Emperor Leo III. The geographical centre of Western Christendom was now Burgundy, where the headwaters of the Rivers Saône, Seine, and Moselle approach most closely to each other and to the south-westward angle of the Rhine. This centre of Transalpine West European communications was the area in which St. Columbanus's monasteries at Luxeuil and Annegray, and then the new-model monasteries at Cluny and Cîteaux, with Cîteaux's illustrious daughter-house Clairvaux, had all been planted. Rome's geographical location had been made more eccentric than ever by the north-eastward and northward expansion of Western Christendom during the half-century beginning in 966. The Normans' conquests to the south-east of Rome were no more than a slight offset to this. To control the ecclesiastical administration of Western Christendom from one of its most remote corners was a *tour de force*.

Rome was Western Christendom's principal common shrine, oracle, and pilgrimage-resort. Its role was the counterpart of the god Pacha-cámac's shrine in the contemporary Andean World and of the god Apollo's shrine at Delphi in the former Hellenic World. Yet Rome was also one of the assets of the local nobility of the Ducatus Romanus. Since the irruption of the Lombards into Italy in 568, the Ducatus Romanus had been left, for most of the time, to fend for itself, except for the brief interventions of the Transalpine empire-builders Pippin III and Charlemagne. As the Roman nobles saw it, the sacredness of Rome and the prestige of the Papacy were their legitimate perquisites. From the standpoint of the rest of Western Christendom the Roman nobles' exploitation of the City and the Papacy was a scandal.

The first champions of the ecumenical Western Christian standpoint were the German holders of the rehabilitated Imperial title. Otto I, Otto III, and Henry III all deposed native Roman popes and installed Transalpine appointees of their own. Otto III's most distinguished appointee was the French scholar Gerbert of Aurillac, who became Pope Silvester II (999–1003); Henry III's was his own Alsatian cousin Bruno (Pope Leo IX, 1048–54). With Henry III's encouragement, Leo IX staffed the Papal Curia with eminent clerics who represented, not the nobles of the Ducatus Romanus, but the clerical 'establishment' of Western Christendom as a whole. But these new masters of the Curia held that they, not the emperor, ought to have the last word in the conduct of the Papacy's affairs.

The moving spirit in the reformed Curia's war on two fronts—with the emperor now, as well as with the local Roman nobles—was Hildebrand who became Pope Gregory VII (1073–86), a Roman at least by adoption, if not by birth, but no friend of the nobles of the Ducatus Romanus. From 1057 onwards the Pope was no longer appointed either by the Roman nobles or by the West Roman Emperor. He was elected by the College of Cardinals, acting as the representatives of the whole of Western Christendom. (This prerogative of the College of Cardinals was not established conclusively till 1179). The Papal Curia was forged into an efficient instrument of government between 1057 and Pope Urban II's death in 1099. But the reformed Papal Curia shared one fatal vice with the Roman nobles and with the rehabilitated West Roman emperors: its objective was power, and, in pursuit of this objective, the Papal Curia broke with the Patriarch of Constantinople, Michael Cerularius, in 1054, and with the West Roman Emperor Henry IV in 1075. The reform of the Papacy and of the Western Church as a whole was a noble ideal and the reformers themselves were sincere, but the outcome was tragic. This reform brought, not peace, but the sword.

[64]

THE ISLAMIC WORLD, 1110–1291

In the twelfth and thirteenth centuries Islam not only survived; it continued to spread. This was a remarkable achievement, considering that the Islamic World was now dismembered politically and that it was assailed, first in the Mediterranean basin by the Western Christians, and then in Asia by the Mongols. The Western Christians' only permanent political gains at Islam's expense were in the Iberian Peninsula and in Sicily, and, in these two areas, a Muslim population survived under Christian rule. As for the Mongols, they failed to conquer Syria and Egypt, and the rulers and their nomad followers in the three western-most appanages of the House of Genghis Khan were converted to Islam: the Golden Horde, in the western half of the Eurasian steppe, in 1257 (and definitively in 1313); the Il-Khans of Iran and Iraq in 1295; the Chaghatayids in Transoxania and in the Tarim basin and the adjoining section of the steppe in 1326 (though not unanimously). Before the Mongol conquest of the western half of the Eurasian steppe, its Qipchaq Turkish nomad occupants had been pagans, and the Volga Bulgars, to the north of them, had been an isolated Muslim community. In 1237 the Mongols sacked Bulghar-on-Volga on their way to Russia and to Europe; but, in the sequel, Islam, so far from being extirpated in this quarter, was able to extend its range immensely. The Muslim conquest of northern India, from the Khyber Pass to Bengal, between 992 and 1202, has been mentioned already. In the west the Murabits failed to reconquer Toledo, which the Christians had taken in 1085; but, in the opposite direction, the Murabits won for Islam in 1086 a foothold to the south of the Sahara, in what is now northern Nigeria.

The establishment of Western Christian beach-heads along the coast of Syria in 1098–9, with an advanced post, to the east of the Euphrates, at Edessa (Urfah), was a serious menace to the Islamic World. The adventurers who took part in the First Crusade were few in numbers (perhaps less than 20,000 strong), and, after the conquest of Jerusalem in 1099, still fewer stayed to hold the territory that had been conquered. Yet they managed to consolidate their holdings. Tripoli (Tarabulus), which had held out in the tenth century against the East Roman Emperors Nicephorus II Phocas and John Tzimisces, capitulated to the Franks in 1109. When, in 1116, the Frankish King of Jerusalem, Baldwin I, occupied Aqabah and the Isle de Graye in the Gulf of Aqabah, he had severed the overland communications between the Asian and the African portions of the Islamic World.

The situation was retrieved for Islam by a Turkish officer in Saljuq employ, Imad-ad-Din Zengi, who was appointed governor of Mawsil (Mosul) in 1127. By 1144 Zengi had annexed Aleppo, Homs, and the Crusaders' outpost Edessa. In 1154 Zengi's son Nur-ad-Din took Damascus. In 1161–70 he won a competition with King Amaury of Jerusalem for the command of Fatimid Egypt. In 1171 Nur-ad-Din's Kurdish officer Salah-ad-Din (Saladin) liquidated the Fatimid dynasty and re-established the Sunnah as the official religion of Egypt. Nur-ad-Din's empire disintegrated at his death in 1174, but Salah-ad-Din reconquered it for himself with the Abbasid Caliphate's blessing. In 1187 he defeated the Franks at Hattin in Galilee and recaptured Jerusalem. The Third Crusade (1189–92) failed to dislodge Salah-ad-Din, though Frederick I and the kings of France and England all served in it (but Frederick was drowned en route). Salah-ad-Din's empire survived its founder's death in 1193 and also survived the extinction of his dynasty in 1250—the year in which the Franks failed, for the third time, to repeat King Amaury of Jerusalem's exploit of occupying Egypt, which was now Islam's citadel and arsenal.

In 1250 Salah-ad-Din's heritage was taken over from his dynasty by a consortium of the dynasty's Turkish military slaves. The succession now passed, not from father to son, but from former slave ruler to slave. A regime with the same constitution had been established at Delhi already. Here the conqueror of northern India to the south-east of the Punjab, Muhammad Ghori, had appointed a slave-viceroy, and this viceroy's second slave-successor became sovereign of the Ghoris' dominions in India when, in 1215, the Ghori dynasty itself was liquidated by the ruler of Khwarizm, an ex-vassal of the Saljuqs.

Transoxania and north-eastern Iran, which had prospered under the rule of the Abbasids and their Iranian successors the Samanids, had then suffered in the early decades of the eleventh century from the influx of Türkmen nomads led by war-lords of the House of Saljuq. In 1141 Transoxania was occupied by a refugee detachment of the Khitan (the Qarakhitay), who in 1124–5 had been supplanted in northern China and Manchuria by the Jürched. The Qarakhitay were not Muslims, but they were a civilized power. Transoxania suffered less from them than from the Muslim rulers of Khwarizm, who ejected the Qarakhitay from Transoxania in 1210. The whole of the north-eastern quarter of the Islamic World was devastated and depopulated when the Mongol war-lord Genghis Khan overran the Khwarizmshah's dominions in 1220–1.

Genghis Khan's intervention had saved Iraq from a threatened invasion by the Khwarizmshah that might have been as destructive as his and Genghis's devastation of Transoxania. The extinction of the eastern branch of the Saljuqs by their ex-vassal the Khwarizmshah in 1194 had left the Abbasid Caliph Nasir (ruled 1180–1225) genuinely independent. He used his freedom of manoeuvre to re-occupy territory in south-western Iran, to give his moral support to Salah-ad-Din and to his successors, and to turn a popular movement, the *futuwwah*, into an order of chivalry under Abbasid patronage.

The *futuwwah* was one of several new Islamic institutions that enabled Islam to survive the ordeal of the Mongol conquest. Another was the host of fraternities of dervishes, of which the earliest was the Qadiriyah, founded in the twelfth century by Abd-al-Qadir of Gitan. Most of the founders of dervish fraternities came from the north-eastern quarter of the Islamic World. Their practice of religion took the form of the inducement of ecstasy, and, whether or not they were disguised Türkmen shamans, they certainly won an influence over the Türkmen converts to Islam, whose practice of their adopted religion was at first no more than nominal. The most eminent creator of a dervish order was Jalal-ad-Din, the founder of the Mevlevis. He was born at Balkh in Tokharistan in 1207, just before the Khwarizmian and Mongol tornados swept over this region. He spent most of his life (1207–73) at Qoniyah, the capital of the Saljuq sultanate of Rum, and it was here that he wrote, in New Persian, his mystical poetry. Another Persian poet, Sa'di of Shiraz, lived (*c.* 1184–1291), not in a secure retreat, but perpetually on the run. He lived to be a centenarian in the stormiest century of the Islamic World's history.

The offshoot of the Saljuq Empire in Asia Minor (Rum) had greater staying-power than this empire's main body to the east of the Euphrates. Saljuq Rum weathered the storm of the First Crusade; in 1176 it defeated a belated attempt, on the East Roman Empire's part, to re-conquer it; and it survived its defeat by the Mongols in 1243, though it had to submit to an onerous Mongol suzerainty. Rum built up in Asia Minor a sedentary Turkish-speaking society imbued with the Islamic civilization in its Iranian version. The Sultans of Rum managed to relegate to the frontier between the Islamic World and the East Roman Empire the horde of nomad Türkmens whom the Saljuqs had carried with them, and also a further horde that flowed in during the thirteenth century in flight from the Mongols. Though Rum, unlike Mamluk Egypt and Syria, was later defeated by the Mongols and fell under their suzerainty, it too provided a shelter for Islam at this crisis in Islamic history.

Thus, when, in 1256, the reigning Mongol Great Khan Möngke commissioned his brother Hülegü to complete Genghis Khan's unfinished conquest of the Islamic World, Islam was able to survive the devastation of Iraq, the capture and sack of Baghdad, and the liquidation of the Abbasid Caliphate in 1258.

In 1261 the slave (Mamluk) successors of Salah-ad-Din's dynasty demonstrated that the Mongols were not invincible by annihilating in Palestine an advance-guard of Hülegü's previously victorious army. The Mongol general, who was killed, was a Nestorian Christian, and he was accompanied by the Christian King of Cilician Armenia and by the Christian Prince of Antioch; but the Franks at Acre gave passage to the Mamluk army. The Mamluks repulsed three more invasions of Syria by the Mongol Il-Khans of Iran and Iraq, and they took Acre, the last remaining Western Christian beach-head in Syria, in 1291.

Both the Western Christians and the Nestorian Christians in the Il-Khans' dominions had hoped that the whole Islamic World might be conquered, and Islam itself extirpated, by a grand alliance between Western Christendom and the Mongol Empire. Papal and French envoys reached the Mongol Great Khan's capital Qaraqorum, near the eastern end of the Eurasian steppe, and the Mongols, on their side, made some overtures to the Western Christians, but nothing came of this project. The rulers of the western appanages of the Mongol Empire opted, not for Christianity, but for Islam. After the conversion of the Il-Khan Ghazan to Islam in 1295, his Muslim subjects made reprisals against his Christian subjects. In the Asian part of the Islamic World the mass-conversions of Christians to Islam, which had started in the eleventh century at the time of the Türkmens' *Völkerwanderung* under Saljuq leadership, now gained a fresh impetus, and the Nestorian and Monophysite Christian communities, once a majority of the population of the Fertile Crescent, dwindled in numbers till they became mere diasporas.

At the opposite end of the Islamic World, the Muslim population in the areas conquered by Western Christians likewise dwindled and was eventually extinguished. Neither the nomad Berber Murabits from the Sahara nor their supplanters the highland Berber Muwahhids from the Atlas succeeded in arresting the Western Christians' military advance in the Iberian Peninsula. Cordoba fell in 1236 and Seville in 1248. Thereafter, Muslim rule in the Peninsula was confined to a natural fastness round Granada. However, the Muwahhids did succeed in evicting the

Norman masters of Sicily from the beach-heads that they had occupied in Ifriqiyah after the collapse of the Murabits there in the 1140s. At this stage, no African Islamic territory fell more than momentarily under Western Christian rule.

However, the western region in which the Islamic civilization flowered after the eleventh-century turn of the tide on the military plane was not Africa; it was the Iberian Peninsula. Here the break-up of the Umayyad Caliphate of Cordoba had the same stimulating cultural effect as the break-up of the Abbasid Caliphate of Baghdad had had in Iran. In the Peninsula likewise the multiplication of local courts increased the number of potential patrons of art and literature. In the Cordoban Caliphate's successor-states there was a brilliant flowering of poetry. On the eve of the Christian conquest of Andalusia, the Peninsula gave Islam a philosopher, Ibn Rushd (Averroes) (1126–98), who was the peer of Ibn Sina (Avicenna), and a mystic, Ibn Arabi (1165–1240) who confirmed Ghazzali's *tour de force* of making mysticism an acceptable component of Sunni Islamic orthodoxy. The Peninsula's contribution to Islamic culture had the same fortune as Ifriqiyah's earlier contribution to Western Christian culture. It survived the amputation of the region in which the makers of this contribution had done their work.

[65]

THE BYZANTINE WORLD, 1071–1240

DURING the ten years 1071–81, which began with the defeat and capture of the Emperor Romanus IV Diogenes by the Saljuq war-lord Alp Arslan and ended with the accession of the Asian aristocrat Alexius I Comnenus to the East Roman Imperial throne, the East Roman 'establishment' made a present to the Turks of Asia Minor—the heart of the East Roman Empire—which their ancestors had defended against Arab assaults indefatigably for three centuries. Factiousness, as reckless as the factiousness in contemporary China, was responsible for the East Roman Empire's débâcle during this decade. By 1081 the greater part of the Empire had been overrun by the Saljuq Turks from the east, by the Normans from the west, and by the Pechenegs and Ghuzz from the north. (These Ghuzz who broke into the Empire from the western extremity of the Eurasian steppe to the north of the lower course of the Danube were pagan kinsmen of the Saljuq Türkmens, and, like them, they had been driven from behind by the westward migration of another Turkish nomad people, the Qipchaq.)

Alexius I (ruled 1081–1118) was a worthy successor of Diocletian and Heraclius. Like them, he rescued the Empire from destruction, and, in John II (ruled 1118–43) and Manuel I (ruled 1143–80), Alexius I had two able and energetic successors. But none of these three emperors succeeded in checking the growth of the large landowners' economic and political power at the Imperial Government's expense or in ejecting the Saljuq and Danishmend Turks from Asia Minor. The nomad Türkmens were elusive; the Christian Greek peasantry was alienated from the Empire. The peasantry suffered severely at the nomads' hands; but, in so far as the Saljuq rulers of the Sultanate of Rum succeeded in protecting the peasants from the Saljuqs' own nomad followers, the Turkish Muslim sultans' yoke was found by the peasantry to be lighter than that of the East Roman Imperial Government.

Alexius I had to cope with the First Crusade. The Islamic World had coped with the Türkmens by transmitting them to East Roman Armenia and Asia Minor; Alexius I retorted by transmitting the Western Crusaders to Syria. But Alexius and the Crusaders were at cross-purposes. Alexius would have preferred to employ the Crusaders as mercenaries to be used for the eviction of the Turks from Asia Minor, but the Crusaders' objective was Jerusalem, and they did not want to be the East Roman Empire's agents or vassals. Consequently, both parties failed to attain their objectives. The East Roman Empire never re-conquered the interior of Asia Minor; the Crusaders did take Jerusalem, but they never succeeded in conquering the interior of Syria. They thus failed to secure for their Syrian beach-heads a defensible frontier on the landward side against the vast Islamic hinterland. The Saljuqs of Rum were able to build up in Asia Minor an organized state with a sedentary population, while Zengi, Nur-ad-Din, and Salah-ad-Din were able to encircle the Franks' beach-heads along the Syrian coast and to evict the Franks from Jerusalem.

Manuel I dissipated his efforts and squandered the East Roman Empire's diminished resources by launching out on a policy of expansion that was far more ambitious than the aims of Nicephorus II Phocas and John Tzimisces and Basil II—aims that had been beyond the Empire's power to achieve at a date when its heartland in Asia Minor was still intact, and when the Imperial Government had not yet been definitively defeated in its struggle with the large landowners for the control of the peasantry. Manuel could not maintain the Empire's command over Serbia, yet he waged war with Hungary. He attempted to reconquer the Empire's lost dominions in Apulia by intervening in the warfare between Frederick I Barbarossa and the North-Italian city-states. Manuel's death in 1180 was followed by a collapse that culminated in a supreme disaster.

Manuel's relations with the Western Christians had been cordial, but his Francophilism was not shared by the majority of his countrymen. The economic privileges with which the East Roman Government had purchased the maritime Italian city-states' naval aid in the course of the previous two centuries had enabled the Italians to capture from the Greeks the East Roman Empire's domestic trade. At Constantinople in 1182 there was a massacre of Western businessmen. The Sicilian Normans retaliated in 1186 by taking and sacking Thessalonica. In 1180 Serbia shook off the East Roman Empire's suzerainty. In 1185 the Bulgars, who had been subjects of the East Roman Empire since 1018, revolted and re-established an independent state—this time in partner-ship with the local Vlakhs. Unlike the Bulgar revolt of 1041, the revolt of 1185 was not quelled. In 1185 Cyprus seceded—only to be conquered in 1191 by a Western Crusader, Richard I of England, and to be handed over by him in 1192 as a consolation prize to Guy de Lusignan, the Frankish King of Jerusalem who had been evicted by Salah-ad-Din in 1187 and whom the Third Crusade had failed to re-instate.

The supreme disaster overtook the East Roman Empire in 1203–4. Constantinople was now twice taken by assault by a combined expeditionary force of Venetians and French 'Crusaders', acting first on behalf of a claimant to the East Roman Imperial throne and then, in the second assault, on the assailants' own account. This was the first time that Constantinople had fallen to an enemy attack since its foundation in 330. The city was barbarously looted, and the victors made a compact with each other for partitioning the Empire among themselves. They proved unable to carry out the whole of their design. Venice achieved the greatest success. She had selected, for her share of the spoils, Crete and other islands, together with some defensible beach-heads at strategic points on the coast of the mainland. Greek successor-states of the defunct East Roman Empire established their independence in north-western Asia Minor, at the east end of the north coast of Asia Minor, round Trebizond, and in Epirus. The city of Constantinople was assigned to a French Crusader, who assumed the title of emperor.

The sequel demonstrated that the possession of Constantinople was now a liability, not an asset. Militarily, it had been an impregnable citadel for the East Roman Empire from 330 to 1204, but it had also been a social and economic incubus since the loss of Syria, Palestine, and Egypt in 633–42. Ever since then, Constantinople had been too big a capital for the Empire's diminished size, and the incubus had been aggravated by the loss of the interior of Asia Minor in and after 1071. The fragment of the Empire's dominions that was acquired in 1204 by a French emperor was utterly inadequate for the maintenance of Constantinople, and, from first to last, Constantinople was a bed of thorns for the French emperors who squatted there from 1204 to 1261.

By contrast, all the local Greek successor-states of the Empire showed greater vitality than the Empire itself had shown at any date since the death of Basil II. The Greek states in north-western Asia Minor and in Epirus were in competition with each other, as well as with the Franks, and the Asian state was the winner against all its competitors, both Frank and Greek. (The remote Greek Empire of Trebizond was not drawn into this struggle.) The Greek state in north-western Asia Minor claimed to be the East Roman Empire's legitimate heir. Its ruler assumed the Imperial title, and his legitimacy was recognized by the Orthodox Patriarch of Constantinople, who installed himself provisionally at Nicaea, which was the refugee Empire's capital. The Nicaean East Roman Empire was more successful in combating the Saljuq Turkish Sultanate of Rum than the Constantinopolitan East Roman

Empire had been in the time of the three Comnenian emperors (1091–1180). The Nicaean Empire pushed its eastern and southern frontiers forward at the expense of Rum. It also prospered economically, and distinguished itself in the field of literature and the visual arts. In 1235 the Nicaean Emperor John III Vatatzes gained a foothold in Europe by capturing a Venetian beach-head at Kallipolis (Gallipoli), on the European shore of the Dardanelles. In 1234 he had made an alliance with Bulgaria, and in 1235 the Nicaean Greeks and the Bulgars, in concert, laid siege to Constantinople from the landward side. From 1235 onwards, the French Empire of Constantinople was encircled by the Nicaean Greek Empire; Frankish Constantinople's only remaining line of communications with Western Christendom was now by sea, and its Frankish rescuers had to run the gauntlet of the Dardanelles (both shores were now in Nicaean Greek hands).

By 1237 the Eastern Orthodox countries in south-eastern Europe were all on the upgrade. Both the resuscitated Bulgarian Empire and the Nicaean Greek Empire had proved more than a match for the French Empire of Constantinople. Serbia, which had formerly been on the fringe of Eastern Orthodox Christendom and, on the ecclesiastical plane, had been a debatable territory between the Eastern Orthodox and the Roman churches, had now opted definitively for Eastern Orthodoxy. The Nicaean Greek Imperial Government had wisely recognized the resuscitation of the Patriarchate of Bulgaria and had created an autonomous archbishopric for Serbia. Yet the cluster of Eastern Orthodox states in south-eastern Europe, together with the cluster in Caucasia, was surpassed by Russia in both extent of territory and size of population, and the Greeks and Bulgars and Georgians were now challenged by the Russians even in the fields of architecture and visual art and literature.

The ecclesiastical history of Russia during the first fifty years after her conversion is obscure, and the interpretation of the historical evidence is in dispute, but it seems clear that, at any rate from 1039 onwards, Russia was a metropolitanate of the Patriarchate of Constantinople. The acquisition of Russia extended the Constantinopolitan Patriarchate's domain enormously, for Russia was already vast, and she was expanding north-eastwards. The seat of the Suzerain Prince of Russia was transferred in 1169 from Kiev-on-Dnepr to Vladimir on the Kiasma tributary of the Volga.

The Georgians, Abkhazians, and Alans were Eastern Orthodox Christians, but they had maintained their independence when their Greek co-religionists had subjugated the Georgians' Monophysite Armenian neighbours during the first half of the eleventh century, and in 1071 Georgia was not implicated in the East Roman Empire's disaster. She survived the Saljuqs' assaults and in the twelfth century she partitioned Armenia with the ephemeral Saljuq Empire's Muslim successor-states. In Queen Thamar's reign (1184–1212) the territory under Georgia's direct and indirect rule extended from the Black Sea coast to the Caspian coast of Caucasia.

The fortunes of the diverse parts of the Byzantine World were affected in different ways by the Mongols' eruptions out of the Eurasian steppe. Georgia was the first Eastern Orthodox country to suffer. She was devastated by the fugitive Khwarizmian prince Jalal-ad-Din in 1225 and by the Mongols themselves in 1236. The Mongols imposed their suzerainty on Georgia. Russia was devastated by the Mongols in 1237 en route, via Bulghar-on-Volga, to Europe, and again in 1240 (when Kiev was sacked). Mongol suzerainty was imposed on the easternmost of the Russian principalities, but Galicia (Halicz) in the south-west, and Pskov and Novgorod in the north-west, maintained their independence, and Novgorod began to outflank the Mongol Empire and its Russian dependencies by expanding, to the north of them, eastwards beyond the Ural Range. The Nicaean Greek Empire profited by the Mongols' defeat and subjugation, in 1243, of the Saljuq Sultanate of Rum.

The East Roman Empire's catastrophe in 1180–1204, and Russia's catastrophe in 1237–40, did not blight the development of Byzantine civilization, and did not check its spread. Serbia was anchored to Eastern Orthodox Christendom by the building of churches, decorated with mural paintings, in the Byzantine style. The architecture of the twelfth-century churches at Vladimir and Suzdal combines Greek with Armenian and Georgian features. Nicetas Choniates, who has bequeathed to us his vivid and moving first-hand account of the sack of Constantinople in 1204, is the last link in a chain of historians who have left a continuous record of East Roman history running from 959 to 1204. The philosopher Michael Psellus, who covered the years 976–1077, is more perfunctory than his predecessor Leo Diaconus in recording facts and dates, but is acute in his analysis of character. These Byzantine Greeks write pedantically in the Attic *koinê*, but Greek was not the only language in which the history of Eastern Orthodox Christendom was written during these years. The Russian Primary Chronicle was composed in Macedonian Slavonic at an early date in the twelfth century, when this was still a living language.

WESTERN CHRISTENDOM, 1099–1321

DURING the second half of the eleventh century Western Christian civilization burst into flower. During the twelfth and thirteenth centuries it displayed an increasing vitality in all fields of activity, but, during the first quarter of the fourteenth century, it suffered a set-back. The population explosion that had started in Western Christendom in the eleventh century was already abating before the genocidal visitation of the Black Death in 1348. The Greeks' recapture of Constantinople in 1261 and the Muslims' recapture of Acre in 1291 set the seal on the failure of the Western Christians' forcible intrusion into the Levant, which had been started in the First Crusade. The Papacy's hegemony over Western Christendom, which had been inaugurated by Pope Gregory VII, was overthrown by the French Crown when its agents physically assaulted Pope Boniface VIII in 1303.

Meanwhile, Western Christendom's twelfth-century and thirteenth-century florescence had been signalized by mighty works, both evil and good. Conspicuous Western public crimes in this age were the conquest and sack, by 'Crusaders', of Eastern Orthodox Constantinople in 1204 and of Cathar Languedoc in 1208–29; the conquest and expropriation of the Slav lands along the south shore of the Baltic Sea, which was consummated in the course of the twelfth century; and the Papacy's war to the death against Frederick II and his heirs. Yet the same two centuries of Western Christian history were illuminated by the lives of four supremely great men: a saint, Francesco Bernardone of Assisi (1182–1226), a philosopher, St. Thomas Aquinas (c. 1225–74), a poet, Dante Alighieri of Florence (1265–1321), and a painter, Giotto Bondoni, from Florence's rural territory (1267–1337). These four great men were Italians, but Western Christian sculpture reached its medieval zenith in thirteenth-century France, and the so-called 'Gothic' style of medieval Western architecture, which was introduced into Western Christendom in the twelfth century from Saljuq Turkish Asia Minor, is represented by magnificent surviving monuments on both sides of the Alps which embody the medieval ideals of Western Christendom as a whole.

A majority of the finest monuments of Gothic architecture—cathedrals modelled on Saljuq khans (caravanserais)—are Transalpine, and this is not surprising; for, in Italy, in spite of her tribulations in the sixth century, there had not been so great a break with the Graeco-Roman past as in other parts of Western Christendom ,and therefore, in Italy, the Romanesque style of architecture was more firmly founded and was less readily abandoned. Moreover, at Ravenna and at Venice, which had once been outposts of the East Roman Empire, there were churches built by East Roman architects in the Byzantine style. The present St. Mark's, for example, which was completed in 1071, is modelled on the former Church of the Holy Apostles at Constantinople. It is, however, remarkable that the adjacent Doge's Palace should have been reconstructed on the Gothic style, and it is also remarkable that Giotto should have broken away from the Byzantine tradition to become the father of the modern Western naturalistic style of painting.

Dante's decision to compose the *Divina Commedia* in stanzas of rhyming lines of Tuscan verse instead of in Latin hexameters has been momentous for the subsequent inspiration of poetry in all the vernacular languages of the Western World. Dante was conscious that, in using the vernacular, he was following a lead given by earlier Transalpine poets; but, for a Tuscan, it was a greater feat to liberate himself from the spell of the Latin language and literature than it had been for poets whose mother-tongues were the Langue d'Oc and the Langue d'Oil—not to speak of poets whose mother-tongues were, not Romance, but Teutonic. The medieval Italians might have remained prisoners of their ancestral Latin language. They might have compromised by writing serious Latin poetry in the metres and style of the contemporary popular poetry in the vernacular. Some exquisite Latin poetry of this genre was, in fact, written in the twelfth and thirteenth centuries. In liberating themselves from a linguistic servitude to the Graeco-Roman past, the medieval Italians were more successful than their Greek contemporaries, and their audacity gave free play to their creativity. By Dante's day, Italy had developed a precocious regional form of Western civilization. It took the rest of Western Christendom two centuries to attain the cultural level at which Italy stood in the year 1300.

Throughout the two centuries ending *c.* 1300, the whole of Western Christendom was advancing economically. It was becoming more populous, more productive, and more efficient in its technology.

The growth of the West's population during this period is attested by the increase in the area of land under cultivation, by the increase in the

number and the size of towns, and by the colonization of subject territories. The increase in the size of towns is recorded in the history of
town-walls. In many cases, a wall built *c.* 1100 was replaced, *c.* 1250–
1350, by a new wall enclosing a larger space. Northern Italy and
Flanders were still the two regions in which towns were thickest on the
ground.

In the production of woollen textiles, Flanders forged ahead in the
twelfth century, and it was not till the close of the thirteenth century
that Florence drew abreast of her. Flanders enjoyed the advantage of
having the raw materials for her industry at her doors, in the Low
Countries themselves and in England. The Italian towns, especially
those on the coast, enjoyed the advantage of conducting the maritime
trade between Western Christendom and the Levant. Italian and Flemish
businessmen met, during the twelfth and thirteenth centuries, at annual
fairs at four places in Champagne, a convenient half-way house.

The increase in population worked together with the rise of the towns
and the colonization of the Baltic shore to modify the social structure of
rural life. The insecurity of life in Western Christendom in the ninth and
tenth centuries had caused large estates (manors) to spread at the expense of small holdings. There had also been a decline in population,
and a manor was therefore operated by letting portions of it to tenants
on condition that they should spend several days in the week on cultivating the demesne (home farm) whose produce the lord of the manor
reserved for himself. So long as there was a shortage of man-power, this
was the best way of ensuring that the demesne should continue to be
cultivated, but the system was economically inefficient and socially
invidious. A serf or slave does a minimum amount of work by comparison
with a wage-earner. Consequently, when population increased, lords of
manors were glad to substitute money-payments for labour-services, and
the serfs found money-payments less aggravating than task-work. Moreover, serfs whose services were not commuted could escape them by
absconding to a town where they would find industrial employment or
to the colonial region to the east of the River Elbe (originally a land of
freeholds, though eventually the last European citadel of serfdom).

The colonization of the Baltic region was both rural and urban. The
first German town with a frontage on the Baltic was Lübeck, founded in
1143. Danzig was founded *c.* 1200, Riga in 1201, Reval in 1219. The
Baltic became a German lake, with Scandinavia and Russia as its commercial hinterlands. By the thirteenth century the Scandinavian peoples,
who had once terrorized Christendom, were being victimized by the
German maritime city-states, as the Greeks and the Muslims were by the
Italian city-states. The Baltic was becoming a counterpart of the Mediterranean on a smaller scale. In the century 1250–1350, the Flemish cities

were importing their grain from the Baltic instead of from Germany and France.

The increasing pressure of population on the land was partly offset by technological improvements. Though the extension of arable at the expense of pasture caused a dearth of manure for use as a fertilizer, the rotation of crops made it possible to substitute a three-field for a two-field system of cultivation, and this reduced the ratio of land lying fallow at any given moment, besides allowing greater opportuneness in the timing of ploughings and sowings. The heavy plough, drawn by rationally harnessed horses, had been perfected by 1200. The number of water-mills in Western Christendom increased during the twelfth and thirteenth centuries, and windmills began to be installed there *c.* 1162–80.

Unlike wind and running water and muscle-power, minerals are a non-replaceable commodity. Since the invention of metallurgy in the fourth millennium B.C., one source of minerals after another has been exhausted. In the tenth century A.D., Germany and Bohemia became the principal source of minerals for Western Christendom, but, by the fourteenth century, the surface seams and shallow mines has been worked out, and more sophisticated and costly mining-techniques had become necessary for reaching seams at deeper levels.

The political life of Western Christendom in the twelfth and thirteenth centuries was dominated by a resumption of the struggle for power between the Papacy and the Empire. In the first bout of this struggle, which had ended in 1122 with a compromise over the issue of investitures, power-politics had been camouflaged by being practised in the name of ethical principles. In the second bout (1158–1268), power-politics emerged naked as a competition between the Papacy and the resuscitated Western Empire for the control of Italy, which had now become the key region of Western Christendom. The *tertii gaudentes* were the North-Italian city-states and France. Both the Empire and the Papacy were losers.

In 1158–83 the Hohenstaufen Emperor Frederick I tried and failed to impose an autocratic imperial regime on the Lombard city-states. The Papacy supported the city-states against the Empire in their struggle for independence, since the city-states provided a territorial screen for the Papacy against Transalpine imperial power. For this reason the Papacy tolerated city-state autonomy not only in Lombardy and Tuscany but also in the Italian territories awarded to the Papacy by Pippin III and by Charlemagne. In the twelfth and thirteenth centuries the Papacy's paramount objective was an ecumenical hegemony over the whole of Christendom, and this ambitious Papal aim was given priority over Papal claims to local sovereignty. Hence the Papacy in this age acquiesced in the autonomy of city-states not only in the Romagna (i.e. the territory of the former East Roman Exarchate of Ravenna) but also in the Ducatus Romanus, including the city of Rome itself. Moreover, the Papacy and some of the Italian city-states became financial as well as political partners. By 1250–1300 Florentine banks were making profits by collecting Papal taxes on the Papacy's behalf.

Another ally of the Papacy was France, whose interest lay in diminishing the Empire's power. During the struggle between the Empire and the Papacy, one Pope after another found asylum in France, from Urban II (1088–99) to Innocent IV (1243–54). In 1194 Frederick I's son and successor Henry VI compensated for his father's failure to subjugate the Lombard city-states by making himself master of the Kingdom of the Two Sicilies. By this stroke the Hohenstaufen dynasty caught both the Papacy and the North-Italian city-states in a vice between the Two Sicilies and Germany. Henry VI's son and successor Frederick II was a genius who was as much at home in the Greek and Arabic culture of the cosmopolitan Kingdom of the Two Sicilies as he was in the Italian version of the Western culture; but Frederick II's genius was defeated by the strength of the opposition that he aroused and by the prematureness of his death.

The Papacy's retort to Frederick's bid for the command over the whole of Italy was to wage a war of extermination against the Hohenstaufens, and in this Urban IV (1261–4) and Clement IV (1265–8) were eventually successful; but they succeeded only by the expedient of persuading a French prince—Charles of Anjou, the brother of Louis IX of France—to conquer the Kingdom of the Two Sicilies from Frederick II's heirs. In overthrowing one secular power, the Papacy had placed itself at the mercy of another. In 1303 the French Crown put an end to the Papal hegemony over Western Christendom as effectively as the Papacy, with French aid, had previously shattered the prestige of the Empire.

For the Empire, the consequence of its long-drawn-out losing battle for the command of Italy was a loss of command over Germany, which was the Empire's home-territory. In the tenth and eleventh centuries, the Crown of East Francia (Germany) had exercised a more effective authority over its subjects than had the Crown of West Francia (France). By 1303 Philip IV of France was able to win the support of the notables of his kingdom, clerics as well as laymen, for defying the pretension to Papal hegemony over secular Western Christian rulers that was being asserted, in rashly provocative terms, by Pope Boniface VIII. By that date, the notables of the Kingdom of Germany had become virtually sovereign rulers who could defy the Emperor with impunity.

The relative increase in France and decline in Germany of the power of the Crown can be measured by the regional differences in the history of the institution of feudalism. Like serfdom, feudalism is a social relation in which the grant of the use of land is paid for by the performance of personal services (feudal services being military, whereas a serf's services are economic). In granting a feudal tenure, a sovereign derogates from his sovereign prerogative by making a contract with one of his subjects instead of exacting his full sovereign rights. If and when a feudal tenure becomes hereditary, the sovereign's loss of sovereignty becomes extreme. Hereditary feudal tenures made their appearance in West Francia as early as the ninth century, but from the close of the tenth century onwards the French Crown progressively recovered its power. In East Francia, hereditary feudal tenures were later in making their appearance, but in the thirteenth century the process went with a run. The cause was the German Crown's persistent but unsuccessful attempt to assert its authority in the Kingdom of Italy. In pursuing a Transalpine objective beyond its grasp, the German Crown lost command of its home-territory. The Imperial Crown was too heavy an additional load, and this was an incubus which a wearer of the French Crown was not called upon to assume.

In the conflict between the Empire and the Papacy, the price paid by both combatants was a loss of authority. The authority that was lost by the Empire was political; the authority lost by the Papacy was moral— but this moral loss brought with it a loss of political power as well; for, since the days of Gregory VII, the Papacy had sought to exercise political power indirectly by virtue of its rehabilitated moral prestige, and this moral flaw in the ideal of a Papal hegemony over Western Christendom was made manifest by the Papacy's conduct of its war with the Empire.

In order to fight the Empire the Papacy needed money, and it devised invidious means of raising funds. It built up an efficient administrative system for taxing the clergy throughout Western Christendom. This source of revenue became so lucrative that secular sovereigns who were powerful enough exacted a share in the proceeds, while Italian bankers found it profitable to serve as the Papacy's financial agents. Another source of Papal revenue was the fees exacted by the Curia for serving as a final court of appeal, and, to an increasing extent, as a court of first instance, in suits that were held by canon lawyers to fall within their province. The rediscovery of Justinian I's code of civil law had been countered by the compilation of an ecclesiastical law to match it. When Frederick I asserted his sovereign rights as Justinian's successor, he was opposed by two Popes, Alexander III (1159–81) and Lucius III (1181–5), who had started their careers as canon lawyers.

The Papacy's appetite for power, and its resort to finance and to law as instruments for serving its purpose, shocked the noblest spirits in Western Christendom. St. Bernard (1090–1153), the abbot of Clairvaux, Cîteaux's daughter-house, protested against the Papacy's legalism and rapacity. St. Bernard was not impeccable. He was passionate and impulsive. He was excessively intolerant of religious unorthodoxy wherever he found it: in the provocative philosopher Abelard, in the ascetic Cathars of Languedoc, in the pagan Baltic Slavs (he lent his eloquence to the preaching of a crusade against these), in the Muslims (he preached on behalf of the Second Crusade in the Levant). He involved himself in a dispute between rival claimants to the Papacy. But he did not seek high ecclesiastical office for himself, and his sincerity was manifest. He was of aristocratic birth, yet he renounced secular well-being in order to become a monk of the austere Cistercian Order. He made personal sacrifices for the sake of principle. On this account he was the most highly revered and influential Western Christian of his generation. His criticism of the Papacy's defection from its own professed principles was authoritative, and it was damning.

St. Bernard was fanatically orthodox (in Western, not Eastern Orthodox, terms). Other twelfth-century and thirteenth-century critics of the Papacy were shocked into adopting heterodox forms of Christianity or the anti-Christian Bulgarian religion of Bogomilism (known as Catharism or Patarenism in the West). The leaders of these movements of protest against Papal misdemeanours agreed with each other in embracing voluntary poverty—voluntary, because these leaders were not poor by birth; like St. Bernard, they were making a sacrifice in order to set an example for counteracting the worldliness of the Papacy and of the Christian clerical 'establishment' in general. (The eleventh-century Western ecclesiastical reformers had imposed celibacy on the Western Christian clergy, but they had not imposed a renunciation of property on the secular clergy, nor a renunciation of corporately-owned property on monastic houses.)

St. Francis of Assisi, the son of a successful wholesale cloth-merchant, defied his father by espousing the Lady Poverty. He became as austere as a Carthusian monk or as a Cathar *electus*; he set himself to lead the life lived by Christ as Christ's life is recounted in the Gospels. When his first adherent, Bernard of Quintavalle, asked Francis to allow him to join Francis in leading a life of poverty, Francis rejoiced, because he believed that the Christlike way was the right way for human beings to live. But Francis had also espoused humility. He had no thought of criticizing the Papacy, even implicitly, or of starting an anti-Papal movement or of becoming the Minister General of a new religious order. To follow Christ was the aim to which Francis was totally dedicated. However, this might not have saved Francis from sharing the Cathars' and the Waldensians' fate, for his espousal of poverty was a practical criticism of the Papacy which was the more damaging for having been inadvertent. Pope Innocent III (1198–1216) and his great-nephew and second successor Cardinal Ugolino (Pope Gregory IX, 1227–41) recognized that Francis's single-minded imitation of Christ had put the Curia in a quandary. They were painfully aware of the swelling chorus of satirical voices that was assailing the Curia from all quarters of Christendom. They decided to enlist St. Francis instead of blasting him. This decision did credit to their intelligence, though the motive was not disinterested.

St. Francis himself would have been saved acute spiritual agony if he had been martyred at his first encounter with the Curia, instead of living to receive the stigmata and also to see the Franciscan Order take a shape, in Cardinal Ugolino's and Brother Elias's hands, that was no longer in tune with Francis's own conception of the Christlike way of life. However, Francis espoused suffering, both spiritual and physical, as well as poverty and humility, and, if Ugolino and Elias had not cut him to the heart by their worldly-wise interventions, the Franciscan spirit might not have outlived St. Francis himself, whereas it is still alive today, nearly three-quarters of a millennium after the date of his death, constricted, but not stultified, by its institutional container, the Order of Friars Minor.

Institutionalization is the price of durability. This is one of the blemishes of the social facet of human life, but the institutionalization of something that has great spiritual value for posterity is a lesser evil than the total loss of the volatile spiritual treasure. St. Francis did not recognize this hard truth. Ugolino and Elias understood it and took the responsibility for acting in the light of it. They salvaged an alloy of Francis's treasure at the price of bringing odium on themselves.

St. Francis's Castilian contemporary St. Dominic (Domingo de Guzman, 1170–1221), the founder of the Order of Friars Preachers, had an easier passage. He made the same commitment to poverty; the two saints were both combating greed. But St. Dominic's spirit could be reconciled to institutionalization more readily than St. Francis's. The rising cities of Western Christendom were enriched spiritually by Franciscan as well as by Dominican houses, libraries, and lecture-rooms, though, for St. Francis, masonry and books were anathema, because he saw in them perilous impediments to the leading of a Christian life. Brother Elias never forfeited St. Francis's confidence; yet assuredly St. Francis would have been excruciated if he could have foreseen Brother Elias's virtuosity as a fund-raiser for building a church at Assisi in St. Francis's honour. The beauty of the architecture and of Giotto's paintings would not have reconciled St. Francis to this outrage against the poverty and the humility with which he had been in love.

Elias and Ugolino had perceived what needed to be done for the Franciscan Order. St. Francis had divined what needed to be done by a Western Christian. In the generation before St. Francis's, a Calabrian,

Giovanni dei Gioacchini (Joachim) of Fiore (1145–1202)—a nobleman who, like St. Bernard, had become a Cistercian monk—had predicted that, after the climax of a time of troubles, the year 1260 would inaugurate the third stage in the coming of the kingdom of heaven on earth. The Age of the Spirit was to succeed the Age of the Son, as, at the birth of Christ, this age had succeeded the Age of the Father. The year 1260 did indeed prove to be a critical one. In 1260 it became manifest that the Papacy could not wrest the Kingdom of the Two Sicilies out of the hands of Frederick II's heirs without military aid from France. But the Age of the Spirit did not dawn; for it could have been attained only if the spirit of St. Francis had prevailed. Meanwhile, Joachim of Fiore, who, in his lifetime, had approached Pope Innocent III with the same impunity as St. Francis later, had been blighted posthumously by the publication in 1254 of a new edition of some of his works at which the Curia had taken alarm. In 1323 the Pope of the day ruled that it was untrue that Christ and his Apostles had possessed no property, and then the 'Spiritual' party among the Franciscans, who stood for St. Francis's conception of what the imitation of Christ entailed, suffered the martyrdom that had not been granted to St. Francis himself or to Joachim of Fiore.

Urbanism, as well as affluence, alienates Man from Mother Earth. Both these maladies were beginning to afflict Western Christendom in St. Francis's day. Posterity is indebted to St. Francis, not only for his deliberate espousal of poverty, but also for his innate fellow-feeling for all living creatures. The reality of the relation of mutual confidence between St. Francis and wild birds and animals can be inferred from the famous legends, even if the legends themselves are not authentic records of historical facts. This mutual confidence has been rare in the Old-World Oikoumenê in any region to the west of India. St. Francis's own canticle stopped short originally at the Shinto-like praise of God for Mother Earth and for the Vegetable Kingdom. The stanzas praising God for the goodness of unvindictive human beings and for his gift of the death of the body were after-thoughts. The stanza praising him for the Sun might have been written by Akhenaton; the stanzas praising him for the elements might be Zoroastrian. From the lips of a Judaic monotheist, these praises are precious.

[67]

EASTERN ASIA, 1126–1281

THE Sung dynasty's military collapse in 1126 had been inglorious. The Empire's Jürched assailants had conquered the whole of the original cradle of the Chinese civilization in the basin of the Yellow River, including Kaifeng, the Sung dynasty's capital. The Sung Empire was saved from total conquest, not by the valour of its troops, but by natural obstacles to the advance of the Jürched cavalry: the maze of waterways round the lower courses of the Rivers Hwai and Yangtse, and the mountainous hinterland. Officially the refugee Sung dynasty's new capital at Lin-an (Hangchow) was a temporary asylum, but the Sung never succeeded in reconquering the North.

However, in the South, the Sung survived for 153 years (1127–1279); Lin-an grew to be one of the greatest and most impressive and attractive cities in the Oikoumenê; throughout the truncated domain of the Sung Empire, there were remarkable increases in population, agricultural productivity, urbanization, trade (foreign as well as domestic), and financial facilities. Paper money was put into circulation first by private banks and then by the Sung Imperial Government itself. The development of Chinese arts and crafts in the Sung Age has been mentioned in Chapter 59. During the century and a half of the truncated Sung Empire's existence, it was more populous and more prosperous than either the Han or the T'ang Empire had been when its territorial extent and its military power had been at their maximum. The one serious set-back to Chinese civilization in the later Sung Age was the decline in the status of women. The introduction of the practice of foot-binding was an atrocity.

The disaster in 1126 did not check the development of the neo-Confucian philosophy. In order to present Confucianism as being a valid alternative to the Mahayana, the neo-Confucians had had to set foot in the uncongenial realm of metaphysics, and in this field the Ch'eng brothers had parted company with each other. For Ch'eng Yi, human nature was one of the phenomenal manifestations of ultimate reality; for Ch'eng Hao, human nature and ultimate reality were identical with each other. Ch'eng Yi's metaphysics were worked out methodically by Chu Hsi (1130–1200); Ch'eng Hao's stand was taken by Chu Hsi's contemporary Liu Chiu-yüan (Liu Hsiang-shan) (1139–93). Chu Hsi was a consummate systematizer, like St. Thomas Aquinas, and, perhaps partly for this reason, his system became the official version of Confucianism for candidates for the civil service and for their examiners, though the school of Ch'eng Hao and of Liu Chiu-yüan continued to have distinguished representatives. However, the disagreement among the neo-Confucians over metaphysics was of minor importance compared to the points on which all neo-Confucians were unanimous. They were all hostile to Taoism and to Buddhism (though they had been constrained to steal some of the Mahayana's metaphysical thunder), and they all felt that ethics were more important than metaphysics. They all condemned, as being anti-social, the Buddhist sage's withdrawal from mundane social life. Ch'eng Hao and Chu Hsi, for instance, not only took their degrees; they also spent part of their working lives as active civil servants. If the Chinese neo-Confucians had been aware of the controversies in the contemporary West, they would assuredly have deprecated the ideals of SS. Francis and Joachim of Fiore, and would have approved of Cardinal Ugolino's and brother Elias's policies.

In Japan the period 935–1185 saw a progressive transfer of power and wealth from the exotic Imperial Court at Kyoto to provincial barons, and a concomitant lapse from domestic peace into civil disorder. The peace of the capital itself was disturbed more and more frequently and rudely by incursions of the armed forces of adjacent Buddhist monasteries. A civil war between two provincial families of Imperial descent, the Taira and the Minamoto, culminated in 1185 in the victory of Yoritomo Minamoto and his establishment of an effective dictatorship over the whole of Japan from a base at Kamakura—just beyond the south-western extremity of the Kanto, the biggest of the rare plains on the main island, Honshu. The Imperial Court and its sophisticated culture were allowed to survive at Kyoto, but the Kyoto Government was deprived of effective power. *De facto*, the Imperial Government at Kyoto had been controlled by regents belonging to the Fujiwara family since at least as early as 858, and, after Yoritomo Minamoto's death in 1199, the regency for the Bakufu (military government) of the Shogun (Commander-in-Chief) at Kamakura was acquired in 1203 by the Hojo family, who stayed in the saddle till 1333 and maintained effectively, till about 1284, the regime that Yoritomo Minamoto had instituted.

Japan had never before been so efficiently governed as she was from 1185 to 1284, and the gross national product increased, though there was also an increase in the inequality of its distribution. Japan was fortunate in having a strong government during this century; for the Mongols invaded Japan in 1274, and again in 1281, after the completion of their conquest of the Sung Empire in 1279. On both occasions Japanese valour was assisted by storms that made havoc of the invaders' ships. In 1274 the Mongols' expeditionary force was small, and it broke off its attack after only one day's fighting. In 1281 the invading force was on a large scale, and the attack was kept up for two months. The repulse of these two Mongol assaults on Japan had as momentous an effect on mankind's history as the repulse of the two Persian assaults on European Greece in the fifth century B.C. and as the failure of the two Muslim Arab sieges of Constantinople.

The military government of Kamakura was more in tune than the civil government at Kyoto with the cultural and social conditions of twelfth-century and thirteenth-century Japan. Yoritomo Minamoto and the Hojo regents who carried on his regime at Kamakura had contemporaries who played a corresponding role in the field of religion. The earliest forms of Mahayana Buddhism that were introduced into Japan via China and Korea were abstruse in their metaphysics—though some monasteries of these sects became crudely militaristic in their practice on Japanese soil. In the twelfth and thirteenth centuries, Buddhism was presented to the Japanese people in simplified forms in which it was comprehensible and congenial to wider circles. A sect of Zen (Ch'an, Dhyana) Buddhism was introduced into Kamakura in 1191. The Zen spiritual technique of achieving sudden enlightenment through severely disciplined meditation was attractive to the soldiers. Honen (1135–1212) and Shinran (1173–1262) appealed to the masses by concentrating on the repetition of the name of the bodhisattva Amida (Amitabha) as a talisman for securing admission, after death, to the 'Pure Land', Amida's paradise. Nichiren (1222–82) concentrated on chanting the praise of the Lotus Sutra. He was more akin to the ninth-century-B.C. Israelite prophets Elijah and Elisha than to any traditional Buddhist sage. Nichiren combated all other Buddhist sects, intervened actively in politics, got into trouble with the Bakufu, but won popularity by preaching resistance to the Mongols. Each of these twelfth-century and thirteenth-century Japanese simplified forms of Buddhism still had numerous adherents in the 1970s.

[68]

THE MONGOLS AND THEIR
SUCCESSORS

THE Mongols were a small pastoral nomad people whose ancestral pastures lay in the extreme north-eastern corner of the Eurasian steppe. In the thirteenth century A.D. they suddenly erupted out of the steppe. By 1241 their armies had ridden westwards as far as the River Oder and the north-eastern shore of the Adriatic, carrying all before them. In 1260 they invaded Syria. In 1297 they occupied Upper Burma. Their progressive conquests, which began at the eastern end of the Eurasian steppe and penetrated deep into all the adjoining regions inhabited by sedentary populations, were planned and executed under a single command from 1203, when Temüchin (c. 1162–1227), known as Genghis Khan from 1206 onwards, became a sovereign independent ruler, until the death of his grandson and third successor Möngke in 1259.

By 1259 the Mongol Great Khan was ruling, directly or by delegation, from his capital Qaraqorum on the eastern steppe, a larger empire than had ever been put together before. At that date the Mongol Empire extended, east and west, from the north-west shore of the Pacific Ocean to the headwaters of the River Volga and the north bank of the lower course of the River Danube. North and south, it extended from Lake Baikal to North Vietnam. The Mongol Empire did not yet include the whole of the Sung dynasty's dominions in China; but eventually the only parts of the Continent that escaped temporary Mongol rule were the Continent's European, African, Arabian, and Indian peninsulas. The Mongols are the only Eurasian nomads who have ever succeeded in conquering the whole of China.

The political unity of the Mongol Empire on this scale was short-lived (1241–59), but it was unprecedented; it was effective while it lasted; and it brought into immediate contact with each other regional civilizations that previously had each been developing on lines of their own with little contact, or even knowledge, of the contemporary civilizations with which they were potentially linked by the conductive Eurasian steppe.

In the fourth and fifth centuries A.D., the Huns had anticipated the Mongols in erupting out of the Eurasian steppe in all directions and in temporarily imposing their rule on some of the sedentary peoples round about. Attila's dominions extended farther westward into Europe than Batu's; the Ephthalite Huns invaded India, which the Mongols shunned, and the Ephthalites made a permanent lodgment there; other Huns participated with non-Hun barbarians in carving out for themselves successor-states, in northern China, of the Chinese Western Chin dynasty. But these were all separate enterprises of different sections of the Hun people. There was no moment at which all the Huns' conquests in all quarters were united politically. On the other hand, from 1241 to 1259 the whole of the Eurasian steppe's 'dry sea' was, in political terms, a Mongol 'dry lake', bordered by the territories of sedentary populations under the rule of a unitary Mongol Empire. From end to end, the steppe, during those years, was effectively policed and its potential conductivity was made actual by the organization of an efficient posting service.

The primary purpose of this was to enable Mongol notables to attend, at short notice, Mongol national councils held at Qaraqorum; but the same facilities brought to Qaraqorum from all quarters the princes of subject sedentary peoples, prisoners of war, voluntary adventurers (skilled artificers, commercial travellers, candidates for administrative posts in the Mongol service), and envoys from independent powers. For instance, in 1254 King Hayton of Cilician Armenia set out for Qaraqorum, and he had been preceded in 1247–8 by his brother the Constable Sempad. Cilician Armenia had readily submitted to Mongol suzerainty, and it was the only Levantine Christian state that tried seriously to seize the opportunity of crushing the Islamic World by a concerted converging movement of the Mongols and the Western Christians. In 1245–7 a Franciscan friar, Giovanni del Piano di Carpine, travelled from Lyons to Qaraqorum and back as an emissary of Pope Innocent IV. In 1253–5 another Franciscan friar, William of Rubruck, travelled from Acre to Qaraqorum and back as an emissary of the crusading Louis IX of France. But these two missions from Western Christendom were not followed up by any effective action on either side, and Islam survived, though it had never been in such great jeopardy at any date since its birth.

The cultural effects of this traffic across the temporarily well-policed Eurasian steppe were more important than the political outcome. Rubruck describes the concourse of Christians of many different regions, denominations, and nationalities who met at Qaraqorum at Eastertide 1254. In 1251 Qubilay, Genghis Khan's grandson and fourth successor, had been commissioned by his brother, the reigning Great Khan Möngke, to conquer the Sung dynasty's dominions, and in 1279 Qubilay

completed this task as Möngke's successor. Like their barbarian predecessors who had conquered northern China in the fourth century, the
Mongols were reluctant to administer China through the agency of
Chinese Confucian civil servants. The fourth-century barbarian conquerors of North China had enlisted Buddhists, Chinese and foreign.
Qubilay and his successors in the Mongol (Yüan) dynasty in China
enlisted Muslims and Christians.

Qubilay's strategy for conquering the Sung Empire was the same as
Ch'in state's had been for conquering Ch'u state in the fourth and third
centuries B.C. Qubilay outflanked the Sung dominions from the west
before attacking them directly. In 1253 he conquered the Thai state
Nan-chao and converted it into the Chinese province Yunnan. Qubilay's
agents here were Muslims from the Mongol dominions in Central Asia;
they established a Muslim community in Yunnan which still survives.
In 1275 30,000 Eastern Orthodox Alans from the northern slopes of the
Caucasus were serving under Qubilay in China. The Venetian Marco
Polo served Qubilay as an administrator in China for perhaps seventeen
years (*c.* 1275–92), and the Transoxanian Muslim Sayyid Ajall from
1274 to 1279. The Sayyid organized for Qubilay the new Chinese
province of Yunnan. Medieval Christian influence in China, unlike
contemporary Muslim influence, was ephemeral. In both Yunnan and
north-western China, Islam came to stay. Reciprocally, Chinese art
influenced Iranian art, permanently, as a result of the conquest of Iran
by the Mongols between 1220 and 1257.

Qubilay's Muslim and Christian soldiers and administrators in China
were brought from far afield, but, from the outset of the Mongols' career
of conquest, the Mongols had enlisted talent and skill from nearer home,
and this had been one of the causes of their sensational success. The
Mongol eruption, like the Muslim Arab and Scandinavian eruptions,
was sudden, but, also like these, it was the sudden effect of a long continuing previous radiation of stimulating influences from adjacent
civilizations.

The pastoral nomads at the eastern end of the Eurasian steppe were
in direct contact with the northern Chinese state Yen at least as early
as the fourth century B.C. Since the tenth century A.D. the Tibetan–
Chinese state Hsi Hsia, bestriding the north-western border between
China and the steppe, and the Khitan (Liao) Empire, and its successor
the Jürched (Kin) Empire, bestriding the north-eastern border between
China and the steppe, had been channels through which the Chinese
civilization had been conveyed to the independent nomads beyond these
semi-Chinese empires' steppe-frontiers.

The Kin Imperial Government, like the East Roman, had kept its
Eurasian nomad neighbours in check by enlisting one nomad people to

chastise another. At some date in the 1160s, the Kin had enlisted the Tatars—the Mongols' south-eastern next-door neighbours—to chastise the Mongols. *Circa* 1202 they enlisted the Karayits (Keraits)—the Mongols' Nestorian Christian nomad next-door neighbours to the south-west—to chastise the Tatars. In this campaign, Temüchin, the son of a minor Mongol chief, served as a subordinate ally of the Khan of the Karayits. In 1203 Temüchin defeated the Karayits and incorporated them in his own horde. The Kin's intervention in nomad power-politics had given Temüchin the opening for building up an independent power of his own.

However, Temüchin, like his grandson Qubilay, took care not to put himself in the hands of the Chinese. But Temüchin recognized the value of knowledge and of intellectual ability; he was willing to take advice; and this was one of the causes of his success. He was able to find non-Chinese councillors and clerks. There were some Muslim merchants in his country already before 1203. The Mongols themselves and the Tatars were still Shamanists, but the Önkuts to the south-east of the Tatars, and the Naimans and Merkits to the north and north-west of the Karayits, had, like the Karayits, been Nestorian Christians since 1009. After Temüchin had overthrown the Karayits in 1203, these other Nestorian Christian nomad peoples combined against him in 1204, and he defeated and incorporated them in their turn. The slain Naiman Khan's Uighur seal-keeper (secretary) Tashatun transferred his services to Temüchin. The Uighur Turkish people, who were the Naimans' south-western and the Hsi Hsia Empire's north-western neighbours, voluntarily submitted to Temüchin, probably soon after the Naimans' defeat in 1204.

The Uighurs, like the Khazars, were an ex-nomad Turkish-speaking people who had taken kindly to various elements of non-nomadic civilization. The Uighurs had become Manichaeans in 763, but there were also Nestorian Christians and Buddhists among them. They were literate in the Syriac alphabet, which they used for conveying their own Turkish language as well as for the conveyance of the Manichaean and Nestorian Christian liturgies and scriptures in the Syriac language. Temüchin, who was now known as Genghis Khan, set his Uighur seal-bearer to work to adapt the Syriac script for conveying the Mongol language and for putting into writing the Mongols' customary law (Yasa). When Genghis Khan took the Kin Empire's capital Ta-hsing (Peking) in 1215, he acquired the service of Yeh-lü Ch'u-ts'ai (1190–1244), a Khitan civil servant previously working for the Kin dynasty. Yeh-lü Ch'u-ts'ai, like Tashatun, transferred his services to Genghis willingly. The Khitans who had become the Jürcheds' subjects felt no loyalty towards their defeated ex-masters.

Genghis's assets were the skill of his Uighur and Khitan and Muslim advisers, the martial virtues and military discipline that were inculcated into pastoral nomad fighting-men by the way in which they made their living, and his own commanding personality and sure judgment in picking able men to serve him in both war and peace. His body-guard, like Alexander the Great's, was a kind of staff-college from which the ruler picked men, whom he had tested personally, to carry out important tasks. Genghis's personality and organizing power, in combination with the Mongols' aptitude for war and with the tincture of civilization that had been acquired gradually by the Mongols' and Tatars' immediate neighbours, explain the astonishing military and political achievements of the Mongols under the impetus given by Genghis's leadership.

Probably Genghis's most difficult task was the initial one of incorporating in his Mongol horde, in 1203–4, all the other nomad peoples at the eastern end of the Eurasian steppe. Genghis then conquered the Hsi Hsia Empire in 1205–9, started on the conquest of the Kin Empire in 1211, and in 1218 overthrew Küchluk, the refugee son of the late Khan of the Naimans, who had usurped the domains of the Qarakhitay astride the T'ien Shan Range. In 1220–1 Genghis conquered the dominions of the Khwarizmshah (Soghd, Tokharistan, and Afghanistan, besides Khwarizm itself). After Genghis's death in 1227, Korea was conquered in 1231 and the conquest of the Kin Empire was completed in 1234.

The campaigns of 1236–41 added to the Mongol Empire the whole western half of the Eurasian steppe, together with the Volga Bulgars and the Russian principalities (all of these except Novgorod, Pskov, and Galicia). The Saljuqs of Rum were defeated and were made tributary in 1243. The conquest of the Sung Empire, started in 1251, was completed in 1279. Meanwhile, Nan-chao was annexed in 1253 and North Vietnam (temporarily) in 1257–8. South-western Iran and Iraq were conquered by Genghis's grandson Hülegü in 1256–8. (In 1258 Baghdad was taken and was sacked, and the Abbasid Caliphate was extinguished.) In the far south-east, Champa (a Hinduized state to the south of North Vietnam) was made tributary in 1283–5. Northern Burma (Mien) was occupied from 1287 to 1303.

The Mongols' conquests did little damage to their fellow nomads. These lost neither their lives nor their pasturelands. They merely underwent a change of leadership. On the other hand, for the Mongols' sedentary victims, the Mongol conquest spelled genocide and devastation. The worst atrocities were committed in Genghis's campaigns in the Khwarizmshah's dominions in 1220–1, in Batu's western campaigns in 1231–41, and in Hülegü's campaign in Iraq in 1258. From 1215 to 1241 Yeh-lü Ch'u-ts'ai did his best to convince his Mongol masters that the extermination of potential tax-payers was contrary to Mongol interests, but Yeh-lü Ch'u-ts'ai did not survive the interregnum during the years 1242–6.

The Mongols, like previous empire-builders, were not invincible. The failure of the naval expeditions against Japan in 1274 and 1281 has been mentioned already. A naval expedition against Java in 1292 was likewise beaten off. More serious for the Mongols was the defeat in 1260 on land, in Syria, of Hülegü's advance-guard by the Mamluk successors of the Ayyubid dynasty. Hülegü's successors, the Il-Khans, in the Mongol Empire's appanage in Iran and Iraq, were defeated again by the Mamluks in Syria in 1281, 1299–1300, and 1303. More adverse still to the Mongols' ambition to complete their conquest of the Oikoumenê was the outbreak of civil war in 1264 between the Il-Khan Hülegü and Berke, the Khan of the vast appanage, embracing the western half of the steppe, that had been won in 1236–41 for the House of Jochi, Genghis's eldest son, by Jochi's son and Berke's brother and predecessor Batu. Berke's 'Golden Horde' and the Mamluks became allies; the Genoese made a profit by exporting slave-recruits for the Mamluks from the Golden Horde's dominions; and this combination was more than a match for the Il-Khans.

Hülegü's elder brother Qubilay, who succeeded Möngke as Great Khan in 1260, was also challenged, both by another brother of theirs, Arik-Böke, from 1259 to 1264, and by Kaidu, a grandson of the Great Khan Ögedei, and then by Kaidu's son Chapar, from 1259 to 1308. When, in 1271, Qubilay adopted for his dynasty the Chinese name Yüan, after having transferred his capital from Qaraqorum to Peking in 1260–7, the Mongol Empire became an avatar of the Chinese Empire endowed with far more extensive western dependencies than any previous avatar of the Chinese Empire had possessed. However, the Golden Horde's allegiance to the Great Khan (*alias* the Yüan Emperor) was only nominal, and the Great Khan's authority was contested in his own direct dominions by Kaidu and his son.

Moreover, the Mongols and the Chinese were antipathetic to each other. The Mongols were the first alien conquerors of China who were not captivated by the Chinese civilization. When, in 1368, the Yüan dynasty was overthrown and its Mongol garrisons were expelled to their ancestral pastures on the far side of the Great Wall, they withdrew, still un-Sinified—in contrast to the Khitan refugees who had established and maintained a Sinified regime in Muslim Central Asia for nearly a century after their expulsion from China. The Khitans had never ruled more than sixteen districts within the north-eastern fringe of China; the Mongols had ruled the whole of China from 1279 to 1368, and had possessed as big a foothold in northern China from 1215 onwards as had ever been possessed by the Khitan.

The Mongol Yüan dynasty made one positive permanent mark on China. In 1289 Qubilay completed the extension of the Grand Canal northwards to Peking from Hangchow. The Mongol regime in China also produced a temporary negative effect which opened the way for a permanent positive result. Under the Yüan regime the Confucian literary tradition fell into such extreme adversity that two new genres of literature, novels and plays written in the contemporary living language, were able to establish themselves. Some of the authors were Confucian litterati. These were ashamed to confess their paternity of such vulgar products, but the two new genres were popular, and they survived the rehabilitation of the Confucian tradition after the eviction of the Mongols from China. The coy creators of these new genres did for Chinese literature what their Tuscan contemporary Dante did for Western literature and what Akhenaton had done for Pharaonic Egyptian literature.

Neither the Chinese civilization nor the Russian version of the Eastern Orthodox civilization captivated the Mongol rulers of China and overlords of the greater part of Russia. On the other hand, both the Mongol masters of Iran and Iraq and the Mongol leaders of the Turkish-speaking Golden Horde were captivated by Islam—a cultural victory for the civilization of the conquered sedentary populations over their pastoral nomad military conquerors.

The eviction of the Mongols from China in 1368 had been preceded by the extinction in 1335 of the Mongol Il-Khans of Iran and Iraq and the extinction in 1359 of the descendants of Batu, who hitherto had been the rulers of the Golden Horde. During the second half of the fourteenth century the sedentary subjects of the Golden Horde and of the Chaghatay Khans asserted themselves against their Mongol masters.

The Golden Horde's south-western frontier—and, with it, the pastoral nomadic way of life—was pushed back from the north bank of the lower Danube to the west bank of the Dnestr by Rouman settlers from Hungary who founded the principalities of Wallachia and Moldavia. Between the Dnestr and the Dnepr, the pagan Lithuanians from the forests in the hinterland of the Baltic momentarily reached the north shore of the Black Sea. In 1386 Lithuania was converted to the Western form of Christianity, and was associated in a personal union with Poland. But this new Western Christian great power was preoccupied with stemming the aggression of the Western Christian Teutonic Knights, and it missed its opportunity of becoming the Golden Horde's successor-state.

In 1371 the Russian princes ventured to refuse to pay their tribute and to do their homage at the court of the Khan of the Golden Horde at Saray-on-Volga, and in 1380 the reigning Khan was defeated by the Prince of Moscow; but the Golden Horde was not yet a spent force, and in 1381 Moscow was sacked by a new Khan, Toktamish, who had been installed by Timur Lenk (Tamerlane). The Russians had not succeeded in liberating themselves from the Golden Horde's domination. They could not yet aspire to enter into the Golden Horde's heritage.

The apparent successor both of the Golden Horde and of the Chaghatay Khanate was Timur Lenk ('the Lame'), a Turkish champion and leader of the sedentary population of the Chaghatay Khans' dominions in Transoxania. In 1362–7 Timur liberated Transoxania from the Chaghatay Khans; in 1369–80 and again in 1383–4 he chastised the Chaghatay Khans' nomad henchmen on their native steppe, and by 1380 he had also liberated Khwarizm on the lower course of the Oxus, which was part of the Golden Horde's appanage. When, in 1338, Timur's protégé Toktamish attempted to reconquer Khwarizm for the Golden Horde, Timur retorted by invading the Qipchaq steppe in 1391, and again in 1395, and in this second campaign he traversed the steppe and raided Russia. Timur was the first leader of a sedentary people to invade the western half of the Eurasian steppe with impunity. Darius I had withdrawn just in time; Alexander's general Zopyrion had perished.

In 1405 Timur died en route for China. If he had not dissipated most of his energies on attacks, accompanied by Mongol-like atrocities, on the interior of the Islamic World, Timur might perhaps have re-assembled the fragments of the Mongol Empire and have ruled them from Samarqand. In the fifteenth century, Timur's descendants made some amends for Timur's atrocities by patronizing men of letters and astronomers, but they were militarily and politically weak. Their ancestor Timur's career had left unanswered the question who were to be the Mongols' successors in the dominion over the heartland of the Old-World Oikoumenê.

69

THE ISLAMIC WORLD, 1291–1555

IN 1555 the Islamic World was larger than it had been in 1291, and the greater part of it was now embraced politically in three large empires: the Osmanli (Ottoman) Turkish Empire in the Levant, the Safavi Empire in Iran, and the Timurid (mis-named Mughal) Empire in India. This was a remarkable sequel to the tribulations that the Islamic World had suffered between the year 1220 (the date of Genghis Khan's invasion of Transoxania) and 1405 (the date of Timur Lenk's death).

In 1555 the Deccan, which the Muslim rulers of northern India had started to conquer in 1294, was under Muslim rule as far south as the line of the rivers Kistna and Tungrabhadra. At the same date, south-eastern Europe was under Muslim rule up to a line that included all but the westernmost strip of Hungary. These extensions of the Islamic World had been made, like its previous extension into northern India, by force of arms, and in India as a whole, and likewise in south-eastern Europe, the great majority of the conquered population remained unconverted to Islam. However, in the heart of the Islamic World, mass-conversions in the twelfth and thirteenth centuries had reduced the former non-Muslim majority of the population here to a small minority, and in several directions the Islamic World had been extended by conversion and not by conquest.

For instance, Nubia, which, by the year 1291, had been Monophysite Christian for about eight centuries, was converted to Islam gradually as a result of an infiltration of Arab tribes from Egypt in and after the fourteenth century. Even those Nubians who retained their ancestral language adopted Islam. In the western Sudan, Islam had continued to win converts since the eleventh century, the date at which it had gained its first foothold to the south of the Sahara. In the Malay Peninsula and Indonesia, Islam won converts in the fifteenth century as peacefully as its predecessors Hinduism and Buddhism. In this region, Islam did not replace the Indian cultural influence that had been at work there for more than a millennium; Islam merely overlaid Hinduism as a veneer. In China, the Muslim communities in Yunnan and Kansu had survived the ephemeral Mongol regime under which they had been founded.

The oldest of the three Islamic empires that co-existed in 1555 was the Ottoman Empire. Its nucleus was in existence by 1300; in 1353 it had gained its first foothold in Europe, where it was to make its fortune. By 1402 it had established its direct or indirect rule over most of the area in Asia, as well as in Europe, that had been held by the East Roman Empire before 1071. In 1402 the Ottoman power had been shattered in Asia Minor by Timur and had then broken up into three competing fragments, but its European, and parts of its Asian, territories had been re-assembled by Sultan Mehmet I (ruled 1402–21). His monument is the exquisite Green Mosque at Bursa. Mehmet II (ruled 1451–81) 'the Conqueror' (of Constantinople) had consolidated the Ottoman Empire's territory and institutions. Selim I (ruled 1512–20) had transformed the Empire by expanding it eastwards and southwards. He had made it into a successor-state of the Mamluk Kingdom as well as of the East Roman Empire. In 1555, under Süleiman I, the Empire had reached its zenith and had not yet passed it.

The Safavi Empire had a meteoric rise in the years 1500–13, but in 1513 it reached its north-eastern limit over against the Uzbek nomads, a West-Siberian section of the Golden Horde that had conquered the Oxus–Jaxartes basin from the Timurids bit by bit in the course of the fifteenth century. For four years (1511–14) the founder of the Safavi Empire, Shah Isma'il, threatened the Ottoman Empire with a repetition of the disaster that had been inflicted on it by Timur in 1402. But in 1514, at the Battle of Chaldiran, to the north-east of Lake Van, the Osmanlis had dealt the Safavis a blow under which, in 1555, the Safavi Empire was still reeling. The Osmanlis had annexed Diyarbakr in 1516 and Iraq in 1534–6. However, in 1555 the Safavis still held all but the north-west corner of Iran.

In 1555 the Timurid Humayun reconquered the Kingdom of Delhi, which his father Babur had conquered in 1526 after having failed in 1512–13 to reconquer from the Uzbeks his House's ancestral dominions in Transoxania. In 1512–13 Babur had had Isma'il Safavi as his ally, but in 1513 Isma'il, now threatened by Selim I Osmanli in the opposite quarter, had made peace with the Uzbeks on terms that left Khorasan to Isma'il and Transoxania and Tokharistan to them. Babur had had to withdraw to Kabul and to wait there for his chance to find in India a compensation for his failure to recover Transoxania.

The building of each of these three empires was a *tour de force*. A state cannot exist without having agricultural and industrial and commercial tax-payers and without having a disciplined and loyal army. But, since a date about half way through the eleventh century, the Islamic World had been afflicted by intrusions of Muslim pastoral nomads. North-West Africa and Andalusia had been overrun by nomad Berbers and Arabs; Iraq and the Jazirah (Mesopotamia) by other nomad Arabs; the Oxus–Jaxartes basin, Iran, Armenia, and Asia Minor by nomad Türkmens. It has been mentioned that these Türkmens had come in two waves, the first wave headed by the Saljuqs in the eleventh century and the second wave fleeing from the Mongols in the thirteenth century. The sedentary population's productivity and tax-paying capacity had suffered from the presence of these Muslim pastoral nomads; from the atrocities committed by the Mongol pastoral nomads; and from the subsequent atrocities committed by Timur Lenk in the interior of the Islamic World between 1380 and 1405.

Timur and his soldiers were not nomads; they were sedentary Transoxanian Muslims; yet Timur behaved with Mongol-like brutality, and, except for his incursion into Russia in 1395, all his victims were Muslims. Besides chastising the Muslim nomads of the Chaghatay Khanate and the Golden Horde, Timur had sacked Baghdad in 1393, had sacked Delhi, the capital of Muslim northern India, in 1398/9, had sacked Aleppo and Damascus in 1401, and had broken up the Asian dominions of the Ottoman Empire in 1402. Timur's performance was destructive and negative. After his death in 1402, his own empire slowly dwindled to vanishing-point, leaving the work of reconstructing the Islamic World politically to be done by more constructive hands.

At the date of Timur's death, the only states in the Islamic World that were still 'going concerns' were the Mamluk Kingdom in Egypt and Syria and the Bahmanid Kingdom in the Deccan. Iraq had not recovered from the Mongol conquest in 1258. Till that date, Iraq had been on a par with Egypt economically. It had been one of the two principal food-producing areas in the Old-World Oikoumenê. In 1358 Iraq's irrigation system had been put out of action, and it had not been rehabilitated.

Northern India, like Egypt, had escaped the Mongols, but it had not escaped Timur, and, even before Timur's destructive invasion, the Kingdom of Delhi had failed to hold Muslim India together. After the northern Indian Muslims' conquest of the Deccan, which had begun in 1294, the King of Delhi, Muhammad b. Tughluq, had made an abortive attempt in 1327–9 to move the capital of a unitary Islamic Indian Empire from Delhi to Deogari in the Deccan. After his return to Delhi his empire broke up. *Circa* 1336 the tip of the peninsula, to the south of the Kistna and Tungrabhadra rivers, was united in the anti-Muslim Hindu Empire of Vijayanagar. In 1347 the Islamic dominions in the Deccan, to the north of this line, were formed into an independent Islamic Empire ruled by the Bahmanid dynasty. Between 1482 and 1512 the Bahmanid Empire broke up into five discordant successor-states.

In 1564 four of these five Muslim states made an alliance with each other against Vijayanagar, and they succeeded in overthrowing this last surviving independent Hindu state in 1565. On the political plane, Hinduism was now submerged almost everywhere throughout the sub-continent, but on other planes Hinduism was still full of life. It responded creatively to Islam's religious impact. In the fifteenth century Kabir presented, in Hindi verse, his intuition of the ultimate spiritual reality that is adumbrated in both Hinduism and Islam. Kabir was a precursor of Nanak (1469–1539), the founder of the Sikh religion and community. The Timurid Mughal Emperor Akbar (ruled 1556–1605) had a Hindu subject, Tulsi Das, who composed a *Ramayana* in Hindi, the living language of a majority of the population of northern India. This poem became as familiar to Hindi-speakers as the poetry of the four major New-Persian poets became to Farsi-speakers.

In 1405 Mamluk Egypt was still intact. The Mongols and Timur, in turn, had invaded Syria, which was Egypt's glacis, but they had not reached Egypt itself. Egypt's irrigation system was still in working order. The country had a dense, productive, tax-paying civil population, and it was governed and defended by a comparatively well equipped, trained, and disciplined army of slave-soldiers imported first from the Qipchaq steppe and then from the Caucasus. The population had been converted progressively from Monophysite Christianity to Islam till the Christians had become a small minority; but under the Mamluks, as under previous Islamic regimes, the Egyptian Christians had continued to play an important part in public affairs as tax-collectors. Thus, in Mamluk Egypt, the Muslim majority of the population was defended and governed by imported aliens and was taxed by non-Muslim natives.

In the Asian portion of the Islamic World outside the domains of the Egyptian Mamluks and the Indian Muslim rulers, the problem, in and after 1300, was how to re-establish stable political structures in spite of the presence, in force, of Türkmen nomads. The potential founders of new Islamic states in this region were the leaders of these nomad tribes. The tribesmen's martial prowess was the basis of their leaders' power, and the leaders must continue to depend on it unless and until they could find an effective substitute for it. Pending this, the leaders must try to dispose of their nomad followers by taming them, by moving them on, and by eventually inducing them to abandon their ancestral calling of pastoral nomadism and to become peasants and artisans.

In Asia Minor, this problem had been partially solved by the Saljuq Sultans of Rum in the twelfth century. These had parked their Türkmen followers in the Asian borderland between Rum and the shrunken East Roman Empire, to wage there the Islamic holy war (jihad) against non-Muslims. The Saljuq sultans had built up a sedentary society in the interior of their dominions. The human materials for this had been partly local ex-Christian and ex-Greek-speaking peasants who had survived the Türkmens' passage through their country, and partly immigrants from Iran. But in the thirteenth century the Saljuqs of Rum had suffered a series of set-backs. The refugee East Roman Empire, which had established its capital at Nicaea after the capture of Constantinople in 1204 by Western Christian adventurers, paid attention to the Asian remnant of its dominions and even re-extended this at the Rum Saljuqs' expense. Rum was then flooded by the second wave of westward-migrating Türkmen nomads. In 1243 the sultanate of Rum was defeated by the Mongols and was made tributary to them, and in 1271 an insurrection here against the Mongols was savagely repressed, and the Mongol Il-Khans' control over Rum was tightened. Meanwhile, the Nicaean Greeks' re-occupation of Constantinople in 1261 had diverted their attention from their possessions in Asia Minor. Consequently, between 1261 and 1300, the Türkmens gained control of almost the whole of Asia Minor at the expense of both the East Roman Empire and the Saljuq Sultanate of Rum. This sedentary Turkish state in Asia Minor had been extinguished either by the local Türkmens or by its Mongol Il-Khan overlords or by both before the extinction, in 1335, of the Il-Khans themselves and the replacement of their regime by the rule of other local Türkmen tribes that, previously, had been the Il-Khans' nominal subjects.

The leaders of the Türkmen tribes who had thus stepped into the shoes of the Il-Khans and the Rum Saljuqs all aspired to become rulers of sedentary principalities of the Rum type. The most successful of all these ambitious leaders were the Osmanlis. Towards the close of the thirteenth century, these had been parked by the Saljuq sultans of Rum in a key position in the lower valley of the River Sangarios (Sakkaria), over against the three Greek cities Nikomedheia (Ismit), Nicaea (Isnik), and Brusa (Bursa). The Osmanlis took Bursa in 1326, Isnik in 1331, Ismit in 1337. The capture of Ismit opened the way to the Asian shore of the Bosphorus; the capture of Bursa opened the way for the conquest in 1344 of Karasi, the next Türkmen principality to the west. Karasi already held the Asian shore of the Dardanelles. When in 1353 the Osmanlis seized a beach-head in Europe at Gallipoli (Kallipolis), they were following in the wake of the Nicaean Greek Emperors, who had invaded Thrace in 1235 and who, by 1247, had encircled Constantinople from the landward side, as the Osmanlis did in their turn, when in 1361 they took Adrianople (Edirne).

The Osmanlis built up their power partly by taming their Türkmen tribesmen and partly by winning a few militarily valuable converts, and many more economically valuable unconverted Christian productive workers and tax-payers, in the territories that they conquered from Christendom. These conquests gave the Osmanlis a supply of sedentary Christian subjects which was comparable in magnitude to the Indian Muslim empire-builders' supply of sedentary Hindu subjects. This source of economic power was not at the disposal of any of the other principalities founded elsewhere in Asia Minor by leaders of Türkmen tribes. Nor was it at the disposal of the Safavis.

The Türkmens were tamed for their leaders by representatives of the Muslim religious (dervish) orders, but, for secular Muslim empire-builders, this was a dangerous expedient. The dervishes were welcomed by the Türkmens because they took the place of the Türkmens' pre-Islamic shamans, but these shamans in Muslim dress were heretical in the eyes of the Sunni Muslim religious 'establishment', and sometimes, instead of taming the Türkmens, they re-activated their traditional turbulence. For instance, in 1416, when the Sultan Mehmet I had not yet finished reconstituting the Ottoman Empire after its temporary overthrow by Timur in 1402, formidable simultaneous insurrections in Ottoman territory in north-eastern Bulgaria and in western Asia Minor (in the re-subjugated Asian Türkmen principalities Sarukhan and Aydin) were engineered by Sheikh Bedreddin of Simar in Germiyan. Bedreddin was a doctor of the Sunni Islamic law who had become a highly unorthodox and revolutionary mystic. He called on Muslims and Christians to join forces in following him against the Ottoman regime. Bedreddin's insurrection was suppressed, but his sect survived into the seventeenth century. In 1416 the majority of the insurgents were discontented Türkmens.

The non-Osmanli Türkmen tribes in Asia Minor had resented being conquered by the Osmanlis in the fourteenth century and being re-conquered by them after having been temporarily liberated by Timur. In 1511 the Ottoman Empire was nearly overthrown once again by a widespread revolt in Asia Minor of Twelve-Imam Shi'i Türkmen partisans of Shah Isma'il, the founder of the Safavi Empire. This revolt was repressed savagely by Selim I in 1512–13. The original Safavi army was composed of corps of Shi'i émigrés from the Türkmen principalities in Asia Minor that had fallen under Ottoman rule. After Shah Isma'il's death in 1524, the turbulence of these Qizilbash ('Red-heads', so-called from the colour of their headgear) became a plague for Isma'il's successors, though the Shahs of the Safavi Empire were *ex officio* the spiritual heads of the Sufi religious order in which the tribal regiments of Qizilbash soldiers were enrolled.

The Osmanli empire-builders did not rely on any Türkmen tribes-men—not even on their own. They encouraged their Türkmens to move on into the expanding Ottoman dominions in Europe, but, for holding their dominions in both Europe and Asia, and for manning their field-armies, the Osmanlis drew upon other sources of man-power. A militia of feudal cavalrymen was maintained out of the revenues from non-heritable fiefs, in which the revenue-producing tenants, as well as the revenue-receiving cavalrymen, had rights prescribed and enforced by the state. Also, following Abbasid and Ayyubid precedents, the Osmanlis maintained a standing army of slaves. Originally these were either purchased, like the Abbasids' and the Ayyubids' slave-soldiers, from abroad or were recruited from prisoners of war, but, before the close of the fourteenth century, the Osmanlis had begun to staff the Padishah's slave-household by conscripting native peasant Christian boys, mostly Serbs, Croats, and Albanians. This inhuman but efficient institution was developed by Murad II (ruled 1421–51).

Originally these native slave-conscripts were employed only as soldiers (the janizaries, *Yeni Çeri*, meaning 'new troops'). Ottoman civil administrators had been recruited at first from among the Empire's free Muslim subjects. Mehmet II started to recruit his administrative officials, too, from among his slaves; and we may infer that by that time it was already the practice to divide a draft of boy-conscripts into *ichoghlanlar* ('interior boys') and *ajemi oghlanlar* ('alien boys'). The *ichoghlans* served as the Padishah's pages, and they were given a long and thorough education—intellectual as well as physical and military—which qualified them for holding the highest offices of state or, at the lowest, for serving in the household cavalry. The *ajemi oghlans* eventually became janizaries.

The training of imperial slaves of both grades was intensely com-petitive and selective. All members of the slave-household were paid, though at differential rates. Conversion to Islam was not compulsory, because it was inevitable. Free-born Muslim Ottoman subjects, includ-ing the sons of imperial slaves, were debarred from admission into the imperial slave-household. So, when the administration of the Empire became the slave-household's monopoly, free-born Muslim Osmanlis were excluded from sharing in the government of their own country. The government was now in the hands of carefully educated and rigidly disciplined ex-Christian slaves. This was one of the principal causes of the Ottoman Empire's success.

The eponymous ancestor of the Safavi dynasty was Sheikh Safi-ad-Din Ishaq (1252–1334) of Ardebil in the south-eastern corner of Azerbaijan. He was the founder of a religious order, not of a state, and there is no evidence that he was a Shi'i. The first of his descendants and successors who was unquestionably a Shi'i was his grandson Khwaja Ali. He was a Shi'i of the Twelve-Imam sect, not of the unpopular seven-Imam Isma'ili sect which had been represented in the tenth century by the Fatimid dynasty and by the Carmathians, and later by the Assassins. The Assassins in western Iran had been extirpated in 1257 by the Mongol war-lord Hülegü. The first Safavid who took to politics and war was Sheikh Junaid, Safi-ad-Din's great-great grandson and Shah Isma'il's grandfather. His accession year 1447 was the year of Timur's son and successor Shah Rukh's death, which was followed by the disintegration of the Timurid Empire. Junaid married the sister of Uzun Hasan, Khan of the Aq Qoyunlu ('White-Sheep') Türkmens, who were the Timurids' successors in Azerbaijan and Diyarbakr.

The Aq Qoyunlu had an Iranian *wazir* (chief administrator), and Shah Isma'il took him over when in 1502 he liquidated this official's Aq Qoyunlu employers, but Shah Isma'il himself and his Qizilbash followers were, like the Aq Qoyunlu, Turkish-speaking—as indeed, by this date, was the whole population of Azerbaijan. Before Shah Isma'il's day, the principal centres of Twelve-Imam Shi'ism had been south-western Iraq and the Jabal Amil (the southern end of the present Republic of Lebanon). Iran had been predominantly Sunni. The four most famous New-Persian poets—Firdawsi, Sa'di, Hafiz, Jami—had all been Sunnis. However, Shah Isma'il forcibly imposed Twelve-Imam Shi'ism on all his subjects; the Iranians accepted their compulsory new religion with surprising docility, and eventually it became the distinctive mark of a new Iranian nationalism, though the Turkish-speaking empire-builder Shah Ismai'l's intention had been simply to extend his dominions and to propagate his ancestral religion.

By 1555 the Ottoman Empire was being governed by the Padishah's slave-household. In Iran, Shah Isma'il's grandson and namesake and second successor was at the mercy of his Qizilbash Türkmen soldiery. The Timurid Humayun had just reconquered northern India with an army of adventurers from many parts of the Islamic World. Humayun and his father Babur were Sunnis, but each in turn had sought aid from the Shi'i Safavis. The Muslim 'ascendancy' in India was so formidably outnumbered by its Hindu subjects that it could not afford to indulge in domestic sectarian quarrels. In Islamic India, Muslim reinforcements of any denomination were always welcome.

In the Islamic World to the west of India, the surprising creation of a Twelve-Imam Shi'i empire in Iran and Iraq in 1500–13 had the effect of insulating the Sunnis in the Levant from those in Central Asia. In 1475 the Ottoman Empire had annexed the Genoese colonies in the Crimea, and Ottoman suzerainty had been accepted by the Crimean 'Tatar' successor-state of the Golden Horde, but the Muscovite Russian

Emperor Ivan IV (the Terrible) cut the communications, across the Eurasian steppe, between the Ottoman Empire and the Sunni Uzbek Khanates in the Oxus–Jaxartes basin by annexing Kazan in 1552 and Astrakhan in 1556. In 1516–17 the Ottoman Empire conquered and annexed the Egyptian Mamluk Kingdom, but, between 1498 and 1515, the Portuguese had seized the naval command over the Indian Ocean, and the Osmanlis were no more successful than the Mamluks had been in 1508–17 in trying to wrest sea-power out of Portuguese hands, though the Osmanlis, like the Mamluks, enjoyed the advantage of operating from the interior lines. In 1538 an Ottoman fleet failed to take Diu from the Portuguese, and in 1539 the Muslim Sultan of Gujerat, who had been first the Mamluks' and then the Osmanlis' ally, made peace with the Portuguese perforce. The Osmanlis gave up in 1551 their attempt to wrest from the Portuguese the command over the Indian Ocean.

In 1542 Osmanli and Portuguese musketeers fought each other in Abyssinia as auxiliaries, respectively, of contending local Muslims and Christians. Abyssinia had played hardly any part in international affairs since she had given asylum to some of Muhammad's Meccan converts to Islam before Muhammad's migration to Yathrib. The Muslim Arabs' subsequent conquest of Egypt had insulated the Monophysite Christians in Nubia and Abyssinia from the rest of Christendom. But when, in and after the fourteenth century, Nubia was converted to Islam, Monophysite Christianity survived in Abyssinia. Since the seventh century, the language of the Semitic-speaking settlers (from the Yemen) at the northern end of the Abyssinian plateau had spread southwards. Monophysite Christianity spread concurrently with the language, but Christianity had to compete with Judaism, which had forestalled Christianity in gaining a foothold here. Since the thirteenth century, the Monophysite Christian Kingdom of Abyssinia had become dominant over Judaism on the plateau, but Islam had spread round the plateau's eastern and southern foot, and in 1529–42 Muslims from the south-east had conquered almost the whole of Christian Abyssinia. Her fate seemed to be sealed by the Osmanli musketeers' victory over the Portuguese in 1542, but the Osmanlis then withdrew, and in 1543 the Abyssinian Christians won a decisive victory with the aid of the Portuguese survivors. Abyssinia emerged devastated and depopulated, and large parts of it were then overrun by a *Völkerwanderung* of Galla pagans moving up on to the plateau from the south-east and the south.

In 1555 the three great Islamic empires dominated, between them, the centre of the Old-World Oikoumenê from Algeria to northern India. The Ottoman Empire was the oldest and the best-built of the three, but it had not saved the Kingdom of Granada, the last surviving Muslim beach-head in the Iberian Peninsula, from being conquered in 1492 by the Western Christian united kingdom of Castile and Aragon. Nor had the Osmanlis annexed Morocco, the westernmost of the Muslim states in North-West Africa. Instead of intercepting the Portuguese in Atlantic waters off the coast of Morocco, the Osmanlis had been defeated by the Portuguese off the coast of Gujerat. Moreover, the Osmanlis had failed to forestall the Russians in occupying the course of the Volga from Kazan down to the Caspian Sea, and had therefore failed to make contact with their fellow Sunnis in the Oxus–Jaxartes basin.

All the same, the Islamic World had performed a remarkable feat in surviving the Mongol cataclysm, and its recovery was not confined to the political plane. Within the years 1300–1555, Iran produced the last two of the four major New-Persian poets, Hafiz (d. 1389) and Jami (1414–92), and North-West Africa produced an outstanding inquirer into the structure of human history, Ibn Khaldun (1332–1406), though, in his lifetime, North-west Africa was in a state of political chaos. It must be noted, however, that not one of these three representatives of Islamic culture was an Osmanli, and that the two last great New-Persian poets lived and died before the Safavi conquest and conversion of Iran.

70

EASTERN ORTHODOX
CHRISTENDOM, 1240–1556

THE Nicaean Greek Empire in north-western Asia Minor and the Greek and Slav Eastern Orthodox states in the Balkan Peninsula escaped the Mongol cataclysm that overwhelmed Russia in 1237–40 and deluged the Saljuq Sultanate of Rum in 1243. In the Balkan Peninsula only Bulgaria was raided. But by 1556 there had been a reversal of the respective fortunes of these two wings of Eastern Orthodox Christendom. In 1556 the Osmanlis were masters of all the southern Eastern Orthodox peoples, including the Roumans who had founded the principalities of Wallachia and Moldavia in the fourteenth century. On the other hand, by 1556 the north-eastern half of Russia was not only free from the Golden Horde's overlordship; the ruler of Moscow had become Grand Duke of Vladimir and had annexed all the principalities of eastern Russia; he had assumed the title Tsar in 1547; and he had conquered two of the now extinct Golden Horde's successor-states: Kazan in 1552 and Astrakhan in 1556.

In 1240 the Nicaean Empire was on the rise. It had won a beach-head in Europe already in 1235. In 1259 it defeated at Pelagonia in Macedonia a coalition between the rival Greek successor-state of the East Roman Empire in north-western Greece and two Frankish powers: the French Principality of the Morea and the Hohenstaufen Kingdom of the Two Sicilies. After that, the Nicaean Greeks took Constantinople from the last of the French emperors there in 1261. However, the sequel to these sensational successes was an anticlimax. In 1282–99, Serbia conquered the northern half of the Macedonian territory that the Nicaean Greek Empire had won in 1246. In 1345 the Prince of Serbia, Stephen Dušan, took Serrhes, and in 1346 he had himself crowned as 'Emperor of the Serbs and the Romans'. By that date the whole of Macedonia, outside the walls of Thessalonica, was in Serbian hands. The price of the Nicaean Greeks' re-occupation of Constantinople in 1261 had been the

loss of their Asian territories to Türkmen tribes, of whom the nearest and
the most menacing were the Osmanlis. By 1346 the rehabilitated East
Roman Empire was doomed. The open question was whether the Serbs
or the Osmanlis would be its heirs.

The East Roman Empire's decline did not sap the vitality of Byzantine art and Byzantine religious experience. The early-fourteenth-
century mosaics in the Chora Church (now the Kahriye Camisi) in
Istanbul are a match for the paintings of the contemporary Florentine
artist Giotto. Simultaneously on Mount Athos there was a revival of
Eastern Orthodox mysticism in which, through quietude (Êsykhía), the
mystic sought a union with the godhead (the declared objective of
devout Eastern Orthodox Christians since the generation of St. Athanasius of Alexandria). In the fourteenth century this mystical union was
pursued by the practice of Hindu-like physical yoga. The orthodoxy of
the implicit theology was questioned by Western Christian theologians
and by some Eastern Orthodox theologians too. But in 1351 Hesychasm
was declared to be orthodox by an Eastern Orthodox church council.
Politics as well as theology were involved. The Eastern Orthodox
pronouncement of 1351 was a retort to a Western Christian attack on
Hesychasm, and it was also a consequence of the victory of the Emperor
John VI Cantacuzenus in the East Roman civil war of 1341–7.

This civil war was the death of the rehabilitated East Roman Empire.
The war was accompanied by a social revolution, as well as by a theological dispute. In the Empire under the long-lived dynasty of the
Palaeologi (1259–1453) the continuing growth of large rural estates and
the increasing misery of the peasantry had gone to intolerable lengths.
John VI stood for the large landowners; he provoked a violent reaction.
The revolutionaries ('the Zealots') held Thessalonica for most of the
time from 1342 to 1350. In the remnant of the Empire during those
years the large landowners met with savage reprisals.

The anti-Western feeling that was manifested by the Greeks in the
fourteenth-century controversy over Hesychasm had begun to show
itself as early as the First Crusade. It had been exacerbated by the
Western Christians' sack of Constantinople in 1204 and by the progres-
sive capture of the domestic trade in the Greeks' home waters by the
Italian maritime republics. Michael VIII Palaeologus, the Nicaean
Emperor who had re-taken Constantinople, had recognized that the
East Roman Empire he had rehabilitated could not survive without
Western Christian good will and military support, and that the price
that would be exacted was the acknowledgment by the Eastern Ortho-
dox churches of the Papacy's ecclesiastical supremacy over them.
Michael VIII himself acknowledged Papal supremacy in 1274, and so
again did John V in 1369 and John VIII at the Council of Florence in

1439, and in 1453 Constantine XI, the last East Roman Emperor, died in communion with the Roman Church.

At Florence in 1439 the Act of Union was signed not only by the Emperor but by all but one of the members of the Eastern Orthodox ecclesiastical delegation; but this time, as on the previous occasions, union on Roman terms was repudiated by the mass of the Eastern Orthodox clergy and laity. After the occupation of Adrianople by the Osmanlis in 1361, Constantinople was insulated, except via the precarious sea-passage through the Dardanelles, and the city was permanently under blockade overland. From then onwards, it was manifest to all Greeks that the last politically independent enclaves of Greek territory were bound to fall to the Osmanlis if they were not salvaged by the Western Christians on Western terms. The Greeks consciously chose to expose themselves to Ottoman political domination because they felt it to be a lesser evil than Papal ecclesiastical and Genoese and Venetian commercial domination.

Muslim governments are bound by the Koran to allow submissive Christian subjects to practise their religion. Western Christian powers, with the important exception of Venice, could not be trusted to refrain from putting pressure on their Orthodox subjects to acknowledge the Papacy's supremacy. The Greeks who had not yet fallen under Western domination were unwilling to pay this price for escaping Muslim domination, and they were also sceptical about the likelihood of the Western Christians' giving them effective military aid, even if they did accept the West's conditions. Above all, they resented the fact that the Westerners, who in Greek eyes were the Greeks' cultural inferiors and also schismatics, had nevertheless now far surpassed the Greeks in wealth and power.

One of the signatories of the Act of Union at Florence in 1439 was the metropolitan of the Eastern Orthodox Church in Russia, Isidore. He was rewarded by being made a Roman Cardinal. The Metropolitan of Russia was still a subordinate of the Patriarch of Constantinople, and Isidore himself was a Greek. The Russian bishops repudiated and ejected Isidore, and in 1448 they elected a native Russian metropolitan—without having obtained the agreement of the Patriarch of Constantinople—on the initiative of the Muscovite Grand Duke of Vladimir and with the concurrence of the Grand Duke of Lithuania and of his West-Russian subordinate, the prince of Kiev. However, the Russian hierarchy did not contest the Patriarch of Constantinople's supremacy over the Metropolitan of the Eastern Orthodox Church in Russia, so, nominally at least, all Russia still remained under the Patriarch's ecclesiastical jurisdiction, in spite of the differences in the political status of the various local Russian principalities.

The principality of Moscow had made its fortune in 1328 by performing a service for the Golden Horde. On the Horde's behalf, Moscow had chastised the principality of Tver, which had revolted against the Horde in 1327. In 1332 Prince Ivan Kalita of Moscow had been rewarded by his Mongol masters by being made Grand Duke of Vladimir. He had continued to reside in his own city, Moscow, and the Metropolitan of the Eastern Orthodox Church in Russia had therefore made Moscow his seat too. The use of the principality of Moscow as the Golden Horde's executioner against other Russian principalities was convenient for the Horde, but it was short-sighted. Moscow proceeded to annex, one by one, the other Russian principalities that were under the Horde's suzerainty. The Muscovite regime was autocratic, in contrast to the regime in Russian principalities that were not yet under Muscovite rule.

The two north-westernmost Russian states, Pskov and the commercial city-state Novgorod, had preserved their independence. Novgorod had become an associate of the North-German Hansa towns, and had established its control north-eastwards over a vast hinterland extending to the shore of the Arctic Ocean from the eastern edge of Norway to the mouth of the River Ob. Moscow incorporated Novgorod in 1478 and Pskov in 1510, and this doubled Muscovy's area, wealth, and power.

In the course of the fifteenth century, Muscovy was liberated *de facto* by the Golden Horde's disintegration. About half way through the fifteenth century, the Horde split into four successor-states: Kazan, the Crimea, Astrakhan, and Kasimov. Kasimov was established in 1452 under Muscovite suzerainty. The Crimean Tatars who had come under Ottoman suzerainty in 1475 extinguished the last remnant of the Golden Horde in 1502. Muscovy's eventual annexation of Kazan (in 1552) and of Astrakhan (in 1556) was inevitable.

A problem had been created for the Russians in 1386 by the election of the pagan prince of Lithuania Iagailo (Jagellon) to be King of Poland, and his simultaneous conversion from paganism to Roman Catholic Christianity. The Lithuanians had taken advantage of Russia's prostration, since the Mongol irruption in 1237–40, to impose Lithuanian suzerainty on the western Russian principalities, except for Galicia, which was annexed by Poland in 1352. The Lithuanians had left the western Russian princes autonomous; they had not interfered with their subjects' Eastern Orthodox religion; and they had placed the seat of their government at Vilna, an Eastern Orthodox city in White Russian territory. Thus the pagan Lithuanian regime was not obnoxious to the western Russians, and it was a safeguard against the greater evil of domination by the Golden Horde. The situation changed for the worse when in 1386 the western Russians' Lithuanian suzerain became a

Roman Catholic Christian and King of Poland, and when in 1404 Lithuania enlarged its holding of Russian territory by taking Smolensk. However, the nobles in the Russian principalities under Lithuanian and Polish rule appreciated the licence that they enjoyed under this regime, in contrast to the autocracy that would have been imposed on them if they had fallen under the rule of their Muscovite fellow-Russians.

Thus in 1556 the Muscovite Russian Tsardom was not master of western Russia; yet it had become a great power, and the door was open for it to expand eastwards. By contrast, the Greeks at that date were in adversity politically. Constantinople had fallen to the Osmanlis in 1453. After the Ottoman Empire's annexation of the Empire of Trebizond in 1461 there was no remnant of Greek territory that was not under either Ottoman or Western Christian rule. However, the imposition of Ottoman rule had brought the Greeks advantages on the ecclesiastical and economic planes.

The Ottoman Padishah Mehmet II had organized his non-Muslim subjects in autonomous communities (*millets*)—Eastern Orthodox, Gregorian Armenian, and Jewish—each of which was headed by an ecclesiastical dignitary who was an Ottoman subject and was held responsible by the Ottoman Imperial Government for his Ottoman co-religionists' behaviour. The area of each *millet*-head's jurisdiction was conterminous with the Ottoman Empire itself. The Patriarch of Constantinople was head, *ex officio*, of the whole Ottoman Orthodox Christian *millet* (Rum-*milleti*), and consequently, after the Ottoman conquest of the Mamluk Empire in 1516–17, the Patriarch of Constantinople, in his capacity as an Ottoman *millet*-head, was the civil head, not only of his own ecclesiastical subjects, but also of the ecclesiastical subjects of his *confrères* the Eastern Orthodox Patriarchs of Antioch, Jerusalem, and Alexandria. The Patriarch of Constantinople also had non-Ottoman ecclesiastical subjects in eastern Georgia, Alania, and Russia. The Russian portion of the Patriarch of Constantinople's ecclesiastical dominions was immense and it was expanding. Moreover, the politically divided Russians' only bond of unity was their common allegiance to the Eastern Orthodox Church as the Patriarch of Constantinople's ecclesiastical subjects. Thus the Patriarch of Constantinople, as well as the Tsar of Muscovy, was a great power in Eastern Orthodox Christendom in 1556, though the Patriarch was the political subject of a Muslim sovereign.

By the same date the tide had turned in the Greeks' favour in the economic competition between the Greeks and the northern Italians. From the close of the tenth century till after the opening of the fifteenth century, the Italians had been gaining ground economically in the Levant at the Greeks' expense, but the Italians had suffered economically as well as politically from the Ottoman annexation of the Genoese colonies at Pera, the northern suburb of Constantinople (1453), from the Turco-Venetian war of 1463–79 (the first of many), and in the Crimea (1475). The gainers had been the Ottoman Greeks, in spite of the competition of Jewish refugees from Spain. The rising new class of prosperous Ottoman Greek businessmen consorted with the Patriarch of Constantinople and his establishment. The position of both these Greek parties was precarious, but, in combination, they already wielded considerable power.

[71]

WESTERN CHRISTENDOM, 1321–1563

DURING the quarter of a millennium *c.* 1050–1300, Western Christendom had maintained its religious and cultural unity and had also made economic progress. Its population and its production had increased. Early in the fourteenth century this material growth abated, and then the attacks of the Black Death, in and after 1348, drastically reduced both the population and the area under cultivation. On the other hand, by 1563 Western Christendom had won a global command of sea-power; yet by the same date its south-eastern land-frontier had receded from the line along which it had run in 1300. Moreover, by 1563, Western Christendom had become a house divided against itself, and this on both the religious and the political planes. This domestic division was accentuated by the fact that the dividing lines on the two planes coincided with each other to a large extent. The rulers of the local states— monarchies, principalities, and city-states—among which Western Christendom was now partitioned had agreed that it was a ruler's prerogative to decide for his political subjects their religious as well as their political allegiance.

There had already been an economic recession in Western Christendom before 1348; the Black Death turned a decline into a catastrophe. The plague entered Western Christendom at Marseilles by sea from the Genoese trading-posts in the Crimea. It must have originated either on the Eurasian steppe or in some region beyond the steppe's more distant borders. It had not been endemic in Western Christian countries, and it killed off at least one third of the population in this first onset and kept on returning to the attack before the survivors began to develop some powers of resistance to it. The population of Western Christendom, and the area of the land under cultivation there, probably did not rise again to the peak at which they had stood *c.* 1300 till some time after the opening of the sixteenth century. The economic consequences were revolutionary. The peasantry benefited by the scarcity of labour, though not so much as they had expected and, even so, not permanently. The depletion of agricultural man-power worked together with the spread of the woollen textile industry from Flanders to England and to Florence to change the balance between arable and pasture in pasture's favour.

In the field of technology the fourteenth century saw the introduction of the use of fire-arms in Western Christendom; *c.* 1440–90 there was a revolution in the build and rig of Western ships; and during the second half of the fifteenth century the technique of printing was adopted in all Western countries. Gunpowder and printing were Chinese inventions. The Mongols had used gunpowder during their conquest of the Sung Empire in the thirteenth century. The technique of printing had been practised in China since the ninth century.

Chinese printers had anticipated the Westerners in using movable type, but the multitude of the Chinese characters had made the use of movable type less convenient than block-printing for Chinese purposes. In Korea, however, printing with movable type had been started on a large scale in 1403, and a phonetic script for conveying the Korean language, consisting of only a small number of signs, had been adopted officially in 1446. In Korea this promising invention was still-born. It was stifled by the age-old prestige there of the Chinese language and characters. Fifteenth-century Western printers were not saddled with this incubus; both Latin and the various local vernacular languages were conveyed in the Latin alphabetic script, which runs to only twenty-six letters; and the Latin alphabet in both classical capital letters and Carolingian minuscules, opportunely revived by fourteenth-century Italian scholars, was admirably suited for printing with movable type. Westerners were soon printing books in the Greek, Hebrew, and Arabic alphabets as well. We do not know whether Gutenberg's technique of printing was an independent invention of his own, or whether the idea came to him from China ultimately. The steppe is conductive. In the fourteenth century it had conveyed to Western Christendom the germs of the Black Death. It is conceivable that it also conveyed the idea of printing about a hundred years later.

The Westerners' mastery of the art of printing was a domestic affair. Their mastery of the use of fire-arms and their invention of a new type of ship were ecumenical affairs. The fifteenth-century Western ship's global conquest of the Ocean is dealt with in Chapter 75. The possession of fire-arms gave the Western maritime adventurers a decisive military superiority over all non-Western peoples within the Westerners' reach from the sea who did not possess fire-arms already or did not acquire them promptly. The Chinese did possess them already; the Osmanlis, the Muscovites, the Timurid conquerors of northern India, and the

Japanese acquired fire-arms promptly. The Aztecs and the Incas succumbed.

The adoption of the technique of printing in Western Christendom during the second half of the fifteenth century gave an impetus to a cultural florescence which had started in northern Italy in the fourteenth century and which spread throughout the rest of Western Christendom in the sixteenth century. Between 1266, when Charles of Anjou passed through on his way to conquer the Kingdom of the Two Sicilies, and 1494, when Charles VIII of France crossed the Alps, northern Italy had been free from the invasions by foreigners with which, during the millennium ending in 1266, it had been plagued incessantly. In the course of these years, 1266–1494, northern Italy created, within Western Christendom, a regional sub-culture of its own. Western Christendom's eighth-century cultural advance had originated in Northumbria, and its twelfth-century cultural advance in France. In the fourteenth century, Italy took the lead.

The extent of the gulf that had been opened between Italian culture and Transalpine culture by the turn of the fifteenth and sixteenth centuries can be measured visually, in King Henry VII's chapel in Westminster Abbey, by observing the contrast between the work there of the Florentine sculptor Pietro Torrigiano (1472–1522) and the native workmanship of the vaulting and of the statuary up aloft. Both schools of art are superb, but, though they are contemporary chronologically, they are ages apart from each other in spirit.

The visual difference is due to the resuscitation in northern Italy, since the fourteenth century, of the Graeco-Roman style—and this not only in sculpture and architecture but in painting and in literature as well. Sculptors and painters and architects modelled themselves on the surviving works of the Graeco-Roman civilization. Writers of Latin sought to reproduce the language of Cicero, not that of St. Jerome or of St. Thomas Aquinas. In the fourteenth century, northern Italians began to master the Greek language and literature of the Hellenic Age, which had passed out of currency in the West between the third and the sixth centuries A.D. Petrarch (Francesco Petrarca, 1304–74) and Giovanni Boccaccio (1313–75) learnt Greek only imperfectly, but, when in 1439 a Greek delegation came to Florence to attend an ecclesiastical council there, they met North-Italian scholars who were well enough versed in Greek to be able to discuss pre-Christian Greek literature and philosophy with them. On this account the Italian cultural florescence was labelled in the sixteenth century the 'Renaissance', meaning a re-birth of the Graeco-Roman civilization, and its exponents were labelled 'humanists', meaning students and admirers of the pre-Christian Graeco-Roman civilization, in contrast to students and devotees of Western Christian theology.

Yet the name 'Renaissance', used in this sense, is a misnomer; for the resuscitation of the Graeco-Roman style was merely an accompaniment and consequence of a second spontaneous flowering of the Western civilization in a different form from that of its first spontaneous flowering in the eleventh century. The second flowering was started, not by Erasmus (1466–1536) when he achieved the feat of writing almost fault-less Ciceronian Latin, but by Dante when he decided to write the *Divina Commedia* in his Tuscan mother-tongue, in which he had already written his earlier poems. Dante was following the practice of his Transalpine predecessors who had written poetry in their native Langue d'Oil and Langue d'Oc.

The early modern Westerners' relation to the Graeco-Roman civiliza-tion was ambivalent. The relation was stimulating when a Graeco-Roman model moved the 'moderns', in emulating it, to create some-thing new that was an asset for the contemporary Western way of life; but the same Graeco-Roman influence was debilitating when it tempted the 'moderns' merely to ape the 'ancients'. Filippo Brunelleschi (1377–1446) enriched his own world when he built his dome at Florence (1420–34) after studying the dome of Hadrian's Pantheon at Rome. (Brunel-leschi did not have the chance to compare notes with the contemporary Osmanli architect of the less high-humped dome of the Green Mosque at Bursa, built in 1421.) Andrea Palladio of Vicenza (1518–80) likewise enriched the life of the modern Western World when he created a classical style of his own after studying the ruins of Rome and Vitruvius' treatise on architecture. On the other hand, Sigismondo Pandolfo Malatesta (1417–68) perpetrated a folly in 1447 when he started to transform one of the churches at Rimini into a travesty of a Greek temple. Again, Niccolò Machiavelli (1469–1527) made a creative use of his study of Livy when he applied this to the production of practical manuals for the conduct of modern politics and warfare, and Erasmus made creative use of his mastery of Ciceronian Latin when he addressed the limited circle of contemporary Latin-readers on the major moral, social, political, and intellectual questions of his day. But literary *tours de force* in more pedantic Latin by 'humanists' who lacked Erasmus's genius were frivolous.

The medieval Western logicians' handling of the Latin language had been more robust. They had not hesitated to coin necessary neologisms, and in this they had followed the example of Cicero himself. The anti-humanist religious revolutionary Luther was more truly a follower of Dante (and of Petrarch and Boccaccio too) than the Ciceronian humanist Erasmus when Luther addressed, in the vulgar tongue, a wider public than Erasmus ever reached. Luther's translation of the Bible into German is a monument of the same modern western cultural florescence that had been heralded by the composition, in Tuscan, of the *Divina Commedia*.

Till about half way through the fifteenth century the focus of the modern Western Renaissance was northern Italy; within this region, Tuscany; and, within Tuscany, Florence. However, neither Florence nor Italy had the monopoly of the new style of Western culture—a monopoly which the Italians claimed when they retorted to the foreign invasions that started again in 1494 by pedantically stigmatizing the invaders as 'barbarians'.

Florence's contribution to the florescence of the modern West was as outstanding as Athens's contribution had been to the florescence of the Hellenic Greek civilization after 480 B.C. Dante, Petrarch, Brunelleschi, the Platonist Marsilio Ficino (1433–99), Lorenzo de' Medici (1449–92) —banker, despot, and patron of artists and scholars—Machiavelli, and Torrigiano were Florentines. Boccaccio was half Florentine, half French. Vinci, the birthplace of Leonardo (1452–1519), lay within the territory of Pistoia, which had been annexed by Florence a century before the date of Leonardo's birth. Arezzo, the birthplace of the pioneer archaeologist Poggio Bracciolini (1380–1459), had been annexed definitively by Florence when Poggio was only four years old. Caprese, the birthplace of Michelangelo Buonarroti (1475–1564), lay in the territory of Arezzo, on one of the headwaters of the River Tiber. Lorenzo de' Medici drew to Florence the scholars Angelo Ambrogini ('Politianus', 1454–94) from Montepulciano in the territory of Siena and Giovanni Pico from Mirandola, a minute principality on the frontier between Reggio di Emilia and Modena. The one non-Florentine titan was Raphael (Raffaello Sanzio, 1483–1520), who was born and brought up at Urbino in Umbria.

However, neither Florence nor even the whole of northern Italy was the sole focus of the modern Western cultural florescence. Flanders balanced northern Italy as the second pole of Western life on the cultural as well as on the economic plane. Fra Angelico (1387–1455) of Fiesole, the ancient city that overhangs Florence and was the first of Florence's neighbours to fall under the upstart power's dominion, was matched by his Flemish contemporary Jan van Eyck (1390–1441); Erasmus of Rotterdam was a match, as a Latinist and as a publicist, for any Italian of his own or of any other generation; and between Tuscany and the Netherlands there were cultural as well as commercial stepping-stones.

The landscape and climate of the Adriatic coast of northern Italy, between the eastern ends of the Appennines and the Alps, have more affinity with the Netherlands than with Tuscany or Umbria, and this difference in the physical environment is reflected in the style of the Venetian school of painting. 'Tintoretto' (Jacopo Robusti, 1518–94) and Paolo Veronese (1528–88) were matched by their Flemish contemporary

Pieter Brueghel I (1525–69). Between the Adriatic and the northern seas, Nuremberg is the half-way house, and Michelangelo's and Raphael's contemporary, the Hungarian Nuremberger Albrecht Dürer (1471–1528), was a match for any Italian artist except the four titans who are so famous that they are known, like kings, by their Christian names without their surnames. (The fourth kingly titan is the Venetian painter Titian (Tiziano Vecelli, 1477–1576).)

In the Transalpine Western countries, as in northern Italy, the city-states were the nurseries of the modern Western cultural florescence, but, by 1563, the peoples of the kingdom-states were also participating fully in this movement. The multiplication of universities gives the measure of this. Between 1350 and 1500 the number of universities in Western Christendom more than doubled, and, within this period, twenty-three were founded in central Europe (the earliest of these twenty-three was the University of Prague, founded in 1347).

On the political plane the quarter of a millennium running from *c.* 1300 saw the posthumous triumph of the thirteenth-century Western emperor, Frederick II. The West's rediscovery of Justinian I's code of law towards the end of the eleventh century, and the acquisition of the Kingdom of the Two Sicilies—a successor-state of the East Roman Empire—by Frederick II's father Henry VI in 1194, had fired Frederick II with the ambition to make himself the autocratic ruler, not only of his own kingdom, but also of all Italy and then perhaps of the Transalpine parts of the Western Empire too. Frederick failed to subjugate the North-Italian city-states, but he inspired a swarm of imitators in northern Italy who were successful because they pursued Frederick II's objective on a less ambitious scale. In the course of the fourteenth and fifteenth centuries, most of the North-Italian city-states were replaced by auto-cratically-governed principalities. Some of these (e.g. Milan) included more cities than one, and a city that remained republican (e.g. Venice) might likewise acquire an empire by bringing other previously inde-pendent North-Italian cities under its rule.

As a result, the number of the separate states in Italy decreased and their average size increased. However, even the largest of the North-Italian states that had taken shape by the close of the fifteenth century (for instance, Milan, Venice, Florence, and the Papal State) were small and weak by comparison with the potential strength of the Western kingdom-states, outside Italy, which were on the political map by the year 1563. These included the kingdoms of France and England, which had both been in existence since the tenth century; the united kingdom of Castile and Aragon (united in 1474–9); and the Danubian Habsburg Monarchy, which was brought into existence by the union, in 1526, of the Habsburgs' Austrian patrimony with the Hungarian and Bohemian

Crowns, after the overthrow by the Osmanlis of the kingdom of Hungary, which had previously been able to serve, single-handed, as Western Christendom's south-eastern march-state, first against the East Roman Empire and then against the Ottoman Empire. Those fifteenth-century Western kingdom-states, which produced statesmen of the ability of Louis XI of France (ruled 1461–83), Ferdinand and Isabella (co-sovereigns of Castile and Aragon, 1479–1504), and Henry VII of England (ruled 1485–1509), outclassed the North-Italian principalities and republics.

Republican states had not disappeared from the political map of Western Christendom by 1563. Venice was then still a sovereign power, with an empire both on the Italian mainland and in the Levant; Genoa still ruled the Italian Riviera and Corsica; Switzerland was a confederacy of republics; the German city-states were sovereign in all but name, and two of them—Nuremberg and Augsburg—were centres of international trade and finance. The Habsburgs had been kept afloat financially by loans from the Fuggers of Augsburg. A leading part in the Protestant secession from the Roman Church had been played by two German city-states—Augsburg and Strasburg; by three Swiss city-states—Zürich and Berne and Basel; and by the Swiss Confederation's ally Geneva.

Conversely, the union of the three Scandinavian kingdoms, formed in 1397 as a retort to the domination of Scandinavia by the North-German league of Hansa towns, had been broken by the secession of Sweden in 1512–23; and the union of Lithuania with Poland, which had been established in 1386 and which was tightened in 1501 and in 1569, had not sufficed to make Poland–Lithuania an effective great power. Nevertheless, it had become clear in the course of the fourteenth century that the predominant type of Western state was going to be the kingdom-state, not the city-state and not even an association of city-states in a league or under the rule of a despot or of a suzerain republic. By 1563 Lombardy and Flanders, which had once been the focal areas in the constellation of Western city-states, had become battlefields for kingdom-state powers.

The North-Italian states had put themselves at the mercy of the non-Italian great powers of Western Christendom by keeping each other in check; and, after the partition, in 1477–82, of the possessions of the Burgundian House between France and the Habsburgs, the device of the balance of power, which had prevented the political unification of Italy by Milan, was applied in a wider arena. Charles V (ruled 1519–56) almost succeeded, in 1525, in uniting the whole of Western Christendom under his rule after having defeated and taken prisoner Francis I of France; but Charles V was frustrated by the strength of French national feeling and then by the politically disruptive force of the Reformation in

Germany, and in 1556 he abdicated, disillusioned. Yet Charles combined, under his and his brother Ferdinand's rule, a unique assemblage of territories: the Habsburgs' hereditary dominions in Austria, augmented by the lands of the Bohemian Crown, together with a remnant of Hungary; the bulk of the ex-Burgundian dominions, including the Netherlands, which were one of Western Christendom's two economic power-houses; Milan, which was the heart of the second power-house, northern Italy; the Kingdom of the Two Sicilies; and Spain, which, during Charles V's reign, acquired, overseas beyond the Pillars of Hercules, an empire 'on which the sun never set'.

In 1563 the political unification of Western Christendom was not in sight. The Western great powers were keeping each other in check, in accordance with the former Italian powers' fourteenth-century and fifteenth-century practice. Even the greatest among the Western powers were only local, and they were in competition with each other. Yet these rival local secular powers, minor as well as major, had been having the last word in the affairs of Western Christendom since 1303, the date of Philip IV of France's humiliation of Pope Boniface VIII.

The Popes resided at Avignon from 1309 to 1378 not for the logistical reason that Avignon was nearer than Rome to the node of fourteenth-century Western Christendom's system of communications, but for the political reason that the French Crown wished to have the Pope on France's doorstep and therefore in her power. In the Great Schism of 1378–1417, which shocked Western Christians, the issue was not ethical or doctrinal; it was the question whether the Papacy was to continue to be a French political asset or was to become an Italian political asset again. The local secular powers and the Papacy were greedy, alike, for tax-money; since the thirteenth century the Papal Curia had worked out efficient methods for levying taxes; simultaneously, the secular governments had impounded an increasing share of the Papal taxes levied in their respective dominions as the condition on which they permitted the Curia to pocket the remainder.

The scandal of the Great Schism evoked the Council of Constance (1414–18) and the Council of Basel (1431–49). These councils tried, but failed, to turn the Papal government of the Western Christian Church from an absolute into a limited monarchy with a parliamentary constitution in which the prelates of bishoprics and religious houses and the representatives of the universities would have the last word. This project failed, and the reason for its failure was that the local secular powers did not support it. If the conciliar movement had succeeded, it would probably have strengthened the Western Church, and this prospect was not to the secular powers' liking. Some of them had extorted as much from the Papacy as they wanted; some of them extorted more now in concordats, as their price for allowing the Papacy still to assert, though no longer to exercise, its 'plenitude of power' in the government of the Western Church. The local secular rulers knew that in truth, since 1303, the plenitude of power had been possessed by themselves, within their respective dominions. By this time the Pope's 'plenitude of power' was really confined to the territories over which he exercised a temporal sovereignty. These territories consisted of a tiny enclave round Avignon, together with part of the Italian 'Donation of Charlemagne', of which the Pope had become the effective local sovereign at last in 1353–63. The Pope had thus become a minor local prince *de facto*.

The major political change in Western Christendom in the course of the quarter of a millennium 1303–1563 was the transfer of power and revenue from the Papacy, and from other organs of the Western Church (e.g. monasteries), to local secular governments. From being a dominant ecumenical institution, presiding over, and holding together, the whole of the Western *Respublica Christiana*, the Papacy had dwindled into being one of the minor local principalities of the Western World, and, in fighting a losing battle with stronger local powers, it had forfeited the spiritual allegiance of the Western Christian community; its ecclesiastical authority had weakened, even in those Western states that still acknowledged it. John Wycliffe's life-span (*c.* 1329–84) was approximately contemporary with the period of the Papacy's residence at Avignon (1309–78). So would have been the life-span of William of Ockham (*c.* 1303–49) and of Marsilius of Padua (*c.* 1290–1343), if these two other castigators of the Papacy had not died prematurely (William of Ockham was one of the victims of the Black Death). Jan Hus's life-span (*c.*1369–1415), which was cut short, not by bacteria but by human action, was approximately contemporary with the Great Schism (1378–1546).

These names, and the still more famous names of Luther (1483–1546), Zwingli (1484–1531), and Calvin (1509–64), are reminders that the protection and patronage of princes was merely the enabling condition for the religious revolutionaries' work. These revolutionary protégés of princes were not princes themselves; they were private individuals, and their work might have been abortive if it had not won the support of the people, as well as of the princes and the oligarchs, in a large part of Western Christendom. When Philip IV of France and Henry VIII of England challenged the Papacy, each of them was the sovereign of a powerful local state and each had also secured the support of his subjects, including the local clergy. For a private individual to challenge the Papacy, even when the Papacy had passed the peak of its prestige, required extraordinary courage, and therefore Luther's stand, first at Wittenberg in 1517 (when the University of Wittenberg was only fifteen years old) and then at the Diet of Worms in 1521, had an electrifying effect; but it was electrifying because the media in which the secessionists from the Papal Church produced their shocks were highly conductive. Hus's fellow Czechs followed his lead because they were already both anti-Papal and anti-German; Luther's fellow Germans followed his lead because they were already anti-Papal. Lutheranism spread like wildfire through Germany, as far south-eastwards as the Tirol and Styria in the Habsburg dominions, before the tide was turned by the Roman Catholic Counter-Reformation. The civic nationalism of Zürich, Strasburg, and Geneva gave Zwingli, Bucer (1491–1551), and Calvin their openings.

Luther was the pioneer. If he had not led the way, his fellow revolutionaries might perhaps have lacked the nerve to make a complete breach with the Papal Church. However, Lutheranism did not spread beyond Germany and Germany's cultural dependency, Scandinavia. On the other hand, Calvinism, which never became dominant, and ultimately suffered defeat, in its homeland, France, spread far and wide from Geneva, its French-speaking city of refuge. After coalescing with the Zwinglian Protestantism of Zürich, Calvinism spread eastwards into Hungary and Poland–Lithuania and north-westwards into north-western Germany, the northern Netherlands, England, and Scotland. Calvinism captured the western fringe of Protestant Germany from Lutheranism, and it partially captured England, in the reign of Edward VI (1547–53), from Henry VIII's national Romish religion. Calvinism was defeated by the Counter-Reformation in Hungary partly, and in Poland–Lithuania wholly but it retained its hold on north-western Germany, the northern Netherlands, and Scotland.

The Protestant religious revolution brought with it a number of political revolutions. It confirmed the *de facto* sovereign independence of the local princes and city-states in Germany (though, officially, they remained subjects of 'the Roman Empire of the German People'). But there was no concomitant social revolution. During the half-century following the arrival of the Black Death in Western Christendom in 1348, there were abortive revolts of peasants in England and France and of industrial workers in the Flemish and Rhenish cities and at Florence. There was another abortive peasant revolt in England in 1450 and one in Germany in 1525, and a militant wing of the Anabaptists set up a communist republic in Westphalia at Münster, the seat of a Catholic prince-bishop, in 1534–6. Luther concurred with the secular political authorities, both Protestant and Catholic, in opposing these revolutionary social movements. In 1525 he declared against the peasants in favour of the princes.

In principle, Luther held that the Lutheran Church ought to abstain from intervening in politics. In Luther's view, politics were the province of the secular authorities in Lutheran states. By contrast, Calvin's view of the proper relations between church and state were more like the views of Pope Gregory VII and even of Boniface VIII. Calvin did not claim that the Calvinist Church ought to conduct the government of a Calvinist state, but he did demand that the secular government of the city-state of Geneva should satisfy the Calvinist Church that it was governing in accordance with the Church's standards. This requirement led to Calvin's banishment from Geneva in 1538 after two years' experience of his regime (1536–8). But in 1541 he was recalled with acclaim, and, from that year till his death in 1564, Calvin had his way at Geneva.

At Florence in 1494/5 the Dominican monk Girolamo Savonarola had been empowered by a republican regime, like Calvin at Geneva in 1536, to reform the people's morals, and Savonarola had ended in 1498, not by being banished and subsequently recalled in triumph, but by being burnt at the stake. In fifteenth-century Western Christendom, northern Italy was precocious; yet, even here, Savonarola's mission was premature, and for this he paid an atrocious penalty. However, before Luther's denunciation of Papal abuses in 1517, a group of Italian ecclesiastics and laymen, led by bishop Giovanni Pietro Caraffa, had started a movement for reforming the Papal Church from within. They began, as St. Francis of Assisi had done, by dedicating themselves to poverty, holy living, and good works. Like St. Francis, and unlike Savonarola and Luther, these were not revolutionaries, and they did not draw fire from the Papacy. So far from that, Caraffa himself was elected Pope (Paul IV, 1555–9).

The founding fathers of Protestantism were revolutionary in their denunciation and defiance of the Papacy and in their secession from the Papal Church, but, like their Roman Catholic predecessors and contemporaries, they were authoritarian and intolerant. Though they themselves individually had followed their own judgment and conscience in taking their anti-Papal stand, they were no more willing than the Catholics to allow liberty of conscience in the states in which they converted the political authorities. The revolutionaries declared that the authority of the Bible overrode the authority of Popes and Councils. Luther himself translated the Bible into German, in order that every German-reader should be able to have direct access to this scriptural fount of authority. Every Christian was to interpret the Bible's statements and injunctions for himself, and Luther, Zwingli, and Calvin each availed himself of this right in formulating his theology; but they did not allow their adherents the same freedom of interpretation.

Sixteenth-century Protestant and Catholic clergy and governments agreed with each other in holding that it was the prerogative of a local government to dictate the religion of its subjects (*cuius regio, eius religio*). Dissenters must migrate or else run the risk of being put to death—

probably by being burnt alive. The Anabaptists were the only sixteenth-century sect that was tolerant on principle. The only sixteenth-century Western states in which the toleration of a number of different religions was practised were Venice and Poland–Lithuania (two Roman Catholic states that tolerated the religions of their Eastern Orthodox subjects), the part of Hungary that was under Ottoman rule, and the autonomous principality of Transylvania, which was alternately under Ottoman and Habsburg suzerainty. In Transylvania from 1571 onwards four religions Catholicism, Lutheranism, Calvinism, and Unitarianism—were all recognized as being legitimate and could all be practised with impunity.

Since the thirteenth-century war to the death between the Papacy and Frederick II and his heirs, sensitive Western Christians had become increasingly alienated from the Papal ecclesiastical 'establishment'. In the fourteenth and fifteenth centuries, some Western Christians had transferred their spiritual activity from participation in institutional religion to the cultivation of the relation between the individual soul and God.

The German Dominican friar Meister Eckhart (*c.* 1260–1327) experienced, like some of the Buddha's contemporaries in the sixth century B.C., the identity of his own self with the ultimate spiritual reality. The mystic's experience is incompatible with a religion in which the ultimate reality is conceived of as being a divine counterpart of a human person; for two persons cannot transcend their separateness without each losing his individual personality. Eckhart got into trouble with the Western ecclesiastical authorities, and the orthodoxy of the contemporary mystical movement (Hesychasm) on Mount Athos was also impugned by Western theologians, although Hesychasm had been approved by a council of the Eastern Orthodox Church in 1351.

The Brethren of the Common Life (the Devotio Moderna) founded by a Netherlander, Gerhard Groote (1340–84), who was an ex-Carthusian monk, were not heretical in terms of Western Christian orthodoxy, and were not anti-social either. Among their various activities they were educationists, who fostered the revival of classical learning and welcomed the introduction of the printing-press. Their most famous, though not their most amenable, pupil was Erasmus. The Brethren practised a devotional form of religion which, though not unorthodox, resembled Eckhart's mysticism in falling outside the official framework of the Western Church. However, Thomas à Kempis (1379/80–1471), the author or compiler of the Devotio Moderna's most influential publication, *The Imitation of Christ*, spent the last fifty years of his life as the inmate of an Augustinian monastery.

Fifteenth-century Western Christians were obsessed with a horror of death (the antithesis of the Pharaonic Egyptians' pleasurable anticipation of a post-mortem eternity), and they were fascinated by the physical suffering of Christ on the Cross. Contemporary Western painters, engravers and sculptors—especially in the Transalpine countries—exerted their art to portray these themes with gruesome realism. This morbid atmosphere of an outgoing age led Luther—who, in most of his moods, was a man of sanguine temperament—to brood over his sinfulness and to despair of overcoming it by his own efforts. Hence he joyfully took refuge in his eventual conviction that he could be saved, solely but surely, by faith in the redemptive power of Christ's sacrifice to God the Father.

This was a Christian counterpart of the Mahayanian Buddhist belief in the possibility of salvation by faith in the power of the bodhisattva Amitabha (Amida) to bring his devotees, after their death, to his 'Pure Land' paradise. This 'Pure Land' version of Buddhism—introduced into Japan in the tenth century—was popularized there at the turn of the twelfth and thirteenth centuries. In Japanese history, this was a painful period of social and psychological transition, as the turn of the fifteenth and sixteenth centuries was in Western Christendom. In transferring from the sinner's own shoulders to Christ's the responsibility for the sinner's redemption, the Augustinian friar Luther resembled his adversary, the Dominican friar Tetzel, when Tetzel offered to transfer the same burden to the shoulders of the Pope. Tetzel's monetary bargain, unlike Luther's act of faith, was repulsively mercenary, but both Luther and Tetzel were providing a more facile substitute for the arduous imitation of Christ, as practised in either St. Francis's or Thomas à Kempis's way.

For Mahayana Buddhists of the 'Pure Land' sect, the bodhisattva Amida was compassionate and benign. For Luther, and for Calvin too, the God of the Christians, Jews, and Muslims was an inscrutable, unaccountable, and omnipotent tyrant, as he was for Muhammad and for the writers of the pre-Prophetic books of the Jewish scriptures (the Christian 'Old Testament'). In Muhammad's belief, God had at least transmitted to mankind a series of warnings which had given them a chance to avert punishment by mending their ways. Luther's and Calvin's God had arbitrarily predestined some of his human creatures to salvation and some of them to damnation. This was St. Augustine's interpretation of St. Paul's theology. Luther had been an Augustinian friar, and St. Paul was the almost inevitable patron for an opponent of the Papacy, since Paul was the only Apostle who was the peer of the Papacy's founder and patron St. Peter.

The belief in predestination seems incompatible with the belief in salvation by faith, since faith is Man's act, not God's. These two fundamental beliefs of the founding fathers of Protestantism can be reconciled

with each other only on the hypothesis that a human being is an auto-
maton and that his act of faith, if he performs this act, is, like all other
acts of his, predestined. It is less difficult to reconcile the Mahayanian
Buddhist belief in salvation by faith in Amida with the Theravadin
belief in *karma*; for, though karma is destiny, it is a man-made destiny,
and it can be altered, for better or for worse, by a human being's action
in any of his successive incarnations.

The Protestants' other departures from contemporary Papal Western
Christian practice had pre-Protestant precedents. In China, Buddhist
monasteries and convents had been dissolved, their property expropriated, and their inmates forced to return to secular life, in 842–5. In
Western Christendom, Philip IV of France had expropriated the property of the Order of the Temple in his kingdom and had persecuted its
members atrociously, in 1307–14, and Edward II of England had followed suit. Images had been banned in Eastern Orthodox Christendom
in the eighth and ninth centuries. The requirement of celibacy, which
had been imposed on the Western Christian secular clergy in the
eleventh century, had been waived in 1439 at the Council of Florence
for Uniates from non-Western churches in which the clergy was not
celibate. The Czech *Utraquists* had restored the laity's right to communicate 'in both kinds'. Zwingli denied 'the real presence' of Christ's
body and blood in the 'elements'; Calvin admitted it only in a non-
corporeal sense; but Luther affirmed it, and Protestants of all sects retained the Western Church's schismatic interpolation of the *filioque* in the
Creeds.

The Protestants' portrayal of the Jewish–Christian–Muslim God, and
in particular their attribution to him of the appalling practice of predestination, alienated 'humanist' Western Christians such as Erasmus
and Sir (today St.) Thomas More. These scholars had recognized and
had criticized the abuses in the life of the Papal Church, but in their
judgment these abuses were a lesser evil than Luther's doctrine and
spirit. Protestant theology was in truth a regression both from Erasmus's
reasonableness and from St. Thomas Aquinas's rationalism. Yet, except
for Luther, the founding fathers of Protestantism were humanists as well.
Zwingli and Calvin were keen classical scholars. Luther's colleague
Philip Melanchthon (a Graecization of 'Schwarzert') was Professor of
Greek at the University of Wittenberg. Melanchthon shared some of the
misgivings of his non-Lutheran fellow humanists over Luther's doctrine
of predestination, and, after Luther's death, he persuaded the Lutheran
Church to soften this doctrine's rigour (eventually Luther's original
version of the doctrine prevailed). Though Luther was singular among
the founding fathers of Protestantism in not being also a humanist,
Luther was nevertheless a mighty man of letters. His translation of the

Bible into German would have immortalized him, even if he had never defied the Papacy.

The makers of the Roman Catholic Counter-Reformation embraced humanism whole-heartedly. St. Ignatius Loyola (1491–1556) put himself through a university education as a preparation for his lifework, and his Jesuit Order (founded in 1540) believed in, and practised, education as earnestly as the Brethren of the Common Life in the preceding century. However, St. Ignatius had started as a soldier; the dominant feature of his Order was its discipline and its dedication of itself to the service of the Papacy. In the sixteenth century, as in the thirteenth and in the eleventh, a great man saved the Papacy from suffering the uttermost retribution for its previous misdemeanours. St. Francis's spirit was the antithesis of the spirit of Gregory VII and of St. Ignatius, but the Papacy profited from the devotion that was the common characteristic of its three successive saviours. The Council of Trent, which was in session intermittently from 1545 to 1563, confirmed the Pope's monarchical rule over the remnant of the Roman Catholic Church, but it also reformed some of this church's worst abuses. If these reforms had been enacted and implemented, as they could and should have been, at some date between 1414 and 1517, Luther might never have been provoked into taking his momentous stand.

[72]

SOUTH-EAST ASIA, 1190–1511

THE three centuries 1190–1511 saw great political, ethnic, and religious change in South-East Asia: the failure of Mongol assaults; the spread southward of the settlements and the political rule of peoples speaking continental East-Asian monosyllabic languages—above all, the Thai; the spread of Sinhalese Theravada Buddhism and of Islam; and the arrival of seafarers from Western Christendom, the Portuguese.

In South-East Asia the Mongol invaders were unsuccessful on the mainland, as well as overseas. They occupied what is now North Vietnam in 1257, 1285, and 1287, but, each time, the Vietnamese compelled them to withdraw. The Chams likewise defeated, in 1285, a Mongol attempt to conquer Champa via northern Vietnam. In 1287 the Mongols did succeed in occupying the Kingdom of Pagan (Mien) in Upper Burma, but they evacuated it in 1303. In continental South-East Asia, as in Syria in the course of the years 1261–1303, the Mongols were worsted by the distance of this theatre of operations from their base at the north-eastern extremity of the Eurasian steppe when they met, in these logistically disadvantageous circumstances, with a determined military resistance. The Mongols' naval expedition against Java in 1292–3 ended as disastrously for them as their naval expeditions against Japan in 1274 and 1281.

The Mahayanian Buddhist Javanese victor founded in 1293 the Empire of Majapahit—the last pre-Islamic empire in Indonesia. The long-lived Sumatran Empire of Srivijaya played no part in the repulse of the Mongols from Indonesia. It had been weakened by Thai military pressure on its dominions in the Malay Peninsula, and it was weakened further by the rise of the Majapahit Empire in Java, and by the introduction of Islam, *c.* 1295, into the north-western end of Sumatra itself. However, there is no sure evidence that Sumatra fell under Majapahit's rule or even under its suzerainty.

The Empire of Majapahit was overthrown, *c.* 1513–28, by a coalition of local Javanese states that had been converted to Islam. In 1403 a Sumatran Shailendra prince, Paramesvara, who had married a princess of the Majapahit dynasty, had founded Malacca, on the continental shore of the straits that are now named after this famous city. By 1414 Paramesvara had been converted to Islam under the name Muhammad Iskandar Shah, and Malacca had become the base from which Islam was propagated in Indonesia. Since as far back as the eighth century, Muslim Arab and Iranian mariners from ports round the shores of the Persian Gulf had been navigating the seas between the Islamic World and China and had been planting commercial settlements and making native converts along the continental and insular coasts en route; but, in Indonesia, a new impetus was given to this process by the foundation and conversion of Malacca. However, in continental and insular South-East Asia, in contrast to the experience of the Indian subcontinent, Islamic rule was not imposed by force of arms. Islam spread here through its voluntary adoption by native rulers and their subjects, but this conversion was only skin-deep. The Indonesians reconciled their adhesion to Islam with the retention of the Indian culture that they had been acquiring during the previous thousand years. Beneath an Islamic veneer, their traditional Indianism still remained alive. The *Mahabharata* still had more power than the Koran to warm Indonesian hearts and excite the imagination.

The Sinhalese Theravada Buddhism which had been introduced into Burma in 1190 spread in the course of the thirteenth century from the Mons and Burmans to the Shans, Thais, Laotians, and Cambodians. Blending with these peoples' native religions, the Theravada became, for each of them, a popular national religion. As such, it ousted the Mahayana Buddhism and the Hinduism which had gained entry into South-East Asia from India long before, but had remained confined to an élite. The substitution of the Theravada for these previous South-East-Asian forms of Indian religion left the greater part of South-East Asia still within India's cultural orbit. Indian culture lost ground only in Indonesia and continental Malaya, where it was superficially overlaid by Islam, and along the east coast, where the Vietnamese, expanding southwards, carried their Chinese Confucianism and Mahayana Buddhism with them.

The southward spread of northern peoples had changed the ethnic map of South-East Asia by the early decades of the sixteenth century. The Burmans consummated in 1535–9 their conquest, begun in the eleventh century, of the Mons in the lower basin of the Irrawaddy River. The Vietnamese had begun to bear down upon Champa less than forty years after 939, when they had shaken off Chinese rule over their homeland, the present-day North Vietnam. By 1000 the Vietnamese had annexed Champa's three northernmost provinces. In 1312 they imposed their suzerainty upon the remainder of Champa. In 1471 Vietnam annexed outright the whole of Champa except for a remnant in the south, and in the seventeenth century the Vietnamese overwhelmed this remnant too and pressed on still farther southwards to occupy and colonize the Mekong delta at the expense of Cambodia. The surviving Chams became Muslims.

The Thais, Shans, and Laotians speak closely related languages belonging to the Chinese-Thai branch of the continental East-Asian monosyllabic family. The Thai Kingdom of Nan-chao, in what is now Yunnan, the south-westernmost province of China, had conquered the Irrawaddy basin in the eighth and ninth centuries, before the Burmans' arrival there, and they had raided China, including present-day North Vietnam, which at that time was a Chinese province. Thereafter, Thai migrants began to descend the valleys of the Salween and the Mekong and to establish themselves round the headwaters of the Menam. Nan-chao had been conquered by the Mongols in 1253. This original homeland of the Thais then became Sinified; Islam struck root there; and these developments gave a fresh impetus in the second half of the thirteenth century to the southward migration of the Thais into the Menam basin and into the northern part of the Malay Peninsula at the expense of the local Mon population in the Menam basin and of the Khmer Kingdom of Cambodia.

If the Thais had carried the Chinese civilization with them, as the Vietnamese did, their southward expansion would have shifted the boundary between the Chinese and the Indian civilizations in the Chinese civilization's favour. Instead, the Thais became converts to the Theravada Buddhism that had established itself in Burma in 1190, and this brought the Thais within the ambit of the Indian civilization.

Thus, by 1511, when the Portuguese took Malacca, South-East Asia had come to be divided into the domains of four religions, two of which —namely Theravada Buddhism and Islam—were relatively recent arrivals. The Theravada had conquered all continental South-East Asia except for Vietnam, the remnant of Champa, and the southern extremity of the Malay Peninsula. The Vietnamese were Mahayana Buddhists of the Chinese school. The Chams and the continental Malays had become Muslims. The insular Malays had become Muslims on the surface but had remained Hindus below their Islamic veneer. In the island of Bali they were still avowedly Hindus. In Borneo they were becoming Muslims on the coast but were still pagans in the huge interior.

73

EASTERN ASIA, 1281–1644

In 1279 China, for the first time in her history, had fallen wholly under the rule of foreign conquerors, without the survival of any politically independent Chinese government anywhere except in North Vietnam— and this former province of China had seceded as far back as 939 and, since then, had developed its own local version of the Chinese civilization on ever more distinctive lines. China's experience in 1279 was like India's at the fall of the Empire of Vijayanagar in 1565, though the Mongols' conquest of China (1205–79) was more rapid and more complete than the Muslims' progressive conquest of India beyond the Punjab (1202– 1565).

Japan's experience in the thirteenth century presents a contrast to China's. In 1281 Japan had successfully repulsed the second and more formidable of the two Mongol assaults on her; but this preservation of freedom from foreign rule, which had been made possible by the effectiveness of the Hojo regency at Kamakura, was followed by the decline and fall of the Hojo regime. The period 1281–1614 was the most anarchic of any in Japanese political history to date. On the other hand, the completion of the Mongol conquest of China in 1279 had re-established China's political unity—albeit under foreign rule. The political unity of China had been whittled away progressively since the final breakdown of the unitary T'ang regime in 874. From 1279 to 1911, the re-established political unity of China was maintained, though this re-united China was under the rule of an indigenous Chinese regime only from c. 1382 to c. 1631 de facto.

China, politically re-united under Mongol rule, became the centre of gravity of the short-lived but far-flung Mongol Empire. The Mongol Great Khan Qubilay (ruled 1260–94) had transferred his capital from Qaraqorum to Peking in 1260–7, and in 1289 he completed the extension of the Grand Canal to Peking from Hangchow. This feat of engineering made it possible to transport Peking's necessary provisions of rice from southern China by inland navigation. In 1271 Qubilay inaugurated a new Chinese dynasty, the Yüan, which was to be hereditary in Qubilay's family.

Among the Mongol Empire's western appanages, the Il-Khanate in Iran and Iraq was the most closely associated with China, since this appanage was established by Qubilay's brother Hülegü on Qubilay's initiative. This is why Chinese art had an enduring influence on Iranian visual art and pottery. In the pre-Mongol Age, Chinese technology (e.g. the technique of paper-making) had already spread westward through the Islamic World to Western Christendom. The Mongol Age saw the westward dissemination of explosives and printing, which were eagerly adopted in Western Christendom.

The Mongol rulers of China and their Chinese subjects of all social classes remained aloof from each other. The Mongols employed Muslim and Christian foreign administrators in China, and unemployed Confucian scholars endowed the Chinese civilization with two new genres of literature, the drama and the novel. The difference between the Chinese and the Mongol peoples' ancestral ways of life generated a mutual antipathy that inhibited cultural assimilation in either direction. Consequently the Mongol regime in China was inevitably ephemeral. Local revolts started all over China in the 1340s. The winner among the rival Chinese insurgents was Chu Yüan-chang (1328-98). This fourth unifier of China, like the second unifier Liu P'ang, was a man of humble origin from the Hwai valley, the border zone between southern and northern China. In 1368 Chu Yüan-chang founded the Ming dynasty as the Emperor Hung-wu. By 1382 he had not only evicted the Mongols from intramural China but had also eliminated all his native Chinese competitors.

Hung-wu retained Nanking ('southern capital'), which he had occupied in 1356, as the capital of a re-united China; but in 1421 his fourth son and second successor Yung-lo (ruled 1403-24) moved the capital back to Peking ('northern capital'), which had been the capital of the Yüan and, before that, of the Kin (Jürched), and had previously been the southern capital of the Liao (Khitan). The experience of Mongol conquest and domination had made the Chinese xenophobic, and the adoption of their hated barbarian masters' capital, Peking, at the extreme north-eastern corner of intramural China and at the maximum distance from the southern rice-paddies, indicated that Yung-lo's and his successors' paramount concern was to ward off the ever-present Mongol menace.

The Mongols had been expelled from China, but they survived on their native steppe, and from there they might invade China again. The easternmost Mongols, the Oirats, were particularly aggressive. Yung-lo conducted five campaigns on the steppe, but the Mongols eluded him as successfully as the Skyths had eluded Darius I and the Hsiung-nu had eluded Han Wu-ti and his successors. In 1449 the Oirat Khan Esen defeated and captured the reigning Ming emperor and besieged Peking. But the city's walls baffled Khan Esen, as Constantinople's walls had baffled the Bulgar Khan Symeon. The Ming's military disaster in 1449 did not have the same catastrophic sequel as the Sung's disaster in 1126 and the East Roman Empire's twin disasters in 1071.

The Ming dynasty rehabilitated for the second time the system of selecting civil servants by competitive examination in the Confucian classics. (This system had been instituted in the second century B.C. by Han Wu-ti and had been rehabilitated for the first time, towards the close of the sixth century A.D., by the Sui dynasty.) This institution now set hard in a form that it retained till the abolition of the public examinations in 1905 and of the imperial regime itself in 1911. The number of Confucian officials in active service was always minute for coping with the size of the Empire's area and population. Their task was made practicable by the assistance of non-Confucian-educated provincial clerical staffs and by the co-operation of the numerous provincial Confucian degree-holding gentry, who conducted local government on their own initiative and without receiving official salaries. (They financed both their family life and their public works out of their takings as local landlords.)

Success in passing the public examinations was not the only means of acquiring a Confucian degree. This could be conferred as an honour, and it could also be bought. However acquired, it gave the recipient a highly prized prestige, and it also imposed an unwritten obligation to perform public service either as a salaried public servant or as an unremunerated landowning local notable.

The restored indigenous Chinese imperial regime was even more conscious of, and more attached to, China's cultural past than its pre-Mongol predecessors had been. In 1403–7 Yung-lo sponsored the production of an encyclopaedia that, in its revised version, ran to 22,877 books filling 11,095 volumes, not counting the sixty books of the table of contents. This colossus remained in manuscript; to print it was beyond even China's technological and economic capacity.

Yung-lo's encyclopaedia was backward-looking; but in the Ming Age Chinese literature and philosophy were still alive. The production of novels and plays continued to flourish, and Chu Hsi's twelfth-century formulation of Confucianism continued to be challenged. As an examination-subject it held the field in virtue of its being incomparably systematic and comprehensive. But the split in the new-Confucian school, which had opened in the eleventh century between the two brothers Ch'eng Hao and Ch'eng Yi, had not been closed by Chu Hsi when he elaborated Ch'eng Yi's system.

The most distinguished exponent of Ch'eng Hao's system was Wang Yang-ming (Wang Shou-jen, 1472–1529). In Wang Yang-ming's view, a human being's mind and the sum total of ultimate reality are identical with each other. In Chu Hsi's view, ultimate reality is the aggregate of principles embodied in persons and things, and these principles exist independently of any human minds. The difference between these two metaphysical standpoints is manifestly important, and it was also felt to be important because of the Buddhist metaphysical background that was common to both schools of neo-Confucianism. But, with the signal exception of the Taoists, all Chinese philosophers, in all periods of Chinese history, were more concerned with ethics and action than with metaphysics and contemplation.

Wang Yang-ming was the last great Chinese philosopher whose views were coloured by Buddhism only, and not by Western philosophy as well. The first Portuguese seafarers reached China in 1514, fifteen years before Wang Yang-ming's death.

Among China's successive foreign conquerors, the Mongols were the least amenable, and the Manchus the most amenable, to the Confucian way of life. Consequently the Mongols were the least congenial, and the Manchus the most congenial, to the Chinese scholar civil servants. The Manchus were not pastoral nomads from the Eurasian steppe; like the founders of the Kin dynasty, they were Jürched hunters and food-gatherers from the forest-clad mountains of north-eastern Manchuria. The Ming Emperor Yung-lo had incorporated Manchuria in China by organizing the Jürched tribes into a number of commanderies under the hereditary leadership of their own respective chiefs.

The Manchus had voluntarily Sinified themselves before they began to occupy territory containing a Chinese population. In 1599 Nurhachi (1559–1626), the founder of the Manchu state, had the Mongolian version of the Syriac alphabet adapted for conveying the Jürched (Manchu) language, and Chinese classics were then translated into Manchu; but literate Manchus soon preferred to read and write the Chinese language itself in the Chinese characters. Nurhachi had created a tri-national army that included Chinese and Mongol as well as Manchu units. In 1618 he annexed part of a Chinese-inhabited extra-mural salient of China, Liaotung; in 1626 he moved his capital to Mukden, on Chinese ground; and he enlisted Chinese administrators.

Nurhachi's son Abahai gave his dynasty the name Ch'ing in 1636. In 1644 the last of the Ming emperors committed suicide in Peking when the city was being seized by a Chinese insurgent. In the same year the

Manchus occupied Peking with the aid of a Chinese general and with the support of Chinese civil servants who preferred a Manchu regime to the rule of the Chinese usurper who had momentarily supplanted the Ming dynasty. The establishment of Manchu sovereignty over the rest of China was not unopposed. Taiwan was not occupied by the Manchus till 1683. However, the Manchu conquest of China was less devastating materially, and was also less traumatic psychologically, for the Chinese people of all classes, than the Mongol conquest had been, four centuries earlier.

In Japan, an abortive coup in 1331 by the Emperor Go-Daigo (ruled 1318–39) led to the overthrow of the Hojo regency and the destruction of Kamakura itself in 1335. In 1338 the seat of the Shogunate was transferred to Kyoto, and the office was invested in the Ashikaga family; but this new regime never won the effective authority over the whole of Japan that had been established by Yoritomo Minamoto in 1185 and had been maintained by the Hojo regents of the Shogunate at Kamakura till after the repulse, in 1281, of the second Mongol invasion.

The Ashikaga Shogunate did not even succeed immediately in establishing its control over the environs of Kyoto. Go-Daigo, ejected by Takauji Ashikaga from Kyoto and replaced there by a puppet emperor, maintained an independent regime in the mountains to the south of Kyoto. This schism in the Imperial dynasty lasted from 1336 to 1392. Meanwhile, the *daimyo* in the provinces became independent princes *de facto*, and the Ashikaga regime's authority became completely ineffective after the ten years' civil war of Onin (1467–77), fought in the streets of Kyoto. The Nichiren and Shinshu Buddhist sects carved out for themselves territorial domains in the provinces, side by side with those of the local secular princes. From 1532 to 1536 there was warfare in the Kyoto district between the adherents of the Shinshu and the Nichiren sects and the armed forces of the monasteries belonging to older sects. In this inter-Buddhist monastic warfare, each belligerent was at war with every other.

Paradoxically, the political anarchy during the period of the Ashikaga Shogunate (1338–1573), like the period of the Warring States in pre-unitary China, was accompanied by an outburst of economic and cultural vitality. The Japanese retort to the unsuccessful Mongol naval assaults on Japan had been maritime private enterprise against the coasts of China, and this Japanese irritant was inherited from the Yüan by the Ming dynasty. In 1404 the Ashikaga regime recognized China's nominal suzerainty over Japan and acquiesced in the Chinese Imperial Government's attempted imposition of restrictions on the volume of Sino-Japanese trade. In practice, private Japanese trader-pirates ignored the agreement between the two governments and continued their activities with some private Chinese collaboration.

In the Japanese domestic field, there was an increase in economic activity and a rise in the material standard of living, and the monopoly of power, which the provincial military class had held since the latter part of the twelfth century, was eroded by the increasing importance of the role of peasant infantry in Japanese civil warfare and by the emergence of industrial and commercial guilds and free cities—particularly Sakai, just to the south of present-day Osaka. However, the same period saw the creation in Japan of a depressed class of 'untouchables' (Eta).

On the cultural plane the Ashikaga Age saw not only an abiding interest in Zen, a form of Mahayana Buddhism which appealed particularly to the aristocratic warriors; the later years—the most anarchic years—of the Ashikaga period also saw the elaboration of the Tea Ceremony. This was promoted by the regime as a cultural device for counteracting the warriors' ever-increasing ferocity. In the field of the visual arts, the Ashikaga period produced Japanese virtuosi in the Sung Chinese style of landscape painting, and also landscape-gardening (a distinctively Japanese art). A grander cultural achievement was the creation of the Nō genre of drama *c.* 1350–1450. The plots of these plays were traditional and familiar; the actors wore masks; the action, diction, intonation, singing, and music were highly stylized. In all these respects the fourteenth-century Japanese Nō drama was an East-Asian counterpart of the Attic Greek Dionysiac drama of the fifth-century B.C.

After political anarchy in Japan had reached its sixteenth-century acme, the country was re-unified and re-stabilized politically by the successive operations of three war-lords: Oda Nobunaga (1534–82), Toyotomi Hideyoshi (1536–98), and Tokugawa Ieyasu (1543–1616). These unifiers and their opponents fought with fire-arms, which came into general use in Japan within twenty years of their introduction, in 1542 or 1543, by the first Portuguese who landed there.

Nobunaga occupied Kyoto in 1568 and extinguished the Ashikaga Shogunate there in 1573. In 1582 Nobunaga's life was cut short in a mutiny by one of his captains, but Hideyoshi, another of Nobunaga's captains, promptly defeated and killed the mutineer. By 1590 Hideyoshi was master of the whole of Japan, in concert with Ieyasu, whom he installed, in the same year, in the Kanto. In 1592–3 and again in 1597–8, Hideyoshi invaded Korea, but the Koreans' resistance was energetic and resourceful. Hideyoshi's Korean campaigns were intended by him to be the prelude to an invasion of China, and Hideyoshi's death on the march in 1598, like Timur Lenk's in 1405, relieved Ming China of a serious impending danger. The contest for inheriting Hideyoshi's power was won by Ieyasu in 1600 at the Battle of Sekigehara. In 1603 Ieyasu obtained the title of Shogun from the shadowy Imperial Government at Kyoto. In 1615 Ieyasu made himself the undisputed master of all Japan by capturing Osaka castle, where Hideyoshi's son Hideyori had held out till then.

Like Han Liu P'ang and Augustus, in contrast to Ch'in Shih Hwang-ti and Julius Caesar, Ieyasu secured effective *de facto* sovereign power with the maximum of face-saving and the minimum of overt political change. The emperor at Kyoto was allowed to remain the titular sovereign, but Ieyasu's seat of government at Edo (the present-day Tokyo), like Yoritomo Minamoto's and the Hojo regents' former seat at Kamakura, dominated the Kanto, which was Japan's economic centre of gravity. The local princes (*daimyo*) were not deposed, but they were subordinated and debilitated by skilful arrangements for preventing them from combining against the Tokugawa regime and for gradually ruining them financially. The political map of Japan under the Tokugawa regime (1600–1868) resembles the political map of Peninsular Italy between 264 and 90 B.C.

The regime's control over Japan was reinforced, between 1622 and 1641, by the almost complete extirpation of Christianity and insulation of Japan from the rest of the Oikoumenê. These measures are dealt with in Chapter 75.

74

THE MESO-AMERICAN AND ANDEAN CIVILIZATIONS, 1428–1519

ALMOST simultaneously in the fifteenth century the Meso-American and Andean societies were each encapsulated politically in an empire that embraced the greater part of the society's domain. In each case the empire-building was done by a community that had arrived relatively recently in the location from which it subsequently expanded its political dominion. The Aztecs (alias Mexicas) had descended on the valley of Mexico from the northern desert; the provenance of the Incas is unknown, but the archaeological evidence shows that they were not the earliest occupants of Cuzco. So far as we know, the Aztecs were the first conquerors in the Meso-American World to create there an empire that came near to being all-embracing. In the Andean World the Inca Empire may have had precedents, if the wide dissemination of the Chavín and the Tiahuanáco styles of architecture, visual art, and other material vehicles of culture was accompanied by a political unification that was co-extensive geographically with these two previous Andean cultural 'horizons'. However, archaeology does not provide evidence for political conditions.

The opportunity for empire-building that the Aztecs seized in the fifteenth century was presented to them by the previous collapse, in the twelfth century, of the Toltec Empire whose capital city had been Tula. The lake-district at the southern end of the high valley of Mexico had been an asylum for refugees of broken civilized communities since at least as early as the destruction of the city of Teotihuacán c. A.D. 600. The lake-district received another wave of refugees after the Toltec Empire's débâcle; but the northern barbarian wreckers followed at the refugees' heels. Consequently, by about the mid-point of the thirteenth century, the lake-district housed a number of politically independent city-state communities of mixed ethnic origin and variegated culture. Their principal link with each other was the Nahuatl language, an import from the barbarian north which, by the thirteenth century, had come to be the language of most of the valley of Mexico's inhabitants.

The Aztecs were a band of vagrant barbarian interlopers who entered the lake-district when it was already occupied by established city-state communities. The post-'Classic' Meso-American society's addiction to war and to non-combatant human sacrifice was shared, or was acquired, by the Aztecs to an extreme degree. They were unwanted intruders, and in the second quarter of the fourteenth century they eventually settled on some unoccupied islands in the south-western bay of Lake Texcoco.

The Aztecs made this novel and inhospitable environment habitable by cutting swathes through the dense water-vegetation, piling up the spoil into closely-matted floating rafts, and making these into fertile food-producing gardens by coating them with mud from the lake-bottom, which the swathes had made accessible. Under the pressure of want, the Aztecs became skilful agriculturalists and town-planners. Subsequently they also became long-distance traders, who combined commerce with military intelligence-work. The Aztecs took over the accurate Meso-American calendrical system, and they combined their ancestral religion with that of their local predecessors to create a pantheon and a ritual of Hindu-like complexity. Like the Hindus, the Aztecs saw time as a succession of eras of vast chronological magnitudes. They also created a script composed of pictograms and of punning phonemes, that was handier than the traditional Meso-American glyphs, and they produced some subtle introspective poetry. Yet, from first to last, they remained addicted to human sacrifice by the horrible method of tearing out the hearts of living victims, and addicted to war as the necessary means of capturing the huge numbers of sacrificial victims that their religion demanded. A corollary of human sacrifice was ritual cannibalism.

The Spanish conquerors of Meso-America were horrified at the spectacle of human sacrifice. (This rite had not been practised in Spain since the liquidation of Carthaginian Canaanite rule there in 206 B.C., though Spaniards had continued to kill their fellow human beings in war, and had also taken to putting religious dissenters to death.) The Spaniards proved their sincerity by compelling their earliest Meso-American ally to stop making human sacrifices, at the risk of alienating him. Christians and Muslims, in their Cis-Atlantic wars, were eager, like Meso-Americans, to take prisoners in battle, but they wanted them, not for providing sacrifices to the gods, but for earning ransoms to line their own pockets. In Meso-America the motive for taking prisoners was economically disinterested; it sprang from a belief that, if the gods were not constantly fed with human hearts, these gods might lose their ability to keep the Universe in being.

Greed made West-European Christian belligerents treat prisoners more humanely. Yet the same greed also impelled them to torture Aztec and Inca prisoners in order to extort information about hidden treasure. By the 1970s the greed exhibited by Western Christians in the New World in the sixteenth century and, before that, at their sack of Constantinople in 1204, had grown *pari passu* with the growth of their technological power to indulge their paramount passion. By the 1970s their self-indulgence was threatening to make the biosphere uninhabitable by polluting it and by using up its irreplaceable natural resources. Westerners were, in fact, now doing their worst to bring on mankind the catastrophe that the Meso-Americans had dreaded. In Meso-American eyes, the Spaniards' veto on human sacrifice had been an insensate abuse of power. The issue between the Meso-Americans and their Western Christian conquerors has to be looked at through Meso-American, as well as through Western Christian, eyes.

The Aztecs made their way to military and political power by serving as mercenaries for an empire-building ruler of the city-state Atzcapotzalco, which, in 1230, had been taken over by Tepanec barbarians from the descendants of refugees from Teotihuacán. In 1428 the Aztecs of Tenochtitlán, one of the two Aztec island-cities, usurped the Tepanec Empire in the lake-district which they had helped, as mercenaries, to build up. The moving spirit was Tlacaélel, who survived as political adviser to three successive rulers of Tenochtitlán. (An Aztec ruler of Tenochtitlán, like an Arab Umayyad caliph, was styled officially, not 'king', but 'President of the Council'.) Tlacaélel began by annexing and incorporating Tenochtitlán's Aztec twin-city and northern next-door neighbour Tlatelolco. He also made an alliance with two other local city-states: the Acolhua state Texcoco, to the east of Lake Texcoco, and Tlacopán, to the west of the lake.

This concentration of power under Tenochtitlán's hegemony enabled the Aztecs to build up an empire which, by 1519, the year in which Cortés landed, extended across Meso-America from coast to coast, held both the Atlantic and the Pacific end of the Isthmus of Tehuántepec, and, to the east of the Isthmus, included a stretch of the Pacific coast extending just to the west of the present-day frontier between Mexico and Guatemala.

This Aztec–Acolhua Empire was extensive, but it was not comprehensive. The city-state Tláxcala, to the east of the lake-district, was no match militarily for the Aztec–Acolhua coalition, but Tlacaélel deliberately left it politically independent under an arrangement by which the two unequally matched powers waged with each other periodical 'flower wars', in which the objective on both sides was the capture of the prisoners that each of them needed in order to maintain its supply of victims for human sacrifices. There were other independent enclaves of territory that the imperial coalition tried, but failed, to conquer. The Aztec–Acolhua Empire's most signal military failure was its inability to subdue its western neighbours the Tarascans, who, unlike the Aztecs, had copper weapons.

Peoples that did fall under Aztec–Acolhua domination found this hard to bear. These subject peoples were held down partly by the stationing of permanent garrisons in their territories, but mainly by terrorism. Under duress, they were compelled to pay a heavy tribute, which included boys and girls for sacrifice as well as foodstuffs, textiles, precious stones and metals, and other valuable inanimate commodities. The Empire's constituent city-states—both the dominant minority of them and the subject majority—had well-developed domestic social and political constitutions, but the imperial administrative service was rudimentary: the itinerant Aztec traders served also as intelligence-officers, and the Imperial Government's principal representatives in the subject territories were the tax-collectors.

About ten years later than the inauguration in 1428 of the Aztec Empire in Meso-America, the Incas started to impose their rule on the Andean World. Down to the reign of the eighth Inca ruler of Cuzco, Hatun Tupac (better known as Viracocha, the name of the Incas' creator god, which Hatun Tupac assumed), Cuzco had been merely one among a number of local states in the Andean highlands. Viracocha Inca had extended his dominions south-eastwards, but other local states had simultaneously been extending theirs. To the west of Cuzco the Chancas had conquered the Incas' next-door neighbours and kinsmen the Quechuas. *Circa* 1438 the Chancas attacked Cuzco; Viracocha Inca and his heir-apparent withdrew to a fastness; and Cuzco was saved from capture, in desperate street-fighting, by two other sons of Viracocha Inca, Cusi Yupanqui (better known as Pachacuti) and Roca.

After winning this crucial victory, Pachacuti assumed the Inca crown and set out to conquer and annex not only the territory of the defeated Chancas, but the whole of the rest of the Andean World. His lieutenants were first his brother Capac Yupanqui and then, from about 1460 onwards, Pachacuti's own son and eventual successor, Topa Inca Yupanqui (ruled *c.* 1471–93).

These Inca empire-builders first conquered and incorporated the rest of the highlands, from the basin of Lake Titicaca on the Altiplano in the south-east to Quito, today the capital of Ecuador, in the north-west. From here, Topa Inca descended to the coast of Ecuador, made a maritime expedition to some islands, and then invaded and conquered Chimú, the northernmost, largest, and most populous of the three coastal states, across Chimú's unfortified northern frontier. Chimú's resistance was feeble compared with that of the Cañaris and the Quitos in the

Ecuadorean highlands, and the two coastal states to the south of Chimú probably submitted soon after Chimú's surrender.

After Topa Inca had become emperor, through his father's abdication, *c.* 1471, he made an abortive expedition against the peoples in the tropical forests on the Atlantic slope of the Andes. Recalled by a rebellion of the subject peoples on the Altiplano round Lake Titicaca, Topa Inca resubjugated them and then went on to conquer the highlands of what are now Bolivia and north-western Argentina, as well as the whole of what is now Chile, as far south as the north bank of the Maule River. Topa's son and successor Titu Cusi Hualpa (Huayna Capac, ruled *c.* 1493–1525/7) conquered the northern Ecuadorean highlands, but here the resistance was so vigorous that the Emperor had to remain in this outlying war-zone and to administer his vast dominions from there. He died there without ever returning to Cuzco, which was not only the Inca Empire's political nucleus and capital but was also the central node of its communications-network.

The Inca Empire dwarfed the Aztec Empire in area, though it may not have surpassed it to the same degree in the size of its population, considering how much of its territory was uninhabitable. In area the Inca Empire was comparable to the First Persian, the Chinese, and the Roman Empires. But the Incas had no wheeled vehicles, and, though they were better equipped than the Aztecs in having a beast of burden, the llama, a llama's maximum load is light by comparison with a packhorse's. The Incas were worse equipped than the Aztecs in not having even an elementary script. They had only quipus: strings of knotted cords. The cords differed in colour; the knots had different numbers of twists; and these differences had meanings but these meanings were intelligible only to an expert, and he had to be instructed orally and to transmit his expertise orally to his successors. The quipus were not self-explanatory, as a script is for anyone who has mastered a written system of notation. Yet, with this imperfect mnemonic equipment, the Incas managed to administer the population and resources of their huge empire in minute detail.

The Incas' means of locomotion were good, in spite of the difficulties of the terrain. In the highlands there were high passes and deep gorges. Along the coast, the irrigated river valleys were separated from each other by broad stretches of desert. The roads were carried over the gorges on suspension bridges composed of cables made of twisted vegetable fibres or tendrils. At intervals along the roads there were rest-houses stocked with provisions. Messages and goods were carried by relays of runners. The Empire's shape was long and narrow. There were two parallel main roads, one over the highlands—a fine feat of engineering, even for a footpath. The second main road followed the coastline. There were transverse connecting roads in the river valleys that descend from the highlands to the coast.

The Inca governing class was expanded by giving Inca status to notable members of friendly incorporated foreign peoples, in order to provide additional civil administrators and military officers. The Inca army was reinforced by the enrolment of conquered opponents—for instance, the warlike Chancas and Cañaris. The annexed territories were kept under control by extensive transfers of population. Colonies of loyal subjects were planted among disaffected subject peoples, and portions of these were deported to districts where the surrounding population was loyal. But care was taken to enable these migrants to keep in touch with their parent communities, and they were not sent to regions where the climate was different from their homeland's. (In the Andean World the difference of climate between the highlands and the coastal plain is extreme.) A still more effective device for binding the Empire together was to bring the local gods of the conquered peoples to reside permanently in Cuzco, attended there by their native priests, and to found local temples for the Inca Sun-god in the annexed territories.

The tribute levied from the subject population seems to have been less heavy in the Inca Empire than in the Aztec Empire, but, as in both the Aztec and the Ottoman Empires, the tribute included children as well as inanimate commodities. The sons of subject chiefs were brought to Cuzco to be educated in company with the sons of Inca grandees. Compulsorily levied tribute-girls were allocated partly to the Inca Emperor and his magnates as wives and partly to convent-like institutions where celibacy was the rule. These counterparts of Buddhist and Christian nuns were occasionally sacrificed, but in the Inca Empire there was not the constant sacrifice of human victims *en masse* which had become the rule by this date in Meso-America and which was the fate of all the tribute-children who were levied by the Aztecs. The sons of non-Inca notables who were given an Inca education were counterparts of the *ichoghlanlar* in the contemporary Ottoman Empire. The Ottoman *ajemi oghlanlar* had their Inca counterparts in the *yanaconas*, who were conscript-slaves.

The Quechua language was the Incas', as well as the Quechua people's, mother-tongue. After the establishment of the Inca Empire, Quechua became a lingua franca for the Empire's polyglot population, and the Aymará language of the inhabitants of the Altiplano round Lake Titicaca became a second lingua franca for the Empire's south-eastern quarter.

These imperial languages, together with the imperial demographic policy and the imperial roads, were potent bonds. Yet it was a *tour de force* to hold together such a large area and population with so modest a material equipment. Topa Inca had expanded the Empire to the limits of the extent that was logistically practicable for Inca empire-builders.

Huayna Capac over-extended the Empire that he had inherited. Consequently, when Huayna Capac died prematurely, there was a civil war between the army of the north, which supported the dead Emperor's bastard son Atahualpa, and the Inca magnates in the juridical capital city, Cuzco, who supported Huayna Capac's legitimate son Huascar. The northern army, hardened by many years of warfare, was the winner. It occupied Cuzco and took Huascar prisoner. At this juncture, Pizarro landed on the Pacific coast of South America for the third time.

75

THE COALESCENCE OF THE OIKOUMENÊ, 1405–1652

In the course of the century and a half *c.* 1400–1550, Mankind's traditional mental picture of Man's habitat, and of its place in the Universe, was transformed. For peoples that were within reach of almost all of the shores of the Ocean, the size of the Oikoumenê now suddenly expanded. Simultaneously, for a small but gradually growing minority which was convinced by the Polish astronomer Copernicus's revolutionary discovery, the size of the Oikoumenê had suddenly contracted in terms of the size of the Universe.

Since the emergence of the earliest regional civilizations about 4,500 years earlier, the planet Earth had been assumed to be the centre of the Universe, and each regional civilization had had a notional location of its own for the centre of the Earth. In the East-Asian peoples' eyes, China had been 'The Middle Kingdom'. In Indian eyes the centre had lain in what are now the states of Uttar Pradesh and Bihar. In Muslim eyes, the centre had been Mecca, while in Jewish and Christian eyes it had been Jerusalem. The civilizations that were extinct by A.D. 1400 had likewise been self-centred. In Hellenic Greek eyes, the centre of the Oikoumenê had been Delphi; in Pharaonic Egyptian eyes it had been the apex of the Nile delta; in Sumerian eyes it had been the city of Nippur in the lower Tigris–Euphrates basin.

Regional civilizations that were adjacent to each other had had contacts with each other, hostile or friendly. The far-flung but ephemeral Mongol Empire had brought Eastern Asia and Western Christendom into direct contact with each other temporarily, via the Eurasian steppe. Africa had been circumnavigated from east to west at least once in the seventh century B.C. At the turn of the tenth and eleventh centuries A.D., Norsemen had planted a settlement along the west coast of Greenland, without knowing that they had reached the threshold of an immense 'New World'. But, so far as we know, no navigator before Columbus in

1492 had crossed the Atlantic in a low latitude in either direction. If any ships had ever crossed the Pacific from Eastern Asia to the 'New World' or in the inverse direction, those trans-Pacific voyages had been both unintentional and rare. So far as we know, Vasco da Gama in 1498 was the first navigator to achieve the feat of circumnavigating Africa from west to east—an enterprise that had been attempted, without success, in the fifth century B.C. by an emissary of the Persian Emperor Xerxes. It is virtually certain that the *Victoria*—the survivor of Ferdinand Magellan's squadron of five vessels—was the first ship that ever circumnavigated the globe (1519–22).

The crew of Magellan's ship the *Victoria* had demonstrated, *navigando*, what the third-century-B.C. Greek astronomer Eratosthenes had known by inference. Eratosthenes' calculation of the length of the circumference of the globe was approximately correct, whereas Columbus's guess— which gave him the nerve to launch out into the Atlantic—was a grossly erroneous under-estimate. (The great-circle distance between Europe and Japan is 10,600 nautical miles, and Columbus had reckoned it to be less than 3,000.) Another third-century-B.C. Greek astronomer, Aristarchus, had divined that the Earth is a satellite of the Sun and that, besides revolving round the Sun once a year, the Earth rotates round its own axis once in every twenty-four hours. Aristarchus' discovery had been rejected by his Greek successors in the second century B.C., but, by A.D. 1512, one Westerner, Nicholas Copernicus (1473–1543), knew the truth, and his rediscovery of it was published in 1540 in his *Narratio Prima* and in 1543, more fully, in his *De Revolutionibus Orbium Coelestium*.

Copernicus's rediscovery of the true relation between the stars in our solar system, in combination with the effect of the *Victoria*'s circumnavigation of the water-surface of the planet Earth, had the effect of making Man's habitat both bigger and smaller. In the course of the thirty years 1492–1522, the oikoumenai that had been centred respectively on Peking, Benares, Mecca, Jerusalem, Tenochtitlán, and Cuzco coalesced into one single Oikoumenê that was far larger than any of its regional predecessors; but, whereas these superseded oikoumenai had been bounded, in some directions, by unexplored lands and seas of unknown extent, the new unitary Oikoumenê, being global, was known, even *a priori*, to be finite.

In 1493 Pope Alexander VI divided the entire globe, outside the limits of Western Christendom, between Spain and Portugal longitudinally, and in 1494 the two oceanic global Western Christian powers concluded a treaty with each other, agreeing a line 270 leagues farther to the west than the Pope's line. The agreed line placed Brazil, on which a Portuguese squadron stumbled in 1500, within the Portuguese hemisphere. In 1529 a new treaty between Spain and Portugal changed the longitude of the dividing line in Portugal's favour in the Pacific. The Portuguese obtained the Moluccas; Spain acquired the Philippines. A global Oikoumenê that could be partitioned, even if only notionally, between two maritime powers was smaller than the Oikoumenê had appeared to be previously, when viewed from one or other of its former regional centres. The unified Oikoumenê had no opaque horizons.

Moreover, the unified Oikoumenê was, and is, the best part of the 'biosphere'. The 'biosphere' is the film of dry land, water, and air that envelops the planet Earth's surface; the Earth itself had now been reduced to being one of the Sun's satellites; the Earth was no longer a centrally placed fixed star; it had been shown to be one of the 'planets' ('vagrants'), and these were now seen to have been misnamed, since all of them, including the Earth, had been proved to perambulate recurrently round the Sun in regular orbits. As for the Sun, it had been proved to be one of the fixed stars, and, distant as the Sun was from the Earth, the myriads of other fixed stars were all vastly more remote. The Earth was a gyrating ambulatory speck of dust in a stellar cosmos that, for all that an observer could tell, might extend to infinity beyond the limits of human vision through the most powerful of the telescopes constructed by Galileo (1564–1642). The global surface of the terrestrial speck of dust was finite; the speck's cosmic environment had no visible or demonstrable bounds. This was the new picture of the Universe in the age in which, on Earth, Man's habitat, the Oikoumenê, coalesced.

The coalescence of the Oikoumenê was sudden, and it brought with it sudden changes of fortune, for weal or for woe, to the previously segregated sections of the human race. It was an unmitigated catastrophe for the Aztecs and the Incas and for West Africans within reach of Western Christian slave-traders. Some of the Aztecs' and the Incas' subjects welcomed their release from the regional empire-builders' recently imposed domination, only to discover that they had not been liberated but had merely undergone a change of masters; and though, for Meso-American peoples, the substitution of Spanish for Aztec rule may have been a change for the better, for Andean peoples the substitution of Spanish for Inca rule was certainly a change for the worse.

Within Western Christendom in its European homeland, the mastering of the Ocean changed the balance of wealth and power in favour of countries with Atlantic and North-Sea seaboards to the disadvantage of countries with only Baltic or Mediterranean seaboards. The thieving, melting, and coining of the Inca emperors' treasure by the Spanish conquerors had the same economic effect as the rape of the Persian emperors' treasure by the Macedonian Greeks. The influx of precious metals, without any countervailing increase in the production of other commodities, caused a rise in prices, and, within each West-European

country, the fortunes of the various social classes were affected differenti-
ally. The pioneer Ocean-faring West-European peoples, the Portuguese
and the Spaniards, were affected the most rapidly and most severely,
but, before the close of the sixteenth century, the wave of inflation had
travelled beyond the eastern borders of Western Christendom and was
upsetting the economy of the Ottoman Empire. An observer experiencing the effects of a rise in prices of the same order of magnitude in the
1970s will guess that the arbitrary impoverishment of some sections of
society and enrichment of other sections, and the consequent increase in
uncertainty, anxiety, and resentment, during the century running from
1519, when Cortés landed on the mainland of Meso-America, may
account in large measure for some of the atrocities that were committed
so demonically in Western Europe during this century in the name of
religion and of *raison d'état*.

In the move out into the open sea, the Chinese were twelve years
ahead of the herrings, and the herrings were three years ahead of Prince
Henry the Navigator. The Chinese Emperor Yung-lo despatched his
first flotilla westwards in 1405; the herrings transferred their spawning-
grounds from the Baltic to the North Sea in 1417; Prince Henry
launched his first maritime expedition southwards in 1420.

Yung-lo's admiral the Yunnanese Muslim eunuch Cheng Ho made
seven westward voyages between 1405 and 1433. He reached Hormuz,
in the throat of the Persian Gulf, and Aden, at the mouth of the Red Sea,
at least twice, and individual vessels from his flotillas reached the east
coast of Africa. The size of the Chinese ships, the number of ships in each
successive flotilla, and the aggregate strength of the ships' companies
were very much greater than the Portuguese equivalents. In the very
first Chinese expedition (1405–7), which reached India, there were sixty-
two vessels carrying 28,000 men. The ships had the compass (a Chinese
invention) and watertight compartments. The biggest were about 400
foot long.

These Chinese ships were the best in the World before the Portuguese
naval architects' inventions later in the fifteenth century. The rulers of
the places they visited were awe-stricken. The Chinese had it in their
power, if they had persevered, to make China 'The Middle Kingdom' of
a global Oikoumenê. They could have forestalled the Portuguese in
taking possession of Hormuz and in rounding the Cape of Good Hope,
and they could have anticipated the Spaniards in discovering and conquering the Americas.

There is no record of the reason why, after 1433, the Chinese maritime
expeditions were not continued. The Ming Imperial Government was
not constrained to make a choice between naval and military exertions.
It is true that Yung-lo's first concern was his northern frontier over

against the Eurasian steppe. He conducted in person his five expeditions against the Mongols. But a politically unified China had ample resources for carrying on simultaneous operations on both fronts. Possibly China's affluence accounts for her rulers' loss of interest in overseas exploration and expansion. As late as 1793, when the Industrial Revolution in Britain was already well under way, the Ch'ing Emperor Ch'ien-lung indicated to a British envoy that the Chinese Empire was economically self-sufficient. West-European rulers were stimulated by their countries' poverty to encourage and support overseas enterprises. Fifteenth-century Chinese traders were as energetic and efficient as their West-European contemporaries, but they were allowed less opportunity for private commercial activity, since they were the subjects of a bureaucratically-governed state whose rulers and officials felt commercial-mindedness to be beneath their dignity. In the modern Chinese Empire, as in the medieval East Roman Empire, a population with a natural aptitude and inclination for trade was inhibited by its government's lack of sympathy with the national genius. Viewed in retrospect in the 1970s, this official prejudice has a (no doubt, delusive) semblance of being prescience.

The Portuguese did persevere. Bartholomew Dias rounded the Cape of Good Hope in 1487. Vasco da Gama made a landfall on the west coast of India in 1498. Alfonso de Albuquerque put the Indian Ocean in Portuguese fetters by seizing Goa in 1510, Malacca in 1511, and Hormuz (never permanently occupied by the Chinese) in 1515. Albuquerque's oceanic strategical planning emulated the thirteenth-century Mongols' land-operations in the magnitude of its geographical scale. A Portuguese ship reached Canton in 1514, and one reached the Japanese islet Tane-gashima, off the southern tip of Kyushu, in 1542 or 1543. The discomfiture of the Muslim powers by the Portuguese between 1503 and 1551 in the contest for the command over the Indian Ocean was considerable.

The sensational success of the Portuguese was the reward of inventiveness as well as courage. In the course of the half-century *c.* 1440–90 their shipwrights devised a build and rig of sailing-vessel which commanded the seas for the next four centuries and was perfected, at the close of its history, during the half-century *c.* 1840–90. Throughout its long *floruit*, this model was known simply as *the* ship. It had three masts (four masts in the first and last days only of its history) and a mixed rig. The foremast and mainmast carried square sails, which gave driving power; the mizzenmast carried a lateen sail, which gave manoeuvrability and the capacity to sail in the eye of the wind. This advantage was increased when, towards the end of the seventeenth century, the Dutch substituted fore-and-aft sails for the lateen sail on the mizzenmast, with jibs between the foremast and the bowsprit. Early in the sixteenth century, port-holes were pierced on both sides of the ship between-decks to enable a row of guns to fire a broadside. Unlike the mechanically-propelled vessels that replaced this classical sailing-ship in the course of the nineteenth century, the ship could keep the seas for weeks and months on end. Its propeller was the inexhaustible wind; it needed no supplies of fuel.

The Spaniards, too, persevered. Columbus made his first landfall in the New World in 1492. Vasco Núñez de Balboa reached the Pacific coast of the Isthmus of Panama in 1513. The Spanish city of Panama was founded in 1519. Hernando Cortés conquered the Aztec Empire in 1519–21; Francisco Pizarro conquered the Inca Empire in 1532–5.

The Spaniards conquered these two great empires, each ruled by a warlike and self-confident imperial people, with numerically tiny forces of Spanish troops. Both of them enjoyed singular good fortune.

Cortés landed on the very day in one of the years, forecast in the Mexican prognostic religious calendar, on which Quetzalcoatl, the god who had been incarnated in an evicted twelfth-century Toltec king, was expected to make his promised—or threatened—return. If the reigning Aztec 'President of the Council' at Tenochtitlán, Moctezuma II, had not believed that Cortés was in truth Quetzalcoatl *redux*, he would never have put himself in the power of a foreign human aggressor who, in truth, had no title whatsoever to replace Moctezuma on the Aztec throne. Also, if Cortés had not previously picked up at Tabasco a Mexican girl—renamed, by the Spaniards, Doña Marina—who was not only bilingual in Nahuatl and Maya but was also unusually quick-witted and conversant with Mexican mentality, Cortés would have arrived in Mexico virtually deaf, dumb, and politically in the dark.

As for Pizarro, he plunged into the interior of the Inca Empire just after the end of a civil war, when the victor, Atahualpa, had not yet had time to confirm his hold. If Pizarro had marched inland on his first expedition (1524–5), he would have collided with Inca Huayna Capac, still alive, still undisputedly the sole sovereign of the Inca Empire, and still encamped in the north with the main body of the Inca Imperial Army, not sitting in the imperial capital, Cuzco, far away to the south-east. If Pizarro had struck inland on his second expedition (1526–7), it is possible, though not certain, that he would still have found Huayna Capac alive. The year—1532—in which Pizarro, in his ignorance, chanced to make his audacious move was the most favourable of any that could have been chosen by a fully-informed foreign invader since the date, *c.* 1438, of Pachacuti's victory over the Chancas.

The Spaniards profited greatly by dissensions in the regions that they had set out to conquer. The Aztecs were hated by their subjects and by their still unsubdued neighbours; the Incas were disliked almost as much; and the Incas were also at daggers drawn with each other. Huascar's defeated partisans were not reconciled to the victory of the bastard usurper Atahualpa's faction. The historic capital city Cuzco resented the rivalry of upstart Quito. These dissensions were fortunate for the Spaniards—but this only because the Spaniards were quick to become aware of them and to exploit them. Cortés enlisted the Tlaxcalans against the Aztecs, and Pizarro the Cañaris and the partisans of Huascar against the partisans of Atahualpa. Pizarro, who had no Marina to serve him as an expert native political adviser, showed the same political discernment as Cortés.

However, the Spaniards' trump cards were their equipment, audacity, and ferocity. After their victims had recovered from the temporary shock of the terrible invaders' surprise attack, they resisted heroically. The Aztecs fought to the death and were almost exterminated; the Incas counter-attacked again and again, and they held out till 1572 in the montaña, the Atlantic slope of the Andes, where the tropical forest provides natural cover. Their last refuge here, Machu Picchu, was discovered (intact, but long since deserted) in 1911. But even the bravest and best-equipped inhabitants of the West-Europeans' 'New World' were unable to withstand gunpowder, steel, and, above all, horses (an unknown animal to them, though the horse had evolved in North America before the arrival there of human beings from north-eastern Asia). The Spaniards secured their conquests by founding autonomous cities at strategic points and garrisoning these with veterans and mestizos. This had been the practice of the Macedonian Greek conquerors of the First Persian Empire.

The sixteenth-century Spaniards, like the ninth-century Norsemen, were mobile on two elements. When they had to disembark, they mounted, and the distances that they traversed on horseback in the Americas did not fall far short of those that had been traversed by the Mongols in the Old-World Oikoumenê.

Before the close of the sixteenth century the Russians were emulating in northern Asia the Spaniards' feats in the Americas. In 1568–9, the Osmanlis tried and failed to take Astrakhan and to dig a canal from the Don to the Volga at the point where these two rivers approach nearest to each other. They proved unable to break through the Russian barrier between the Ottoman Empire and the Osmanlis' fellow Sunni Muslims in the Oxus–Jaxartes basin. This barrier was now strengthened by the Cossacks ('Kazaks', meaning, in Turkish, 'diggers', i.e. outsiders from a nomad horde's standpoint). These were Ukrainian Eastern Orthodox watermen who had established themselves first on an island in the cataracts of the Dnepr, at some date after the Golden Horde had been pushed back eastwards from here by the Lithuanians' descent to the north shore of the Black Sea in the fourteenth century. In 1571 a Cossack community established itself along the River Don, and another, perhaps at about the same date, along the River Yaik (Ural).

In 1581 a Cossack Russian adventurer, Yermak, crossed the Urals from west to east and conquered the Khanate of Sibir, whose Turkish-speaking inhabitants had recently been converted to Islam. Yermak's followers, like the Spanish conquerors of the Americas, had fire-arms, which their West-Siberian victims did not possess. Travelling through the Siberian forests by boat along the rivers, and discovering and traversing the portages, Yermak's successors reached the north-western shore of the Pacific Ocean at Okhotsk in 1637 or 1638. They had by-passed the Buddhist Mongol Buriats round Lake Baikal, who had offered a vigorous resistance. The Russians overcame the Buriats, and founded Irkutsk in their country, in 1651. Meanwhile, the Russians had invaded the Amur basin, and in 1643 a Russian raiding-party had reached the Amur's right-bank tributary, the Sungari, in Manchuria.

Here the Russians met their match in the Manchus, who also possessed fire-arms. After conquering China, the Manchus drove the Russians back westwards and confined them to the Amur's westernmost headwaters in 1658. The limit thus set to the Russians' advance south-eastwards was confirmed by treaty in 1689. In the Amur basin the Russians were far from their home base, whereas the Manchus were near to theirs, and the Manchus' logistical advantage was decisive. The date of the first clash between Russians and Manchus *c.* 1652 is historic. When these two non-nomadic but mobile empire-building peoples thus met in the Amur basin, the Eurasian pastoral nomads found themselves completely encircled, for the first time, by sedentary powers.

The Manchus had begun to impose their suzerainty on the eastern Mongols in 1634–5, before they had entered intramural China and before they had encountered the Russians. The Buriats were the only eastern Mongols who fell under Russian rule. Meanwhile, the eastern Mongols had been converted to the Tibetan form of Mahayana Buddhism *c.* 1576–7 and the western Mongols soon after. The western Mongols (Ölöds, Dzungars, Calmucks) were now astride the gap between the Altai Mountains and the T'ien Shan—a key position commanding the passage from the steppe's eastern section to its central section. At about the turn of the sixteenth and seventeenth centuries, a section of the Calmucks erupted westwards; they elbowed their way through the Turkish-speaking Muslim Kazakhs on the central section of the steppe, and crossed the lower course of the Volga *c.* 1613, the last year of Russia's 'Time of Troubles' (1604–13). Encamped between the lower Volga and the lower Don, these Calmuck migrants were ensconced in a no-man's-land between the Russian and Ottoman Empires —a political vantage-point for Buddhists who had no commitments either to Eastern Orthodox Christianity or to Sunni Islam.

Before the close of the seventeenth century the Portuguese and the Spaniards had fallen into adversity. In 1578 the Portuguese met with a military disaster in Morocco. In 1580 Portugal was united with Spain under the sovereignty of Philip II, and in 1588 a Spanish attempt to conquer England ended in a naval disaster comparable in magnitude to the Mongols' disasters in Japan in 1281 and in Java in 1292. After that, even the combined naval strength of Spain and Portugal was impotent to preserve the two hemispherical maritime empires from encroachments by the Peninsular powers' ravenous and envious north-west-European neighbours—the Dutch, French, and English.

These three buccaneering peoples now seized a number of islands in the Caribbean, which they had already been raiding. English settlers landed in Virginia in 1606 and in New England in 1620. The French settled in Acadia in 1605 and founded Quebec in 1608. The Dutch founded New Amsterdam (today New York) in 1612. Spain lost little of the effectively occupied parts of its vast 'Empire of the Indies' (i.e. the Americas). Portugal's losses were much greater. The Dutch took from the Portuguese Malacca in 1641 and coastal Ceylon in 1658. Between 1609 and 1623 the Dutch defeated the English in a competition for ousting the Portuguese from Indonesia. Between 1621 and 1654 the Dutch attempted to conquer Brazil, but the scale of this ambitious enterprise was beyond the capacity of Dutch military resources.

More ominous for Portugal—and indeed for all West-European empire-building powers on a long view—was the eviction of the Portuguese by Asian and African powers. The Safavi Emperor of Iran, Shah Abbas (ruled 1588–1629), took Hormuz from the Portuguese in 1622 with English naval aid. In 1632 the Abyssinians (present-day Ethiopians) expelled the Portuguese and also Jesuits of all European nationalities, and insulated themselves from the rest of the Oikoumenê, without any foreign help. Almost simultaneously the Japanese did the same. Hidey-oshi had ordered the expulsion of Christian missionaries as early as 1587. An edict banning the practice of Christianity in Japan was promulgated by the Tokugawa government in 1614. Christianity was persecuted savagely in Japan during the years 1622–38, and the out-break and suppression (with some Dutch naval aid) of a Japanese Christian insurrection in 1637–8 was followed in 1638 by the expulsion from Japan of Portuguese traders. This move had been preceded in 1636 by an edict forbidding Japanese subjects to go abroad. Dutch traders, who had been admitted into Japan in 1603, were allowed to stay but were confined to Deshima, an artificial island in Nagasaki harbour.

The Abyssinians and the Japanese had found the presence of the Portuguese intolerable for an identical reason. The Portuguese were fanatically sincere Roman Catholics, and they were concerned to propagate their religion, as well as to make profits from trade. In Abyssinia in 1626 the Jesuits had cajoled the reigning emperor into recognizing the Pope's supremacy over the Monophysite Church in his dominions and into attempting to abolish, *in toto*, the local Monophysite rite, which included some Jewish practices (Judaism had reached Abyssinia before Christianity). Though the Abyssinians were indebted to the Portuguese for saving them from being conquered by the Muslims in the sixteenth century, the subsequent Portuguese attempt to impose Roman Catholicism on them provoked an outburst of hostility. In Japan there had been numerous voluntary conversions to Roman Catholic Christianity since the arrival in 1549 of the first Jesuit missionary, St. Francis Xavier, in Kyushu. But the Spanish conquest of the Philippine Islands in 1571, followed in 1580 by the union of the Spanish and Portuguese crowns, made Hideyoshi and his Tokugawa successors fear that the Spaniards might try to use the Japanese converts to their religion as a 'fifth column' for attempting to conquer Japan, and this was why, like the Abyssinians, the Japanese forestalled the menace from Western Europe by precautionary measures that went to the length of voluntary self-insulation from the rest of the Oikoumenê.

The reason why the Japanese Government allowed Dutch traders to stay was that the Dutch had convinced them that they were interested solely in trade, and that they had no intention of trying to convert any Japanese to the Calvinist form of Christianity. The English traders, too, deliberately abstained from trying to convert their non-West-European trading partners, and even the Roman Catholic French were cautious about this, though to some extent they followed the provocative Portuguese and Spanish practice, with an eye to using Roman Catholic missionaries as French political agents.

Consequently there was a difference in the forms in which the Western civilization was exported by successive waves of Western traders and empire-builders. The Spanish-Portuguese first wave tried to export Western civilization integrally, including the native religion, which, in any civilization, is the key to the civilization as a whole. This attempt was resisted successfully by all non-West-European peoples that had the power. Accordingly the Dutch-French-English second wave of West-Europeans operating *in partibus infidelium* exported only an expurgated version of West-European civilization, and Dutch and English private traders and public authorities frowned upon missionary activities. The paramount element in this expurgated Western civilization that began to pervade the Oikoumenê in the seventeenth century was not religion; it was technology and, first and foremost, the technology of warfare.

In Japan, Roman Catholic Christianity survived surreptitiously on some of the islets off the coast of Kyushu until the abrogation in 1873 of the death penalty for being convicted of being a crypto-Christian. By that date the Roman Catholicism of the latent 'Kirishtan' had become blended with indigenous Japanese popular beliefs and practices, and the same thing happened in the Spanish dominions overseas, where the conquered populations had been converted *en masse* compulsorily, and therefore only nominally.

Empire-builders of all West-European nationalities alike exploited, or alternatively exterminated, their overseas victims. The Spanish conquerors' greed and brutality were emulated by their rivals without ever being surpassed, but the Spaniards were singular in facing promptly and frankly the moral issue that the conquest had raised. As early as 1514 the Spanish conquerors' victims found a determined and persistent champion in the Dominican friar Bartolomé de Las Casas; he moved the Spanish Government to enact legislation prohibiting the worst abuses, and this legislation was partially enforced, in the teeth of the conquerors, who took up arms in opposition. The Spaniards and Portuguese also mitigated their oppression of their victims by intermarrying with converts. In their eyes, community of religion was a spiritual bond that transcended any differences of physical race. The effect of conversion in lowering the barrier between the conquerors and the conquered is displayed visually in the colour and costume of post-Cortesian New Spain's tutelary goddess the Virgin of Guadalupe.

The Portuguese started to enslave Black Africans as soon as they had reached the coast of sub-Saharan Africa, and all later West-European Empire-builders took to this atrocious practice. When the West-Europeans acquired territories overseas, they imported Black slaves, captured in Africa, to provide them with forced labour in lieu of the natives whom they had exterminated or decimated. The mortality among the victims was great; the profits of the traders were proportionate; the survivors of the enslaved Black African deportees managed, thanks to their race's vitality, to produce a progeny in the Americas to share the acquisition of this 'New World' with the West-European Whites who had transplanted them.

The migration and inter-breeding of different races of human beings was not the only effect of the Oikoumenê's coalescence on the biosphere's fauna and flora. There were beneficial gifts of independently domesticated animals and plants from each of the two previously segregated hemispheres to the other. There were also baneful disseminations of bacteria and viruses. Smallpox germs were conveyed westward to the Americas by human carriers following in Columbus's wake. A host of these germs may have been the invisible vanguard of Pizarro's tiny band of human invaders of South America if smallpox was the disease that cut short the life of the Inca Huayna Capac. Conversely, venereal disease—

first reported in Western Europe in 1495, i.e. within three years of Columbus's first landfall—may have been the 'New World's' revenge for the wrongs that the 'Old World' was inflicting on it. The catastrophic rise in prices in Western Europe during the century beginning in 1519 was certainly a retribution for the importation of the bullion which the Spaniards had stolen from the Aztecs and the Incas and which they subsequently extracted from American mines by conscripting native American labour. Thus one result of the coalescence of the Oikoumenê was that each of three dire visitants—smallpox, venereal disease, and the inflation of the currency—won an empire that dwarfed even Charles V's empire in the range of its geographical extension. These, too, were empires of the novel kind on which the Sun never set.

[76]

THE WESTERN CIVILIZATION,
1563–1763

In the course of the two centuries 1563–1763 Western civilization made a greater mental and spiritual revolution than any that had ever been made by this society at any previous date since it had arisen among the local débris of the Roman Empire. Western thinkers now refused to take their heritage from their predecessors on trust. They decided that henceforward they would test inherited doctrines by examining the phenomena independently, and that they would do their own thinking. They also reconciled themselves to co-existing peacefully with heterodox minorities. They no longer felt an obligation or an impulse to impose a majority's creed and rite by force. Neither of these revolutions was instantaneous. In both, there were pauses and setbacks. In 1686 Fontenelle published *Entretiens sur la pluralité des mondes*, a doctrine which had cost Giordano Bruno his life in 1600; yet Fontenelle lived to be a centenarian and died, in 1757, in his bed. In 1687 Newton (1642–1727) published his *Principia*, without being compelled by any ecclesiastical authorities to retract, as Galileo had been compelled to do in 1633. On the other hand, the Edict of Nantes, which had granted toleration to the Protestant minority in France, was revoked by Louis XIV in 1685.

The Westerners' servitude to authority, from which they now liberated themselves, was age-old. All non-Christian religions had been suppressed forcibly by the Roman Imperial Government before the close of the fifth century, and in some of the Roman Empire's Western successor-states—for instance Spain in the course of the years 1391–1492 and Portugal in 1497—all Jews who failed to find asylum abroad had been converted compulsorily to Christianity. The Hellenic-Age Greek philosopher Aristotle's tenets had been imposed on Western Christian theologians and philosophers since the thirteenth century. The style of Ciceronian-Age and Augustan-Age Latin-writers had been imposed on modern Western Latin-writers since the fifteenth century.

The authority of Christianity, with the Western interpolation of the *filioque* in its creeds, had not been impugned by the Protestant revolt against the Papal government of the Western Church. The Protestants had substituted the authority of the Bible for the authority of the Papal Curia. Protestant princes had been as intolerant as Roman Catholic princes in imposing their own version of Western Christianity on their subjects. The split within the bosom of Western Christendom had merely made both contending parties behave even more fanatically and atrociously than their unanimous Roman Catholic predecessors.

The aping of the style of the 'classical' Latin writers had been more frivolous than the former intellectual subservience of Western Christian thinkers to Aristotle. On the other hand, the printing, in the West, of Hellenic-Age Greek mathematical and scientific works had provoked independent thought; for these 'ancient' interpretations of physical phenomena had been refuted, in a number of cases, by subsequent technological inventions and geographical discoveries. In this field, the 'renaissance' of 'ancient' information had led to new departures.

The West's emancipation of itself from the intellectual tyranny of its Graeco-Roman predecessors was dramatized in Fontenelle's *Une Digression sur les anciens et les modernes* (1688) and in William Wotton's *Reflections upon Ancient and Modern Learning* (1694), but the attack had been opened by Jean Bodin (1530–96), and had been carried farther by Francis Bacon (1561–1626) and by René Descartes (1596–1650), before the partisans of the Moderns had won their definitive victory. Moreover, the victors had to concede that the panegyrists of Louis XIV were not better poets than Homer, and they did not endorse, and therefore did not revive, the Christian claim that a Christian civilization was better than a pre-Christian one. The fields in which these champions of Modern Western achievements were victorious were physical science, technology, and philosophy.

Christianity had been discredited by the Western 'wars of religion', which had started in 1534 and which continued spasmodically till 1648. These wars were both fanatical and hypocritical. The motives and objectives of the belligerent princes were political, but it suited them to assume the mask of religious conviction, and the animosity of the belligerents was envenomed by clerical zeal that was genuine, though rancorous and benighted. The Royal Society was founded in England in 1660 by a group of people interested in physical science whose aim was, not to subvert Christianity, but to rehabilitate it morally. Their policy was to divert their contemporaries' thoughts and feelings from theological controversies that were both unedifying and inconclusive and to direct attention to questions concerning natural phenomena that could be discussed dispassionately and could be answered conclusively by observation or by experiment.

At the same time, there were other critics and victims of the 'wars of religion' who did seek to loosen Christianity's hold on Western hearts and minds; and, since this was still a dangerous game, they worked surreptitiously—except in regions beyond the bounds of Christendom, where, for example, the Dutch in Japan secured continued permission to trade by abstaining ostentatiously from Christian missionary activity. Fontenelle inserted dicta that were hardly compatible with Christianity into his *éloges* (oral obituary notices) of deceased men of science. In his *Histoire des oracles*, published in 1688, he was more daring. Pierre Bayle (1647–1706), a French Protestant refugee in the Northern Netherlands, published, at Rotterdam in 1695–7, a *Dictionnaire historique et critique* which was the prototype of Diderot's and d'Alembert's *Encyclopédie*, published in France in 1751–65. Bayle copied the format of contemporary Western annotated editions of Greek and Latin authors. His text is anodyne; his notes on his own text, printed unobtrusively in smaller type but frequently occupying the greater part of a page, are in some cases subversive—if the author's intention, in these enigmatic comments, is correctly interpreted as being ironical.

Edward Gibbon, writing about eighty years later, adopted Bayle's device, but this did not save him from being castigated for the chapters in *The History of the Decline and Fall of the Roman Empire*, published in 1776–88, in which he offered a non-miraculous explanation of the Roman Empire's conversion to Christianity. Among the Western countries, England was a pioneer in establishing religious toleration but was slow in becoming indifferent to the expression of anti-Christian beliefs and sentiments. John Wesley (1703–91) had started on his evangelical mission in 1739, when Gibbon (1737–94) was an infant. Gibbon's French contemporaries, Voltaire (1694–1778) and the Encyclopaedists, were able to be more frank with impunity; yet, even in the eighteenth century, Voltaire found it prudent to live just on the Swiss side of the Franco-Swiss frontier.

In France in the seventeenth century, Blaise Pascal (1623–62) had combined scientific genius with an ardent faith in Jansenist Christianity, and Bishop Bossuet (1627–1704) had published a *Discours sur l'histoire universelle* in which mankind's history was still presented, as it had been by Eusebius of Caesarea (*c.* 264–340), in terms of the providence of a unique and omnipotent god, the Judaic Yahweh. Voltaire retorted to Bossuet by writing a cultural and social history of mankind in which he gave pride of place, not to the Jews, but to the Chinese whose civilization had been made known in the West by Jesuit missionaries.

In the history of the establishment of religious toleration in the West, the literary landmarks are *A Letter on Toleration* (1689 seqq.) by the repatriated English exile John Locke (1632–1704), and his *Treatises on*

Civil Government (1690). The practical landmarks were acts of Leopold I, the sovereign of the Roman Catholic Danubian Habsburg Monarchy. In 1690 Leopold published a proclamation to all Christian peoples formerly subject to the Hungarian Crown and to all those still under Ottoman rule, offering them religious liberty and communal autonomy, up to Ottoman standards, under Habsburg rule. In 1690–5 Leopold gave asylum to a refugee Eastern Orthodox Serb community on terms that preserved for them, in Habsburg territory, the privileges of an Ottoman *millet*. As recently as 1664, people in Silesia—one of the Bohemian crownlands reconquered by the Habsburg Monarchy in the Thirty Years War (1618–48)—had been openly expressing their longing to be liberated by an Ottoman conquest. The Danubian Habsburg Monarchy had been converted, within the intervening twenty-five years, to a policy of religious toleration by the necessity of competing with Russia for the political allegiance of the Ottoman Eastern Orthodox Christians over whom the Ottoman Empire was then beginning to lose its grip as a result of the disastrous failure, in 1682–3, of the second Ottoman siege of Vienna.

Yet toleration, like intellectual independence, was achieved by Westerners only slowly. In France the Edict of Nantes was revoked in 1685. In China the Jesuit missionaries had won a foothold by mastering the Confucian culture, introducing useful knowledge of Western astronomical and military technology, and allowing their converts to continue to venerate their ancestors in the traditional Chinese way on the plausible ground that this rite was civil, not religious. Matteo Ricci (1552–1610), the pioneer Jesuit in China, had been adopted by the Chinese Confucian scholars into their fraternity, under a Chinese *nom de plume*, in recognition of his proficiency in Confucian scholarship. The Jesuits had translated *Deus* as *T'ien* ('Heaven'). Intransigent Roman Catholic authorities sabotaged the Jesuits' work by forbidding Chinese converts to practise the traditional rites for venerating ancestors and by insisting that *Deus* should be translated *T'ien-ti*, to signify that the Christians' god is not supra-personal but is a human-like person. The Roman Church thus provoked a controversy with the Chinese Imperial Government that ended, after thirty years (1693–1723), in the banning and suppression of Christianity in China. The Curia had not learnt the lesson of what had happened in Japan in 1587–1638. In Europe, forty-two years after the Danubian Habsburg Monarchy had conceded toleration to Eastern Orthodox Christians, Protestant Christians were expelled from the adjoining prince-bishopric of Salzburg in 1731–2.

The seventeenth century saw the death, in Western countries, of the superstitious belief that the appearance of a comet was a miraculous event contrived by God as a warning of imminent chastisements. The comet of 1680 still caused alarm. In 1682 Bayle published *Pensées diverses sur la comète*, asserting that the 1680 comet and all others were normal natural phenomena. When another comet appeared in 1682, the astronomer Edmund Halley identified it with those that had appeared in 1456, 1531, and 1607, and he calculated its orbit, periodicity, and speed. Halley also did the same for the comet of 1680. Another Western superstition, the belief in witchcraft, died harder. Two hundred years (1563–1762) passed between the first published challenge to this belief in Western Christendom and the last execution of a 'witch' that was perpetrated there. Meanwhile, thousands of innocent people were shamefully put to death.

The rejection of authority, intolerance, and superstition was an intellectual and moral triumph that left gaps in the cultural and social structure of the Western society. These gaps were filled, with different degrees of success in different departments of life, by more or less deliberate replacements.

The religious polemics that had instigated such atrocities as the massacres in Paris on St. Bartholemew's Day 1572 and at Drogheda in 1649 were successfully replaced by an interest in mathematics and physical science that was stimulated by a hope of increasing human welfare through the systematic application of mathematicized science to technology. This hope, expressed precociously by Leonardo da Vinci, was cherished by Francis Bacon, and it inspired Bacon's disciples, the founders of the Royal Society. William Harvey (1578–1657), an English alumnus of the University of Padua, published his *De Motu Cordis et Sanguinis* in 1628. Robert Boyle (1627–91) extricated the science of chemistry from alchemy. Isaac Newton revolutionized Western physics and astronomy. Charles Linnaeus (1707–78) initiated the systematic classification of the biosphere's flora and fauna. Linnaeus believed in the immutability of the species and genera that he had classified. Nature, as he saw it, was static. Linnaeus's contemporary G. L. Leclerc, Comte de Buffon (1707–88), found evidence that Nature has come to be what it now is through a long-drawn-out process in the course of time, and he expected that this process would continue in the future.

In the domain of philosophy, the gap left by the rejection of Aristotle's authority had not been filled by the humanists' cult of Plato. Seventeenth-century Western thinkers sought to fill this gap by making a clean break and a fresh start. René Descartes tried to do this for epistemology. His *Discours de la méthode* (1637) remained an intellectual landmark even for successors who contested his claim to have achieved finality. John Locke sought to handle epistemology empirically. Spinoza (1632–77) and Leibniz (1646–1716) sought to lay new foundations for metaphysics. In the domain of sociology, Thomas Hobbes (1588–1679) underpinned his hypothesis of a social contract by making a preliminary reconnaissance into the realm of psychology. Locke, who worked in this field too, did not delve so deep. Giambattista Vico (1668–1744), in his *Principi d'una scienza nuova* (1718), broke new ground in the domain of cultural history. His work was so novel that its importance was not appreciated by his contemporaries. Vico was inspired by the Hellenic-Age Greek theory of cyclic recurrences, but, unlike his Hellenic mentors, he had two cultures, the Hellenic and the Western Christian, within his ken, and, armed with this more ample information, he made the first Western essay in the comparative study of civilizations.

Medieval Western Christendom had been held together by the Papacy's presidency over a Western *Respublica Christiana* and by the use of Latin as a lingua franca for diplomacy, for scholarship, and even for poetry, side by side with poetry in the numerous Western local vernaculars. The ecclesiastical *Respublica Christiana* was replaced to some extent by a literary and scientific 'Republic of Letters'. Its founding father had been Erasmus, but Bayle endowed it, in 1684, with a periodical, *Nouvelles de la République des Lettres*. Intellectual exchanges between both men of letters and men of science were facilitated by the improvement of public postal services and by the opening of these for use by private correspondents as a means of enabling the services to pay their way. Private correspondence generated newsletters, and these generated newspapers. The first Western printed periodical started publication in 1609, the first daily newspaper in 1702. By the seventeenth century most Western universities, with the outstanding exceptions of the University of Padua and the Scottish universities, had lost their medieval vitality and creativity. This gap was partially filled by academies founded or supported by the governments of local sovereign states, and, in eighteenth-century Paris, also by the private salons of cultivated ladies.

The gap left by the foundering of the Papal *Respublica Christiana* was also partially filled by the social network of the Western royal family and the Western aristocracy. These two social classes at the summit of the Western society were knit together by marriages that transcended the frontiers between states and by a command of diverse vernacular languages which transcended the barriers between nationalities. The solidarity of the Western royal family and the Western aristocracy survived the religious schism in Western Christendom. Changes of religion for *raison d'état* were condoned. A Calvinist kinglet of Navarre turned Roman Catholic in order to become Henri IV of France. William, the Calvinist prince of the Northern Netherlands, and George, the Lutheran Elector of Hanover, became adherents of the Episcopalian Protestant Church of England in order to become, respectively, William III, King of England, and George I, King of the United Kingdom of

England and Scotland. Since in Scotland Calvinism was the established religion, William III had to adopt only one extra form of Protestantism in addition to his own; but the four Georges and William IV had to be Calvinist Presbyterians in Scotland and Episcopalians in England, while continuing to be Lutherans in Hanover.

The living vernacular languages of the Western peoples had begun, as early as the twelfth century, to assert themselves in poetry side by side with a contemporary Latin poetry in which the vernacular style showed through a Latin veneer. When the vernaculars won the upper hand completely, the first effect was to give licence for an exuberance that provided a hotbed for genius. An example of this in prose is Rabelais (1494?–1553) and in poetry Shakespeare (1564–1616). The Age of the Western 'wars of religion' was also a great age of Western poetry. The cultural price of discarding religious superstition and persecution was a descent from poetry to prose—not in music, but in genres in which the medium was a vernacular language.

Sixteenth-century Transalpine Western poets had written, like their Italian predecessors and contemporaries, under the spell of 'classical' Latin and Greek models. French examples are Joachim du Bellay (1522–60), Pierre de Ronsard (1524–85), and the other five members of the 'Pléiade'. Their English counterparts are the pioneers Sir Thomas Wyatt (1503?–42) and Henry Howard, Earl of Surrey (1517?–47), followed by the galaxy of Elizabethan-Age poets and their successors down to the restoration of the monarchy in England and Scotland in 1660. The radiant light of Shakespeare and Milton (1608–74) takes the shine out of many English and Scottish poets of this age who would have shone brightly if they had not been outshone by these two great luminaries. After the dawning of the Enlightenment, Western poets deliberately became prosaic. The initiative in this change of mood and style was taken by the seventeenth-century French dramatists: Corneille (1606–84), Molière (1622–73), Racine (1639–99). These geniuses confined their verse within sober forms. They had been given a new linguistic instrument by contemporary French prose-writers—for instance, Pascal.

The French prose style that was fashioned in the course of the seventeenth century was simple, lucid, and precise. It was far better suited than any 'classical' Latin or Greek style to Indo-European languages which, by this date, had gone as far as English and the Romance languages had gone in changing over from an inflexional structure to an analytical one in which detachable particles, prepositions, and auxiliary verbs had replaced the less handy device of welding suffixes and prefixes on to the stems of verbs and substantives. The new French prose style also renounced the Latin-like and Turkish-like smothering of sentences under a load of subordinate clauses; the new French sentence-structure was paratactic. The writer left it to the reader to divine the logical relation between one short single sentence and another.

This French stylistic revolution took English literature by storm, and here the change, being not of native origin, was sharp, and the revolutionaries were self-conscious. Dryden, for instance, was confident that his style, in both prose and verse, was a notable improvement on Milton's.

The export of the French style of writing and of French Protestant émigrés to other Western countries won for France a cultural ascendancy throughout the Western World in all fields except music. In this field, Germany now won the lead from Italy. In Northern Germany after the Thirty Years War, the prolific Bach family eclipsed the princes who were its patrons. Johann Sebastian Bach (1685–1750) and Georg Friedrich Handel (1685–1759) were the most eminent Germans of their generation. Frederick II 'the Great' King of Prussia (ruled 1740–86) achieved the *tour de force* of raising his small and indigent kingdom to the status of a great power, yet he also managed to find funds for financing opera at Berlin. All the same, Frederick's principal non-military ambition was to write French verse that would pass muster in French literary circles. Gibbon, too, wrote in French before deciding, like Dante, to use his mother-tongue as the vehicle for his masterpiece. In the Western wars of 1667–1713, France only just failed to cap her cultural ascendancy with a political domination. She was defeated with difficulty by a coalition of weaker Western states in which the northern Netherlands bore the brunt.

In the first bout (1494–1559) of the contest between France and the Burgundian-Habsburg power, France had been the weaker party, and in 1525 she had been brought momentarily to her knees. The trial of strength between the two Roman Catholic super-powers was then interrupted by civil wars, the so-called 'wars of religion'. The earliest of these had been waged in Germany in 1534–55. It was followed by civil wars in France (1562–98), in the Netherlands (1569–1609), in Germany for the second time (1618–48), and in England (1642–8).

All these civil wars gave openings for foreign intervention—to a minimum extent in the English civil war, to a maximum in the Thirty Years War in Germany. Catholic France had already supported the Protestant German princes against the Habsburg Emperor Charles V in the German civil war of 1534–55. In the Thirty Years War, France co-operated with Protestant Sweden to prevent the Habsburgs from subjugating the Protestant German states. This French policy was conducted by two statesmen who were cardinals of the Roman Church: Richelieu (1585–1642), who came into power in 1624, and Mazarin (1604–60) who was Richelieu's immediate successor.

In the Thirty Years War, France was the principal gainer. The Danubian Habsburg Monarchy came off second best. It reconquered the Bohemian crown-lands and it survived. Sweden exhausted herself by engaging in an adventure that was beyond her strength. Spain collapsed. She had failed to take advantage of the paralysis of France in 1562–98. The union of Portugal with Spain in 1580 had appeared to raise Spain to a pinnacle of power; but, by then, her strength was being sapped by the war in the Netherlands. Besides being a civil war between Protestant and Catholic Netherlanders, this was a national revolt of the Protestant Netherlanders against Spanish rule; and Portugal's political association with Spain exposed the Portuguese overseas empire to damaging Dutch assaults. Spain's resumption in 1621 of her attempt to reconquer the northern Netherlands revived the drain on Spain's resources. The annihilation of a Spanish armada by the Dutch in 1639 confirmed the results of Spain's previous naval defeat by the English in 1588. On land, in the Old World, Spain was crippled by the revolts of Portugal and Catalonia in 1640.

Notwithstanding Spain's loss of her sea-power, her huge overseas empire remained almost intact, and the silver from her Andean and Mexican mines continued to reach her. But these assets did not avail to save her from decline. Spain was no match for France in the extent of her agricultural land, and her agriculture was hampered by a large-scale nomadic animal husbandry. Consequently, Spain, like Sweden, did not have a big enough population to sustain the role that she tried to play, and Spain's and Sweden's and Germany's exhaustion gave France an opportunity that she seized. Already in 1552 she had acquired the three fetters of Lorraine: Metz, Toul, and Verdun. In the Thirty Years War she acquired Alsace.

France survived the wars of 1667–1713, as the Danubian Habsburg Monarchy had survived the Thirty Years War. France even survived the emigration in and after 1685 of the greater part of the Protestant minority of her population. France was so populous that this loss did not have the debilitating effect on her that the expulsion of the Spanish Jews and Muslims had had on Spain. On the other hand, the accession of these skilful and industrious Protestant French émigrés strengthened France's present and future adversaries: the northern Netherlands, England, and, above all, Brandenburg, as well as Württemberg, the Dutch settlement at the Cape of Good Hope, and the English settlement in South Carolina.

Moreover, in the later stages of the war of 1667–1713, after England had joined forces with the Dutch, and in the subsequent Anglo-French wars of 1740–8 and 1756–63, France was the loser in a competition with Britain for the command over North America, to the north of the

Spanish Empire, and for the command over India. The British won North America from France in 1690–1763 and India (except for a few small and isolated enclaves of territory) in 1746–61. In 1767 Hume took Gibbon to task for writing in French. He forecast that North America was going to be occupied by an English-speaking population, and Hume's forecast was endorsed by Gibbon himself in a passage written in English after the outbreak of the American Revolutionary War.

France failed to win North America and India; yet, among the Western states that had been great powers in 1621, France and the Danubian Habsburg Monarchy were the only two that still retained this status a century later. Spain's power had been broken by her participation in the Thirty Years War, the northern Netherlands' by the wars of 1667–1713, and Sweden's by her defeat in the Russo-Swedish War of 1700–21. By 1721 the Netherlands' place had been taken by Britain, and Sweden's by Russia and Prussia. The Danubian Habsburgs had, once again, fared well. They had inherited the Spanish Habsburgs' dominions in Lombardy and in the southern Netherlands, and the Monarchy had expanded eastwards at the Ottoman Empire's expense after the failure, in 1682–3, of the second Turkish siege of Vienna.

The West's reversion, half way through the seventeenth century, from the so-called 'wars of religion' to wars that were fought frankly in pursuit of political power and economic advantage, was accompanied by a mitigation of the brutality of the conduct of war. Wars between Western states were now waged, not as struggles *à outrance* between mutually hostile peoples and sects, but as 'temperate contests' (Gibbon's phrase) between governments employing uniformed and disciplined professional troops. The lives and property of civilians were now supposed to be spared. Armies were required to supply themselves by providing their own commissariat, and no longer to 'live off the country'. Civilian populations that were transferred from one state's sovereignty to another's were supposed to be entitled to exemption from spoliation, eviction, and massacre.

Western governments did not always live up to these new humane standards. War itself is an atrocity; abolition is the only cure; and even sincere attempts to humanize war cannot be more than partially successful palliatives. The French deliberately devastated the Rhenish Palatinate in 1674 and again in 1688, and, if a fortified city was taken by assault after its military garrison had rejected a summons to surrender, the victorious enemy troops still felt themselves entitled to rob and rape the civilian inhabitants. All the same, between 1688 and 1792, war was successfully reduced, in the Western World as a whole, to the relatively low degree of barbarity that had been achieved in the fifteenth century locally in northern Italy.

EASTERN ORTHODOX
CHRISTENDOM, 1556–1768

SINCE the conversion of Russia to Eastern Orthodox Christianity in 989, Eastern Orthodox Christendom had consisted of two parts: its old domain in south-eastern Europe, Asia Minor, and the Caucasus, and a new Russian domain that was insulated from the old domain physically by the western bay of the Eurasian steppe to the north of the Black Sea. In spite of the interposition of this geographical obstacle, Russia was united with the older part of Eastern Orthodox Christendom by a common religion, and she was receptive to the Byzantine civilization both in its Greek and in its Bulgarian versions. Russia was, however, independent, and she was expanding. Between 1552 and 1637 or 1638 she expanded eastwards from the upper waters of the Volga basin to the north-western shore of the Pacific Ocean, and her expansion was neither arrested by the Osmanlis nor rolled back by the Calmucks.

By contrast, the whole of the southern part of Eastern Orthodox Christendom was now subject to either Ottoman or Western Christian rule. The Ottoman Empire was gaining ground at the expense of the Western Christian colonial empires in the Levant. For instance, the island of Chios, which had been ruled by a Genoese chartered company since 1346, was annexed by the Ottoman Empire in 1566, and in 1645–69 the island of Crete was conquered by the Osmanlis from the Venetians, who had held Crete since 1204. But these changes of masters left the southern Orthodox Christians still subjected. A few Ottoman Greek communities were allowed some degree of local self-government; but within the Ottoman dominions there were only six fully autonomous Eastern Orthodox principalities: four Georgian statelets in the Caucasus and the two Roumanian principalities, Wallachia and Moldavia, to the north of the lower course of the Danube.

However, the Greeks' situation was not so unfavourable, and the Russians' was not so favourable, as might appear. Though Russia was expanding eastwards across the northern hinterland of the steppe, she was still exposed to nomad raids across the steppe's western end; the Khanate of the Crimea, which was the south-westernmost of the Golden Horde's successor-states, had survived thanks to its having submitted to Ottoman suzerainty in 1475. In 1671 Crimean Tatar raiders burned Moscow. Moreover, Muscovy was landlocked. Except for Murmansk, which was not yet accessible from the interior of Russia, Russia's only ice-free seaboard was along the north shore of the Caspian, and that 'sea' is only a lake, though it is a vast one. The Ottoman fortress Azov, at the mouth of the River Don, debarred Muscovy from access to the sea of Azov and therefore also from access to the Black Sea, the Mediterranean, and the Atlantic.

Muscovy was also debarred from access to the Atlantic via the Baltic and the North Sea. The former Russian republic of Novgorod, annexed by Muscovy in 1478, had held a short stretch of Baltic coastline at the head of the Gulf of Finland, but in the years 1558–83 Ivan the Terrible (1530–94) lost this Baltic seaboard in trying to extend it. During a bout of anarchy in Muscovy ('The Time of Troubles', 1604–13) the Swedes occupied Novgorod in 1611 and the Poles Moscow in 1610–12. The peace-settlement of 1618 left Muscovy still barred out by Sweden from access to the Baltic, while the eastern frontier of Poland-Lithuania was now pushed forward again as close to Moscow as it had been in the fifteenth century.

From 989 to 1589 the whole of the Russian portion of Eastern Orthodox Christendom was under the ecclesiastical jurisdiction of the Patriarchate of Constantinople, and thus, though since 1453 the Patriarch of Constantinople had been an Ottoman subject and civil servant resident in Ottoman territory, the major part of his ecclesiastical domain lay outside the Ottoman Empire's frontiers. In 1589, however, the Metropolitanate of Moscow was raised to the status of an ecclesiastically independent Patriarchate. The Polish-Lithuanian Crown retorted in 1594–6 by coercing most of the Eastern Orthodox Christians under its rule into becoming Uniate Roman Catholics. Union with the Roman Church was successfully rejected only by those Ukrainian subjects of the Polish-Lithuanian Crown that were controlled by the Dnepr Cossacks, and the Patriarch of Constantinople lost even these last of his northern ecclesiastical subjects when, in 1648–54, the Dnepr Cossacks transferred their political allegiance from Poland-Lithuania to Muscovy.

The Eastern Orthodox Church continued to be as hostile to the West as it had been in the fifteenth century. It was unwilling to fraternize with the Western Protestants, though these had followed suit to the Eastern Orthodox Christians in rejecting the Papacy's claim to ecclesiastical supremacy. The Patriarchate of Constantinople did not co-operate with the Polish Protestants in resisting the Counter-Reformation in Poland-Lithuania, and this was one of the causes of its failure in 1594–6 to prevent the imposition of Uniatism on a majority of those of its ecclesiastical subjects who were under Polish-Lithuanian rule. Cyril Lucaris, Patriarch of Constantinople, 1620–35 and 1637–8, who did incline towards Calvinism, was followed in this by only a small minority of his fellow Greek Eastern Orthodox clerics. In the eighteenth century a Greek educationist, Eugenius Vulgaris (1716–1806), was persecuted by the Greek ecclesiastical authorities because he had been educated in Germany and was well versed in contemporary Western philosophy.

The Patriarchate of Constantinople provided a rallying-point for the Ottoman Greeks—laymen as well as clerics—after the extinction of the East Roman Empire in 1453; but in the course of the next two centuries the Eastern Orthodox Greek laity, unlike the clergy, came to feel friendly towards the West. It has been mentioned already that, in the sixteenth century, Ottoman Greek businessmen were making profits by trading with the West. Ottoman Greek maritime trade in the Mediterranean was supplemented by overland trade with Central Europe when the failure in 1682–3 of the second Ottoman siege of Vienna was followed by an eastward expansion of the Danubian Habsburg Monarchy at the Ottoman Empire's expense.

Greeks who came into commercial or political contact with the West were also attracted by Western culture. Ottoman as well as Venetian Greeks studied at the University of Padua, and the Cretans produced, under Venetian rule, a literature in colloquial Modern Greek in the current Western style. The production of this Cretan Greek literature was cut short in Crete itself by the fall of Candia in 1669, but Cretan refugees carried their literary heritage to the Ionian Islands, which remained under Venetian rule.

The Ottoman Greeks' acquaintance with the West benefited them politically when, in the seventeenth century, the tide began to turn against the Ottoman Empire in its perennial warfare with the Western Christian states. The Ottoman Imperial Government now found that it needed diplomatists who would be competent to negotiate with Westerners. In 1669 the office of Dragoman of the Porte (tantamount to a Minister for Foreign Affairs) was created for Western-educated Ottoman Greeks. From 1711 onwards, the rule over the two Roumanian principalities, Wallachia and Moldavia, was conferred on Greek Ottoman subjects. The Ottoman Government was bound by treaty to allow the principalities to be governed by Christian princes. In 1711 the native prince of Moldavia had turned traitor to the Ottoman Empire when his principality had been invaded by Peter the Great. The Osmanlis reckoned that they could trust their Greek subjects, since these were

domiciled in the Ottoman Empire and were therefore at the Osmanlis'
mercy. The Roumanian principalities were rich, and the appointments to
the office of prince were lucrative both for the Greek appointees and for
the Turkish officials whom the Greek candidates had to bribe.

The Greeks induced the Ottoman Government to abolish the Serbian
Patriarchate of Peć in 1766 and the Bulgarian Metropolitanate of
Okhrida in 1767, and to place these two non-Greek Eastern Orthodox
churches under the command of exarchs appointed by the Patriarch of
Constantinople. By this time the Western-educated Ottoman Greek lay
'establishment' was becoming a junior partner of the Turkish 'establishment' in the government of the Ottoman Empire's non-Greek Christian
subjects. The Greeks were beginning to dream of becoming one day the
Osmanlis' senior partners or even their legatees.

The major event in the history of Eastern Orthodox Christendom in
the seventeenth and eighteenth centuries was the revolutionary Westernization of Russia by Peter the Great (ruled *de jure* 1682–1725, *de facto*
1694–1725). Peter did not initiate the process. Western influences had
already been seeping into Russia through the port of Archangel on the
White Sea (founded in 1585, after Muscovy had lost her seaboard on the
Gulf of Finland) and also through the Ukrainian Eastern Orthodox
Church, which had come under Western influence while the Ukraine
had been under Polish-Lithuanian rule. By Peter's day there was already
a settlement of Western residents outside the walls of Moscow, to which
Peter resorted. Peter neither initiated the Westernization of Russia nor
completed it. In 1700 he let the Patriarchate of Moscow fall into
abeyance, and then in 1721 he replaced it by a synod that was a department of state, but he did not eradicate the religiosity of the peasant
majority of the Russian people. He changed the style of the Muscovite
monarchy from a traditional Byzantine to the contemporary Western
pattern, but he left its powers and practice autocratic.

Peter inherited a huge empire whose only seaboards were ice-bound
coasts. He was bound to seek access to open seas. This had been sought
already by his predecessor Ivan the Terrible; but Peter succeeded in an
enterprise in which Ivan had failed. Peter won for Russia a seaboard on
the Baltic, and from 1696 to 1711 he held Azov as well. Peter was
successful because he recognized that even a second-rate Western power,
such as Sweden now was, could not be defeated without a mastery of
Western military and naval technique, and that a Western-style Russian
army and navy could not be created without the Westernization of
Russia's civil administration and of the industrial sector of her economy.

Peter had a passion and a gift for technology that would have been
precocious even in a contemporary Netherlander. In the preceding
generation in England the founders of the Royal Society had recognized

that technicians and men of science had much to learn from each other. Peter was a practising technician; he worked with his own hands. This was a matter of course for an Ottoman Padishah; to master some practical trade was a compulsory part of a Padishah's education; but it was not in the tradition of a Byzantine-style Muscovite autocrat whose dynasty's founding father had been a Patriarch of Moscow.

The bent of Peter's genius was highly individual, and its appearance in the heir to the Muscovite Tsardom was an unforeseeable coincidence. It was also a coincidence that Peter was born in the first generation in which it was feasible—thanks to a recent spiritual revolution in the Western World—for non-Westerners to adopt Western techniques without being compelled to swallow the Western civilization whole, including its religion. A century earlier, an attempt to Westernize Russia might have ended, as the attempts to Westernize Japan and Abyssinia had ended, not in even a partial success, but in a radical anti-Western reaction. Thus Peter's personality, appearing when and where it did, had a momentous effect on the course of mankind's history.

[78]

THE ISLAMIC WORLD, 1555–1768

FOR a century and a half, 1555–1707, three great Islamic empires—the Ottoman, the Safavi, and the Timurid Mughal—co-existed with each other and embraced, between them, the greater part of the Islamic World. The Ottoman Empire was about 200 years older than the Safavi Empire and about 250 years older than the Timurid Mughal Empire, if we date the foundation of this third of the post-Mongol Islamic empires from Humayun's re-entry into Delhi in 1555, and not from his father Babur's invasion of India in 1525–6. In the year 1555 the Ottoman Empire was at its zenith and was on the point of declining. The Timurid Mughal Empire in India was at its zenith in the reigns of Akbar (1556–1605) and Jahangir (1605–27). Shah Abbas I's reign (1588–1629) was the zenith of the Safavi Empire.

The Ottoman Empire's decline was caused by a simultaneous inflation of the monetary currency and of the personnel of the Padishah's slave-household. The monetary inflation created an economic crisis and a consequent outbreak of disorder among public employees who found that their pay was losing its purchasing power. This economic and social derangement was due to the influx into the Old-World Oikoumenê of silver from the mines in the Spanish Empire in the Americas, and this influx was beyond the Ottoman Government's control. However, the consequent disorders in the Ottoman Empire might have been less violent if the discipline of the Padishah's slave-household had not already been impaired by the progressive relaxation of the rule that the sons of imperial slaves were disqualified, by having been born as freemen and Muslims, for entry into their Christian-born enslaved fathers' career.

Originally the sole exception to this rule had been the admission of the sons of household cavalrymen. Süleiman I (ruled 1520–66) had begun to extend this privilege to the sons of janizaries. This concession was confirmed in 1566 by Selim II, and Murad III (ruled 1574–95) made all free Muslims eligible. Consequently, between 1566 and 1598, the number of janizaries on the pay-rolls rose from about 12,000 to 101,600–not to speak of 150,000 unpaid candidates waiting for places. The *ichoghlanlar*, who staffed the higher administrative service, were still recruited by the conscription of Christian children, but the practice was abandoned in the course of the seventeenth century, and the Ottoman Government now had to enlist the ability of its Christian subjects without enslaving them or converting them. Meanwhile, the janizaries ceased to be an efficient military force and turned into a turbulent urban mob.

Nevertheless, Ottoman military power did not immediately collapse. Baghdad, recovered in 1623 for the Safavi Empire by Shah Abbas I, was reconquered in 1638 for the Ottoman Empire by Murad IV (1623–40). In 1682–3 the Osmanlis were able to besiege Vienna for the second time. Their failure, once again, to take Vienna brought upon them the greatest reverse that they had suffered since the overthrow of Bayezid I by Timur Lenk in 1402. In 1689 the Habsburg Empire's counter-offensive reached the headwaters of the River Vardar; and, though the Osmanlis rallied in 1690, they had to cede Ottoman Hungary and Croatia to the Habsburg Monarchy, and the Peloponnesos to Venice in 1699, and Azov (already taken in 1694) to Russia in 1700. Yet the Ottoman Empire recovered Azov in 1711 and the Peloponnesos, with the addition of Tenos, in 1715. In 1768 the Ottoman Empire still held Bosnia and Belgrade and exercised an effective suzerainty over the two Roumanian principalities to the north of the lower course of the Danube. In fact, the Ottoman Empire emulated its predecessor the East Roman Empire in its ability to recuperate from disasters that had looked as if they were irretrievable.

Moreover, the Ottoman Empire's military and administrative decline did not blight its architectural creativity. The Mosque of Sultan Ahmet I in Istanbul, built in 1609–18, has a grandeur of its own. It is not put out of countenance by its confrontation with the Ayia Sophia. However, no Ottoman public monument except Mehmet I's Green Mosque at Bursa can compare with Shah Abbas's Masjid-i-Shah at Isfahan, built in 1612–37, or with Shah Jahan's Taj Mahal at Agra, built in 1632–53. The Masjid-i-Shah is not only beautiful in itself; its harmonization with the older beautiful buildings adjoining the Maidan-i-Shah is unique. There are also beautiful buildings in Akbar's new city Fathpur Sikri, built in 1569–76. But Fathpur Sikri resembles the acropolis of Athens. It is a congeries of buildings that are beautiful individually but do not harmonize with each other, as the constituents of the Maidan-i-Shah do.

The Timurid Mughal and Safavi Empires did not surpass the contemporary Ottoman Empire in their architecture only. In the Emperors

Shah Abbas I and Akbar they produced two rulers whose vision was not matched by any contemporary Ottoman Padishah's.

Akbar recognized that a Muslim regime in India could not survive for long if it failed to win the assent of its Hindu subjects. In 1564 he abolished the poll-tax on non-Muslims. He demonstrated his power to the Rajput descendants of the Huns and Gurjaras by taking Chitor in 1567–8 (this once impregnable rock was not proof against artillery), but, having intimidated the Rajputs, Akbar conciliated them, and this was wise, since they were the most martial of the Hindu peoples before the rise of the Marathas and the Sikhs, and Rajasthan, where the Rajputs had congregated since the Muslim conquest of the Jumna–Ganges basin in the twelfth century, was the nearest to Delhi of all the regions in India in which the Hindus had preserved their autonomy.

However, Akbar's conciliatoriness to his Hindu subjects was not prompted solely by political considerations; it was partly inspired by an ambition to break down the traditional barriers between the historic higher religions. Akbar initiated a series of debates between representatives of Islam, Hinduism, Zoroastrianism, and Roman Catholic Christianity, and in 1582 he promulgated a new religion of his own, the Din-i-Ilahi ('the Divine Religion'), which, so he hoped, would unite all the older religions by transcending each of them.

The first call on Akbar's time and energy was necessarily the organization and expansion of his empire. Akbar profited by the administrative and financial ability of the Bengali Afghan Emperor Sher Shah Sur, who had evicted Akbar's father Humayun from India in 1539–40. In his brief reign (1540–5), Sher Shah had created an excellent administrative and fiscal organization and postal service, and these assets were inherited from him by Akbar.

Shah Abbas I was less fortunate than Akbar. He had to rebuild the Safavi Empire's structure from the foundations. He had inherited a Farsi-speaking urban and agricultural population that had been converted to Shi'ism forcibly by his ancestor Shah Isma'il, and an unruly expatriate Türkmen soldiery, who were Shi'i refugees from the Ottoman and Mamluk Empires. He brought his Türkmens to heel partly by winning the loyalty of a portion of them and partly by creating a new army on the model of the Ottoman Padishah's slave-household, including regiments of musketeers and artillerymen. These were inferior to their Ottoman counterparts, but, now that the Ottoman Empire was in decline, Abbas I's new model was sufficiently effective to succeed in recovering much of the territory that the Safavis had lost to the Osmanlis since 1514. In 1622 Abbas I also recovered Hormuz from the Portuguese. He replaced Hormuz by a new port, Bandar Abbas, on the mainland.

In 1598 Abbas I had given his empire a new capital at Isfahan. This was out of range of the Ottoman army, but it was not out of range of the Safavis' Afghan subjects in the north-east corner of their empire. Like the Kurds in the debatable borderland between the Safavi and Ottoman Empires, the Afghans were warlike highlanders whose mother-tongue was a non-Farsi Iranian language. Neither of these two peoples had yielded to Shah Isma'il's pressure to embrace Twelve-Imam Shi'ism; neither of them was friendly to the Safavi regime, and in 1722 a band of Afghan insurgents occupied Isfahan. The Safavi Empire disintegrated, and in 1724 the Ottoman and Russian Empires agreed to partition their fallen neighbour's derelict western provinces. However, in 1729 a Khorasani Türkmen soldier, Nadir Quli, drove the Afghans back into their highlands and eventually recovered all the ex-Safavi territory that the Russians and Osmanlis had occupied.

In other directions, Nadir took the offensive. In 1739 he sacked Delhi; in 1740 he occupied Uzbekistan up to the south bank of the River Oxus. In 1736 he had had himself crowned Shah and had sought to reconvert Iran to the Sunnah; but the Ottoman Government rejected his terms for religious reunion, and his Iranian subjects remained faithful to the Shi'ism that had been their national religion for the last two centuries. In 1747 Nadir Shah was assassinated and Iran was left in political chaos.

The Timurid Mughal Empire had disintegrated already. Akbar's second successor, Shah Jahan (ruled 1628–58), had abandoned Akbar's policy of conciliating the Hindus and had at the same time taken the offensive against the independent Muslim states in the Deccan. Shah Jahan's successor Aurangzeb (ruled 1659–1707) had gone farther. He had put to death the ninth Sikh guru, Teg Bahadur, in 1675; he had re-imposed the poll-tax on non-Muslims in 1679; and he had driven the Rajputs, hitherto the Mughals' allies, to take up arms against him in 1680–1.

In 1689–91 Aurangzeb imposed his suzerainty on the south of Peninsular India, right down to the tip. Meanwhile, he had brought upon himself a formidable Hindu counter-offensive. The Marathas possessed abundant natural fastnesses in the Western Ghats, and they found a national leader in Shivaji (1627–80). In 1670 the elusive Marathi light cavalry levied tribute in Mughal territory for the first time. In 1674 Shivaji had himself crowned as an independent Hindu ruler. After Aurangzeb's death in 1707, the disintegration of the Mughal Empire was rapid. The Marathas came within range of Delhi in 1737; Nadir Shah sacked Delhi in 1739; the Abdali Afghan Ahmad Shah Durrani— the founder of an enduring successor-state of Nadir Shah's ephemeral empire—sacked Delhi in 1757 and defeated the Marathas in a trial of strength in 1758–61.

For the next phase of Indian history, the defeat of the Marathas by the Afghans was less decisive than the contemporaneous defeat of the French by the British. Even before the British had completed the virtual elimination of their French competitors, they had taken the first step towards making themselves the Mughals' heirs. In 1757–65 the British East India Company became the virtual sovereign of Bengal, Bihar, and Orissa under the camouflage of serving as the Mughal Imperial Government's provincial revenue-collector.

The Mughal Empire's successor in India was the British East India Company and eventually the British Crown, but, astride the Hindu Kush, the Abdali Afghan state, founded by Ahmad Shah in 1747, still held in the 1970s a bunch of territories that had once belonged to the Mughals and to Nadir Shah. At the opposite end of the Islamic World, Morocco had managed to maintain its independence against both the Ottoman and the Spanish Empires. In 1579 the Moroccans had annihilated an invading Portuguese army. In 1591 they had crossed the Sahara and had conquered for themselves a colonial empire in the western Sudan. This feat was still more remarkable than the Cossacks' contemporary feat of crossing the Urals.

The Moroccans, like the Cossacks, were victorious because they were equipped with fire-arms, which their opponents lacked. Superiority in fire-power—in this case in artillery as well as in small-arms—also accounts for the Osmanlis' military ascendancy over the Safavis. The military prowess of the Moroccans in the western Sudan and the naval prowess in the Mediterranean of the Ottoman ruling minorities in the virtually independent Ottoman dominions Algeria, Tunisia, and Tripolitania was largely due to the local Muslims' reinforcement by foreign recruits who were masters of the contemporary technological skills of Western Christendom. These recruits included Muslim refugees from Spain, converted Western Christian prisoners of war, and Western immigrants who had 'turned Turk' because this opened for them careers that would not have been within their reach at home.

It has been noted already that Peter the Great's victory over the Swedes was his reward for having raised Russian technology to the contemporary Western level. However, Western technology had not yet reached a level at which it could prevail against less well equipped adversaries who were favoured by their terrain. The Mughal artillery, even though it was partly serviced by Western mercenaries, could not subdue the Marathas' natural fastnesses in the Ghats. The Osmanlis, who were still holding their own against Western, Russian, and Iranian armed forces, were unable to prevent the rise of the Wahhabi power in central Arabia, which was insulated from the Ottoman dominions by a ring of deserts. Muhammad b. Abd-al-Wahhab (1703–92) was a fanatical adherent of the puritanical Hanbalite school of Sunni Islamic law who made the fortune of the House of Saʿud—petty rulers of one small central Arabian oasis—by converting its reigning representative in 1745. By 1773 the Wahhabi Saʿudis had subjected the rest of central Arabia to their rule.

EASTERN ASIA, 1644–1839

Of all the non-Western regional civilizations, the East Asian was the last to experience the impact of modern Western civilization forcefully enough to produce a revolutionary effect on the course of the assaulted civilization's history. During the years 1622–41 Japan insulated herself almost completely. Japanese subjects were debarred from going abroad; the only foreigners who were still allowed to reside in Japan were Chinese and Dutch businessmen; and these were confined to a single Japanese port. In China Westerners were still allowed to transact commercial business and to reside in the Portuguese settlement at Macao and on an islet adjoining Canton, but, from 1760 onwards, Western traders were not admitted to any other Chinese port, and Chinese subjects were forbidden in 1723 to profess Christianity (as Japanese subjects had been forbidden in 1597 and in 1606). Obdurate Chinese Christians were then persecuted. In China Christianity was not suppressed as effectively as it had been in Japan in 1612–38, but, from 1723 onwards, China, too, insulated herself from the West, even though her self-insulation was not so rigorous as Japan's and Abyssinia's.

Though the volume of China's trade with the West during the years 1644–1839 was greater than that of Japan, not only absolutely, but also relatively to the scale of China's wealth and population, China, during this period, had even less need than Japan for commercial relations with the West. China continued to be virtually self-sufficing economically, and the eventual increase of facilities in China for foreign trade was imposed on the Chinese Government, against its will, as the penalty for China's defeat in the Anglo-Chinese War of 1839–42. As for Japan, her gross national product increased greatly during the period of her economic self-isolation (1641–1853).

On the cultural plane, China under the Ch'ing (Manchu) dynasty continued to be as inward-looking and as backward-looking as she had been under the Ming dynasty. Under the Ming this had been the Chinese cultural reaction to the experience of having been conquered and ruled by the pastoral nomad Mongols. The Manchus, unlike the Mongols, were non-pastoral barbarians who embraced Chinese culture whole-heartedly and successfully. The only non-traditional genres of Chinese literature that continued to flourish in the Ch'ing Age were the novel and the drama—a legacy from the Yüan (Mongol) Age of Chinese history which had survived the Ming Age's archaistic bent.

In the Ch'ing Age Chinese Confucian scholars carried archaism to its logical conclusion. They rejected both the current varieties of neo-Confucianism—Chu Hsi's version of it, which had been the officially established one, and Wang Yang-ming's. The Ch'ing-Age scholars' objective was to disinter and re-establish the Confucianism of the Emperor Han Wu-ti's day, when Confucianism had been first 'established' as the Chinese Empire's official philosophy. Ch'ing-Age scholars did critical work on the current versions of the texts of the Confucian canon of scripture. Their scholarship is comparable to that of contemporary Western students of the pre-Christian Greek and Latin literature. But the Ch'ing scholars did not perceive how far the Han-Age version of Confucianism had departed from the original philosophy of Confucius and Mencius.

While neo-Confucianism of both varieties was being impugned in China, Chu Hsi's version of it was being promoted in Japan by Ieyasu and his successors in the Tokugawa Shogunate because they believed that the inculcation of Confucian ethics would fortify their own political regime. The Tokugawa disapproved of Wang Yang-ming's neo-Confucianism on the same criterion, but nevertheless Wang Yang-ming won disciples in Japan in the Tokugawa Age, and there were also some Tokugawa-Age Japanese Confucianists who followed their Chinese contemporaries in seeking to revert to the Confucianism of Han Wu-ti's time.

Though Confucianism was favoured by the Tokugawa, Buddhism was not repressed. Indeed, the Shogun Iemitsu (1623–51) required every Japanese subject to register as a lay associate of some Buddhist temple as a proof that he was not a Christian. Moreover, there was a continuing spontaneous loyalty to the various sects in which Buddhism had been acclimatized culturally in Japan. At the same time there was a revival of interest in, and sentiment for, Shinto, which was attractive to nationalist-minded Japanese because it was a native Japanese religion, not a Chinese or Indo-Chinese import.

The Ch'ing (Manchu) Emperors K'ang-hsi (ruled 1672–1722) and Ch'ien-lung (ruled 1736–96) followed the example of the Ming Emperor Yung-lo in making collections of extant Chinese literature of all ages. K'ang-hsi's collection, which was a compendium, though a massive one, was printed in 5,000 volumes in 1728. Ch'ien-lung's collection was un-abridged; it ran to 36,000 volumes; and seven fair copies of this, in addition to the original rough copy, were made in manuscript. This assemblage of Chinese literature gave Ch'ien-lung an opportunity for stigmatizing and suppressing books that were politically objectionable from his point of view. K'ang-hsi produced a dictionary, and Ch'ien-lung a number of encyclopaedias in which he presented his version of Chinese political institutions.

The Ch'ing dynasty successfully accomplished three military tasks: the suppression of the anti-Manchu resistance-movement in the south, the checking of the Russians' advance in the Amur basin, and the crushing of the pastoral nomad western Mongol (Dzungar, Ölöd, Calmuck) empire in the north-west. The frontier within which the Russians had been confined in 1658 was confirmed by Sino–Russian treaties in 1689 and 1727. The western Mongols were the Manchus' most formidable military adversaries in the age that ended in 1839.

The western Mongols had followed suit to their eastern kinsmen in becoming converts to Tibetan Tantric Mahayana Buddhism at some date in the last quarter of the sixteenth century. The Mongols had been converted by the Yellow-Hat sect, and in 1641–2 one of the western Mongol tribes had installed the head of this sect, the Dalai Lama, in Lhasa under Mongol rule, after having crushed the Tibetan supporters of the rival Red-Hat sect. The war-lord of the Dzungar western Mongols, Galdan, annexed, in and after 1670, the Turkish-speaking Muslim population in what is now the Chinese province of Sinkiang (the Tarim basin, together with some strategically important territory to the north-east of it); in 1696 Galdan invaded eastern Mongolia, which was under Manchu suzerainty, but he was defeated by K'ang-hsi's artillery. Galdan's aggression was supported by the western Mongols' Tibetan agent at Lhasa; this provoked a competition between the Dzungars and the Manchus for the control of the Dalai Lama; and the competition was won by the Manchus in 1750.

Ch'ien-lung then attacked the Dzungars in their home country in the gap between the T'ien Shan and the Altai Mountains. He crushed them in 1755–7, and in 1758–9 he subjugated the Dzungars' former Muslim dependency in present-day Sinkiang. The Dzungar steppe-empire was the last explosive one of the Eurasian steppe, though on the Arabian steppe the Wahhabis continued to be explosive until after the First World War. The fate of Eurasian pastoral nomadism had been sealed in 1652, when the encirclement of the Eurasian steppe was revealed by a collision in the Amur basin between two sedentary powers, the Manchu and the Russian Empires, each equipped with fire-arms.

The Manchus' victory over the main body of the western Mongols was confirmed in 1771 by the eastward migration, from Russian to Manchu territory, of part of the Calmuck horde which, *c.* 1613, had established itself in the area between the lower courses of the rivers Volga and Don. The remnant of the western Calmucks that stayed to the west of the Volga was impotent. In the Russo–Turkish peace-treaty of Küçük Kainarca (1774) the suzerainty over the Khanate of the Crimea, which was the last surviving successor-state of the Golden Horde, was transferred from the Ottoman Empire to the Russian Empire, and in 1783 the Crimea was annexed to the Russian Empire outright. Meanwhile the conversion of the Mongols to Buddhism was reducing this people's bellicosity, and was easing its population pressure, by opening for its young men a career as celibate monks. In combination, these changes in the fortunes of the Eurasian pastoral nomads reduced them to quiescence, and this eliminated from the life of the Old-World Oikoumenê a dynamic element that had been playing a major role in history for nearly 4,000 years.

From 1757 onwards China was relieved of the Eurasian nomad barbarian menace to which she had been subject for at least 2,000 years. Thereafter, Ch'ien-lung indulged in southward offensive campaigns: against Burma (1766–70), against Vietnam (1788–9), and against Nepal (1790–2). But Ch'ien-lung's military expansion masked, like Aurangzeb's, his empire's contemporary domestic social and economic weaknesses.

The most serious of these weaknesses was a portentous increase in the size of China's population during the century ending in 1839. The recorded figures may not be correct, but it is certain that, during these hundred years, the increase in the population outran the increase in China's food-supply that had been achieved during the preceding century. The food-supply had been increased by the introduction from the Americas of crops that could be grown on soils which had previously been unused because they were unsuitable for growing rice. However, some of these soils were on hill-sides that eventually became denuded as a result of their having been stripped of their natural forest cover. Before the close of Ch'ien-lung's reign, the real income per head of the Chinese peasantry must have begun to decline.

In Japan during the first century of the Tokugawa regime the population increased by perhaps fifty per cent. By 1721 it had risen to nearly 30,000,000, but, from that date till the ending of Japan's self-insulation in the sixth and seventh decades of the nineteenth century, the population remained almost stationary, though agricultural production continued to grow and the commercial and industrial sectors of the Japanese economy continued to expand. The reason why, in Tokugawa Japan, population did not increase *pari passu* with the increase of wealth was that the distribution of wealth was becoming more and more unequal. The increase in the productivity of agriculture was accompanied by the commercialization of agriculture, and this turned a majority of the rural population into landless and impoverished wage-earners, rural and urban. The feudal lords (*daimyo*) and their retainers (*samurai*) were compelled by the Tokugawa Government to live beyond their means. They were deliberately ruined by being required to spend part of every year in the Tokugawa's capital Edo (present-day Tokyo)—one of the Tokugawa's contrivances for keeping them in check.

The beneficiaries were the businessmen. These were a despised new class. Consequently they escaped the heavy taxation that was assessed on agricultural land. Japan's increasing wealth therefore came into the businessmen's hands. The former peasants who had been pushed out of agriculture became the businessmen's industrial employees; the *daimyo* and the *samurai* became the businessmen's debtors. The firm of Mitsui, which is still one of the World's largest business organizations in the 1970s, rose, in the course of about seventy years, to become in 1691 the official bankers for both the Tokugawa Shogunate and the Imperial Court.

When in 1793 an envoy from George III of Britain presented a letter from his sovereign to Ch'ien-lung, the Emperor composed a reply which reveals that he imagined that China was still the World's self-sufficient, impregnable, and dominant 'Middle Kingdom'. Evidently Ch'ien-lung was unaware of the shift in the balance of military power in the West's favour since the first appearance of Westerners in China five and a half centuries earlier. On the other hand, there was at least one man in Japan, Hayashi Shihei (1738–93) who already had some inkling of this. In 1786 he had published a book with the title *A Discussion of the Military Problems of a Maritime Country*. Hayashi Shihei had taken alarm at the maritime activities of the Russians in the northern Pacific. The Russians were Westerners only by adoption. The British, French, and American kinsmen of the Dutch had not yet appeared above Japan's southern horizon.

[80]

THE BIOSPHERE, 1763–1871

In the eventful century 1763–1871, by far the most important event was a sudden vast increase in human power both over human beings themselves and over non-human Nature. This increase in human power was achieved by the combination of a social innovation with a technological one. The efficiency of soldiers and of industrial workers was increased by subjecting them to a strict discipline, by setting them to work with machinery and weapons of an unprecedented potency, and by organizing their work intensively. Disciplined professional armies began to be created in the West towards the close of the seventeenth century. In the later decades of the eighteenth century, the regimentation already imposed in military parade-grounds was applied in civilian factories, and a technique that had been invented for boring cannon-barrels was applied to the fitting of pistons for steam-engines. In the non-military field, the suddenness of this increase in human power justifies its being called a revolution, though the beginning of a technological and economic revolution cannot be dated as precisely as the outbreak of a political revolution or of a war.

The technological and economic revolution that began in Britain in the course of the third quarter of the eighteenth century transformed agriculture, livestock-breeding, and industry. By 1871 this revolution had spread beyond Britain into continental Europe and was starting in North America and in Japan. In the 1970s its momentum is still increasing. No end to this is yet in sight, but by now it is evident in retrospect that the Industrial Revolution reversed the relation between Man and the biosphere.

Man had, of course, already made his mark on the biosphere, but hitherto, Man, like all other animate constituents of the biosphere, had had to keep within the confines of a niche within which the biosphere had tolerated his presence. Any species that trespassed beyond tolerable limits had exposed itself in the past to the risk of being extinguished. In fact, all species, Man included, had lived hitherto at the biosphere's mercy. The Industrial Revolution exposed the biosphere to the risk of being extinguished by Man. Since Man is rooted in the biosphere and could not survive apart from it, Man's acquisition of the power to make the biosphere uninhabitable is a threat by Man to Man's own survival.

The increase in human power during the later decades of the eighteenth century was achieved locally in Britain, but this British achievement had been emulated in other Western countries by 1871, and this had given the West as a whole a temporary ascendancy over the rest of the Oikoumenê. The domination of the World by the West is the second important event of the century 1763–1871. The third important event of this century is the reaction in some non-Western countries against Western pressure. In citing the events of this century in the order of their relative importance, the fourth and last place must be assigned to the West's domestic affairs. The Industrial Revolution cannot be reckoned to be just one of these. Though it started in a Western country, the Industrial Revolution is an event of a biospherical magnitude.

The objective of the British makers of the Agricultural and Industrial Revolutions was to achieve a maximum increase in the production of material wealth. This was timely; for, in the immediately preceding generation, the population of Britain and of some other Western countries had begun to increase at an accelerating rate, like the population of China since the seventeenth century. The innovators' intention, however, was not to meet a collective need; it was to benefit themselves individually. They did increase the gross national product to a dramatic degree, but they also increased both the inequality of the shares in which the gross product was distributed and the inequality in the distribution of the ownership of the land and the plant that were the instruments of production.

Some traditional but relatively inefficient ways of working—for instance, small-scale subsistence-farming and the combination of this with small-scale industrial work—mainly spinning and weaving—were put out of action permanently. Production, both agricultural and industrial, was now organized in elaborately and expensively equipped large-scale units. These simultaneous changes started a flow of population out of the countryside into the new industrial cities. At the same time it deprived most of the migrants of any shadow of economic independence that they may previously have retained. In the rapidly increasing population the percentage of employees whose only means of subsistence was the sale of their services rose steeply by comparison with the percentage of employers and of self-employed persons.

These changes in the conditions of life and work and in the distribution of income and property increased the gross national product at the cost of inflicting injustice as well as suffering. There is no objective standard for assessing what would have been the equitable allocation of the former common land that was enclosed and was transferred to private ownership by successive Acts of Parliament. The equitable shares of entrepreneurs, investors, and employees in the profits of industry are also disputable. But it is certain that the enclosures made it impossible for many rural small-holders to continue to earn a living on the land, and that, when these former peasants became industrial workers, they were barely able to subsist on their wages.

These were paradoxical and unhappy human consequences of an increase in the production of material wealth. The cause of this social miscarriage was the motive of the entrepreneurs by whom the Industrial Revolution was launched. Their stimulus was greed, and greed was now released from the traditional restraints of law, custom, and conscience. In an influential book, *An Inquiry into the Nature and Causes of the Wealth of Nations*, published in 1776, the Scottish professor, Adam Smith, declared that, if every individual were set free to pursue his own personal economic interest, this would produce the best economic result for society as a whole. The reservations with which Adam Smith himself presented his thesis were ignored, and anyway the thesis itself was implausible. The increase of productivity through the freer play given to greed was accompanied by the waste and chaos of competition, and unrestricted economic competition made many more victims than victors.

The industrial workers became a new social class which was alienated from the society that had called it into existence but had not given it a fair deal. The only weapon at the industrial workers' disposal for self-defence was combination for collective bargaining with their employers. The necessary condition for successful collective bargaining was a monolithic solidarity. The workers therefore subjected themselves to a tyranny of their own in order to combat the tyranny that their employers had imposed on them. 'Blacklegs' who broke the ranks were intimidated into conforming. In Britain, combination, prohibited by law in 1799, was made legal in 1824–5. The class-war had begun, and it spread, with the Industrial Revolution itself, from Britain to other countries.

The workers' employers and opponents, the entrepreneurs, were, on the whole, ruthless, but they were also quick-witted, daring, and indomitable. Richard Arkwright (1732–92), who made a fortune by patenting inventions that were probably not his own, was more typical than James Watt (1736–1819), an inventor who was fortunate in finding successive partners who enabled him to reap for himself some material reward from his genius. Most of the makers of the inventions that were of capital importance for the Industrial Revolution lost the material reward to entrepreneurs who were more businesslike. Most of them also groped their way to their inventions empirically. Watt was exceptional: in him science and technology were fruitfully mated. His inspiration at the University of Glasgow came to fruition in Matthew Boulton's factory at Birmingham. Watt had not had a university education, but he had profited intellectually by his friendship with a professor of chemistry, Joseph Black (1728–99). In the nineteenth century, academic chemists, especially at German universities, began to apply their science to industrial processes directly and systematically.

Watt's decisive improvements in the steam-engine made it serviceable for industrial production and for traction, as well as for pumping, which had been its earlier use. The first steam-ship plied in 1807, the first steam-driven locomotive ran on rails in 1829. A steam-engine is a machine, and the use of machinery is the Industrial Revolution's salient technological feature. Man's tools are coeval with mankind itself, but a tool merely augments human muscle-power without taking its place. For instance, a human hand's power is augmented by using a spear-thrower, spade, oar, or bow; but these tools work only while they are being wielded. A machine relieves Man from doing any of the physical work himself. The machine does this for him and does it on a scale and at a speed beyond Man's own physical capacity. When a man has constructed a machine, he has only to set it to work, to superintend it, and to keep it in working order. A rowing-boat is propelled by the physical power of human arms augmented by the use of oars. A sailing-ship is propelled by the wind, and the steersman who is needed to guide it would not have the physical strength to propel it himself. A sailing-ship is a machine, and so, by the same definition, is a gun, in contrast to a bow.

Sailing-ships were invented about 5,000 years before the start of the Industrial Revolution in Britain, but, until the Industrial Revolution, the use of machinery, as distinct from the use of tools, was still rare. It now became normal; and the forms of inanimate physical energy that were harnessed in machines did not remain confined to winds, running water, explosives, and steam. In 1844 electricity was used successfully to transmit a message by telegraph. The invention of metallic tools had called into existence a new profession, the smith's. The invention of steam-driven machines now called into existence another new profession, the engineer's.

Wind-power and water-power have two merits: they are clean and they are inexhaustible. Steam has to be generated by burning a fuel, and the smoke that is a by-product of burning coal-fuel pollutes. This was immediately evident and obnoxious, but it was tolerated as being no more than a local nuisance. It was not till the Industrial Revolution had been in progress for two centuries that mankind realized that the effects of mechanization were threatening to make the biosphere uninhabitable for all species of life by polluting it, not locally, but globally, and uninhabitable for Man in particular by using up non-replaceable natural resources that had become indispensable for him.

Before the Industrial Revolution, Man had devastated patches of the biosphere. For instance, he had caused mountain-sides to be denuded of soil by felling the trees that previously had saved the soil from being washed away. Man had cut down forests faster than they could be replaced, and he had mined metals that were not replaceable at all. But, before he had harnessed the physical energy of inanimate nature in machines on the grand scale, Man had not had it in his power to damage and despoil the biosphere irremediably. Till then, the air and the ocean had been virtually infinite, and the supply of timber and metals had far exceeded Man's capacity to use them up. When he had exhausted one mine and had felled one forest, there had always been other virgin mines and virgin forests still waiting to be exploited. By making the Industrial Revolution, Man exposed the biosphere, including Man himself, to a threat that had no precedent.

The Western peoples had begun to dominate the rest of mankind before the Industrial Revolution. In the sixteenth century the Spaniards had subjugated the Meso-American and Andean peoples and had annihilated their civilizations. In the course of the years 1757–64 the British East India Company had become the virtual sovereign of Bengal, Bihar, and Orissa. In 1799–1818 the British subjugated all the rest of the Indian subcontinent to the south-east of the River Sutlej. They had a free hand because they held the command of the sea and because in 1809 they made a treaty with Ranjit Singh, a Sikh empire-builder, in which the two parties accepted the line of the Sutlej as the boundary between their respective fields of conquest. In 1845–9 the British went on to conquer and annex the Sikh empire in the Punjab. Meanwhile, in 1768–74, Russia had defeated the Ottoman Empire decisively; in 1798 the French had temporarily occupied Egypt, and in 1830 they had started to conquer Algeria; in 1840 three Western powers and Russia had evicted the insubordinate Ottoman viceroy of Egypt, Muhammad Ali, from Syria and Palestine. In 1839–42 the British had defeated China dramatically. In 1853 an American naval squadron compelled the Tokugawa Government of Japan to receive a visit from it. The Japanese recognized that they were powerless to prevent this unwelcome visit by force of arms.

These military successes of Western powers and of one Westernized Eastern Orthodox power, Russia, were won at the cost of occasional reverses. In the seventeenth century, the Portuguese were evicted forcibly from both Japan and Abyssinia. A British army that invaded Afghanistan in 1839–42 was annihilated. Yet by 1871 the Western powers and Russia were dominant throughout the World.

Even before the Industrial Revolution in Britain the Tsar of Russia, Peter the Great, had recognized that the only means by which a non-Western state could save itself from falling under Western domination was the creation of a new-model army on the pattern of the Western armies that were being created in Peter's time, and Peter also saw that this Western-style army must be supported by a Western-style technology, economy, and administration. The signal military triumphs of the Western powers and of a Westernized Russia over non-Westernized states between 1757 and 1853 moved the rulers of some of the threatened states to do what Peter the Great had done.

Eminent examples of Westernizing statesmen in the first century after the beginning of the Industrial Revolution in Britain are Ranjit Singh (ruled 1799–1839) the founder of the Sikh successor-state, in the Punjab, of the Abdali Afghan Empire; Muhammad Ali, the Ottoman Padishah's viceroy in Egypt from 1805 to 1848; the Ottoman Padishah Mahmud II (ruled 1808–39); King Mongkut of Thailand (ruled 1851–68); and the band of Japanese statesmen that, in the Emperor's name, liquidated the Tokugawa regime and took the government of Japan into its own hands in 1868. These Westernizing statesmen have had a greater effect on the history of the Oikoumenê than any of their Western contemporaries. They have kept the West's dominance within limits, and they have done this by propagating, in non-Western countries, the modern West's way of life.

While the achievements of all the Westernizers mentioned above are remarkable, the Japanese makers of the Meiji Revolution were outstandingly successful. They themselves were members of the hitherto privileged, though impoverished, traditional military class, the *samurai*; the Tokugawa Shogunate succumbed after offering only a minimal resistance; a majority of the *samurai* acquiesced peacefully in the forfeiture of their privileges; a minority of them that rebelled in 1877 was easily defeated by a new Western-style Japanese conscript army composed of peasants who, before 1868, had been prohibited from bearing arms.

Muhammad Ali and Mahmud II did not have so smooth a start. Like Peter the Great, they found that they could not begin to build up a Western-style army till they had liquidated a traditional soldiery. Peter had massacred the Muscovite *Streltsy* ('Archers') in 1698–9; Muhammad Ali massacred the Egyptian Mamluks in 1811, and Mahmud II massacred the Ottoman janizaries in 1826. The new Western-style armies all gave a good account of themselves in action. Muhammad Ali began building his new army in 1819 and a navy in 1821; in 1825 his well-drilled Egyptian peasant conscript troops almost succeeded in re-sub-jugating for his suzerain Mahmud II the valiant but undisciplined Greek insurgents. The Greeks were saved only by the intervention of France, Britain, and Russia, who destroyed the Egyptian and Turkish fleets in 1827 and compelled Muhammad Ali's son Ibrahim to evacuate Greece in 1828. In 1833 Ibrahim conquered Syria and was only pre-vented from marching on Istanbul by Russia's intervention on Mahmud II's behalf. Muhammad Ali's army was more than a match for Mah-mud's because he had been able to make an earlier start in building it up. Mahmud could not start before 1826, the year in which he destroyed the janizaries; yet, in the Russo–Turkish war of 1828–9, his new-model peasant conscript army put up a much stiffer resistance than the old Ottoman army in the Russo–Turkish wars of 1768–74, 1787–92, and 1806–12.

Ranjit Singh, like his contemporary Muhammad Ali, engaged former Napoleonic officers as instructors. The British succeeded in defeating the Western-trained Sikh army in 1845–6 and again in 1848–9, but these two wars cost the British a greater effort and heavier casualties than their previous conquest of the whole of India outside the Punjab.

Rulers who set out to Westernize non-Western countries could not do this solely with the aid of a few Western advisers and instructors. They had to discover or create, among their own subjects, a class of Western-educated natives who could deal with Westerners on more or less equal terms and could serve as intermediaries between the West and the still un-Westernized mass of their own fellow-countrymen. In the seventeenth and eighteenth centuries the Ottoman Government had found this newly needed class, ready to hand, among Greek Ottoman subjects who were acquainted with the West through having been educated there or having had commercial relations with Westerners. Peter the Great in Russia, Muhammad Ali in Egypt, and the British in India had to create the intermediary class that they, too, needed. In Russia this class came to be called the *intelligentsia*, a hybrid word composed of a French root and a Russian termination. During the years 1763–1871, an intelligentsia was called into existence in every country that either fell under Western rule or saved itself from suffering this fate by Westernizing itself suffici-ently to succeed in maintaining its political independence. Like the industrial entrepreneurs and the wage-earning industrial workers who made their appearance in Britain in the course of this century, the non-Western intelligentsia was a new class, and by the 1970s it had made at least as great a mark on mankind's history.

The intelligentsia was enlisted or created by governments to serve these governments' purposes, but the intelligentsia soon realized that it held a key position in its own society, and in every case it eventually took an independent line. In 1821 the ex-Ottoman Greek Prince Alexander Ypsilantis's invasion of the Ottoman Empire taught the Ottoman Government that its Greek intelligentsia was a broken reed. In 1825 a conspiracy of Western-educated Russian military officers against Tsar Nicholas I was defeated and was suppressed, but it was a portent of things to come, and this not only in Russia but in a number of other Westernizing countries.

To live between two worlds, which is an intelligentsia's function, is a spiritual ordeal, and in Russia in the nineteenth century this ordeal evoked a literature that was not surpassed anywhere in the World in that age. The novels of Turgenev (1818–83), Dostoyevsky (1821–81), and Tolstoy (1828–1910) became the common treasure of all mankind.

Compared with the Industrial Revolution in Britain and with the contemporary impact of the West on non-Western countries, the domestic cultural and political affairs of the West in 1763–1871 were of secondary importance—portentous though they might appear to be if they were viewed in isolation from their global context. In this century the leaders of Western civilization in the arts were Germans. Immanuel Kant (1724–1804) was the greatest Western philosopher, and Goethe (1749–1832) was the greatest Western poet of this age. This German luminary outshines two brilliant English shooting-stars, Shelley (1792–1822) and Keats (1795–1821). Mozart (1756–91) and Beethoven (1770–1827) carried Western 'classical' music to its zenith. It is noteworthy that Germany's cultural eminence in the modern age of Western history has been in inverse ratio to her political power and economic prosperity. German music blossomed after the close of the Thirty Years War, and it wilted after the foundation of the Second Reich.

In the field of science, Edward Jenner (1749–1823) demonstrated in 1798 that immunity from smallpox could be obtained by vaccination, and in 1857 Louis Pasteur (1822–95) demonstrated the existence of bacteria. So long as they had remained unknown, these predators on Man and on his domesticated animals had taken more lives than the carnivores over whom Man had won his ascendancy in the Upper Palaeolithic Age. When bacteria had been identified, they too could be, and were, combated by Man successfully. No deadly enemy of Man now survived in the biosphere except Man himself. The application of science to technology was making Man more and more formidable; the application of it to preventive medicine was causing an accelerating increase in the biosphere's human population by reducing the death-rate faster than the birth-rate was being reduced by contraception. In the same year 1798 in which Jenner demonstrated the efficacy of vaccination against smallpox, T. R. Malthus published his *Essay on Population*, and this book suggested to Charles Darwin (1809–82) his concept of 'the struggle for life' which figures in the sub-title of *The Origin of Species* (1859).

A century before Darwin's time, Buffon had dissented from the Judaic religions' traditional doctrine that the various species of living beings had been created once for all, as distinct and immutable entities, by the fiat of an omnipotent god. Buffon's thesis that the diverse extant species were the product of a process of change in time had been followed up on the geological plane by Charles Lyell (1797–1875), whose *Principles of Geology* (1830–3) had also been read by Darwin. Darwin's thesis shocked orthodox Christians; yet the words 'selection' and 'the preservation of favoured races' reveal that it was a version of the Jewish myth of a 'chosen people'; and, though Darwin eliminated the postulate of a creator god, he replaced this by the hypothesis of an impersonal selective action of Nature on a series of mutations that are observed but are not explained.

Darwin's revolutionary achievement was not his account of the mechanism of biological change; it was his demonstration that life in the biosphere is dynamic, not static. Darwin did in biology what Hegel (1770–1831) had done in philosophy. Hegel had portrayed life in process of change in the time-dimension by converting into the intellectual terms of thesis, antithesis, and synthesis the phenomenon of a sexual act that procreates offspring endowed with features derived from each of its parents. Mendel (1822–84) discovered the laws of genetics; he was able to formulate these laws in quantitative terms, and he published his findings in 1864–6, but these remained unknown to Darwin; they continued to be overlooked until the year 1900.

On the military and political plane, this century saw the achievement of the independence of the United States in the Revolutionary War (1776–83); the restoration of its unity in the Civil War (1861–5); and its geographical expansion across North America from coast to coast (1783–1853). The same century also saw France's repetition, in 1797–1815, by Napoleon, of the attempt to unify the Western World politically under the domination of France that had been made by Louis XIV in the wars of 1667–1713. The aftermath of Napoleon's failure was the creation of an Italian national state in 1859–70 and of a German national state in 1866–71. Thus, in the course of this century, the political organization of the Western part of the World as a congeries of sovereign, independent national states made further progress, and the attempt to unify the West politically suffered a further set-back.

Napoleon's temporary territorial aggrandizement of France was on a much larger scale than Louis XIV's, but, in the interval between the dates of these two successive French military enterprises, the size of the Western World and its annexes had increased more than proportionately.

Louis XIV came nearer to dominating the smaller Western World of the year 1700 than Napoleon came to dominating the far larger Western World of the year 1800. In the meantime, Russia and India and North America had been drawn into the West's ambit; Russia's geographical extent was, in military terms, virtually endless; the West's overseas annexes had grown to be of decisive economic importance; and, during the Napoleonic Wars, these annexes were all at Britain's economic command thanks to her naval ascendancy over France.

Britain's former colonies in North America had won their political independence, but they still found it profitable to trade with Britain, and so did Spain's and Portugal's subjects in the Americas when they won a free hand as an incidental consequence of Napoleon's invasion of the Iberian Peninsula. The material resources of the overseas World were Britain's sinews of war and fruits of victory in her contest with Napoleon. By 1821 the former Spanish dominions in the Americas and the former Portuguese dominion, Brazil, had followed suit to the United States in winning their political independence, but on the economic plane the Latin American states had become, and the United States had continued to be, a part of the overseas market for the products of British mechanized industry.

In 1823 the President of the United States, Monroe, proclaimed his famous doctrine. This was a guarantee, by the United States, of the independence of the recently established Latin American states. The Monroe Doctrine was in accord with Britain's interests. Britain's ambitions in Latin America were exclusively economic. She therefore stood to gain by the United States' veto on the political intervention of European powers in Britain's Latin American field of economic enterprise.

The several revolutions that broke out in the Western World in the course of the period 1763–1871 were different in kind from each other. The Industrial Revolution in Britain was technological, economic, and social, not political, though it had a non-revolutionary political sequel when in 1832 the passage of a reform bill by Parliament began the transference of political power in Britain from the rural landowners to the urban middle class. The revolution that turned Britain's former colonies in North America into the United States was not technological, economic, or social; it was solely political. The French Revolution that started in 1789 was political and economic and social. It transferred political power from the Crown to the urban middle class and it transferred the ownership of rural land from the aristocracy to the peasantry in large measure. In Britain contemporaneously the rural small-holders were being either reduced to becoming wage-earning agricultural labourers or were being pushed right out of the countryside to become wage-earning industrial workers in urban factories. By contrast, in the United States the rural freeholders survived and spread into virgin land to the west, where they were followed by land-hungry rural immigrants from Europe. The United States remained, and France became, a community of self-employed citizens, with the major exception of the ex-African Black slaves in the southern states of the American Union and the minor exception of the not yet numerous urban workers in France.

The enslavement of Africans and their importation into the European settlements in the Americas was as wicked a sequel to Columbus's discovery of Western Europe's 'New World' as was the subjugation or extermination of the Americas' pre-Columbian inhabitants. During the period 1763–1871 the juridical status of slavery was abolished in most American countries: in Haiti between 1793 and 1803, in the whole French colonial empire in 1848 and in the British colonial empire in 1833, in the United States in 1863, and in Brazil by stages between 1871 and 1888. Abolition cost Haiti ten years of revolution and war, and it cost the United States the civil war of 1861–5; but, whether slavery was abolished peacefully or by force, it left a legacy of economic and social maladies.

In the United States, and in France down to 1871, the wage-earning industrial employees were still only a minority of the population. The opening-up of virgin soil in the United States and the acquisition of much of the land by the peasantry in France saved these two Western countries from the massive migration of ex-rural workers into the cities that in Britain was the consequence of the Enclosure Acts. But in the United States, France, and Britain alike, the industrial workers remained alienated from the middle-class 'establishment', and they did not succeed in improving their position either by peaceful or by violent action.

The middle-class makers of the French Revolution of 1789 exploited the discontent of the urban proletariat, but they did nothing to relieve its plight. So far from that, they behaved, in this field, like their British opponents. The French middle class, too, swept away the traditional restrictions on the freedom of private economic enterprise which had previously provided some protection for the economically weaker members of society. The slogans *laissez-faire, laissez-passer*—i.e. 'remove restrictions on industrial production and abolish tolls on the transport of goods'—were coined in France, and a law prohibiting combination was enacted in France in 1791, eight years before the enactment of the corresponding law in Britain. In France, attempts by the Parisian proletariat to convert a political revolution into a social one were crushed by military forces in 1795 and 1848 and 1871. The French urban workers were foiled by the concerted action of the middle class and the peasantry. In Britain, the industrial workers placed their hopes in trades unionism and in the progress of political reform beyond the modicum that had been achieved in 1832. The Chartist movement of 1837–48 had a purely political programme, and, though Chartism petered out, a further instalment of political reform was enacted in Britain in 1867–72. However, the partial political enfranchisement of the British industrial working class, like the juridical emancipation of the slaves in the Americas, disappointed the beneficiaries by failing to produce any substantial immediate improvement in their condition.

The spectacle of the industrial workers' tribulations and of the middle class's acquiescence in this social injustice aroused the indignation of Karl Marx (1818–83) and moved him to create the fourth of the Judaic religions. Marxism, like Buddhism, is theoretically atheistic; but, like Darwinism, Marxism provides a substitute for Yahweh, the god of Judaism, Christianity, and Islam. Darwin's substitute is Nature, whose selective action is deemed to preserve 'favoured races'. Marx's substitute for Yahweh is 'historical necessity', and his 'chosen people' is the industrial proletariat. Marx sought to console the proletariat for its present plight by proclaiming the inevitability of an eventual righteous revolution in which the conflict between the proletariat and the middle class would be ended by the establishment of a classless society.

Though Marx did not live to see social injustice redressed, a contemporary Genevan philanthropist, Henri Dunant (1828–1910), did bring about an alleviation of the sufferings of combatant soldiers by securing in 1864 the conclusion of the first Geneva Convention and the establishment of the International Committee of the Red Cross.

During the century 1763–1871 Britain played a leading role, for good or evil, not only in the West but in the World as a whole. In the immediately preceding phase of Western history, Britain had been the winner in a contest with France for the command over North America and over India. By her victory, Britain had opened the way for her own former colonies in North America to throw off British sovereignty and to become an independent United States on the geographical scale of the Russian Empire. Britain herself now unified the whole of the Indian subcontinent politically for the first time in its history, and she succeeded in retaining her hold when the East India Company's Indian troops mutinied in 1857–9. Britain also shared with Russia and Spain the credit, or responsibility, for having defeated Napoleon, and this frustration of the latest attempt to unify the Western World politically condemned the West to remain partitioned among a number of local sovereign independent states in an age in which the Industrial Revolution was equipping states with armaments of unprecedented destructive power. In attacking and defeating China in 1839–42, Britain dealt a mortal blow to a regime that had given peace and stability to the huge Chinese section of mankind for most of the time during the previous two millennia. These were mighty deeds, but Britain's mightiest deed of all in this period was the launching of the Industrial Revolution. In doing this, Britain tipped the balance of power between the biosphere and Man in Man's favour, and this eventually put it in Man's power to make the biosphere uninhabitable for all forms of life, including mankind itself.

[81]

THE BIOSPHERE, 1871–1973

By the 1970s it looked as if the biosphere was in danger of being over-whelmed, polluted, and perhaps ultimately made uninhabitable for any form of life by one of the biosphere's own creatures and denizens, Man. Retrospectively it could be seen that Man's power over the biosphere had been increasing progressively. By the time that Man had become human, he had been stripped of all built-in physical weapons and armour, but he had acquired a conscious intellect which could think and plan, and two physical organs, his brain and his hands, which were the material instruments for his thinking, his planning, and his attempts to achieve his purposes by physical action.

It has been noted already that tools are coeval with human conscious-ness. The capacity to make and use tools enabled Man to hold his own in the competitive arena of the biosphere during the Lower Palaeolithic Age, which embraces by far the greater part of human history to date. Since the beginning of the Upper Palaeolithic Age, perhaps 70,000/ 40,000 years ago, Man has been taking the offensive against the rest of the biosphere; but it is only since the beginning of the Industrial Revolution, no more than two hundred years ago, that Man has become decisively dominant. Within the last two centuries, Man has increased his material power to a degree at which he has become a menace to the biosphere's survival; but he has not increased his spiritual potentiality; the gap between this and his material power has consequently been widening; and this growing discrepancy is disconcerting; for an increase in Man's spiritual potentiality is now the only conceivable change in the constitution of the biosphere that can insure the biosphere—and, in the biosphere, Man himself—against being destroyed by a greed that is now armed with the ability to defeat its own intentions.

In the 1970s the devastating effect of Man's impact on the biosphere is being demonstrated by a number of symptoms. The biosphere's human population is increasing at an accelerating rate, and this growing population is concentrating itself in gigantic cities. Since the majority of mankind is still indigent, the growth of the cities mainly takes the form of a proliferation of parasitic shanty-towns, inhabited by unemployed, and perhaps unemployable, migrants from the rural areas in which the majority of mankind has lived and worked since the invention of agriculture at the beginning of the Neolithic Age. The cities are spreading tentacles round the globe in the form of speed-ways for mechanized overland vehicles and air-lanes for planes. The minority producing industrial commodities, or food-stuffs and organic raw materials, by more and more sophisticated and high-powered mechanical processes is polluting the biosphere's water-envelope and air-envelope with the waste-products of its pacific activities, even when it was not defoliating the flora and killing the fauna (human and non-human alike) by intentionally destructive military operations.

In 1871 and perhaps even as recently as 1944, before the achievement of the technological feat of splitting atoms, it would have seemed incredible that the biosphere's ocean and atmosphere as a whole could ever be polluted lethally by the action of such a puny product of the biosphere as Man. Man's capacity to make the whole biosphere uninhabitable is apparent in the extermination of a number of undomesticated non-human species of living beings, but Man himself and his domesticated animals are not immune. Some of these, too, are being poisoned by unintended consequences of deliberate human activities.

The physical growth of cities has been enormous within the lifetime of someone who was born, as was the writer of the present book, in 1889. I have seen Ankara and Athens transformed from small towns into megalopolises since 1922. Since 1929 the once lovely Japanese countryside adjoining the Shimonoseki Straits has been obliterated under a load of streets and houses. Since the Second World War the locality in London in which I was born and brought up has been transformed, like some localities in Japan, out of all recognition. After this site in London was cleared of houses by German bombs, it was occupied by an elevated throughway for mechanized traffic, and this was a piece of English handiwork.

For a Londoner born in 1889 in a middle-class family, the month of August 1914 made a traumatic break in the century 1871–1973. In contrast to the years 1871–1913, the years 1914–73 were a time of self-inflicted tribulation for all mankind. There were two world wars, in which war—itself a crime—was unprecedentedly lethal and devastating. Genocide was committed by Turks against Armenians, by Germans against Jews, by Hindus and Indian Muslims against each other. The Palestinian Arabs, the Tibetans, and the native African majority of the population of southern Africa were victimized. One of the so-called 'wars of religion' is still being waged savagely in Northern Ireland. The Western middle class, like the non-Western migrants from the country-side into the shanty-towns, has suffered a conspicuous relative deterioration in its way of life. By contrast with the baneful years 1914–73, the years 1871–1913 may wear the appearance of a golden age in the memories of middle-class Westerners who were already adult in 1914 and who survived till the 1970s. However, when the whole century 1871–1979 is reviewed in retrospect, it is evident that the optimism which was the prevailing mood during the years 1871–1913 was unwarranted.

A middle-class Englishman born in 1889 supposed—from the date at which he became conscious of the world around him, until August 1914—that the Earthly Paradise lay only just round the corner. The industrial workers would be given their fair share in mankind's gross product; the installation of responsible parliamentary government would be completed in Germany and would be achieved in Russia; the Christians still left under Ottoman Turkish rule would win their political liberation; and then the millennium would have arrived. In this new Golden Age the non-Christian subjects of Christian empires would remain under Christian rule, but this was better for them than the chaotic conditions of their life before they had forfeited their political independence.

Westerners did not expect to see the abolition of war; some Westerners —for example, some in Germany and some in the Balkan states—not only expected a recurrence of war but positively looked forward to it. But the wars that even the most bellicose-minded German envisaged were short wars of the Bismarckian kind, not counterparts of the long-drawn-out Napoleonic wars or of the devastating Thirty Years War of 1618–48 in Germany or of the more recent devastating civil war of 1861–5 in the United States.

The Sino-Japanese War of 1894–5, the Spanish-American War of 1898, the South-African War of 1899–1902, and the Balkan Wars of 1912–13 were, in fact, local and short, and even the Russo-Turkish War of 1877–8 and the Russo-Japanese War of 1904–5 were only regional conflicts that did not embrace the rest of the World. The immense devastation and destruction of life caused by the outbreaks and the suppressions (1850–73) of the T'ai-p'ing and other rebellions in China against the discredited Manchu regime were discounted by contemporary Westerners as being characteristic of the misery of the life of Oriental peoples where and when these peoples had not yet been reduced to order by the imposition on them of Christian rule. To a middle-class English child of the present writer's generation it seemed in 1897, the year in which the British were celebrating Queen Victoria's diamond jubilee, as if the world into which he had been born had transcended history, since history signified a past age of injustice, violence, and suffering which the 'civilized' nations had left behind, never to recur, so it was naively assumed. Western civilization *was* 'Civilization'. It was unique. Its rise and its world-wide dominance were the inevitable and well-deserved rewards of its merits. 'Civilization' had come to stay. That was why history was now obsolete.

The achievements that were the grounds for this optimism were in truth impressive; yet each of these achievements was imperfect and contained within itself the seeds of future trouble. In the 1970s the flaws seem patent; but between 1871 and 1914 they were not so easy to discern.

For instance, the emancipation of the serfs in Russia in 1861 and the abolition of slavery in the United States in 1863, and the beginning, in 1871, of the abolition of slavery in its last remaining domain, Brazil, looked like glorious milestones on the road towards the millennium. But the emancipation of the Russian serfs had not satisfied their hunger for the ownership of land, and the juridical emancipation of Black slaves had not abolished racial prejudice, discrimination, and conflict. As for the juridically free industrial workers, these had not yet made a Marxist social revolution anywhere, but in Western countries their relative economic position was gradually improving, and this improvement in their conditions of life had been accompanied by an improvement in their physical conditions of work. Yet mechanized work was becoming more and more unsatisfying spiritually with every fresh advance in technology. The invention of the conveyor-belt and the assembly-line had increased productivity and had reduced financial costs at the spiritual price of turning men and women into 'scientifically managed' components of machines. The industrial workers were now better off in material terms, but, now that they were bribed to serve as galley-slaves, they still remained alienated spiritually from the society that had called this new social class into existence to serve the middle class's purposes.

The completion, in 1870–1, of the creation of a German and an Italian national state appeared to have stabilized the political structure of the Oikoumenê. The local sovereign national state was now recognized to have become the standard political unit, and, since 1871, there had been no war, except the Russo-Japanese War of 1904–5, in which two or more great powers had come into conflict with each other. Russia's war with Turkey in 1877–8 and her war with Japan in 1904–5 had each been brought to an end without involving Britain. The Oxus–Jaxartes basin and Türkmenistan, up to the north-western borders of Afghanistan, had been annexed by Russia in 1865–85, and this time, too, a Russo-British war had been averted. Between 1881 and 1904, all but two of the African countries that had still been exempt from West-European rule in 1871 were brought under the direct or indirect control of Britain, France, Germany, Belgium, or Portugal without any war between these West-European competitors for the acquisition of African territory. Abyssinia (having assumed the name Ethiopia, which originally signified the present-day eastern Sudan) took part in the scramble for African territory, and she inflicted a humiliating defeat on Italy in 1896. Liberia, a colonial settlement of liberated American Black slaves, survived thanks to her being virtually a protectorate of the United States. All other African states and peoples lost their independence. After the signal defeat of China by Japan in 1894–5, Britain, Russia, Germany, and France began to partition China among themselves, as they were already partitioning Africa. In Eastern Asia, as in Africa, they avoided falling into war with each other over the division of the spoils.

These seemed to be good auguries for the preservation of peace between the great powers. After the Emperor of Germany, William II, had dismissed Bismarck in 1890, he began to make provocative gestures; yet it still looked as if the Oikoumenê were going to continue to be kept at peace, and at the same time to be kept in order, by co-operation between the powers. There were now eight of these, and only three— Russia, the United States, and Japan—lay outside Europe. Though the European states were sovereign, the present writer found in 1911 that none of them except Roumania and Turkey required a traveller to carry a passport, and in Greek villages he was able to change gold sovereigns and napoleons into silver coins that were as likely to be French or Italian or Belgian as to be Greek. Political frontiers had not yet become either monetary barriers or obstacles to the movements of private persons.

There were, however, some sinister features in the picture. France was not reconciled to the loss of the territory that she had been compelled to cede to Germany in 1871; the inhabitants of this territory were not reconciled to their having become subjects of the Second German Reich. The ceded territory was still being administered as a 'Reichsland'; the German Imperial Government had not ventured to give it the status of one of the Reich's constituent autonomous states. Bismarck had been haunted by 'the nightmare of coalitions', and, after his fall, his nightmare quickly became a reality. France and Russia made an entente, supplemented by a military convention, in 1892–3; France and Britain made an entente in 1904, and Russia and Britain made one in 1907. In 1898 Germany had begun to compete with Britain in naval power. Competitive plans for mobilization and for subsequent naval and military operations were being worked out by the five European powers and Russia.

Since the completion of the establishment of an Italian and a German national state in 1870–1, it had come to be assumed that this was the

natural, normal, and rightful political unit; but this assumption was unsettling; for, though the West-European peoples, including the bilingual
Belgians and the quadrilingual Swiss, had all now secured national states
for themselves, the East-European peoples had not. The Poles, for
instance, had no independent state of their own; they were Russian,
Prussian, or Austrian subjects. The Greek, Bulgarian, Serbian, and
Roumanian national states looked forward to acquiring 'unredeemed
territories' that still remained under Ottoman or Habsburg rule. The
multinational Habsburg Monarchy, which was one of the eight great
powers, had become an anomaly in a world in which national states had
become the standard political units. In the Russian Empire, about one
third of the population were not Great Russians by nationality. The
German national state included unassimilated Polish, Danish, and
French minorities. Italy still had 'unredeemed territories' (the term was
Italian in origin) on the far side of her frontier with the Habsburg
Monarchy. In short, 'the principle of national self-determination', which
had given political stability to Western Europe after its satisfaction there
in 1871, was now an explosive and subversive ideal in Eastern Europe.

Thus the political structure of the Oikoumenê on the eve of the outbreak of the First World War was strained by its failure to conform in
eastern Europe to the pattern of the West-European national state,
which had now become the accepted norm. But the structure would have
remained precarious even if, before 1914, all 'unredeemed territories'
had been united with the national states of their choice, and even if all
subject territories had been transformed into sovereign national states.
The Oikoumenê would still have continued to be partitioned politically
into mutually independent local units, and there would therefore still
have been an unresolved conflict between mankind's political demands
and its economic needs.

The local national state was the political ideal of the Western peoples
and of an increasing number of other peoples that were adopting
Western institutions. The strength of the Western peoples' attachment to
nationalism had been demonstrated by their successful resistance to the
successive attempts of Charles V, Philip II, Louis XIV, and Napoleon
to reimpose on Western Christendom the political unity that it had
possessed in Theodosius I's time and in Charlemagne's. Yet the political
ideal of the national state had been an economic anachronism ever since
the coalescence of the Oikoumenê through the mastering of the technique of oceanic navigation by the Chinese and the Portuguese and the
Spaniards in the fifteenth century; and the economic unification of the
Oikoumenê, which the Portuguese and the Spaniards had begun, had
been carried a long step farther by the Industrial Revolution in Britain.

Till then, most of the goods exchanged in world trade had been luxuries; as a result of the Industrial Revolution the goods exchanged had come to include more and more of the necessities of life. The British entrepreneurs who had launched the Industrial Revolution had won a profitable return on their costly investment in machinery by making Britain 'the workshop of the World'. Thenceforward, Britain exported manufactures, and imported raw materials and food, on a global scale; and world trade retained these global dimensions when, after 1871, Germany, the United States, and other countries deprived Britain of her monopoly by following her lead.

The beginning of the economic unification of the Oikoumenê had been signalized by the invention of the Portuguese ocean-going sailing-ship; its completion was signalized by the inauguration of the International Telegraphic Union in 1864 and of the International Postal Union in 1875. By that time mankind had come to rely on global unification on the economic plane but remained unwilling, on the political plane, to abandon national segregation. This misfit still persists in spite of the havoc it has caused since 1914. The consequent dislocation of human affairs has become so extreme that it now threatens to paralyse the whole of human society except the small surviving minority of farmers, hunters, and food-gatherers who subsist on what they produce or collect for themselves, without being implicated in the world-market.

The modern Western sailing-ship reached its acme in build, rig, and speed during the half-century 1840–90, when it was fighting a losing battle with the steam-ship, a competitor that had been called into existence by the Industrial Revolution. This was also the latest age of the 'classical' style of Western music, which had reached its acme at the turn of the eighteenth and nineteenth centuries in Beethoven's works. The Modern Western style of painting had passed its acme when, after 1600, the primacy had been taken over from the Italians and the Flemings by the Spaniards and the Dutch. The 'classical' sailing-ship was put out of action by Watt's decisive improvement of the steam-engine; the naturalistic style of painting was stultified by the invention of photography. During the outwardly placid and prosperous forty-three years 1871–1913, painters and composers were already deliberately breaking with a long tradition and were groping after radically different forms of expression. Evidently they felt that the 'classical' style of their art had been worked out to a dead end, like an exhausted coal-mine or an effete Chinese dynasty. In the 1970s it could be seen in retrospect that Western artists had been pre-cognizant, during a spell of calm weather, of the storm that hit Western society in the next generation. Artists have psychic antennae that are sensitive, in advance, to portentous coming events.

If we attempt to present a balance-sheet of mankind's experiences and actions in the period 1871–1973, the first feature that we are bound to record is the multitude and magnitude of discoveries and inventions. Western Man had been making notable discoveries and inventions throughout the preceding three centuries, but in the century ending in 1973 he surpassed his previous achievements in these fields. Freud (1856–1939) brought up into consciousness the behaviour of the subconscious levels of the human psyche. Einstein (1879–1955) demonstrated that Newton's physics correspond to reality only within limits. Einstein gave physics a wider range by recognizing that observation is interaction. The observer himself is a part of the physical cosmos whose motion through time and space he is observing. The discovery of the existence and the nature of electrons by J. J. Thomson in 1897 showed that the word 'atom' is a misnomer. An 'atom' proved to be not an indivisible entity; it is a miniature solar system. Its structure was divined by Ernest Rutherford (1871–1937) in 1904. He identified the atom's nucleus, and he succeeded in splitting a nucleus in 1919. The composition of the nucleus itself was revealed by James Chadwick's discovery of the existence and the nature of neutrons in 1932. Meanwhile, these discoveries in the realm of physics had led physicists, on the initiative of Niels Bohr (1885–1962), to recognize an epistemological truth. An identical event is experienced in two ways that not only differ but are incompatible and cannot be experienced simultaneously, yet are both valid and both indispensable.

Rubber had been used for making balls for sinister games in Meso-America before Cortés landed there, and petrol had been a secret component of the East Roman Empire's deadly weapon 'Greek fire'. The years 1871–1973 saw these two raw materials used respectively for making tyres and for fuelling internal-combustion engines. This made it possible to construct viable automobiles and aeroplanes, and the achievement of aviation gave Man the entrée to an element in the biosphere that had previously been the preserve of insects, birds, and bats.

A dramatic advance in geographical and historical exploration was made. Westerners reached both Poles of this planet and landed on Earth's satellite the Moon, and they disinterred eight Troys piled one upon another, besides discovering the Minoan, Mycenaean, and Indus civilizations and detecting that the language conveyed in the 'Linear-B' script is Greek.

The most notable of all the discoveries and inventions that have been made in the course of the last hundred years are those in the fields of medicine and surgery. Progress in the use of anaesthetics (discovered in the 1840s) enabled surgeons to perform previously inconceivable operations, culminating in the transplantation of organs. Mosquitos were discovered to be the carriers of yellow fever and of malaria, and these discoveries, made respectively in 1881 and in 1897–9, enabled preventive medicine to take the offensive against these two diseases. DDT, discovered in 1942, gave Man another weapon against insects, who are Man's principal non-human competitors for the command over the biosphere.

These Western discoveries and inventions were mighty feats of courage and imagination as well as intelligence, but their effects on human affairs were ambivalent. For instance, the new Western technique of aviation, combined with the older Chinese invention of explosives, enabled belligerents to drop bombs from the air, and the use of this blind weapon wiped out the human distinction between combatants and civilians that had been established with so much effort since the close of the seventeenth century. Less than half a century after the discovery of the existence of electrons in 1897, and only thirteen years after the discovery of the existence of neutrons in 1932, two bombs charged with the titanic force released by the fission of the nuclei of atoms were dropped on Hiroshima and Nagasaki. Motor cars gave human beings an unprecedented mobility at the cost of extending the tentacles of the cities into the countryside and congesting the traffic on the roads, as well as in the streets. By 1973 the fumes emitted by cars and planes were threatening to make the biosphere's atmosphere unbreathable.

The reduction of the death-rate and the prolongation of the expectation of life by the triumphant progress of medicine and surgery were benefactions with a backlash. The reduction of the death-rate, shooting ahead of any reduction of the birth-rate, reinforced the acceleration of the increase in the biosphere's human population. Medicine's new capacity for prolonging an individual human being's life make it feasible to prolong life undesirably; and the question whether its prolongation might or might not be desirable in this or that particular case confronts physicians, their patients, and the patients' relatives and friends with previously undreamed-of moral problems.

Before the Industrial Revolution, the two principal functions of governments had been to maintain domestic law and order and to make war on the governments and peoples of foreign states. The inhuman conditions of work and life that the Industrial Revolution imposed on a new social class, the workers in mechanized factories, compelled governments to undertake a third function: the provision for social welfare. The first legislation for the protection of factory workers had been enacted in Britain in 1802. In Germany between 1883 and 1889, Bismarck extended the social field of governmental action by securing the passage of legislation that provided insurance against sickness, accidents, and incapacitation by old age and other causes. These novel German humanitarian measures were being copied in Britain before the outbreak of the First World War.

This recognition that governments have a duty to provide for their subjects' welfare was a beneficent ethical advance in the field of politics. The state has now become a welfare organization, besides continuing to be a law-enforcing and a war-making organization, in most of the World's industrialized countries. However, the welfare state is still a controversial issue. The provision of public services for the benefit of the indigent majority of the population requires the raising of additional public revenue by a steeply graded taxation of the affluent minority. This minority's opposition to welfare legislation is therefore not disinterested, and consequently its declared objection, which is an ethical and psychological one, is suspect. The objection is that the welfare state demoralizes its beneficiaries, and by the 1970s experience has shown that this specious objection has been partly borne out by events. In some of the countries in which public provision for welfare has been carried far, the feeling that it is a man's duty to earn his own living has been weakened, the standard of workmanship has declined, and—more disconcerting still—a rise in the average standard of living has been accompanied by a decline in the standard of honesty. Moreover, there is a residual indigent minority—partly consisting of temporary or permanent immigrants from poorer foreign countries—whose conditions of life, and in particular their housing, continues to be scandalously bad.

In countries in which the private sector of the economy is still predominant and in which the political regime is 'democratic' (i.e. parliamentary), welfare legislation, working together with trades union organization, has enabled the majority of industrial workers to tilt, in their own favour, the balance of power between them and the middle class. Employees in public services which provide for the population's daily material needs are in a particularly strong bargaining position. Cases in point are dockers, miners, and workers in installations for supplying light and heat and water and for disposing of sewage. By comparison, the teaching profession's bargaining-power is weak, since educators cannot paralyse the community's life immediately by striking, though on a longer view their social value is at least as great as that of workers in any other profession.

The trades with great instant bargaining power have become the foremost champions of the economic regime of private enterprise. They have opposed proposals for restricting the freedom of collective bargaining. Their wish to exploit their growing power for their own sectional advantage is natural, and it is also in accordance with the philosophy of *laissez-faire,* which was first invoked by middle-class entrepreneurs to the industrial wage-earners' detriment. Yet it is now apparent that the progressive mechanization of the World's work would make life intolerable for everyone if it were not accompanied by a progressive increase in governmental intervention (that is to say, socialism, an ideology to which industrial workers have always paid lip-service).

While trades unions in trades that hold strategic bargaining positions are asserting their power in countries that have parliamentary political regimes, in the Soviet Union both the industrial and agricultural workers are regimented by an authoritarian government. The Soviet Government subscribes to Marx's ideology but has not departed from the practice of its Tsarist predecessor. Lenin (Vladimir Ilyich Ulianov), 1870–1924, one of the great men of the century, overthrew a regime founded on force by imposing a more potent regime of the same character. Lenin and his successors in the Kremlin also followed Peter the Great's example in modernizing Russia's technology at the maximum possible speed. The Russian revolution of October 1917 was engineered by the Bolshevik ('majoritarian') wing of the Marxist minority of the intelligentsia and received co-operation from the peasantry. The Russian peasants had hoped to gain possession of the land. The French peasants had gained this during the French revolution of 1789–97, but in Communist Russia the land was quickly nationalized and is now being cultivated in large-scale units. The objective was the same as that of the Enclosure Acts in Britain; it was to increase productivity; but in the Soviet Union, to date, this policy has suffered from the peasants' passive resistance.

In its own authoritarian way the Soviet Union, like the contemporary United Kingdom, is a welfare state, in contrast to the previous Tsarist regime in Russia. For instance, literacy has been greatly extended and wealth has been more evenly distributed. But all states alike, whatever their ideological colour, have continued to be war-making institutions. The two world wars, waged in 1914–18 and in 1939–45, surpassed the Chinese civil wars of 1850–73 in the magnitude of the slaughter and devastation that they inflicted. All wars are atrocities, including Bismarckian short wars with limited objectives. The atrociousness of the two great twentieth-century wars was aggravated by 'genocide' (i.e. the wholesale extermination of civilian populations). In the First World War the Turks committed genocide against the Armenians; in the Second World War the Germans committed genocide against the Jews.

The only incidents in the two world wars to which posterity might perhaps be able to look back without being abashed at the spectacle of human wickedness and folly were the Turkish people's resistance in 1919–22 to the recent victors in the First World War and the British people's resistance in 1940–1 to a temporarily victorious Germany. These two peoples had the spirit to resist though they were facing fearful odds and though they had no apparent prospect of escaping defeat and destruction. Both peoples were fortunate in finding leaders—Mustafa Kamal Atatürk and Winston Churchill—who inspired them to rise to the occasion.

Atatürk not only led the Turkish people to victory in a war for self-preservation; he also put them through a Westernizing revolution in which he carried Mahmud II's work to completion. Atatürk, like Lenin, was a member of the intelligentsia who swept away the regime that had called the intelligentsia into existence in his country. Atatürk also acted like Lenin in resorting to the ruthless use of force for performing an urgent task. The Mahatma Gandhi (1869–1948) too was a member of the intelligentsia who accomplished a political revolution; but Gandhi's strategy was non-violent non-cooperation, and his economic objective was, not to complete the incorporation of India in the mechanized world, but to sever India's existing economic ties with it.

Gandhi's countrymen did not respond to his call to revert to pre-mechanical methods of industrial production, and eventually they failed to live up to Gandhi's ideal and practice of eschewing the use of violence. When, in 1947, Britain abdicated and the former British Indian Empire was partitioned between the Indian Union and Pakistan, Hindus and Muslims committed genocide against each other while they were in the act of segregating themselves. This was, in the end, the price of the liquidation of Western imperialism in the Indian subcontinent.

What, then, is the balance-sheet of Western Imperialism, which is one of the salient features of the history of the Oikoumenê during the century ending in 1973?

Western rulers over non-Western peoples have been guilty of atrocities—for instance, the slaughter of Indians by the British at Amritsar in 1919, and the barbarous humiliations that were inflicted on the survivors. But the liquidation of these empires was also accompanied by atrocities committed by the empires' liberated subjects. In the Indian subcontinent the reciprocal slaughter of Muslims and Hindus in 1947 was followed eventually in Bangladesh by the reciprocal slaughter of Urdu-speaking and Bengali-speaking Muslims; and before the Indian Army's operations against the Pakistani Army in Bangladesh there had been hostilities on the western frontier between the British Indian Empire's two original successor-states. The vacuum left elsewhere by the liquidation of the West-European colonial empires opened the way for civil wars, and for atrocities against civilians, in Vietnam, in the Southern Sudan, in Burundi, in the Congo, in Nigeria. These outbreaks of violence were the price of political liberation. The empires had been imposed on their subjects for the empire-builders' own purposes, but an incidental effect had been to give the subject peoples domestic peace so long as the forcibly imposed alien regimes lasted.

By 1973 the non-European territories still under the rule of West-European states had been reduced to a few beach-heads and islands, except for Portugal's possessions on the mainland of Africa. In Southern Africa, however, politically independent settlers of European origin are still ruling over subject African majorities, and in Palestine the homes and property of the indigenous Palestinian Arabs have been expropriated by the immigrant Israelis. Moreover, in a number of African countries, West-European rule has been replaced by the domination of one local African people over its weaker neighbours. The former Russian and Chinese Empires' rule over non-Russian and non-Chinese Asian subject peoples survived the introduction of Communist regimes. The overland empires of these two continental nations have outlived the West-European nations' ephemeral transmarine empires.

Mention has already been made of the discrepancy between the political partition of the Oikoumenê into local sovereign states and the global unification of the Oikoumenê on the technological and economic planes. This misfit is the crux of mankind's present plight. Some form of global government is now needed for keeping the peace between one local human community and another and for re-establishing the balance between Man and the rest of the biosphere, now that this balance has been upset by Man's enormous augmentation of human material power as a result of the Industrial Revolution.

However, the magnitude and the impersonality of operations on the global scale are daunting; and the generation responsible for securing the survival of the human race is jeopardizing it by trying to split the unity of life into an ever greater number of ever smaller compartments. The increase in the number of local sovereign states is matched by a contemporaneous increase in the number of academic 'disciplines', and this progressive fission is making business unmanageable and information unintelligible. The plethora is not being dispelled by this evasive action; on the contrary, it is being allowed to swell to a magnitude at which it might come to be completely out of hand.

Mankind is in a crisis as grave as the two world wars and the outlook is perplexing. Manifestly mankind has a prospect of continuing to survive in the biosphere for perhaps a further 2,000 million years, if human action does not make the biosphere uninhabitable at some earlier date; but Man now possesses the material power to make the biosphere uninhabitable in the near future, and it is therefore possible that people who are already alive might have their lives cut short by a man-made catastrophe that would wreck the biosphere and would destroy mankind together with all other forms of life. Evidently these are two possibilities; but they are certainly not the only two alternatives.

The future is undiscernible because it has not yet come into existence; its potentialities are infinite, and therefore the future cannot be predicted by extrapolating from the past. Anything that has occurred in the past may, no doubt, recur, if conditions remain the same. But a past occurrence is not bound to recur; it is merely one among an unknown number of possibilities; some of these possibilities are unforeseeable because they have no known precedents; and there is no precedent for the power that Man has acquired over the biosphere in the course of the two centuries 1763–1973. In these bewildering circumstances, only one prediction can be made with certainty. Man, the child of Mother Earth, would not be able to survive the crime of matricide if he were to commit it. The penalty for this would be self-annihilation.

[82]

A RETROSPECT IN 1973

THE future does not yet exist; the past has ceased to exist, and therefore, in so far as a record of the past survives, the recorded events are immutable. However, this immutable past does not present the same appearance always and everywhere. It looks different at different times and places, and either an increase or a decrease in our information may also change the picture. Our view of the relations of past events to each other, of their relative importance, and of their significance, changes constantly in consequence of the constant change of the fugitive present. The same past viewed in the same country by the same person, first in 1897 and then in 1973, presents two very different pictures; and no doubt the self-same past will look still more different when viewed in China in 2073 and even more different again when viewed in Nigeria in 2173.

In the present chapter, the writer of this book has picked out, for mention, features in the record of the past that looked salient and significant to him in 1973 and that seemed to him likely (a hazardous guess) to present the same appearance when viewed at later dates in other places.

Since our ancestors became human, mankind has lived, during all but the last fraction—perhaps the last sixteenth part—of its time-span to date, in the Lower Palaeolithic way. A band of Lower Palaeolithic food-gatherers and hunters had to be small in numbers and to give a wide berth to other bands. At this stage of technology and economy, a concentration of population would have spelled starvation. In the Lower Palaeolithic Age, technology was almost static, and each band was small enough for all its members to be acquainted with each other personally. This was the setting of human social life till recently.

Perhaps 40,000 years ago, or, at the utmost, not more than 70,000 years ago, there was a relatively sudden and rapid advance in technology.

The event is well attested by archaeological evidence, though the cause of it is unknown. Lower Palaeolithic tools were replaced by a series of Upper Palaeolithic improvements. Since then technology has gone on advancing. Its advance has not been continuous. There have been successive bursts of technological invention, with intervening pauses. The principal bursts, to date, have been the Upper Palaeolithic (improved tools, bows and arrows, domestication of the dog), the Neolithic (still better tools, together with the domestication of more species of animals and plants, and the invention of spinning and weaving and pottery-making), the fifth millennium B.C. (sails, wheels, metallurgy, writing), and the Industrial Revolution (a vast increase in mechanization) which started two hundred years ago and is still in progress. Thus the progression of technology has not been uninterrupted, but it has been cumulative. The loss of an acquired technique has been rare. In the Aegean area, the technique of writing was lost in the twelfth century B.C., but this was an exceptional event.

Technology is the only field of human activity in which there has been progression. The advance from Lower Palaeolithic to mechanized technology has been immense. There has been no corresponding advance in human sociality, though advances in this field have been called for by the changes in social conditions that have been imposed upon mankind by its technological progress.

The most important of Man's successive technological advances to date has been the domestication of other animals, besides the dog, and the invention of agriculture, in the Neolithic Age. Agriculture and animal husbandry have provided the base for all subsequent technological progress, including the current Industrial Revolution, and also the base for the way of life of all the civilizations that have risen and fallen to date.

The Neolithic-Age village-community was larger in numbers than the pre-agricultural food-gathering and hunting band, but it was not so large that the personal relations between its members had to be eked out by the introduction of impersonal institutions, and Neolithic technology was not so complex as to require any appreciable amount of specialization and division of labour beyond the physiological differentiation between the functions of the two sexes. Moreover, though the Neolithic village-community was sedentary, it was insulated from other village-communities by intervening stretches of virgin wilderness. Thus, though the change in the technological and economic conditions of life between the Upper Palaeolithic Age and the Neolithic Age was great, the measure of sociality to which mankind had been conditioned during the immensely long-drawn-out Lower Palaeolithic Age could be stretched to meet the needs of the Neolithic-Age way of life. This is why, in the fourth century B.C., more than a thousand years after the replacement of this way of life by civilization in China, Taoist philosophers in the Age of the Chinese Warring States looked back to the conditions of the Neolithic Age nostalgically. Their experience of life in their own age made them feel that the subsequent progress of technology, and the social consequences of this, had been misfortunes.

In 1973 peasants living in village communities of the Neolithic-Age style still constituted a majority of the living generation of mankind, but they were rapidly drifting out of the countryside into shanty-towns enveloping the cities, while, conversely, the mechanization that had been invented for processing inanimate matter in factories was being applied to agriculture and to animal husbandry. Moreover, for the past 5,000 years, the Oikoumenê's peasantry had been saddled with the burden of having to support a superstructure of civilization.

This had been possible because, in the fourth millennium B.C., the advance of technology had begun to produce a surplus of production over and above what was needed for bare subsistence, while Man's Palaeolithic heritage of sociality had proved to be morally inadequate for allocating the use of this surplus beneficently. Part of the surplus had been misspent on war; the rest had been appropriated inequitably by a minority of the members of society whose collective work had produced it.

The advance of technology in the fourth millennium B.C. had required specialists (miners, smiths, and the planners, inspirers, and organizers of large-scale public works, e.g. for drainage and irrigation). The specialists' contribution to the production of the surplus was greater than that of the unskilled majority of the workers, and a differential distribution of the economic reward, though not amiable, was perhaps not unjust in principle, and anyway was probably inevitable, considering that Man, like every other species of living being, is innately greedy, and that the restraint imposed on his greed by his Lower-Palaeolithic degree of sociality no longer sufficed in Man's new technological and social situation. The 'differentials' in the distribution of the surplus were inequitably great, and they also tended to become hereditary. Thus social injustice and war were the price of collective affluence. These two congenital social maladies of civilization still afflict mankind today.

Since the dawn of civilization there has been a disparity between Man's technological progression and his social performance. The advance of technology, particularly the most recent advance during the two centuries 1773–1973, has vastly increased Man's wealth and power, and the 'morality gap' between Man's physical power for doing evil and his spiritual capacity for coping with this power has yawned as wide open as the mythical jaws of Hell. During the last 5,000 years, the widening 'morality gap' has caused mankind to inflict on itself grievous disasters.

Man's spiritual inadequacy has set a limit to his social progress and therefore to his technological progress too; for, as technology has grown in scale and in complexity, it has increased its requirement of social co-operation among the producers of wealth. Since the beginning of the current Industrial Revolution, mechanization has introduced a second limitation on technological progress. Mechanization has been making industrial work more productive materially at the cost of making it less satisfying psychologically, and this has made the workers restive and has tended to lower the standard of workmanship.

Productivity was increased at the dawn of civilization through the draining and irrigation of the jungle-swamps in the lower basins of the Tigris and Euphrates and of the Nile. This required an increase in the scale of technological operations; this in turn required an increase in the numerical strength of communities that went far beyond the limits of a sociality based on personal relations between the members of society. When the requirements of technology constrained the founders of the earliest civilizations to assemble man-power in excess of the narrow limits of pre-civilizational communities, they invented a new social device: impersonal institutions. These can sustain larger communities because they can generate co-operation between human beings who have no personal acquaintance with each other. But institutionalized social relations are both frigid and fragile. Human beings have never felt at home in them as they do feel at home in personal relations. Institutions are always in danger of losing grip and breaking down, and consequently the persons in authority who are responsible for maintaining them are always under temptation to resort to coercion as a substitute for the voluntary co-operation that institutions often fail to evoke.

Since the dawn of civilization, Man's master institution has been states—in the plural, not in the singular; for, to date, there has never been one single state embracing the whole living generation of mankind all round the globe. There has always been a multitude of states co-existing side by side, and, unlike the Palaeolithic bands and the Neolithic village-communities, the states of the Age of the Civilizations have not been insulated from each other; they have collided with each other, and their collisions have precipitated the wars that have been one of the maladies of civilization.

The usual type of state has been a local sovereign state juxtaposed with a number of other states of its own kind. There are about 170 of these in the present-day global Oikoumenê; its political configuration is the same as that of Sumer in the third millennium B.C.

Local sovereign states are an awkward institution. They fall between two stools. Even a city-state, not to speak of a nation-state or a federation of city-states or of nation-states, is far too large to be capable of being based socially on the personal relations in which human beings feel at home. On the other hand, the largest local state is still only one of a number of states of the same kind. It has the ability to make war, but not the ability to provide peace. Wherever and whenever there has been a set of local sovereign states juxtaposed to each other, they have always fallen into warfare with each other, and, in the past, this warfare has always ended in the imposition of peace by the forcible establishment of an empire embracing as much of the Oikoumenê as has lain within the horizon of the liquidated set of warring local states. The Pharaonic Egyptian civilization was singular in having been united politically by force at the dawn of its history, without the protracted preliminary bout of warfare between local states. It is significant that this civilization was the most stable and the most durable of all the civilizations that have arisen so far.

The present-day global set of local sovereign states is not capable of keeping the peace, and it is also not capable of saving the biosphere from man-made pollution or of conserving the biosphere's non-replaceable natural resources. This ecumenical anarchy on the political plane cannot continue for much longer in an Oikoumenê that has already become a unity on the technological and economic planes. What has been needed for the last 5,000 years, and has been feasible technologically, though not yet politically, for the last hundred years, is a global body politic composed of cells on the scale of the Neolithic-Age village-community—a scale on which the participants could be personally acquainted with each other, while each of them would also be a citizen of the world-state. However, the Oikoumenê cannot now be united politically by the barbarous and ruinous traditional method of military conquest. In 1945 an Oikoumenê that was still un-unified politically was overtaken by the invention of the nuclear weapon, and the Oikoumenê could never be united by the use of this deadly weapon; annihilation, not unification, would be the inevitable outcome of a nuclear world war.

The record of Sumerian, Hellenic, Chinese, and medieval Italian history demonstrates that a set of local sovereign states can be no more than a transitory political configuration. In the age in which mankind has acquired the command over nuclear power, political unification can be accomplished only voluntarily, and, since it is evidently going to be accepted only reluctantly, it seems probable that it will be delayed until mankind has brought upon itself further disasters of a magnitude that will induce it to acquiesce at last in global political union as being the lesser evil.

At this point in our history, we human beings might be tempted to envy the social insects. These have been conditioned by Nature to co-operate with each other on the grand scale. The individual bee or ant or termite subordinates and sacrifices itself in the service of its community, and its self-surrender is neither voluntary nor enforced by external compulsion; it is inherent in the constitution of the insect's psyche. It is going to be harder for Man the amphibian to stretch his sociality from the modicum required of him, and acquired by him, in the Lower Palaeolithic Age till an enhanced human sociality embraces the whole of the biosphere; for Man, unlike the termite, ant, and bee, is not just an inherently social psychosomatic organism; he is also a soul which possesses consciousness and which therefore can, and must, make choices, either for good or for evil.

Fortunately, Man's sociality is not confined within the narrow compass of personal relations that was adequate for pre-civilizational human societies. A human being does have a sense of compassion for any other human being whom he finds in distress, even if, in tribal parlance, this fellow human being is an 'alien'. A human being will take pity on any sick person and on any lost child, and will come to the sufferer's aid. In empires, such as the Chinese Empire and the Roman Empire, whose rulers equated their dominions with the whole of the Oikoumenê, the rulers' subjects came, in the course of time, to look upon themselves as being, not victims of alien conquerors, but citizens of an ecumenical state. The missionary religions set out to evangelize the whole of mankind, and the Chinese philosopher Mo-tzu held that a human being ought to love and serve all his fellow human beings with an impartial devotion. Confucius' most authoritative interpreter, Mencius, rejected Mo-tzu's precept as being impracticable; he stood for the Confucian ideal of a graduated order of loyalties; but experience shows that love inspired by personal acquaintance and love for all fellow human beings simply in virtue of a common humanity need not be mutually exclusive expressions of sociality. In India, the range of love has been restricted by the barriers of caste, but it has also been extended to include Man's fellow living beings of every species. In the Oikoumenê in the Age of the Industrial Revolution, human love needs to be extended to include all components of the biosphere, inanimate as well as animate.

These were the reflexions, in 1973, of one British observer who had been born in 1889. What, in 1973, were the reflexions of the writer's fellow human beings? How far were they aware of the past? And how vigorously were they acting on lessons that they had derived from a retrospective survey of history?

Evidently few people are ready to recognize that the institution of local sovereign states has failed repeatedly, during the last 5,000 years, to meet mankind's political needs, and that, in a global society, this institution is bound to prove to be transitory once again and this time more surely than ever before. Since the end of the Second World War the number of local sovereign states in the Oikoumenê has more than doubled, in spite of the fact that, at the same time, all the politically sundered fractions of mankind have become more and more closely interdependent, on the technological and economic planes.

The Chinese people, who once equated the Chinese Empire with 'All that is under Heaven', have now resigned themselves to seeing their country play its role as a member of a set of warring states in a global arena. Implicitly, the Chinese are ignoring the grim chapter of their own history when China herself was an arena for local warring states. On the other hand, the Chinese appear to be alive to the history of China since her political unification in 221 B.C.; for they are making energetic efforts to avoid a recurrence of the estrangement of the civil service from the peasantry that was 'China's sorrow' ever since the reign of the Emperor Han Wu-ti.

In the second century B.C. this emperor had inaugurated the recruitment of the Chinese civil service by merit, and the assessment of the candidates' merit by examination. The Chinese Imperial civil service had been the best of any in the Oikoumenê; it had held together a larger number of human beings in peace and order for a greater number of years than any other civil service anywhere. Yet, time after time, the Chinese civil servants had betrayed their trust and had brought China to grief by abusing their power for their own personal advantage. China's leaders have taken steps to prevent this from happening again. Whether they will be more successful than earlier Chinese reformers remains to be seen, but at least the vigour of their current action is a good augury.

If the Chinese take to heart the lesson of past Chinese errors, and if they succeed in saving themselves from repeating these errors, they may do a great service, not only to their own country, but to the whole of mankind at a critical stage in mankind's enigmatic course.

Man is a psychosomatic inhabitant of the biosphere that coats the surface of the planet Earth, and in this respect he is one among the species of living creatures that are children of Mother Earth. But Man is also a spirit, and, as such, he is in communication with—and in the mystics' experience, is identical with—a spiritual reality that is not of this World.

As a spirit, Man possesses consciousness, he distinguishes between good and evil, and in his acts he makes choices. In the ethical field, in which Man's choices are either for evil or for good, his choices produce a moral credit-and-debit account. We do not know whether this account is closed at the death of each short-lived human being or whether (as Hindus and Buddhists believe) it runs on through a potentially endless series of reincarnations. For the network of relations between incarnate human beings that constitutes human society, the account is still open and will remain open so long as mankind allows the biosphere to remain inhabitable.

Will mankind murder Mother Earth or will he redeem her? He could murder her by misusing his increasing technological potency. Alternatively he could redeem her by overcoming the suicidal, aggressive greed that, in all living creatures, including Man himself, has been the price of the Great Mother's gift of life. This is the enigmatic question which now confronts Man.

INDEX

Abbas, Shah: Safavi Emperor of Iran (ruled 1588–1629), 532, 551, 552, 553

Abbasid Caliphate, 124, 373, 390–94, 400, 426–30, 447, 448; liquidation of (1258), 449, 450, 472

Abdali Afghan state: founded (1747) by Ahmad Shah, 555

Abd-al-Malik, Caliph (ruled 685–705), 372

Abd-ar-Rahman III, Caliph (ruled 929–61), 393

Abelard, Peter (1079–1142), 462

Abkhazians: Eastern Orthodox Christians, 454

Abolition of slavery: in Haiti (1793–1803), in French colonial empire (1848), in British colonial empire (1833), in U.S. (1863), in Brazil (1871–88), 572. *And see under* Slavery

Abraham (*c.* 18th cent. BC), 126

Abu Bakr (573–634), 332; Muhammad's successor, 370; his wars, 370

Abu Muslim: agent of the House of Ali, 392

Abu'l-Abbas, Caliph, 'the Butcher' (d. 754), 374

Abydos, 73

Abyssinia (Ethiopia), ix, 32, 363, 484, 532, 533, 550, 579

Acadia (Nova Scotia): French in (1605), 532

Achaeans: intrusion into Egypt, 108; Achaean Confederation, 201, 202

Achaemenes, House of, 164, 185, 190

Achaeus (cousin and opponent of Antiochus III), 255

Acre, 449, 456

Acrotatus: Spartan prince, 236

Actium: Octavian's defeat of Antony and Cleopatra at (31 BC), 278

Adad-Nirari I (ruled 1307–1275 BC): Assyrian leader, 100

Aden, 527

Adonis myth: in Canaan, 72; in Greek mythology, 298

Adoptionists (holders of the belief that the human Christ was the *adoptive* not the true son of God), 345

Adrianople (Edirne), 480, 488

Adriatic, 395, 396, 468, 496, 497

Aegean, 27, 33, 48, 83, 101, 108, 111–12, 166, 190, 395, 396, 590

Aegina: lived by trade, 173; conflict with Athens, 173

Aeschylus (525–456 BC): Greek tragic dramatist, 286

Aetolian Confederation, 199, 200, 201, 254, 256

Affluence, collective: price of, 591

Afghanistan; Afghans, ix, 33, 34, 164, 263, 273, 428, 472, 554–5, 567

Africa: North-West, 27, 334, 335, 337, 429; *homo sapiens* first appearance in (?) East Africa, 31, 35, 36; North African steppe, 34, 35; tropical forests in, 35; languages in West Africa, 35; circumnavigated by Necho II, 160; circumnavigated by Vasco da Gama, 525; white rule in southern Africa, 586

Agade: city founded by Sargon on un-identified site near Babylon, 67. *See* Sargon

Agathocles: despot of Syracuse, 232, 233, 253

Ager Romanus (ancient Roman territory, 5th cent. BC), 338

Aghlabid dynasty (Sunni Arab), 392, 393, 426

Agony, Age of, 202

Agriculture: invention of, 40, 590; development and progress of, 45; irrigation for, 45, 46; rain-fed, 46; dawn of, 49; vagrant type

used for the inscriptions, 227; propagated an ethical standard, 128; concern for the alleviation of suffering of all sentient beings, 229; decline of Mauryan Empire after his death, 262, 350

Asia, Eastern, xii; Neolithic Age in, xii, 47; Central, 27; migrants to America, 31; route to Australia, 31; its most prominent peninsulas, 32; S.-W. Asia as a 'geopolitical hub', 33; leading role in Neolithic Age, 36; prospect of leadership in present Age, 37; motherland of husbandry and metallurgy, 45; its cultural influence on Egyptian life, 97; the Fertile Crescent in S.-W., 103, 108, 121, 128, 277, 310, 363, 364, 372, 382, 390, 391, 427, 441. *And passim throughout. See also under constituent countries*

Asia Minor, 45, 46, 60, 68, 72, 77, 267. *And passim*

Assassins, the (secret society organized *c.* 1090 by the Isma'ilis), 428, 483

Asshur: male celibate god (Assyrian), 290

Asshur: Assyrian city, rebellion of, 150

Asshurbanipal, King of Assyria (d. 626 BC), 150, 153, 154, 164

Assisi: church of St. Francis at, 463

Assyria; Assyrians, xi, 11, 36, 68, 108; successor-state of 3rd dynasty Ur, 86; downfall and destruction (612–608 BC), 85; expansion of trading area, 87; reconciled to Mittani's suzerainty, 95; re-emerges as aggressively militant, 100, 120; repeatedly at war with Babylon, 101, 122; Aramaeans conquered, 122; final bout of militarism, 149–54, 168; brutal empire-building, 149–50; last remnant annihilated, 150; last stand at Harran, 154, 160; expired 605 BC, 154

Astrakhan, 484, 486, 489, 530

Astrology, Babylonian, 299

Asturias, 345

Astyges, Median Emperor (6th cent. BC), 164, 284

Atahualpa (illegitimate son of Huayna Capac): victor in Inca civil war, 529–30

Atheno–Peloponnesian War (431–404 BC), 232

Athens: acropolis massively fortified in 13th cent. BC, 102; sudden adoption of Proto-geometric style in pottery (*c.* 1250 BC), 138; pre-eminent city-state, but temporary setback from *c.* 750 BC, 171; escapes from Spartan control and adopts democratic system (*c.* 507 BC), 172; co-operates with Sparta to resist Persian invasion, 173; reforms by Solon, 173; Persians repulsed

by, 190; naval victories at Salamis and Mycale, 191; victory on land at Plataea, 191; sinks to political nadir but rises to cultural zenith, 195; supremely beautiful works on acropolis, 195; the Parthenon, 196; how financed, 195; Athens denounced as 'a tyrant city', 196; receives Delos as a gift from Rome, 264; war on two fronts, 286

Athens, University of, 377

Athos, Mount, 487, 503

Atlas Mountains, 392, 449

Atlantic, 7, 33, 34, 35, 81, 400, 405, 485, 525, *and passim*

Atom: nucleus split by Rutherford (1919), 576, 582

Atom bombs, 583

Atomic energy: released by uranium, 16; myth of Phaethon an allegory of risk of manipulating, 16

Aton: the sun disk, 9; Akhenaton's One-God, 98; conceived as lord of the Universe, 99

Atrocities, 11, 27, 196, 472, 475, 478, 527, 586

Attic Drama: outcrop from ritual, 197; as an instrument for commenting on political issues and spiritual depths, 197; as a cultural asset, 206; the chief tragedy and comedy writers, 206; part of the public cult of Dionysos, 295

Attica: social tension in, 173

Attila, Hun war-lord (ruled 433–53): attacks West Roman Empire; defeated at Orleans (AD 451); invades North Italy; dies, 321, 338; extent of dominions, 469

Attis (mythological deity); in Asia Minor, 72, 130, 290; self-castrated, 298

Augsburg: a centre of trade and finance and of Protestantism, 498

Augustus (Gaius Julius Caesar Octavianus, 63 BC–AD 14), 258, 271, 280, 281–2, 283–4, 306, 327, 401, 404

Aurangzeb, Mogul emperor (ruled 1659–1707), 554

Aurelian, Emperor (Lucius Domitius Aurelianus, *c.* 212–75; ruled 270–75), 9, 306, 307, 311, 340

Australia: route from Asia to, 31; first human settlers in, 47

Australopithecus, 24–6

Austrasia (Eastern Frankland), 383

Avalokita (a Buddhist bodhisattva): changes sex to become Kwan Yin, 293

Avaris: the Hyksos capital, 99

Averroes. *See* Ibn Rushd

Aviation, 582, 583

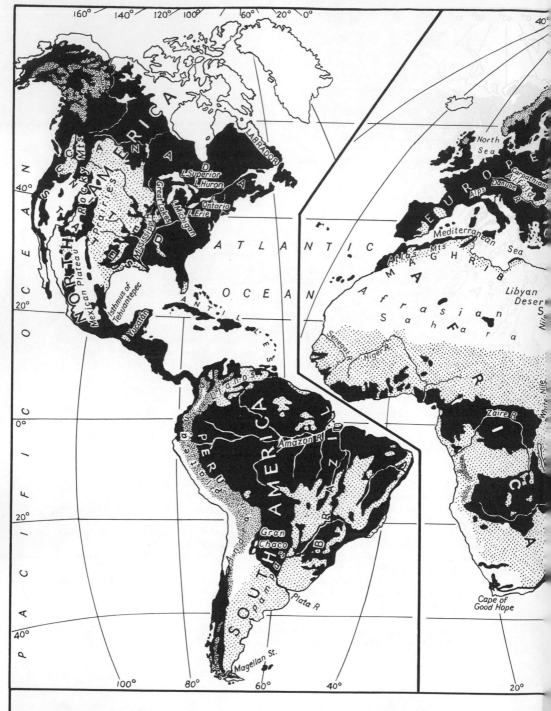

THE PHYSICAL SETTING OF
THE CIVILIZATIONS

| Desert & tundra | | Steppe & grassland | | Mountain vegetation | | Forest | |

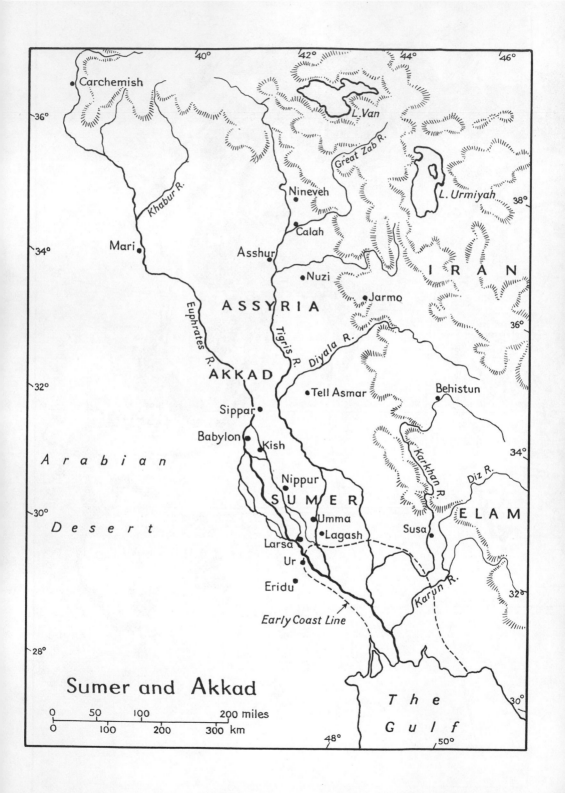

Carchemish

L. Van

Khabur R.

Nineveh

Great Zab R.

L. Urmiyah

Mari

Calah

Asshur

I R A N

Nuzi

A S S Y R I A

Jarmo

Euphrates R.

Tigris R.

Diyala R.

A K K A D

Tell Asmar

Behistun

Sippar

Babylon

Kish

A r a b i a n

Karkhan R.

Nippur

Diz R.

D e s e r t

S U M E R

E L A M

Umma

Susa

Larsa

Lagash

Ur

Eridu

Early Coast Line

Karun R.

Sumer and Akkad

0   50   100   200 miles

0   100   200   300 km

T h e

G u l f

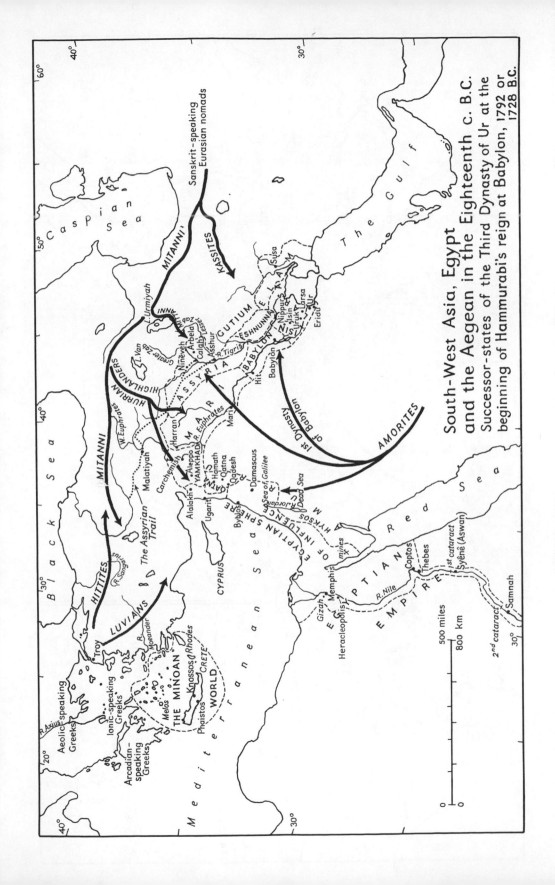

South-West Asia, Egypt and the Aegean in the Eighteenth c. B.C. Successor-states of the Third Dynasty of Ur at the beginning of Hammurabi's reign at Babylon, 1792 or 1728 B.C.

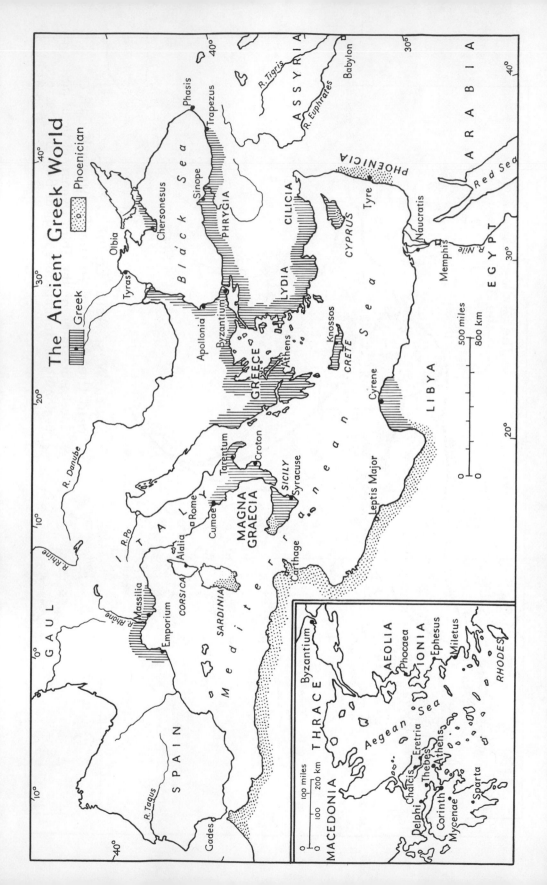

The Ancient Greek World

Greek

Phoenician

GAUL

SPAIN

Gades

R. Rhine

R. Rhône

Emporium

Massilia

CORSICA

SARDINIA

ITALY

R. Po

Rome

Cumae

Alalia

MAGNA
GRAECIA

Tarentum

Croton

SICILY

Syracuse

Carthage

Mediterranean Sea

Leptis Major

LIBYA

Cyrene

R. Danube

R. Rhône

R. Taqus

40°

10°

0°

10°

20°

Tyras

Olbia

Black Sea

Chersonesus

Sinope

Phasis

Trapezus

PHRYGIA

Apollonia

Byzantium

GREECE

Athens

LYDIA

CILICIA

Knossos

CRETE

Aegean Sea

CYPRUS

Tyre

PHOENICIA

Naucratis

Memphis

R. Nile

EGYPT

ASSYRIA

R. Tigris

R. Euphrates

Babylon

ARABIA

Red Sea

30°

40°

30°

30°

40°

20°

20°

500 miles

800 km

0

MACEDONIA

THRACE

Byzantium

AEOLIA

Phocaea

IONIA

Ephesus

Miletus

Aegean Sea

Delphi

Chalcis

Eretria

Thebes

Athens

Corinth

Mycenae

Sparta

RHODES

100 miles

200 km

0

100

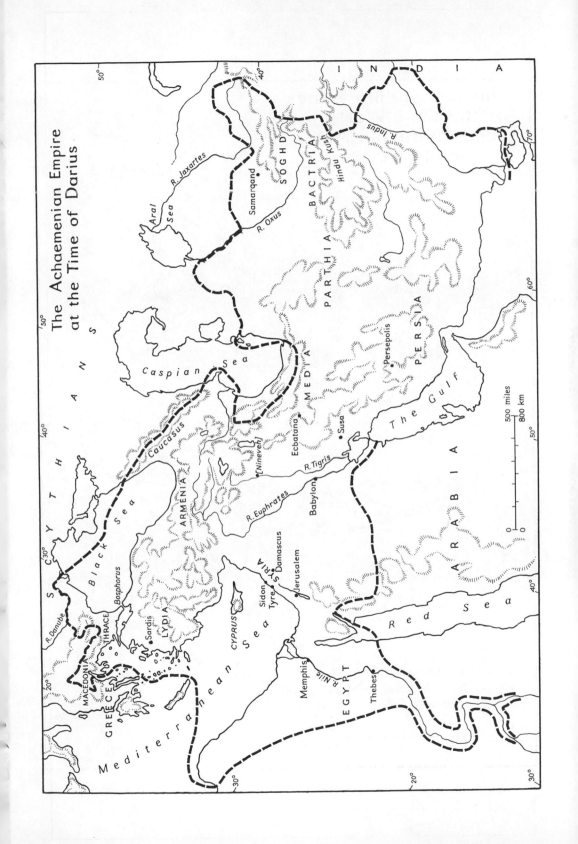

The Achaemenian Empire
at the Time of Darius

S C Y T H I A N S

R. Jaxartes

Aral
Sea

Samarqand

R. Oxus

S O G H D

B A C T R I A

I N D I A

Hindu Kush

R. Indus

P A R T H I A

Caspian Sea

M E D I A

P E R S I A

Persepolis

Susa

Ecbatana

The Gulf

Caucasus

[Nineveh]

R. Tigris

A R M E N I A

R. Euphrates

Babylon

A R A B I A

Black Sea

Bosphorus

Damascus

S Y R I A

Jerusalem

Sidon
Tyre

Red Sea

THRACE

Sardis

L Y D I A

CYPRUS

MACEDONIA

GREECE

Mediterranean Sea

Memphis

R. Nile

E G Y P T

Thebes

R. Danube

500 miles

800 km

50°

50°

40°

30°

20°

30°

20°

70°

60°

50°

40°

30°

20°

30°

40°

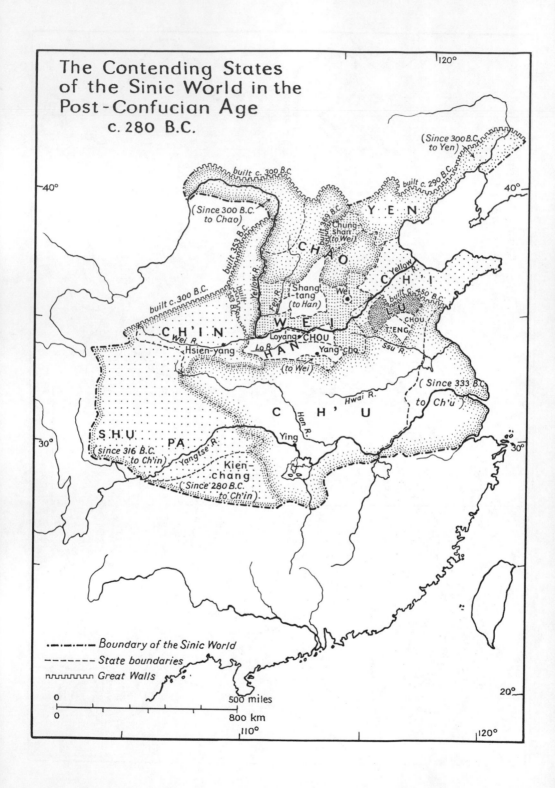

The Contending States
of the Sinic World in the
Post-Confucian Age
c. 280 B.C.

(Since 300 B.C.
to Yen)

built c. 300 B.C.

built c. 290 B.C.

(Since 300 B.C.
to Chao)

built 353 B.C.

YEN

Chung-
shan
(to Wei)

CHAO

built c. 300 B.C.

built 333 B.C.

Yellow R.

Fen R.

Wei

C Yellow

CHI

built c. 450 B.C.

CH'IN

Shang-
tang
(to Han)

LU

CHOU

T'ENG

Wei R.

Hsien-yang

WEI

Loyang CHOU

ssu R.

Lo R.

HAN

Yang-cho

(to Wei)

(Since 333 B.C.

to Ch'u)

Hwai R.

SHU

PA

CH'U

Han R.

(since 316 B.C.
to Ch'in)

Yangtse R.

Ying

Kien-
chang
(Since 280 B.C.
to Ch'in)

Boundary of the Sinic World

State boundaries

Great Walls

0   500 miles

0   800 km

40°

40°

30°

30°

20°

110°

120°

120°

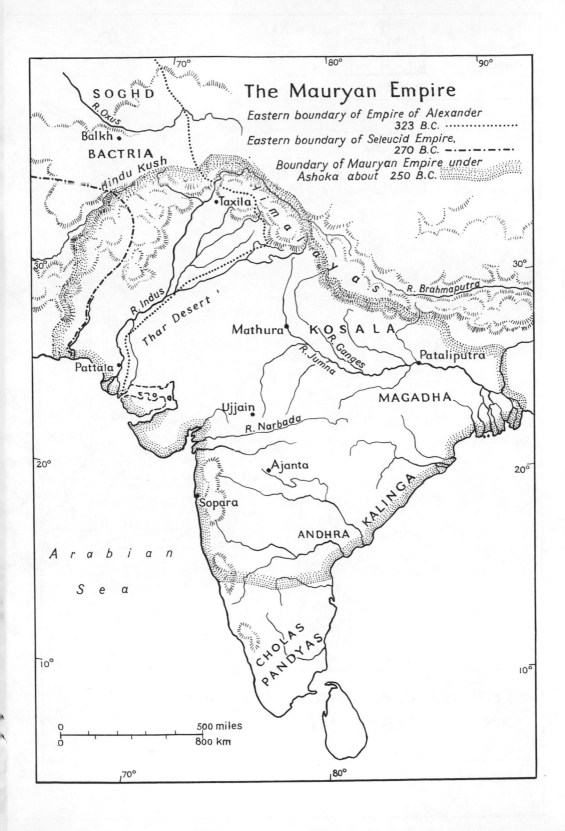

The Mauryan Empire

Eastern boundary of Empire of Alexander
323 B.C. ....

Eastern boundary of Seleucid Empire,
270 B.C. —·—·—·—·—

Boundary of Mauryan Empire under
Ashoka about 250 B.C.

SOGHD

R. Oxus

Balkh •

BACTRIA

Hindu Kush

• Taxila

H i m a l a y a s

R. Indus

R. Brahmaputra

Thar Desert

Mathura •

K O S A L A

R. Ganges

R. Jumna

Pataliputra

Pattala

S Z O

MAGADHA

Ujjain •

R. Narbada

• Ajanta

20°

KALINGA

Sopara

A r a b i a n

ANDHRA

S e a

CHOLAS

PANDYAS

0   500 miles
0   800 km

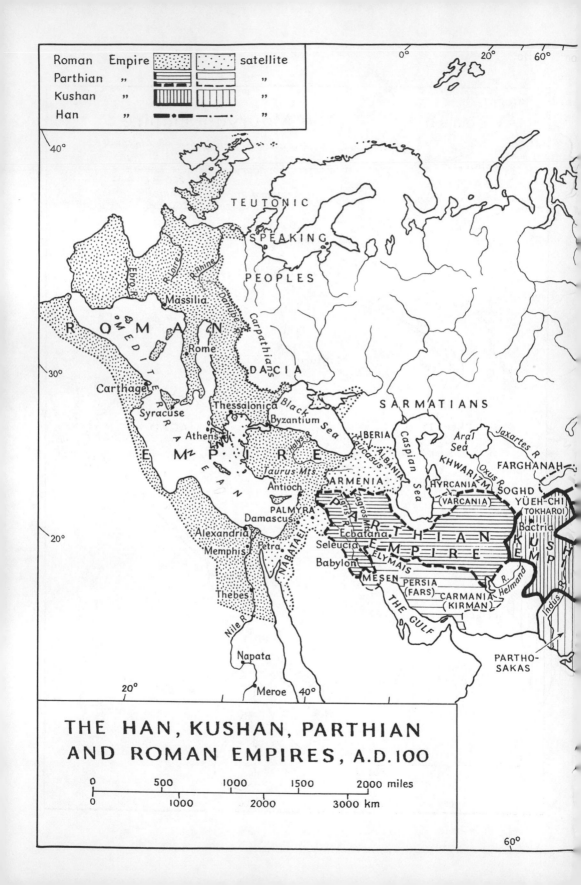

THE HAN, KUSHAN, PARTHIAN
AND ROMAN EMPIRES, A.D.100

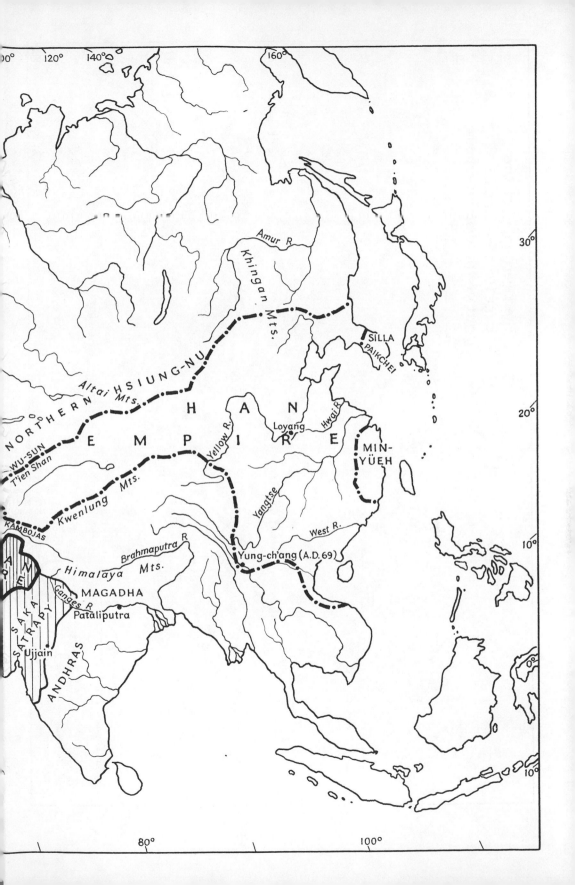

120° 140° 160°

30°

Amur R.

Khingan Mts.

Altai Mts. HSIUNG-NU

NORTHERN

WU-SUN

T'ien Shan

H A N

Yellow R.

Loyang

Hwai R.

20°

E M P I R E

SILLA
PAIKCHEI

MIN-
YÜEH

Kwenlung Mts.

Yangtse

KAMBOJAS

West R.

10°

Brahmaputra R.

Himalaya Mts.

Yung-ch'ang (A.D. 69)

MAGADHA

Ganges R.

Pataliputra

SAKA
SATRAPY

Ujjain

ANDHRAS

0°

10°

80° 100°

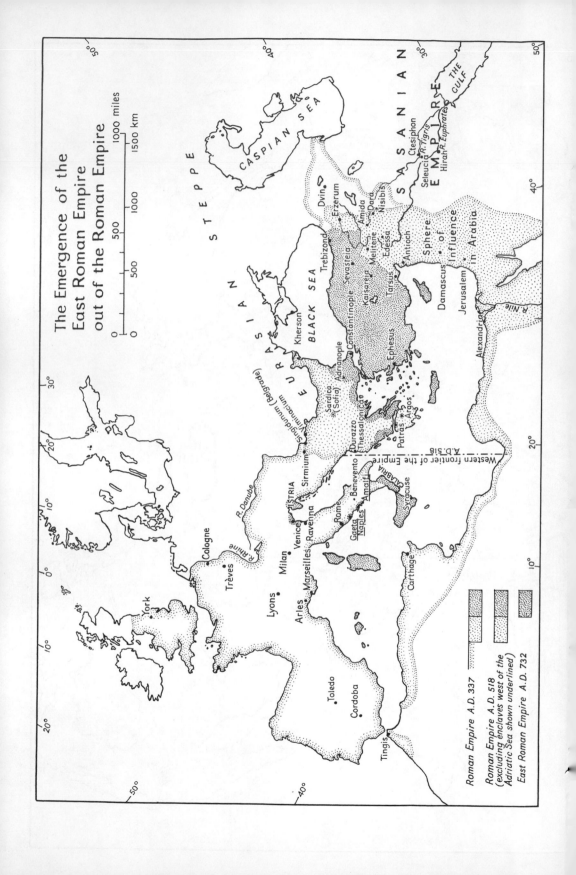

The Emergence of the
East Roman Empire
out of the Roman Empire

1000 miles
1500 km
1000
500
500
0
0

STEPPE

CASPIAN SEA

SASANIAN EMPIRE

THE GULF

Ctesiphon
Seleucia R.Tigris
Hirah R.Euphrates

Dvin
Erzerum
Amida Dara
Nisibis
Trebizond
Sevasteia Melitene Edessa
Sphere
Constantinople Kaiseri Tarsus Antioch of
Adrianople Ephesus Damascus Influence
Sardica Jerusalem in Arabia
(Sofia) Thessalonica
Durazzo Alexandria
Patras Argos R. Nile

BLACK SEA

EURASIAN

Kherson

Singidunum (Belgrade)
Viminacium

R. Danube

Sirmium
ISTRIA
Venice
Ravenna
Milan
Benevento
Rome CALABRIA
Gaeta Naples Syracuse
Amalfi
Marseilles
Arles
Lyons
Cologne
Trèves
R. Rhine

York

Toledo
Cordoba

Carthage

Tingis

Western frontier of the Empire
A.D. 518

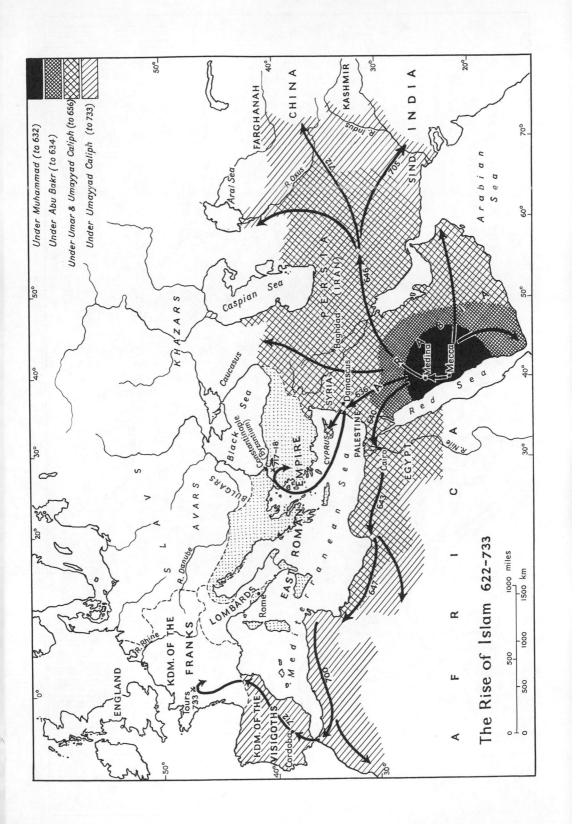

The Rise of Islam 622–733

Under Muhammad (to 632)
Under Abu Bakr (to 634)
Under Umar & Umayyad Caliph (to 656)
Under Umayyad Caliph (to 733)

ENGLAND

KDM. OF THE FRANKS

KDM. OF THE VISIGOTHS

Tours 733

Cordoba 712

Mediterranean Sea

Rome

LOMBARDS

R. Danube

R. Rhine

SLAVS

AVARS

BULGARS

EAST ROMAN EMPIRE

Constantinople (Byzantium)

717–18

CYPRUS

Black Sea

KHAZARS

Caucasus

Caspian Sea

Aral Sea

FARGHANAH

CHINA

R. Oxus

717

646

KASHMIR

R. Indus

SIND

705

INDIA

Arabian Sea

PERSIA (IRAN)

Baghdad

SYRIA

Damascus

635

PALESTINE

630

Red Sea

Medina

Mecca

Cairo

643

647

700

EGYPT

R. Nile

A F R I C A

0   500   1000 miles
0   500   1000   1500 km

0°   20°   30°   40°   50°   60°   70°

50°   40°   30°   20°

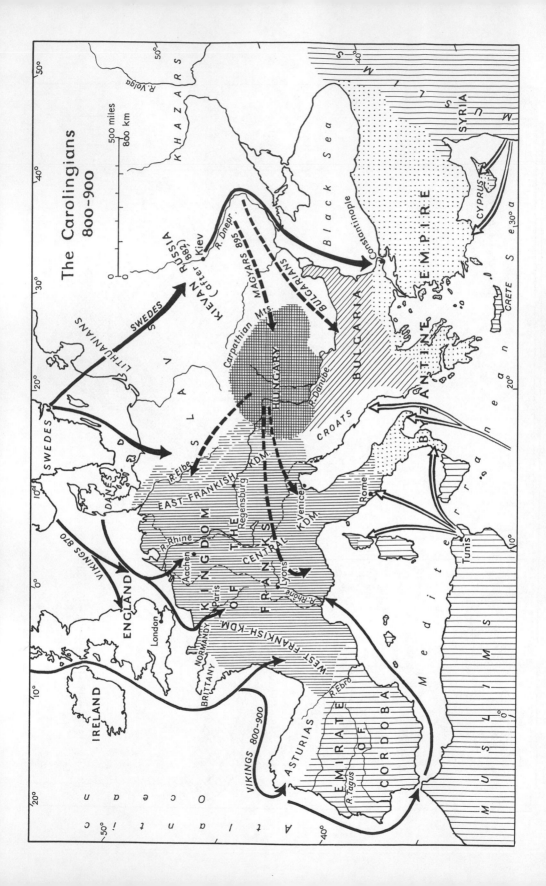

The Carolingians
800–900

500 miles
800 km

KHAZARS

R. Volga

Black Sea

SYRIA

BYZANTINE EMPIRE

CYPRUS

CRETE

Mediterranean Sea

MUSLIMS

Atlantic Ocean

IRELAND

ENGLAND

London

VIKINGS 870

SWEDES

LITHUANIANS

SWEDES

RUSSIA (after 882)

Kiev

R. Dnepr

KIEVAN

MAGYARS 895

BULGARIANS

Carpathian Mts.

HUNGARY

BULGARIA

Constantinople

CROATS

R. Danube

Venice

KDM.

Rome

Tunis

EAST-FRANKISH KDM.

R. Elbe

Regensburg

R. Rhine

Aachen

Paris

KINGDOM OF THE

CENTRAL

FRANKISH

KDM.

Lyons

R. Rhône

WEST FRANKISH KDM.

NORMANDY

BRITTANY

ASTURIAS

R. Ebro

R. Tagus

EMIRATE OF CORDOBA

VIKINGS 800–900

SLAVS

DANES

SWEDES

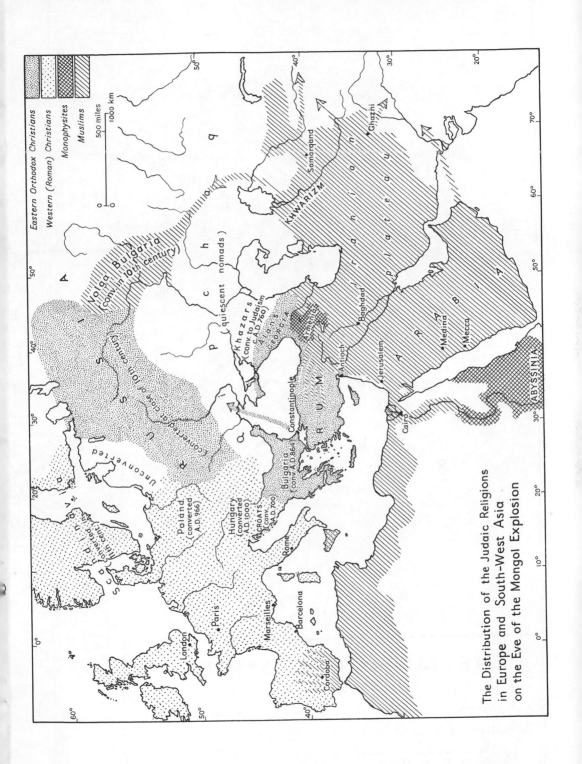

The Distribution of the Judaic Religions
in Europe and South-West Asia
on the Eve of the Mongol Explosion

Eastern Orthodox Christians
Western (Roman) Christians
Monophysites
Muslims

500 miles
1000 km

A   l   a   n   s
Volga Bulgaria
(conv. in 10th century)

converted close of 10th century

Khazars
(conv. to Judaism
A.D. 760)

Petcheneg (quiescent nomads)

Unconverted

R U S S I A N S

Scandinavians
converted close of 10th century

Poland
(converted
A.D. 966)

Hungary
(converted
A.D. 1000)

CROATS
(conv.
A.D. 700)

Bulgaria
(conv. A.D. 864)

Constantinople

R U M

Georgians

Armenians

London
Paris
Marseilles
Barcelona
Cordoba
Rome

KHWARIZM
Samarqand
Ghazni

I r a n i a n   p l a t e a u

Antioch
Jerusalem
Cairo
Baghdad

A R A B I A

Medina
Mecca

ABYSSINIA

0°   10°   20°   30°   40°   50°   60°   70°

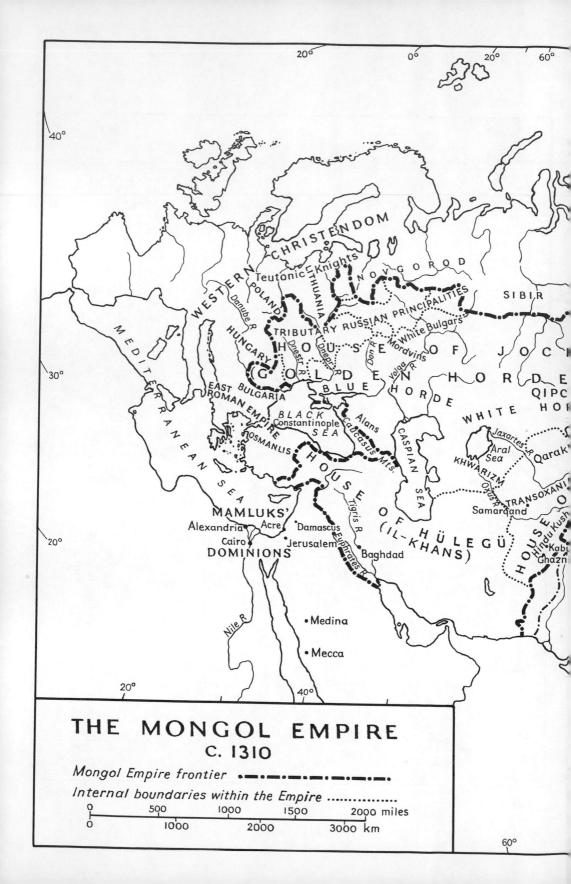

WESTERN CHRISTENDOM

Teutonic Knights

LITHUANIA

NOVGOROD

SIBIR

POLAND

Danube R.

HUNGARY

HOUSE

TRIBUTARY RUSSIAN PRINCIPALITIES

White Bulgars

OF

JOC

GOLDEN

Dniestr R.

Dnieper R.

Don R.

Mordvins

HORDE

EAST
ROMAN EMPIRE

BULGARIA

BLUE

Volga R.

QIPC
HOR

BLACK
SEA

Constantinople

Caucasus Mts.

Alans

CASPIAN

WHITE

HOR

OSMANLIS

HOUSE

CASPIAN SEA

Jaxartes R.

Aral
Sea

Qarak

KHWARIZM

Oxus R.

MAMLUKS'

Alexandria

Acre

Damascus

Tigris R.

OF

HÜLEGÜ

Samarqand

TRANSOXANI

HOUSE O

Cairo

Jerusalem

Euphrates R.

Baghdad

(IL-KHANS)

Hindu Kush

Kabl

DOMINIONS

Ghazn

MEDITERRANEAN SEA

Nile R.

• Medina

• Mecca

THE MONGOL EMPIRE
C. 1310

Mongol Empire frontier ▄▬ ▬ ▬ ▬

Internal boundaries within the Empire ....

0	500	1000	1500	2000 miles
0	1000	2000	3000 km	

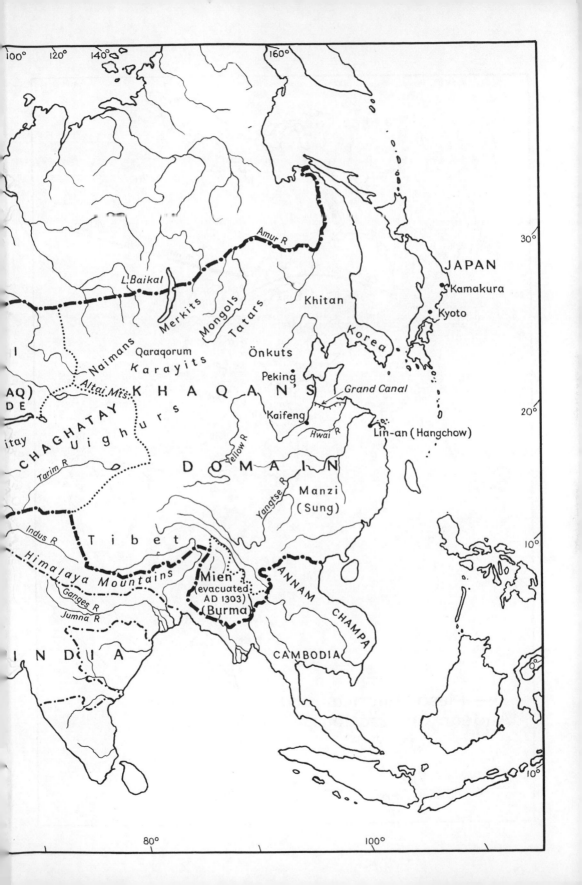

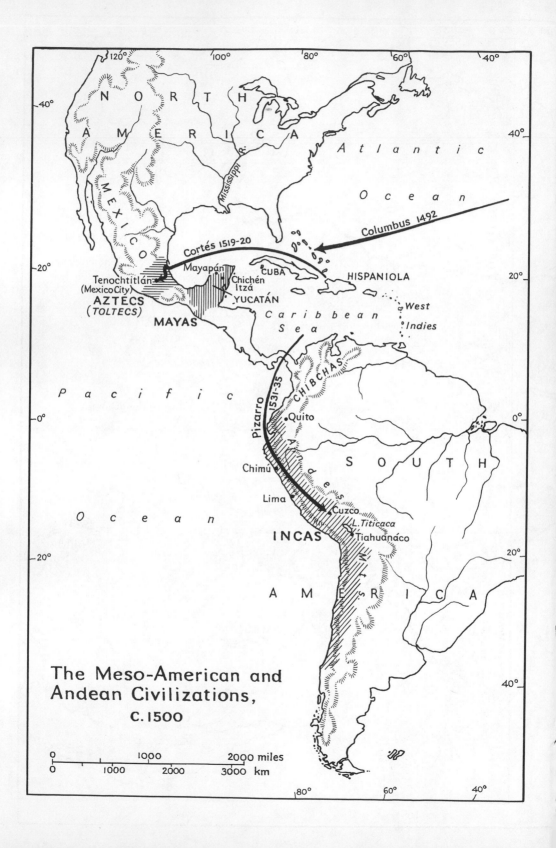

The Meso-American and
Andean Civilizations,
C.1500

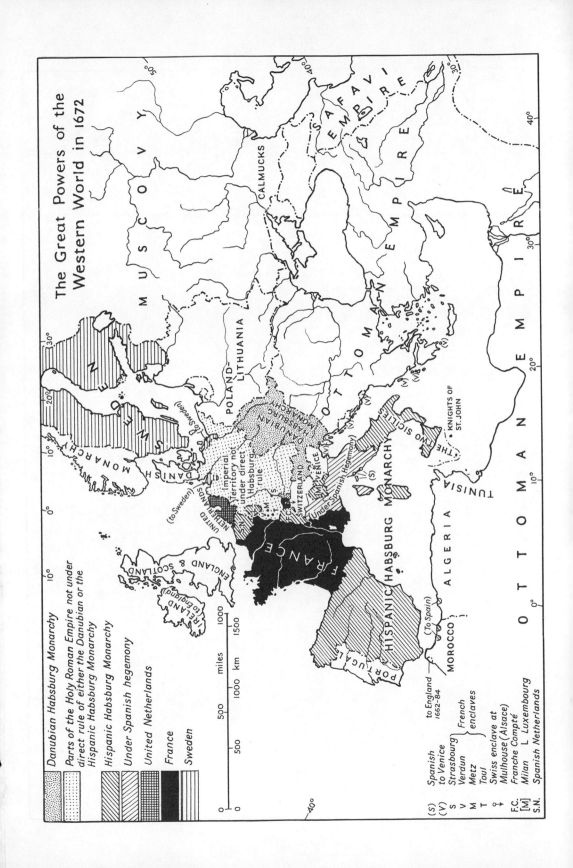

The Great Powers of the
Western World in 1672

Danubian Habsburg Monarchy

Parts of the Holy Roman Empire *not under
direct rule of either the Danubian or the
Hispanic Habsburg Monarchy*

Hispanic Habsburg Monarchy

Under Spanish hegemony

United Netherlands

France

Sweden

(S)   Spanish   to England
(V)   to Venice   1662-84
s   Strasbourg ⎤
v   Verdun   ⎥ French
M   Metz   ⎥ enclaves
T   Toul   ⎦
⚓   Swiss enclave at
       Mulhouse (Alsace)
F.C. Franche Compté
[M]   Milan   L. Luxembourg
S.N. Spanish Netherlands